# HOLMAN ILLUSTRATED BIBLE HANDBOOK

# HOLMAN ILLUSTRATED BIBLE HANDBOOK

Nashville, Tennessee

Holman Illustrated Bible Handbook


DEWEY: 220.02
SUBHD: BIBLE—HANDBOOKS, MANUALS, ETC.

ISBN: 978-0-8054-9587-4

Printed in China
4 5 6 7 8 9 10 18 17 16 15 14

## Maps



## Illustrations/Paintings

## Charts



## Acknowledgments

***Holman Illustrated Bible Handbook*** draws on a number of B&H resources. The core of the ***Handbook*** is taken from Kendell H. Easley's ***QuickSource Guide to Understanding the Bible***. Summaries of each the Bible's sixty-six books is taken from ***Holman Concise Bible Commentary***, David S. Dockery Editor; ***Holman Illustrated Bible Dictionary***, Chad Owen Brand, Charles W. Draper, Archie W. England, and Trent C. Butler, editors; ***HCSB Apologetics Study Bible***, Ted Cabal, Chad Owen Brand, Ray Clendenen, Paul H. Copan, and J. P. Moreland, editors; ***HCSB Study Bible***, Edwin A. Blum and Jeremy Royal Howard, General Editors.

**Genesis:** Eugene H. Merrill. Charles W. Draper, E. Ray Clendenen, Kenneth A. Mathews, A. Boyd Luter, Jr. , Robert D. Bergen; **Exodus:** Eugene H. Merrill, Trent C. Butler, Robert D. Bergen, Dorian G. Coover-Cox; **Leviticus:** Eugene H. Merrill, W. H. Bellinger, Jr., Mark F. Rooker, Kenneth A. Mathews, Tiberius Rata;

**Numbers:** Eugene H. Merrill, Douglas K. Wilson, Jr. , R. Dennis Cole; **Deuteronomy:** Eugene H. Merrill, Daniel I. Block; **Joshua:** Kenneth A. Mathews, Stephen J. Andrews, Len Fentress, Richard S. Hess; **Judges:** Kenneth A. Mathews, Daniel I. Block, Barry C. Davis, Iain M. Duguid; **Ruth:** Kenneth A. Mathews, Daniel I. Block, Barry C. Davis, Iain M. Duguid; **1,2 Samuel:** Kenneth A. Mathews, Robert D. Bergen, Bryan E. Beyer; **1,2 Kings:** Kenneth A. Mathews, Pete Wilbanks, Phil Logan, Kirk E. Lowery, Andrew C. Bowling; **1,2 Chronicles:** Kenneth A. Mathews, John H. Traylor, Jr., Kirk E. Lowery, Winfried Corduan; **Ezra-Nehemiah:** Kenneth A. Mathews, D.C. Martin, Barrett Duke, Carl R. Anderson; Esther: Kenneth A. Mathews, Kirk Kilpatrick, Barrett Duke, Carl R. Anderson; **Job:** Duane A. Garrett, Harry Hunt, Richard D. Patterson; **Psalms:** Duane A. Garrett, David M. Fleming, Russell Fuller, Allen P. Ross, Kevin R. Warstler, Sherri L. Klouda; **Proverbs:** Duane A. Garrett. Raymond C. Van Leeuwen, Edward M. Curtis, David K. Stabnow; **Ecclesiastes:** Duane A. Garrett, Stephen R. Miller; **Song of Songs:** Raymond C. Van Leeuwen, Sherri L. Klouda, Craig Glickman; **Isaiah:** Robert B. Chisholm, Harold Mosley, Steve Bond, Gary Smith, Tremper Longman III; **Jeremiah:** Robert B. Chisholm, Hans Mallau, E. Ray Clendenen, David K. Stabnow, Walter C. Kaiser; **Lamentations:** Robert B. Chisholm, David K. Stabnow, Walter C. Kaiser; **Ezekiel:** Robert B. Chisholm, Daniel I. Block, Lamar E. Cooper, Sr., Mark F. Rooker**; Daniel:** Robert B. Chisholm, Stephen R. Miller, Michael Rydelnik; **Hosea:** E. Ray Clendenen, Billy K. Smith, Thomas J. Finley; **Joel:** E. Ray Clendenen. Alvin O. Collins, Thomas J. Finley, Shawn C. Madden; **Amos**: E. Ray Clendenen, Roy L. Honeycutt, Thomas J. Finley, Duane A. Garrett; **Obadiah:** E. Ray Clendenen, Leslie C. Allen, Thomas J. Finley, Gregory W. Parsons; **Jonah:** E. Ray Clendenen, Thomas J. Finley, Joe Sprinkle; **Micah:** E. Ray Clendenen, Scott Langston, Thomas J. Finley, Kevin Peacock; **Nahum:** E. Ray Clendenen, Scott Langston, Thomas J. Finley, Gregory W. Parsons; **Habakkuk:** E. Ray Clendenen, John H. Tullock, Thomas J. Finley, Joe Sprinkle; **Zephaniah:** E. Ray Clendenen, Paul L. Redditt, Thomas J. Finley, Gregory W. Parsons; **Haggai:** E. Ray Clendenen, Thomas J. Finley, Gregory W. Parsons; **Zechariah:** E. Ray Clendenen, Thomas J. Finley, D. Brent Sandy; **Malachi:** E. Ray Clendenen, Thomas J. Finley; **Matthew:** Craig L. Blomberg, Oscar Brooks, Alan Hultberg, Charles L. Quarles; **Mark:** Christopher L. Church, Rodney Reeves, Alan Hultberg, Ross H. McLaren; **Luke:** Darrell L. Bock, T. R. McNeal, Alan Hultberg, A. Boyd Luter; **John:** James Emery White, C. Hal Freeman, Jr., Craig L. Blomberg, Andreas Köstenberger; **Acts:** John Polhill, Charles W. Draper, Stanley E. Porter; **Romans:** David S. Dockery, Charles L. Quarles, William W. Klein, Edwin A. Blum; **1 Corinthians:** David S. Dockery, R. E. Glaze, Paul W. Barnett, F. Alan Tomlinson; **2 Corinthians:** David S. Dockery, R. E. Glaze, Paul W. Barnett, Kendell H. Easley; **Galatians:** David S. Dockery, C. Hal Freeman, Jr., Walter Russell, A. Boyd Luter; **Ephesians:** David S. Dockery, Ray Summers, William W. Klein; **Philippians:** David S. Dockery, Michael Martin, Richard R. Melick, Jr.; **Colossians:** David S. Dockery, Michael Martin, Clinton E. Arnold, Andreas Köstenberger; **1,2 Thessalonians:** David S. Dockery, Leon Morris, Michael W. Holmes, James F. Davis; **1,2 Timothy:** David S. Dockery, Mark E. Matheson, Charles L. Quarles, Ray Van Neste; **Titus:** David S. Dockery, Terry L. Wilder, Charles L. Quarles, Ray Van Neste; **Philemon:** David S. Dockery, Kenneth Hubbard, Clinton E. Arnold, Murray J. Harris; **Hebrews:** Thomas D. Lea, Charles A. Ray, Terry L. Wilder, Malcolm B. Yarnell III; **James:** Thomas D. Lea, Paige Patterson, Terry L. Wilder, R. Gregg Watson; **1,2 Peter:** Thomas D. Lea, Thomas R. Schreiner, Terry L. Wilder; **1,2,3 John:** Thomas D. Lea, Daniel L. Akin, Robert W. Yarbrough; **Jude:** Thomas D. Lea, Thomas R. Schreiner, Terry L. Wilder; **Revelation:** Robert B. Sloan, Daniel L. Akin, A. Boyd Luter, Jr.

Understanding made the difference then—and it does now.

October days are typically beautiful in Jerusalem. On October 8, nearly 450 years before Christ, a large crowd gathered in the square at the Water Gate during the Festival of Booths. Ezra, the priest, mounted a high wooden platform, carrying a scroll of the Books of Moses (Genesis–Deuteronomy). As he opened the scroll to the passage to be read, all the people came to their feet out of reverence for the Scriptures. Ezra praised God whose Word he was about to read. The people lifted their hands to heaven and said, "Amen! Amen!" They then bowed down, their faces to the ground.

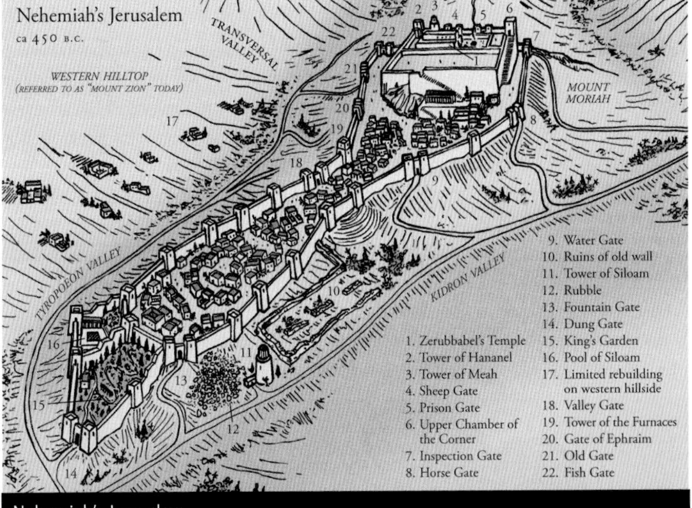


Nehemiah's Jerusalem.

Ezra read in Hebrew. Since most of people spoke only Aramaic at this time, interpreters translated as Ezra was reading. Not only that, Levites walked among the people explaining and clarifying what Ezra was reading. The response of the people was profound. They wept as those who grieve. They had become aware of their failure to measure up to God's expectations.

Seeing this heartfelt response, Ezra and the Levites further instructed the people, "This day is holy to the LORD your God. Do not mourn or weep. . . . Go and eat what is rich, drink what is sweet, and send portions to those who have nothing prepared, since today is holy to our LORD. Do not grieve, because the joy of the LORD is your stronghold" (Neh 8:1–18, specif. 7–12).

explained to them" (v. 12).

This profound engagement with God's Word began with expectant awe, gave way to great sorrow, and was turned to joy as the Scriptures were explained to the people. Whether you read from a hand-held digital reader, a printed page, or listen to an audio rendition of the Bible, you are encountering God's Word, a Word that can transform your life.

The *Holman Illustrated Bible Handbook* can do for you some of what the Levites walking among the people of Jerusalem were doing on that October day some 450 years before Christ—provide explanations that will better enable you to understand the Scriptures.

One of the most effective keys to reading comprehension is background knowledge. The richer your store of background knowledge, the greater your understanding of a text. That's what the Levites walking among the citizens of Judah were doing on that October day. They were providing background knowledge that enriched the people's understanding and turned sorrow to joy.

That's the aim of the *Holman Illustrated Bible Handbook*—to provide a richer store of background knowledge that will yield greater understand and joy.

*Holman Illustrated Bible Handbook* opens with Dr. George Guthrie's article "How to Read and Understand the Bible." Dr. Guthrie is a gifted interpreter of Scripture whose joy it is to lead others to grow in their ability to understand and engage Scripture in life-changing ways. This is of great value to those who have begun their journey with the Bible and with those who have been on this journey for years.

One of the questions most asked about the Bible is, "How can I know that the Bible contains the right books?" Dr. Jeremy Howard, a Christian apologist, responds to this question in two articles, "The Origin, Transmission, and Canonization of the Old Testament Books" and "The Origin, Transmission, and Canonization of the New Testament Books." In his article on the Old Testament, Dr. Howard addresses another question that many people ask about the Bible: "What is the Apocrypha and why do most Protestants not view it as Scripture?"

## FEATURES

For each of the 66 books of the Bible, the *Holman Illustrated Bible Handbook* provides the following features:

- **Key Texts (Bible verses)**
- **Key Term**
- **One Sentence Summary**

- **Author and Date of Writing**
- **First Audience and Destination**
- **Occasion**

- **Summary of the Book's Content**
- **The Reliability of the Book**

- **How the Book Fits into God's Story**
- **Christian Worldview Elements**
    - **God**
    - **Humanity**
    - **Salvation**

- **Genre and Literary Style**

- **A Principle to Live By**

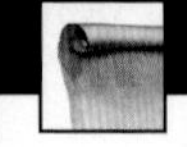

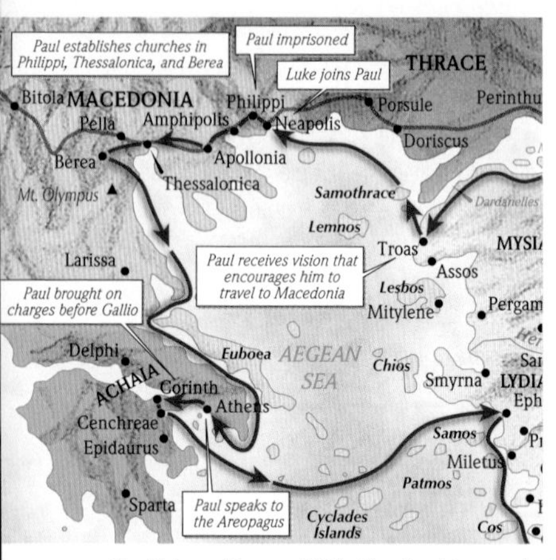


In addition to having background knowledge with words, *Holman Illustrated Bible Handbook* provides a wealth of visual resources that can be enjoyed and contribute to understanding the Scriptures. Photos, maps, reconstructions, and illustrations complement verbal explanations and together illuminate the biblical text. Terry Hulbert says interpreting the Bible apart from knowing the geographical, historical, and cultural contexts in which it is set is like watching a Shakespearean drama in an empty warehouse. You hear the lines of the actors but there is so much missing.

The *Holman Illustrated Bible Handbook* is no substitute for a direct experience of the lands in which the events of the Bible took place. But the *Handbook* does give a glimpse of the settings in which God placed His people, into which He came to live as a man, and across which the good news was delivered by the apostles.

The Euphrates is one of the most important rivers in the Bible. It was known as "the great river" (Gn 15:18; Jos 1:4) or "the river" (Nm 22:5). It formed the northern boundary of the land promised by Yahweh to Israel (Gn 15:18; Dt 1:7).

A replica of the Temple of Artemis in Istanbul, Turkey. The original Temple was in Ephesus and was one of the seven wonders of the world.

An Israeli man broadcasting seed at Petah Tikva.

The Bible is unique among the books of the world. Its "release date" is centuries old, yet it still dominates the best-seller lists, confronting moderns with messages as fresh as today's news headlines. At times the Bible is so crystal clear that a child can understand it, yet its difficulties can humble the most learned of scholars. Diverse in theme and literary genres, it conveys a unified story, a message that climaxes in the person and work of Jesus Christ. It was delivered through human writers, yet it truly is God's Word. The Bible can seem as familiar as a walk next door or as foreign as a distant country.

This article aims to help you hear from God through daily interaction with the Bible. Hearing God in the pages of the Bible takes time and effort; spiritual listening stances much removed from our own.

## WHY SPEND TIME IN THE BIBLE?

Perhaps your past has been marked by starts and stops in reading the Bible, and you are wondering whether you have the discipline to engage the Bible consistently. Well, join the club. Most of us have struggled with the discipline of Bible reading and study. So is it worth giving consistent Bible reading and study another try or a first try? Most believers know intuitively that it is.

This is *God's* Word. The God who spoke the world into being has spoken His truth about life through the Bible so that we might know what He intends for this world and how we might live for His fame. He calls us to be "Word people," people who are countercultural in the ways we approach life. Thus the Bible serves as the foundation for understanding who we are and what we should be doing in this world.

In the next few pages I offer a number of suggestions you can start applying daily in less time than it takes you to watch a sitcom on TV.

## BEGIN WITH THE HEART

In the parable of the seeds and soils (Mk 4:3–20), Jesus used a word picture to describe the different levels of receptivity people have toward God's Word. He tells of a farmer broadcasting seed along the edge of a field. Some seeds fall on the hard-packed path beside the field; some fall on rocky ground that has little topsoil; some fall in the weeds; and some fall in fertile soil that offers a good environment for growth. The various places they fall provide images of the human heart as it is confronted with God's Word.

Some people have hearts that are hard packed, like a frequented footpath. God's Word does not get through to these hearts. Others have shallow hearts that seem open to God's Word. The Word comes and they respond, but the moment things get tough, the pressures of life override the principles of God's Word, and the spiritual life withers. A third type of person engages God's Word at a deeper level, but worries and desire for worldly things squeeze out the Word, choking it from the person's life. Finally, there are those who receive the Word with a heart like a well-tilled field. This is the picture of a person fully receptive to God's Word, and God's Word brings exponential growth to their spiritual life.

Which pattern of response describes the condition of your heart today? Perhaps you have never committed to following Christ as Lord of your life. I encourage you to talk to a Christian or a minister whom you trust and ask them about following Christ as Lord. First Corinthians 2:14 tells us that a person who is not a Christ fol-

lower cannot engage spiritual truth in a way that is life changing, so this would be the beginning place for you. Turn to Christ, asking Him to bring His good news to life in you.

Or perhaps you have committed your life to follow Christ, but your heart is not receptive to God's Word at this time. You may be plagued by a heart that is consumed with worry or material things. Sin and self-absorption can eat the heart out of your Bible study. Begin your path back to a healthy relationship with God by crying out to Him right now, asking Him to forgive you for your hard-heartedness, expressing your desire to hear and live His Word.

## MOTIVATIONS

Once our hearts are receptive to the Word, we can hear the motivations offered us in Scripture. Among other motives, we read the Bible . . .

- to experience consistent joy (Ps 119:111)
- to sort out our thoughts and motivations (Heb 4:12)
- to guard ourselves from sin and error (Eph 6:11–17; 1 Pt 2:1–2)
- to know God in a personal relationship (1 Co 1:21; Gl 4:8–9; 1 Tm 4:16)
- to know truth and think clearly about what God says is valuable (2 Pt 1:21)
- to be built up as a community with other believers (Ac 20:32; Eph 4:14–16)
- to reject conformity to the world as we renew our minds (Rm 12:1–2; 1 Pt 2:1–2)
- to experience God's freedom, grace, peace, and hope (Jn 8:32; Rm 15:4; 2 Pt 1:2)
- to live well for God, expressing our love for Him (Jn 14:23–24; Rm 12:2; 1 Th 4:1–8)
- to minister to Christ followers and to those who have yet to respond to the gospel, experiencing God's approval for work well done (Jos 1:8; 2 Tm 2:15; 3:16–17)

## 12 PRACTICAL SUGGESTIONS FOR READING WELL

We want to approach our reading of the Bible in a way that will lead to a fulfilling, faithful, and fruitful pattern of life. Below are 12 suggestions to make your Bible reading more effective and fulfilling.

1. *Read the Bible prayerfully.* Engaging the Bible regularly is a spiritual exercise, and you need spiritual power and discernment to do it well. As you begin your Bible reading, ask God for a receptive and disciplined heart, ask Him to speak to you through the Word, and use the passages you read as providing you with thoughts and words you can use as you pray to God.

2. *Read expectantly and joyfully.* As you pray over your Bible reading, also read it expecting to hear from God, being joyful and thankful for what you find in the Scriptures. Allow the "music" of the Word to give you joy in your walk with God.

3. *Meditate on what you are reading.* To meditate means to mentally "chew" on what we are reading, to think about what the passage means as well as its implications for belief and practice. Just as food chewed and swallowed too quickly gives indigestion, so we will not be able to digest our Bible readings unless we slow down and consider the "meat" we find there.

4. *Read for transformation.* The Bible is not meant merely to inform; it is meant to transform us in accordance with God's truth (Rm 12:1–2). Therefore, read with expectation that you will hear from the Lord. Be thinking about ways to apply God's truth to your life as you read.

5. *Read with perseverance.* Commit yourself to being consistent for the next 10 to 12 weeks, which is about how long it takes to form a long-term habit. As you are faithful with your Bible reading and begin to see it make a difference in your life, you will begin to hunger for your time in the Word.

6. *Be realistic about the goals you set and have a good plan.* If you take just 20 to 30 minutes per day, you can read through the whole Bible in a year. In just 10 to 15 minutes per day, you can read through the whole Bible in two years. The key is not volume but consistency and a clear plan.

7. *Set aside a consistent time and place to read and study the Bible.* Make it a time and place that guards you from distractions and allows you to be consistent, missing no more than a handful of times per month. When you do miss a day, just pick back up the next day.

8. *Read with a few good tools at hand.* Along with this handbook, have a good Bible dictionary on hand. These typically provide outlines and message summaries of each book of the Bible, plus quick entries on theological, historical, and cultural elements.

9. *Read with a pen in hand.* Underline key passages and make notes in the margins as you read. As the saying goes, the lightest ink is stronger than the strongest memory. If you prefer a keyboard to an ink pen, store your notes on your computer.

10. *Read in light of the immediate context.* Not only do we need the "big picture" of the Bible's overarching story; we also need the "little picture" of the immediate context. So read with an awareness of where you are in the development of a particular book.

11. *Do your Bible reading and study as part of a community.* It helps if you have family or friends who also are reading the Bible, for they can encourage you and discuss the Bible with you. Become part of a community of Christians, a church, so you can have a place to celebrate what you are learning, to pose questions that come up in your study, and to use your spiritual gifts in ministering to others.

12. *Read in light of the overarching story of the Bible.* Reading the Bible is much more meaningful if you read it in light of its overarching story. As you read, notice great interwoven themes such as how creation in Genesis 1–2 relates to creation

themes in Psalm 8; Isaiah 65:17–25; John 1; Romans 8:19–22; and Revelation 21. Read book introductions in your *Illustrated Bible Handbook*, noting where each book fits in the overall development of God's story. That story can be outlined in seven scenes.

1. Prologue: Creation, Fall, and the Need for Redemption
2. God Builds His Nation (2000–931 BC)
3. God Educates His Nation (931–586 BC)
4. God Keeps a Faithful Remnant (586–6 BC)
5. God Purchases Redemption and Begins the Kingdom (6 BC to AD 30)
6. God Spreads the Kingdom Through the Church (AD 30-?)
7. God Consummates Redemption and Confirms His Eternal Kingdom
8. Epilogue: New Heaven and New Earth

## GOING DEEPER: THE BASICS OF SOUND BIBLE STUDY

Think for a moment about a trip you have taken. You left home, traveled to your destination, and had various memorable experiences. Perhaps you experienced a culture different from your own and found that the greater the cultural differences between home and destination, the greater the effort needed to communicate and to learn in your new environment. Yet you persevered, experienced new people and places, and were enriched by it all.

The Bible is God's Word to us; we are not simply "reading someone else's mail." Yet Bible study can be like taking a trip to another culture. The language at times seems foreign. You might have difficulty finding your way around the history or the literature. You see new things that are beautiful or even strange. You then gather up what you have gained from your study time and hopefully you grow by the experience.

Since reading the Bible is a cross-cultural experience, we need a vehicle that can take us to where we can hear what God is saying to us through those experiences, and I suggest that the right vehicle is *a sound process of listening to the text of Scripture*. Through a sound process of Bible reading, we see "the sights" God wants us to see. We learn to navigate the unfamiliar territories of biblical history and literature, read the "road signs" that mark the main points to which we must pay attention, and understand the language of the Bible.

After we have lived in the world of the biblical text for a while and become familiar with what is going on there, persevering through challenges and hearing what God wants us to hear, we then "travel back home" to our life contexts, bringing with us changed hearts and minds. The vehicle that can bring us home is *discerning the principles and significance* of what we have encountered in the Bible and then finding specific ways to apply God's truth to our lives.

Using this word picture, let's look at five main stages for doing a more thorough study of a Bible passage.

**FIVE STAGES OF THOROUGH BIBLE STUDY**

| 1 | 2 | 3 | 4 | 5 |
|---|---|---|---|---|
| Pack Your Bags | Read the Maps | Read the Road Signs Carefully | Learn to Speak like a Local | Head Home |
| Choose a passage | Study the broad historical context of the book | Read the passage in several translations | Choose key words to study | Identify the main points and principles of the passage |
| Gather your tools | Study the literary genre | Look for key dynamics in the passage | Consult word study tools | Identify how these address original and modern contexts |
| Pray | Study the immediate literary context of the passage | Make a provisional outline of the passage | Consult a concordance | Make specific application for your own life |

## STAGE 1: PACK YOUR BAGS

One of the most important aspects of a trip is what happens *before* the trip. Preparation and packing can make all the difference.

*Choose a passage.* Just as when traveling you need to start out with a destination in mind, when studying the Bible you must first decide what specific passage you will address. Be sure to choose a passage you can cover well in your designated period of time. For instance, if you are doing a detailed study of a passage from one of Paul's letters, four to seven verses (e.g., 2 Co 2:14–17) are plenty to tackle in one session. If you have a longer passage you want to study (e.g., all of Romans 8), break it down into smaller segments and study the whole of the chapter over an extended period of time. Trying to study too large a section all at once will lead to frustration. However, if you are studying a section of biblical narrative, your passage can be longer since narratives do not depend on detailed argumentation.

As you attempt to do Bible study over the coming weeks, you will get a sense of how much ground you can cover in a week's time. Over time you will become more familiar with your tools and processes, allowing you to study more efficiently. But remember, just as you would not want to hurry past important historical sites just to get to the end of a trip, the key in Bible study is not speed but rather an approach that takes you deeper into God's Word and transforms you in the process.

*Gather your tools.* In addition to a study Bible, which includes a variety of features to take you deeper into the Word, it helps to have several types of translation on hand. Some translations are more "formal," following the patterns of the original words as closely as possible, even if the results are not always readily understandable to modern readers. Others are more "functional," trying to communicate the author's meaning even if that means departing from the exact pattern of words in the passage. Still other translations attempt to strike a balance between these two approaches, which is the tactic taken in the HCSB.

A strong Bible dictionary has much to offer, including an outline and introduction to each book of the Bible, plus entries on people, places, culture, theological issues, and key events mentioned in the Bible. It is also helpful to have dictionaries specifically covering the original languages of the Old and New Testaments. These show you the range of possible meanings a given word can have. There are many Bible study software programs available. Some may be had for free on the Internet. While the Internet can be an amazing resource for Bible study, not all Web sites are created equal. Therefore, do your best to assess the quality of the site. You might ask a minister or mature Christian to help you discern a site's trustworthiness. Also, while free Internet sites can be helpful, they often use outdated tools that are public domain. These tools still have value but need to be used in conjunction with tools based on recent study by evangelical scholars.

The best Bible commentaries provide a treasure trove of information, including an introduction to the book, an outline of the book, theological reflection, deep word studies, thoughtful interpretive insights, and application. Ask a trusted Christian or minister to help you evaluate the usefulness, trustworthiness, and accessibility of the commentaries that are available.

*Pray.* Once you have chosen your passage and gathered your tools, begin your time of study with prayer. You might begin by praying something like this:

*Lord, thank You for Your Word. I pray that You will give me the discipline to study this passage carefully. Please also give me the discernment to understand the details. Lord, please guide me by Your Spirit and lead me into Your truth. I am committed to applying what I find here, and I pray that You will change me by Your Word, bringing my life in line with Your will and ways of thinking. Thank You for this time.*

## STAGE 2: READ THE MAPS

Maps are vital to navigation—you must know where you are to understand how to get to where you want to go. In Bible study, knowledge of the historical and literary contexts provides orientation. Like maps, they give us the layout of the biblical "neighborhood." The historical context can give us a clearer backdrop in terms of historical events or cultural dynamics of the time, and the literary context can help

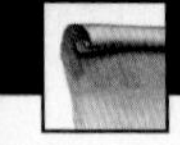

Understanding cultural, historical, and literary contexts enables us to navigate the "biblical neighborhood."

us understand how these words function, given where the author placed them in the book.

*The broad historical context of the book.* In studying the historical context of a book, you want to understand the following facts:

Who authored the book?

Who were the original recipients?

Where were the author and the recipients located?

When was the book written?

What is the purpose of the book?

You can find this kind of information for each book of the Bible in the *Holman Illustrated Bible Handbook*. You can also find it in Bible dictionaries, commentaries, and study Bibles.

*The literary genre.* Another aspect of the context of a passage has to do with "genre," or the kind of literature with which we are dealing. The kind of literature of a given passage will determine how we approach the text and what kind of questions we might ask of it. If I pick up a novel, I understand that its purpose is not

primarily to communicate historical facts. If, however, I read a book detailing the history of America, the purpose is to communicate and interpret historical facts.

Different parts of the Bible reflect different literary genres and, therefore, are intended to accomplish different purposes and must be interpreted by different rules. Our goal with each is to understand what God intends to communicate through the human author, but to do so we must understand how the author intended his writing to communicate with his original audience.

This brings us to vital questions we must ask of the text. For narrative literature, for instance, we want to ask: "What is the significance of this part of the story? How does it fit into the grand story of God in the Scriptures?" The biblical authors had much material from which to choose, and they chose to include the stories they did for a reason.

Psalms and other poetic literature, on the other hand, often communicate emotions expressed in worship. These might include celebration, thanksgiving, sadness, reflection, or anger. Therefore, an important interpretive key when studying a psalm is to ask, "What is the emotion expressed?" and "How is the emotion being expressed?" The Psalms often use figurative language, for instance.

Finally, proverbs are meant to communicate general guidelines for living. Consider the following passage from Proverbs 4:10–12:

> Listen, my son. Accept my words, and you will live many years. I am teaching you the way of wisdom; I am guiding you on straight paths. When you walk, your steps will not be hindered; when you run, you will not stumble.

Some mistakenly take this passage as a promise that an obedient child will be guaranteed a long life free of impediments. Many wonderful promises in Scripture are intended to give comfort and hope to God's people, but neither the human author nor the Divine Author intended for proverbs to be promises. This proverb is saying, in effect, that the best way for a child to live is by seeking wisdom; this is the path of success in life, and, generally speaking, will lead to a long and effective life.

*The immediate context of the passage.* By the immediate literary context we mean how the passage under consideration fits into the overall development of the book. Words need a context to have a specific meaning. Think about the English word *hand*. It has more than a dozen possible meanings. It can be used for your physical hand, "give him a hand" (meaning either "applause" or "help"), the hand of a clock, etc. Yet you normally have no trouble following the meaning of the word in specific contexts. Someone might say, "I cut my hand with a knife," and you know they are not talking about the "hand" on a wall clock.

In the same way, the words of the Bible often could be understood to mean different things, but the authors used their words to communicate in specific contexts.

So reading a Bible passage in its correct context is foundational for understanding what a given word means. One way to identify the context is to track the themes in a section of Scripture. Write in the margins the main topics covered, and constantly reflect on these as you progress through the passage.

When we consider the immediate context in a narrative passage, we are looking for any aspect of a historical situation indicated by the passage itself. What do we mean by the immediate historical situation? In studying the story of Elijah and the prophets of Baal in 1 Kings 18:1–46, for example, the immediate historical situation has to do with Ahab as king of Israel, a time of punishing drought, Elijah the prophet, and the location of Mount Carmel. The historical situation of the book as a whole, on the other hand, would have to do with when and why 1 Kings was written and the fact that the book spans from the reign of Solomon down through the death of the wicked king Ahab.

## STAGE 3: READ THE ROAD SIGNS CAREFULLY

When you travel, it is critical that you read the road signs well. As we study the Bible, many clues to the author's intentions are built right into any given passage. So one important aspect of Bible study is slowing down and reading the passage carefully.

When you are driving down a road at 65 miles per hour, how many roadside details do you catch? Not many. You might be able to *see* interesting objects on the roadside, but they blur and then fade quickly as you speed by.

Many of us are "drive by" readers of Scripture, never slowing down to explore and

The landscape is a virtual blur when we travel fast.

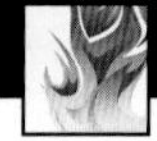

enjoy the details of God's Word; consequently there is much that we miss in the process. Choose to slow down and read with care. Read a passage repeatedly if you sense you've yet to catch all the elements. One way to ensure that you are reading slowly enough to catch the details is to underline key phrases or words, or write notes in the margin.

*Read the passage in several translations.* Doing a comparison of modern English Bible translations can be a helpful way to highlight key interpretive issues in a passage. Why? Because translation, by its nature, requires interpretation. With almost any verse of Scripture, translators have to choose, given the context and grammatical constructions, between various possible word meanings. Therefore, the differences reflected in the various translations represent various interpretations of the passage.

*Look for key dynamics in the passage.* Now read through your chosen passage again in your main translation. Look for the features listed below and circle, underline, or highlight them, perhaps using different color pens. This exercise will give you a much clearer picture of the passage. Common features to look for include:

*Subject*—Who or what is the passage focusing on?

*Verb*—Is it a statement, an exhortation, a question or answer, an action, explanation, or illustration?

*Conjunctions*—and, but, or, so, for, both . . . and, neither . . . nor, either . . . or, not only . . . but also

*Time*—after, before, when, while, since, until

*Cause*—because, since, in order that, so that

*Condition*—if, in case, even if, unless

*Concession*—although, even though, whereas

*Means*—How is the action accomplished?

*Agent*—Who does the action?

*Result*—What is accomplished?

*Purpose*—Why was the action done?

When reading narrative material, identify the following:

*Introduction and conclusion*—The author often tips off the intended impact of a narrative in his introduction and conclusion.

*Setting*—details on place, time (historical era and duration of the event), and social situation (Who is involved?).

*Character information*—Identify the protagonist and antagonist, note prevailing emotions and actions, and pay close attention to dialogue and character descriptions.

*Narrative dynamics*—Identify the conflict, its escalation, and eventual resolution.

*Teaching forms and figures of speech*—Look for the presence of allusions to or quotations of the Old Testament, plus figures of speech such as hyperbole, simile, metaphor, riddle, pun, parable, object lesson, illustration, parabolic act, paradox, irony, amen formula, and prophecy.

Don't get overwhelmed with searching for these dynamics. Take a few at a time, reading the passage with those dynamics in mind. Then read again, looking for a few more of the dynamics listed above. "Filtering" the passage in this way will give you great insight into the passage. If when reading the passage you see just two or three features that you had not seen before, you are making progress!

*Make a provisional outline of the passage.* The outline is provisional since you still have a good bit of study to do on the passage. However, it is helpful to make a tentative outline at this point to begin to assess the general structure of the passage.

## STAGE 4: LEARN TO SPEAK LIKE A LOCAL

One of the most interesting aspects of traveling has to do with learning how people in different places use words. For instance, the German phrase "Guten Tag" literally means "good day," yet it is normally used as a greeting only in the afternoon and thus is equivalent to an English speaker saying, "good afternoon."

To understand the biblical text, we need to have an accurate understanding of *how* words are used. Word meanings are determined by the contexts in which they are used. When studying a word in the biblical text, we want to (a) know the possible meanings for that word in the ancient world, (b) determine, based on the context, which meaning the author most likely intended, and (c) see whether insight on an author's use can be gained by noting how the same word is used elsewhere in the Bible.

This hiker on Mount Tabor is able to explore and savor this site.

*Choose key words to study.* Identify key words in the passage. These may be terms that are repeated, terms that are unclear or puzzling, or terms that seem to be theologically important.

*Consult word study tools.* Get at the Hebrew or Greek words behind our English translations by using an exhaustive concordance, Bible software programs, or various types of expository dictionaries. Once you have accessed the range of possible meanings for the

Hebrew or Greek word, consider those possible meanings in the context of the passage you are studying. This gives you a look at the various nuances of the Greek or Hebrew word behind the translation you are using, deepening your understanding of what the biblical author might have been trying to say.

This is also an excellent point in your Bible study to consult good commentaries. They will discuss the key words of the passage against the backdrop of literary context, background issues, the author's theology, and other factors.

*Consult a concordance.* You can use a concordance to look for other uses of the same Hebrew or Greek term you are studying. Identify places where the word is used similarly to the way it is used in the passage you are studying. Such cross-references can provide you with greater understanding of the passage on which you are doing your word studies.

Word studies can be helpful, but they can also be abused, and we want to avoid word study fallacies. A few of the most common fallacies include:

*Cross-reference fallacy*—Insisting that a word as used in one passage must be used the same way in another passage, simply because the same word is being used.

*Root fallacy*—Insisting that a word's true meaning is tied to its root meanings, or the parts of the word. But this is not always how language works.

*Multiple meanings fallacy*—Insisting that all the possible meanings of a word occur in a given use in a particular passage. Most of the time an author had a particular meaning in mind.

## STAGE 5: HEAD HOME

As with any trip, a time comes to travel home. Bible study is analogous in that applying the Bible to our lives is "bringing it home." We were never meant to read and study the Bible simply to learn a list of facts. Rather, we were meant to experience transformation by the Word (Rm 12:1–2), and transformation takes place as we embrace the Word, applying it to our everyday lives. Commenting on the command to love one's neighbor, James says:

> What good is it, my brothers, if someone says he has faith but does not have works? Can his faith save him? If a brother or sister is without clothes and lacks daily food and one of you says to them, "Go in peace, keep warm, and eat well," but you don't give them what the body needs, what good is it? In the same way faith, if it doesn't have works, is dead by itself. (Jms 2:14–17)

Faith without deeds, without application, is dead. James was addressing those who had disconnected belief in the Christian life from active obedience.

At times the application may be a right belief, the adjusting of one's understanding to fit what God says is true. At other times application might be to worship God. Often application will involve active obedience that puts into practice what has been learned. But the movement from understanding the Word to its application in obedience is nonnegotiable from the Bible's standpoint.

How then can we apply the things we learn in the Bible to our lives in responsible ways?

*Identify the main points and principles of the passage.* What truth claims is the Scripture passage making? Identify them. Search for the principles as well. A principle is a "universal truth" that applies in all places at all times.

*Identify how these address original and modern contexts.* Notice how the principle is applied to the situation dealt with in your passage and think through parallel situations in your life.

*Make specific applications to your life.* Work at moving beyond vague generalities like, "I need to love people more!" Write down *whom* you need to love and *how* you need to express love to them. As noted above, applications might be an *action* to do (e.g., "wash the dishes"). Yet they could also involve the change of a belief, or even to respond to God's Word by worshipping Him.

## A SIMPLE PLAN

I hope you have enjoyed the "trip" as we have discussed how to read and study the Bible more effectively. Begin your new commitment with a definite reading plan. Commit to taking 15–30 minutes per day, and read through the Bible over the next year or two. Take one or two longer blocks of time per week to study the Bible in greater depth.

Bible reading and study can give us great joy and fulfillment as we open our lives to God's Word. May you be blessed as you pursue being a "Word person" led by the Spirit, transformed by the Scriptures, and effective in advancing God's agendas in the world.

The term *canon* is used to describe the list of books approved for inclusion in the Bible. It stems from a Greek word meaning "rod," as in a straight stick that serves as a standard for measuring. Hence, to speak of the biblical canon is to speak of authoritative books, given by God, the teachings of which define correct belief and practice. Obviously, only books inspired by God should be received as canonical. The Bible before you includes 39 books in the Old Testament (OT). Are these the right books? Who wrote them? What were their sources of information? These questions are asked by friends and foes of biblical faith. The present essay will touch on such issues with an aim to bolster Christian confidence in the OT.

## SOURCES FOR THE EARLIEST HISTORIES

Genesis chapters 1–11 are referred to as "primeval history" because they cover events that occurred far back in the shadows of earliest time. Genesis chapters 12–50 are in turn called "patriarchal history" since they recount the lives of Israel's founding fathers from Abraham down to Joseph. From the creation of the world to Joseph's establishment in Egypt, all the events retold in Genesis occurred long before Moses was born. This is significant because the Bible and longstanding Jewish tradition assert that Moses wrote the first five books of the Bible (the Pentateuch). Most likely he composed them between 1440 and 1400 BC while he and the Israelites sojourned outside Canaan. Many events in Exodus through Deuteronomy coincided

Moses. A mosaic from Cathedral Basilica of Saint Louis.

him supernaturally. In this scenario God's inspiration of Moses would include God supplying Moses with historical details about far-gone people, places, times, and even conversations—information Moses would not have known had God not told him. This possibility cannot be ruled out in principle since God is capable of working such miracles, but careful analysis reveals the Pentateuch nowhere hints that the historical narratives were given to Moses in this manner. For instance, Genesis never says anything like, "The word of the Lord came to Moses, saying, 'This is the history of Abraham.'" Instead, the Genesis narratives about Abraham and other historical figures read like straightforward accounts that have been handed down in the usual way: through oral and written records, with the oral records presumably originating soon after the events occurred. In this case, we would add that God superintended the transmission of the early oral and written accounts so that Moses received reliable histories worthy of inclusion in Genesis.

That Moses possibly used such sources may seem surprising at first. People often assume the Bible is the product of divine dictation, but it is more accurate to view Bible composition as having involved both supernatural and natural means, with the result that the original Bible manuscripts were fully reliable and stemmed simultaneously from divine inspiration as well as regular human approaches to writing. This model is supported by Luke 1:1–4, where Luke says he did a lot of research before writing his Gospel. A similar example is found in Numbers 21:14, where a quote is lifted from the now lost "Book of the Lord's Wars." From these examples we see that Bible writers were free to draw reliable historical data from nonbiblical sources. Thus it seems Moses was able to write about historical events that occurred long before his birth by drawing upon information found in preexisting sources, all while God's Spirit inspired him in penning Genesis.

How did these written sources come down to Moses? For the primeval history it is reasonable to suggest that from earliest times people passed down carefully preserved oral accounts about key events and significant persons. Later, when elementary writing arose, many of these would have been committed to writing. The transfer to written format may have happened earlier than is commonly supposed. Rudimentary alphabets are known to have circulated in the early second millennium BC, and with the discovery of the Palermo Stone, we have solid evidence that the Egyptians wrote detailed historical records (in hieroglyphic text) at least as far back as 2600 BC, a time that predated Moses by over 1,100 years. The rich details inscribed on the Palermo Stone reach back toward the dawn of Egypt, naming kings from 3100 BC and even earlier. In light of this example, it is fitting to suppose

that key remembrances of early human history were preserved and passed down to later generations.

That the earliest writings have not survived to our day is no surprise, for they would have been rare to begin with and would have perished long ago as the acids of time worked their destruction. But they survived long enough to bequeath vital facts to later societies who learned to write the histories in more permanent formats. Some of the greatest modern archeological digs have uncovered ancient nonbiblical texts that resemble the biblical accounts of Noah's flood and the Tower of Babel. These texts date from 1600 BC and earlier, and in broad strokes they corroborate Genesis. Their points of departure from Genesis may reflect corruptions that slipped in as cultures pulled farther and farther away from knowledge of God. By contrast people who kept alive a faith like Noah's preserved the stories uncorrupted, and these accounts came down to men like Moses in later generations.

A fragment of the Palermo stone, on display at the Petrie Museum, London.

As for the patriarchal histories, it goes without saying that men such as Abraham would pass down close accounts of their remarkable experiences with God. Once God interrupted Abraham's life and promised to create a nation through him, he knew his life was unique. This heritage was repeatedly confirmed to his descendants as God kept up His habit of revealing Himself and confirming His covenant of blessing. Somewhere down the line Abraham's descendants began writing down these stories. This may have begun most earnestly with Joseph, the son of Israel who became a great political figure in Egypt. Writing was an old art in Egypt by the time Joseph ascended to power. Having achieved a royal-like status and having married a well-placed Egyptian, Joseph and his family would have had every opportunity to learn the Egyptian writing craft. As a chief bearer of Abraham's lineage, Joseph would have been keen to preserve the family traditions and the link to the one true God.

In the years after Joseph's death, the Hebrews grew in number but came to be suppressed by the Egyptians. This suppression highlighted the need to preserve the histories. One theory holds that one of the Israelite families, possibly the Levites, became the official preservers of the old stories. If so, these materials would have been available to Moses (a Levite) when he became leader of the Hebrews. This inheritance, plus God's commission of Moses and the fact that he was raised and educated in Pharaoh's household, put Moses in a fine position to write an early history of humankind from the Hebrew perspective. A possible exception would be the portions of the creation accounts (Genesis 1–2) that could not stem from human eyewitness testimony. These accounts bear close resemblance to visionary revelations that were later given to prophets such as Isaiah and Ezekiel, as well as John in the book of Revelation. Hence, it is plausible to suggest that God gave Moses a revelatory vision for the first two chapters of Genesis. But in his writings generally, whether he was making use of oral accounts, written histories, or relying on God's Spirit for the unveiling of the creation accounts, Moses often wrote more than he knew. In other words, Moses could not plumb the depths of everything he wrote, for an Author greater than he breathed profundity and prophecy into the works of his pen.

## WHO WROTE THE BOOKS AND WHEN?

The OT books do not have copyright dates on them, and few of them explicitly identify their author. Nevertheless, by aid of biblical testimony and Jewish history, we know the approximate time at which the books were composed. We also know in many cases who the author was or who was likely to have been chiefly responsible for a book's content. For thousands of years now, scholarly people of faith have studied the matter and have concluded that the OT books and their earliest recipients have reliably portrayed the authorship and dates for the sacred writings, yet today critics say the books were written many hundreds of years *after* the dates and authors traditionally assigned to them. For instance, it is claimed that the Pentateuch was actually written nearly 1,000 years after Moses. In its extreme version this theory even says men such as Moses and Abraham never existed; they and their histories were allegedly invented by priests who sought to provide hope-inspiring stories during the tough years when the Hebrews were exiled in Babylon in the sixth century BC.

Such theories are chiefly built on the slim supports of (1) skepticism, which presupposes that God does not exist and/or that the Bible is just a human book, and (2) the occasional anachronisms scattered throughout the early portions of the OT. Skepticism is itself a faith of sorts, for the assertions that God does not exist or did not inspire the Bible if He does exist cannot be proven from the data at hand. Ironically skeptics, who insist we should form beliefs only on the basis of evidence, contradict their own mantra. But what about the anachronisms found in the OT? The Pentateuch occasionally includes such things as place-names or vocabulary that did not belong to the era described. In other words, some of these only came into usage hundreds of years after men like Abraham died. Skeptics take this as

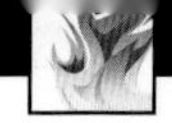

proof that the books (and all the stories they contain) originated much later than popularly believed and that the priests who invented these stories occasionally slipped up and placed contemporary names and words into ancient settings.

But this radical theory is firmly against the evidence. In reality the early OT books consistently bear the mark of ancient contexts—contexts that suit times long before national Israel arose. For instance, the laws, customs, and political situations described in the Pentateuch fit naturally with the second millennium BC and earlier. This is proven by the discovery of many nonbiblical texts and artifacts from that era. It is unlikely that unethical priests a thousand years or more removed from the historical situations described in the Pentateuch could have gotten things so right. Also, the concerns that dominated the Hebrew mind-set during the Babylonian exile are not addressed by the Pentateuch. Hence, how could priests hope to encourage their downtrodden fellow Hebrews in Babylon by inventing stories that bore no semblance to their situation? Further, it is unimaginable that the mass of Hebrews would fall for such a ruse, choose to base their entire worldview on false histories passed off on them by a band of inventive clergymen, and then succeed in selling the hoax to their children for generations to come.

So what should we conclude about the anachronisms? Simply this: in the years after the Pentateuch was written, inevitable changes in place-names, vocabulary, and political situations made these old books harder to comprehend. To alleviate this problem, priestly guardians of the sacred oracles updated the texts at key junctures to reflect contemporary word usage and geopolitical situations. Such changes as these (e.g., Jdg 1:10; 1 Sm 9:9) would have been undertaken soberly and with great care to preserve the meaning and intention of the holy text. Thus, under strict guidelines the books underwent helpful editing, with the result that the texts remained accessible with the passage of time.

On the whole, however, virtually all the scribes who ever touched the sacred scrolls did so only to read them or copy them word for word. Literary copying was an important skill in the ancient world since there was no means of rapid duplication, such as modern printing presses or photocopiers. Believing that the writings in their care were authoritative and inspired by God, the Hebrew scribes took exceptional care when copying the scrolls.

In conclusion, we can be confident in the traditional beliefs about the date and authorship of the OT books. We can also rest assured that the books were carefully copied and preserved and that all editorial updates of the books were done in a strictly conservative fashion.

## DO WE HAVE THE RIGHT BOOKS?

Are the 39 books of our OT really the ones God meant for us to revere? The first step to answering this question is to address the issue of collection: Who originally

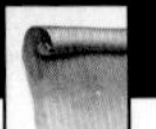


collected the sacred writings? Solid evidence indicates that the priests undertook this duty. In Deuteronomy 31:24–26, Moses commanded that the book of the law be kept with the ark of the covenant, where the Ten Commandments were stored. This put Moses' writings at the center of Jewish religious life just as soon as they were complete. Further, in Deuteronomy 4:2 we read the command to preserve the commandments of God faithfully. Taken together, these passages indicate that the priests were to keep charge of God's written revelations and that these were to be safeguarded against perversion.

Since Moses was the author of the earliest biblical books, and since Moses himself charged the priests with the duties to store and protect God's words, the high value of identifying, collecting, and protecting the sacred writings was established when the Pentateuch originated. When other prophets and holy men arose in Israel subsequent to Moses and were given revelations by God, their teachings (whether written by them or by their close associates) would have been gathered quickly by the community of the faithful. At some later point the books came to be stored at the Jerusalem temple. We know this because in a time of national backsliding the unused books collected dust in the temple's storerooms (2 Kg 22:8–13). At a much later time in history the books were still kept in the temple, for Josephus (a repu-

The ark of the covenant, a replica.

table Jewish historian) received the Scriptures from his Roman benefactors who had sacked the temple in AD 70.

We have seen that the Jews identified, collected, and preserved the sacred writings as a matter of course. Next we must ask if or when they believed the production of sacred writings had ceased. Josephus is helpful for elucidating this matter. He tells us (*Against Apion*, 1.37–43) that the Jews widely recognized that the succession of the prophets ended in the time of Artaxerxes, when Latter Prophets such as Haggai and Malachi fell silent and left no successors. Hence, says Josephus, books written after about 400 BC were not regarded as Scripture even if they were valuable on other terms. In 164 BC Judas Maccabaeus reconsolidated the Scriptures in the temple after the fires of the Antiochene persecution died out, and it appears that the scrolls were harbored there in a long stretch of safety that did not end until the above-mentioned Roman aggressions. There can be no doubt of the identity of the Scriptures held at the temple throughout this time: There were 22 books (or 24, depending on how they were divided and counted), and they were lumped into three major divisions: the Law (Pentateuch), the Prophets, and the Writings. Though we divide them into 39 books rather than 22 or 24, the Protestant OT canon is identical to those books that were safeguarded at the temple before the time of Christ. The two most significant religious bodies in Israel (Pharisees and Sadducees) both accepted this body of books as the canon of Scripture, though one often hears it mistakenly asserted that the Sadducees accepted only the Pentateuch.

What about the books of the Apocrypha? This is a diverse set of books—most of which were written between 200 BC and early in the first century AD—that treat various aspects of Jewish religious and national life in the intertestamental period, which ranged from 400 BC to the time of Christ. They offer important windows into the Jewish context, and many Jews of that time regarded them as valuable religious literature. However, they were never received as Scripture by mainstream Judaism, and even fringe groups such as the Essenes reckoned them valuable but *not* scriptural. The books of the Apocrypha were never stored in the temple, a sure sign that they were not thought to be inspired by God.

This is not to say there were no struggles among the Jews about the identity of the canon. In fact, five of the books that were counted as canonical had a hard time winning unilateral acceptance. The books of Proverbs, Ecclesiastes, Esther, Song of Songs, and Ezekiel were subjected to scrutiny because they seemed secular in outlook or else promoted teachings that initially seemed inconsistent with the Pentateuch. Jewish leaders debated the merits of these books from time to time, as Christian leaders would do in the centuries to come, but all in all their status in the canon was well established.

Following Jesus' example, early Christians adopted the Jewish consensus on the OT canon. During His ministry Jesus showed that He was in line with the standard

## THE HEBREW CANON OF THE OLD TESTAMENT

| CLASSIFICATION OF THE BOOKS | HEBREW NAMES FOR THE BOOKS | ENGLISH NAMES FOR THE BOOKS |
|---|---|---|
| THE LAW (Torah) | In the beginning<br>These are the names<br>And He called<br>In the wilderness<br>These are the words | Genesis<br>Exodus<br>Leviticus<br>Numbers<br>Deuteronomy |
| FORMER PROPHETS | Joshua<br>Judges<br>1 Samuel<br>2 Samuel<br>1 Kings<br>2 Kings | Joshua<br>Judges<br>1 Samuel<br>2 Samuel<br>1 Kings<br>2 Kings |
| LATTER PROPHETS | Isaiah<br>Jeremiah<br>Ezekiel<br>The Book of the Twelve<br>(which includes)<br>Hosea<br>Joel<br>Amos<br>Obadiah<br>Jonah<br>Micah<br>Nahum<br>Habakkuk<br>Zephaniah<br>Haggai<br>Zechariah<br>Malachi | Isaiah<br>Jeremiah<br>Ezekiel<br><br><br>Hosea<br>Joel<br>Amos<br>Obadiah<br>Jonah<br>Micah<br>Nahum<br>Habakkuk<br>Zephaniah<br>Haggai<br>Zechariah<br>Malachi |
| THE WRITINGS (HAGIOGRAPHA) | Praises<br>Job<br>Proverbs<br>Ruth<br>Song of Songs<br>The Preacher<br>How!<br>Esther<br>Daniel<br>Ezra<br>Nehemiah<br>1 The words of the days<br>2 The words of the days | Psalms<br>Job<br>Proverbs<br>Ruth<br>Song of Solomon<br>Ecclesiastes<br>Lamentations<br>Esther<br>Daniel<br>Ezra<br>Nehemiah<br>1 Chronicles<br>2 Chronicles |

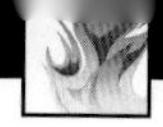

Jewish assessment of the canon by quoting from all three divisions of the OT. Furthermore, He demonstrated that the OT included many prophecies and veiled allusions to Himself, the Messiah. Thus, Christians learned to read the Jewish holy books with a view to seeing Jesus in them. In fact, for the first few decades of the church, the majority of Christians had little access to the New Testament (NT) writings that were starting to emerge. The OT was the only Bible many of them knew, and they valued it greatly as they read it from a Christ-centered vantage point. Interestingly, they tended to hold the Apocrypha in high esteem as well—higher than most Jews did, in fact. A little background information helps us understand how this situation arose.

Several centuries before Christ the Jews living in Alexandria commissioned a Greek translation of the Hebrew OT. They did this because they increasingly spoke and read Greek rather than Hebrew. Known as the Septuagint, this Greek translation was the Bible of choice for many Jews and early Christians. In addition to the authoritative Holy Scriptures, the Septuagint included Greek translations of some key Jewish apocryphal books. The reason they were added is clear: Jews living in predominantly Greek-speaking areas wanted access to all the important Jewish writings, both canonical and noncanonical. As the early church grew and experienced ever greater tensions with traditional Judaism, Christian and non-Christian Jewish communities were increasingly isolated from one another socially and religiously. For this reason the Jewish assessment that the Apocrypha was noncanonical was perhaps somewhat lost on many Christians as they picked up the Septuagint and noted that the books of the Apocrypha were included along with the canonical OT books. This is an important fact because Greek was the dominant language of the early church, which means few Christians gave close attention to the Hebrew OT. Thus, every time they took up the OT, they took it up in its Greek version, and in doing this they took up the Apocrypha as well. Additionally, early Christians noted that the NT authors most often quoted from the Septuagint, not the Hebrew OT. Finally, many Christians had high regard for the Apocrypha because its books were deemed useful for kindling religious affections. In summary, the early church automatically adopted the Jewish OT canon, most often read the Septuagint version of the OT rather than the Hebrew, and held the Apocrypha to be valuable.

Does this mean the early church took the Apocrypha to be on par with the canonical books? It is best to start by taking note of the NT approach. Jesus *never* quoted any of the books of the Apocrypha, and neither did His disciples in their writings. While Jude 9 apparently alludes to an event described in a minor noncanonical book, nowhere in the entire NT is any book of the Apocrypha cited. Given the fact that neither Jesus nor His apostles quoted from the Apocrypha, it would be remarkable if early Christians trumped their example and counted these books as Scripture. Nevertheless, the early church developed a custom of giving the

Apocrypha a place in religious life, and admittedly some misinformed leaders through the early centuries seemed to think of the Apocrypha as Scripture. The two chief causes of this misidentification are that the books were included in the beloved Septuagint and that they were thought to be genuinely conducive to religious devotions. For such reasons as these, the Apocrypha maintained a steady but unofficial presence in the church for well over a millennium.

Even the early Reformers included the Apocrypha in their English and German translations of the Bible, though they set it off in sections that were separate from the canonical OT books and introduced it with a note saying that throughout church history the Apocrypha had not been received as Scripture. Thus the Reformers initially kept alive the old tradition of packing the Apocrypha into the Bible, though as in a seatless balcony reserved for bystanders. As they continued to debate Roman Catholic leaders over the proper bases for doctrinal formation, the Reformers eventually concluded that for the sake of clarity the Apocrypha should be dropped altogether from the Bible. As inheritors of the Reformation movement, Protestant Bibles today exclude the Apocrypha, signifying that while those books may be useful, they are nonbiblical.

## CONCLUSION

We have solid reasons for believing that the OT books include only true history and that they were written by men who were appointed by God to deliver Spirit-inspired writings to humanity. Further, the Jews of old clearly received these books with awe and a sense of responsibility. Hence, the sacred books were identified, collected, preserved, and transmitted through the generations by men approved for such high tasks. The 39 books of the Protestant OT are assuredly the books God would have us venerate as scriptural. The books of the Apocrypha are valuable (indeed, more valuable than most Protestants realize) but should be consulted for their historical value and not for instruction in doctrine or religious practice.

## THE APOCRYPHA

| TITLES (listed alphabetically) | APPROX-IMATE DATES | LITERARY TYPES | THEMES | IN SEPTUAGINT? | IN ROMAN CATHOLIC CANON? |
|---|---|---|---|---|---|
| Baruch | 150–60 BC (composite) | Wisdom & narrative promise of hope, opposition to idolatry | Praise of wisdom, law | Yes | Yes |
| Bel and the Dragon | 100 BC | Detective narrative at end of Daniel | Opposition to idolatry | Yes | Yes |
| Ecclesiasticus (Wisdom of Jesus Sirach) | 180 BC in Hebrew; 132 BC Greek Translation | Wisdom | Obedience to law; praise of patriarchs; value of wisdom; patriotism; temple worship; retribution; free will | Yes | Yes |
| I Esdras | 150 | History (621–458 BC) | Proper worship; power of truth | Yes | No |
| 2 Esdras | AD 100 | Apocalypse with Christian preface & epilogue | Preexistent, dying Messiah: punishment for sin; salvation in future; inspiration; divine justice; evil | No | No |
| Additions to Esther (103 verses) | 114 BC | Religious amplification | Prayer; worship; revelation; God's activity; providence | Yes | Yes |
| Letter of Jeremiah | 317 BC | Homily added to Baruch based on Jer. 29 | Condemn idolatry | Yes | Yes |
| Judith | 200–100 BC | Historical novel | Obedience to law; prayer; fasting; true worship; patriotism | Yes | Yes |
| 1 Maccabees | 90 BC | History (180–134 BC) | God works in normal human events; legitimate Hasmonean kings | Yes | Yes |
| 2 Maccabees | 90 BC | History (180–161 BC) | Resurrection; creation from nothing; miracles; punishment for sin; martyrdom; temple angels | Yes | Yes |
| 3 Maccabees | 75 BC | Festival legend | Deliverance of faithful; angels | Some mss. | No |
| 4 Maccabees | 10 BC; AD 20–54 | Philosophical treatise based on 2 Macc. 6–7 | Power of reason over emotions; faithfulness to law; martyrdom; immortality | Some mss. | No |
| Prayer of Azariah and Song of Three Young Men | 100 BC | Liturgy; hymn & additions to Dan. 3:23 | Praise; God's response to prayer | Yes | Yes |
| Prayer of Manasseh | 200–201 BC | Prayer of penitence based on 2 Kings 21:10-17 2 Chron. 33:11-19 | Prayer of repentance | Yes | No |
| Psalm 151 | ? | Victory hymn | Praise to God who uses young & inexperienced | Yes | No |
| Susanna | 100 BC | Detective story at end of Daniel | Daniel's wisdom; God's vindication of faithfulness | Yes | Yes |
| Tobit | 200–100 BC | Folktale | Temple attendance; tithing; charity; prayer; obedience to Jewish law; guardian angel; divine justice and retribution; personal devotion | Yes | Yes |
| Wisdom of Solomon | 10 BC in Egypt | Wisdom personified; Jewish apologetic | Value of wisdom and faithfulness, immortality | Yes | Yes |

The English title is based on the name given by the Greek translators of this book in the second century BC. The name could be translated "source" or "generation." The original Hebrew title is simply the first word of the book, *Bereshith*, "In the beginning."

## KEY TEXTS: 1:1 AND 12:3

*"In the beginning God created the heavens and the earth."*

*"I will bless those who bless you, I will curse those who treat you with contempt, and all the peoples on earth will be blessed through you."*

## KEY TERM: "BEGINNING"

This book tells the beginning of many things: the creation of the world, the origin of the human race and marriage, the rise of sin and death. The book also shows the beginning of God's glorious plan to build a kingdom of redeemed people.

## ONE-SENTENCE SUMMARY

The God who created mankind and punished disobedience with death began His great plan of redemption with His covenant to Abraham, whose descendants arrived in Egypt as God's cherished people.

Maffei 2 Spiral Galaxy.

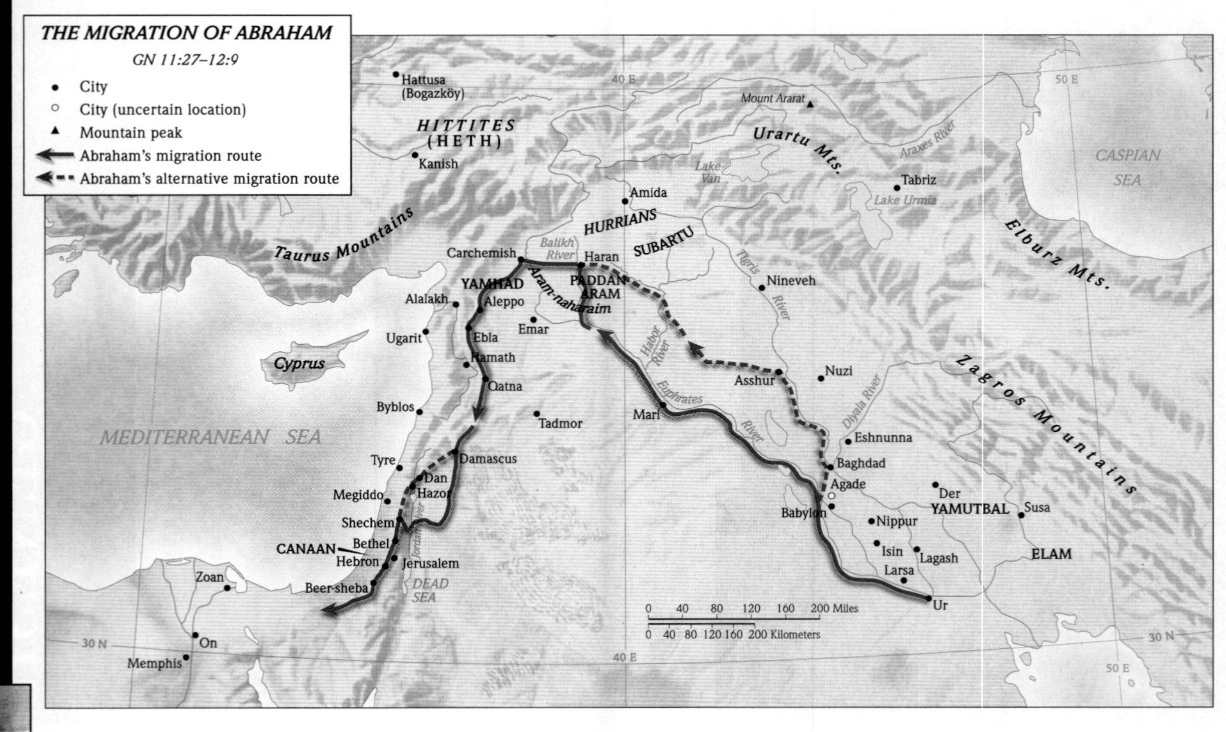
THE MIGRATION OF ABRAHAM
GN 11:27–12:9
City
City (uncertain location)
Mountain peak
Abraham's migration route
Abraham's alternative migration route
Hattusa (Bogazköy)
Kanish
HITTITES (HETH)
Taurus Mountains
Cyprus
MEDITERRANEAN SEA
Ugarit
Alalakh
Carchemish
YAMHAD
Aleppo
Ebla
Hamath
Qatna
Byblos
Tyre
Damascus
Dan
Hazor
Megiddo
Shechem
Bethel
CANAAN
Hebron
Jerusalem
Jordan River
Beer-sheba
DEAD SEA
Zoan
On
Memphis
Emar
Tadmor
Balikh River
Haran
PADDAN-ARAM
Aram-naharaim
HURRIANS
SUBARTU
Amida
Habor River
Mari
Euphrates River
Asshur
Tigris River
Nineveh
Lake Van
Mount Ararat
Urartu Mts.
Araxes River
Lake Urmia
Tabriz
CASPIAN SEA
Elburz Mts.
Zagros Mountains
Nuzi
Diyala River
Eshnunna
Baghdad
Agade
Babylon
Der
YAMUTBAL
Susa
Nippur
Isin
Lagash
Larsa
ELAM
Ur
0 40 80 120 160 200 Miles
0 40 80 120 160 200 Kilometers
30 N
40 E
50 E

## AUTHOR AND DATE OF WRITING

**Moses, Perhaps Around 1445 BC**

Although Genesis was written by an anonymous author, its integral part in the Pentateuch (Genesis–Deuteronomy) suggests that the author was the same person who wrote the other four books. Internal evidence in the five books reveals their common plot, common theme (divine promises), central figure (Moses), and specific literary interconnections. Jewish and Christian traditions attribute the Pentateuch to Moses, whose life paralleled the events of Exodus–Deuteronomy (e.g., 2 Ch 23:18; Lk 16:29,31; Ac 28:23).

## FIRST AUDIENCE AND DESTINATION

**The Israelites at Mount Sinai**

The original hearers and destination are not stated but believed to be the Israelite nation in the wilderness on their way to Canaan.

## OCCASION

Genesis sets the birth of Israel at Sinai in the context of both family history (Gn 12–50) and cosmic history (Gn 1–11). As such it enabled this people to understand who they were and Whose they were. Knowing was vital to their fulfilling the purpose for which God had called them.

Reconstruction of the Great Ziggurat of Ur based on a drawing by Leonard Wooley. The ziggurat was built close to the time Abraham lived. It served as both an administrative center for Ur and as a shrine to the moon god Nanna. God called Abraham to leave this polytheistic context and come to a land God would show him.

## PURPOSE

Genesis lays the historical and theological foundation for the rest of the Bible. If the Bible is the story of God's redemption of His people, Genesis 1–11 tells why redemption is necessary: humans are rebels, unable to redeem themselves. Further, Genesis 12–50 shows the steps God initiated to establish a redeemed people and to make a way for the Redeemer to come. He did this through His unconditional covenant with Abraham, Isaac, and Jacob and with His providential care through Joseph's life. God's people who study Genesis today should view it with this original purpose in mind.

## FIRST PASS

**God, the Creator**

God is the central character of Genesis. He is sovereign Lord and Creator of all things. Genesis assumes the fact of divine creation but does not try to prove it (1:1–2:3). Genesis does not specify when creation occurred or exactly how long it took. Genesis eloquently teaches that God created all things, including Adam and Eve, by special creation for fellowship with Himself.

**Sin and Its Consequences**

Adam and Eve were created innocent and with a capacity to choose. Freely they chose to disobey God, fell from innocence, and lost their freedom (3:1–24). The freedom of human beings is limited by fallen human nature. Death came because of sin and humanity was so corrupt that God wiped them out in a great flood and started over with Noah and his family (6:1–9:17). The second humanity also proved corrupt, and God confused their languages and scattered them (11:1–9).

**God Calls a Man, a Family, a Nation**

God's plan of redemption began to unfold by His calling one man to establish a family, one family chosen from among all the families of the earth (12:1–3). That family would be God's instrument of blessing and salvation for all peoples. Through each generation in Genesis, God demonstrated that the promise depended only on His sovereign power and that no circumstance, person, family, or nation could thwart His purposes (11:27–50:26). Human sin could not destroy God's plan but rather provided Him opportunity to demonstrate His glory. Joseph may lie dead in a casket in Egypt, but his dying command was that his bones be carried home to Canaan when, not if, God brought His people again into the land He promised Abraham, Isaac, and Jacob (50:25).

## THE RELIABILITY OF GENESIS

Since the events of Genesis preceded Moses, this raises the question of where he got his information. Prior to the nineteenth century, the principal explanation was

divine revelation coupled with the availability of written records, such as genealogies and stories.

By the nineteenth century a new consensus arose among "critical" scholars that became the starting point of all future study. They understood that the Pentateuch was the product of a series of unnamed Jewish editors who progressively stitched together pieces of preexisting sources dating from the tenth to the sixth centuries BC. Instead of being "Mosaic," the Pentateuch was viewed as a "mosaic." Such scholars today often view the stories as simple fabrications conceived hundreds of years after the supposed events, perhaps during the exile.

There is significant evidence, however, that Genesis reflects the political and cultural setting of the second millennium, the era in which Abraham and his heirs lived. The structure and contents of chapters 1–11 generally parallel the Babylonian epic *Atrahasis* (c. 1600 BC). Social and religious practices among the patriarchs correlate better in the earlier period than the first millennium. For example, Abraham's marriage to his half-sister Sarah was prohibited under the Mosaic law (20:12; Lv 18:9). It's unlikely that the Jews of the exilic period would fabricate offensive events or preserve such stories unless they were already well-entrenched traditions. Also, the prevalent use of the *El* compounds for the name of God (e.g., *El Shaddai* = God Almighty, 17:1) in Genesis contrasts with their virtual absence in first millennium texts. The tolerant attitude toward Gentiles and the unrestricted travels of the patriarchs do not suit the later setting. The evidence, when considered as a whole, supports the position that Genesis presents authentic events.

A reproduction of tablet eleven of the Epic of Gilgamesh, a Babylonian account of the great flood.

The parallels between chapters 1–11 and creation and flood myths have elicited the question, Is the Bible merely a Hebrew version of myths about beginnings? When weighing the importance of parallels, three general principles should be kept in mind. First, not all parallels are equally significant. Second, the identity of who is borrowing from whom cannot be definitively concluded. Third, the functions of the stories are much different. For example, the flood story of the Babylonian Gilgamesh Epic is incidental to the main idea of telling how Gilgamesh sought immortality. In the Bible the flood narrative is central to the development of the theme. That the Bible's theology is divergent from the polytheism of antiquity argues against dependence. The author of Genesis was aware of the cultural milieu of the nations and often crafted his accounts to counter the prevailing view. The historical framework of chapters 1–11 (e.g., "these are the records of," 2:4; 5:1) and the genealogies (chaps. 4–5; 10–11) indicate that the author presented a historical account, not a literary myth.

## HOW GENESIS FITS INTO GOD'S STORY

1. Prologue: Creation, Fall, and the Need for Redemption
2. God Builds His Nation (2000–931 BC)
3. God Educates His Nation (931–586 BC)
4. God Keeps a Faithful Remnant (586–6 BC)
5. God Purchases Redemption and Begins the Kingdom (6 BC to AD 30)
6. God Spreads the Kingdom Through the Church (AD 30-?)
7. God Consummates Redemption and Confirms His Eternal Kingdom
8. Epilogue: New Heaven and New Earth

## CHRIST IN GENESIS

Creation is the first theme of Genesis, and Christ is the agent of creation. "For everything was created by Him" (Col 1:16). Christ as Redeemer is first promised in Genesis 3:15. When God commanded Abraham to offer Isaac as a sacrifice, He provided a substitute for Isaac (Gn 22:8) in the same way He provided Christ as our substitute through His sacrificial death. Through Abraham's seed, Jesus Christ, all peoples of the earth will be blessed.

## CHRISTIAN WORLDVIEW ELEMENTS

### Teachings About God

Genesis reveals God first as Creator. He is righteous in His commands, and He judges when mankind disobeys Him. Genesis further reveals God as the One who

makes His covenant with undeserving people (see Gn 15:1–6). The first promise of Christ is given in Genesis 3:15; the Spirit of God is mentioned in Genesis 1:2 and 6:3.

### Teachings About Humanity

Genesis shows the glory of humanity by emphasizing that mankind alone of all creation was made in "the image of God." On the other hand Genesis shows the shame of humanity by recounting three incidents involving the whole race: the fall, the flood, and Babel. All three events portray humans as sinners in need of a Savior.

### Teachings About Salvation

Genesis introduces critical truths about salvation developed in later parts of Scripture. In particular, the incident of the death of a ram instead of Isaac points to a substitutionary understanding of sacrifice. Further, the New Testament makes much of Abraham as a pattern of salvation for all the redeemed: "Abram believed the LORD, and He credited it to him as righteousness" (Gn 15:6).

## GENRE AND LITERARY STYLE

### A Historical Narrative Written in Excellent Hebrew

Although Genesis was "The First Book of the Law," it recorded relatively few divine commands (but see 2:16–27; 9:6–7). Genesis has preserved two historical narratives. Chapters 1–11 contain a selective history of the entire human race. Chapters 12–50 tell the story of the direct ancestors of the Israelites. Genesis also contains a few passages of poetry (see 3:14–19) and important genealogies (see chap. 5). The Hebrew style of Genesis is like that of the rest of the Pentateuch. The writer composed his account carefully.

## A PRINCIPLE TO LIVE BY

### God's Mercy (Gn 11:27–12:3, *Life Essentials Study Bible*, p. 17–18)

Since God reached out to us before we reached out to Him, we should always thank Him for saving us by His sovereign grace.

To access a video presentation of this principle featuring Dr. Gene Getz, use a Smartphone or iPad to connect to this QR code or go to http://www.bhpublishinggroup.com/handbook/genesis

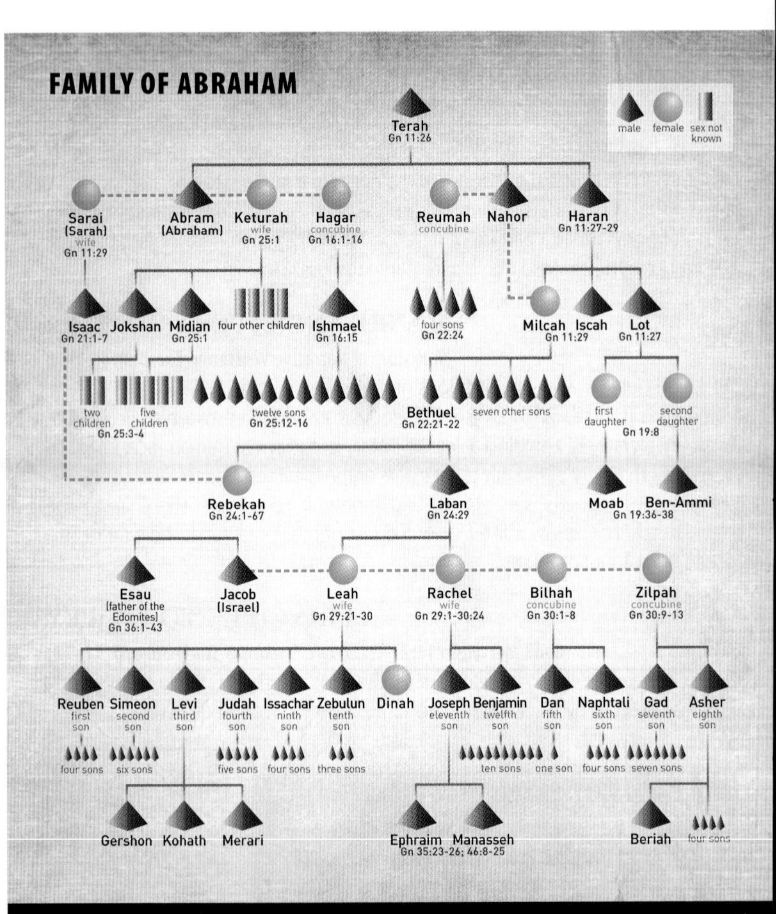


God promised Abraham an heir when he was 75 and Sarah, his wife, was 10 years younger. The child, Isaac, was born 25 years later (Gn 12:2; 17:1,17,21; 21:5).

In the Hebrew text, the book's first two words are its title, *We'elleh Shemot*, "These are the names." The English title is the name first used by the book's Greek translators (second century BC). "Exodus" could be rendered "going out" or "departure."

## KEY TEXTS: 14:30-31

*"That day the LORD saved Israel from the power of the Egyptians, and Israel saw the Egyptians dead on the seashore. When Israel saw the great power that the LORD used against the Egyptians, the people feared the LORD and believed in Him and in His servant Moses."*

## KEY TERM: "REDEEM"

Exodus shows how the Lord for His name's sake redeemed His people Israel by buying them out of slavery through payment of a price, the death of the Passover lambs (see 6:6). Further, it records God's commands to those redeemed people.

## ONE-SENTENCE SUMMARY

When God redeemed His chosen people Israel through His servant Moses, He entered a covenant relationship with them and instituted His dwelling with them, the tabernacle.

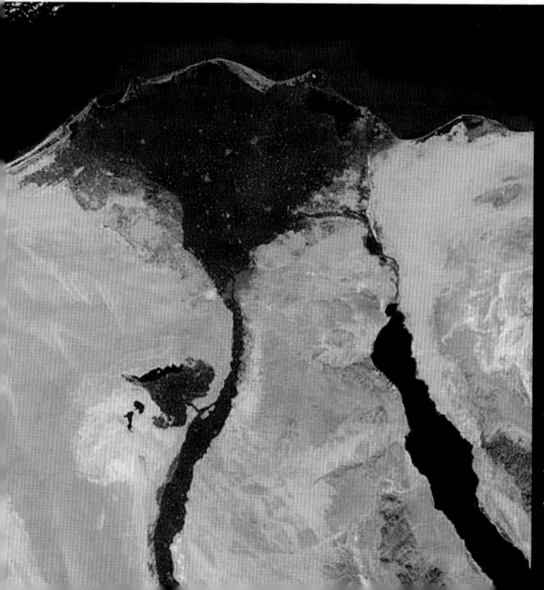

This NASA satellite photo shows in dramatic fashion the Nile as the basis of Egypt's life and wealth. The Nile is the only river to flow northwards across the Sahara. Egypt was unique as an agricultural community in not being dependent on rainfall. The secret was the black silt deposited on the fields by an annual flood caused when the Blue Nile was swollen by the runoff from winter rains in Ethiopia. God's people came to Egypt as a family (Gn 41–50) and left as a nation (Ex 13:17–14:31).

## AUTHOR AND DATE OF WRITING

**Moses, Perhaps Around 1445 BC**

The book is anonymous. Because Moses is the central character, however, everything in the book is compatible with the traditional belief that he was its author. The book refers to Moses as physically writing down some of God's commands (24:4; see also 34:28). Scholars who accept the testimony of Scripture at face value continue to affirm that Moses wrote Exodus. Assuming an early date for the exodus and that Moses wrote while Israel camped at Mount Sinai, this book was written in the middle of the fifteenth century BC.

## FIRST AUDIENCE AND DESTINATION

**The Israelite People at Mount Sinai**

The original hearers were the children of Israel living in the wilderness on their way to the Promised Land.

## OCCASION

Although the book does not say so, the need for Israel to have a permanent historical record of the events that brought it into existence as a nation surely is what prompted the composition. If one believes that Moses received the Ten Commandments by divine revelation, then one can just as readily believe that God also prompted him to write down everything recorded in Exodus.

# GOD'S MESSAGE IN EXODUS

## PURPOSE

Exodus serves two broad purposes. First, it narrates God's greatest redemptive act of the Old Testament, Israel's exodus from Egypt. The life and travels of Moses provide the organizing principle for the book. The action occurs wherever Moses is present. The first half is mainly narrative, chapters 1–18 (Israel's deliverance from Egypt and journey to Sinai) as is the last fourth, chapters 32–40 (Israel's violation of the covenant, the restoration, and the building of the tabernacle). Sandwiched between the historical sections are law chapters 19–24 (the covenant at Sinai) and 25–31 (rules concerning the tabernacle and the priesthood). If the overall Bible tells the story of God's kingdom, then Exodus tells how the first phase of that kingdom came into being by God's mighty power. God's people who read and study Exodus today should also view it in light of the ultimate Redeemer, who purchased people by His own death (John 1:29).

## FIRST PASS

### The Plight of Israel

Exodus builds on the narrative of creation, human sin, divine punishment and renewal, the call of Abraham to bless the world, and the struggles of Isaac and then Jacob to carry out God's call. This struggle ends with Joseph taking his father's family into Egypt to avoid the harsh sufferings of famine. Exodus takes up the story of the children of Jacob in Egypt, now under a new pharaoh and seen as feared foreigners instead of welcomed deliverers from famine. Israel thus became slave laborers in Egypt (chap. 1).

### God Raises Up a Deliverer

God's saving presence is clear in the early life of Moses, the human agent of God's deliverance. Moses' Levite parents saved him from a cruel death by hiding him in a basket in the Nile (2:1–10). Rescued by Pharaoh's daughter, Moses was reared by his mother, who introduced him to the God of Israel. Though Moses enjoyed the privileges of the Egyptian court, he never forgot his Israelite heritage. Trying to protect a Hebrew, Moses killed an Egyptian. As a result, he had to flee to the wilderness of Midian where he helped seven endangered shepherd girls. He settled among their family and married one of the girls. One day as Moses was shepherding his father-in-law's sheep, God called him at a burning bush near Mount Horeb and sent him back to rescue Israel from Egypt (chaps. 2–4). God's revelation of Himself to Moses as the LORD (Yahweh) stands as one of the most profound passages in all Scripture.

### Confronting Pharaoh

With his brother Aaron, Moses faced a stubborn pharaoh, who refused to release the Israelites. When Pharaoh made life harder for Israel, the Israelites complained about Moses. God took this as opportunity to reveal Himself to Israel, to Pharaoh, and to the Egyptians. God brought 10 plagues on Egypt. Pharaoh stubbornly refused to let Israel go until his firstborn son and the eldest sons of all Egypt died in the final plague. This tenth plague became the setting for Passover, the first of Israel's three annual festivals, that celebrated the exodus from Egypt and rejoiced at God's supreme act of salvation for His people (chaps. 5–13).

### Deliverance

As Israel fled Egypt, Pharaoh again resisted and led his army after them. The miracle of the Red Sea (or perhaps more literally, the Sea of Reeds) became the greatest moment in Israel's history, the moment God created a nation for Himself by delivering them from the strongest military power on earth. God led Israel through the divided waters of the sea and then flooded the sea again as the Egyptians tried to follow (chap. 14).

### Grumbling

After celebrating the deliverance in song and dance (15:1–21), Israel followed God's leadership into the wilderness, but soon the difficult wilderness life proved too hard.

The Israelites cried for the good old days of Egypt, even after God supplied their food and drink and after He defeated the Amalekites (15:22–17:15). Moses' father-in-law Jethro brought Moses' wife and children back to him in the wilderness and praised God for all that He had done for Moses and the people. Jethro also advised Moses how to organize a more efficient judicial system, relieving Moses of stress (chap. 18).

**Sinai**

Then Israel came to Sinai, where God called them to become His covenant people, a holy nation to carry out Abraham's mission of receiving God's blessing and passing that blessing on to the nations. God gave the Ten Commandments and other laws central to the covenant (chaps. 19–23) and then confirmed the covenant in a mysterious ceremony (chap. 24). Moses went to the top of the mountain to receive the remainder of God's instructions, especially instructions for building the sacred place of worship, the tabernacle (chaps. 24–31). The Sinaitic covenant was a "suzerain-vassal" covenant in which the master (suzerain) promised to protect and bless the subjects (vassals) as long as they obeyed and submitted to him. This contrasted with the "royal grant" unconditional covenant, such as the one in which God categorically promised to make Abraham into a worldwide blessing (Gn 12; 15).

**Intercession for a Rebellious People**

Even before Moses could descend from the mountain with the tables of stone and other covenant texts, the people, with Aaron's consent, violated the covenant terms by casting an idol of gold and bowing down to it. This act of apostasy brought God's judgment and even a threat of annihilation. Only Moses' intercession prevented the annulment of the covenant with the larger community. The Lord was attentive to Moses' cry and did not utterly destroy the idolaters immediately. God did renew His promise to bring His people into the land of promise. Yahweh, however, declared that He could not go with Israel lest He destroy the stubborn, rebellious people. Twice Moses interceded with God on behalf of rebellious Israel. Yahweh twice revealed Himself to Moses as a God of mercy and compassion. God's mercy and compassion—not Israel's faithfulness—formed the basis for renewal of the broken covenant. Descending from the mountain with the tablets of the covenant, Moses appeared before his people, his face aglow with the reflection of the glory of God (chap. 34).

**God's Presence**

Moses then led Israel to celebrate the Sabbath and to build the tabernacle (chaps. 35–39). Moses set up the tabernacle and established worship in it. God blessed the action with His glorious presence (chap. 40). This provided the sign for Israel's future journeys, following God's cloud by day and by night (40:36–38).

## THE RELIABILITY OF EXODUS

The internal evidence suggests that Moses kept a record of Israel's experiences in the desert (Ex 17:14; 24:4,7; 34:27; Nm 33:1–2; Dt 31:9,11). Furthermore, many statements in the OT credit the Pentateuch to Moses (e.g., Jos 1:8; 8:31–32; 1 Kg 2:3; 2 Kg 14:6; Ezr 6:18; Neh 13:1; Dn 9:11–13; Mal 4:4), and the NT identifies the Torah closely with him (Mt 19:8; Jn 5:46–47; 7:19; Ac 3:22; Rm 10:5). A series of additional features within the text point to an early date for its composition: (1) the forms of the names and many of the actions of the patriarchs make best sense in a second millennium BC environment; (2) the narratives suggest a thorough acquaintance with Egypt; (3) Egyptian loanwords appear with greater frequency in the Pentateuch than anywhere else in the OT; (4) the name "Moses" itself suggests an Egyptian setting for the story; (5) the general viewpoint of the narrative is foreign to Canaan; (6) the seasons are Egyptian; the flora and fauna are Egyptian and Sinaitic; (7) in some instances the geography reflects a foreign viewpoint (e.g., Gn 33:18, "Shechem in

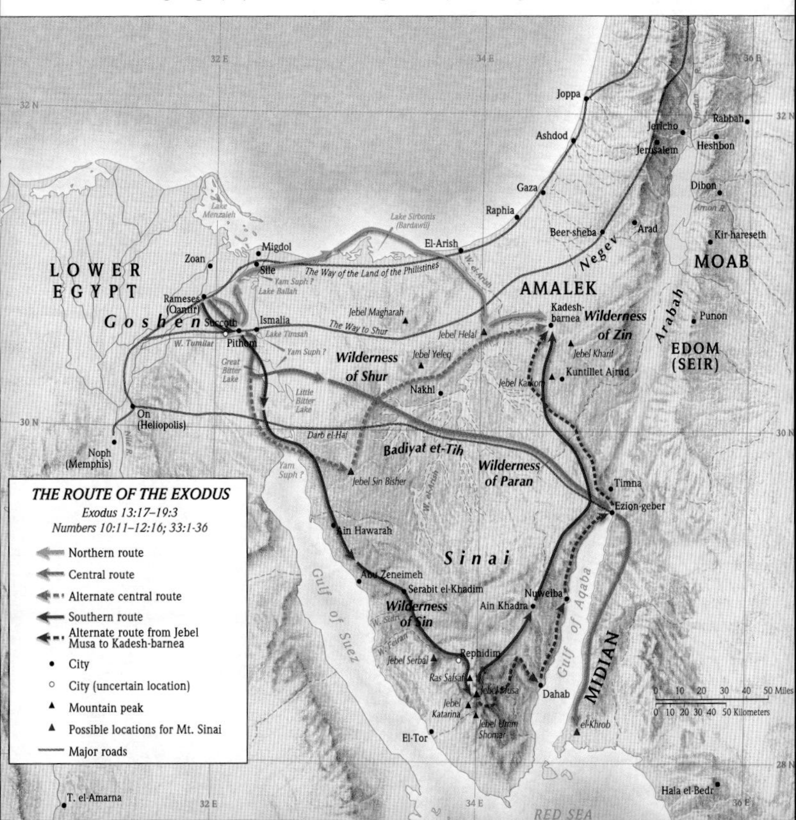

the land of Canaan," is unlikely after the exile because by then Israel had been in the land for 900 years); and (8) archaisms in the language (like the use of the third-person singular pronoun, *hi*, for both genders), all point to an early date.

There is no reason to doubt that Moses wrote down the speeches he delivered (Dt 31:9–13), or that when he came down from Mount Sinai, he arranged for the transcription of the revelation he had received on the mountain, if he did not write it all himself. Just as the pieces of the tabernacle were constructed and woven by skilled craftsmen and finally assembled by Moses (Ex 35–40), so literary craftsmen may have composed some bits and pieces of the Pentateuch, submitted them to Moses, who then approved them. When exactly the Holy Spirit guided an author to put together the pieces in their present form we may only speculate (Deuteronomy suggests sometime after the death of Moses), but it seems likely that by the time David organized temple worship, the contents of the Torah were fixed.

1. Prologue: Creation, Fall, and the Need for Redemption
2. God Builds His Nation (2000–931 BC)
3. God Educates His Nation (931–586 BC)
4. God Keeps a Faithful Remnant (586–6 BC)
5. God Purchases Redemption and Begins the Kingdom (6 BC to AD 30)
6. God Spreads the Kingdom Through the Church (AD 30-?)
7. God Consummates Redemption and Confirms His Eternal Kingdom
8. Epilogue: New Heaven and New Earth

## CHRIST IN EXODUS

Exodus is a book of redemption. God's freeing His people from Egyptian slavery is a picture of Christ's delivering sinners from their sin and its consequences. Christ was with Israel as the rock that followed them through their journey from slavery to the

Reconstruction of the tabernacle and its court (Ex 26:1–35). The tabernacle was always set up to face east. This view is from the northeast. The tabernacle was a sanctuary where Yahweh met His people. God told Moses on the Mount, "You must make it according to all that I show you---the pattern of the tabernacle as well as the pattern of all its furnishings" (Ex 25:9).

Promised Land (1 Co 10:4; Ex 17:6). The Passover lambs are a picture of Christ's death for sinners (Jn 1:29; 1:36) and His providing access to God.

## CHRISTIAN WORLDVIEW ELEMENTS

### Teachings About God

Exodus reveals the Lord as Redeemer. Because of His love and for His name's sake, He takes the initiative to save His people from bondage. Exodus further reveals Him as the one who expects His redeemed people to live according to the provisions of the covenant made at Sinai. Christ is prefigured both by Moses and by the Passover lambs. Exodus 31:3; 35:31 mention the Spirit as empowering a person for special service.

### Teachings About Humanity

Exodus highlights the universality of human evil by showing rebellion against God in a variety of ways. Pharaoh's wickedness (chaps. 4–14) and redeemed Israel's shameful idolatry in the golden calf incident (chap. 32) are perhaps the clearest examples. On the other hand, Exodus shows the great value God puts on humanity through the high price paid at the time of Israel's deliverance from Egypt.

### Teachings About Salvation

Until Christ's coming and His death on the cross, the exodus was the greatest divine redemptive act. In the exodus God provided a clear picture of substitutionary atonement in the Passover lamb's death: "When I see the blood, I will pass over you" (12:13). This, however, only prefigured the coming One, "the Lamb of God who takes away the sin of the world!" (Jn 1:29).

## GENRE AND LITERARY STYLE

Although Exodus was "the second book of the Law," it preserved more historical narrative than law. Chapter 15, "The Song of Moses," is poetry rather than prose and the first extensive poetry in Scripture. The Hebrew style of Exodus is like that of the rest of the Pentateuch.

## A PRINCIPLE TO LIVE BY

### Christ, the Passover Lamb (Ex 12:21–22, *Life Essentials Study Bible*, p. 92)

To inherit eternal life, we must receive the Lord Jesus Christ as our personal Savior and experience the redemption that comes through His shed blood.

To access a video presentation of this principle featuring Dr. Gene Getz, use a Smartphone or iPad to connect to this QR code or go to http://www.bhpublishinggroup.com/handbook/exodus

The English title is based on the name given by the Greek translators of this book in the second century BC. The name could be translated "pertaining to Levites." The original Hebrew title is the first word of the book, *Wayyiqra'*, "and He called."

## KEY TEXT: 11:45

*"For I am Yahweh, who brought you up from the land of Egypt to be your God, so you must be holy because I am holy."*

## KEY TERM: "HOLINESS"

Holiness throughout Scripture, but especially in Leviticus, is first an attribute of God. It refers to His glorious moral perfections as the One who is the standard of ethical purity. Second, holiness is commanded by God to His redeemed people. This holiness includes both moral living (submitting gladly to God's laws) and being separated from common use (intentionally set apart to God and His service).

## ONE-SENTENCE SUMMARY

God forgives sin and makes people holy through blood sacrifice; further, He then expects His people to live in fellowship with Him by following His regulations concerning separated living.

# ORIGINAL HISTORICAL SETTING

## AUTHOR AND DATE OF WRITING

**Moses, Around 1445 BC**

From both literary and theological perspectives, the connection between Exodus and Leviticus is seamless. Exodus closes on the first day of the first month of the second year. Numbers begins on the first day of the second month of the second year. In the intervening month, Yahweh gives Moses instruction that constitutes most of Leviticus. Over 30 times Yahweh speaks directly to Moses. Assuming an early date for the exodus and that Moses wrote while Israel camped at Mount Sinai, this book was written in the middle of the fifteenth century.

## FIRST AUDIENCE AND DESTINATION

**The Israelite People at Mount Sinai**

The first hearers were the Israelites camped around Mount Sinai.

## OCCASION

Apparently what prompted Leviticus to be written was the need to preserve permanently for Israel the oral commands God gave Moses. Even the brief narrative sections deal with the application of God's laws concerning the priesthood.

| SACRIFICIAL SYSTEM | | | |
|---|---|---|---|
| **NAME** | **REFERENCE** | **ELEMENTS** | **SIGNIFICANCE** |
| Burnt Offering | Lv 1; 6:8–13 | Bull, ram, male goat, male dove, or young pigeon without blemish. (Always male animals, but species of animal varied according to individual's economic status.) | Voluntary. Signifies propitiation for sin and complete surrender, devotion, and commitment to God. |
| Grain Offering. Also called Meal or Tribute Offering | Lv 2; 6:14–23 | Grain, flour, or bread (always unleavened) made with olive oil and salt; or incense. | Voluntary. Signifies thanksgiving for firstfruits. |
| Fellowship Offering. Also called Peace Offering, which includes: (1) Thank Offering, (2) Vow Offering, and (3) Freewill Offering | (1) Lv 3; 7:11–36; 22:17–30; 27 | Any animal without blemish. (Species of animal varied according to individual's economic status.) (1) Can be grain offering. | Voluntary. Symbolizes fellowship with God. (1) Signifies thankfulness for a specific blessing; (2) offers a ritual expression of a vow; and (3) symbolizes general thankfulness (to be brought to one of three required religious services). |
| Sin Offering | Lv 4:1–5:13; 6:24–30; 12:6–8 | Male or female animal without blemish—as follows: bull for high priest or congregation; male goat for king; female goat or lamb for common person; dove or pigeon for slightly poor; tenth of an ephah of flour for the very poor. | Mandatory. Made by one who had sinned unintentionally or was unclean in order to attain purification. |
| Guilt Offering | Lv 5:14–6:7; 7:1–6; 14:12–18 | Ram or lamb without blemish. | Mandatory. Made by a person who had either deprived another of his rights or had desecrated something holy. Made by lepers for purification. |

## PURPOSE

Leviticus was God's word to Israel to teach two essential truths about how a sinful people may sustain a right relationship with God who is holy. First, people enter a relationship with God based on forgiveness of sins, obtained by offering the right sacrifices the right way by the right priest. Second, forgiven people maintain fellowship with God by living according to His regulations. This means that His people are separate and therefore different from others. The specific laws in Leviticus are both precise and peculiar.

Of all the books of the Old Testament, Leviticus is the most challenging for Christians to apply. First, the New Testament, especially Hebrews, teaches that the right sacrifice offered the right way by the right priest has been truly fulfilled once and for all in Jesus. Second, the entire thrust of the New Testament is that fellowship with God is no longer based on *external* matters such as circumcision, keeping dietary laws, or following Israel's holy days. Today, fellowship with God and holy living are essentially *internal*. God's people who read and study Leviticus today should remember that its two essential principles are certainly still true but that God intended its particular rules to be in effect only until Christ came (Gl 4:24–25).

## FIRST PASS

### Need for Sacrifice

The first major section of Leviticus (chaps. 1–7) deals with the nature, purpose, and ritual of sacrifice. The summary statement that concludes this section sets the entire sacrificial system in the context of God's covenant with Israel at Mount Sinai. God freed Israel from Egyptian slavery so that they would be free to worship.

### Need for Mediators

Moses' role as mediator on behalf of rebellious Israel (Ex 32:30–32; 33:12–17; 34:8–9) points to the need for God-ordained mediators to continue his ministry of intercession throughout Israel's history. Exodus 28–29 specifies that these mediators will be the priests. The second major part of Leviticus—chapters 8–10—describes the establishment of the priesthood in answer to this need.

### Need for Separation

God had called Israel to be a people separated for service (Ex 19:5–6). Israel was, however, constantly tempted to conform to the standards of its neighbors in Egypt and Canaan (Lv 18:3). The laws of clean and unclean witness the "separateness" of Israel and remind God's people that there can be no compromise of His standards. The Lord had charged Aaron directly to distinguish between the holy and the profane (10:10). Leviticus 11–15 provides examples.

### Need for Atonement

The greatest act of purification—one involving the entire nation—was that achieved on the Day of Atonement. On this day the high priest first offered up sacrifice for himself. He then slaughtered one goat as a sin offering for all the people and expelled another goat (the scapegoat) from the camp as a symbol of the removal of sin from the community. Following a whole burnt offering, the camp was purified of the blood and animal remains by ceremonies of bathing and burning outside the camp. The writer of Hebrews developed images from the Day of Atonement to stress the superiority of Christ's priesthood (Hb 8:6; 9:7,11–26). Hebrews 13:11–12 uses the picture of the bull and goat burned outside the camp as an illustration of Christ's suffering outside the Jerusalem city walls.

### Need for Holy Living

The longest section of Leviticus (chaps. 17–25) is sometimes called the "Holiness Code" because it contains an exhaustive list of miscellaneous regulations pertaining to the acquisition and maintenance of holiness in Israel. The previous sections of Leviticus have been concerned primarily with holiness as "position." In chapters 17–25 (especially chap. 19) the focus shifts to holiness as moral condition.

### Blessing and Curse

The essentially covenantal nature of Leviticus is made crystal clear in the summary statement of 27:34, which sets the whole book in the context of the Sinai covenant. The lists of blessings and curses that make up Leviticus 26 reinforce this view of Leviticus as a covenantal text.

### Dedication Offerings

Leviticus closes with regulations concerning offerings of dedication (chap. 27). Placed here, these laws perhaps suggest appropriate ways to respond to the lifestyle choice posed by the blessing and curse.

## THE RELIABILITY OF LEVITICUS

The practice of slaying an animal for a sacrifice was not unique to the Israelite tradition. The slaughtering of an animal as a "religious" expression was a common practice in the ancient world, particularly in the ancient Near East. However, the purposes for offering sacrifices in Israel could not have been more different from the motivations for sacrifice among Israel's neighbors. Israel was worshipping an omnipotent, sovereign God and offering a blood sacrifice for sin that foreshadowed God's provision in the Messiah. The rationale for pagan sacrifices in the ancient world was confined to the maintenance and sustenance of the gods, as the gods were believed to have the same appetites and desires as humans. The motivation to present food to the god was to gain a god's favor. Pagan worship was self-serving at its core because the person presenting the offering was using the gift for his own advantage. The offering was actually a form of magic, a mechanism employed to effect a supernatural intervention. It is thus not surprising that in Mesopotamia, for example, the magician was as important as the priest. Adherence to the Old Testament sacrificial system made the nation of Israel a holy nation and distinct from other nations.

Plate of pure gold with inscription: "HOLY TO THE LORD." Ex 28:36

Turban or mitre Ex 28:36-38

The shoulder straps for the breastplate capped with two onyx stones bearing the names of Israel's twelve sons, six on each, in order of their birth Ex 28:9-10

Twelve gemstones, each bearing a name of one of the twelve tribes Ex 28:17-21

Sash Ex 28:4,39,40

Ephod, woven and reflecting the colors of the sanctuary Ex 28:5-15,31

Fringe composed of alternating pomegranates and gold bells; the pomegranates are woven from blue, purple, and scarlet yarn Ex 28:33-35

Artist's rendition of the high priest's garments (Ex 28:1–38; Lv 8:1–10:20).

## HOW LEVITICUS FITS INTO GOD'S STORY

1. Prologue: Creation, Fall, and the Need for Redemption
2. **God Builds His Nation (2000–931 BC)**
3. God Educates His Nation (931–586 BC)
4. God Keeps a Faithful Remnant (586–6 BC)
5. God Purchases Redemption and Begins the Kingdom (6 BC to AD 30)
6. God Spreads the Kingdom Through the Church (AD 30-?)
7. God Consummates Redemption and Confirms His Eternal Kingdom
8. Epilogue: New Heaven and New Earth

## CHRIST IN LEVITICUS

The specific sacrifices (for example, chap. 16) described in Leviticus suggest the multiple aspects of Christ's atoning sacrifice. The chapters on the priesthood (chaps. 21–22) foreshadow Christ's perfections as the ultimate high priest.

## CHRISTIAN WORLDVIEW ELEMENTS

### Teachings About God

Leviticus teaches that in His holiness God has the absolute right to instruct His people in what holiness demands, down to the minute details of life. Sinful people may approach Him for forgiveness only through the sacrifices He has ordained.

### Teachings About Humanity

God has made complete provision for forgiving the sins and failures of people, if only they make use of His means. Further, humans can enjoy full fellowship with God but only if they live according to the way He has revealed.

### Teachings About Salvation

"Blood" occurs more than 60 times in Leviticus. Readers are overwhelmed with the truth that in God's design blood outpoured through ritual sacrifice is the key to atoning for sins (17:11). This is critical for understanding the necessity of Christ's violent death as the atoning sacrifice for people's sins.

## GENRE AND LITERARY STYLE

### Ancient Laws, with a Little Narrative, Composed in Hebrew

The laws in Leviticus were stated in two forms. First was "command law" (or "apodictic law"), often introduced with the formula "you must . . ." (positive) or "you must not . . ." (negative). This parallels modern constitutional law or legislative acts. Second was "case law" (or "casuistic law"), often using the formula "if a man . . . ." These introduced examples or situations are parallel to modern verdicts of judges that then become the basis for later judicial rulings. The Hebrew in Leviticus is like that of the rest of the Pentateuch.

## JEWISH FEASTS AND FESTIVALS

| NAME | MONTH | DATE | REFERENCE | SIGNIFICANCE |
|---|---|---|---|---|
| Passover | Nisan | (Mar./Apr.): 14–21 | Ex 12:2–20; Lv 23:5 | Commemorates God's deliverance of Israel out of Egypt. |
| Festival of Unleavened Bread | Nisan | (Mar./Apr.): 15–21 | Lv 23:6–8 | Commemorates God's deliverance of Israel out of Egypt. Includes a Day of Firstfruits for the barley harvest. |
| Festival of Harvest, or Weeks (Pentecost) | Sivan | (May/June): 6 (seven weeks after Passover) | Ex 23:16; 34:22; Lv 23:15–21 | Commemorates the giving of the law at Mount Sinai. Includes a Day of Firstfruits for the wheat harvest. |
| Festival of Trumpets (Rosh Hashanah) | Tishri | (Sept./Oct.): 1 | Lv 23:23–25; Nm 29:1–6 | Day of the blowing of the trumpets to signal the beginning of the civil new year. |
| Day of Atonement (Yom Kippur) | Tishri | (Sept./Oct.): 10 | Ex 30:10; Lv 23:26–33; | On this day the high priest makes atonement for the nation's sin. Also a day of fasting. |
| Festival of Booths, or Tabernacles (Sukkot) | Tishri | (Sept./Oct.): 15–21 | Lv 23:33–43; Nm 29:12–39; Dt 16:13 | Commemorates the 40 years of wilderness wandering. |
| Festival of Dedication, or Festival of Lights (Hanukkah) | Kislev and Tebeth | (Nov./Dec.): 25–30; and Tebeth (Dec./Jan.): 1–2 | Jn 10:22 | Commemorates the purification of the temple by Judas Maccabaeus in 164 BC. |
| Feast of Purim, or Esther | Adar | (Feb./Mar.): 14 | Est 9 | Commemorates the deliverance of the Jewish people in the days of Esther. |

## A PRINCIPLE TO LIVE BY

**Living Holy Lives (Lv 19:2;20:7–8,26, *Life Essentials Study Bible*, p. 154–55)**

We are to reflect God's holiness in all relationships.

To access a video presentation of this principle featuring Dr. Gene Getz, use a Smartphone or iPad to connect to this QR code or go to http://www.bhpublishinggroup.com/handbook/leviticus

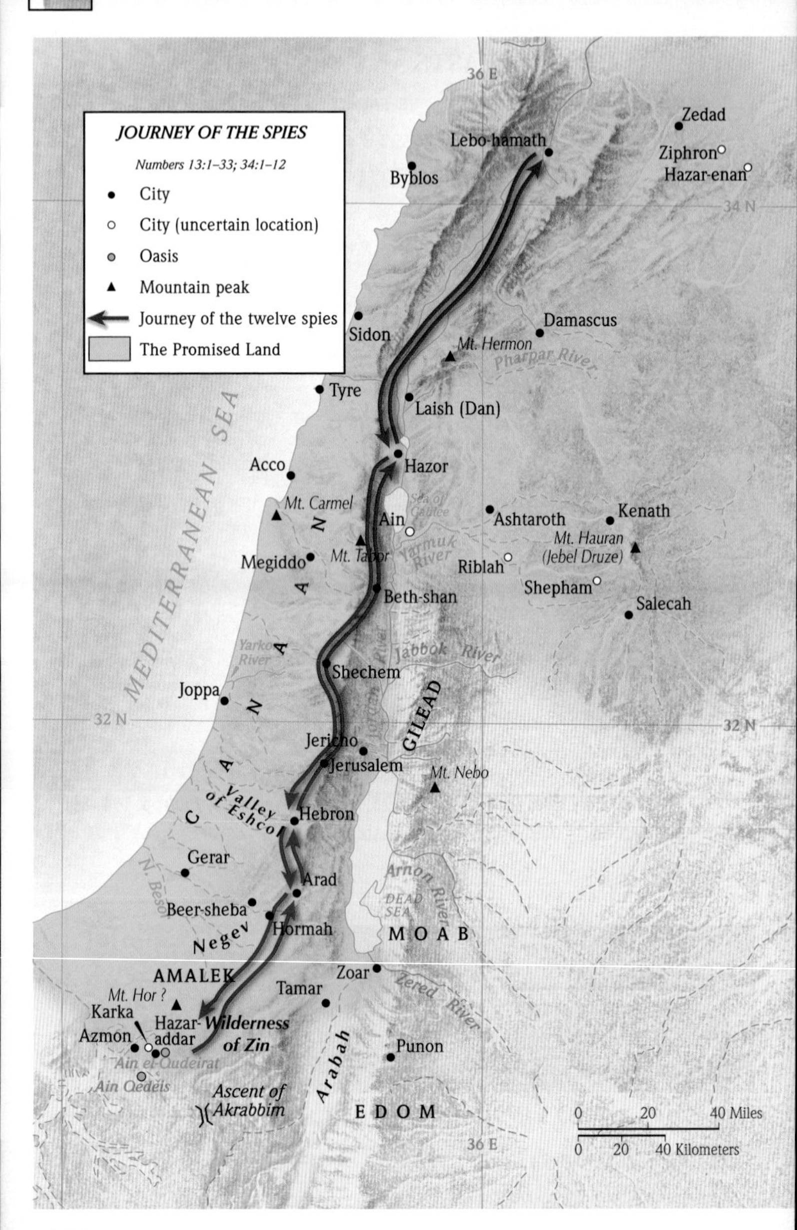
JOURNEY OF THE SPIES
Numbers 13:1–33; 34:1–12
City
City (uncertain location)
Oasis
Mountain peak
Journey of the twelve spies
The Promised Land
36 E
34 N
32 N
Zedad
Lebo-hamath
Ziphron
Hazar-enan
Byblos
Sidon
Damascus
Mt. Hermon
Pharpar River
Tyre
Laish (Dan)
MEDITERRANEAN SEA
Hazor
Acco
Mt. Carmel
Sea of Galilee
Ain
Ashtaroth
Kenath
Mt. Hauran (Jebel Druze)
Mt. Tabor
Yarmuk River
Megiddo
Riblah
Shepham
Beth-shan
Salecah
CANAAN
Yarkon River
Jabbok River
Shechem
Joppa
Jordan River
GILEAD
Jericho
Jerusalem
Mt. Nebo
Valley of Eshcol
Hebron
Gerar
N. Besor
Arad
Arnon River
DEAD SEA
Beer-sheba
Hormah
Negev
MOAB
Zoar
AMALEK
Tamar
Zered River
Mt. Hor ?
Karka
Hazar-addar
Wilderness of Zin
Azmon
Punon
Ain el-Qudeirat
Ain Qedeis
Ascent of Akrabbim
Arabah
EDOM
0 20 40 Miles
0 20 40 Kilometers

The English title is based on the lists of numbers in the book and is the name given by its Greek translators in the second century BC. The Hebrew title is more apt, *Bemidbar*, "in the wilderness," a word taken from the opening verse.

## KEY TEXT: 9:17

*"Whenever the cloud was lifted up above the tent, the Israelites would set out; at the place where the cloud stopped, there the Israelites camped."*

## KEY TERM: "WILDERNESS"

This book explains what happened to the Israelites during the 38 years they traveled through the wilderness from Mount Sinai to the border of Canaan. The term "wilderness" appears more than 40 times.

## ONE-SENTENCE SUMMARY

God used Moses to lead Israel from Sinai to Kadesh, but even after they rejected Him there, resulting in the wilderness years, He remained faithful to them and led a new generation to the edge of the Promised Land.

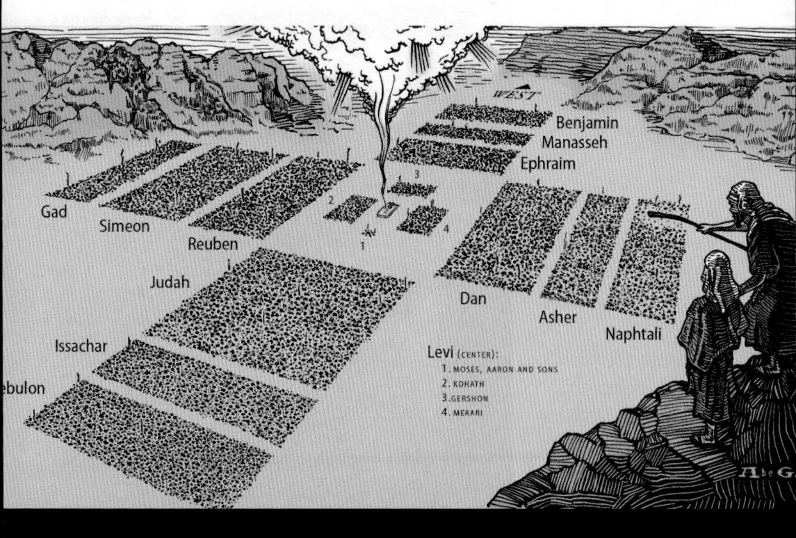


The Lord prescribed a specific arrangement for the Israelites to camp (Nm 2:1–34). "They camped by their banners in this way and moved out in the same way, each man by his clan and by his ancestral house" (v. 34).

## AUTHOR AND DATE OF WRITING

**Moses, About 1407 BC**

The book is anonymous, but like Exodus and Leviticus, Moses is the central human character. Further, 33:2 notes that Moses kept a journal of the Israelite travels. The exact words, "the LORD spoke to Moses," occur 31 times. There are many good reasons to affirm that Moses wrote Numbers.

The book may have been slightly edited after Moses' death. For example, 21:14–15 seems to insert a citation from an otherwise unknown "Book of the LORD's Wars." Further, many Bible students believe that if Moses himself penned comment about his meekness (12:3), it would disprove the point. Under divine inspiration the end product of Numbers is entirely true and exactly what God intended it to be.

## FIRST AUDIENCE AND DESTINATION

**The Israelite People, Camped at the Jordan River**

The original hearers and destination are not stated directly but were apparently the Israelite nation camped on the plains of Moab shortly before they crossed the Jordan River into the Promised Land.

## OCCASION

Although the book does not say so, Israel needed a permanent historical record of the events that shaped their national existence from the time of the covenant ratification at Sinai to the edge of the Promised Land. If one believes that Moses received the divine commands recorded in this book, then one can just as readily believe that God also prompted him to write down everything recorded in Numbers.

Moses' sister, Miriam.

## PURPOSE

Numbers mainly answers the questions, How did Israel get from Mount Sinai to the border of Canaan? and Why did the journey take so long? The book contrasts God's faithfulness with Israel's disobedience. Ultimately, however, Numbers shows the progress of God's people in moving toward the goals He had promised. Because God accomplished this despite His people's waywardness, He received all the glory. Those studying Numbers today should view it with this original purpose in mind.

## FIRST PASS

### Taking the Promised Land

The diverse materials in Numbers point toward a common goal—the possession of the land God promised the patriarchs. Most of Numbers is arranged chronologically, but there are places where the order is topical. Numbers opens with a census that reveals God had blessed Israel with the strength necessary for the conquest of the Promised Land (1:1–2:34). Organization for worship (3:1–4:49), instructions for preserving the purity of God's people (5:1–6:27), and the building of the tabernacle (7:1–8:26) all made possible God's dwelling with this people (9:15)—a necessary condition for reaching the land.

### Rejecting God's Promise

Though God equipped His people for conquest (10:11–36), their hearts repeatedly longed for Egypt (11:1–35; 14:2–4; 20:2–5; 21:4–5). They rejected Moses, the leader God had appointed to bring them to the land (12:1–15). Ultimately, Israel rejected God's gift of the land (12:16–14:45).

### Wandering

Having spurned God's gift, Israel was condemned to wander in the desert (15:1–22:1). Again and again Israel rebelled against God's chosen leaders and suffered judgment (16:1–50). Even Moses failed to trust in the power of God's word (20:1–29) and was excluded from the land of promise.

### Encountering Obstacles

God, however, is true to His promises. God overcame obstacles to Israel's possession of the land—the external threat of Balaam's curses (22:2–24:25) and the internal threat of Israel's idolatry and immorality (25:1–18).

### Preparing for Conquest

After the death of the rebellious generation, God again blessed Israel with a force capable of conquering the land (chap. 26). God rewarded the daughters of Zelophehad who, unlike the previous generation, earnestly desired their share in the land (27:1–11; 36:1–13). God's provision of Joshua as Moses' successor prepared for the successful conquest of the land.

## THE RELIABILITY OF NUMBERS

Ascribing the Pentateuch to Moses would place the date of the book of Numbers in the late fifteenth century or late thirteenth century BC. Based on ancient archaeological and historical evidence, several parallels to this era exist internally in the book of Numbers. The census lists in chapters 1 and 26 show parallels with those found in texts from Egypt, Mari, Ugarit, and Alalakh of the second millennium BC, and the organization of the Israelite tribal camps in a rectangular fashion around the central shrine is similar to the encampment of the armies of Ramses II of the thirteenth century BC. Gordon Wenham notes several other second millennium parallels among the people of the ancient Near East, including (1) the Late Bronze Age (1550–1200 BC) design of the lampstand (Nm 8); (2) tasseled garments (Nm 15); (3) the positioning of the Levites as guardians of the tabernacle (Nm 2–4); (4) the bronze serpent (Nm 21), which is similar to one found in the excavation of a Midianite shrine at Timna; and (5) the holy day calendar (Nm 28–29), which finds parallels at both Ugarit and Emar from the fifteenth to the fourteenth centuries BC.

Some scholars assert that most of the material in the Pentateuch that relates to the duties of priests and Levites comes from a period after the return of the exiles from Babylonia (538 BC). Yet the job descriptions of the Levites in Numbers 3–4 apply primarily to the period of the mobile sanctuary, prior to the eras of both the first (c. 962 BC) and second (c. 515 BC–AD 70) Jerusalem temples. Another reason given for rejecting the historical setting is the complexity of the priestly structure, which some critics claim must have developed over many centuries. But other Near Eastern peoples of the third and second millennia BC, such as those of Sumer, Old Assyria, and Old Babylonia, had priestly systems even more diverse and complex in structure and more detailed in their prescribed rituals.

## HOW NUMBERS FITS INTO GOD'S STORY

1. Prologue: Creation, Fall, and the Need for Redemption
2. **God Builds His Nation (2000–931 BC)**
3. God Educates His Nation (931–586 BC)
4. God Keeps a Faithful Remnant (586–6 BC)
5. God Purchases Redemption and Begins the Kingdom (6 BC to AD 30)
6. God Spreads the Kingdom Through the Church (AD 30-?)
7. God Consummates Redemption and Confirms His Eternal Kingdom
8. Epilogue: New Heaven and New Earth

## CHRIST IN NUMBERS

Christ is foreseen both as the water-giving rock (1 Co 10:4) and as the raised serpent that gives life to those who look (Jn 3:14–15). He is foretold as a star that will come out of Jacob and a scepter out of Israel (24:17). The first fulfillment of this prophecy is in David, who brought down a wicked nation (Moab). The perfect fulfillment of this prophecy is in David's Son, Jesus Christ, who will subdue all the enemies of God.

## CHRISTIAN WORLDVIEW ELEMENTS

### Teachings About God

Numbers emphasizes two attributes of God: His sovereign power and His covenant faithfulness. He is faithful to Israel on account of the covenant He made with Abraham (32:11). God's Spirit is present as the One enabling service and inspiring true prophecy (11:25–26; 24:2).

### Teachings About Humanity

This book shows how painfully sinful and flawed all humans are. The rebellion at Kadesh led by Korah and the story of Balaam demonstrate this. Moreover, even Moses the lawgiver, to whom God spoke directly, sinned and was not allowed to enter Canaan. Without divine mercy, all perish.

### Teachings About Salvation

Exodus (redemption through the death of the Passover lambs) and Leviticus (forgiveness provided through many blood sacrifices) teach more extensively about salvation than Numbers. The incident concerning the brass serpent on the pole, however, shows the centrality of faith in receiving God's provision: "Then the LORD said to Moses, 'Make a snake image and mount it on a pole. When anyone who is bitten looks at it, he will recover.' So Moses made a bronze snake and mounted it on a pole. Whenever someone was bitten, and he looked at the bronze snake, he recovered" (21:8–9).

## GENRE AND LITERARY STYLE

**Narrative and Laws (Written in Hebrew Prose) with Some Prophecies (Written in Hebrew Poetry)**

The narrative portions of Numbers continue along the lines of the narrative of Exodus and Leviticus. As "the fourth book of the Law," its laws are also similar to those previously recorded. One new feature is the prophetic oracle, given by Balaam (chaps. 23–24), written in the poetic parallelism so familiar in such books as Isaiah and Jeremiah. The Hebrew style of Numbers is like that of the rest of the Pentateuch.

## A PRINCIPLE TO LIVE BY

**Looking to Jesus (Nm 21:4–9, *Life Essentials Study Bible*, p. 198–99)**

To receive the gift of eternal life, each of us must put our faith in the Lord Jesus Christ who made atonement for our sins on the cross.

To access a video presentation of this principle featuring Dr. Gene Getz, use a Smartphone or iPad to connect to this QR code or go to http://www.bhpublishinggroup.com/handbook/numbers

Silver amulet containing the blessing Moses gave to Aaron and his sons to use in blessing Israel: "May Yahweh bless you and protect you; may Yahweh make his face shine on you and be gracious to you; may Yahweh look with favor on you and give you peace" (Nm 6:24–26). This artifact contains the oldest known copy of Scripture portions, dating to the late seventh or early sixth centuries. The silver scroll was found August 4, 1979 by Judy Hadley who was then an archaeology student at Wheaton College, working as part of an excavation led by Israeli archaeologist Gabriel Barkay.

# DEUTERONOMY

## THE FIFTH BOOK OF MOSES

The Hebrew title is *'Elleh Haddebarim*, "these are the words," or more succinctly *Debarim*, "words," from the opening of the book. The English title reflects the Greek word *Deuteronomion*, meaning "second law."

### KEY TEXT: 6:4–5

*"Listen, Israel: The Lord our God, the Lord is One. Love the Lord your God with all your heart, with all your soul, and with all your strength."*

### KEY TERM: "COMMANDMENTS"

Keeping the commandments of God out of love for Him lies at the heart of His covenant with Israel, seen especially by the repetition of the Ten Commandments. Forms of the noun or verb "command" occur almost a hundred times in the book.

### ONE-SENTENCE SUMMARY

Through Moses' great speeches near the end of his life, God reminded Israel on the verge of entering the Promised Land about His mighty acts, His covenant, and His many commands.

The area northeast of Mount Sinai, possibly the Wilderness of Paran, through which Israel passed on the journey from Horeb (Sinai) to Kadesh-barnea (1:1–2).

## AUTHOR AND DATE OF WRITING

**Moses, About 1406 BC**

The book refers to Moses' involvement in writing it (1:5; 31:9,22,24). Later Scripture refers to Mosaic authorship (1 Kg 2:3; 8:53; 2 Kg 14:6; 18:12). Both Jesus and Paul confirmed that Moses wrote Deuteronomy (Mk 10:3–5; Jn 5:46–47; Rm 10:19). The book's formal prologue (1:1–5) and the epilogue about Moses' death (chap. 34) were perhaps added by Joshua to round out the book.

Many modern critical scholars believe that Deuteronomy (or at least chaps. 12–26) first came into being as a pious fraud composed by scribes during the 600s BC at the time of King Josiah. These scribes subsequently "discovered" the book and claimed it came from the time of Moses (2 Kg 22–23). This belief became the keystone of the famous Documentary Hypothesis, which holds that the first five books of the Bible were an editorial creation around 450 BC from four primary literary sources, each written independently from a different perspective. Two centuries of modern critical study, however, have not proven that anything in the book could not have been composed during the time of Moses.

## FIRST AUDIENCE AND DESTINATION

**The Israelite People on the Plains of Moab**

Of all the books of the Pentateuch, Deuteronomy is the one that most clearly began as oral communication by a human speaker. Later, Moses put it in written, permanent form. The first audience was the new generation of Israelites listening to their beloved leader of 40 years as they faced the prospect of entering Canaan without him. The religious reforms instituted during the time of King Josiah were an application of the teachings of Deuteronomy for a new audience in another situation.

## OCCASION

Deuteronomy alone of the books of Moses states its precise occasion: "When Moses had finished writing down on a scroll every single word of this law, he commanded the Levites who carried the ark of the LORD's covenant, 'Take this book of the law and place it beside the ark of the covenant of the LORD your God so that it may remain there as a witness against you" (31:24–26).

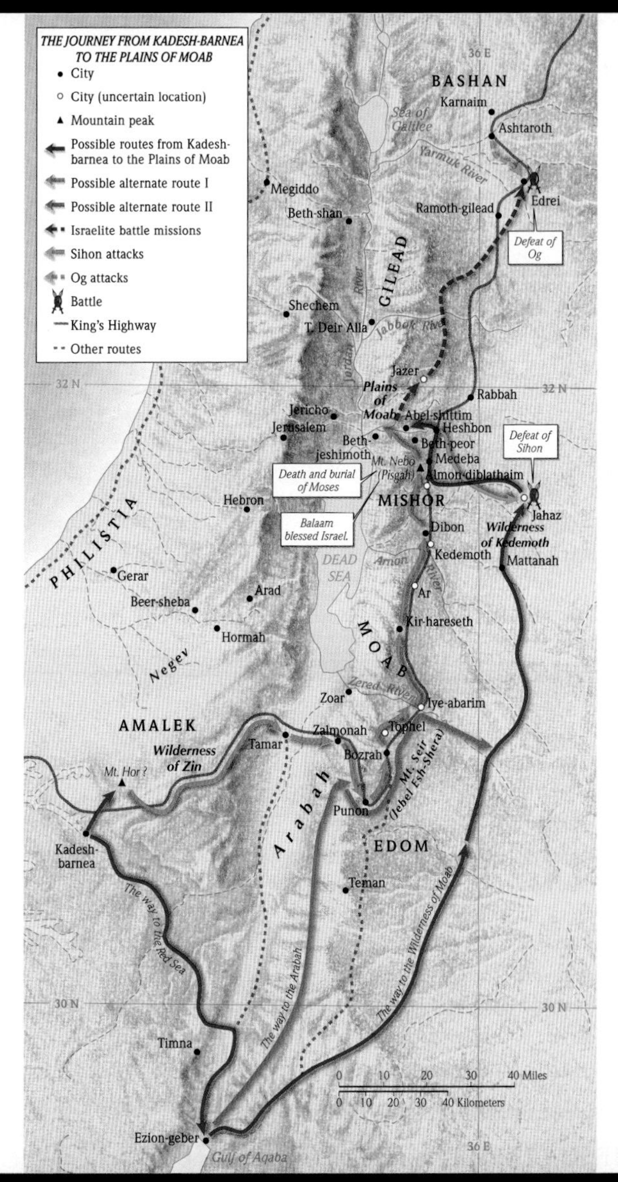


The map shows three possible routes from Kadesh-barnea to the Plains of Moab (Nm 20–21; 33:37–49; Dt 1–2; Jdg 11:12–28). Israel's passage east of the Jordan prompted great concern to Sihon, king of the Amorites and Og, king of Bashan. Both kings suffered defeat at Israel's hands.

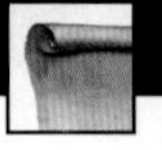


## PURPOSE

According to its own testimony, Deuteronomy originated as farewell messages from Moses to a new generation of Israelites. He pleaded passionately for them to keep God at the center of their national life once they settled in the land. The book is essentially a covenant-renewal document. The large central section mostly repeats laws found earlier in the Pentateuch. The truths in Deuteronomy have a perennial relevance. Jesus knew Deuteronomy well. When Satan tempted Him at the beginning of His ministry, He responded to each of the three temptations with a quotation from Deuteronomy. The NT either quotes or alludes to Deuteronomy nearly 200 times.

## FIRST PASS

### Setting

Deuteronomy 1:1–5 is an introduction, giving the time and place of the addresses. The time is "the fortieth year" (Dt 1:3) of wilderness wandering, "in the eleventh month, on the first of the month." The place is "across the Jordan in the wilderness" (Dt 1:1) and, more particularly, "in the land of Moab" (Dt 1:5).

### Moses' First Address

Deuteronomy 1:6–4:40 is Moses' first address, in which he recounted Israel's journey from Horeb to Moab and urged Israel to be faithful to Yahweh. Moses used Israel's immediate past history to teach the present generation of Israelites the importance of trusting God. Israel's obedience was imperative if they expected to possess the land of Canaan. Moses set up cities of refuge on the east bank of the Jordan (Dt 4:41–43).

### Moses' Second Address

Deuteronomy 4:44–28:68 contains Moses' second address to Israel. In this address Moses teaches Israel lessons from the law. These are not laws to be used in the courts to decide legal cases but instructions for life in the land of Canaan.

### Moses' Third Address

This address (Dt 29:1–30:20) focuses on covenant renewal. Repentance and commitment would assure life and the blessings of God. Rebellion would result in their death as a nation. The choice was theirs.

### Moses' Final Address

Deuteronomy 31:1–29 is Moses' farewell address. The song of Moses is given in Dt 31:30–32:52. Moses' blessing is reported in chap. 33, and his death is recounted in chap. 34.

## THE RELIABILITY OF DEUTERONOMY

The structural similarities between Deuteronomy and Near Eastern treaty texts from the second millennium BC have furnished strong evidence for the unity and antiq-

uity of the book. Comparison to Hittite treaties suggests a date no later than about 1300 BC. Scholars seeking to maintain an eighth- or seventh-century BC (or later) date for Deuteronomy have pointed to similarities to Neo-Assyrian treaties from the seventh century BC. This later treaty form, however, is missing important elements found in Deuteronomy and the Hittite texts, such as the historical prologue (Dt 1:6–4:44) and the list of blessings (Dt 28:1–14). The conclusion is that Moses' authorship of Deuteronomy essentially as we have it is the most reasonable view for the person who accepts the testimony of Scripture.

It is doubtful Moses wrote the account of his death in Deuteronomy 34. Frequently the text provides explanatory notes updating facts for a later audience (e.g., "Esau, that is, Edom," Gn 36:1; the aboriginal inhabitants of the Transjordan, Dt 2:10–12). Furthermore, the form of the cursive Canaanite script that Moses probably used was still in its infancy and was replaced with the square Aramaic script in the postexilic period, and the vowels were added a millennium later. The archaic qualities of the poems (Gn 49; Ex 15; etc.), in contrast to the surrounding narrative, suggest the latter may have been updated periodically in accordance with the evolution of the Hebrew language. These points explain why the grammar and syntax of Deuteronomy in its present form read much like Jeremiah, who lived long after Moses.

A Jewish man praying at the Western Wall in Jerusalem. He wears phylacteries that come from a Jewish tradition dating to the second century BC. A phylactery, or frontlet, is a small black leather or parchment case containing four Scriptures. It is attached to a long, single leather strap by a loop, forming two long straps on either side of the loop. In Moses' second address he reminded Israel of the greatest commandment: "Love the LORD your God with all your heart, with all your soul, and with all your strength" (6:5). They were to talk about the LORD's commands throughout the course of the day and to repeat them to their children. "Bind them as a sign on your hand and let them be a symbol on your forehead. Write them on the doorposts of your house and on your gates" (6:8–9).

## HOW DEUTERONOMY FITS INTO GOD'S STORY

1. Prologue: Creation, Fall, and the Need for Redemption
2. **God Builds His Nation (2000–931 BC)**
3. God Educates His Nation (931–586 BC)
4. God Keeps a Faithful Remnant (586–6 BC)
5. God Purchases Redemption and Begins the Kingdom (6 BC to AD 30)
6. God Spreads the Kingdom Through the Church (AD 30-?)
7. God Consummates Redemption and Confirms His Eternal Kingdom
8. Epilogue: New Heaven and New Earth

## CHRIST IN DEUTERONOMY

Moses tells of a prophet like him whom God would raise up from among Israel (18:15–22). Christ is seen as a fulfillment of that prophecy (Ac 3:22; 7:37). The law states that whoever is hung on a tree is under God's curse (Dt 21:23). Christ has redeemed us from the curse of the law by Himself becoming a curse for us (Gl 3:13).

## CHRISTIAN WORLDVIEW ELEMENTS

### Teachings About God

Deuteronomy emphasizes the unity of God in the famous *Shema*, "Listen!" (see *Key Text* above). God's love as the basis for His covenant, His acts on Israel's behalf, and His commands are also prominent. On the other hand, idolatry or apostasy is so serious an affront to God's glory that the book commands the most severe penalties against those who insult God by turning away from Him.

### Teachings About Humanity

Deuteronomy faithfully records Israel's failures and gives solemn warnings of divine curse on disobedient and rebellious people. Yet the tenor of the book is that living according to God's commands is a true delight and that obedience is no drudgery but the response of love and faith—an easy yoke. "But the message is very near you, in your mouth and in your heart, so that you may follow it" (30:14; see Mt 11:29).

### Teachings About Salvation

Deuteronomy emphasizes that salvation is entirely God's provision. He sets His covenant love on people solely out of His love. The remarkable text in Deuteronomy 7:1–10 denies that God's redemption of Israel from Egypt was based on any quality in Israel but only "because the LORD loved you" (7:8)—His sovereign choice. This book also shows that redeemed people demonstrate their love and faith by their obedience.

## GENRE AND LITERARY STYLE

**A Record of Moses' Final Speeches, Composed in Hebrew**

Many scholars have noted the sermonic style of Deuteronomy, which sets it apart from the other books of Moses. The speeches are a combination of narrative (reminders of God's acts) and repetition of God's laws. Together they serve to renew the covenant for a new generation. At the end of the book, the extraordinary "Song of Moses" (chap. 32) and his "Final Blessing on Israel" (chap. 33) show Moses to be a poet of considerable skill. The Hebrew of Deuteronomy is similar to that of the rest of the Pentateuch.

## A PRINCIPLE TO LIVE BY

**Love and Obedience (Dt 11:1, *Life Essentials Study Bible*, p. 237–38)**

To love God sincerely and fully, we must obey what He commands.

To access a video presentation of this principle featuring Dr. Gene Getz, use a Smartphone or iPad to connect to this QR code or go to http://www.bhpublishinggroup.com/handbook/deuteronomy

View of Mount Nebo from the east. Nebo is about 12 miles east of the mouth of the Jordan River from which Moses viewed the Promised Land (Dt 32:49). It rises over 4,000 feet above the Dead Sea and gives an excellent view of the southwest, west, and as far north as Mount Hermon. Israel captured the area around Mount Nebo as they marched toward Canaan. They camped in the area of Mount Nebo opposite Jericho when the Balaam incident occurred (Nm 22–24).

Joshua 13–21 describes the distribution of the Promised Land among the tribes of Israel. This land was God's gift to His people. The detailed boundary descriptions and lists emphasize God's ownership of the land and His authority to distribute the land as He chooses.

The English (and Hebrew) title is based on the name of the central character. Moses changed his original name *Hoshea* ("salvation") to *Yehoshua* ("Yahweh Is salvation"), traditionally spelled "Joshua" in English. The Greek equivalent is "Jesus."

## KEY TEXT: 21:44–45

*"The LORD gave them rest on every side according to all He had sworn to their fathers. None of their enemies were able to stand against them, for the LORD handed over all their enemies to them. None of the good promises the LORD had made to the house of Israel failed. Everything was fulfilled."*

The Jordan River (shown here) was at flood stage when God commanded Joshua to lead the people across (Jos 3:14–17). Just as when God opened the Red Sea, He provided a dry path through the Jordan River when the priests, bearing the ark of the covenant, touched the edge of the river. For people seeing the Jordan today, it's difficult to imagine what the river was like at the time Joshua led Israel across. Up until the 1950s, more than three billion cubic feet of water flowed through the stretch of the Jordan between the Sea of Galilee and the Dead Sea annually. With the construction of a number of dams on the Jordan north of the Sea of Galilee and on rivers that feed the Jordan, that volume has been reduced to 300 million cubic feet of water each year.

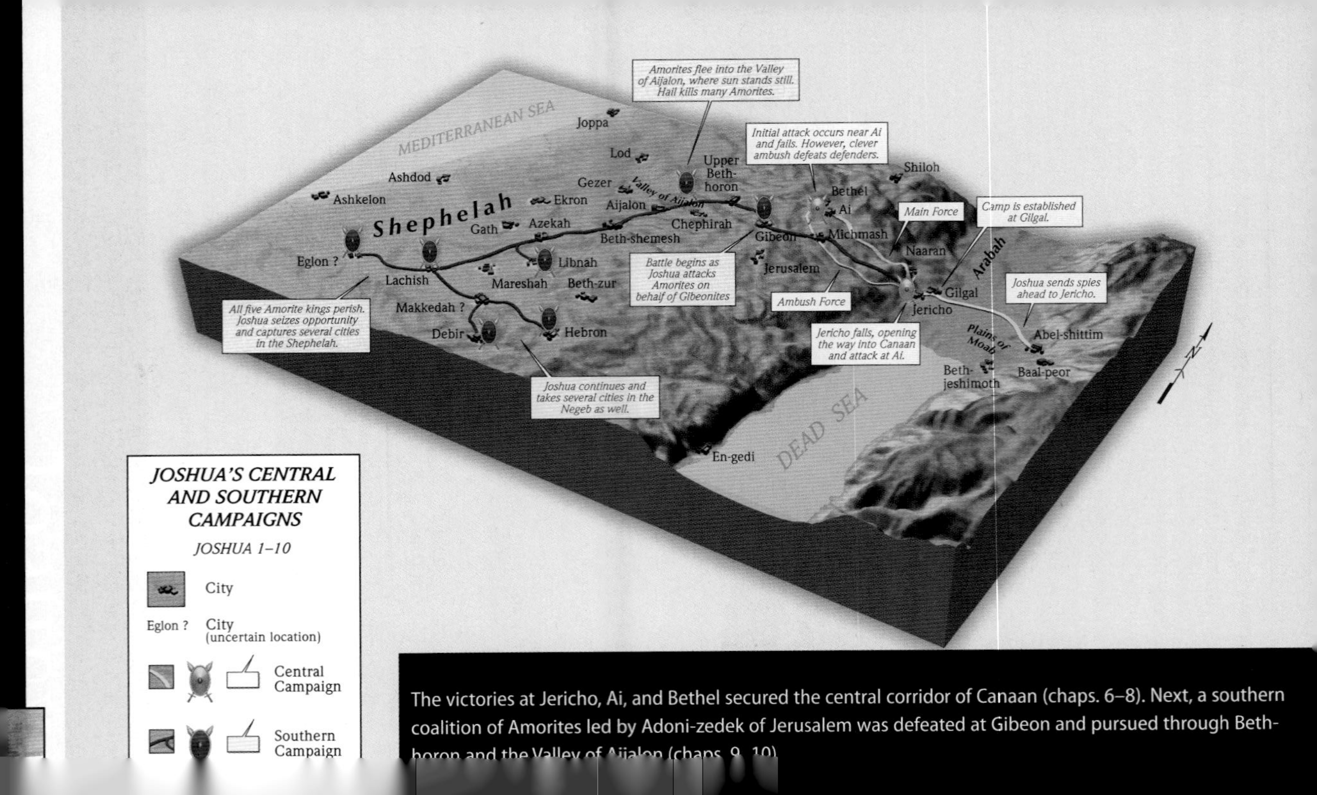


The victories at Jericho, Ai, and Bethel secured the central corridor of Canaan (chaps. 6–8). Next, a southern coalition of Amorites led by Adoni-zedek of Jerusalem was defeated at Gibeon and pursued through Beth-horon and the Valley of Aijalon (chaps. 9–10).

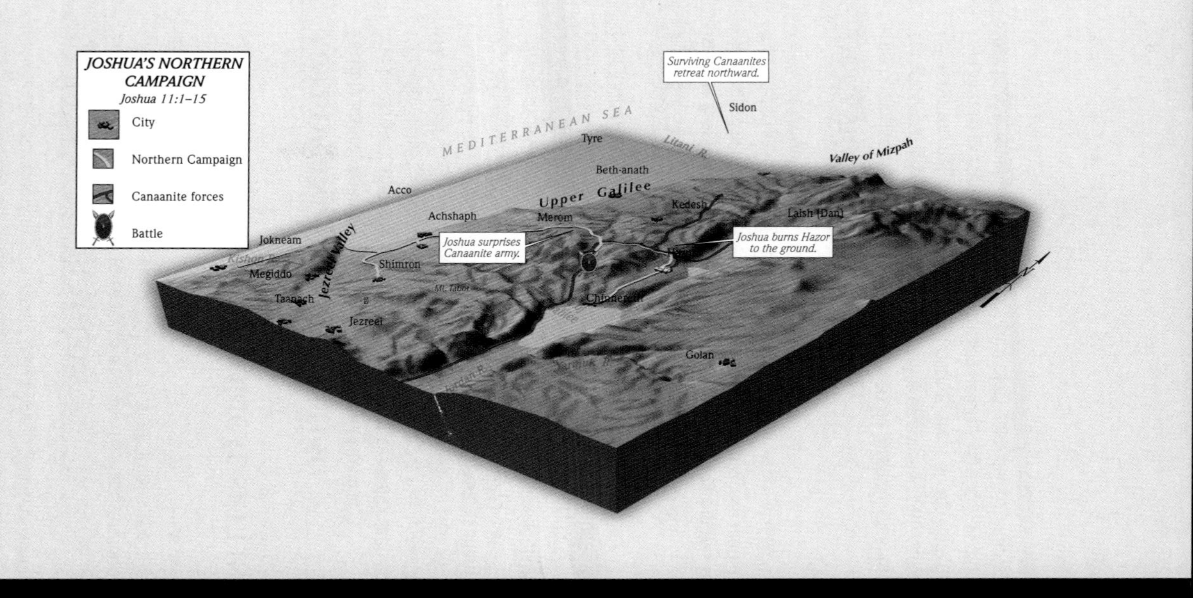


A powerful northern coalition led by Jabin the king of Hazor encamped together at the waters of Merom to fight against Israel (chap. 11). A list of conquered kings rounds out the record of the conquest (chap. 12).

When Joshua and the Israelites defeated this northern coalition, there was no power left in Canaan strong enough to pose a large-scale threat to Israel. The book of Joshua indicates that only Jericho, Ai, and Hazor were destroyed by fire. Many of the fortified cities were left standing, and the task of completing the conquest fell to the individual tribes who would inherit select portions of the land.

## KEY TERM: "CONQUEST"

This is a book of victory and conquest. It shows God's people on the march throughout Canaan, subduing their enemies and claiming their promised possession.

## ONE-SENTENCE SUMMARY

God fulfilled His promises to Israel to give them a land through the conquest of Canaan and through the allocation of the land among the tribes, all under the leadership of Joshua.

# ORIGINAL HISTORICAL SETTING

## AUTHOR AND DATE OF WRITING

**Possibly Joshua, Around 1380 BC, or Samuel, Around 1050 BC**

The book is anonymous. Because Joshua is the central character, Jewish tradition held him to be the author. Joshua's writing activity is mentioned twice in the book (18:8; 24:26). Everything in the book could have been written by Joshua except for the last few verses that tell of his death. On the other hand, many students believe several instances of the phrase "unto this day" (for example, 4:9; 5:9) point to a time after Joshua's lifetime. The reference to the "Book of Jasher" (10:13; see also 2 Sm 1:18) may also suggest a later date. If the book was not written by Joshua, then the next likely candidate is Samuel, who would have used sources were passed on to him from the time of Joshua.

## FIRST AUDIENCE AND DESTINATION

**Israelite People After They Settled in Canaan, Before Kingship Was Established**

The first audience was the Israelite nation living in its own land. The book—which first existed in scroll form, as did all the biblical books—was deposited with the five books of Moses at the tabernacle (24:26).

## OCCASION

The book does not tell what prompted it to be written. If Joshua was the primary author, then he was continuing the pattern established by Moses. He put into written form the mighty acts God accomplished through his leadership. If the author was Samuel or some writer living shortly before kingship was established, the need was to give Israel a permanent account of its early days of triumph in the land.

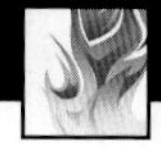

## PURPOSE

The covenant God made with Abraham included a promise that his descendants would take possession of Canaan (Gn 12:7). For long ages the promise lay unfulfilled. The book of Joshua shows how God—in His time and way—fulfilled the land aspect of the Abrahamic covenant. Yet the New Testament book of Hebrews speaks of a greater Joshua who gives His people ultimate rest (Hb 4:8–9). God's people who read and study the book today should view it with both Joshuas in mind: the Israelite general and the King of kings.

## FIRST PASS

The book of Joshua documents the conquest and settlement of the land of Canaan. The book naturally divides itself into four main divisions with each section built around a particular Hebrew concept: "going over" (1:1–5:15); "taking" (6:1–12:24); "dividing" (13:1–21:45); "worshipping" (22:1–24:33).

### Going Over

The first five chapters focus on the preparations made by Joshua and Israel to cross over the Jordan and invade the land. Highlights include God's charge to Joshua (chap. 1), the encounter of the spies with Rahab (chap. 2), the miraculous crossing of the Jordan River at flood stage (chaps. 3–4), and the celebration of the Passover (chap. 5).

### Taking

Chapters 6–12 record the three-part campaign of Joshua and the Israelites to claim the Promised Land as their inheritance. The military strategy of the conquest is rather simple, and it reflects the political circumstances of the region during the Amarna period at the end of the late Bronze Age (1400 BC). Canaan at the time contained a mixture of powerful fortified city-states and coalitions of smaller city-states. Egypt held nominal control, but no unified political power existed.

First, the victories at Jericho, Ai, and Bethel secured the central corridor of Canaan (chaps. 6–8). Next, a southern coalition of Amorites led by Adoni-zedek of Jerusalem was defeated at Gibeon and pursued through Beth-horon and the Valley of Aijalon (chaps. 9–10). Finally a powerful northern coalition led by Jabin the king of Hazor encamped together at the waters of Merom to fight against Israel (chap. 11). A list of conquered kings rounds out the record of the conquest (chap. 12).

When Joshua and the Israelites defeated this northern coalition, no power left in Canaan was strong enough to pose a large-scale threat to Israel. The book of Joshua indicates that only Jericho, Ai, and Hazor were destroyed by fire. Many of the fortified cities were left standing, and the task of completing the conquest fell to the individual tribes who would inherit select portions of the land. As can be seen in the book of Judges, many of the tribes were not able to secure their own territory.

**Dividing**

Chapters 13–21 document the inheritance and distribution of the Promised Land to Israel. God is the great "land giver." The detailed boundary descriptions and lists emphasize the fact that God is the owner of this land and has the authority to distribute it as He chooses. Emphasis is placed on the inheritance of Judah (chaps. 14–15) and of Joseph (chaps. 16–17). Provision is also made for the cities of refuge (chap. 20) and the Levitical cities (chap. 21).

**Worshipping**

The final section of the book focuses on the farewell speeches of Joshua and the consecration of the land through the great covenant renewal ceremony at Shechem (chap. 24). Joshua blesses the people, calls on them to follow the Lord, warns them of the consequences of disobedience, and challenges them to reaffirm their covenant with God. Here Joshua expresses his personal commitment to the covenant Lord (24:15). After Joshua dies, he is given the title "the servant of the LORD" just like Moses (24:29).

## THE RELIABILITY OF JOSHUA

The events recorded in the book of Joshua took place during the second millennium BC in the period immediately following the 40 years of Israelite wilderness wanderings. The date of the exodus has been the subject of much scholarly debate. Joshua apparently supports an early date for the exodus. The book refers to places and peoples best situated in the middle of the second millennium BC (e.g., the mention in Jos 13:6 of the Sidonians rather than the later more powerful people of Tyre). If the early date for the exodus (c. mid fifteenth century BC) is correct, then the events of Joshua occurred approximately in the late fifteenth century BC (c. 1400 BC).

Critics often cite the book's three dramatic miracles (the stopping of the Jordan River in 3:15–17; the collapse of Jericho's wall in 6:20; and Joshua's long day 10:12–14) as evidence of its legendary or fictional character. Biblical narratives do not portray an indiscriminately large number of miracles. The Bible does not read like the pagan mythologies of antiquity in which gods are constantly interrupting and disrupting ordinary human affairs. The relative infrequency of biblical miracles may be seen in the fact that they constitute a small, albeit important, part of the narratives spanning approximately two millennia from the time of Abraham through the apostolic era. Biblical miracles always have a clear objective. Purposive timing is a characteristic of some miracles providing evidence God is up to something.

Certain critical turning points in biblical history are marked by more intense spiritual warfare and miracles. The life and ministry of Jesus Christ is the most obvious of these periods, and the exodus of Israel from Egypt with the subsequent conquest of Canaan represents another. The book of Joshua records the events at

the close of this strategic era, and its three major miracles reveal Yahweh's sovereign work to install Israel in the land of promise.

## HOW JOSHUA FITS INTO GOD'S STORY

1. Prologue: Creation, Fall, and the Need for Redemption
2. God Builds His Nation (2000–931 BC)
3. God Educates His Nation (931–586 BC)
4. God Keeps a Faithful Remnant (586–6 BC)
5. God Purchases Redemption and Begins the Kingdom (6 BC to AD 30)
6. God Spreads the Kingdom Through the Church (AD 30-?)
7. God Consummates Redemption and Confirms His Eternal Kingdom
8. Epilogue: New Heaven and New Earth

## CHRIST IN JOSHUA

The name *Joshua* is a variation of *Jesus*. Joshua's leadership of God's people in taking possession of the Promised Land is a foreshadowing of Christ's leading the people of God to their eternal inheritance. Joshua is one of only a few Old Testament heroes pictured without major character flaws or sins. The "commander of the LORD's army" (5:15) was doubtless Christ in preincarnate form.

## CHRISTIAN WORLDVIEW ELEMENTS

### Teachings About God

The two attributes of God most on display in Joshua are His faithfulness to fulfill His promises and His ultimate judgment on evil. If the promise made to Abraham concerning land for Israel was kept only after many centuries, then today's believers should not be surprised if the promise He made concerning the return of Christ is kept after many centuries.

### Teachings About Humanity

Although the book is careful to report Israel's occasional failures during the conquest, it is optimistic in its view that God's people can "live in victory" as they trust in Him. For this reason Joshua has been popular in Christian pulpits with the positive principles it contains.

### Teachings About Salvation

The account of Rahab the harlot (chaps. 2 and 6) profoundly illustrates salvation by "grace through faith." So thoroughly was she converted that she was considered an Israelite and became a biological ancestor of Jesus (Jos 6:25; Mt 1:5; Heb 11:31). Although most of the victories in Joshua are military, the entire tenor of the book is that salvation—of whatever kind—comes only from God's hand.

## GENRE AND LITERARY STYLE

### A Historical Narrative Composed in Hebrew

Joshua is mainly a report of the military conquest and settling of Canaan, recounted with a great deal of skill. The dialogues and the farewell speech of Joshua add vividness and excitement. In the Hebrew Scriptures this book is positioned as the first of the four "Former Prophets." (The others are Judges, Samuel, and Kings.) Together these books describe the 800-year period from Israel's entry into Canaan (about 1406 BC) to the destruction of the temple and Jerusalem and the exile to Babylon (about 586 BC). See comments on *Genre and Literary Style* in **2 KINGS** for further material about the possible literary relationship of the "Former Prophets."

## A PRINCIPLE TO LIVE BY

### Finishing Well (Jos 24:1,14–16, *Life Essentials Study Bible*, p. 296–97)

To follow God fully throughout our time on earth, we must obey the Word of God and keep our eyes focused on the Lord Jesus Christ..

To access a video presentation of this principle featuring Dr. Gene Getz, use a Smartphone or iPad to connect to this QR code or go to http://www.bhpublishinggroup.com/handbook/joshua

The name translates the Hebrew title, *Shofetim*, which could also be rendered "leaders" or "chieftains." It refers to the style of government in Israel from Joshua's death to Saul's kingship. The judges did not preside over courts as the English term might suggest.

### KEY TEXT: 21:25

*"In those days there was no king in Israel; everyone did whatever he wanted."*

### KEY TERM: "DELIVERED"

Whenever the Israelites fell into apostasy, God delivered them to their political enemies. Then after they cried out to God, He raised up a leader who delivered them from their oppressors. In both situations God delivered His people because He is the ultimate Judge (11:27).

### ONE-SENTENCE SUMMARY

Israel experienced the repeated cycle of apostasy, oppression, repentance, and restoration by divinely appointed judges throughout the long period following Joshua's death.

## ORIGINAL HISTORICAL SETTING

### AUTHOR AND DATE OF WRITING

**Unknown, Perhaps Samuel, About 1050 BC**

The book is anonymous. It could hardly have been completed until after all its events, and the repeated refrain "in those days there was no king in Israel" (17:6; 18:1; 19:1; 21:25) suggests the author wrote at a time when there was a king. Jewish tradition identified Samuel as the author. There is no reason Samuel could not have written from the early days of Saul's kingship, in which case this is his companion to the book of Joshua. The text of Judges bears the mark of eyewitness accounts of the events narrated that were accessible to the author. In addition, the author used ancient sources, such as "The Song of Deborah" (chap. 5).

### FIRST AUDIENCE AND DESTINATION

**Israelite People After They Settled in Canaan, After Kingship Was Established**

The first audience was the Israelite nation living in its own land. No doubt the

The author of Judges sets the stage by summarizing the fortunes of the respective tribes as they claimed the land the Lord had allotted them (1:1–36). He reported the results in a deliberate orde[r] beginning with the successes of Judah and ending with the utter failure of Dan. This pattern anticipates the structure of the narratives that follow, as the portrait of the nation begins rather positively with Othniel (3:7–11), but with each cycle the picture becomes ever bleaker.

book—which first existed in a scroll form, as did all the biblical books—was deposited with the growing canon of Hebrew Scripture at the tabernacle in Shiloh.

## OCCASION

Judges captured for a later generation the story of earlier national failure. It was perhaps prompted by the need to give a thorough historical explanation to the question first asked by Gideon: "If the LORD is with us, why has all this happened?" (6:13). Some scholars believe Judges originated as a long prophetic sermon.

# GOD'S MESSAGE IN JUDGES

## PURPOSE

Judges serves two main purposes. Historically, it sketches the dark period in Israel's history between the exciting days of Moses and Joshua to the promising time of Samuel and Saul. Sadly, there were only fleeting times when Israel truly fulfilled its role as God's people. Theologically, the author presented a convincing case for the fundamental degeneration of Israel during the period of the judges. Each part of the book makes a vital contribution to the development of this theme.

## FIRST PASS

### Israel's Failure in the Holy War

The author set the stage by summarizing the fortunes of the respective tribes as they claimed the land the Lord had allotted them (1:1–36). He reported the results in a deliberate order, beginning with the successes of Judah and ending with the utter failure of Dan. This pattern anticipated the structure of the narratives that followed, as the portrait of the nation began rather positively with Othniel (3:7–11), but with each cycle the picture became ever bleaker.

This historical introduction is followed by a heavily theological preamble (2:1–3:6). The fundamental problem is Israel's loss of the memory of the Lord's redemptive work on their behalf (2:1–10). This resulted in the sorry truth expressed in a refrain that is repeated seven times in the book: The Israelites did evil (literally "the evil") in the sight of the Lord; they served the Baals and abandoned the Lord their Redeemer (2:11–12; cp. 3:7,12; 4:1; 6:1; 10:6; 13:1).

### The Judges

The following narratives of the individual judges, which take up the bulk of the book (3:7–16:31), describe the consequences of this apostasy. The preamble (2:1–3:6) invites the reader to interpret these accounts not merely as cyclical recurrences of the same problem but as illustrative of an intensification of the evil in Israel

(2:17–19), offering the reader the key to understanding both the people of Israel and the judges who led them.

Because of the theological nature of the narrative and the author's selective use of data, it is difficult to reconstruct the history of Israel during the period of the judges from the accounts in the heart of the book (3:7–16:31). The events are deliberately arranged so that each judge is presented in a worse light than the previous, beginning with Othniel, an exemplary character (3:7–11), and ending with Samson, who embodies all that is wrong with Israel. Each cycle is structured after a literary pattern signaled by a series of recurring formulas:

1. "The Israelites did what was evil in the LORD's sight" (2:11; 3:7,12; 4:1; 6:1; 10:6; 13:1).
2. "He handed them over to . . . the enemies around them" (2:14; 6:1; 13:1).
3. "The Israelites cried out to the LORD" (3:9,15; 4:3; 6:6; 10:10).
4. "The LORD raised up judges, who saved them" (2:16,18; 3:9,15).
5. "So X [the oppressing nation] was subdued before the Israelites" (8:28; cp. 3:30; 4:23).
6. "Then the land was peaceful N years" (3:11,30; 5:31; 8:28).
7. "Then X [the judge] died" (2:19; 3:11; 4:1b; 8:32; 12:7).

Spring of Harod at Ainharod at the foot of Mount Gilboa. This is where Gideon's men were tested on how they drank water. Using this test, Gideon was able to identify the men who were qualified to fight against the Midianites (Jdg 7:4–8).

From these formulas it is evident that the Lord is the most important character in the book, and the author's attention is fixed on His response to the increasing corruption of His people by the Canaanite culture. In judgment He sends in foreign enemies (as Lv 26 and Dt 28 predicted). Then in mercy He hears their cry, raises up a deliverer, and provides victory over the enemy. But the

Israelites do not learn the lesson; on the contrary the spiritual decline goes deeper and deeper into the soul of the nation. In the end Gideon acts like an oriental despot (8:18–32); like the pagans around him, Jephthah tried to win the good will of God by sacrificing his daughter (11:30–40); and Samson's life and death looked more like that of a Philistine than one of the people of the Lord (chaps. 14–16).

### Symptoms and Consequences of Israel's Apostasy

Many interpret Judges 17–21 as more or less independent appendices. However, once we realize that the overall concern of the book is Israel's spiritual degeneration and God's response to it, we discover that, far from being an awkward add-on, these chapters represent the climax of the composition. The tone is set by four variations of the refrain, "In those days there was no king in Israel; everyone did whatever he wanted" (17:6; 18:1; 19:1; 21:25). Far from being an ethical community of faith, the Israelites became like the worst of the Canaanites. And instead of exposing the immoral criminals in their midst, the Benjaminites defended them. The book closes with Israel in total disarray politically, spiritually, and morally, with one tribe all but eliminated, leaving the reader to wonder what will become of this people of God.

## THE RELIABILITY OF JUDGES

Controversy surrounds the book of Judges. Even a cursory reading of this book causes many to question the validity of its inclusion in the Scriptures, the content being deemed by some as unworthy of God or of little or no value to twenty-first-century readers. The book includes: (1) graphic depictions of violence (such as the slaughter of seemingly innocent people by the command of God, maiming, human sacrifice, and gloating over the deaths of one's enemies); (2) heroes who are anything but role models and who engage in deceit, lies, mockery, and self-centered behavior; (3) illicit sex and sexual innuendo; (4) a degrading depiction of women; and (5) a writing style that seemingly includes exaggeration or fabrication.

Regarding the controversial matters of the content, a closer reading of the text reveals that, by being written as straightforward accounts, Judges displays a higher degree of credibility than if it presented a sanitized history. It does not attempt to gloss over any of the sins, foolishness, or errors of the people described in it. Despite conclusions skeptics might draw from a cursory assessment of the text, the book never places blame for sin, foolishness, or error on God. God was not guilty, and the so-called innocent were, in fact, not innocent at all. Instead they deserved judgment.

The events and customs fit precisely into the story line of Judges and align well with what is known from ancient sources of information outside the Bible. The stories may not make us feel comfortable, but this book was not designed to comfort. Rather, it presents hard-hitting truth designed to disturb, to inform, and to challenge.

## HOW JUDGES FITS INTO GOD'S STORY

1. Prologue: Creation, Fall, and the Need for Redemption
2. God Builds His Nation (2000–931 BC)
3. God Educates His Nation (931–586 BC)
4. God Keeps a Faithful Remnant (586–6 BC)
5. God Purchases Redemption and Begins the Kingdom (6 BC to AD 30)
6. God Spreads the Kingdom Through the Church (AD 30-?)
7. God Consummates Redemption and Confirms His Eternal Kingdom
8. Epilogue: New Heaven and New Earth

## CHRIST IN JUDGES

The judges were God's agents for delivering His people from a variety of enemies. In a much greater way, Christ confronts and defeats Satan and his forces, thereby delivering the people of God from their enemies. This theme is seen in Matthew, Mark, and Luke, in Paul's letter to the Ephesians, and in the Revelation.

## CHRISTIAN WORLDVIEW ELEMENTS

**Teachings About God**

Judges shows the severity of God, who does not take it lightly when people claiming His name forsake His ways (2:11–15). It also shows the mercy of God, who is moved with pity when His children cry out to Him, even when their troubles are caused by their own sins (2:16–18). The Spirit's power in enabling certain judges to perform mighty works is noteworthy in the book.

**Teachings About Humanity**

This book paints an embarrassing picture of human fickleness. Israel was seemingly ready to turn away from God to serve idols at the drop of a hat. The shameful incident of the Levite's concubine (chap. 19) demonstrates how degraded the times of the judges were. Even the three most memorable judges (Gideon, Jephthah, and Samson) were seriously flawed.

**Teachings About Salvation**

Judges teaches that salvation involves more than just an individual's forgiveness from sin. Sin has consequences that are social and can affect an entire society. Therefore, when God brings salvation, He dramatically changes societies and nations as well as individuals. Further, this book teaches that salvation—deliverance—is always from the Lord and never because someone (or some group) deserves it.

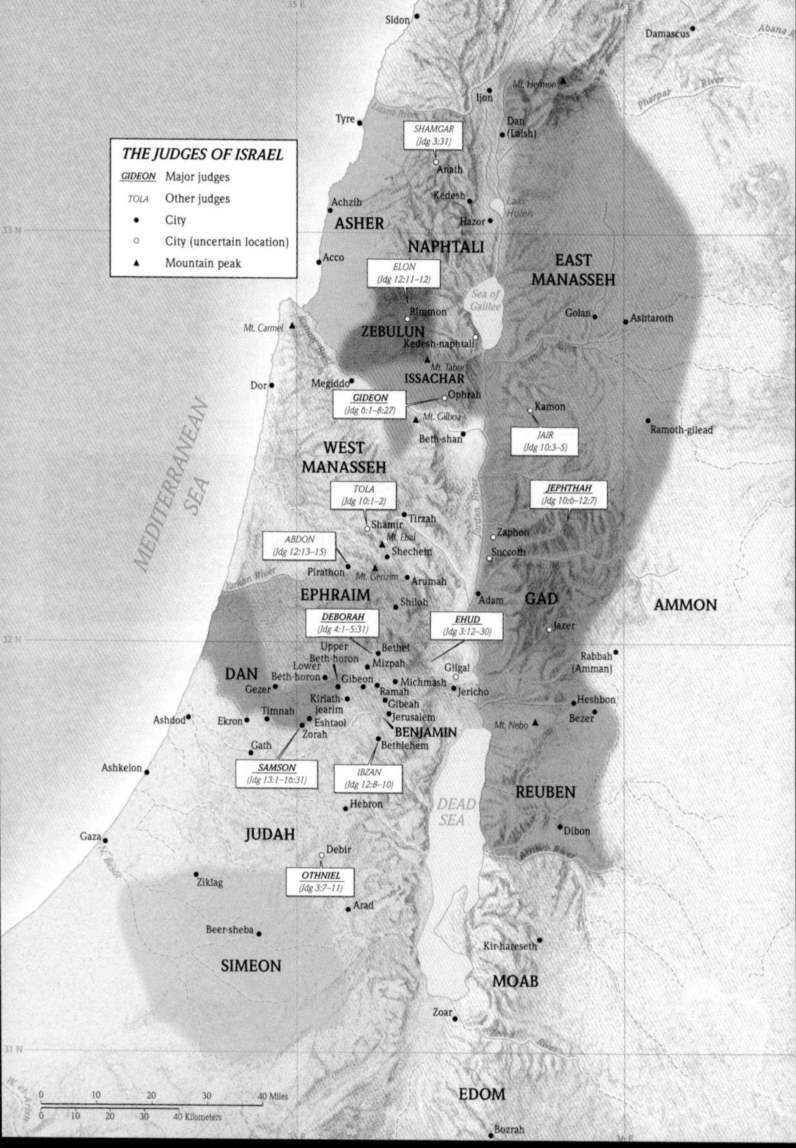


Over a period of 400 years Israel experienced seven periods of apostasy, oppression by other nations, and remarkable deliverance at the Lord's hand. Shown are the geographical locations of 12 of the 13 judges God raised up during this era.

## GENRE AND LITERARY STYLE

**A Narrative with a Long Prologue and Epilogue, Composed in Hebrew**

More than most of the historical books, Judges has a tightly knit narrative plot. "The Song of Deborah" (chap. 5) is a superb example of early Hebrew poetry. In the Hebrew Scriptures this book is positioned as the second of the four "Former Prophets." (The others are Joshua, Samuel, and Kings.) Judges, like Kings, tells the story of several centuries with only a few episodes given any detail. Joshua and Samuel lavish attention on central characters: Joshua, Samuel, Saul, and David.

## A PRINCIPLE TO LIVE BY

**Stories That Teach (Jdg 13–16, *Life Essentials Study Bible*, p. 323–24)**

When we read biblical stories of people's lives, we should look for the lessons we can learn from both their successes and their failures.

To access a video presentation of this principle featuring Dr. Gene Getz, use a Smartphone or iPad to connect to this QR code or go to http://www.bhpublishinggroup.com/handbook/judges

The English title is the name of the heroine of the story. The title carries over from the Hebrew Bible.

## KEY TEXT: 4:14

*"Then the women said to Naomi, 'Praise the* LORD, *who has not left you without a family redeemer today. May His name become well known in Israel.'"*

## KEY TERM: "KINSMAN"

Boaz willingly fulfilled the responsibility of the *go'el*, "kinsman" or "redeemer" for Ruth as well as for Naomi. As such he beautifully illustrates God, who gladly redeems His people. Ruth and Boaz became ancestors of Jesus, the ultimate Redeemer.

## ONE-SENTENCE SUMMARY

Ruth, a Moabite widow, found love and fulfillment through Boaz, a rich Israelite bachelor who redeemed the ancestral land and the name of Ruth's deceased husband, thereby restoring Naomi, Ruth's mother-in-law, from emptiness to fullness.

## AUTHOR AND DATE OF WRITING

**Unknown, Any Time 1000–500 BC**

The authorship of Ruth is unknown. The book is named for its chief character, not necessarily for its author. A late Jewish

The Merneptah Stele or Israel Stela is the first inscription outside the Bible that mentions Israel. This stone slab was found at Thebes, Egypt in 1896 and is dated to the late thirteenth century BC. On one reckoning of Israel's history, this would have been during the era of the judges, the setting for the book of Ruth. The next inscriptions mentioning Israel come 400 years later—one from Assyria, the other from Moab.

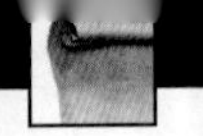



tradition ascribes the book to the prophet Samuel. It was written after David's rise to power, but beyond that little is certain. The author's skill in writing is matchless in the Old Testament.

## FIRST AUDIENCE AND DESTINATION:

### Israelites Living Sometime After David Came to Power

The golden age of Israelite culture during the days of Solomon would serve admirably as the original setting for the book's composition. It is, however, strikingly different from the Song of Songs, the other Old Testament book that tells an individual love story.

## OCCASION

The beauty of a story told well is sufficient reason to bring it into being. Because nothing is known for certain about its original author or audience, no one can be sure what first prompted it to be written.

Field of Boaz near Bethlehem (Ru 2:1–3).

## PURPOSE

Biblical scholars have debated the original purpose of this book, for the author may have been teaching a number of lessons—for example, the need for a society to take care of its childless widows or the importance of racial tolerance. More obvious than these, however, is its portrayal of God's providential care of people committed to Him in the midst of overwhelming challenges to their faith. This charming account of faith in God contrasts sharply with the faithlessness displayed in Judges, the other Bible book that tells of the same time period. God's people who read and study Ruth today should enjoy it for its own sake in its Old Testament setting.

## FIRST PASS

The story is framed by a historical prologue of Naomi's sorrows (1:1–5) and a forward-looking epilogue of Naomi's renewal (4:13–22). Between these are four deftly drawn scenes: Naomi's affliction (chap. 1); Ruth meets Boaz (chap. 2); Ruth's appeal to Boaz (chap. 3); and Naomi's renewal (chap. 4).

### Naomi's Affliction

A famine was the occasion of Elimelech, Naomi, and their two sons moving from Bethlehem to Moab during the dark era in Israel's history ruled by the judges. Elimelech died in Moab. His sons, who married Moabite women, also died there. Faced with little hope, Naomi decided to return to her homeland in Bethlehem. Ruth, one of her daughters-in-law, strongly insisted on going with her. They arrived at Bethlehem as the barley harvest began (1:22).

### Ruth Meets Boaz

Boaz was a relative of Naomi's husband, Elimelech. He was a man of importance and wealth. According to Mosaic law, the poor could glean the corners of the fields. Ruth looked for work as the barley was being harvested. She happened to come to the field of Boaz. Boaz invited Ruth to work exclusively in his fields. Ruth was surprised by Boaz's generosity, particularly since she was a Moabitess, a foreigner. Boaz explained that he had already heard a good report about her commitment to Naomi. He commended Ruth for her faithfulness and prayed that God might bless her (2:12).

### Ruth's Appeal to Boaz

Naomi was concerned about finding long-term security for Ruth (3:1). She instructed Ruth to prepare herself properly and approach Boaz during the night at the threshing floor. She obeyed Naomi's instructions carefully. Ruth secretly approached Boaz. By lying at his feet, Ruth humbled herself as one of his servants. She trusted God to use Boaz to answer her needs and to protect her. Ruth startled Boaz since women were usually not with the men at night. She made her request: "Spread your cloak over me, for you are a family redeemer" (3:9). By this expression Ruth was asking Boaz for marriage (see Ezk 16:8).

### Naomi's Renewal

Boaz took the next step. He informed an unnamed kinsman that Naomi's fields were the kinsman's to redeem. The kinsman agreed to buy the fields, but Boaz added that whoever bought the land ought to marry Ruth to "perpetuate the man's name on his property" (4:5). The kinsman declined because that marriage would jeopardize his own inheritance. Boaz happily announced that he would redeem the property and marry Ruth himself. The elders witnessed it and offered a prayer of blessing. They asked God to give Boaz children as He did the wives of Jacob and the house of Judah through Tamar, who bore Perez. God rewarded the couple by giving them the child Obed. The women of the city praised God and recognized that Obed would sustain Naomi and possess Elimelech's property. Through Ruth, who continued the lineage of her husband and provided Israel with its greatest king, David, Naomi gained far more. Naomi experienced a complete reversal in her life from emptiness to fullness.

## THE RELIABILITY OF RUTH

The time of composition is disputed: Ruth has been dated to either the early monarchy (about 950 BC) or the postexilic period (about 450 BC). Linguistic arguments have not been decisive since they can be used to date the book either early or late. Also scholars are divided about whether the story fits better with the concerns of the monarchy or the setting of the postexilic period—whether it defends the Davidic dynasty or it simply promotes the faithfulness of Naomi, Ruth, and Boaz. Recently, however, many biblical scholars have adopted the traditional view of Ruth, accepting it as the historically trustworthy work of one writer from about 950 BC. These scholars argue that it is unlikely that David would have been linked to a Moabite ancestress unless he was in fact her descendant. Ruth's insistence on converting to the worship of Yahweh (1:16–17) and her good reputation (2:11–12) combine with Boaz's noble character (2:1) and his integrity (3:12–13) to demonstrate how a good king like David could emerge from the dark period of the judges.

## HOW RUTH FITS INTO GOD'S STORY

1. Prologue: Creation, Fall, and the Need for Redemption
2. **God Builds His Nation (2000–931 BC)**
3. God Educates His Nation (931–586 BC)
4. God Keeps a Faithful Remnant (586–6 BC)
5. God Purchases Redemption and Begins the Kingdom (6 BC to AD 30)
6. God Spreads the Kingdom Through the Church (AD 30-?)
7. God Consummates Redemption and Confirms His Eternal Kingdom
8. Epilogue: New Heaven and New Earth

## CHRIST IN RUTH

Boaz's role as kinsman-redeemer is fulfilled in greater measure by Christ who is both our Brother and our Redeemer. Ruth is in the genealogy of Christ. She is the great-grandmother of Israel's Messiah figure, King David.

## CHRISTIAN WORLDVIEW ELEMENTS

### Teachings About God

The sovereign hand of God in all circumstances is prominent throughout Ruth. The famine and the deaths of three husbands at the beginning of the book were not random acts that "just happened." They were the divinely arranged circumstances to incorporate Ruth into God's family and to bring her joy. God's bringing about Naomi's journey from emptiness to fullness parallels the way He brings all His people in the end to eternal fullness of joy. Many scholars recognize Boaz's role of kinsman-redeemer as a prefiguring of Jesus Christ.

### Teachings About Humanity

One of the virtues held up throughout the Old Testament is *chesed*, "loving kindness" or "acts of loyal friendship." Ruth, Boaz, and Naomi did memorable deeds based on *chesed*. Further, although human life inevitably includes pain and loss, it becomes purposeful when people see themselves living under God's protective care. Also, people find great blessing when they live according to God's commands, illustrated by Boaz's blessing because he followed both the law of gleaning and the law concerning levirate marriage.

### Teachings About Salvation

In this story a most unlikely person was reached by God's grace and gained full membership in the community of God's people. This shows that, even in the Old Testament, God's grace was not limited only to the descendants of Jacob. Further, Ruth's famous declaration of loyalty to Naomi (1:16–17) includes the concept that conversion and commitment to the Lord is a way of life, not just a point of decision.

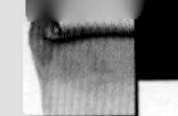



## GENRE AND LITERARY STYLE

**A Compact Narrative Written in Excellent Hebrew**

Many call Ruth a short story, and it may be called this with the understanding that its events really happened. In the Hebrew Scriptures it was placed in the third section, the Writings or *Kethuvim* (the other two sections are the Law and the Prophets). Among the Writings it was one of the Five Scrolls. Each of these Five Scrolls became associated with one of the Israelite festivals and was read publicly during that festival. Ruth was identified with *Shavuoth*, "Weeks" or "Pentecost," which celebrated the end of the barley harvest and the beginning of the wheat harvest. Its Hebrew is so carefully polished that Ruth has been likened to a precious jewel.

## A PRINCIPLE TO LIVE BY

**The Family of God (Ru 4:13–22, *Life Essentials Study Bible*, p. 340–41)**

We should use this beautiful love story to remind ourselves that through faith in Jesus Christ, we become spiritual brothers and sisters.

To access a video presentation of this principle featuring Dr. Gene Getz, use a Smartphone or iPad to connect to this QR code or go to http://www.bhpublishinggroup.com/handbook/ruth

The book is named for Samuel, the judge who anointed Saul and David, the first two kings of Israel, of whom 1 and 2 Samuel tell the story. In the Hebrew Bible 1 and 2 Samuel were originally one book. The Greek translators (second century BC), who divided the book, used the titles 1 and 2 Kingdoms.

## KEY TEXT: 18:7

*"As they celebrated, the women sang: Saul has killed his thousands, but David his tens of thousands."*

The Valley of Elah where David killed Goliath, the Philistine (1Sm 17:2,19).

## KEY TERM: "MONARCHY"

This book describes the beginning of the monarchy in Israel. The first king, Saul, was a failure; the second king, David, succeeded but struggled to survive Saul's bitter jealousy.

## ONE-SENTENCE SUMMARY

After Samuel's leadership as judge, the people of Israel turned to Saul as their first king, whom God later rejected and instead chose David, who had many adventures as a renegade from Saul's court.

# ORIGINAL HISTORICAL SETTING

## AUTHOR AND DATE OF WRITING

**Unknown, Perhaps Around 950 BC (During Solomon's Reign)**

The book (1 and 2 Samuel together) was composed by someone who used sources, for none of the characters in it could have been an eyewitness to all the events mentioned. Some scholars think a clue to authorship is found in 1 Chronicles 29:29: "As for the events of King David's reign, from beginning to end, note that they are written in the Events of Samuel the Seer, the Events of Nathan the Prophet, and the Events of Gad the Seer." The author's repeated use of the phrase "to this very day" (see 1 Sm 30:25) suggests a time of composition somewhat removed from when the events occurred. If the purpose of the composition was to answer questions about the legitimacy of Israel's kingship (see *Purpose* below), then a date during Solomon's reign but before the divided monarchy fits. Other scholars suggest that the historical note in 1 Samuel 27:6 requires a date after the monarchy divided, but this could be an editorial comment added later.

## FIRST AUDIENCE AND DESTINATION

**Israelites Living in Their Land During the Monarchy**

The book does not state its original audience or destination. Perhaps the original "Scroll of Samuel" was deposited in a book depository in Solomon's temple when it was first completed. There it would have joined the growing collection of Israel's sacred Scriptures.

## OCCASION

Since the authorship and date of composition are unknown, the occasion cannot be surmised. Because of its ultimate position in the Hebrew canon of Scripture as the third of the "Former Prophets," 1 and 2 Samuel may have been prompted by the

author's desire to continue the story of God's people Israel that the books of Joshua and Judges began. Some scholars believe that the author was propelled by discovering long passages originally composed by someone else and which stood on their own. These include the "Ark Narrative" (1 Sm 4:1–7:1), "David's Rise to Power" (1 Sm 16:14–2 Sm 5:10), and "Absalom's Revolt" (2 Sm 13–20).

## GOD'S MESSAGE IN 1 SAMUEL

### PURPOSE

Since this book was originally the first half of a single composition, the purpose for the books now called 1 and 2 Samuel must be considered together. This work answered important questions for Israelites (probably living in the days of Solomon) about the true nature of the Davidic dynasty. If the people had been wrong to ask for a king and if God had rejected Saul as king, then why should they now suppose that the monarchs of the Davidic line would continue? The work is filled with narrative tension between the dangers of a king (1 Sm 8) and the hope for an enduring dynasty (2 Sm 7). The answer is that despite human evil God worked to bring about His plan for an everlasting kingdom with an everlasting King (2 Sm 7:16). God's people who study the books of Samuel today should view them with this original purpose in mind.

### FIRST PASS

First Samuel tells of the transition in leadership from the period of the judges to the rise of the monarchy. The book continues the story of Israel's wars with the Philistines begun in the book of Judges (see Jdg 13–16). First Samuel is organized around three great men and tells their stories successively.

#### Samuel: Judge and Prophet

In the opening section the godly life of Samuel is distinguished from the failures of the high priest Eli and his sons, Hophni and Phinehas. Although Samuel and the sons of Eli were reared in the same house, their dedication and destinies were different. The Philistine wars led to the end of Eli's family, but Samuel prevailed over the Philistines and led Israel as judge and prophet (chaps. 1–7).

#### Saul: Israel's First King

Israel's disappointment with the priesthood of Eli and the sin of Samuel's sons led Israel to turn to a new form of leadership. The people, following the example of the nations around them, demanded a king (1 Sm 8). God granted their desires, and Samuel reluctantly appointed a king. Saul's reign had a promising beginning. King Saul, however, proved to be unlike Samuel because he did not listen to the word of the Lord. The Lord thus rejected Saul just as He had the house of Eli.

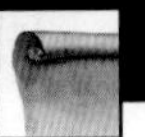



### David: From Shepherd to King

The book's final section focuses on the personalities of Saul and David. Although Saul is king until the end of the book (chaps. 16–31), the narrative turns to his successor's rise. David's story is told from the viewpoint of Saul's continued failures. Saul's reign was chaotic, marred by personal problems and the threat of Philistine oppression. While it became clearer that Saul was unfit for leadership, David emerged before the nation as God's champion to defeat the Philistines and rule the land. In the end Saul would take his own life.

## THE RELIABILITY OF 1 AND 2 SAMUEL

Critical scholarship in the twentieth century repeatedly questioned the historical reliability of the OT by asserting that extrabiblical evidence to verify the biblical accounts was either sparse or nonexistent. As recently as 1994, P. R. Davies expressed a widely held appraisal of the historical value of the OT's historical books when he said, "King David is about as historical as King Arthur."[1] A widely held view is that the kingdom of David and Solomon is fictional, giving a small nation a sense of a glorious past.

Since 1993, however, three artifacts with references to David have come to light. The first is the Tel Dan Stele found in the ruins of ancient Dan in Northern Israel. The inscription on this stone slab refers to two kings mentioned in the Bible: "Jehoram (Joram) son of Ahab, King of Israel" and "Ahaziahu (Ahaziah) son of Jehoram (Joram), king of the House of David" (2 Kg 9:23).

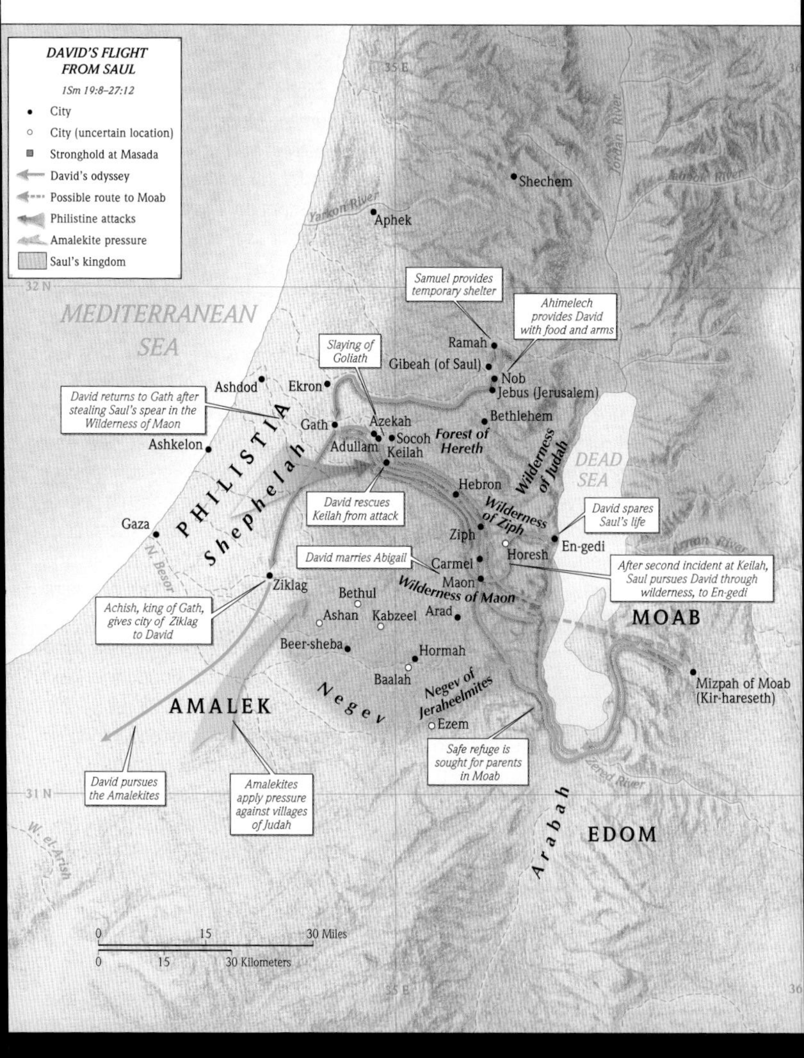


David's success in battle and the people's love for him made Saul wildly fearful for his kingdom. Saul tried in numerous ways to have David killed.

The second is the Mesha Stele or Moabite Stone. This stone, which bears an inscription from the reign of the same King Mesha mentioned in 2 Kings 3, was discovered in 1868, near the ruins of ancient Dibon, by a German missionary. Known also as The Mesha Inscription, the monument reports the major accomplishments of King Mesha's reign. He boasts especially of having recovered Moabite independence from Israel and of having restored Moabite control over northern Moab. The phrase "House of [Da]vid" is part of the inscription. This artifact was badly damaged following its discovery as different local factions tried to take possession of it. The reassembled stele can now be seen in the Louvre.

The third inscription is found in a list of Pharaoh Shoshenq's military victories recorded on the wall of Amun's temple at Karnak, near Luxor, Egypt. Shoshenq (Shishak) invaded Judah during the fifth year of Rehoboam's reign (2 Ch 12:1–12). In his list of victories, he included the phrase "highlands/heights of David."[2]

The existence of a strong centralized government that developed following a period of destruction has been confirmed in such cities as Hazor, Megiddo, and Gezer; this agrees well with the Bible's claims regarding the Israelite conquest of Canaan and the development of a national government during the kingship period.

The promises God made to David in 2 Samuel 7 created hopes and expectations that the New Testament writers understood to have been fulfilled by Jesus the Messiah. The Lord promised David that He would establish the kingdom of one of David's descendants (2 Sm 7:12); in the New Testament Jesus was identified as that descendant of David (Mt 1:20; 21:9) who brought the kingdom of God to humanity (Mt 12:28; Lk 11:20). God said David's descendant would build a house for God's name (2 Sm 7:13); the New Testament writers portrayed Jesus as the One who built the ultimate temple of God in three days (Mt 26:61; Jn 2:19). God promised David that one of his descendants would have a throne that would last forever (2 Sm 7:13); the New Testament declares that such a throne belongs to Jesus (Heb 1:8). God said that one of David's descendants would be a "son to Me"

The relief of Shoshenq I's campaign list at the southern exterior walls of the temple of Karnak, north of Luxor, Egypt.

(2 Sm 7:14); Jesus came as the ultimate Son of God (Mt 16:16; Mk 1:1; Lk 1:35).

## HOW 1 SAMUEL FITS INTO GOD'S STORY

1. Prologue: Creation, Fall, and the Need for Redemption
2. **God Builds His Nation (2000–931 BC)**
3. God Educates His Nation (931–586 BC)
4. God Keeps a Faithful Remnant (586–6 BC)
5. God Purchases Redemption and Begins the Kingdom (6 BC to AD 30)
6. God Spreads the Kingdom Through the Church (AD 30-?)
7. God Consummates Redemption and Confirms His Eternal Kingdom
8. Epilogue: New Heaven and New Earth

## CHRIST IN 1 SAMUEL

First Samuel presents Israel's first two kings, Saul and David. These kings of Israel foreshadow Israel's true King, Jesus Christ. Jesus is in the lineage of David and is called Son of David, a term equivalent to Messiah. Samuel's model of priest, prophet, and political leader foreshadows Jesus' role as Prophet, Priest, and King. First Samuel includes the first mention of a person being called the anointed of Yahweh. This is significant because the word *Messiah* or *Christ* means "anointed one."

## CHRISTIAN WORLDVIEW ELEMENTS

### Teachings About God

God was responsible for shaping Israel's destiny. He allowed Israel's choice of Saul to stand, but He judged Saul for his disobedience. He chose David, who by the end of 1 Samuel was not yet secure in his position as king. The Spirit of God is seen as the divine enabler: He came upon both Saul and David to empower their service.

### Teachings About Humanity

This book teaches about mankind through telling the stories of three heroes: Samuel, Saul, and David. Samuel was a dedicated servant of God who nevertheless failed as a parent. Saul was a handsome, talented leader who failed in his primary task: glad obedience to God's revealed will. David's life (in 1 Samuel) demonstrates that those whom God chooses may come as a surprise to other humans, and that they may face great difficulties and yet serve Him wholeheartedly.

### Teachings About Salvation

This book shows that a right relationship with God inevitably brings with it obedience from the heart and that God values heart obedience much more than external conformity to religious rituals: "Then Samuel said: Does the LORD take pleasure in burnt offerings and sacrifices as much as in obeying the LORD? Look: to obey is better than sacrifice, to pay attention is better than the fat of rams" (15:22).

## GENRE AND LITERARY STYLE

**A Historical Account Written in Hebrew**

First Samuel narrates the rise of monarchy in Israel by giving the biographies of three men: Samuel, Saul, and David. When secondary characters such as Hannah and Jonathan enter the story, they are important only as they relate to the major characters. Although the Hebrew writing style is acceptable, the hand-copied Hebrew manuscripts of 1 and 2 Samuel have occasional defects in which words are missing—for example Saul's age and length of reign in 1 Samuel 13:1. (Compare the HCSB with the KJV at this point.) In these cases scholars rely on other ancient versions of the book. In the Hebrew canon this was included in the "Former Prophets." See comments on *Genre and Literary Style* in **2 KINGS** for further material about the possible literary relationship of the "Former Prophets."

## A PRINCIPLE TO LIVE BY

**Prideful Behavior (1Sm 15:22–23, *Life Essentials Study Bible*, p. 368)**

We must be on guard against prideful behavior, which Satan wants to use to lead us into rebellion against God.

To access a video presentation of this principle featuring Dr. Gene Getz, use a Smartphone or iPad to connect to this QR code or go to http://www.bhpublishinggroup.com/handbook/1samuel

## ENDNOTES

1. P. R. Davies, "'House of David' Built on Sand," *BARev* 20, no. 4 (1994:54–55, on 55, quoted in *A Biblical History of Israel*, Iain Provan, V. Philips Long, and Tremper Longman III (Louisville: Westminster John Knox Press, 2003), 216.

2. I. Provan, V. P. Long, T. Longman III, *A Biblical History of Israel* (Louisville: Westminster John Knox Press, 2003), 216.

The book is named for Samuel, the judge who anointed Saul and David, the first two kings of Israel, of whom 1 and 2 Samuel tell the story. In the Hebrew Bible 1 and 2 Samuel were originally one book. The Greek translators (second century BC), who divided the book, used the titles 1 and 2 Kingdoms.

## KEY TEXT: 7:16

*"Your house and kingdom will endure before Me forever, and your throne will be established forever."*

ome view David's moving the Israel's capital from Hebron to Jerusalem as the most important eographical decision in the Bible. Shown here is Warren's Shaft, an almost 50-foot vertical chan-el through which water came into the fortified Jebusite citadel from the Gihon Spring (2Sm :7–8). David and his men took this heavily fortified Jebusite stronghold by making entry through his shaft, discovered in 1867 by Sir Charles Warren, a British Army officer and archaeologist.

## KEY TERM: "DAVID"

The name "David" appears more than 200 times in this book. It focuses entirely on the time he was king of Israel.

## ONE-SENTENCE SUMMARY

David's reign over Israel included times of elation, such as his conquest of Jerusalem and the Lord's promise of an everlasting dynasty, as well as times of failure, such as his adultery with Bathsheba and the treason of his son Absalom.

# ORIGINAL HISTORICAL SETTING

## AUTHOR AND DATE OF WRITING

**Unknown, Perhaps Around 950 BC (During Solomon's Reign).**

Because 1 and 2 Samuel first existed as a single composition, see the discussion on *Author and Date of Writing* in **1 SAMUEL**.

## FIRST AUDIENCE AND DESTINATION

**Israelites Living in the Land of Israel During the Monarchy**

## OCCASION

**Unknown**

Water shaft at Gibeon. Following Saul's death a crucial meeting occurred in Gibeon involving Abner and Joab, the respective generals of Saul and David (2Sm 2:12–17). A "sporting" battle (v. 14) by the pool of Gibeon ensued in which the men of Joab proved to be victorious. Archaeologists have discovered a spiraling shaft and tunnel with circular stairway leading to water and providing the city a way to get water inside the city walls during enemy attacks. Gibeon also played host to part of Sheba's rebellion against David (2Sm 20:8–13).

## PURPOSE

Because 1 and 2 Samuel first existed as a single composition, see the discussion in the *Purpose* section for **1 SAMUEL**.

## FIRST PASS

### God Establishes

Second Samuel continues the story of how God established His kingdom through the leadership of Israel's monarchy. The book begins by tracing the triumphs of David's reign, first over the tribe of Judah (2:1–32) and then over all Israel (5:1–12). David secured the borders of Israel, subjugated its enemies, and brought prosperity to the fledgling kingdom. The Davidic covenant is the theological centerpiece of the book (chap. 7). God promised David and his heirs an eternal lineage that would rule over an everlasting kingdom (7:12–16). The Davidic king was God's adopted son who ruled in the name of the Lord and enjoyed God's providential care. This covenant promise became the messianic hope of God's people. This promise is fulfilled by David's greater Son, Jesus Christ (Lk 1:31–33).

### God Chastens

The sin of David and Bathsheba changes the tenor of the story from David's triumphs to his mounting troubles (11:1–27). Nathan the prophet delivered a divine oracle of judgment against David for his sin with Bathsheba (12:1–23). Unlike Saul, who tried to excuse his sin, David confessed his sins before the Lord (12:13). The child that was conceived died. God, however, gave Bathsheba the child Solomon, whom the Lord loved (12:24–25). God continued to reveal His will to David through the prophets Nathan and Gad and the priests Zadok and Abiathar (12:1–14; 15:24–29; 24:11–14). Also, He was merciful by safeguarding David during the rebellions of Absalom and Sheba (chaps. 18; 20).

### God Preserves

The last section of the book is an appendix to David's career as the Lord's anointed. Here the emphasis falls on David's praise for God's sovereign mercies and the mighty warriors the Lord used in the service of the king (21:1–24:25). The stories of famine, war, and pestilence resulting from Israel's sin were fitting reminders that no king was above the word of the Lord.

## THE RELIABILITY OF 2 SAMUEL

**See *The Reliability of 1 and 2 Samuel* in 1 SAMUEL**

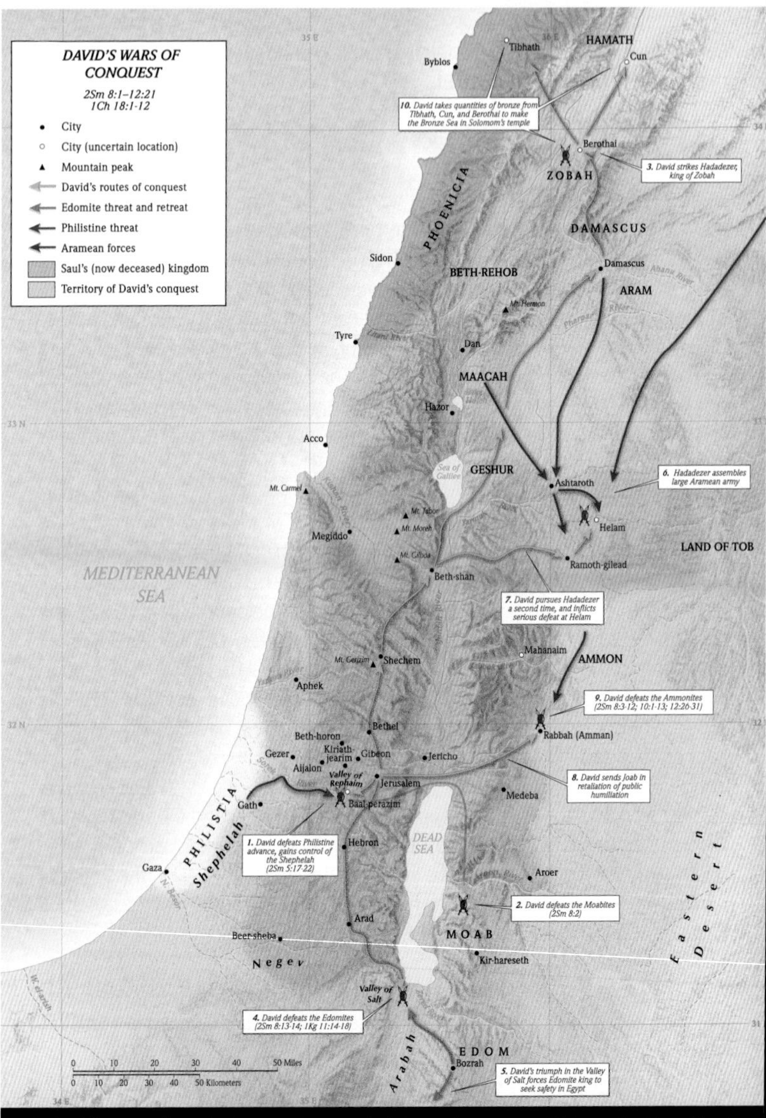


David's skill as a military leader greatly extended the territory over which a united Israel had control.

## HOW 2 SAMUEL FITS INTO GOD'S STORY

1. Prologue: Creation, Fall, and the Need for Redemption
2. God Builds His Nation (2000–931 BC)
3. God Educates His Nation (931–586 BC)
4. God Keeps a Faithful Remnant (586–6 BC)
5. God Purchases Redemption and Begins the Kingdom (6 BC to AD 30)
6. God Spreads the Kingdom Through the Church (AD 30-?)
7. God Consummates Redemption and Confirms His Eternal Kingdom
8. Epilogue: New Heaven and New Earth

## CHRIST IN 2 SAMUEL

As founder of the dynasty of which Jesus ("Son of David") is the eternal King, David illustrates Christ's kingship in many ways. His compassion and loyalty to Mephibosheth (9:1–13) was one example of the undeserved love we receive from God.

## CHRISTIAN WORLDVIEW ELEMENTS

### Teachings About God

God is sovereign in carrying out His kingdom plans. His unconditional covenant with undeserving David (chap. 7) is as magnificent as His covenant with Abraham. This book also says a great deal about approaching God in worship. He desires the worship of His people, but only in the ways He has revealed, as the material about the ark of the covenant emphasizes.

### Teachings About Humanity

Second Samuel throws the spotlight on one individual, David, who modeled magnificently that humans can accomplish great tasks for God when their hearts are passionately turned to pleasing him. On the other hand, David's sins and failures show that redeemed humans still must deal with the effects of the fall in their lives.

### Teachings About Salvation

The account of David's adultery, Nathan's confrontation with the king, and David's subsequent repentance and restoration stand as a profound paradigm of salvation. The following exchange distills the message of redemption even today: "David responded to Nathan, 'I have sinned against the LORD.' Then Nathan replied to David, 'The LORD has taken away your sin; you will not die'" (12:13). David's reflection on this experience, Psalm 51, stands unsurpassed in Scripture on the relationship between confession of sin and divine forgiveness.

## GENRE AND LITERARY STYLE

**A Historical Narrative Written in Hebrew, with a Few Passages of Poetry**

The narrative of 2 Samuel focuses on David's exploits as king. His relationship to God, Israel's true King, also receives attention. The writer portrayed him realistically and was careful not to gloss over David's faults. The memorable poetic sections were David's compositions: "The Song of the Bow" (1:19–27); "Psalm of Praise" (22:1–51, which is also Psalm 18); and "David's Last Words" (23:1–7). Second Samuel in the Hebrew canon was part of the "Former Prophets." See comments on *Genre and Literary Style* in **2 KINGS** for further material about the possible literary relationship of the "Former Prophets."

## PRINCIPLE TO LIVE BY

**God's Sovereign Plan (2Sm 7:1–17, *Life Essentials Study Bible*, p. 398–99)**

Though our journey through life includes many human factors, we must remember that God's sovereign plan for each one of us continues to unfold.

To access a video presentation of this principle featuring Dr. Gene Getz, use a Smartphone or iPad to connect to this QR code or go to http://www.bhpublishinggroup.com/handbook/2samuel

*Melakim*, the Hebrew title, means "kings." Originally a single work, 1 and 2 Kings was first divided into two books by the Greek translators (second century BC), and English Bibles follow this pattern. The Greek version used the titles 3 and 4 Kingdoms.

## KEY TEXT: 11:35-36

*"I will take 10 tribes of the kingdom from his son's hand and give them to you. I will give one tribe to his son, so that My servant David will always have a lamp before Me in Jerusalem, the city I chose for Myself to put My name there."*

## KEY TERM: "DIVISION"

This book describes the division of the Israelites into two competing kingdoms. The kings of Israel, the northern kingdom, were invariably idolatrous, while the kings of Judah, the southern kingdom, were sometimes good and sometimes evil.

## ONE-SENTENCE SUMMARY

After Solomon's splendid rule, culminating in the dedication of the temple in Jerusalem, the kingdom divided, and to confront idolatry God raised up prophets, notably Elijah, who opposed the evil Ahab.

# ORIGINAL HISTORICAL SETTING

## AUTHOR AND DATE OF WRITING

**Unknown, Perhaps Jeremiah About 560 BC**

First and 2 Kings are anonymous, but Jewish tradition named Jeremiah, who was also credited with the books of Jeremiah and Lamentations. Most modern scholars discount the traditional view. Whoever the author was cannot now be known. The perspective is that of the exile in Babylon. The writer, however, used sources from an earlier time, incorporating their phrases "to this day" and "still today" (for example, 1 Kg 8:8; 2 Kg 8:22) for matters that did not exist during the exile.

## FIRST AUDIENCE AND DESTINATION

**Probably the Israelites Living in Babylonian Exile**

The original audience is not stated but is judged from reading the book. See the discussion below on *Purpose* for an explanation of how 1 and 2 Kings met the needs of Israelites living after the destruction of Jerusalem and the temple.

## OCCASION

Some official court records from the monarchy were evidently preserved and transported to Babylon. These included "The Book of Solomon's Events" (1 Kg 11:41); "The Historical Record of Israel's Kings" (1 Kg 14:19 and 17 other references); and "The Historical Record of Judah's Kings" (1 Kg 14:29 and 14 other references). The writer selected materials from these records to interpret the era of Solomon and the divided monarchy for people of his own day.

# GOD'S MESSAGE IN 1 KINGS

## PURPOSE

Since this book was originally the first half of a single composition, the purpose for the books now called 1 and 2 Kings must be considered together. This work answered important questions for Israelites (probably living in the years of exile in Babylon) about the period of the kings from God's perspective. If they were now in exile, why had this happened, especially since Solomon's rule had been so splendid? Had the later kings failed militarily? politically? economically? The answer was that the kings and the people under them had all failed religiously. They had abandoned the Lord, their true King, and He had sent three painful lessons to teach them the importance of staying true to Him. First, He divided Israel into two kingdoms (1 Kings 12, about 931 BC); second, He sent the idolatrous northern kingdom into permanent captivity through the Assyrians (2 Kings 17, about 722 BC); third, He sent the idolatrous southern kingdom into temporary exile through the Babylonians (2 Kings 25, about 586 BC).

Thus, the author wrote a highly selective account of the kings, evaluating each one as to whether he did right or evil in the eyes of the Lord. The author's religious perspective is also seen in that about a third of the narrative focuses on the prophetic ministries of Elijah and Elisha. God's people who study the books of Kings today should do so with this original purpose in mind.

## FIRST PASS

### Ruthless Succession

As David's reign came to an end, his son Adonijah attempted to make himself king by acquiring a following and declaring himself to be the king (1:5–10). Nathan the prophet and Bathsheba interceded, and David named Solomon as his successor. Once Solomon was declared king, he exercised "wisdom" and exterminated those who might oppose his kingship (1:11–2:46): Adonijah, Joab, and Shimei. Also, Abiathar the priest, who joined Adonijah's insurrection, was banished from the

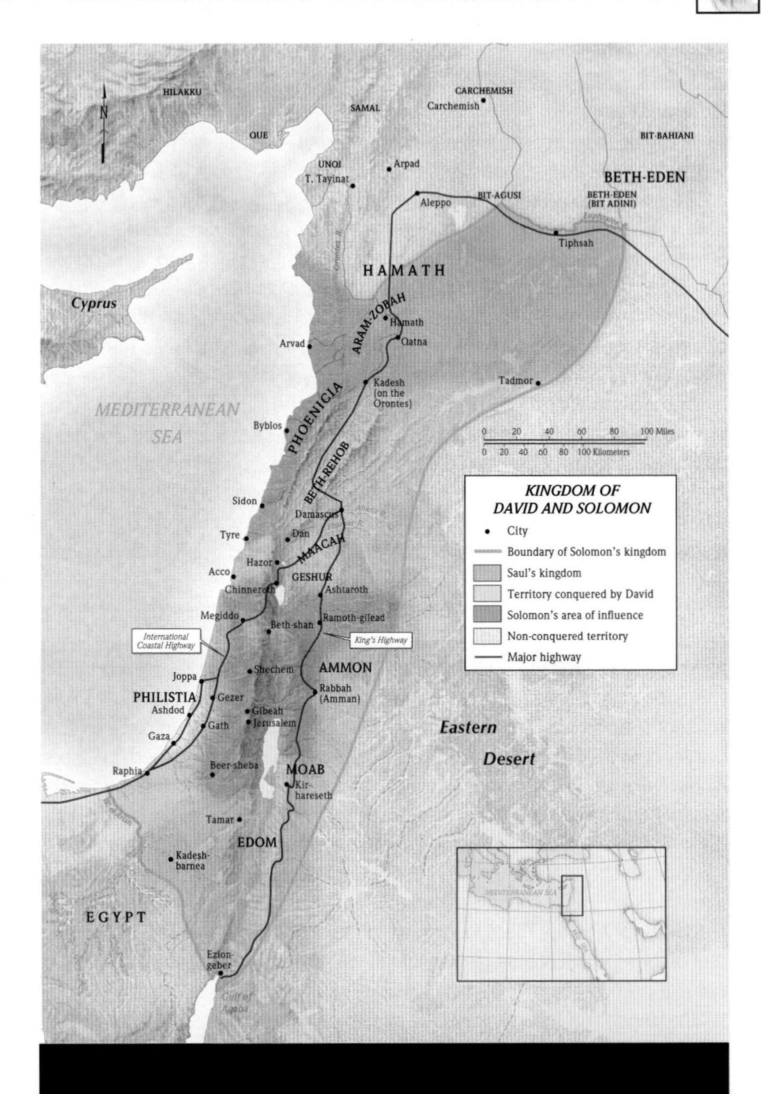


This map shows how Israel's territory grew under David's reign and the increased areas of influence Solomon's kingship brought.

priesthood in fulfillment of the prophecy against the house of Eli in Shiloh (1 Sm 2:27–36; 3:10–14).

**Riches and Ruin**

As he began his reign, Solomon acted decisively but realized that in order to govern he needed more than human wisdom. He humbly asked God for such wisdom. God answered Solomon's request and more (chap. 3). Solomon's classic display of wisdom is seen in his arbitration between the two prostitutes disputing over a child. Solomon was able to assemble an impressive administration and to undertake numerous building projects, in particular the Jerusalem temple. He became an important international figure through wealth, trade, and politics. These accomplishments were God's blessing because of His covenant with David (4:1–10:29). Although Solomon's wealth exceeded that of any king of Israel either before or after him, he still had an "Achilles' heel"—foreign gods. The foreign wives Solomon had married brought other gods into Solomon's life. These wives turned Solomon's heart away from total devotion to Yahweh, and Solomon both worshipped these foreign gods and built shrines to them. This sinful action was a blight on the magnificent reign of Solomon, but true to Deuteronomic form, the author of 1 Kings recorded God's pronouncement of judgment—the tearing away of the kingdom from Solomon (11:1–43). God brought this judgment to pass after Solomon died. Interestingly, no spiritual evaluation of Solomon is present in the text as is so common in 1 and 2 Kings for all the kings after Solomon.

**Judah and Israel Divided**

The once-united nation of Israel then entered a downward spiral (12:1–16:34). Solomon's son, Rehoboam, acted unwisely in stating his intention to place an even heavier burden of labor and taxation on the people than did his father. This action empowered Jeroboam, a former enemy of Solomon, to "break away" from the Jerusalem monarchy. The 10 northern tribes then became the nation of Israel, and the two southern tribes (Judah and Benjamin) became the nation of Judah (c. 930 BC). Jeroboam became the first king of the northern kingdom. He erected idolatrous shrines at Dan and Bethel thus attempting to keep the people from traveling to Jerusalem to worship. These idolatrous shrines contained golden calves, reminiscent of the rebellion of the Israelites at Mount Sinai. Israel suffered the bloodshed of war and political coups. In all, nine dynasties ruled Israel in its 200 years (931–722 BC). The kingdom of Judah enjoyed the stability of only one dynastic house since the Lord preserved the throne of David. Yet its kings also committed the idolatrous sins of their northern counterparts. The kings of Judah continually experienced war, and only righteous Asa had a long, prosperous rule.

**Elijah and Micaiah**

Though most of the kings of Israel have a scant amount of information concerning their exploits, Ahab and Jehu, who reigned during the prophetic ministries of Elijah

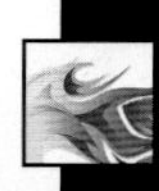

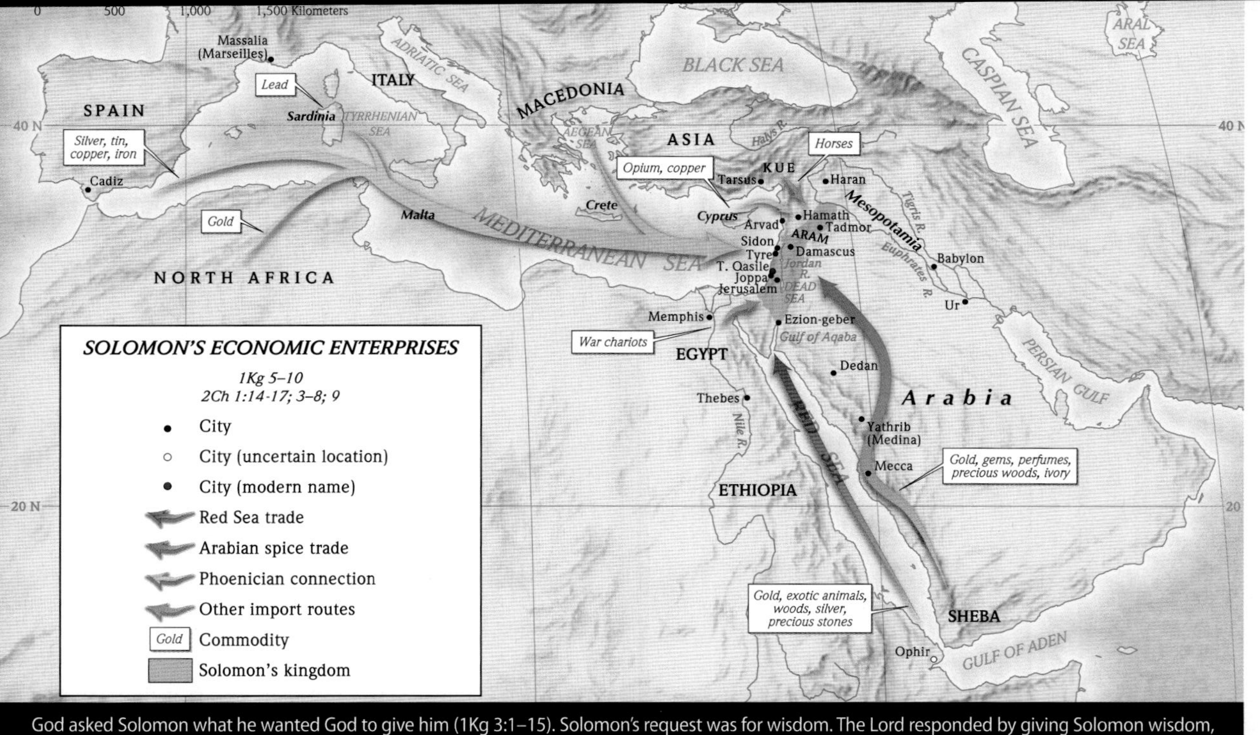


God asked Solomon what he wanted God to give him (1Kg 3:1–15). Solomon's request was for wisdom. The Lord responded by giving Solomon wisdom, understanding, and insight as vast as the sand on the seashore (4:29). One sphere in which that wisdom was expressed was in international trade.

and Elisha, receive additional attention (17:1–22:53). Elijah enters the narrative in 1 Kings 17. By confronting King Ahab (c. 874/73–853 BC), Queen Jezebel, and the prophets of Baal, Elijah appears as a champion for faithfulness to the covenant with Yahweh. Elijah was a miracle-working prophet who remained faithful to Yahweh in spite of persecution. After fleeing from Jezebel to the Negev/Sinai region, Elijah received the word of God regarding the concept of a remnant (1 Kg 19:18). Yahweh told Elijah that 7,000 people had not bowed down to Baal; therefore, God would spare their lives. In fulfillment of God's word at Horeb, Elijah placed the prophetic mantle upon Elisha, who ministered during the ninth century BC. The transition from 1 Kings to 2 Kings is virtually seamless, indicative of these two books being a single document originally.

## THE RELIABILITY OF 1, 2 KINGS AND 1, 2 CHRONICLES

The books of Kings and Chronicles give two perspectives on the history of Israel. In recent years questions have been raised about how much history these books contain. One view is that much of the Old Testament was written between 400 and 200 years before Christ and that, rather than being history, Israel as we see it in the Bible is a fictitious invention. To what extent are the accounts we read in Kings and Chronicles anchored in history of the ancient Near East?

Kenneth Kitchen, an Egyptologist at the University of Liverpool, says two kinds of evidence have a bearing on the question of the historicity alleged in a document: direct or explicit evidence and indirect or implicit evidence.[1]

The books of Kings and Chronicles list some 20 rulers of nations other than Israel and Judah. If these rulers were the invention of someone creating a history, we would not expect to find those same rulers mentioned in documents outside Israel/Judah. But of these 20 rulers, all but three of them are found in records of their own country.

Another test that can be performed is to look at kings of Israel and Judah mentioned in Kings and Chronicles and ask how many of these kings are mentioned in documents of other nations. Nine of 15 of Israel's kings and eight of 15 of Judah's rulers are named in documents of other nations. Credible explanations can be given for many of these kings who are not mentioned. For the era covered by Kings and Chronicles, there was not much contact between Israel/Judah and other nations in the region prior to 853 BC. That began to change with the expansion of the Neo-Assyrian Empire to the northeast. Furthermore, some missing kings of Israel/Judah are attested on seals and bullae found by archaeologists.[2]

Kitchen says the sequence and chronology of both Hebrew and foreign kings is "impeccably accurate" in 1,2 Kings. This is an additional indicator that Israel's history is not just a piece of pious fiction conceived late in the first millennium before Christ.

## HOW 1 KINGS FITS INTO GOD'S STORY

1. Prologue: Creation, Fall, and the Need for Redemption
2. God Builds His Nation (2000–931 BC)
3. God Educates His Nation (931–586 BC)
4. God Keeps a Faithful Remnant (586–6 BC)
5. God Purchases Redemption and Begins the Kingdom (6 BC to AD 30)
6. God Spreads the Kingdom Through the Church (AD 30-?)
7. God Consummates Redemption and Confirms His Eternal Kingdom
8. Epilogue: New Heaven and New Earth

## CHRIST IN 1 KINGS

Solomon, David's son and Israel's third king, is prominent in 1 Kings. Solomon's wisdom and splendor were known far beyond Israel. This shining hour in Israel's history points to the wisdom and glory of Christ. Jesus reminded one of His audiences that the queen of Sheba made a long journey to hear Solomon and One greater than Solomon is now among them (Luke 11:31).

## CHRISTIAN WORLDVIEW ELEMENTS

### Teachings About God

First Kings emphasizes "one God, one temple." Because Israel's God is the one true Lord of all, He can be worshipped properly at the one place He has designated: the temple in Jerusalem. He will not tolerate the worship of rival deities (such as Baal). He will not long endure being worshipped in rival sites such as at the shrines of the golden calves in Dan and Bethel or on the "high places." The Spirit is present to inspire God's prophets.

### Teachings About Humanity

This book looks at humanity by evaluating the kings' lives. The only thing that really mattered was whether a king did "right in the LORD's eyes" (15:5,11; 22:43) or did "evil in the LORD's sight" (11:6).

### Teachings About Salvation

On one hand 1 Kings emphasizes that salvation is entirely due to God's sovereign work. Solomon's temple dedication prayer emphasized this: "For You, Lord GOD, have set them apart as Your inheritance from all the people on earth" (8:53). On the other hand His people were expected to live in loyalty to the covenant, and kings and people are both evaluated according to the terms of the covenant established at Mount Sinai.

## GENRE AND LITERARY STYLE

**A Selective Historical Account Written in Hebrew**

First Kings focuses on the days of Solomon and then tells of the reigns of most other kings with broad strokes. Then when he comes to Ahab, the author provides a number of details once again, in particular describing the role of Elijah as the prophet of the Lord. First Kings in the Hebrew Scriptures was one of the "Former Prophets." See comments on *Genre and Literary Style* in **2 KINGS** for further material about the possible literary relationship of the "Former Prophets."

## A PRINCIPLE TO LIVE BY

**Aged Wisdom (1Kg 12:1–19, *Life Essentials Study Bible*, p. 448)**

When seeking advice, we should value the accumulated wisdom of those who are older than we are.

To access a video presentation of this principle featuring Dr. Gene Getz, use a Smartphone or iPad to connect to this QR code or go to http://www.bhpublishinggroup.com/handbook/1kings

## ENDNOTES

1. Kenneth A. Kitchen, *On the Reliability of the Old Testament* (Grand Rapids: Eerdmans, 2003), 4.
2. Ibid., 62–64.

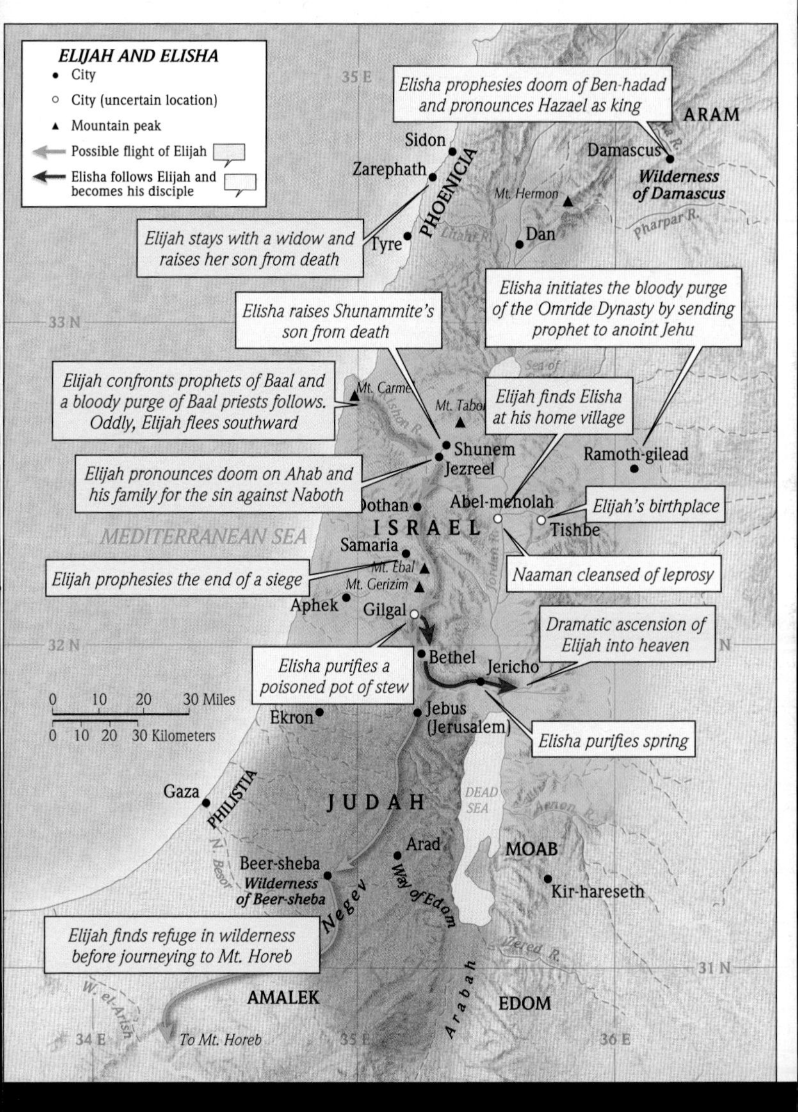


The era of Elijah's (862–852 BC) and Elisha's (?850-?798) ministries was one of great challenges within Israel and with surrounding nations. This era, like that of the exodus and the life and ministry of Jesus, was one in which God worked through these prophets in miraculous ways.

Elijah asked Elisha what he could do for him before he was taken from him. Elisha asked for two shares of Elijah's spirit. "Elijah replied, 'You have asked for something difficult. If you see me being taken from you, you will have it. If not, you won't'" (2 Kg 2:1–15). Elijah's fiery ascension into heaven, witnessed by Elisha, is portrayed here in a sixteenth-century Russian painting from Pskov Museum. Following this event, the sons of the prophets from Jericho met Elisha

*Melakim*, the Hebrew title, means "kings." Originally a single work, 1 and 2 Kings was first divided into two books by the Greek translators (second century BC), and English Bibles follow this pattern. The Greek version used the titles 3 and 4 Kingdoms.

## KEY TEXT: 17:22–23

*"The Israelites persisted in all the sins that Jeroboam committed and did not turn away from them. Finally, the LORD removed Israel from His presence just as He had declared through all His servants the prophets. So Israel has been exiled to Assyria from their homeland until today."*

## KEY TERM: "DISPERSION"

This book tells the ongoing story of the Israelites in two competing kingdoms with its sad conclusion. The northern kingdom fell to Assyria and was dispersed forever. Then the southern kingdom fell to the Babylonians and likewise went into exile.

## ONE-SENTENCE SUMMARY

Even after Elisha's ministry, Israel persisted in idolatry and so went into permanent captivity; yet Judah, despite the prophets and a few righteous kings, continued to be so wicked that God sent Nebuchadnezzar to remove them to Babylon.

# ORIGINAL HISTORICAL SETTING

## AUTHOR AND DATE OF WRITING

**Unknown, Perhaps Jeremiah About 560 BC**

## FIRST AUDIENCE AND DESTINATION

**Probably the Israelites Living in Babylonian Exile**

## OCCASION

**Unknown, but see 1 KINGS**

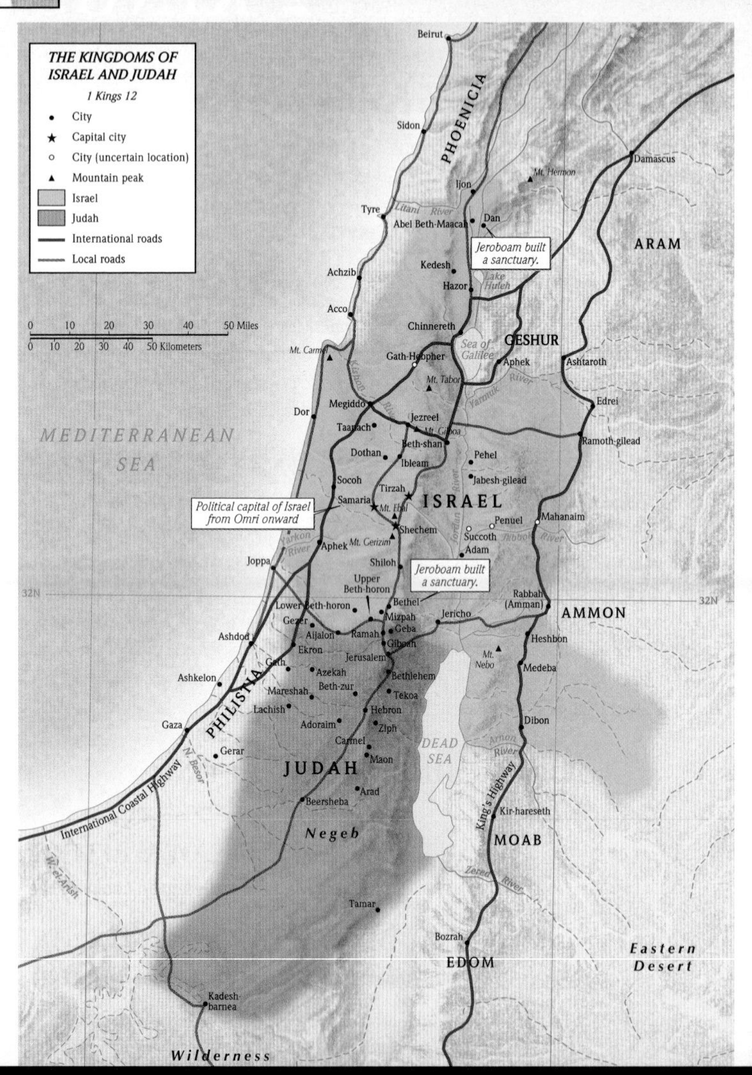


Solomon became one of the most significant monarchs of his era. By the end of his 40-year reign, his kingdom was strong, but his commitment to the Lord had waned, and his latter years were troubled by internal problems. Soon after his death, the united monarchy ended. The united kingdom of the 12 tribes suddenly divided in 931/930 BC. The 10 tribes in the north would henceforth be known as Israel or Ephraim (its most influential tribe). The two southern tribes, Judah and Benjamin, remained loyal to the house of David and was known as Judah.

## PURPOSE

Because 1 and 2 Kings first existed as a single composition, see the discussion in the *Purpose* section of **1 KINGS**.

## FIRST PASS

### Elisha

The introductory section continues the account of the prophets, Elijah and Elisha, who delivered the word of the Lord during this decadent period in the life of the nation. Elijah's ministry closed with his ascent to heaven. But his successor, Elisha, picked up his mantle and performed a double portion of God's wondrous acts. Through Elisha's prophetic ministry, the Lord guided Israel to victories over their enemies, the Moabites and Arameans. God showed that He also is the Lord of all nations and shapes their destinies (1:1–8:29).

### Decline and Destruction of Israel

The second section describes the deterioration and eventual collapse of the northern state of Israel under the weight of its religious paganism and political infighting. Jehu's dynasty rid Israel of its Baalism, postponing God's wrath. But the slide to

A panel on the Black Obelisk of Shalmaneser III, king of Assyria (858–824 BC). Here, Jehu, king of Israel (848–814 BC) is paying tribute to Shalmaneser. Jehu was likely securing his position as king by this alliance with the ever-expanding Neo-Assyrian Empire. This artifact is unique in showing a king of Israel or Judah on a monument of another nation.

destruction came quickly afterwards with the rise and fall of four dynasties within the short span of 30 years. The climax of the account is the final chapter of the section, which explains why Israel did not survive (17:7–41). By disregarding the covenant, Israel chose death (Dt 30:19–20).

Meanwhile, the southern kingdom, the descendants of David, escaped annihilation only by the grace of God. The alliances of Jehoshaphat with Israelite kings (see 1 Kg 22; 2 Kg 3; 2 Ch 20:35–37), sealed by intermarriage (2 Kg 8:18; 2 Ch 18:1), threatened the existence of the Davidic line when Athaliah became queen mother. The reigns of Joash and Amazaiah were the only two periods of stability in the otherwise tottering kingdom to the south.

**Survival and Final Days of Judah**

The final section of Kings traces the survival of Judah after Samaria's collapse. From the perspective of the biblical writer, the reigns of Hezekiah (18:1–20:21) and Josiah (22:1–23:30) brought sweeping moral and religious reforms that prolonged Judah's existence for another hundred years. However, this period also saw Judah's most wicked king, Manasseh (21:1–26). Because of Manasseh's heinous sins, Jerusalem fell under God's final judgment of expulsion.

## THE RELIABILITY OF 2 KINGS

**See *The Reliability of 1, 2 Kings* and *1, 2 Chronicles*, p. 80.**

The Taylor Prism. In 1830, Col. R. Taylor, British Consul General, discovered this six-sided clay prism in ruins of Assyrian King Sennacherib's palace at Baghdad. This prism gives a parallel account of the events narrated in 2 Kings 18:13–19:37. The perspectives of the Bible's account and that of the prism are different. The prism doesn't mention the fact that Sennacherib was unable to take Jerusalem.

## HOW 2 KINGS FITS INTO GOD'S STORY

1. Prologue: Creation, Fall, and the Need for Redemption
2. God Builds His Nation (2000–931 BC)
3. God Educates His Nation (931–586 BC)
4. God Keeps a Faithful Remnant (586–6 BC)
5. God Purchases Redemption and Begins the Kingdom (6 BC to AD 30)
6. God Spreads the Kingdom Through the Church (AD 30-?)
7. God Consummates Redemption and Confirms His Eternal Kingdom
8. Epilogue: New Heaven and New Earth

## CHRIST IN 2 KINGS

Second Kings presents the ministries of Elijah and Elisha, prophets through whom God performed mighty acts. Jesus is described as "a Prophet powerful in action and speech before God and all the people" (Lk 24:19). God preserved Israel's monarch as long as He did because of His promises to David (8:19). Israel may even count on God to preserve a lamp for David forever (Rv 21:23).

## CHRISTIAN WORLDVIEW ELEMENTS

### Teachings About God

Like Judges and 2 Chronicles, 2 Kings shows the severity of God in judging those who rebel against Him. Deuteronomy had promised divine condemnation on those who were unfaithful to the Lord. The story of 2 Kings is largely one of disloyalty, and God's "educational program" meant teaching His people that He values faithfulness to Him above all else, even if that means exiling them. The book ends with a ray of hope: God's promises about an everlasting Davidic dynasty are intact, for the king, Jehoiachin, is still alive.

### Teachings About Humanity

Like 1 Kings, this book evaluates people by just one criterion: did they do "right in the LORD's sight" or not? Tragically, for the most part both kings and people did not (see *Key Text*). The author reached the following verdict about the last king of Judah: "Zedekiah did what was evil in the LORD's sight just as Jehoiakim had done. Because of the LORD's anger, it came to the point in Jerusalem and Judah that He finally banished them from His presence" (24:19–20).

### Teachings About Salvation

God's prophets in 2 Kings (Elijah, Elisha, Jonah, Huldah, and Isaiah are named) called people to repent for their religious apostasy and to worship the Lord alone. Hezekiah is the model of trust in the Lord for salvation (18:5–6). Turning from the sin of idolatry, when accompanied by a desire for God's glory to be displayed, may even bring salvation from military threats (see Hezekiah's prayer and God's response in 19:15–37).

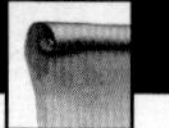



## GENRE AND LITERARY STYLE

**A Selective Historical Account Written in Hebrew**

In describing the period of the divided monarchy, the writer alternated between the kings of Israel and the kings of Judah. He gave attention only to Jehu, the founder of yet another dynasty in Israel, and Joash, the boy king of Judah. After describing the fall of the northern kingdom, the author focused only on two righteous kings, Hezekiah and Josiah. His interpretation of the reason Israel fell (chap. 17) and then Judah (chap. 25) was entirely theological, rather than military, political, or economic.

In the Hebrew Scriptures, the single composition 1 and 2 Kings was placed as the last of the four "Former Prophets." Beginning with Joshua and Judges, and then moving on to Samuel (collectively) and Kings (collectively), these books described the 800-year period from Israel's entry into Canaan (about 1406 BC) through the destruction of the temple and Jerusalem and the exile to Babylon (about 586 BC). Their common theme is that sin brings divine punishment, but obedience brings blessing and peace (in line with the teachings of Deuteronomy, especially chaps. 27–28).

This interpretation is commonly called "Deuteronomic History." Critical scholars have argued that this view arose late in the Israelite monarchy, perhaps at the time of Josiah, yet it is much more believable that Moses himself by divine revelation originated this perspective, as Deuteronomy plainly claims. Then the later historians more or less uniformly used the interpretive lens of Deuteronomy to write their respective parts of Israel's history. Finally, the books reflecting this perspective were gathered into Israel's canon as the first section of "The Prophets."

## A PRINCIPLE TO LIVE BY

**Walking Worthy (2Kg 18:1–6, *Life Essentials Study Bible*, p. 497–98)**

No matter how sinful the environment in which we live, we are to trust God to provide the inner resources to walk worthy of our calling in Jesus Christ.

To access a video presentation of this principle featuring Dr. Gene Getz, use a Smartphone or iPad to connect to this QR code or go to http://www.bhpublishinggroup.com/handbook/2kings

First divided by the Greek translators (second century BC), 1 and 2 Chronicles were originally one book, *Dibre Hayyamin*, "events of the days," in the Hebrew Bible. The English title comes from *Chronicon*, the name given by the Latin translator Jerome.

### KEY TEXT: 28:4

*"Yet the LORD God of Israel chose me out of all my father's household to be king over Israel forever. For He chose Judah as leader, and from the house of Judah, my father's household, and from my father's sons, He was pleased to make me king over all Israel."*

### KEY TERM: "DYNASTY"

First Chronicles focuses on how God established the everlasting dynasty of David, describing David's positive achievements, both religious and military.

### ONE-SENTENCE SUMMARY

After extensive introductory genealogies, the author tells how David ruled for 40 years under the blessing of God, particularly as he lavished attention on Jerusalem, the priesthood, and preparation for building the temple.

## ORIGINAL HISTORICAL SETTING

### AUTHOR AND DATE OF WRITING

**Unknown, Possibly Ezra Around 450 BC**

Scholars refer to the anonymous author of 1 and 2 Chronicles as "the Chronicler." According to Jewish tradition, Ezra was the composer, but this cannot be either proved or disproved. The work was written after the return of the exiles from Babylon. Some scholars date the book in the 300s, but on the whole an earlier date seems more likely.

### FIRST AUDIENCE AND DESTINATION

**Israelites in Jerusalem After They Returned from Exile**

The book does not state its original audience or destination, but see the discussion on the book's purpose below. Perhaps the original manuscript was placed in a book depository in the rebuilt temple. There it would have joined the growing collection of Israel's sacred Scriptures.

## OCCASION

Because the authorship and date are uncertain, no one knows what prompted Chronicles to be written. The author used many sources, including the biblical books of Samuel and Kings. The author mentioned official court documents, called "The Book of the Kings of Judah and Israel" (1 Ch 9:1; 2 Ch 16:11). He also had access to material written by certain prophets, such as "The Events of Samuel the Seer, the Events of Nathan the Prophet, and the Events of Gad the Seer" (1 Ch 29:29); "The Events of Jehu son of Hanani" (2 Ch 20:34); and "The Visions of the Prophet Isaiah son of Amoz" (2 Ch 32:32). Other sources, such as old genealogies and temple lists, appear likely.

# GOD'S MESSAGE IN 1 CHRONICLES

## PURPOSE

Since this book was originally the first half of a single composition, the purpose for the books now called 1 and 2 Chronicles must be considered together. This work answered important questions for Israelites who had returned after years of exile in Babylon. Their times were difficult and disappointing. Did they still fit into God's plan? Were the promises of God still applicable to them? Further, what religious and political institutions were important? Finally, what lessons from the past could they learn to keep from making the same mistakes?

The author answered these questions by compiling a highly selective religious history. The covenant God made with David concerning an eternal dynasty was still in effect. Even with no Davidic king on the throne, they were still God's people and could still wait in hope for restoration of the monarchy. While waiting, they could do the things God required, such as offer the right sacrifices with the right priests at the right place. Finally, although David and Solomon are presented as ideal kings, the apostasy of later kings is noted as the cause of Babylonian exile (2 Ch 36:16). God's people who study the books of Chronicles today should do so with the author's original purposes in mind.

## FIRST PASS

### From Adam to Zechariah, Son of Meshelemiah

First and 2 Chronicles give the history of Israel from its ancestral roots in Adam to the period of restoration after the Babylonian exile (chaps. 1–9). An important function of the genealogies that begin Chronicles is to show continuity in God's plan for Israel. The genealogies are not a sterile recitation of names. They are a significant statement of Israel's place in the whole sweep of God's plan for the world. The

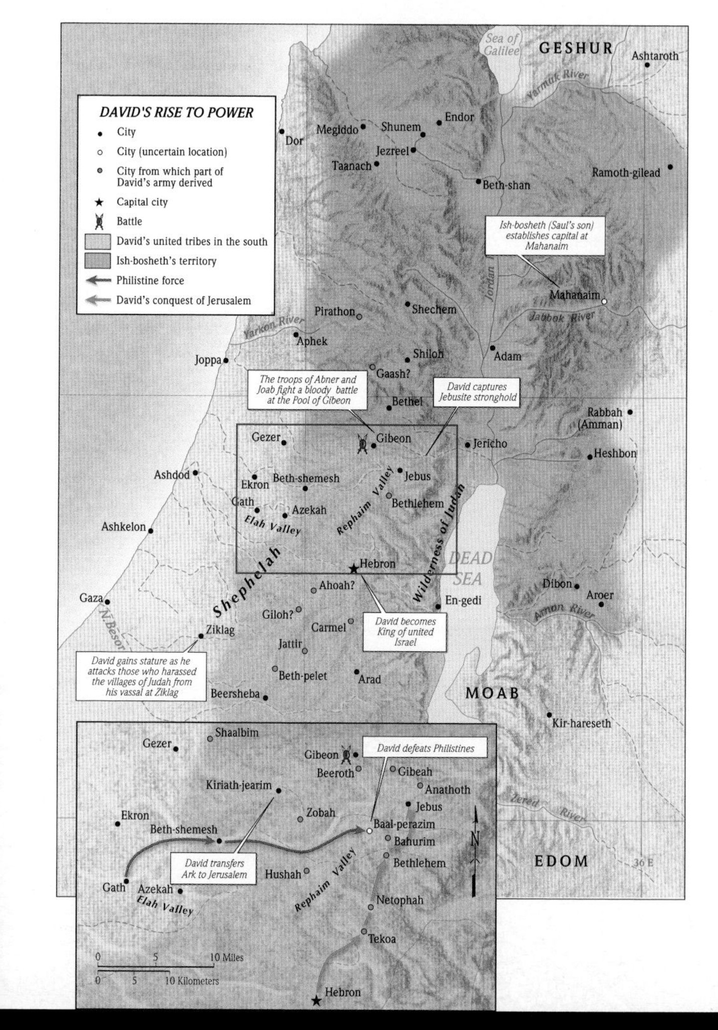


Hearing of the deaths of Saul and Jonathan, David avenged the murderer of Saul and sang a lament over the fallen (2Sm 1). He moved to Hebron, where the citizens of Judah crowned him king (2Sam. 2). This led to war with Israel under Saul's son Ish-bosheth. After much intrigue, Ish-bosheth's commanders assassinated him. David did the same to them (2Sm 4). The northern tribes then crowned David king at Hebron, uniting all Israel under him. He led the capture of Jerusalem and made it his capital. David then organized his administration and subdued other nations who opposed him, finally gaining control of the land God had originally promised the forefathers.

Chronicler found the proper appreciation of universal history in the founding of Israel, the appointment of David, and the building of the temple, where God resided in the world (a foretaste of the true Temple, Jesus Christ, who resided in the world as a man; see John 12).

**David's Rule**

The episode of Saul's death provides the background for David's kingdom (10:1–13). David's rule was glorious, and the pinnacle of his reign was the bringing of the ark into Jerusalem (15:1–29). God honored David's desire to build a temple by granting him an eternal throne (17:1–27). David prospered all the more because of God's blessing and dedicated to the Lord the spoils of his victories (chaps. 18–20).

**David's Preparation for the Temple**

The final section features the preparations David made for the building of the temple (22:1–19). For the Chronicler this was the most important contribution of the king and governed his account of David's reign. The temple site was divinely chosen. David organized the Levites and priests for the temple work, organized the army, and held a national convocation (chaps. 23–29). There the people contributed gifts (29:1–9). Solomon was anointed as king and Zadok as the priest (29:22–25).

## RELIABILITY OF 1 CHRONICLES

**See *The Reliability of 1, 2 KINGS and 1, 2 CHRONICLES*, p. 106.**

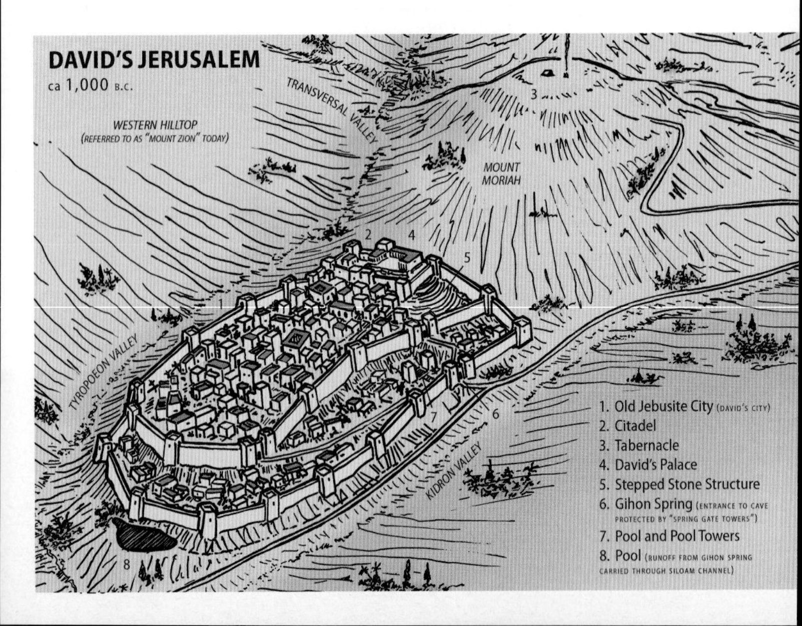

## HOW 1 CHRONICLES FITS INTO GOD'S STORY

1. Prologue: Creation, Fall, and the Need for Redemption
2. God Builds His Nation (2000–931 BC)
3. God Educates His Nation (931–586 BC)
4. God Keeps a Faithful Remnant (586–6 BC)
5. God Purchases Redemption and Begins the Kingdom (6 BC to AD 30)
6. God Spreads the Kingdom Through the Church (AD 30-?)
7. God Consummates Redemption and Confirms His Eternal Kingdom
8. Epilogue: New Heaven and New Earth

## CHRIST IN 1 CHRONICLES

The Messianic promise of a son of David to rule over Israel occupies the center of 1 Chronicles (chap. 17). The family lines of Israel's kings are traced (chap. 3), showing that God has been faithful to maintain a son of David to lead Israel even in the face of exile. This son of David is described as the eternally loved son of God (17:13; Lk 1:32–33; Heb 1:5). David's prayer of praise (29:10–13) is applied to Jesus (Rv 5:12–13).

## CHRISTIAN WORLDVIEW ELEMENTS

### Teachings About God

God is sovereign in carrying out His kingdom plans. His unconditional covenant with undeserving David (chap. 17) is as magnificent as His covenant with Abraham. He desires the worship of His people in the ways He has revealed. (See 1 Ch 28:12 for the Holy Spirit's work in revealing the plans for temple construction.) David's concern for the ark, his preparation for building the temple, and his organizing the priests and Levites properly show this.

### Teachings About Humanity

The long genealogies at the beginning of 1 Chronicles show that God cares for persons as individuals. Each one has worth as created in the image of God. If a historian took the trouble to discover and preserve these lists that may seem tedious, how much more does God care for the "little people" that can appear to be insignificant. Moreover David modeled magnificently that humans can accomplish great tasks for God when their hearts are passionately turned to pleasing Him.

### Teachings About Salvation

The book's clearest teaching on salvation as the gift of God is David's psalm of thanksgiving when the ark of the covenant was finally moved into a tent (chap. 16). The conclusion especially demonstrates that the purpose of salvation is to bring glory to God: "Give thanks to the LORD, for He is good; His faithful love endures forever. And say: Save us, God of our salvation; gather us and rescue us from the nations so that we may give thanks to Your holy name and rejoice in Your praise. May Yahweh, the God of Israel, be praised from everlasting to everlasting" (16:34–36).

## GENRE AND LITERARY STYLE

**Genealogical Tables, Narrative History, and Some Poetry, All Composed in Hebrew**

The genealogical material is the most extensive found in Scripture. The account of David's kingship is focused differently from the account in 2 Samuel. Neither his adultery with Bathsheba nor the treason of Absalom is considered. David is almost perfect in 1 Chronicles; even his taking a census of Israel is attributed to Satan and resulted in the royal discovery of the proper site for the temple (chap. 21). The brief poetic sections preserve prayers of David (chaps. 16; 29). See comments on *Genre and Literary Style* in **NEHEMIAH** for further material about the possible literary relationship of Chronicles, Ezra, and Nehemiah.

## A PRINCIPLE TO LIVE BY

**Building God's Eternal Kingdom (1Ch 29:22b–30, *Life Essentials Study Bible*, p. 543)**

As we live our lives, we should have as a primary goal to build God's eternal kingdom, not our own.

To access a video presentation of this principle featuring Dr. Gene Getz, use a Smartphone or iPad to connect to this QR code or go to http://www.bhpublishinggroup.com/handbook/1chronicles

First divided by the Greek translators (second century BC), 1 and 2 Chronicles were originally one book, *Dibre Hayyamin*, "events of the days," in the Hebrew Bible. The English title comes from *Chronicon*, the name given by the Latin translator Jerome.

## KEY TEXTS: 7:1 AND 36:19

*"When Solomon finished praying, fire descended from heaven and consumed the burnt offering and the sacrifices, and the glory of the LORD filled the temple."*

*"Then the Chaldeans burned God's temple. They tore down Jerusalem's wall, burned down all its palaces, and destroyed all its valuable articles."*

## KEY TERM: "TEMPLE"

The book begins with Solomon's plans to build the temple in Jerusalem and ends with its destruction. Between dedication and destruction (about 384 years, from 959 to 586 BC), the temple was sometimes neglected and sometimes refurbished, but it was always the most important building in Israel.

## ONE-SENTENCE SUMMARY

After Solomon's glorious reign, which culminated in the dedication of the temple, kings of the Davidic dynasty—some righteous and some evil—continued ruling in Jerusalem, ending in the destruction of the temple and the exile.

# ORIGINAL HISTORICAL SETTING

## AUTHOR AND DATE OF WRITING

**Unknown, Possibly Ezra Around 450 BC**

## FIRST AUDIENCE AND DESTINATION

**Israelites in Jerusalem After They Returned from Exile**

## OCCASION

**Unknown, but See *Occasion* for 1 CHRONICLES.**

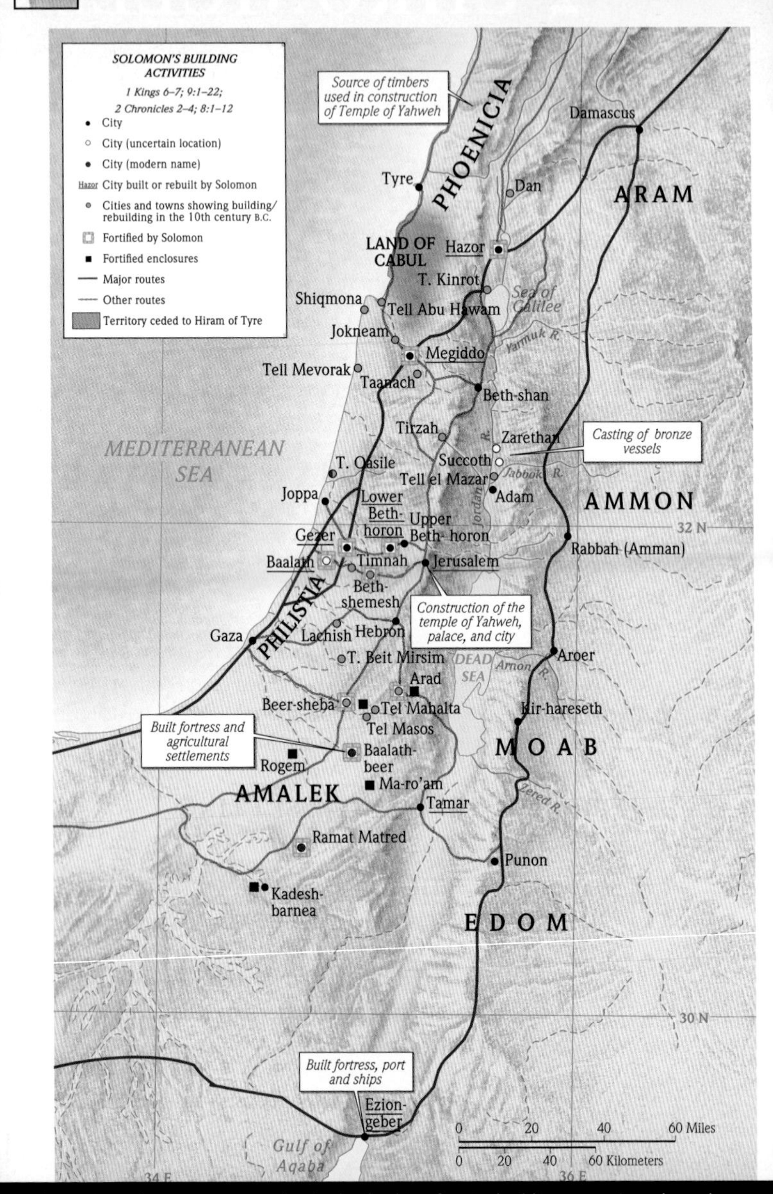


Solomon's wisdom was expressed in his leadership of major building campaigns throughout

## PURPOSE

Because 1 and 2 Chronicles first existed as a single composition, see the discussion in the *Purpose* section of **1 CHRONICLES**.

## FIRST PASS

Second Chronicles continues the story of God's redemptive plan for Israel presented in 1 Chronicles. The break between the books is a convenient one because the first half ends with David's preparations for the temple and the second describes the building and history of the temple under Judah's kings. Second Chronicles covers four and a half centuries, from Solomon's reign (about 971 BC) to Cyrus's edict (539 BC).

### God's Temple

Second Chronicles narrates Israel's past from the standpoint of its religious history. The building of the temple is the central concern (chaps. 2–7). The history of the monarchy is told from the perspective of how temple worship fared under Judah's kings.

One of the most striking features of 2 Chronicles is the way the author connected the temple and the kingship by noting the kings who initiated repairs to the temple and thus initiated religious reform and renewal. The history of Solomon's temple can thus be outlined as follows:

| EVENT | KING | TEXT | YEAR |
|---|---|---|---|
| Temple Dedication | Solomon | 5:1 | c. 959 BC |
| First Repair and Reform | Asa | 15:8 | c. 895 BC |
| Second Repair and Reform | Joash | 24:13 | c. 830 BC |
| Third Repair and Reform | Hezekiah | 29:3 | c. 715 BC |
| Fourth Repair and Reform | Josiah | 34:8 | c. 622 BC |
| Temple Destruction | Zedekiah | 36:19 | c. 586 BC |

### Spiritual Lessons

The second section of the book (10:1–36:13) reviews the spiritual life of the nation under the kings of Judah during the divided monarchy. After the revolt of the northern tribes is recounted (chap. 10), the narrative alternates between periods of spiritual decay and religious reforms. Special consideration is given to the reformers Asa and Jehoshaphat, Joash, Hezekiah, and Josiah. The final period of degeneracy is the last days of Judah's kings.

The kings of Judah are judged on the basis of their fidelity to Moses' commandments (6:16; 7:17–18). Those kings who were faithful prospered in their reigns, such as the reformers Asa (14:4), Jotham (27:6), Hezekiah (31:20–21), and Josiah (34:31–33; 35:26). The kings that were unfaithful to the law of Moses met with disaster. Jehoram experienced disease and defeat (21:12–20), Joash was assassinated (24:24–25), Uzziah suffered leprosy (26:16–21), Ahaz was humiliated (28:19,22), and Manasseh was imprisoned (33:7–11). The presence of a Davidic king by itself did not guarantee God's favor on Israel. Obedience was the Lord's requirement.

**Cyrus's Decree**

The Chronicler's final remarks are a sermon blaming the failure of the priests and leaders to obey the Lord's commands for the temple's and city's destruction. Writing almost two centuries after Kings, the Chronicler included in his story the return of the exiles, adding that Jeremiah predicted this (Jr 25:11; 29:10). The Chronicler commented that the land had its Sabbath rest as the law required (see Lv 26): 70 years from the ruin of the temple (586 BC) to its rebuilding (516 BC). With the ousting of the Babylonians, the Persian emperor Cyrus inaugurated a new policy toward the exiles (36:14–23). Cyrus's edict, published in the famous Cyrus Cylinder (539 BC), was quoted by the Chronicler in its Hebrew version. Cyrus permitted the conquered peoples of Babylon to return to their homelands and revive their religious traditions. For the Jews he ordered the rebuilding of the Jerusalem temple. Although it appeared that God's promises to David were abandoned, the Chronicler showed through his review of history that God remains faithful and can change history to accomplish His purposes. The story of Israel's fortunes was not finished. These last two verses were repeated in Ezra 1:1–3a to indicate that the story of God's redemptive work through the temple continued in the accounts of Ezra and Nehemiah.

## THE RELIABILITY OF 2 CHRONICLES

**See *The Reliability of 1, 2 KINGS and 1, 2 CHRONICLES*, p. 106.**

## HOW 2 CHRONICLES FITS INTO GOD'S STORY

1. Prologue: Creation, Fall, and the Need for Redemption
2. God Builds His Nation (2000–931 BC)
3. God Educates His Nation (931–586 BC)
4. God Keeps a Faithful Remnant (586–6 BC)
5. God Purchases Redemption and Begins the Kingdom (6 BC to AD 30)
6. God Spreads the Kingdom Through the Church (AD 30-?)
7. God Consummates Redemption and Confirms His Eternal Kingdom
8. Epilogue: New Heaven and New Earth

SOLOMON'S TEMPLE, Exterior View (LOOKING WEST)

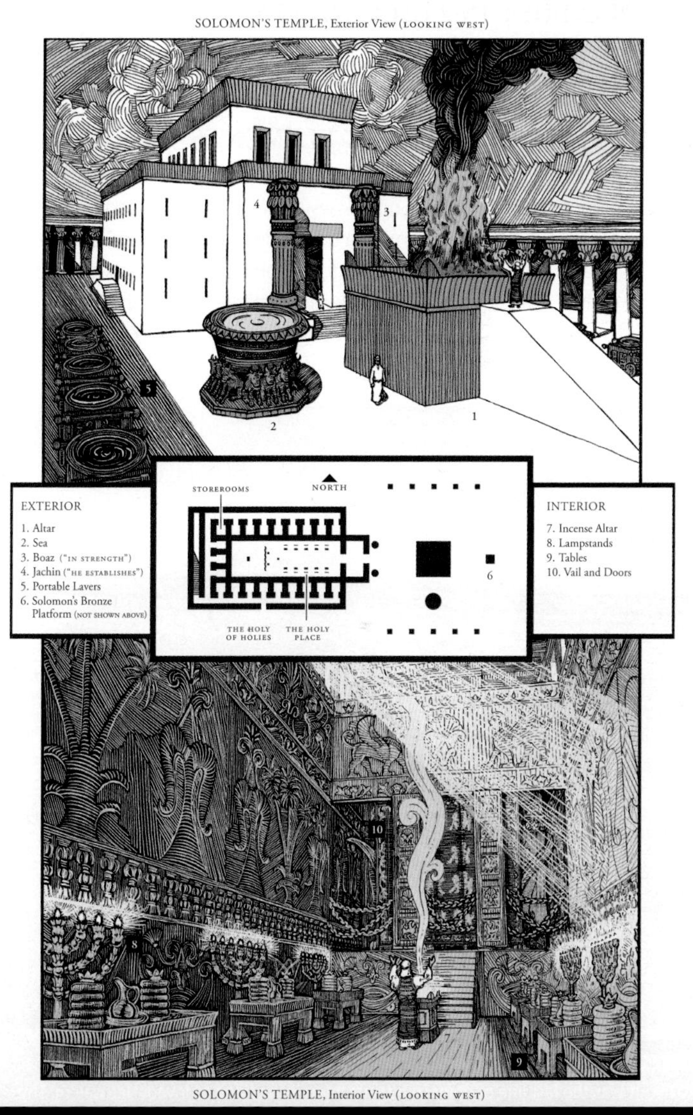


SOLOMON'S TEMPLE, Interior View (LOOKING WEST)

"So all the work Solomon did for the LORD's temple was completed. Then Solomon brought the consecrated things of his father David—the silver, the gold, and all the utensils—and put them in the treasuries of God's temple" (2 Ch 5:1).

## CHRIST IN 2 CHRONICLES

Solomon's glorious reign as third king of Israel is a picture of Christ's eternal reign in the New Jerusalem (Rev. 21–22).

## CHRISTIAN WORLDVIEW ELEMENTS

### Teachings About God

Second Chronicles shows that God blesses faithfulness to Him and punishes His people when they turn away from Him. God's "educational program" meant teaching His people that He values allegiance to Him above all else. The book ends with a note of hope: the Israelite exiles have been permitted to return home in order to rebuild their temple. God's Spirit is noted as inspiring certain priests and prophets.

Assyrian siege ramp at Lachish. "After this, while Sennacherib king of Assyria with all his armed forces besieged Lachish, he sent his servants to Jerusalem against King Hezekiah of Judah" (2 Ch 32:9). Lachish was one of the most strategic of the 46 Judean cities taken by Sennacherib in 701 BC. It was the last line of defense against enemies seeking to invade Jerusalem. The Assyrian siege ramp of rock and dirt was countered by a siege ramp the people of Lachish built inside the wall. The Assyrian tactics and force prevailed and Lachish fell. This makes all the more remarkable the fact that Jerusalem was spared during this Assyrian incursion.

**Teachings About Humanity**

Second Chronicles focuses at length on Solomon, whose splendid rule in Jerusalem was a preview of Christ's everlasting reign in the New Jerusalem (Mt 12:42; Rv 21–22). As in 2 Kings, the worth of the kings is determined only by whether they did right or evil in the sight of the Lord.

**Teachings About Salvation**

As in 2 Kings, God's prophets in 2 Chronicles called both king and people to repent for religious apostasy and to worship the Lord alone. (Isaiah and Jeremiah are known from their writings; Shemaiah, Oded, Micaiah, Eliezer, and Huldah are less familiar.) Four kings led Israel to turn from sin, repair the temple, and recommit to wholehearted worship of the Lord (Asa, Joash, Hezekiah, and Josiah).

The assault on Lachish. Siege-engines lead the way up artificial ramps. Inside, men with ladles pour water to prevent their being set alight by torches thrown from the walls. The artist has anticipated the results of the assault and shows a procession of men and women streaming out of the town gate, ready to go into exile (2Kg 18; 2Ch 32; Is 36). This elaborate bas-relief was found on the wall of the royal palace in Nineveh and is presently housed in the British museum in London. A replica of this relief may be found in the library of The Southern Baptist Theological Seminary in Louisville, Kentucky.

## GENRE AND LITERARY STYLE

### A Selective Historical Account Written in Hebrew

Although 2 Chronicles describes the same time period as 1 and 2 Kings, its approach is distinctive, concentrating only on the kings of Judah. The author's perspective on the northern kingdom is plain: "Israel is in rebellion against the house of David until today" (10:19). Thus, King Hezekiah (who ruled in Judah both before and after the fall of the northern kingdom) invited people from "all Israel and Judah" to his great Passover, and many people came (30:1,6,10). Consequently, from Hezekiah's time until the final destruction of Jerusalem, the Davidic king in Jerusalem ruled "all Israel" (31:1; 35:3). The Chronicler was concerned mainly with the state of the temple and whether the Davidic king was devoutly following the Lord.

In the Hebrew Bible, Chronicles was placed in the third section, the Writings (*Kethubim*), rather than in the Law or the Prophets. In fact it was the last book of the Hebrew Scriptures. Thus, just as modern Christians use the phrase "Genesis to Revelation" to mean the entire canon, Christians living in the first century thought in terms of "Genesis to Chronicles." See comments on *Genre and Literary Style* in **NEHEMIAH** for further material about the possible literary relationship of Chronicles, Ezra, and Nehemiah.

## A PRINCIPLE TO LIVE BY

### Response to God's Word (2Ch 34:14–33, *Life Essentials Study Bible*, p. 587–88)

When Scripture confronts sin in our lives, we should allow God's Spirit to convict us, humble us, and redirect our lives into His will.

To access a video presentation of this principle featuring Dr. Gene Getz, use a Smartphone or iPad to connect to this QR code or go to http://www.bhpublishinggroup.com/handbook/2chronicles

The book is named for Ezra, the leading character. In the Hebrew Bible, Ezra and Nehemiah were initially one book. English Bibles follow the Latin translator Jerome, who named the two parts Ezra and Nehemiah. Others have used the titles 1 and 2 Ezra.

## KEY TEXT: 6:16

*"Then the Israelites, including the priests, the Levites, and the rest of the exiles, celebrated the dedication of the house of God with joy."*

## KEY TERM: "RESTORATION"

The book describes two restorations from Babylonian captivity. First, more than 40,000 Israelites returned under Sheshbazzar (530s BC). Second, a smaller group accompanied Ezra, whose goal was to teach the people the law of Moses (about 458 BC).

The Euphrates River. The Jewish exiles returning from Babylon would have crossed the Euphrates and then traveled parallel to it as they returned to Judah.

## ONE-SENTENCE SUMMARY

The first group of returning exiles restored worship of the Lord, culminating in a rebuilt temple; but Ezra, who led the second group, reestablished Israelite community under Mosaic law, culminating in putting away mixed marriages.

# ORIGINAL HISTORICAL SETTING

## AUTHOR AND DATE OF WRITING

**Unknown, Perhaps Ezra Around 430 BC**

Jewish tradition held that Ezra the priest composed the single work Ezra-Nehemiah. There is no reason he could not have done so, particularly since he was a "scribe skilled in the law of Moses" (7:6). In 7:28–9:15, Ezra is referred to in the first person ("I," "me," "my"). If Ezra was not the composer, then a later composer directly copied his memoirs. (The book of Nehemiah included similar first-person memoirs of Nehemiah.)

## FIRST AUDIENCE AND DESTINATION

**Israelites in Jerusalem After They Returned from Exile**

The book was a permanent record of the events that reestablished Israel's national identity. Perhaps the original "Scroll of Ezra-Nehemiah" was placed in a book depository in the rebuilt temple when it was first completed. There it would have joined the growing collection of Israel's sacred Scriptures.

## OCCASION

What originally prompted the writing of this book is not clear. The author could not have been an eyewitness to all the events of Ezra-Nehemiah since they cover about a century. He could, however, have seen all events of both Ezra's and Nehemiah's ministries. The author skillfully knitted his sources into a powerful account of God's provision and protection of his people.

# GOD'S MESSAGE IN EZRA

## PURPOSE

Since this book was originally the first half of a single composition, the purpose for the books now called Ezra and Nehemiah must be considered together. This work continued the history of Israel at the point that 2 Chronicles ended. It showed Israelites who had come back to their land that they were still God's people, despite the years of exile and the difficulties they had experienced since their return. God was at work through pagan kings such as Cyrus and Artaxerxes (Ezr 1:1; 7:27) to bring about the return from exile and the rebuilding of the temple. God had worked to bring devout teachers (Ezr 7:9) and strong governors (Neh 2:12) to help His people. From an even broader perspective, the second temple, the Jewish community, and a stable Jerusalem were important circumstances for the coming of Jesus more than four centuries later. God's people who read and study Ezra and Nehemiah today should keep the author's purpose in mind.

## FIRST PASS

### Rebuilding the Temple

The first section provides an account of Sheshbazzar, Zerubbabel, and the first Jews who returned to Jerusalem from captivity in 538 BC (chaps. 1–6). The Lord inspired Cyrus to permit the return of the Jews to worship their God. Those who volunteered for the first expedition are listed. Their main objective was to rebuild the temple. Its foundation was laid in 536 BC, but opposition from their enemies stopped the work. Then there was a long delay. Haggai and Zechariah (Ezr 5:1) in 520 BC had encouraged the people to finish the project, which they did in 515 BC (6:14–15), and they "celebrated the dedication of the house of God with joy" (6:16).

### Reform Under the Law

Almost 60 years passed before Ezra went to Jerusalem (458 BC)—six decades of silence. He left Persia with "a copy of the letter that King Artaxerxes gave to Ezra the priest and scribe" (7:11), granting him unusual power and authority (7:12–26). As he went, he "searched among the people and priests, but found no Levites there" (8:15). These were essential for his teaching program to implement the law of God in Jerusalem. During a three-day delay more than 200 ministers "for the house of our God" (8:17) were enlisted. Four months later the group, probably fewer than 2,000, arrived in the holy city.

Soon Ezra was informed of the most glaring sin of the Jews: intermarriage with non-Jews, those not in covenant relation with Yahweh (9:2). Ezra was greatly upset (9:3–4). He prayed (9:6–15). Together, the people reached what must have been a heartrending decision: "Let us therefore make a covenant before our God to send away all the foreign wives and their children" (10:3). The book concludes with the carrying out of this decision.

Ezra's story reaches its climax in Nehemiah 8–10. There he read from "the book of the law of Moses that the LORD had given Israel" (Neh 8:1). A great revival resulted.

## THE RELIABILITY OF EZRA

Prominent in Ezra are official proclamations of the Persian government (e.g., Ezr 1:1–5; 4:8–10,11–16,17–22; 5:6–17; 6:6–12; 7:11–26). Until recently many scholars doubted the authenticity of these proclamations. They claimed that the language sounded too theological or that they didn't follow standard Persian form. However, recent studies have muted these criticisms. Study of the letters from the Jewish community at Elephantine, Egypt, reveals that the theological tone of the royal edicts is probably the result of the interaction of the Jewish people with the king prior to the issue of his edicts. In other words, the king (or his scribe) used language that would be familiar to the recipients. The official letters in the book are now known to be comparable in style to typical letters of the day, varying partly in whether they were written from inferiors to superiors or vice versa.

Some of these proclamations are from Cyrus II, founder of the Achaemenid Empire. Following his conquest of Babylon, he instituted a policy of returning some conquered peoples to their homelands. This policy is reflected toward specific peoples in the so-called Cyrus Cylinder, one of the most important archaeological

The Cyrus Cylinder. Cyrus gives credit to the Babylonian god Marduk for choosing him and enabling him to conquer Babylon. The inscriptions express Cyrus's policy of allowing captive peoples, such as the Jews, to return to their homelands. The biblical writers saw God's hand in these world events (2Ch 36:22–23; Ezr 1:2–4; Is 44:24–28; 45:1).

discoveries of the modern era. While the Cyrus Cylinder doesn't mention the people of Judah specifically, it shows that the proclamations in Ezra attributed to Cyrus are consistent with his more comprehensive policy of repatriation. He also supported the reconstruction of temples in locations where exiles were resettled just as Ezra reports concerning the temple in Jerusalem.

## HOW EZRA FITS INTO GOD'S STORY

1. Prologue: Creation, Fall, and the Need for Redemption
2. God Builds His Nation (2000–931 BC)
3. God Educates His Nation (931–586 BC)
4. **God Keeps a Faithful Remnant (586–6 BC)**
5. God Purchases Redemption and Begins the Kingdom (6 BC to AD 30)
6. God Spreads the Kingdom Through the Church (AD 30-?)
7. God Consummates Redemption and Confirms His Eternal Kingdom
8. Epilogue: New Heaven and New Earth

## CHRIST IN EZRA

Ezra was a priest who played an important role in leading God's people from captivity in Babylon back to Judea. In a sermon at the synagogue in Nazareth, Jesus announced His agenda, part of which was "to proclaim freedom to the captives" (Lk 4:18).

## CHRISTIAN WORLDVIEW ELEMENTS

### Teachings About God

Because God is righteous, He acts on behalf of His people. This includes working through pagan kings (who issue decrees) and godly teachers (who teach His word to His people). Further, as the last two chapters show, God may require His people to forsake family ties for the sake of following His will.

### Teachings About Humanity

As with 1 Chronicles, Ezra has many lists of names. Although such lists may seem tedious today, they show the importance of each individual in God's purposes. If the author made the effort to preserve all these names and numbers, then how much more does God care about individuals! This perspective is strengthened by observing that the work of restoring worship (altar and temple) was a community task. The work accomplished for God was done by people working together more than by a great leader.

### Teachings About Salvation

The people who returned from exile were cured of the idolatry that had taken their ancestors into captivity. Ezra revives an emphasis found in Mosaic law: without the shedding of blood, there is no forgiveness (Lv 17:11). Thus, the first concern of the returning Israelites was to reinstate an altar on which to offer the appointed sacrifices (3:1–6). Only secondarily were they concerned with the temple (6:13–18). As throughout the Old Testament era, personal trust in God is expressed through participation in the right sacrifices and through obeying God's law.

# LITERARY FEATURES

## GENRE AND LITERARY STYLE

**Court Documents, Lists, and Narratives Written in Hebrew, with Some Aramaic Sections**
The author had access to many sources, including official Persian documents, lists, and memoirs. The lists are similar to the lists in Chronicles and may indicate the same historian at work (Ezra?). The Hebrew vocabulary and style are considered "late Hebrew," as is fitting for a postexilic composition.

One striking element of Ezra is the presence of documents untranslated from their original Aramaic form. Aramaic was the international trade language of the ancient Near East under the Persians. The Aramaic parts of Ezra are 4:8–6:18 and 7:12–26. Another feature of Ezra and Nehemiah is the use of lists. The lists and the Aramaic show that the author was determined to use official documents where possible. Establishing the legitimacy of the Jews was an important objective, and these helped do that.

In the Hebrew Bible, Ezra-Nehemiah was placed in the third section, the Writings (*Kethubim*), rather than in the Law or the Prophets. See comments on *Genre and Literary Style* in **NEHEMIAH** for further material about the possible literary relationship of Chronicles, Ezra, and Nehemiah.

## A PRINCIPLE TO LIVE BY

**Our Divine Source (Ezr 6:18, *Life Essentials Study Bible*, p. 601)**
To please God on a consistent basis, we must be committed to living in God's will as recorded in the Holy Scriptures.

To access a video presentation of this principle featuring Dr. Gene Getz, use a Smartphone or iPad to connect to this QR code or go to http://www.bhpublishinggroup.com/handbook/ezra

The book is named for Nehemiah, the leading character. In the Hebrew Bible, Ezra and Nehemiah were initially one book. English Bibles follow the Latin translator Jerome, who named the two parts Ezra and Nehemiah. Others have used the titles 1 and 2 Ezra.

## KEY TEXT: 6:15

*"The wall was completed in 52 days, on the twenty-fifth day of the month Elul."*

## KEY TERM: "WALLS"

In the ancient world a city without walls was helpless before its enemies. For Jerusalem once more to have its walls complete was evidence of divine favor and meant that the inhabitants could carry on life with a measure of security.

## ONE-SENTENCE SUMMARY

Through Nehemiah's leadership God enabled the Israelites to rebuild and dedicate Jerusalem's walls as well as to renew their commitment to God as His covenant people.

# ORIGINAL HISTORICAL SETTING

## AUTHOR AND DATE OF WRITING

**Unknown, Probably Ezra Around 430 BC**

## FIRST AUDIENCE AND DESTINATION

**Israelites in Jerusalem After They Returned from Exile**

## OCCASION

**Unknown, but See *Occasion* for EZRA**

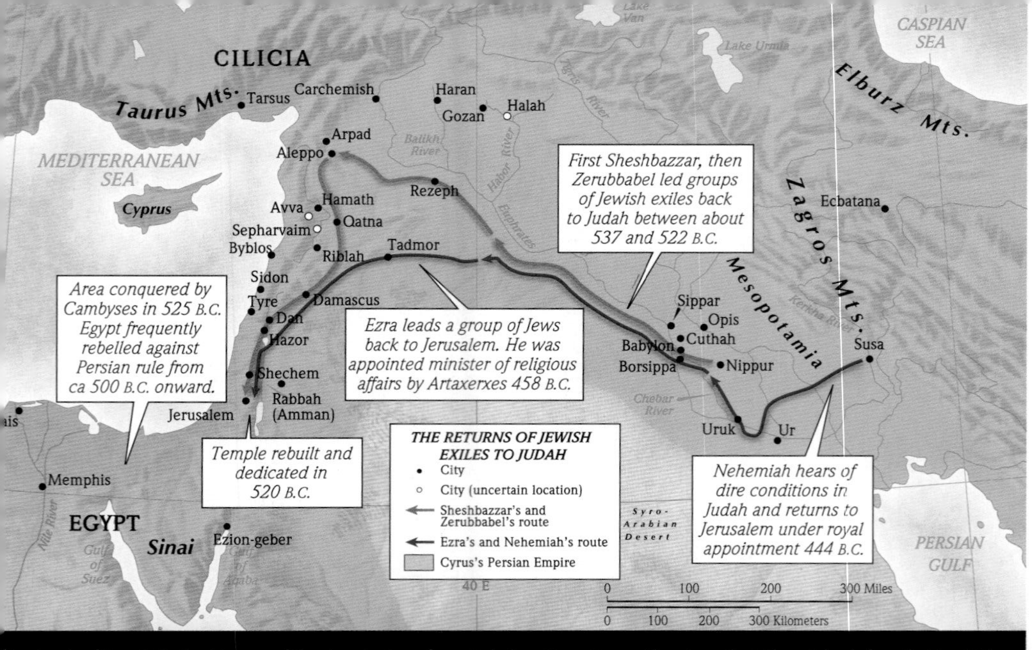


The book of Ezra tells the history of the Jews' return from Babylon. It continues the story that Chronicles left unfinished. The first half of the book (chaps. 1–6) concerns the expedition ordered by King Cyrus (538 BC) to rebuild the temple under Sheshbazzar of Judah. The second half of the book (chaps. 7–10) concerns Ezra's ministry, which began 58 years (458 BC) after the completion of the temple (515 BC).

## PURPOSE

Because Nehemiah and Ezra first existed as a single composition, see the discussion in the *Purpose* section for **EZRA**.

## FIRST PASS

### Nehemiah's Request

Nehemiah held the distinguished position of cupbearer to the king of Persia (1:11). As the book opens, visitors to Susa informed Nehemiah that Jerusalem's walls had been broken down. He was so upset that he cried and "mourned for a number of days" (1:4); his grief led to confession (1:5–11). Artaxerxes read the depression on Nehemiah's face and inquired about the source of his sadness. Before Nehemiah responded to the king's inquiry, he prayed. He then told the source of his sadness and asked for a leave of absence to go to Jerusalem and see the conditions first-hand. Artaxerxes granted his request.

### Inspection and Planning

Nehemiah's first act in Jerusalem was to inspect the walls at night (2:15). He then called an assembly and convinced the people of the need for a building program. He was an excellent leader who demonstrated engineering knowledge and brilliant organizing ability (chap. 3). So the work began.

### Opposition

Trouble arose from without and within. Sanballat, Tobiah, and Geshem tried to stop the work but without success (chap. 4). Trouble from within was economic. Building the walls caused a labor shortage; farms were mortgaged, and high rates of interest were charged. He corrected the problem and even gave financial aid to those in need (chap. 5). As Nehemiah moved into the last phase of construction, Sanballat and other non-Jews made several attempts to lure Nehemiah away from the job with the intent of harming him and preventing his completing the gates of the city, but they failed. Nehemiah proved to be a person of strong will and unusual boldness. "The wall was completed in 52 days" (6:15). The dedication of the wall is described in 12:27–43.

### Revival

The theological climax of the book of Nehemiah and of the life of Ezra is the Great Revival (Neh 8–10). People assembled and requested Ezra to read from the book of the law of Moses (8:1). The book was probably the Pentateuch (Torah) or some part of it. Ezra read, and others helped by "translating and giving the meaning so that the people could understand what was read" (8:8). The translation was probably from Hebrew into Aramaic, the commonly spoken language.

A great celebration occurred, and they observed the Festival of Booths. Results were impressive: they spent a fourth of the day "in confession and worship of the LORD their God" (9:3). Their prayer resulted in action: separating themselves "from the surrounding peoples to obey the law of God" (10:28). They divorced their foreign spouses. They prayed a long prayer of confession (9:6–37). The people responded, "In view of all this, we are making a binding agreement in writing" (9:38). The signers and terms of the covenant were then recorded (chap. 10).

**Repopulating Jerusalem**

Nehemiah was dissatisfied with the small size of the population of Jerusalem. He made an ingenious proposal: to "cast lots for one out of 10 to come and live in Jerusalem, the holy city, while the other nine-tenths remained in their towns" (11:1).

**Final Reforms**

Nehemiah's final chapter cites reforms made during his second visit to Jerusalem in 432 BC. He threw out a Gentile who had been permitted to live in the temple; he restored the practice of tithing to support the Levites; he corrected the lack of obedience of those who bought and sold on the Sabbath; and he dealt forthrightly with those who had married foreigners, those not in covenant relation with God.

## THE RELIABILITY OF NEHEMIAH

Nehemiah's three opponents—Sanballat the Horonite, Tobiah the Ammonite official, and Geshem the Arab—have been attested in sources outside the biblical record. Sanballat is named in a letter from Yadaniah and his associates to the Persian governor of Judah during the seventeenth year of the reign of Darius (408 BC). The letter is seeking help for reconstructing a temple to Yahweh at the fortress of Yeb in Egypt. It mentions that a similar appeal has gone to Deleiah and Shelemiah, sons of Sanballat, governor of Samaria.

In the early 1990s about 15 miles southwest of Amman, Jordan, a team of archaeologists from Jordan and France found a number of caves near some second-century BC buildings. The entrance to one of the caves bears an inscription of the name *Tobiah* in Aramaic. Tobiah the Ammonite was part of a family from this region.

The third opponent of Nehemiah, Geshem the Arab, is mentioned in an inscription on some silver bowls found at Tell el-Maskhuta in Egypt's East Delta and dated to the fifth century BC. The inscription reads, "What Qaynu son of Gashmu the king of Kedar brought in offering to Han-ilat." Han-ilat was an Egyptian goddess. Gashmu is Geshem the Arab. Kedar was one of the 12 sons of Abraham's son Ishmael.[1]

## HOW NEHEMIAH FITS INTO GOD'S STORY

1. Prologue: Creation, Fall, and the Need for Redemption
2. God Builds His Nation (2000–931 BC)
3. God Educates His Nation (931–586 BC)
4. **God Keeps a Faithful Remnant (586–6 BC)**
5. God Purchases Redemption and Begins the Kingdom (6 BC to AD 30)
6. God Spreads the Kingdom Through the Church (AD 30-?)

7. God Consummates Redemption and Confirms His Eternal Kingdom
8. Epilogue: New Heaven and New Earth

## CHRIST IN NEHEMIAH

Nehemiah was a key leader in the restoration of God's people from Babylon to Jerusalem. He called for undivided loyalty to the work at hand in the same way Jesus did when He said, "Anyone who is not with Me is against Me, and anyone who does not gather with Me scatters" (Lk 11:23).

## CHRISTIAN WORLDVIEW ELEMENTS

### Teachings about God

God works on behalf of His people to enable them to accomplish His purposes. He works through kings; He sends good leaders (such as Ezra and Nehemiah). Further, God does not change, even though the circumstances of His people change. The same God who had graciously revealed Himself at Mount Sinai as the covenant-making God a thousand years before (c. 1446 BC) still wanted Israel to be in a covenant relationship with Him (10:29).

### Teachings About Humanity

Nehemiah shows that there are really only two kinds of people: those who oppose God and His purposes and those who identify with God and His purposes. Equally evident in this book (as in Leviticus) is the concept that God's holiness requires His redeemed people to live different from the pagans that surround them. Although Ezra and Nehemiah fulfilled different personal roles, each illustrates someone who was wholly committed to God and whom God used to accomplish kingdom purposes.

### Teachings About Salvation

Nehemiah teaches the doctrine of salvation as clearly as any Old Testament book. It contains no more profound confession of sin at the community level than Nehemiah 9: salvation means acknowledging and turning away from wrongdoing and then clinging steadfastly to God.

## LITERARY FEATURES

## GENRE AND LITERARY STYLE

### Mainly Nehemiah's First-Person Memoirs and Official Lists, Written in Hebrew

The book of Nehemiah has the longest first-person sections (where the writer uses "I," "my," and "me") of any narrative book in Scripture. Chapters 1–7 and 12:27–13:30 appear to be copied from "The Memoirs of Nehemiah." The material in chaps. 8–10 tells about Ezra's preaching, which is further eyewitness material if Ezra in fact wrote this work.

In the Hebrew Bible, Ezra-Nehemiah was placed in the third section, the Writings (*Kethubim*), rather than in the Law or the Prophets. Many Bible scholars believe that 1 and 2 Chronicles (originally one book) and Ezra-Nehemiah were composed by a single author, designated "the Chronicler," perhaps Ezra himself. The books all have a common postexilic perspective, share a fondness for lists, like to describe Israelite feasts, and focus extensively on the temple and the temple workers (priests and Levites). They also share unusual vocabulary features, such as calling the temple "the house of God" (more than 60 times in these books) and the reference to "gatekeepers" more than 30 times. Further, the end of Chronicles is the same as the beginning of Ezra.

## PRINCIPLE TO LIVE BY

**Confession and Repentance (Neh 9:38; 10:28–29, *Life Essentials Study Bible*, p. 626–27)**
When we discover specific areas in our lives that are out of harmony with God's will, we should confess our sins and respond with repentant hearts.

To access a video presentation of this principle featuring Dr. Gene Getz, use a Smartphone or iPad to connect to this QR code or go to http://www.bhpublishinggroup.com/handbook/nehemiah

## ENDNOTES

1. Kenneth A. Kitchen, *On the Reliability of the Old Testament* (Grand Rapids: Eerdmans, 2003), 74–75.

The English title is the name of the heroine of the story. The title carries over from the Hebrew Bible.

## KEY TEXT: 4:14B

*"Who knows, perhaps you have come to your royal position for such a time as this?"*

## KEY TERM: "PROVIDENCE"

This book is famous because it does not directly mention God. Yet one cannot understand the story apart from God's remarkable presence and providence with His people—however invisible He may seem to be at times.

## ONE-SENTENCE SUMMARY

Esther, a Jewish beauty selected by Persian king Ahasuerus to become his new queen, saved the Jews from Haman's wicked plot, so her relative Mordecai established the yearly Jewish feast of Purim.

The Megillah of Esther, a scroll made from parchment, the product of a kosher animal

## AUTHOR AND DATE OF WRITING

**Unknown, Perhaps Mordecai Around 465 BC**

The book is anonymous, but according to Jewish tradition, the author was Mordecai. There is no reason he could not have composed the book since he was an eyewitness to everything that occurred (or had direct access to eyewitnesses). As Ahasuerus's prime minister, he is a likely candidate for adding this incident to the official Persian archives (9:32; 10:2). The writer was gifted in developing plot and narrative tension and wrote with considerable literary skill.

## FIRST AUDIENCE AND DESTINATION

**Jewish Exiles Living in Persia**

The first ones to hear Esther were Jews in Persia, sometime after the feast of Purim had become an established custom. By this time the postexilic people of Israel had adopted the name "Jew," for the term *Jew(s)* occurs more often in the book of Esther than in the rest of the Old Testament combined.

## OCCASION

The book of Esther was prompted in general by the desire to preserve the origins of the feast of Purim. Since the author is not known, the specific occasion is unclear.

# GOD'S MESSAGE IN ESTHER

## PURPOSE

Esther primarily preserves the historical origins of the Jewish festival of Purim. Secondarily it portrays God's providential care of people committed to Him in the midst of overwhelming challenges to their faith. In this sense Esther functions similarly to Ruth, the only other biblical book named for a woman. The characters Esther and Ruth, however, are a study in contrasts: the one was a powerful and wealthy Jew who always lived outside the Promised Land and became the bride of a pagan king; the other was a humble and impoverished Gentile who moved to the Promised Land and became an ancestor of Israelite kings. People who read and study Esther today should enjoy it for its own sake in its Old Testament setting.

## FIRST PASS

**Ahasuerus's Feast**

The events of Esther took place during the reign of Ahasuerus (Hebrew), commonly identified with Xerxes I (485–464 BC). The setting is Susa, the winter resort of Persian kings (Neh 1:1; Dn 8:2). Ahasuerus called an extended feast that lasted for

180 days, during which he displayed the splendor of the Persian Empire. It culminated in a seven-day banquet of luxurious dining. On the seventh day of the banquet, the king, "feeling good from the wine," called for Queen Vashti to come before him and the banquet guests so he could show off her beauty. Vashti refused and so she lost her royal position.

**Esther Becomes Queen**

A search was made for a replacement for Vashti. The woman chosen was Esther, a young Jew whose cousin and legal guardian, Mordecai, may have served the king as a gatekeeper. Mordecai, at an earlier time, had discovered a plot to kill Ahasuerus. The two culprits were hanged on gallows, and Mordecai's heroism was recorded.

**Haman's Plot**

Haman the Agagite (who seems to be identified as a descendant of Agag, king of the Amalekites) was made prime minister of Persia. Infuriated by Mordecai's refusal to bow to him, Haman began to plot against Mordecai and all of the Jews. After Haman had the Persian monarch sign a decree for the destruction of the Jews on an appointed day, Mordecai and all of the Jews lamented their impending doom. Neither Haman nor the King was yet aware of Esther's ethnic background.

**Mordecai Appeals to Esther**

Mordecai called on Esther to approach the king. He reminded her that as a Jew she would not escape and that it might be the case that "for such a time as this" God had allowed her to rise to the position of queen of Persia. Esther, after fasting and prayer, risked her life by entering the king's throne room unbidden. After the king extended the royal scepter to her, she requested the king's presence at a banquet prepared in his honor. Haman was also invited. Meanwhile, Haman was busy plotting Mordecai's death and building a gallows on which he intended to hang him.

**Mordecai Honored**

One night the King suffered from insomnia. He got up and began reading the book that recorded daily events. In that record he read about Mordecai's faithfulness in revealing the earlier plot against his life. The king then purposed to honor Mordecai and obtained Haman's advice concerning what should be done for the man that the king would like to honor. Thinking that he had prescribed his own treatment, Haman found out, to his chagrin, that the high honors he prescribed would be performed by him for Mordecai.

**Haman's Plot Revealed**

At the banquet on the second day, Esther revealed Haman's plot to the king. Haman was then hanged upon the gallows he had prepared for Mordecai. After that, another decree was sent out allowing the Jews to defend themselves. On the appointed day the Jews were victorious.

### The Feast of Purim

An annual feast was established to celebrate these two days. The feast was named Purim because of the *pur* ("lot") cast by Haman to determine the day on which the Jews would be killed. The purpose of the feast was a memorial to Haman's wicked plot, which returned "on his own head." To promote the feast, Esther added her authority to a joint letter distributed with Mordecai.

The book concludes in the way it began by describing the power and influence of Ahasuerus's kingdom. It also pays tribute to Mordecai for his contribution to the welfare of his people and to the Persian Empire. The greatness of Mordecai vindicated the Jews as a people. Their heritage was not a threat to the Gentiles, but rather through Mordecai and the Jews the empire enjoyed peace.

## THE RELIABILITY OF ESTHER

Many scholars doubt the historicity of the events described in the book because there is no evidence outside the Bible for some of the characters, events, and customs described in the book. Consequently these scholars prefer to designate the book as something other than history. Some have suggested that the book of Esther is a wisdom tale, a historical romance, a festival tale, a novel whose central characters are Jews living outside their homeland, a sermon with a moral, a Persian court chronicle, or even a comedy along the lines of Greek comedy.

Many other scholars are not nearly so skeptical about the book's relationship to history. They note that Vashti may well be the Hebrew name for the cruel and self-willed queen Amestris, Xerxes's wife during this time. The difference in spelling has been attributed to the lack of certain vocalizations in Hebrew, making it difficult to pronounce the Greek name. Certainly Vashti's character appears similar to the character of the historical Amestris.

In addition, the historical situation in Persia during this time tracks closely with the events described in Esther. With the help of such important Greek historians as Herodotus and Ctesias and Persian records discovered during archaeological digs, it is possible to reconstruct a history of this period without reference to the biblical record. These records enable scholars to piece together the following order of events.

Revolts in the empire toward the end of Darius's life (Egypt in 486–484 BC and Babylon in 484 BC) required a crushing response from his son Xerxes in 484 BC. Following these victories, Xerxes held a banquet in Susa for the leading people in his kingdom as preparation for his planned invasion of Greece. This may coincide with the banquet mentioned in Esther 1:5. Xerxes failed in his attempt to defeat Greece, assured by the Greeks' naval victory over Persia at Salamis in 480 BC. Xerxes returned home in defeat and engaged in a series of harem intrigues. The search for a new queen described in Esther 2 fits well within this time period. D. J. A. Clines has noted that many details of Persian life recorded in Esther are confirmed by sources

beyond the Bible. These confirmed details include the extent of the empire under Xerxes from India to Ethiopia (Est 1:1), the council of seven nobles (1:14), the efficient postal system (3:13; 8:10), the keeping of official diaries including records of the king's benefactors (2:23; 6:8), the use of impalement as a form of capital punishment (2:23; 5:14; 7:10), the practice of obeisance to kings and nobles (3:2), belief in lucky days (3:7), setting crowns on the heads of royal horses (6:8), and reclining on couches at meals (7:8).

The book of Esther intends the reader to believe the events actually happened as they are described. The author located them within the reign of a specific king, Ahasuerus/Xerxes (Est 1:1). He associated events with specific dates (e.g., the "third year" of Ahasuerus's reign, 1:3; "the tenth month, the month Tebeth, in the seventh year" of Ahasuerus's reign, 2:16; "the first month, the month of Nisan, in King Ahasuerus' s, twelfth year," 3:7). And he tied the establishment of the festival of Purim to the events in the book (9:16). It is difficult to imagine that the author would fabricate a story to explain the origin of Purim.

## HOW ESTHER FITS INTO GOD'S STORY

1. Prologue: Creation, Fall, and the Need for Redemption
2. God Builds His Nation (2000–931 BC)
3. God Educates His Nation (931–586 BC)
4. **God Keeps a Faithful Remnant (586–6 BC)**
5. God Purchases Redemption and Begins the Kingdom (6 BC to AD 30)
6. God Spreads the Kingdom Through the Church (AD 30-?)
7. God Consummates Redemption and Confirms His Eternal Kingdom
8. Epilogue: New Heaven and New Earth

## CHRIST IN ESTHER

Although the name of God is not mentioned in Esther, nowhere in Scripture is the care of God for His people more evident. Prior to His arrest, Jesus prayed, "While I was with them I was protecting them by Your name that You have given Me. I guarded them and not one of them is lost, except the son of destruction, so that the Scripture may be fulfilled" (Jn 17:12).

## CHRISTIAN WORLDVIEW ELEMENTS

### Teachings About God

The book reveals the providence of God in caring for His covenant people. Although many evils—including satanic opposition—may come against God's people, nothing ever happens beyond God's ability to work all things "together for the good of those who love God: those who are called according to His purpose" (Rm 8:28).

**Teachings About Humanity**

The villainy of Haman demonstrates human depravity at its worst; the integrity of Mordecai shows the enormous good that one person can do. Esther's story (like Joseph's in Genesis) demonstrates that when God's people face difficult circumstances they are to act courageously and risk themselves for a righteous cause rather than give in to "fate" or "being unlucky."

**Teachings About Salvation**

God will accomplish His redemptive purposes. If Haman's edict to destroy the Jews had succeeded, the coming of the Jews' ultimate deliverer, Jesus the Messiah-King, would have been imperiled. God's plan to save cannot be thwarted, and He has always taken the initiative to bring about salvation.

## GENRE AND LITERARY STYLE

**A Historical Narrative Written in Excellent Hebrew**

Esther is a carefully crafted narrative, but its events really happened. In English Bibles it is positioned as the last of the historical books of the Old Testament. In the Hebrew Scriptures it was placed in the third section, the Writings or *Kethuvim* (the other two sections are the Law and the Prophets). Among the Writings it was one of the Five Scrolls. Each of these Five Scrolls became associated with one of the Israelite festivals and was read publicly during that festival. Esther was, of course, identified with Purim, a late winter festival that originated in the fifth century BC and that is still celebrated annually by Jewish people as a minor holiday.

Hamantashen are three-cornered pastries with a variety of fillings served during the Jewish holiday of Purim. The pastries are designed to resemble the ears of Haman, defeated enemy of the Jews.

The Hebrew of Esther is carefully polished, but the Greek translators (second century BC) were apparently troubled by the lack of reference to God. Therefore, when they translated Esther from Hebrew to Greek, they inserted more than a hundred verses that frequently refer to God. Protestants, however, have accepted as Old Testament Scripture only texts that had a Hebrew original.

## A PRINCIPLE TO LIVE BY

**Unselfish Acts of Faith (Est 4:10–17, *Life Essentials Study Bible*, p. 640–41)**

Since we claim Christ as our example, we are to be willing to sacrifice our own needs for the good of others.

To access a video presentation of this principle featuring Dr. Gene Getz, use a Smartphone or iPad to connect to this QR code or go to http://www.bhpublishinggroup.com/handbook/esther

First chapter of a handwritten scroll of the book of Esther, with reader's pointer. The book of Esther is read twice on Purim, the fourteenth day of the Jewish month of Adar. The first reading is on the evening of Purim and the second reading is the next morning. Synagogues are normally solemn places, but for Purim children dress up in the costume of their favorite Purim character. As the book of Esther is read, when the name Haman is mentioned, the congregation boos him and shakes noisemakers called gragers.

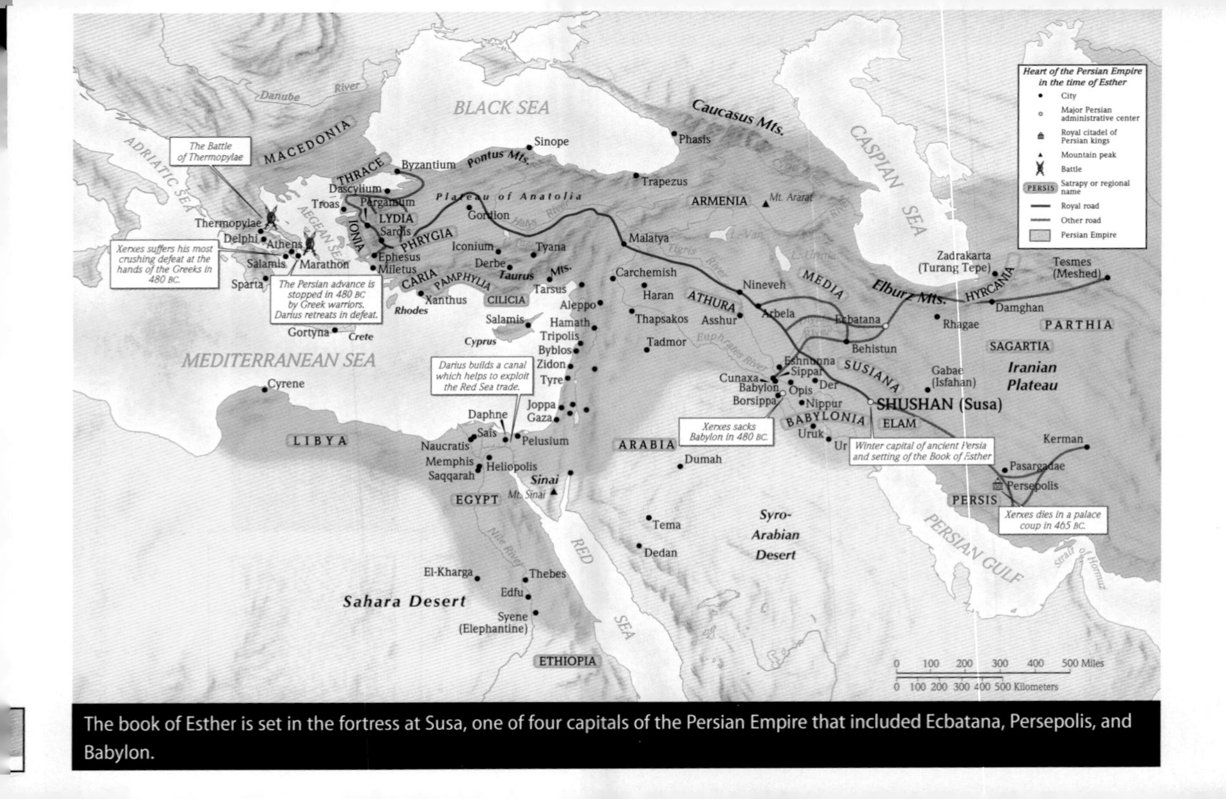


The book of Esther is set in the fortress at Susa, one of four capitals of the Persian Empire that included Ecbatana, Persepolis, and Babylon.

# JOB

The English title is the name of the central character in the narrative and the chief speaker in the poetic dialogues. The title carries over from the Hebrew Bible.

## KEY TEXT: 1:21

*"Naked I came from my mother's womb, and naked I will leave this life. The* LORD *gives, and the* LORD *takes away. Praise the name of Yahweh."*

## KEY TERM: "SUFFERING"

The book of Job explores the issue of human suffering despite God's goodness and power. The questions of why people suffer and why evil continues have been the focus of intense thought throughout the ages. Job is the main biblical treatment of this issue.

Job's 10 children were celebrating in their oldest brother's house when "a powerful wind swept in from the desert and struck the four corners of the house" (1:19).

## ONE-SENTENCE SUMMARY

After the upright Job suddenly lost family, health, and possessions, he and his friends dialogued at length about the reasons for his sufferings, but God alone had the final word and ultimately restored Job's losses.

# ORIGINAL HISTORICAL SETTING

## AUTHOR AND DATE OF WRITING

### Unknown, Perhaps During Solomon's Rule, Around 950 BC

The book is anonymous. The author's frequent use of "the LORD" (Yahweh) in the prose sections suggests that he wrote from an Israelite national perspective. It may have been penned anytime in the millennium between Moses and the end of the Old Testament period (1400–400 BC). The flowering of Hebrew culture under

The Pleiades. Brilliant grouping of six or seven visible stars located in the shoulder of the constellation Taurus (Jb 9:9; 38:31; Am 5:8). The derivation of the name has been traced to the seven daughters of Atlas and Pleione in Greek mythology, the adjective *pleos*, suggesting the "fullness" of the cluster, or to the verb pleo (to sail) from the cluster's usefulness in navigation.

Solomon, particularly in light of Solomon's association with wisdom literature, suggests a date during or shortly after Solomon.

## FIRST AUDIENCE AND DESTINATION

**The Israelite People**

The original hearers are not stated and can only be generally suggested.

## OCCASION

The book does not tell what prompted it to be written. Its events evidently occurred centuries before the writer's birth. Although some records of the various speeches may have survived for the author to use as sources, the material in chaps. 1–2 could only be known by divine revelation.

# GOD'S MESSAGE IN JOB

## PURPOSE

Job is the fullest development in Scripture of the issue referred to by theologians and philosophers as "the problem of evil" or "theodicy." Simply put, the matter is this: since humans, especially the seemingly innocent, suffer pain and evil, then what kind of God must there be? Logic suggests one of three answers: (1) God is righteous, but He is not powerful enough to prevent suffering; (2) God is all-powerful, but He is not truly good and has elements of evil in His nature; or (3) all pain and evil are in fact deserved by the sufferer and sent by God (in other words, the truly innocent do not suffer).

The biblical view finds these answers unacceptable. Job reveals a wider arena than humanity can observe. The conflict of the ages between God and Satan must in the end demonstrate both the righteousness and supremacy of God. He lets the innocent suffer to demonstrate that in His sovereignty He receives glory even when His people suffer and persevere in faith without understanding why. From a merely human point of view, the answer is that there is no answer given to the problem of evil. From a divine perspective the answer is that God's glory is served even when evil is permitted. (Christ's death is God's ultimate answer to the problem of evil.) Those who study Job today should interpret it in view of its original purpose.

## FIRST PASS

The book of Job has the characteristics of a drama with a prologue (1–2) and an epilogue (42:7–17) enclosing three cycles of poetic speeches between Job and his three friends (chaps. 3–27), a beautiful wisdom poem from Job (chap. 28), Job's concluding remarks (chaps. 29–31), the mysterious Elihu speeches (chaps. 32–37), God's whirlwind speeches (38:1–41:34), and Job's response (42:1–6).

### Prologue

The prologue describes the setting for the ensuing drama. Job was a wealthy man of perfect integrity who feared God and turned from evil (1:1–5). God was well pleased with Job. However, Satan challenged the motivation of Job's righteousness, saying in effect, Job is righteous because You've blessed him so greatly. Satan challenged God to remove the hedge of protection and Job will be seen for who he really is. God allowed the challenge but limited Satan's power to Job's family and possessions (1:6–12). In quick succession Satan destroyed all of Job's possessions including even his children. However, Job did not blame God or question His integrity (1:13–22). Satan then challenged God to let him attack Job's personal health. God agreed but did not allow him to kill Job (2:1–6). Without warning, a loathsome disease fell upon Job, yet he still refused to blame God (2:7–10). Job's friends were shocked and dismayed but nevertheless came to encourage him and offer their help (2:11–13). To this point Job displayed a traditional faith accepting suffering as inevitable and patiently enduring it.

### Three Cycles of Speeches

What follows are three cycles of speeches between Job and his friends. From the prologue, readers have a quasi-omniscient perspective. They are aware of the conversation between God and Satan that neither Job nor his friends are aware of.

The three friends reminded Job of a commonly held view. If people are righteous, God will bless them. If they aren't blessed or if they suffer, it is because of sin in their life. This theme is articulated in a variety of ways. The friends urged Job to take a closer look at his life. He was sure to find a sin or sins for which he needed to repent. All the while Job protested that he had not sinned. Job was confident that he could prove his innocence if given the opportunity to make his defense before God (chaps. 3–27).

### Ehihu

At this point a young man named Elihu rose to speak. He gave four speeches, each of which sought to justify God's actions. First, Elihu contended that God speaks to all people, and thus, even though he was a young man, he had every right to speak and even had the understanding to do so (32:1–33:33). Second, he reiterated the view that God was just and thus what had happened to Job was well deserved (34:1–37). Third, he sought to show that God honored the righteous and condemned the prideful (35:1–16). Fourth, he then pleaded with Job to accept what had happened to him as an expression of God's discipline and to humbly repent and seek His forgiveness (36:1–37:24). Finally, Elihu realized that Job really was not listening, so he stopped speaking.

**Out of the Whirlwind**

Suddenly, out of the midst of a whirlwind, God began to speak. God showed Job the marvels of creation. Now in God's presence Job didn't cross-examine God. God, in effect, put Job on the stand and asked if Job would now correct God (38:1–40:2). Job, who had been quick of speech, was now virtually speechless in God's presence

Orion. Constellation bearing the name of a giant Greek hunter who, according to myth, was bound and placed in the heavens. Job 38:31 perhaps alludes to this myth. God is consistently portrayed as the Creator of the Orion constellation (Jb 9:9; Am 5:8). The plural of the Hebrew term for Orion is rendered *constellations* at Isaiah 13:10. In His cross-examination of Job, the Lord asked, "Can you fasten the chains of the Pleiades or loosen the belt of Orion?"

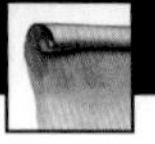



(40:3–5). God asked Job: "Would you really challenge My justice? Would you declare Me guilty to justify yourself?" (40:8). Next God pointed to two of His amazing creatures: Behemoth and Leviathan. This exercise brought Job to the awareness that he had been in way over his head in his view of God and in the demands he had made: "I had heard rumors about You, but now my eyes have seen You. Therefore I take back my words and repent in dust and ashes" (42:5–6).

**Job Restored**

God was pleased with Job and his responses. However, He rebuked the three friends and commanded that they ask Job to pray for them (42:7–9). Then God restored all Job's fortunes and even gave him more children (42:10–17). In the end Job found meaningful life, not in intellectual pursuits or even in himself but in experiencing God and trusting in Him.

## THE RELIABILITY OF JOB

Did Job really live, and did the things the book reports really happen, or is all this just a good story? Is the book of Job pure fiction like some of the stories of innocent sufferers preserved in ancient literature from Mesopotamia, Egypt, and elsewhere? These other stories may be more than fiction; they could be stories of true events.

"Can you hunt prey for a lioness or satisfy the appetite of young lions when they crouch in their dens and lie in wait within their lairs?" (Jb 38:39–40)

Moreover, efforts to equate Job with, or derive the account of Job's trials from, such ancient Near Eastern sources have proved valueless.

The absence of convincing contradictory data suggests that a fair hearing of the evidence points to the existence of a real person named Job. Certainly the style of the opening statement concerning Job (1:1) is much like that of Samuel's father, Elkanah (1 Sm 1:1), whose historical existence is not seriously doubted. Moreover, Ezekiel links Job with two other historical figures, Moses and Daniel (Ezk 14:14,20). Jesus' brother James apparently accepted the history of both Job and the Lord's dealing with him as much as the facts concerning the prophets who suffered in their service for the Lord (Jms 5:10–11).

A further area of criticism concerning Job has to do with its theological outlook, which some have categorized as undeveloped. Critics say that God is portrayed in the book as a sovereign who is interested solely in His power and control rather than in the plight of His creatures. Nor can He be the good and merciful God of the later Hebrew-Christian Scriptures, for He seems uninterested in Job's situation and unwilling to alleviate his suffering until He has demonstrated His mastery over all creation and creatures, including Job.

Such a viewpoint misses a great deal of the presentation of God in the book. From the beginning God is seen to be conscious of Job and his perfect integrity (1:8; 2:3), is concerned for Job's life (1:12; 2:6), and takes delight in Job.

## HOW JOB FITS INTO GOD'S STORY

Job does not fit into the narrative of God's kingdom. It offers timeless insights for God's people in any era of history.

## CHRIST IN JOB

In his great losses and suffering, Job cries out for a mediator to stand between him and God. Christ is the answer to that heart cry. "For there is one God and one mediator between God and humanity, Christ Jesus, Himself human" (1Tm 2:5 ).

## CHRISTIAN WORLDVIEW ELEMENTS

### Teachings About God

Job reveals God in His heavenly court (Is 6 and Ezk 1 may be compared). The book shows that God permits an adversary (Satan) to challenge His sovereign righteousness but that God's glory is served in the end. Job's expectation of a coming Redeemer (19:25) was fulfilled in Jesus Christ. The creative work of God's Spirit is evident in such texts as Job 33:4.

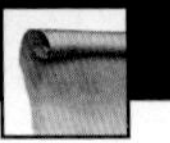



### Teachings About Humanity

The prose sections of Job (chaps. 1–2 and 42) show that human behavior is on display before supernatural powers. The poetic sections (chaps. 3–41) show that, however logical it appears, human reasoning alone can never penetrate the mind of God. Job and his counselors reached only partial truth about suffering, and only when God revealed Himself did the inadequacy of human wisdom become evident.

### Teachings About Salvation

Job 1 is consistent with Genesis in showing a family head offering sacrifices for the sins of his own family members. Job's personal confession of faith anticipated both the coming of Christ and the resurrection (19:25–26).

## GENRE AND LITERARY STYLE

### Wisdom Literature, Emphasizing Dialogues in Poetry, Framed by a Narrative Prologue and Epilogue, Written in Difficult Hebrew

The book of Job belongs to the literary type called "speculative wisdom," which explored the great questions of human existence. A number of other ancient Near Eastern texts have parallels to Job, for example the Egyptian "Admonitions of Ipuwer" or the Mesopotamian "I Will Praise the Lord of Wisdom." Israelite wisdom, however, based on the fear of the Lord, surpassed that of other nations. Job was placed in the third section, "The Writings" (*Kethubim*), of the Hebrew canon.

The narrative prologue (chaps. 1–2) and epilogue (chap. 42) are necessary frames for the extended body of the book. The poetic dialogues and monologues (chaps. 3–41) were composed entirely in the form of Hebrew parallelism found in the other wisdom books and the Psalms (as well as elsewhere in the Old Testament). See *Genre and Literary Style* for **PROVERBS** for more information on Hebrew parallelism.

The Hebrew vocabulary and style were so challenging to the Greek translators of Job (second century BC) that they skipped translating a number of lines, further suggesting an earlier date for the composition of Job.

## A PRINCIPLE TO LIVE BY

### An Eternal Perspective (Jb 19:23–27, *Life Essentials Study Bible*, p. 667)

Though we may never know on earth why bad things happen to good people, we should pray for grace and strength to believe that in eternity everything will be clear.

To access a video presentation of this principle featuring Dr. Gene Getz, use a Smartphone or iPad to connect to this QR code or go to http://www.bhpublishinggroup.com/handbook/job

The English title is based on the name given by the Greek translators of this book in the second century BC. The name could be translated "Songs." The original Hebrew title is *Tehillim*, "Hymns" or "Praises."

## KEY TEXT: 150:6

*"Let everything that breathes praise the* LORD. *Hallelujah!"*

## KEY TERM: "HALLELUJAH"

The Psalter became Israel's hymnal. Not all psalms were hymns (songs honoring or about God), but praise to God was their dominant theme.

## ONE-SENTENCE SUMMARY

God, the true and glorious King, is worthy of all praise, thanksgiving, and confidence—whatever the occasion in personal or community life.

Psalm 1, the gateway to this inspired collection, presents what has come to be called "the two ways." The process of winnowing—separating chaff from the grain—is an apt image of the two ways and their consequences. The other 149 psalms elaborate on this theme in a variety of ways.

## AUTHOR AND DATE OF WRITING

**Many Authors, Perhaps Finally Compiled Around 400 BC**

The titles of more than 70 psalms mention David, a noted musician and poet (1 Sm 16:23; 2 Sm 1:17). Both Asaph and "the sons of Korah" wrote several. Other named authors are Moses, Solomon, Heman, and Ethan. Of these, Moses was the earliest (1400s BC). Some psalms may have been composed after Israel returned from exile.

The collection grew gradually over time. For example, "Book One" (Pss 1–41) could have been completed early in Solomon's time. The "Asaph Collection" (Pss 73–83) and the "Songs of Ascents" (Pss 120–134) were perhaps added as a group. The final compilation probably did not occur until after the second temple had been completed.

Psalm 122, the third of 15 Songs of Ascents. These psalms were likely sung in pilgrimage processions, celebrating three annual festivals. They may also have been sung in ascending the 15 steps leading to the temple.

## FIRST AUDIENCE AND DESTINATION

**The Israelite People Living in Their Land**

Each of the 150 psalms was first intended for a particular audience. Sometimes the psalm title is suggestive, for example the "Songs of Ascents" (120–134; "Songs of Degrees," KJV) were evidently composed as songs for Israelite travelers to sing as they were going up (literally) to Jerusalem. The Psalter in its final form was designed as "The Hymnal of Second-Temple Judaism."

## OCCASION

Only 14 psalms provide a historical occasion in the title (3; 7; 18; 30; 34; 51; 52; 54; 56; 57; 59; 60; 63; 142). For others the content is suggestive but not conclusive. The final editors of the collection were prompted by the need to preserve the psalms they had. Many scholars believe the final editors composed Psalms 1; 2; and 150 as the formal introduction and conclusion to the Psalter.

# GOD'S MESSAGE IN PSALMS

## PURPOSE

The purpose of the individual poems as well as the entire collection process for the Psalter was to preserve the inspired words of Israelite songwriters as they expressed the heights and depths of their relationship with God. Their poems were preserved to guide God's people in later times in how to approach Him no matter what experiences they were undergoing. Thus, there are songs of exultation and high worship, songs of respect for God's Word, songs of trust when evil prevails, songs of confession, and other expressions of true religion. Although the psalms contain doctrine, prophecy, and instruction, above all they were meant to be sung to God as expressions of delight in Him. God's people today should use the psalms in light of their original purpose.

## FIRST PASS

Traditionally the book has been divided into five sections corresponding to the five books of Moses, each section ending with a doxology.

| | |
|---|---|
| Book 1 | Psalms 1–41 |
| Book 1 | Psalms 42–72 |
| Book 3 | Psalms 73–89 |
| Book 4 | Psalms 90–106 |
| Book 5 | Psalms 107–150 |

These divisions may suggest that the "books" were independent for a time. (Note that Pss. 14 and 53 are similar and occur in different "books.") Some psalms also may be grouped according to their function; for example, the Songs of Ascent (Pss 120–134) were probably sung by Israelites on their way to the three required feasts in Jerusalem. Another group of psalms (Pss 93; 96–99) celebrate the Lord's divine sovereignty over the universe.

Scholars have debated the forms and classifications of individual psalms for centuries. The book of Psalms contains hymns (Pss 145–150), laments (Pss 38–39), songs of thanksgiving (Pss 30–32), royal psalms (Pss 2; 110), enthronement psalms (Pss 96; 98), penitential psalms (Pss 32; 38; 51), and wisdom or didactic psalms (Pss 19; 119).

A *lament* can be expressed by the community (e.g., Pss 44; 74; 79) or the individual (Pss 22; 38; 39; 41; 54). Both types of laments are prayers or cries to God on the occasion of distressful situations. Differences are related to the types of trouble and the experiences of salvation. For the community the trouble may be an enemy;

A middle-eastern shepherd leading his sheep. The Bible mentions shepherds and shepherding over 200 times. Shepherds led sheep to pasture and water (Ps 23) and protected them from wild animals (1Sm 17:34–35). Shepherds guarded their flocks at night whether in the open (Lk 2:8) or in sheepfolds (Zph 2:6) where they counted the sheep as they entered (Jr 33:13). The shepherd came to designate not only persons who herded sheep but also kings (2Sm 5:2) and God Himself (Ps 23; Is 40:11). Later prophets referred to Israel's leaders as shepherds (Jr 23; Ezk 34).

with an individual it may be an illness. The basic pattern includes an invocation of God, a description of the petitioner's complaint(s), a recalling of past salvation experiences (usually community laments), petitions, a divine response (or oracle), and a concluding vow of praise.

The *thanksgiving psalms* are also spoken by the community (Pss 106; 124; 129) and the individual (Pss 9; 18; 30). These psalms are related to the laments in that they are responses to liberation occurring after distress. They are expressions of joy and are fuller forms of the lament's vow of praise.

The *hymn* (Pss 8; 19; 29) is closest in form to a song of praise as sung in modern forms of worship. These psalms are uniquely liturgical and could be sung antiphonally; some have repeating refrains (Pss 8; 136). The hymn normally includes a call to praise. Then the psalm describes the reasons for praising God. The structure is not as clear-cut as other types of psalms.

Some psalms are considered *royal psalms* (Pss 2; 18; 20). These psalms are concerned with the earthly king of Israel. Again, these are usually understood as mixed psalms. They were used to celebrate the king's enthronement. They may have included an oracle for the king. In some cases (such as Ps 72), prayers were made to intercede on behalf of the king.

Another mixed type is the *enthronement psalms* that celebrate Yahweh's kingship (Pss 96–99). They are closely related to the hymns; the main difference is a celebration of Yahweh as king over all creation.

*Penitential psalms* are expressions of contrition and repentance. The psalmist pleads to be restored to a right relationship with God (Pss 38; 51).

A final type of psalm is the *wisdom psalm*. This type has poetic form and style but is distinguished because of content and a tendency toward the proverbial. These psalms contemplate questions of theodicy (Ps 73), celebrate God's Word (the Torah; Ps 119), or deal with two different ways of living—that of the godly person or the evil person (Ps 1).

Some mixed psalms indicate that the psalms are not neatly or easily categorized. Nevertheless, identification helps the reader to know what type of psalm is being read, with a possible original context or a fitting present context in worship.

These classifications should not be taken too strictly. They are not rigid molds. The genuine religious feelings and expressions found in the Psalms may at times intersect with many of these classifications, or even transcend these classifications. A few psalms (Pss 25; 34; 37; 111; 112; 119; 145) are acrostically arranged according to the Hebrew alphabet, probably to aid in memorization.

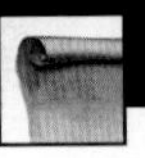



## THE RELIABILITY OF THE PSALMS

The Psalter was not completed until late in Israelite history (in the postexilic era). But it contains hymns written over a period of hundreds of years. Many individual psalms are far older than the whole book.

### Evidence of the Superscripts

A primary source of information regarding the date and authorship of individual psalms are the superscripts found above many psalms. According to these, some of the authors include David, the sons of Korah, Asaph, Moses, and Solomon. Other psalms, including some of the "Psalms of Ascent" (Pss 120–134) and "Hallelujah" Psalms (Pss 146–150) are anonymous. These titles, if taken at face value, would date many of the psalms to the early tenth century (psalms of David) and at least one to the fifteenth century (Ps 90).

### Meaning and Reliability of the Superscripts

Some scholars, however, question whether the superscripts are meant to ascribe authorship to the psalms. The phrase *ledawid* used frequently in the psalm superscripts could mean *by David*, but it also could mean *for David*. But most scholars would admit that the word means *by David*. There is no reason to think it is some kind of dedication. A more serious question is whether the superscripts are reliable. Some scholars believe they were added at a late date and are no more than conjectures that have no real historical value. But there are good reasons to believe the superscripts can be trusted. Many of the psalm superscripts refer to incidents in the life of David about which Samuel and Chronicles say nothing. For example, the superscript of Psalm 60 mentions battles with Aram-Naharaim, Aram-Zobah, and Edom. It would be strange if, in the late postexilic period, rabbis invented this. Another example is the superscript of Psalm 7, which speaks of a certain "Cush the Benjaminite." He is mentioned here only in the OT. If the superscripts were late fabrications, one would expect that they would refer more to incidents from David's life mentioned in Samuel. Many of the psalm titles contain technical musical terms, the meanings of which were already lost by the time the Old Testament was translated into Greek. For example, *lammenasseah*, "for the choir leader," is wrongly translated "to the end" in the Septuagint, the pre-Christian Greek translation of the Old Testament. A number of these terms are still not understood. Obscure or difficult words in the superscripts include: *song titles* ("Do Not Destroy," "A Silent Dove Far Away," "The Deer of the Dawn," "Lilies," "The Lily of Testimony," and "Mahalath"); *musical instruments or technical terms* ("stringed instruments" and "Sheminith"); *musical guilds or singers* ("Asaph," "Sons of Korah," "Heman the Ezrahite," "Ethan the Ezrahite"); and *types of psalms* ("Songs of Ascent," likely sung by those who were making a pilgrimage to Jerusalem; *maskil*, possibly an instructional or meditative psalm; *miktam; shiggayon)*. Ancient terminology and references to old guilds and bygone events all imply that the titles are very old. This supports confidence in their reliability.

### Davidic Authorship of Psalms

Many scholars have asserted that David did not write the psalms attributed to him. But there are no historical reasons why David could not have authored those psalms. David had a reputation as a singer and as a devoted servant of the Lord, and nothing in his life is incompatible with his being a psalmist. One difficulty here is that some of the psalms of David seem to refer to the temple (for example, 27:4), which did not exist in his day. But terms like "House of the LORD," "Holy Place," and "House of God" are regularly used of the tent of meeting and need not be taken as references to Solomon's temple (see Ex 28:43; 29:30; Jos 6:24; Jdg 18:31). Certainly David could have written the psalms attributed to him.

### The Date of the Psalms

Earlier critics dated many of the psalms late in Israel's history, some as late as the Maccabean period. For two reasons, however, this is no longer possible. First, the Ugaritic songs and hymns show parallels to many of the psalms. The grammar and poetic forms are similar. The Ugaritic tradition of hymn writing is ancient (before twelfth century) and implies that many of the psalms may be ancient too. Second, a fragmentary, second-century copy of the biblical collection of psalms was found in the Dead Sea Scrolls. This proves beyond doubt that the psalms were composed well before the second century since it must have taken a long time for the written psalms to be recognized as Scripture and for the psalter to be organized. There is no reason, therefore, to date all the psalms late. Generally speaking, they can be dated to three broad periods: (1) *Preexilic.* These psalms are very much like the Ugaritic songs, the royal psalms, and those that mention the northern kingdom. (2) *Exilic.* This includes the dirge songs that lament the fall of Jerusalem and call for vengeance on the Edomites and others. (3) *Early postexilic.* These psalms, such as Psalm 119, emphasize the written law.

## HOW PSALMS FITS INTO GOD'S STORY

Psalms does not fit into the narrative of God's kingdom. It is a timeless resource for the people of God in their worship of the living God.

## CHRIST IN PSALMS

Both Christ's first and second comings are prophesied. For example, Psalm 22 looks ahead to the crucifixion, and Psalm 2 looks forward to the time that His kingdom is universally acknowledged.

## CHRISTIAN WORLDVIEW ELEMENTS

### Teachings About God

The Psalms display God as Creator. He is also Redeemer and Covenant-maker. Many attributes of God are praised throughout the Psalms. The Spirit is God's active agent in accomplishing His purposes (Ps 51:11 and Is 63:10–11 are the only Old Testament passages referring to the Holy Spirit by name).

**Teachings About Humanity**

The essential teaching of Psalms about the human race is that God desires and enables people to praise and thank Him. Humans reach their highest potential only when they seek joy and fulfillment in the Creator rather than in the creation. The Psalms note the extremes of human existence. Psalm 8 shows the glory of humanity as made by God. On the other hand, the many Psalms that mention enemies of God and of God's people show the shameful sinfulness to which humans may fall.

**Teachings About Salvation**

The quotation of Psalm 32:1–2 by Paul in Romans 4:7–8 demonstrates that justification by faith was the same in Old Testament times as in New Testament times. Other passages, such as Psalm 51, confirm that the perspective of the psalmists was that salvation was initiated by the God of the covenant and was His gift to those who trusted in His *chesed* (usually translated "faithful love" or "kindness").

## GENRE AND LITERARY STYLE

**An Anthology of Poetry in Honor of Israel's God and Israel's Faith, Written in Hebrew**

The poetic style of the Psalms has much in common with the poetry of every culture: the rich use of figurative language and hyperbole that comes from thoughtful use of the imagination. Who can forget the metaphor, "The LORD is my shepherd" (23:1), or the personification, "Let the rivers clap their hands" (98:8)? See *Genre and Literary Style* for **PROVERBS** for more information on Hebrew parallelism. Psalms was the first book in "The Writings" (*Kethubim*), the third section of the Hebrew canon. Jesus referred to this threefold organization in Luke 24:44: "Everything written about Me in the Law of Moses, the Prophets, and the Psalms must be fulfilled."

## A PRINCIPLE TO LIVE BY

**Proclaiming God's Praises (Ps 147, *Life Essentials Study Bible*, p. 825)**

When we worship, we should fulfill a major purpose for which God has called us—to proclaim His praises.

To access a video presentation of this principle featuring Dr. Gene Getz, use a Smartphone or iPad to connect to this QR code or go to http://www.bhpublishinggroup.com/handbook/psalms

"As a father has compassion on his children, so the LORD has compassion on those who fear Him. For He knows what we are made of, remembering that we are dust" (Ps 103:13–14).

▲ "Splitting the Read Sea" by Dr. Lidia Kozenitzky. "The sea looked and fled . . . Why was it, sea, that you fled?" (Ps 114:3,5). Historically and theologically this is the most important event in the OT. More than a hundred times in all parts of the OT except the Wisdom Literature, Yahweh is proclaimed as "the one who brought you up from the land of Egypt, out of the house of bondage." Israel remembered the exodus as God's mighty redemptive act. She celebrated it in her creeds (Dt 26:5–9; 1Sm 12:6–8). She sang of it in worship (Pss. 78; 105; 106; 114; 135; 136).

▶ Gerard Hoet's (1648–1733) illustration of Israel at Mount Sinai. "The mountains skipped like rams, the hills, like lambs. . . . Why was it mountains, that you skipped like rams? Hills, like lambs? Tremble, earth, at the presence of the Lord, at the presence of the God of Jacob, who turned rock into a pool of water, and flint into a spring of water" (Ps 114:4–8).

The longer title translates the name found in Latin Bibles (*Liber Proverbiorum*). In Hebrew the title was "Proverbs of Solomon." Solomon was named as the main contributor. Proverb (*mashal* in Hebrew) may be rendered "maxim" or "wise saying."

## KEY TEXT: 3:5–6

*"Trust in the LORD with all your heart, and do not rely on your own understanding; think about Him in all your ways, and He will guide you on the right paths."*

## KEY TERM: "WISDOM"

This book shows God's people how to live life skillfully: "The fear of the *LORD* is the beginning of knowledge" (1:7). These principles for everyday life combine common sense as well as proper reverence for God, resulting in true wisdom. Wisdom (Hebrew *chokmah*) goes beyond theoretical knowledge into practical guidelines for facing life's challenging issues successfully.

Spanish painter, Pedro Berruguete's "Salomon." Solomon is remembered for having 3,000 proverbs and 1,005 songs in his repertoire (1Kg 4:32). It is difficult to know precisely the role Solomon and his court may have had in starting the process that culminated in the book of Proverbs. This process may be compared to the way psalms of Davidic authorship eventually led to the book of Psalms. In Israel wisdom was considered Solomonic almost by definition. Thus the titles in 1:1 and 10:1 are not strictly statements of authorship in the modern sense. Solomon's wisdom is illustrated in the Bible by the accounts of the two harlots who claimed the single surviving child (1Kg 3:16) and by the visit of the queen of Sheba (1Kg 10).

## ONE-SENTENCE SUMMARY

Those who follow God's wise design for living—particularly in areas of sexual purity and integrity of speech—avoid the perils that others fall into and enjoy life on earth as God meant it to be lived.

# ORIGINAL HISTORICAL SETTING

## AUTHOR AND DATE OF WRITING

**Primarily Solomon, but also Others, Around 950–700 BC**

Solomon ruled Israel about 970–931 BC. He "composed 3,000 proverbs, and his songs numbered 1,005" (1 Kg 4:32). Many of these were preserved in this book. Solomon wrote the first section (1:8–9:18) and the second section (10:1–22:16). More than two centuries later, more of Solomon's proverbs were compiled by scholars working for King Hezekiah (25:1–29:27). Unnamed wise men wrote the proverbs collected in 22:17–24:22. Two others, unknown outside this book, contributed short sections: Agur (30:1–33) and King Lemuel (31:1–9). The final compiler of Proverbs evidently wrote the prologue stating the book's purpose (1:1–7) and the epilogue about the virtuous woman (31:10–31).

Solomon may have put his own proverbs into written form before 930 BC. The later contributions could have been completed by 700 BC. Some scholars believe the book of Proverbs was not edited into its final form until after the Jews returned from their Babylonian exile, perhaps the fifth century BC.

## FIRST AUDIENCE AND DESTINATION

**The Israelite People Living in Their Own Land**

The first hearers were the Israelite people who came to admire the wisdom of their great king Solomon (1 Kg 3:28). According to 1 Kings 4:29–34, representatives of the surrounding nations came to Jerusalem to hear Solomon's divinely inspired wisdom.

## OCCASION

When God asked Solomon at the beginning of his reign to request a gift, he asked for "wisdom and knowledge" to rule the Israelite people well (2 Ch 1:10). God granted this, and over the course of years Solomon's wisdom became legendary so that it "was greater than the wisdom of all the people of the East, greater than all the wisdom of Egypt" (1 Kg 4:30). Perhaps most of Solomon's proverbs were written during his early years as king, before he was led astray by "many foreign women" (1 Kg 11:1).

## PURPOSE

Proverbs gives positive and negative principles for successful living, no matter the situation. The book applies to everyday life the great commandments to love God supremely and to love one's neighbors as oneself (Lv 19:18; Dt 6:5). Because proverbial teachings, by their nature, tell what works in human relationships, they cannot be treated as absolutes or as prophecies. The book assumes (but does not explicitly mention) covenant and redemption or Israel's history. Living well means enjoying successful relationships now, whatever happened in history or whatever the future brings.

## FIRST PASS

As indicated above, Proverbs is a collection of several books. Nevertheless, Proverbs displays a unified, richly complex worldview. Proverbs 1–9 introduces this worldview and lays out its main themes. The short sayings of Proverbs 10–31 are to be understood in light of the first nine chapters.

The beginning and end of wisdom is to fear God and avoid evil (1:7; 8:13; 9:10; 15:33). The world is a battleground between wisdom and folly, righteousness and wickedness, good and evil. This conflict is personified in Lady Wisdom (1:20–33; 4:5–9; 8; 9:1–6) and Harlot Folly (5:1–6; 6:23–35; 7; 9:13–18). Both "women" offer love and invite simple young men (like those in the royal school) to their homes to

"Wisdom calls out in the street; she raises her voice in the public squares. She cries out above the commotion; she speaks at the entrance of the city gates: 'How long, foolish ones, will you love ignorance? How long will you mockers enjoy mocking and you fools hate knowledge?'" (Pr 1:20–22a).

sample their wares. Wisdom's invitation is to life (8:34–36); the seduction of Folly leads to death (5:3–6; 7:22–27; 9:18).

Mysteriously, Lady Wisdom speaks in public places, offering wisdom to everyone who will listen (1:20–22; 8:1–5; 9:3). Wisdom does not hide but stands there for all who seek her. Some scholars consider Wisdom to be an attribute of God, especially shown in creation (3:19–20; 8:22–31). More accurately stated, however, Wisdom is revealed in creation. That is, God has placed in creation a wise order that speaks to mankind of good and evil, urging humans toward good and away from evil. This is not just the "voice of experience" but God's general revelation that speaks to all people with authority. The world is not silent but speaks of the Creator and His will (Pss 19:1–2; 97:6; 145:10; 148; Jb 12:7–9; Ac 14:15–17; Rm 1:18–23; 2:14–15).

This perspective eliminates any split between faith and reason, between sacred and secular. The person who knows God also knows that every inch of life is created by God and belongs to Him. Experiences in the world point the person of faith to God.

Thus the wise person "fears God" and also lives in harmony with God's order for creation. The sluggard must learn from the ant because the ant's work is in tune with the order of the seasons (Pr 6:6–11; cp. 10:5).

## THE RELIABILITY OF PROVERBS

### The Date and Authorship

The text says that the four units that make up Proverbs are by Solomon, by Solomon as edited by Hezekiah's scribes, by Agur, and by Lemuel as learned from his mother. This means that the majority of Proverbs (1–29) is essentially from Solomon. Even so, many modern scholars believe these collections came together long after Solomon. Some believe Proverbs was not written until over 500 years after Solomon, although others would date the collections to the late monarchy, some 300 years after Solomon. But no hard evidence exists that forces us to abandon the Bible's assertion that Solomon wrote most of the book. Some have argued that passages like Proverbs 8 are too advanced in thought to have come from Solomon. Yet other advanced and complex works of wisdom literature that are far older than Solomon's day appear in ancient Near Eastern texts. In addition, we read in the Bible that Solomon's reign was something of a flowering of wisdom in ancient Israel and that Solomon was at the head of its study (1 Kg 10:1–9). That being the case, it is not strange that the greatest Israelite wisdom literature should come from this period.

Kenneth Kitchen, an Egyptologist from the University of Liverpool, has done a structural analysis of Proverbs. One of his conclusions is that Proverbs 1–24 constitutes a single literary unit with characteristics that place it in the early part of the first millennium BC. This claim is further strengthened by parallels to Proverbs

1–9 in early Egyptian wisdom literature. It was earlier believed that chapters 1–9 supported a composition date much later than Solomon.[1]

Agur and Lemuel may be pen names of someone otherwise familiar to us; more likely Agur and Lemuel were simply sages about whom we have no other information. Since we do not know the identities of the writers, we cannot know the dates of composition. But there is no reason to date these sections very late. Also, although we cannot be sure when something like the present book of Proverbs first appeared, the reign of Hezekiah (716–687 BC) may be a reasonable surmise (25:1).

## HOW PROVERBS FITS INTO GOD'S STORY

Proverbs does not fit into the narrative of God's kingdom. It provides timeless wisdom for God's people in any era of history.

## CHRIST IN PROVERBS

Wisdom as an attribute of God is pictured as a person in Proverbs. In light of the New Testament we know that Wisdom as Jesus Christ, the Word by whom the worlds were created and are sustained (Jn 1:1; Heb 1:3).

## CHRISTIAN WORLDVIEW ELEMENTS

### Teachings About God

In Proverbs, God is the One who has set up the world so that those who live by His principles will find blessing and success. The highest virtue is "the fear of the LORD."

### Teachings About Humanity

Proverbs shows that humans may live by a right way or a wrong way, a wise way or a foolish way. The right way is not the easy way, but those who live by it find great reward. All of life's relationships may be governed by the wise teachings of this book.

### Teachings About Salvation

Proverbs assumes God's covenant but does not teach about it directly. This surely serves to demonstrate that the wisdom coming from the people of God is superior to and results in greater blessing than the wisdom coming from others—even without explicitly referring to the mighty acts of God on behalf of His people.

## GENRE AND LITERARY STYLE

### Wisdom Literature Emphasizing Short Maxims, Written Entirely in Hebrew Poetry

People of the ancient Near East greatly admired the wise men who collected and published guidelines for successful living. Wisdom literature was of two types:

proverbial (such as the present book, stating principles for living well) and speculative (such as Job or Ecclesiastes, pondering deep issues of human existence). Both the Mesopotamians and the Egyptians developed wisdom traditions. Israelite wisdom, however, based on the fear of the LORD, surpassed that of other nations. Proverbs was placed in the third section, "The Writings" (*Kethubim*), of the Hebrew canon.

Hebrew poetry characteristically had two (sometimes three) lines that are parallel in thought (rather than in rhyme). In *synonymous* parallelism, the second line repeated the essence of the first in different words (see 5:7). In *antithetic* parallelism, the second line stated the opposite of the first (see 10:3). When the later line built on the first without either repeating or contrasting, it is referred to as *synthetic* parallelism (see 31:15).

## A PRINCIPLE TO LIVE BY

**Heart Knowledge (Pr 1:4; 2:2, *Life Essentials Study Bible*, p. 836)**

To walk in God's will, we must allow His Word to penetrate our innermost being.

To access a video presentation of this principle featuring Dr. Gene Getz, use a Smartphone or iPad to connect to this QR code or go to http://www.bhpublishinggroup.com/handbook/proverbs

## ENDNOTES

1. See http://bible.ucg.org/bible-commentary/Proverbs/Introduction-to-Proverbs-Part-2/default.aspx.

The Greek translators used this name when they titled it in the second century BC. It was their rendering of the Hebrew title, *Qoheleth*, "Preacher" or "Teacher." "Ecclesiastes" means "one who assembles people," akin to *ekklesia*, "assembly."

## KEY TEXT: 1:2 (WHICH IS THE SAME AS 12:8)

*"'Absolute futility,' says the Teacher. 'Absolute futility. Everything is futile.'"*

## KEY TERM: "FUTILITY" (USELESSNESS OR ABSURDITY)

The Hebrew term *hebel* literally meant "breath" or "vapor." It referred to something without meaning or something absurd or useless. The term occurs more than 30 times in the book.

## ONE-SENTENCE SUMMARY

Although human beings can accumulate many things, accomplish much, and achieve great wisdom, these are without profit and ultimately pointless unless one has lived in fear and obedience to God.

## AUTHOR AND DATE OF WRITING

**Probably Solomon, Perhaps Near the End of His Reign, Around 935 BC**

The author called himself Qoheleth, "Preacher" or "Teacher" in the sense of one who assembles people for instruction. He was also "son of David, king in Jerusalem" (1:1). Jewish and Christian tradition alike have identified him as Solomon, and the perspective of an experienced old man is certain (see 12:1–7).

On the other hand, several features of the book point to a writer other than and later than Solomon. The Hebrew style is unusual and considered late; the reference to "all who were before me in Jerusalem" (2:9) seems odd for Solomon, Jerusalem's second Israelite king; and the writer expressed negative views about rulers (see 4:13; 5:8–9; 7:19; 8:2–3) that are hard to imagine coming from Solomon.

It may be, as is clear in the case of Proverbs, that the material was mainly written by Solomon but that it was expanded and revised by an unknown editor at a later time, perhaps as late as the 400s BC. There is nothing in the book that Solomon could not have written, and he certainly is the best Old Testament character to fit the description of one who "taught the people knowledge . . . and arranged many proverbs" (12:9; see 1 Kg 4:32). For more on authorship and date of composition, see *The Reliability of Ecclesiastes* below.

## FIRST AUDIENCE AND DESTINATION

**The Israelite People Living in Their Own Land**

The first hearers were the Israelite people who came to admire the wisdom of Solomon (1 Kg 3:28). According to 1 Kings 4:29–34, representatives from the surrounding nations came to hear Solomon's divinely inspired wisdom.

## OCCASION

Solomon reigned about 970–931 BC. The precise occasion for Ecclesiastes is unknown. The teachings of Ecclesiastes come from late in Solomon's reign—after he had experienced everything life had to offer and was contemplating once again "what's it all about?" (The book of Proverbs was evidently his wisdom from earlier in his reign.)

## PURPOSE

Ecclesiastes answers the question, What is the meaning of life? The way Qoheleth ("the Teacher") argued was to show at length the failure of the answers offered by those who live life "under the sun," that is, apart from revealed religion. *Materialists* find life's object in the abundance of possessions or achievements. *Sensualists* discover meaning in physical pleasure (food, sex, excitement, adventure). *Scholars* seek purpose through intellectual inquiry (wisdom). All these answers are "absolute futility" or "utterly meaningless." Life's meaning cannot be *discovered*; it is only *revealed* by God. Life is brief; judgment is coming; God is sovereign. Qoheleth's answer is that of divine revelation: "When all has been heard, the conclusion of the matter is: fear God and keep His commands, because this is for all humanity. For God will bring every act to judgment, including every hidden thing, whether good or evil" (12:13–14).

## FIRST PASS

Ecclesiastes at first appears to have no structure at all. The book does not follow modern standards of setting topics in a hierarchy. But a careful reading shows that Ecclesiastes carefully moves among a group of selected subjects. These include wealth, politics, wisdom, death, and aging. As the book moves to and fro among these and other topics, a complete statement gradually emerges.

### Introduction (1:1–2)

Verse 1 gives the title of the work, and verse 2 gives its theme. The word *futility*, *vanity*, or *meaningless* translates the Hebrew word *hebel,* which originally meant *breath*. From *breath* comes the idea of that which is insubstantial, transitory, and of fleeting value.

### On Time (1:3–11; 3:1–15a; 11:7–12:7)

All of nature is in constant motion and yet is going nowhere. This is a parable of human life; it is a long flurry of activity that accomplishes nothing permanent. Not only that, but there is nothing new in this world. Our existence in this world is a mixture of joy and sorrow, harmony and conflict, and life and death. Each has its own proper moment, and we, as creatures of time, must conform to the temporal limitations that are built into the cycle of life (3:1–15a).

**On Wisdom (1:12–18; 2:12–17; 6:10–7:6; 7:11–29)**

Education and intellectual pursuits fail to satisfy our deepest needs. The task of the intellectual, the quest to understand life, is itself a hopeless endeavor. Both the wise man and the fool will die. Of course, the wise go through life with better understanding of what lies ahead than do fools, but neither can escape death (2:12–17). Still, it is better to go through life with sobriety and understanding than in inane pleasure seeking (6:10–7:6). Qoheleth compares wisdom to wealth and considers wisdom better because it does not disappear in hard times (7:11–14).

**On Wealth (2:1–11,18–26; 4:4–8;5:10–6:9; 7:11–14; 10:18–20; 11:1–6)**

Many people devote themselves to incessant labor for the sake of their children. But the children may well simply squander all their parents struggled to accumulate (2:18–26). The two proverbs in 4:5–6 are set in opposition to each other in order to provide balance in life. Laziness leads to poverty and self-destruction. But it is better to be content with what one has than to spend life toiling away for more possessions. Work itself has value. The laborer has more peace and better sleep than the affluent man (5:10–6:9). While Ecclesiastes discourages the pursuit of wealth, it favors wise investment and diligent work. Better to recognize that all things are in God's hands and proceed with our work with an eye toward all possible contingencies (11:1–6).

**On Politics (3:15b–17; 4:1–3,13–16; 5:8–9; 7:7–10; 8:1–9:6; 9:13–10:20)**

Ecclesiastes voices dismay at the widespread corruption in places of political power, but it asserts that someday God will judge (3:15b–17). Political power and the popularity that accompanies it are short-lived. Those who have long held power tend to become inflexible and thus vulnerable. But the entire struggle, an endless game of "king of the hill," is pointless (4:13–16).

Corruption of government officials is a universal occurrence and should not surprise anyone. But anarchy is not the answer (5:8–9). Many who have power use it ruthlessly for their own gain. That they often seem to go unpunished aggravates the situation. This is, perhaps, the most troubling problem of life.

**On Death (3:18–22; 8:1–9:6)**

Ecclesiastes states that no one, by comparing the carcass of an animal to a human corpse, can find any evidence that the human, unlike the animal, is immortal. The thought that persons have "no advantage" over the animals astonishes many readers. But it does not mean we are in all respects like the animals, nor does it contradict the rest of the Bible. It means humans can no more claim to have the power to beat death than can any other animal. For Christians this should only drive us closer to Christ, who did conquer death in His resurrection (3:18–22).

**On Friendship (4:9–12)**

In all the hardships and disappointments of life, few things give more real, lasting satisfaction than true friendship. A friend is a comfort in need and a help in trouble.

Verse 11 does not refer to sexual relations but to shared warmth between two traveling companions on a cold desert night. At the same time, it may imply that the best friend for life ought to be one's spouse.

**On Religion (5:1–7; 7:15–29)**

Fools assume they know all about God and are able to please Him. True piety and wisdom recognize the limitations of both our understanding of God and our ability to please Him with our deeds. The attitude of awe toward God that Ecclesiastes recommends (5:7) is in reality dependence on God's grace and recognition that the benefits we have from Him are only by His mercy.

**On Evil (8:1–9:6)**

One of life's most troubling observations is that the good and the bad suffer the same fate. This, however, should not lead to cynicism. Instead, it should provoke deeper faith that only God knows the end from the beginning and only He can finally set all things right.

**On Contentment (9:7–12; 11:7–12:7)**

This section is in two parts: counsel to youth and a poem on aging and death. To the young, Ecclesiastes advises that their brief time of youthful vigor be spent in joy rather than in anxiety. But they are not free to pursue folly and immoral behavior. Awareness of divine judgment and the fleeting nature of youth should always govern their decisions.

**Conclusion (12:8–14)**

True wisdom comes from God and is worth acquiring. But one should be wary of endless academic pursuits. Some readers feel the concluding call to fear God does not follow from all that has gone before, but it is in fact the perfect conclusion. The pursuit of wealth, knowledge, and political power is ultimately unsatisfactory and leads to divine judgment. Life is short and full of mystery. All our attempts to make life meaningful fail. The wise response, therefore, is to cling to God and His grace.

## THE RELIABILITY OF ECCLESIASTES

Two questions often arise in connection with the book of Ecclesiastes: first, whether the book was written by Solomon; and second, whether the book is consistent with the rest of Scripture. Regarding the first question, many scholars consider Ecclesiastes to be a late book, written between 400 and 100 BC, and therefore obviously not by Solomon who lived in the tenth century BC. The main argument against Solomonic authorship of Ecclesiastes is that the book contains a few words that do not appear in any other texts until several hundred years after the time of Solomon. This is not insignificant, but arguments based on linguistic evidence are notoriously difficult to make. Since we have a limited number of texts from the ancient Near East, it is hard to say when a given word may have entered the common speech.

We do have evidence that the author of Ecclesiastes was familiar with certain classic texts from Mesopotamia (*Epic of Gilgamesh*) and Egypt ("The Harper's Song") that were written before the time of Solomon. But the book shows no familiarity with later literature, such as the classic Greek texts from the fifth century BC and following. This lends weight to Solomon's being author of Ecclesiastes and creates problems for the position that Ecclesiastes was written between 400 and 100 BC.

Regarding the second question, many readers are troubled by the book's apparently cynical attitude ("Everything is futile," says 1:2), by its apparent denial of afterlife (e.g., 3:19–20), by its recommendations to eat, drink, and enjoy life (e.g., 5:18; 10:19), and by its seemingly indifferent attitude about morality (e.g., 7:2).

The word translated "futile" in the HCSB could be rendered "fleeting." It literally means "breath" and implies that something only has fleeting value and then evaporates, like a puff of air. In Hebrew the word appears twice in a construction that is translated into English as an intensification ("breath of breaths," or "absolute futility"). The book is not saying that everything is worthless but that everything is short-lived and quickly passing. Nothing under the sun lasts forever.

Ecclesiastes appears to reject the idea of an afterlife. What he is questioning, however, may be the materialistic notions of afterlife that predominated in ancient Egypt, where people thought that after death a powerful man could continue to enjoy his possessions, his women, and the services of his slaves. In short, this theology did not take seriously the finality of physical death (the great pyramids of the Pharaohs were expressions of this view). The Egyptian "Harper's Song," written about 1,000 years before the time of Solomon, criticizes this refusal to face the significance of death and reveals some striking parallels to Ecclesiastes. (Solomon had cultural ties with Egypt, being married to the daughter of an Egyptian ruler; 1 Kg 3:1.) Biblical theology, by contrast with Egyptian "wisdom," takes death seriously as "the last enemy" (1 Co 15:26); it is only by an act of God, the resurrection of Jesus, that we can overcome its finality (1 Co 15:55–56).

In saying that it is appropriate for a person to eat, drink, and find enjoyment in life "because that is his reward" (3:22; 5:18), the author does not mean these are life's only reward and that there is no afterlife. These things are the reward of a person's labor, and one should not neglect to take time out for some simple pleasures.

## HOW ECCLESIASTES FITS INTO GOD'S STORY

Ecclesiastes does not fit into the narrative of God's kingdom. It provides timeless wisdom for God's people in any era of history.

## CHRIST IN ECCLESIASTES

Ecclesiastes gives a graphic picture of life's emptiness and futility apart from God. Jesus uses the image of a vine with branches to underscore this truth: "The one who remains in Me and I in him produces much fruit, because you can do nothing without Me" (Jn 15:5 ).

## CHRISTIAN WORLDVIEW ELEMENTS

### Teachings About God

In Ecclesiastes God is referred to simply as "God" (*Elohim*) or "Creator." He is not called "the Lord" or "LORD" (Yahweh). This emphasizes God in relationship to all humanity—their Creator and the One to whom they are ultimately accountable—as opposed to God in relationship to Israel as the covenant people.

### Teachings About Humanity

Ecclesiastes has an optimistic view of human capacity apart from God. Materialists, sensualists, and scholars alike can reach worthwhile goals that bring temporary satisfaction and the appearance of meaning. Yet the book is pessimistic about the ability of persons to understand their true purpose unaided by divine revelation. Left to themselves, humans never reach right answers to the question, Why am I here?

### Teachings About Salvation

Salvation in Ecclesiastes is spoken of in terms of proper fear (reverence, awe, respect) of God (see 3:14; 5:7; 8:12; 12:13). Ultimately, only those who "fear God and keep His commands" (12:13) give evidence of experiencing salvation, which like existence itself comes from the Creator. The meaning of human life is displayed when redeemed people magnify the glory of God by joyfully fearing and obeying Him.

## GENRE AND LITERARY STYLE

### Wisdom literature Composed in a Mixture of Prose and Poetry, Written in Unusual Hebrew

Ancient wisdom literature was of two types: proverbial (such as the book of Proverbs, stating principles for living well) and speculative (such as Job or the present book, pondering deep issues of human existence). In the Hebrew canon, Ecclesiastes was placed in the third section, the Writings or *Kethubim* (the other two sections are the Law and the Prophets). Among the Writings it was one of the Five Scrolls. Each of these Five Scrolls became associated with one of the Israelite festivals and was read publicly during that festival. Ecclesiastes was identified with *Sukkoth*, "Tabernacles" or "Booths," a happy time that celebrated the completion of all agricultural labors. The Hebrew style is markedly different from anything else in the Old Testament.

## A PRINCIPLE TO LIVE BY

**Life Without God (Ec 1:1–11, *Life Essentials Study Bible*, p. 881)**

Even though we are capable of accomplishing many wonderful things in this life, our primary focus should be on eternity.

To access a video presentation of this principle featuring Dr. Gene Getz, use a Smartphone or iPad to connect to this QR code or go to http://www.bhpublishinggroup.com/handbook/ecclesiastes

"So remember your Creator in the days of your youth: before the days of adversity come, and the years approach when you will say, 'I have no pleasure in them'" (Ec 12:1).

The Hebrew title is *Shir Hashirim*, "Song of Songs," meaning "the finest song." Because 1:1 mentions Solomon, English Bibles have often included his name in the title. *Canticles* is Latin for "Songs."

## KEY TEXT: 6:3

*"I am my love's and my love is mine; he feeds among the lilies."*

## KEY TERM: "LOVE"

Song of Songs is a book of romantic love poetry. The lovers—bride and groom—refer to each other passionately. The bride calls him "love," a term found more than 20 times; the groom calls her "my love."

## ONE-SENTENCE SUMMARY

A bride and groom (or wife and husband) celebrate with exuberant passion God's wonderful gift of the love they share by describing the intimate dimensions of their love—physical, emotional, and spiritual.

"Daughters of Jerusalem, I am dark like the tents of Kedar, yet lovely like the curtains of Solomon. Do not stare at me because I am dark, for the sun has gazed on me. My mother's sons were angry with me; they have made me a keeper of the vineyards" (Sg 1:5–6)

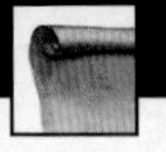



## AUTHOR AND DATE OF WRITING

**Probably Solomon, Perhaps Near the Beginning of His Reign, Around 965 BC**

The author wrote the most exquisite romantic poetry in the Bible, and the perspective of a young couple captivated with each other is transparent. The inscription (1:1) as well as Jewish and Christian tradition identified the author as Solomon. According to 1 Kings 4:32 Solomon's "songs numbered 1,005." Many believe that the pure and passionate words of love described in this book were necessarily written early in his life—before he was married to so many women (1 Kg 11:1–8).

Some scholars have argued that the title is a dedication to Solomon (rather than a statement of authorship) and find it hard to imagine that a polygamous king wrote such a beautiful celebration of monogamous love. Although their arguments for later anonymous authorship have merit, there is no reason that a young Solomon could not have written the song in its entirety. For more on authorship and date of composition, see *The Reliability of Song of Songs* below.

## FIRST AUDIENCE AND DESTINATION

**Israelites Living in Their Own Land**

The first hearers were the Israelite people who admired both the proverbs and the songs of their great King Solomon (1 Kg 4:32).

## OCCASION

Scholars have a variety of opinions about what prompted the composition of this book. Two major suggestions follow. Some believe the book describes an ideal romance and was composed for a royal occasion, such as a state wedding. In this view, the bride and groom were not individuals but "Every-Bride" and "Every-Groom," depicting the possibilities of human romance with all its challenges and glories. Others have argued that this is Solomon's poem about an actual, historical romance and marriage between an unnamed girl (called the "Shulammite," 6:13) and her beloved (either Solomon himself or an unnamed lover). The former view of the occasion appears preferable.

## PURPOSE

Many parts of Scripture address human sexuality, and a number of divine commands regulate marriage, adultery, divorce, and sexual immorality. Other than this book, however, little is noted in Scripture about whether a man and woman should enjoy or merely endure romance. In the tradition of ancient Near Eastern wisdom literature, Song of Songs explores one of the "big issues" of life. It definitively answers the question, Should a husband and wife enjoy the amorous dimension of their relationship? The answer is, Yes indeed! Although people often abuse or distort erotic love, it is a wondrous and normal part of marriage to be savored as God's gift. Strikingly, the dominant speaker is the wife, whose delight in the intimacies she enjoys demonstrates that the biblical view of sex is neither negative nor repressed. It is not claiming too much to call this book "The Bible's Romance Manual for Marriage." God's people should enjoy the Song of Songs today in light of its original purpose.

"Like an apricot tree among the trees of the forest, so is my love among the young men. I delight to sit in his shade and his fruit is sweet to my taste" (Sg 2:3).

## FIRST PASS

Song of Songs is a love song with three roles—a man, a woman, and a chorus of women. In the Song that begins at 1:2, the groom, the bride, and the chorus each take turns singing their parts, but they do not follow a consistent sequence. At times it is difficult to tell who is singing a given line of lyrics.

In the past many called for an allegorical interpretation of the Song because they felt that a simple love song had no place in the Bible and that, unless it was allegorized, no theological message could be found in it. This concern, however, is misguided. Song of Songs conveys important meaning without being turned into something it is not.

First, as the Bible is meant to serve as a guide in every aspect of life, so the Song deals with one universal aspect of human life—love, marriage, and sexuality. People need direction and teaching in the matter of how to nurture love for a spouse just as they need guidance in every other matter. The Song teaches that this love relationship is to be both physical and verbal. Again and again the two lovers speak of their desire for and joy in each other. For many couples the inability to express love is a profound problem.

Second, although the Song teaches by example and not by decree, its message is clear. The love the couple shared was exclusive and binding (7:10). By implication this ideal portrait excludes extramarital sex as well as all perversions and abuses of sexuality, such as promiscuity and homosexuality.

Third, Song of Songs celebrates love between man and woman as something that is valid and beautiful even in a fallen and sinful world. In this way Song of Songs testifies in a significant way to the grace of God. Although we are sinners, God tells us that the love relationship is a thing to be cherished and enjoyed. If the Bible said nothing in this area beyond prohibitions and warnings, we might suppose that all sexuality is innately evil and is to be suppressed entirely except for procreation. But because the Song is in the Bible, we understand that it is not sexuality but the misuse and abuse of sex that is wrong. In the Song we see that genuine love between man and woman, and the physical affection that follows, is a good and tender thing.

Fourth, the Song of Songs is unlike its ancient Near Eastern counterparts in one significant respect: it does not turn sexuality into a sacred ritual. In the ancient world fertility cults and religious prostitution abounded. The sexual act was thought to have religious meaning. None of this is found in Song of Songs. The romantic love between man and woman is a joy, but it is exclusively a joy of this world. In this way the Bible avoids the two pitfalls of human religion. It neither condemns sexual love as innately evil and dangerous (as do legalistic cults) nor elevates it to the status of religious act (as do sensual cults and religions). The Song of Songs, therefore, should be taken as it stands. It is a song of love and an affirmation of the value of the bond

between a man and a woman. In this way it adds greatly to our appreciation of God's creation.

## THE RELIABILITY OF SONG OF SONGS

Traditional scholars affirm Solomon as the author of the Song based on 1 Kings 4:29–34, dating the text to approximately 900 BC. In the Old Testament, Solomon is commonly associated with poetry, wisdom, and horticulture, further supporting the traditional view of authorship. Solomon's name occurs six times in the book.

The title probably implies that Solomon wrote it, but it could be taken to mean that it was simply part of Solomon's collection and was written perhaps by a court singer. Still, many scholars believe the Song was written late in Israelite history (500–100 BC) and therefore could not possibly have been written by Solomon or his contemporaries (961–922 BC). It is important, therefore, to see what evidence there is for dating the book. Most scholars who regard the Song as a late work do so primarily because some of the vocabulary found in it appears to be incompatible with the earlier date. For example, many argue that the Hebrew word for "orchard" in 4:13, *pardes,* is derived either from the Persian word *pairidesa* or the Greek word *paradeisos* (compare the English *paradise*). The argument is that it is difficult to see how Hebrew could have borrowed a word from either Persian or Greek as early as Solomon's day. However, the word *pardes* ("orchard") may come from a Sanskrit root word that is far older than either Persian or Greek. In addition, many words once asserted to be from a late Aramaic background have been found to be more ancient than originally supposed.

The poetic imagery of Song of Songs reflects an age of great prosperity. This also lends support to the belief that it was written in Solomon's day. Only then did Jerusalem possess the spices, perfumes, and luxuries mentioned in the book as well as great quantities of gold, marble, and precious jewels (Sg 5:14–15; see 1 Kg 10:14–22). Of course, one can argue that these are only similes and do not prove that the writer actually lived in an age when such things were common. But it is doubtful that a poet would use imagery described in such detail that was outside his own frame of reference and experience.

## HOW SONG OF SONGS FITS INTO GOD'S STORY

Song of Songs does not fit into the narrative of God's kingdom. It provides timeless wisdom for God's people in any era of history regarding God's plan for love between husbands and wives.

## CHRIST IN SONG OF SONGS

Love between a husband and a wife is taken by Paul as a picture of the love Christ has for His bride, the church (Eph 5:32).

## CHRISTIAN WORLDVIEW ELEMENTS

### Teachings About God

God is not directly named in this book. None of His usual names are found, such as God, LORD, the Lord, or the Almighty. God is affirmed indirectly as the Creator who conceived of romantic love between husband and wife, as in the account of the first man and woman coming together as one flesh (Gn 2:18–25).

### Teachings About Humanity

Song of Songs celebrates the glory of wedded bliss possible for human beings, despite the many obstacles to true love. The climax of the book shows how strong and wonderful romantic love is: "Mighty waters cannot extinguish love; rivers cannot sweep it away. If a man were to give all his wealth for love, it would be utterly scorned" (8:7).

### Teachings About Salvation

The book does not teach directly about redemption. If the love of a husband for his wife can be as rich and satisfying as the book describes, how much greater is the love of God for His beloved people (see Rv 21:9).

## GENRE AND LITERARY STYLE

### Wisdom Literature Emphasizing the Value of Romantic Love, Written Entirely in Hebrew Poetry

Although some scholars have questioned whether this book is properly "wisdom literature," it answers one of the grand questions of life: Should a husband and wife enjoy the erotic dimension of their relationship? (See earlier discussion under *Purpose*.) As such, it belongs to the literary category "speculative wisdom." The poetic imagery is exquisite, lavish, and delicate, even if modern lovers do not fully appreciate the vivid metaphors from the ancient Near East (see 4:1–7; 5:10–16; 6:4–10; 7:1–10). The lines of poetry are short, and the Hebrew style is appropriate to the subject matter.

In the Hebrew canon this book was placed in the third section, the Writings or *Kethubim* (the other two sections are the Law and the Prophets). Among the Writings it was the first of the Five Scrolls, each of which became associated with one of the Israelite festivals and was read publicly during that festival. Song of Songs was associated with *Pesach*, "Passover." Although this connection seems strange, this can be understood in light of the Jewish allegorical interpretation of the book. Its deeper (and truer) meaning was said to be its declaration of God's love for Israel, of which the

greatest historical evidence was the exodus at the first Passover. This view was also taken up by Christians in the medieval period but revised and seen as an allegory of Christ's love for the church. Bible scholars today generally reject such allegorical readings as a misunderstanding of the book's purpose by theologians unwilling to admire as literally true the frankly erotic elements of the book.

## A PRINCIPLE TO LIVE BY

**Intimate Love (Sg 1:1–11, *Life Essentials Study Bible*, p. 895)**

Men and women who are joined in a marital union are to enjoy to the full the sexual dimension of their relationship.

To access a video presentation of this principle featuring Dr. Gene Getz, use a Smartphone or iPad to connect to this QR code or go to http://www.bhpublishinggroup.com/handbook/songofsongs

"Set me as a seal on your heart, as a seal on your arm. For love is as strong as death, ardent love is as unrelenting as Sheol" (Sg 8:6).

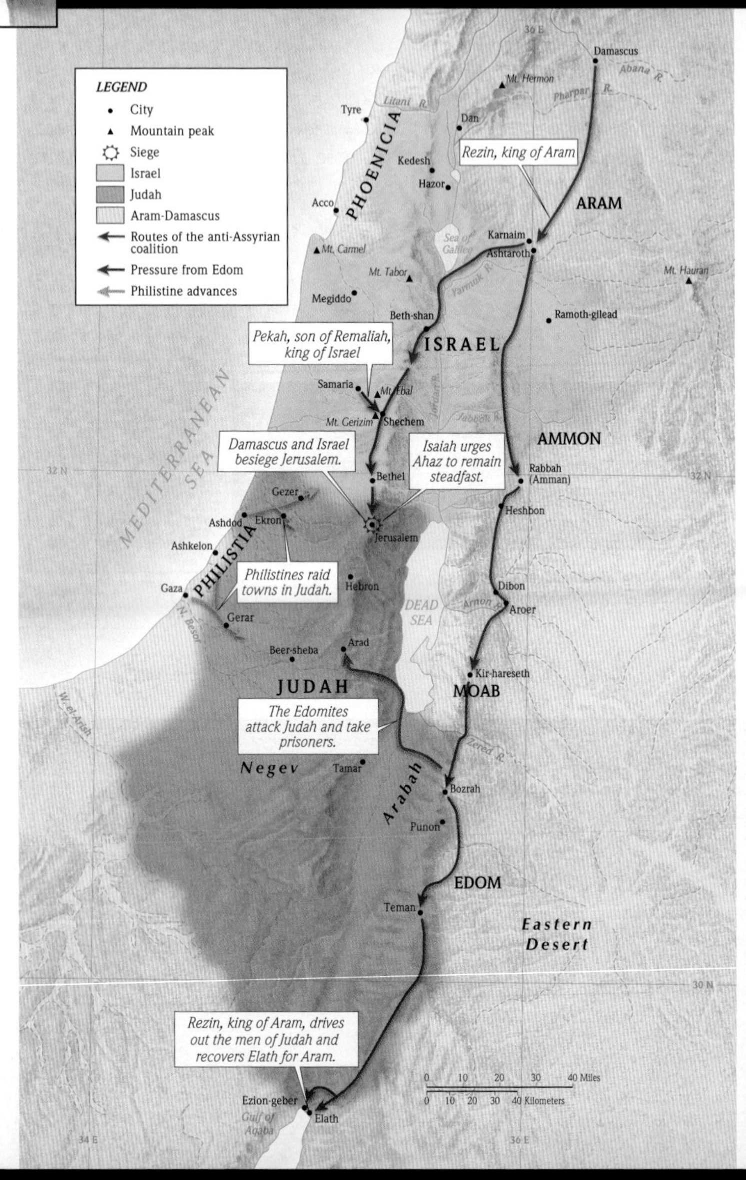


The Syro-Ephraimite War (Is 7). In the context of this crisis, Isaiah gave counsel to Judah's King Ahaz. Rezin, king of Aram, and Pekah, king of Israel, joined forces to attack Jerusalem. Also in that context, Isaiah prophesied the birth of Immanuel (7:10–25).

Isaiah, the eighth-century Israelite prophet from Judah, has given his name to this book as its composer. His name means "Yahweh saves" in Hebrew.

## KEY TEXT: 1:19-20

*"'If you are willing and obedient, you will eat the good things of the land. But if you refuse and rebel, you will be devoured by the sword.' For the mouth of the* LORD *has spoken."*

## KEY TERM: "JUDGMENT"

Isaiah's vision of the heavenly throne compelled him to proclaim God's case against His people before their earthly throne in Jerusalem. Although divine judgment was inevitable, Isaiah offered hope, comfort, and a glorious future for God's kingdom.

## ONE-SENTENCE SUMMARY

Isaiah prophesied that because of continued idolatry God would send Judah into Babylonian captivity, yet He would graciously restore them (through the work of His Servant, who would bear away their sins by His death), so that His kingdom would be unending in the new heavens and the new earth.

# ORIGINAL HISTORICAL SETTING

## AUTHOR AND DATE OF WRITING

**Isaiah, Perhaps Finally Compiled Around 680 BC**

Because of the message of good news in the last section of his book, the author has been called "The Evangelist of the Old Covenant." Isaiah the son of Amoz was evidently from Jerusalem. According to Jewish tradition, he was from a noble family. He had a wife and at least two sons with symbolic names, "A Remnant Will Return" and "Speeding to the Spoil; Hastening to the Plunder" (Shear-jashub and Maher-shalal-hash-baz, 7:3; 8:3). He was possibly martyred by being sawed in half (see Heb 11:37). The kings Isaiah mentioned ruled over a century, from 792 to 686 BC. His years of influence were around 740–700 BC.

For the past two centuries, critical scholars have argued that chapters 40–66 were necessarily written later than Isaiah's lifetime. These chapters focus on return from Babylonian exile (which did not happen until centuries after Isaiah) and name Cyrus (44:28; 45:1), the Persian king who allowed the Jewish exiles to return

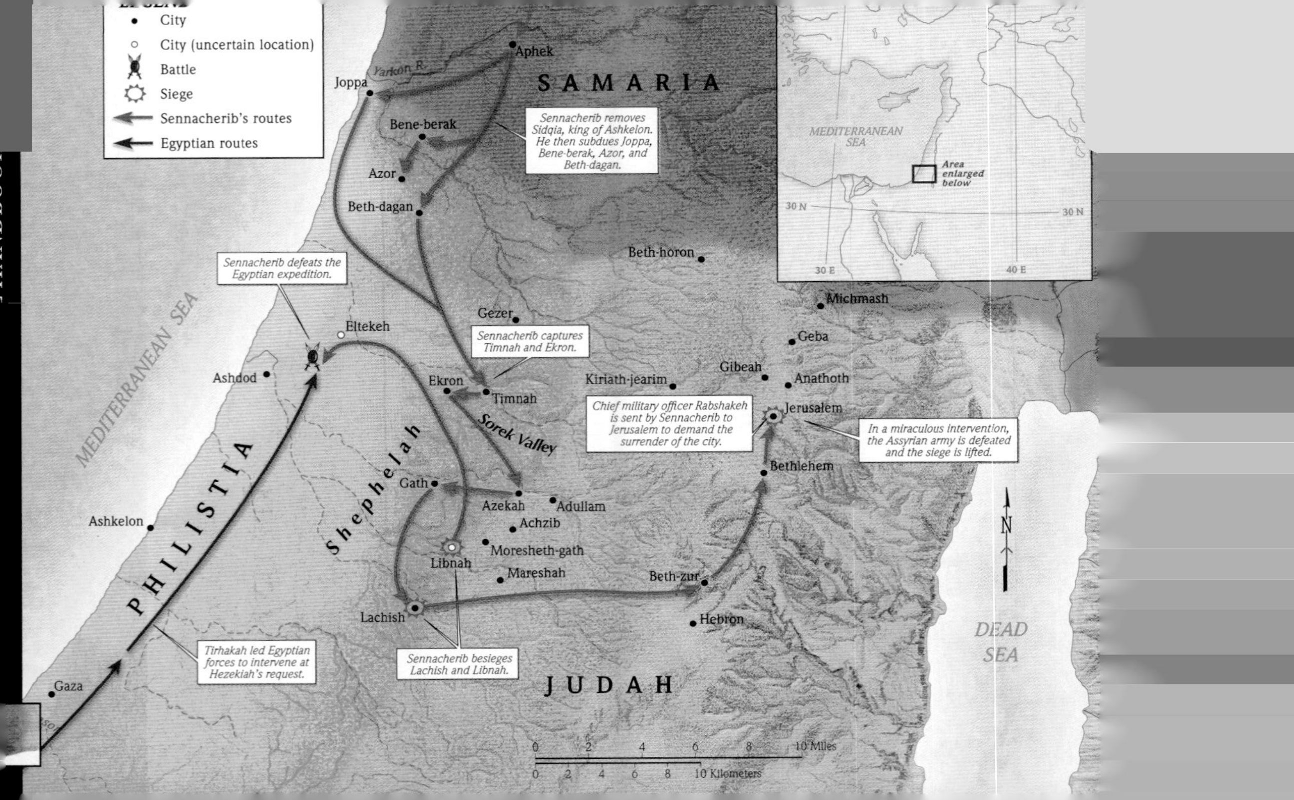
City
City (uncertain location)
Battle
Siege
Sennacherib's routes
Egyptian routes
SAMARIA
PHILISTIA
JUDAH
Shephelah
MEDITERRANEAN SEA
DEAD SEA
Sorek Valley
Yarkon R.
Aphek
Joppa
Bene-berak
Azor
Beth-dagan
Beth-horon
Gezer
Eltekeh
Ashdod
Ekron
Timnah
Kiriath-jearim
Gibeah
Geba
Michmash
Anathoth
Jerusalem
Bethlehem
Gath
Azekah
Adullam
Achzib
Libnah
Moresheth-gath
Mareshah
Lachish
Beth-zur
Hebron
Ashkelon
Gaza
Sennacherib removes Sidqia, king of Ashkelon. He then subdues Joppa, Bene-berak, Azor, and Beth-dagan.
Sennacherib defeats the Egyptian expedition.
Sennacherib captures Timnah and Ekron.
Chief military officer Rabshakeh is sent by Sennacherib to Jerusalem to demand the surrender of the city.
In a miraculous intervention, the Assyrian army is defeated and the siege is lifted.
Sennacherib besieges Lachish and Libnah.
Tirhakah led Egyptian forces to intervene at Hezekiah's request.
MEDITERRANEAN SEA
Area enlarged below
30 N
30 E
40 E
N
0 2 4 6 8 10 Miles
0 2 4 6 8 10 Kilometers

(Ezr 1:1–2). Isaiah 40–55 are thus assigned to "Deutero-Isaiah" (an unknown prophet with an exilic perspective) and Isaiah 56–66 are assigned to "Trito-Isaiah" (an unknown postexilic prophet). The basic assumption of this critical view appears to be that Scripture does not contain true predictive prophecy. For Bible students who accept that God gave specific revelations of the distant future to His prophets, there is no reason to doubt that Isaiah wrote all the book that bears his name. For additional discussion of authorship and date of composition, see *The Reliability of Isaiah* below.

## FIRST AUDIENCE AND DESTINATION

**The People of Judah Living During Isaiah's Lifetime**

The first hearers were people living in Judah near the end of the 700s BC.

## OCCASION

The specific occasion of a few parts of Isaiah are clear; for example chapter 7 was prompted by the Syrian-Israelite coalition against Judah (734–732 BC), and chapters 36–39 were prompted by Sennacherib's invasion of Judah (701 BC). The last event that may be dated in Isaiah's lifetime is the murder of Sennacherib (681 BC). By this time Isaiah was an old man, for he had been commissioned around 740 BC, the year of King Uzziah's death. Isaiah did not tell what prompted his compilation of the entire book.

# GOD'S MESSAGE IN ISAIAH

## PURPOSE

This book preserves the divinely inspired prophecies Isaiah made during his ministry of more than 40 years. These prophecies were originally for the people of Judah facing Assyrian invasions. Because of rebellion and idolatry, their kingdom would be destroyed—even though individuals could still repent and seek the Lord.

The last part of Isaiah (40–66) was really addressed to later generations. On the one hand, it would comfort exiles returning to the land after Babylonian captivity (late sixth century BC); on the other hand it speaks to every later generation of God's people who long for God's kingdom to be revealed to all in its holiness and righteousness.

## FIRST PASS

**The Assyrian Threat**

Isaiah lived and prophesied in a time of seismic change in the ancient Near East. At the beginning of the eighth century BC, both Israel and Judah were prosperous and secure, ruled by Jeroboam II (793–753 BC) in the north and Uzziah (792–740) in the south. The last half of the eighth century saw the Assyrian Empire begin a policy of expansion and conquest. This resulted in the destruction of the northern kingdom and left the southern kingdom vulnerable and paying tribute to Assyria.

**Isaiah's Call**

Changes were no doubt underway before Uzziah's death, but his death is a pivotal moment in Judah's history. That was the year Isaiah, worshipping in the temple, saw the Holy One of Israel in majestic splendor. In God's presence Isaiah realized both the magnitude of his sin and the willingness of God to atone for and cleanse his sin. The result of this encounter was a divine call to Isaiah to be God's prophet to a rebellious people (6:1–13).

**Judgment and Comfort**

Isaiah is often divided into two major sections, "The Book of Judgment," (chaps. 1–39) and "The Book of Comfort" (chaps. 40–66). While there are understandable reasons for such a division, this broad outline fails to capture the dynamic structure of Isaiah. In both halves of Isaiah, the reader will discover an alternating pattern of judgment and comfort.

Isaiah begins with judgment. The setting is a courtroom. God is the prosecutor and Judah is on trial. Heaven and earth are called to witness the charges God brings against His covenant people (1:2–15). But a gracious invitation soon follows (1:18–20). In the next chapter Isaiah casts a vision of peace for Jerusalem and for the nations of the world as they seek the knowledge of God that He has revealed through His covenant people (2:1–4). So both judgment and comfort are seen at the outset of the prophecy.

**Trust**

One of the key themes in Isaiah is the call for people to trust God. During the era of Uzziah, Judah was rich and powerful, so there was a temptation to trust in the nation's military power and economic strength (2:7–8) rather than trusting in God. Later, during the time of Ahaz (chaps. 7–11; cp. 2 Ch 28) and Hezekiah (chaps. 28–39; cp. 2 Kg 18–19), Judah was not as strong, and the Assyrians were exerting their sovereignty over all the nations in the Near East. In these circumstances there was a temptation to trust in political alliances with Assyria (2 Ch 28), Egypt (30:1–6; 31:1–9), or the Babylonians (39:1–8) rather than trusting in God. So, to encourage his audience to trust God, Isaiah recorded a hymn proclaiming that he would trust in God (12:2). An opportunity to model this trust came later when the Assyrian general questioned Hezekiah's trust in God (36:7). Although facing great difficulties, Isaiah and Hezekiah asked God to deliver them (37:16–20). Rather than surrendering, they put their trust in God.

### Obedience

God wants servants who exalt God and follow His instructions. Ahaz was not willing to bend his knee and serve God (7:1–12). Even the righteous king Hezekiah struggled with serving God completely and not leaning on other nations (chaps. 30–31). The rationale for serving God involves His sovereignty over the affairs of the world. His exaltation above all other gods and nations is confirmed in the many passages about wooden idols that cannot talk, walk, speak, or predict the future. God was vastly superior to these pieces of wood (44:6–20). He is the first and the last; there is no other God beside Him (45:5–7,14,18,21). Even the Babylonian gods would be powerless to protect the Babylonian people (46:1–11).

### The Servant

The people of Israel were blind servants who did not follow God (42:18–22), but God would raise up a true Servant who would establish justice in the earth (42:1–4; just like the Messiah in 9:6–7) and serve as a light to and covenant with the nations (42:6–7; 49:6–7). This Servant would be abused and suffer for the sins of others (50:4–9; 53:1–9), bearing their sins in order to bring forgiveness for many others (53:5,10–12). Later, through God's transforming grace, Israel and the other nations will join to worship God and function as His faithful servants (60:1–9; 65:1–16) in God's glorious kingdom.

### Hope and Warning

Throughout this book the pagan nations of this world are seen as rebellious and proud opponents of God (chaps. 13–23). But Isaiah proclaimed that there will be a future day when the nations will come to Zion to worship God (2:2–4; 14:1–3; 19:18–25). They will come with gifts to praise God (60:4–14), and some of them will even serve as priests and Levites (66:18–20). Those nations that do not submit to God and worship Him will experience the terrible effects of God's wrath (34:1–15; 63:1–6), and instead of enjoying the new heavens and the new earth, they will endure the torments of a place where fire and worm never die (66:22–24). These themes inform the reader about God's ways, motivate the trusting soul to exalt God, and warn the sinner to turn from pride. God's kingdom plans are established, so all must choose whom they will serve.

## THE RELIABILITY OF ISAIAH

Despite claims to the contrary, the book of Isaiah contains many indications that it was written by the prophet Isaiah, who ministered in Judah during the reigns of Uzziah, Jotham, Ahaz, and Hezekiah and during the early years when Manasseh was a co-regent with Hezekiah (Is 1:1). The introductions to chapters 1; 2–12; and 13–24 begin with superscriptions that identify the content of these chapters as the words, visions, or oracles of Isaiah. In addition, these chapters describe events in Isaiah's life: his call to ministry (6:1–8); his interaction with Ahaz at the pool in Jerusalem (7:9);

the events surrounding the birth of a child to Isaiah and his wife (8:1–4); a three-year period of functioning as a sign by walking around nearly naked (20:1–6); and his encouragement of Hezekiah during Sennacherib's siege of Jerusalem in 701 BC (36:1–39:8).

In 1892, Bernhard Lauardus Duhm, German Old Testament scholar, published a translation and commentary on Isaiah in which he set forth the view that Isaiah was not the sole author of the book that bears his name. On Duhm's view, Isaiah is not a single work but really three prophecies: First Isaiah (chaps. 1–39), Second Isaiah (chaps. 40–55), and Third Isaiah (chaps. 56–66). Duhm's theory has been enormously influential on subsequent studies of Isaiah. The result has been that these three sections of Isaiah have been studied in isolation from each other.

Recent studies have focused on the significant thematic unity throughout Isaiah. Those who maintain Isaiah has multiple authors explain this thematic and stylistic unity as stemming from skillful editing rather from a single author. Few would argue that Isaiah personally penned every word. Rather, this view holds that the messages themselves derive from the prophet Isaiah, leaving open the possibility that Isaiah's disciples later organized or put the prophet's oracles in writing. Several reasons exist for the single-author view.

One of the arguments for dividing Isaiah into parts has to do with stylistic issues. Proponents of division argue that the style and vocabulary are different from section to section. These stylistic differences do exist; however, the importance of these differences has been overstated. Considering the differences in historical perspective, subject matter, and themes, one would expect stylistic alterations, especially if

The Siloam Inscription. This inscription in Hebrew was discovered in 1880. It gives an account of workers cutting an aqueduct under Jerusalem to bring the waters from the Gihon Spring to the Pool of Siloam. The excavators started on different ends of the massive limestone rock and were able to come within a few inches of meeting by tapping on the rock and perhaps following a natural fissure in this structure.

Hezekiah's tunnel, the channel through which waters from the Gihon Spring flowed into the city.

the sections were from different periods in Isaiah's life. Over the prophet's 40-plus years of ministry, events and perceptions could easily create changes in literary style.

Although differences are present, many similarities also exist between the sections of the book. Several images are used consistently throughout the book: light and dark (5:20,30; 9:2; 42:16; 50:10; 59:9; 60:1–3); blindness and deafness (6:10; 29:10,18; 32:3; 42:7,16–19; 43:8; 44:18; 56:10); human beings as fading flowers (1:30; 40:6–7; 64:6); God as potter and mankind as a vessel (29:16; 45:9; 64:8). Also, the distinctive name for God in Isaiah is "the Holy One of Israel." This expression occurs 31 times in Scripture, with 25 of them appearing in the book of Isaiah. The occurrence in 1 Kings 19:22 was also spoken by Isaiah. In Isaiah the name occurs 12 times in chapters 1–39 and 13 times in 40–66, thus indicating a continuity of thought across the entire book.

The NT includes quotations and allusions from Isaiah on several occasions. In each instance no indication is given that the book should be divided. For example, John 12:38–40 alludes to both Isaiah 53:1 and Isaiah 6:10, indicating both were spoken by Isaiah. Likewise, the Dead Sea Scrolls shed light on the unity of the book. Among the discoveries at Qumran was a complete copy of Isaiah. The particular placement of Isaiah 40 is interesting. Chapter 39 ends on the next to the last line on the page. Chapter 40 begins on the last line. If a break ever existed between chapters 39 and 40, the copyists at Qumran did not indicate it. However, a break of three blank lines does exist after chapter 33, with chapter 34 beginning on the following page. The Dead Sea Scrolls thus do not solve the problem of the division of Isaiah. Rather, they complicate the issue.

For many interpreters, Isaiah's authorship of chapter 40–66 is difficult or impossible to accept, given that the times of which he is prophesying are in the future, long after Isaiah's death. But one of the key characteristics of Yahweh in Isaiah 40–55 is His sovereignty over history, His knowledge of what He will do, and His ability to communicate that through His prophets. This is what sets Yahweh apart from the gods.

> Let them come and tell us
> what will happen.
> Tell us the past events,
> so that we may reflect on them
> and know the outcome
> Or tell us the future.
> Tell us the coming events,
> then we will know that you are gods.
> Indeed, do something good or bad,
> then we will be in awe and perceive. (41:22–23)

If one believes that a prophet of Yahweh can predict events in the distant future (such as the ruin of Jerusalem and the return from exile) without actually living in that time period, then the historical problems with the book of Isaiah do not require additional authors writing in the exilic and postexilic eras.

Jewish tradition concerning Isaiah is expressed in Ecclesiasticus (180 BC):

> With inspired power he saw the future
> And comforted the mourners in Zion.
> He revealed things to come before they happened,
> The secrets of the future to the end of time.[1]

## HOW ISAIAH FITS INTO GOD'S STORY

1. Prologue: Creation, Fall, and the Need for Redemption
2. God Builds His Nation (2000–931 BC)
3. **God Educates His Nation (931–586 BC)**
4. **God Keeps a Faithful Remnant (586–6 BC)**
5. God Purchases Redemption and Begins the Kingdom (6 BC to AD 30)
6. God Spreads the Kingdom Through the Church (AD 30–?)
7. God Consummates Redemption and Confirms His Eternal Kingdom
8. Epilogue: New Heaven and New Earth

## CHRIST IN ISAIAH

Isaiah is the only Old Testament book to prophesy the virgin birth of Christ (7:14). Christ as Suffering Servant is foretold in Isaiah (52:13–53:12).

## CHRISTIAN WORLDVIEW ELEMENTS

### Teachings About God

God expects His people to fulfill His requirements. He is outraged by sin and will judge it. Yet He is also the God of help and hope. Isaiah's portrait of God is thus one of tension that includes both judgment and comfort. The book is famous for its detailed prophecies about Christ, especially His birth (7:14; 9:6–7) and His death (53). The Spirit will empower both the Servant and the servants of the Lord (11:2; 32:15; 42:1; 44:3; 61:1).

### Teachings About Humanity

Aside from its general teachings that humans are fallen sinners whom God must redeem, the book provides personal glimpses into the lives of two persons whom God used. Isaiah shows that God may call and use someone who is well educated.

The section on Hezekiah (chaps. 36–39) shows a ruler who valued trust in God more than military or economic success.

**Teachings About Salvation**

In Isaiah salvation is based on God's forgiveness of sins (1:18; 6:5–6). The passage on the suffering Servant (52:13–53:12) is the most detailed biblical prophecy about Jesus' death as a substitute, and the New Testament writers quoted it often. Ultimately, however, salvation includes the restoration of Zion (chap. 62) as well as the nations (chap. 60). The goal is for the nations to "proclaim the praises of the LORD" (60:6). This will be brought to completion in the eternal state (Is 65:17; cp. Rv 21:1).

## GENRE AND LITERARY STYLE

**Prophecies and a Few Historical Narratives Written in Excellent Hebrew Poetry and Prose**

The genius of Hebrew prophecy was that it both "forth tells" and "foretells." The essence of the prophetic message was its clear "thus says the LORD." Isaiah includes the three classic elements of prophecy: (1) call for people to turn from their sins in the face of divine judgment, (2) predictions of near events (such as the fall of Damascus), and (3) predictions of remote events (such as the coming of the Servant of the Lord).

The book is mainly Hebrew poetry. The main prose section, the narrative about King Hezekiah (chaps. 36–39), skillfully makes the transition from the challenges Judah faced from the Assyrians to those they would later face from the Babylonians. Isaiah was a master of Hebrew vocabulary and style. His book has a larger vocabulary than any other Old Testament book. He particularly used the literary technique of personification, such as the sun being ashamed or the mountains singing (24:23; 44:23). In the Hebrew Scriptures the book of Isaiah was the first of the four "Latter Prophets."

## A PRINCIPLE TO LIVE BY

**God's Redemptive Story (Is 52:13–53:12, *Life Essentials Study Bible*, p. 967)**

When we present the redemptive message, we should use Old Testament passages to support and clarify New Testament truth.

To access a video presentation of this principle featuring Dr. Gene Getz, use a Smartphone or iPad to connect to this QR code or go to http://www.bhpublishinggroup.com/handbook/isaiah

"As a mother comforts her son, so I will comfort you, and you will be comforted in Jerusalem" (66:13).

## ENDNOTES

1. *Ecclesiasticus* 48:24–45, New English Bible version of the Apocrypha) quoted in *The Message of Isaiah*, Barry A. Webb (Downers Grove: InterVarsity Press, 1996), 37.

"This is the word that came to Jeremiah from the LORD: 'Go down at once to the potter's house; there I will reveal My words to you.' So I went down to the potter's house, and there he was, working away at the wheel. But the jar that he was making from the clay became flawed in the potter's hand, so he made it into another jar, as it seemed right for him to do. The word of the LORD came to me: 'House of Israel, can I not treat you as this potter treats his clay?'—this is the LORD's declaration. 'Just like clay in the potter's hand, so you are in My hand, house of Israel'" (Jr 18:1–6).

# JEREMIAH

Jeremiah, the seventh- to sixth-century Israelite prophet from Judah, has given his name to this book as its composer. His name in Hebrew probably means either "Yahweh exalts" or "Yahweh throws down."

## KEY TEXTS: 30:15 AND 31:31

*"Why do you cry out about your injury? Your pain has no cure! I have done these things to you because of your enormous guilt and your innumerable sins."*

*"'Look, the days are coming'—this is the* Lord*'s declaration—'when I will make a new covenant with the house of Israel and with the house of Judah.'"*

Cistern in Avdat, Israel. Jeremiah used the image of a cistern to convey the spiritual condition of Judah. "For my people have committed a double evil: They have abandoned Me, the fountain of living water, and dug cisterns for themselves, cracked cisterns that cannot hold water" (Jr 2:13). Here and in 14:3, broken cisterns symbolize pagan gods that cannot give or sustain life.

## KEY TERM: "CURSE"

Jeremiah was the original "doomsday prophet." He called people to repent, but his main message was that Judah had fallen under the curse of God and was doomed to Babylonian exile because of its refusal to turn from sin.

## ONE-SENTENCE SUMMARY

Anguished by the burden of his prophetic call and the rejection of his message, Jeremiah witnessed what he warned about, the Babylonian captivity, yet he prophesied God's gracious restoration through the new covenant.

# ORIGINAL HISTORICAL SETTING

## AUTHOR AND DATE OF WRITING

**Jeremiah, Perhaps Finally Compiled Around 585 BC**

Because of his personal anguish over the coming captivity, Jeremiah has often been called "The Weeping Prophet." Jeremiah, son of Hilkiah the priest, was from Anathoth, a town near Jerusalem in the territory of Benjamin. God required him to remain unmarried and childless (16:2). His prophetic call came around 626 BC, when he was still young (1:6). His message of coming doom isolated him and exposed him to danger time and again. For 40 years he proclaimed God's Word in Judah and stayed there even after Jerusalem fell. According to chapter 43, finally he was forcibly taken to Egypt and probably died there. Although many critical scholars believe

Replica of one of the 21 letters found in or near the ruins of Lachish between 1935 and 1938. The so-called Lachish Letters were inscriptions on storage jars that date to 588–86 BC, the period during which the Babylonians were attacking the fortified cities of Judah, including Jerusalem. The Lachish Letters provide an account of these events that complements that of Jeremiah.

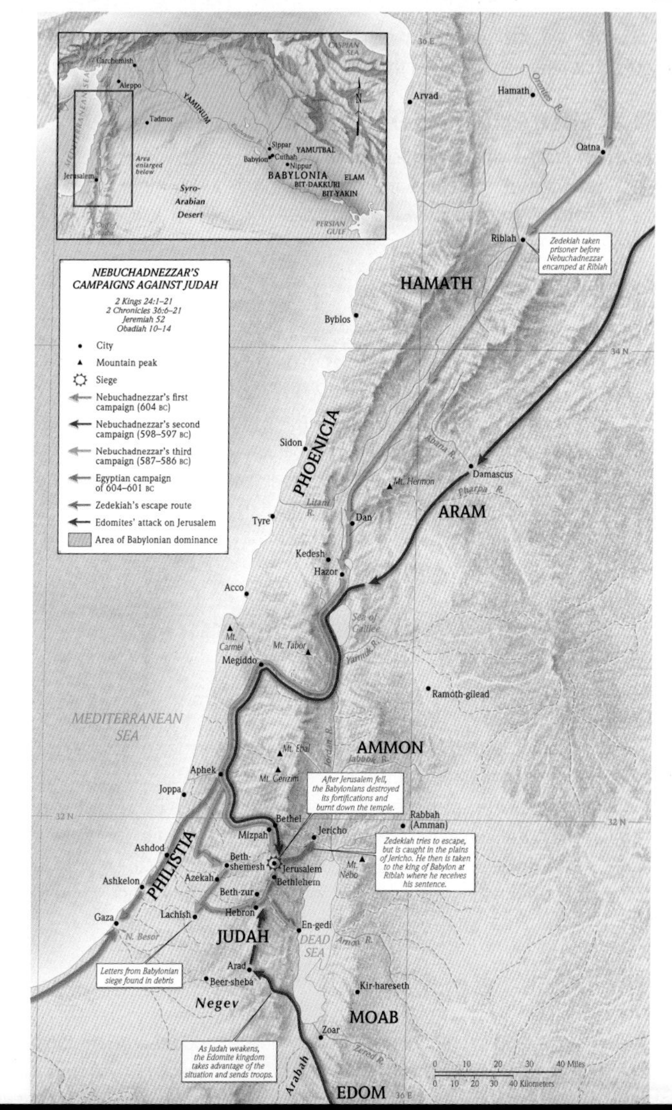


In 605 BC, Nebuchadnezzar, crown prince of Babylon, defeated Egypt at the battle of Carchemish. Babylon was then the dominant power in the region. Judah's rebellion against the stronger Babylon brought three incursions against Judah led by Nebuchadnezzar who assumed the throne when his father Nabopolasser died soon after the battle of Carchemish.

that portions were written by other anonymous prophets, there is no good reason to doubt that Jeremiah authored the entire book.

## FIRST AUDIENCE AND DESTINATION

**The People of Judah Living During Jeremiah's Lifetime**

The first hearers were the kings and people living in Judah during the 40 years before the Babylonian captivity. A few parts were originally for Jews living just after the fall of Jerusalem.

## OCCASION

This book records its origins as a piece of literature more than any other prophetic work. That Jeremiah caused his prophecies to be put in scroll form is explicitly told in several passages, for example, 25:13; 30:2; 36:2; 45:1; 51:60. Of special interest is the bitter story of Jehoakim's contempt for the word of God that he showed by burning one of Jeremiah's scrolls (chap. 36). "Baruch son of Neriah" was Jeremiah's personal assistant, who physically wrote down at least some of the words of the book (45:1). Since he accompanied Jeremiah to Egypt (43:6), the two may have worked together on the final compilation of the book of Jeremiah, the longest book in the Bible composed by a single author.

# GOD'S MESSAGE IN JEREMIAH

## PURPOSE

This book preserves both the divinely inspired prophecies Jeremiah made during his long ministry and a great many of his personal experiences. These prophecies were originally for people of Judah facing invasions and then Babylonian captivity. They were facing the curse that Deuteronomy 27 had predicted for rejecting the covenant. Although he prophesied doom, Jeremiah foretold that the exile would be limited, that Babylon would fall, and that salvation lay on the other side of divine wrath.

## FIRST PASS

**Overview**

Jeremiah is not arranged chronologically as a whole, although some chronological arrangement is apparent. No theory has achieved a consensus, but various devices (such as theme, style, audience, and rhetoric) are summoned to explain certain connections. The book is often considered an anthology of prophetic units that were collected and combined at various times with little intentionality.

### The Structure of Jeremiah: a Proposal

A useful proposal recently made by Richard Patterson is that the prophecies were arranged according to the prophet's divine call to be a prophet to the nations (1:4–19) and to Judah in particular (1:13–19). He identifies a twofold structure to the book that reverses those emphases: chapters 2–24 focus on Jeremiah and his people, and chapters 25–51 focus on Jeremiah and the nations. On either end are the description of the prophetic call and commission in chapter 1 and the historical appendix in chapter 52. The two main sections each begin with a subsection that sets forth the theme (2:1–3:5 and 25:1–38) followed by a subsection that develops the theme (3:6–23:40 and 26:1–51:58) and a sign that concludes the section (24:1–10 and 51:59–64).

The so-called confessions of Jeremiah (11:18–23; 12:1–4; 15:10–21; 17:14–18; 18:19–23; 20:7–18) are scattered through chapters 11–20. Oracles of hope (chaps. 30–31) interrupt the stories about Jeremiah (chapters 26–45). Words against kings (21:11–22:30) and against prophets (23:9–40) appear to be independent collections.

## THE RELIABILITY OF JEREMIAH

It is common these days for critical scholars to dismiss the idea that God might speak directly to someone. They consider prophetic utterances to be mere literary devices, and they assume predictions are impossible. They don't even consider the possibility that what Jeremiah had to say might be true.

Such accusations, however, are nothing new. Jeremiah himself faced significant opposition during his time as a prophet of God, and he saw little or no fruit for any of his labors. His words were discounted by everyone almost as soon as he said them. Yet, despite everything, he persisted in his ministry.

Jeremiah strongly believed that he was delivering a message from God (Jr 1:2–3; 2:5; 34:1). When he was imprisoned (32:2; 37:15) and even threatened with death

Baruch bulla. Baruch, son of Neriah served as Jeremiah's scribe and friend. This bulla or seal is inscribed with Baruch's name. Such clay seals were used to seal and secure papyrus documents. The document was first tied with a string. A flattened piece of clay as seen in the photo was pressed onto the string and stamped with a seal. Papyrus document perish easily through fire and the elements but the clay bullae are so constituted as to become stronger in many environmental conditions, especially in fires.

(26:8), he did not recant his prophecies or reverse his claim that they were a message from God (26:12). A man may be willing to die for something he mistakenly thinks is true, but one will seldom die for something he knows to be false. Jeremiah was in a unique position to know whether or not his words were a revelation from God. Given the way he lived his life in the face of such opposition, we can be sure these words are not the ranting of a madman.

The words about Jeremiah's call to ministry—"I chose you before I formed you in the womb; I set you apart before you were born. I appointed you a prophet to the nations" (Jr 1:5)—have caused some to think that the date of Jeremiah's call and birth is one and the same. However, this is not likely to have been the case. The plain sense of the text is that God was thinking about Jeremiah and planning his life before he was born, and He had already designated Jeremiah as a prophet, but Jeremiah's commissioning took place when he was "a youth" (see v. 6; this Hebrew word most commonly refers to men in their teens). The important point to note is that God chose Jeremiah and God spoke through Jeremiah.

Jeremiah's friend, Baruch son of Neriah, served as his scribe. In 1975 a bulla (clay seal) of Baruch appeared on the antiquities market. It reads,

To/from Baruch //
son of Neriah//
the scribe[1]

The Hebrew word translated *scribe* connotes a royal clerk. The bulla was published by archaeologist Nahman Avigad in the late seventies and is now on display in the Israel Museum, Jerusalem (see photo, p. 207).

## HOW JEREMIAH FITS INTO GOD'S STORY

1. Prologue: Creation, Fall, and the Need for Redemption
2. God Builds His Nation (2000–931 BC)
3. **God Educates His Nation (931–586 BC)**
4. **God Keeps a Faithful Remnant (586–6 BC)**
5. God Purchases Redemption and Begins the Kingdom (6 BC to AD 30)
6. God Spreads the Kingdom Through the Church (AD 30–?)
7. God Consummates Redemption and Confirms His Eternal Kingdom
8. Epilogue: New Heaven and New Earth

## CHRIST IN JEREMIAH

Jeremiah's own sufferings anticipate the sufferings of Jesus, Israel's Messiah. There are numerous parallels between Jeremiah and Jesus. Both wept over Jerusalem

(Jr 9:1; Lk 19:41) and both foretold the imminent destruction of the temple (Jr 7:11–15; Mt 24:1,2).

## CHRISTIAN WORLDVIEW ELEMENTS

### Teachings About God

Jeremiah's understanding of God explicitly included such attributes as His omnipresence (He is everywhere) and His omnipotence (He is all powerful). The classic text is 23:24: "'Can a man hide himself in secret places where I cannot see him?'—the LORD's declaration. 'Do I not fill the heavens and the earth?'—the LORD's declaration." Neither Christ nor the Spirit is explicitly present in the book. Jesus, however, liked to quote Jeremiah and taught that His crucifixion established the "new covenant" that Jeremiah had predicted (31:31–34).

### Teachings About Humanity

The book manifests both the wickedness and the greatness possible in human beings. King Jehoiakim's destruction of the scroll and King Zedekiah's mistreatment of Jeremiah (chaps. 36–38) show the great evil that political leaders can fall into. On the other hand, more is known about the godly Jeremiah than any other writing prophet.

### Teachings About Salvation

Individuals in Jeremiah's own time, at least early in his ministry, could still turn from sin and avoid destruction (7:5–7; 18:7–8). Later on he announced that doom was inevitable. The overall perspective of the book is that redemption will happen only after judgment (29:10–14). The passage on the new covenant (31:31–34), the longest text quoted in the New Testament (Heb 8:8–12), looked forward to what Christ would accomplish by His coming and death, as the argument of Hebrews makes clear.

## GENRE AND LITERARY STYLE

### Prophecies and Historical Narratives Written in a Mixture of Hebrew Poetry and Prose

Jeremiah's prophecies both "forth tell" and "foretell." Jeremiah includes the three classic elements of Hebrew prophecy: (1) call for people to turn from their sins in the face of divine judgment, (2) predictions of near events (such as the fall of Jerusalem), and (3) predictions of remote events (such as the coming of the new covenant).

The majority of the book is poetic. The prose sections are mainly found in chapters 7; 11; 16; 19; 21; 24–29; 32–45; 52. The biographical sections were written in the third person, perhaps evidence of Baruch's input. Jeremiah's style included repetition, such as "sword . . . famine . . . plague" (fifteen times), and the use of cryptograms ("Sheshach" for Babylon in 25:26). Memorable phrases abound, for example, "Can the Cushite change his skin, or a leopard his spots?" (13:23). In the Hebrew canon, Jeremiah was the second of the four "Latter Prophets."

## A PRINCIPLE TO LIVE BY

**Ready to Serve (Jr 1:4–19, *Life Essentials Study Bible*, p. 986–87)**

Though age and experience are normally priorities in God's requirements for spiritual leadership, we are all to be available for God's use to achieve His divine purposes in the world.

To access a video presentation of this principle featuring Dr. Gene Getz, use a Smartphone or iPad to connect to this QR code or go to http://www.bhpublishinggroup.com/handbook/jeremiah

## ENDNOTES

1. *Harper's Bible Dictionary*, Paul Achtemaier, general editor (San Francisco: Harper & Row, 1985), 95.

Palm trees and orchards near the site where Babylon existed (present-day Iraq). Jeremiah wrote a letter to the exiles who had been taken to Babylon: "Build houses and live in them. Plant gardens and eat their produce. Take wives and have sons and daughters. . . . Multiply there; do not decrease. Seek the welfare of the city I have deported you to. Pray to the LORD on its behalf, for when it has prosperity, you will prosper" (29:5–7).

The English title renders the name given by the Greek translators of this book in the second century BC, *Thrénoi*. The original Hebrew title is simply the first word of the book, *'Ekah*, "How!"

## KEY TEXT: 1:1

*"How she sits alone, the city once crowded with people! She who was great among the nations has become like a widow. The princess among the provinces has been put to forced labor."*

## KEY TERM: "LAMENT"

A "lament" or "lamentation" is a formal expression of grief in the face of loss or death. This book expresses the anguish the author felt over the fall of Jerusalem.

## ONE-SENTENCE SUMMARY

A skillful and emotional poet described the devastation of the city of Jerusalem—brought by the Babylonians but ultimately caused by the Lord's anger against His people—and poured out his own personal expressions of sorrow.

*Jeremiah Lamenting the Destruction of Jerusalem* by Rembrandt Harmenszoon van Rijn (1606–1669).

## AUTHOR AND DATE OF WRITING

**Unknown, Perhaps Jeremiah, Written Soon After 586 BC**

The book is anonymous. Jewish and Christian tradition alike affirmed that Jeremiah the prophet wrote this book. According to 2 Chronicles 35:25, Jeremiah was a writer of laments. For more information, see *Author and Date of Writing* for **JEREMIAH**.

On the other hand, both the literary style and some of the content of Lamentations is unlike the book of Jeremiah. In particular, it is hard to imagine that the composer of the longest prophetic book would also write, "Instruction is no more, and even her prophets receive no vision from the LORD" (2:9). If Jeremiah did not write the book, then one of his contemporaries, now unknown, wrote it. Ultimately, there is no reason Jeremiah could not have written the book. If so, this confirms his reputation as "The Weeping Prophet."

Because the book expresses such raw emotions, it was almost certainly composed shortly after Jerusalem's demise. It was necessarily written before the Jews returned from exile in 536 BC. For additional discussion of authorship, see *The Reliability of Lamentations* below.

## FIRST AUDIENCE AND DESTINATION

**Jewish Witnesses to Jerusalem's Fall**

If an unknown author wrote the book, then his audience could have been exiles newly arrived in Babylon. If Jeremiah wrote the book, he composed it for those who had remained in the ruined Jerusalem or else for those who fled Jerusalem for Egypt after Gedaliah's assassination (Jr 40–42).

## OCCASION

The book does not tell what prompted it to be written other than the fall of Jerusalem. It is possible that Lamentations was originally composed in order to be read on "The Ninth of Ab," the annual commemoration of the temple's destruction.

# GOD'S MESSAGE IN LAMENTATIONS

## PURPOSE

This book comes to grips with the destruction of Jerusalem on several levels, especially the emotional and the theological. On one hand, Lamentations shows that bitter grief is a fitting response to loss and death. On the other hand, it shows that the prophets who had warned "repent or be destroyed" had given a true message from God after all. God's people who study Lamentations today should view it with

its original purpose in mind, but it can also help them express their own grief in times of sorrow.

## FIRST PASS

Lamentations 1–4 are alphabetic acrostics. Because there are 22 letters in the Hebrew alphabet, chapters 1; 2; and 4 have 22 verses: each verse begins with a succeeding letter of the alphabet. Chapter 3 has 66 verses because three successive verses are allotted to each letter of the alphabet. (Chapter 5 also has 22 verses, but it is not composed as an acrostic.) The reason the author used the alphabetic acrostic may have been either to control and restrain the grief that would otherwise run rampant or to express his sorrow completely—from A to Z, as we would say.

The facts of the fall of Jerusalem are given in 2 Kings 25 and Jeremiah 52; Lamentations expresses the emotion. Like Job, Lamentations wrestles with the problem of evil. Like Ezekiel, it expresses what results when God leaves His temple, His city, and His people. Throughout, it is acknowledged that Judah deserved its punishment; it is consistent with the curse in Deuteronomy 28:15–68. But along with this admission of guilt is a call for the punishment to end, as in the psalms of lament, and a call for the enemies who carried it out to be punished in return (Lm 4:22), as in the imprecatory psalms and Habakkuk 1:12–17.

## THE RELIABILITY OF LAMENTATIONS

The book does not state who its author was, but from ancient times it has traditionally been ascribed to Jeremiah. While some scholars find reason to doubt this, others defend it.

The following factors favor authorship by Jeremiah: (1) There are similarities between Lamentations and Jeremiah in tenor, theology, themes, language, and imagery (cp. Lm 1:15 and Jr 8:21; Lm 1:2 and Jr 30:14). (2) Like the book of Jeremiah, Lamentations affirms that Judah should submit to the exile because it is deserved (Lm 1:5; 3:27–28; Jr 29:4–10), yet there is hope for restoration (Lm 3:21–33; 4:22; 5:19–22; Jr 29:11–14). (3) Both books suggest that the prophets and priests share with the people the blame for the nation's sin (Lm 2:14; 4:13; Jr 14:14; 23:16).

An eyewitness to the destruction of Jerusalem seemingly wrote Lamentations, and the prophet Jeremiah was an eyewitness (Lm 2:6–12; Jr 39:1–14). We know that Jeremiah wrote a lament over Josiah (2 Ch 35:25); therefore it is entirely possible he also wrote these laments.

The canonicity of Lamentations has never been seriously challenged. The English Bible, like the Greek and Latin, places Lamentations after Jeremiah, probably for reasons of authorship and historical content.

## HOW LAMENTATIONS FITS INTO GOD'S STORY

1. Prologue: Creation, Fall, and the Need for Redemption
2. God Builds His Nation (2000–931 BC)
3. God Educates His Nation (931–586 BC)
4. **God Keeps a Faithful Remnant (586–6 BC)**
5. God Purchases Redemption and Begins the Kingdom (6 BC to AD 30)
6. God Spreads the Kingdom Through the Church (AD 30–?)
7. God Consummates Redemption and Confirms His Eternal Kingdom
8. Epilogue: New Heaven and New Earth

## CHRIST IN LAMENTATIONS

Lamentations shows God's wrath poured out on the city He loves just as His wrath was later poured out on His beloved Son. Lamentations 1:12 has often been used of Christ as He suffered on the cross: "Is this nothing to you, all you who pass by? Look and see! Is there any pain like mine, which was dealt out to me, which the LORD made me suffer on the day of His burning anger?"

## CHRISTIAN WORLDVIEW ELEMENTS

**Teachings About God**

God's holiness resulted in his destroying Jerusalem for her many sins. Yet at the very center of the book, the author emphasized God's mercy and faithfulness (3:22–26). The most often quoted text is 3:22–23: "Because of the LORD's faithful love we do not perish, for His mercies never end. They are new every morning; great is Your faithfulness!" There is no specific reference to Christ or to the Holy Spirit.

**Teachings About Humanity**

Because human beings are moral agents responsible to God, their sins will be punished. The destruction of Jerusalem and the temple is the chief Old Testament event showing that rebellion against God cannot go on indefinitely. Yet because God made mankind in His image, they are capable of emotion, including sorrow and despair. Even when the loss is deserved, intense expressions of grief are a normal part of human experience.

**Teachings About Salvation**

Despite the grief he expressed, the author did not waver in his faith in God (see 3:26). The author's steadfast trust in God in the presence of national catastrophe and personal disaster makes him one of the greatest heroes of faith found in Scripture.

## GENRE AND LITERARY STYLE

### A Lament Written in Hebrew Poetry with Acrostic Features

People of the ancient Near East often composed laments in the face of tragedy. "Lamentation over the Destruction of Ur" (Sumerian) is an early example. The Old Testament has many examples: David's "Song of the Bow" (2 Sm 1:19–27); Psalms of lament (for example, Pss 44; 60; 88); and expressions by the prophets (Is 63–64; Ezk 19; Am 5; Mc 1).

The entire book is Hebrew poetry, and more than in any other book, the poetry seems to have a definite rhythm or meter. Many of the lines follow the *qinah* (lament) meter: lines of five beats, divided into three beats and then two. An example is 5:14:

"The elders / have left / the city gate, (3 beats)
the young men, /their music." (2 beats)

In English Bibles, Lamentations follows the Greek tradition, placing it after Jeremiah. In Hebrew Scripture it was placed in the third section, the Writings or *Kethubim*. Among the Writings it was one of the Five Scrolls (*Megilloth*). Lamentations became the scroll read publicly on "The Ninth of Ab," the solemn annual Jewish remembrance of both the destruction of Solomon's temple (586 BC) and of the second temple (AD 70). The month of Ab corresponds to July-August.

"I call this to mind, and therefore I have hope: Because of the LORD's faithful love we do not perish, for His mercies never end. They are new every morning; great is Your faithfulness!" (Lm 3:21–23).

## A PRINCIPLE TO LIVE BY

**God's Faithfulness (Lm 3:22–27, 31–33, *Life Essentials Study Bible*, p. 1066–67)**
Because of our relationship with God through the Lord Jesus Christ, we are to be confident that we have an eternal inheritance guaranteed by the presence of the Holy Spirit in our lives.

To access a video presentation of this principle featuring Dr. Gene Getz, use a Smartphone or iPad to connect to this QR code or go to http://www.bhpublishinggroup.com/handbook/lamentations

Ezekiel, close-up of the southern portal of the façade of the cathedral Notre-Dame in Amiens, France.

Ezekiel, the sixth-century Israelite prophet exiled to Babylon, has given his name to this book as its composer. His name in Hebrew means "God strengthens."

## KEY TEXT: 38:23

*"I will display My greatness and holiness, and will reveal Myself in the sight of many nations. Then they will know that I am Yahweh."*

## KEY TERM: "VISIONS"

This book is built around the three "visions of God" (1:1; 8:3; 40:2) that Ezekiel received. The first vision revealed God's glory (chaps. 1–3); the second God's judgment (chaps. 8–11); the third God's people and temple idealized (chaps. 40–48).

## ONE-SENTENCE SUMMARY

From exile in Babylon, Ezekiel's stunning visions and startling symbolic acts were prophecies for the Israelites to teach God's sovereign plan over them in the history of His kingdom, so that "they will know that I am Yahweh."

# ORIGINAL HISTORICAL SETTING

## AUTHOR AND DATE OF WRITING

**Ezekiel, Perhaps Finally Compiled Around 570 BC**

Ezekiel, the son of Buzi, was born into a priestly family and grew up in Judah. As a young adult, he was taken captive by the Babylonians in 597 BC and deported, along with King Jehoiachin and 10,000 others (2 Kg 24:14–17). He settled in Tel-abib by the Chebar Canal. At age 30 Ezekiel was called as a prophet (1:1–3). He was married, but his wife died suddenly just before Jerusalem's final fall (24:15–18). God called Ezekiel "son of man" ("human being") more than 90 times.

Ezekiel's strange visions and symbolic actions marked him as unusual both in his own day and by modern standards. His message was not well received (3:25; 33:31–32). Some recent scholars have even suggested he suffered from mental illness. Other scholars accept that Ezekiel wrote parts of the book but that many editorial insertions were made at a later date. Ezekiel is the only prophetic work written entirely in the first person. Scholars who accept the testimony of Scripture at face value continue to affirm that Ezekiel, under divine inspiration, composed the entire book. He perhaps compiled the work shortly after the last dated prophecy (571 BC; 29:17–21).

## FIRST AUDIENCE AND DESTINATION

**Israelite Exiles Living in Babylon**

The first hearers were Israelites who had been taken into exile along with Ezekiel. By the time of Ezekiel's first vision, five years had elapsed, so the people had begun to establish themselves in a foreign land. After the final fall of Jerusalem, recently arriving exiles also heard Ezekiel's message.

## OCCASION

The messages God sent to Ezekiel were at God's initiative, not the prophet's. God sometimes told him to turn his face toward someone and prophesy against him. His references to specific dates on which he received messages are 1:1–2; 8:1; 20:1–2; 24:1; 26:1; 29:1,17; 30:20; 31:1; 32:1,17; 40:1. Ezekiel did not tell what prompted his compilation of the entire book.

## PURPOSE

This book preserves the divinely inspired prophecies that Ezekiel made during his ministry of more than 20 years. These prophecies were originally for Israelites that had been exiled to Babylon shortly before the final fall of Judah. Ezekiel warned that God's destruction of Jerusalem was looming but that God responded to individuals based on their relationship to Him. Ezekiel also foresaw the distant time that God would act decisively so that Israel and all the nations would know that the Lord alone is God.

## FIRST PASS

Although many of Ezekiel's oracles were addressed to the population in Jerusalem or to foreign nations, his primary audience was fellow exiles in Babylon. Prior to 586 BC the elders of the community came to him at his house to hear a word from God (8:1; 14:1; 20:1), hoping for an announcement of their imminent return to Jerusalem. However, the exiles refused to acknowledge that they had been exiled because of their own rebellion against the Lord.

### Judgment on Judah

Ezekiel's rhetorical strategy in chapters 4–24 was to demolish illusions of security by exposing the peoples' sins. He argued that far from being innocent in this "divorce," they were guilty and had brought the calamity on themselves. Although the order in which these major themes are addressed appears to be somewhat random, all his oracles were deliberately aimed at demolishing the four pillars on which they had based their security. Systematically he undermined the validity of their reliance on God's eternal promises of an immutable and unconditional covenant (e.g., 15:1–8; 16:1–60), of eternal and unconditional title to the land (4:1–3; 6:1–14; 7:1–27; 11:1–23), of the Davidic kings as an irrevocable symbol of His commitment to them (12:1–16; 17:1–24; 19:1–14), and of Jerusalem as the eternal dwelling place of God (8:1–10:22; 24:16–27). Courageously he declared they could not sin with impunity. On the contrary, built into the covenant were warnings of judgment if they persisted in rebellion (Lv 26; Dt 28). This was the eternal word that God would certainly fulfill. Not only were the promises eternal, so was judgment for ingratitude and disobedience.

### Judgment on the Nations

When Jerusalem fell in 586 BC, Ezekiel's message changed. Judgment had fallen, and he was vindicated as a true prophet. Not only was Judah judged, but the nations surrounding Judah also would not escape God's judgment. This section contains oracles against seven specific nations. Though all directions of the compass are represented, Tyre (to the north) and Egypt (to the south) receive special attention. The wide geographical distribution of the nations mentioned, as well as the use of the symbolic number seven, convey a sense of completeness. In addition to judging these seven nations, the Lord would ultimately defeat the worldwide conspiracy under the leadership of Gog of the land of Magog (chaps. 38–39). Since this prophecy does not correspond to any known historical event, it is best to understand it as still awaiting fulfillment.

**Restoration**

Ezekiel 36:22–38 is the theological heart of the restoration oracles. Ezekiel summarized the process. After the Lord cleansed the land, He would again gather the people and bring them back to the Promised Land. Then He would replace their hearts of stone with hearts of flesh and put His Spirit within them, so that they might walk in His ways and experience His generous blessing.

**The New Temple**

Ezekiel also declared that God would restore Israel to full status and well-being as His own covenant people. Ironically, he based that hope on the promises of God that he had so systematically shown to be false bases of security in chapters 1–24. His restoration oracles show those ancient promises to be indeed eternal. The deportations were not the last word: Israel must return to the land promised to their fathers, the Davidic kingship would be restored, and God would again dwell in their midst and never abandon them again (chaps. 40–48).

## THE RELIABILITY OF EZEKIEL

Because of the bizarre nature of Ezekiel's opening vision, well-intentioned people often give up reading the book before they even get through the call narratives. While many different theories concerning the significance of this vision have been proposed, the vision makes perfect sense if one interprets it within the context of ancient Near Eastern iconography. Daniel Block says: "Virtually every feature of the heavenly throne chariot has been attested on images and reliefs from the ancient world. While the images may be confusing to us, in Ezekiel's day they made perfect sense."[1] To a community that had lost its spiritual way and its confidence in the Lord, God broke through, declaring that He remained absolutely and gloriously sovereign over all things. Nebuchadnezzar's razing of Jerusalem was not a sign of Marduk's superiority over Yahweh; he came as the agent of Yahweh. God departed from the temple (chaps. 8–11) but appeared to Ezekiel far away in a defiled and pagan foreign land.

## HOW EZEKIEL FITS INTO GOD'S STORY

1. Prologue: Creation, Fall, and the Need for Redemption
2. God Builds His Nation (2000–931 BC)
3. God Educates His Nation (931–586 BC)
4. God Keeps a Faithful Remnant (586–6 BC)
5. God Purchases Redemption and Begins the Kingdom (6 BC to AD 30)
6. God Spreads the Kingdom Through the Church (AD 30–?)
7. God Consummates Redemption and Confirms His Eternal Kingdom
8. Epilogue: New Heaven and New Earth

## CHRIST IN EZEKIEL

The expression "son of man" is used more than 90 times in Ezekiel. God uses the term to address Ezekiel. "Son of Man" is the expression Jesus uses most frequently to refer to Himself. The phrase has two different meanings. First, it simply designates a human being. Second, it refers to a divine being. When used of Jesus, it carries both of these meanings.

## CHRISTIAN WORLDVIEW ELEMENTS

### Teachings About God

All that God does on behalf of people is ultimately for the sake of His name or glory (39:7). He is absolutely sovereign in the affairs of all people and all nations. Prophecies of a coming Davidic king, fulfilled by Christ, are scattered throughout the book (17:22–24; 37:24–28). In the future the Spirit will enable God's people to obey His laws from their heart (36:27; 39:29).

### Teachings About Humanity

One of the clearest biblical passages about the responsibility of each individual before God is Ezekiel 18. This is famously stated in 18:4: "The person who sins is the one who will die." Ezekiel illustrates one whom God used in a time of crisis and whose intimate family life became a symbol of God's dealing with His people (24:15–18).

### Teachings About Salvation

Ezekiel teaches both the individual and the corporate dimensions of salvation. Chapter 18 teaches that the wicked child of a righteous parent will die (18:10–13). A person showing the fruit of righteousness—even if the parents are wicked—will live (18:14–17). Corporately, salvation is the sovereign act of God's Spirit, who breathes on spiritually dead people ("dry bones"), giving them spiritual life and enabling them to follow God's ways.

## GENRE AND LITERARY STYLE

**Prophecies, Including Visions and Symbolic Actions, Written Mainly in Hebrew Prose but with Some Poetry**

Ezekiel's prophecies both "forth tell" and "foretell." Ezekiel includes the classic elements of Hebrew prophecy: (1) call for people to turn from their sins, (2) predictions of near events (such as the destruction of the temple, chap. 24), and (3) predictions of remote events (such as the coming of the new temple, chaps. 40–48).

Ezekiel's three visions (chaps. 1–3; 8–11; 40–48) are a special kind of prophecy. The first "forth tells" God's glory; the second "foretells" a near disaster; the third "foretells" a remote blessing. More than any other prophet, Ezekiel performed actions with symbolic meaning, which he then interpreted. The best known of these include his lying on one side (chap. 4), shaving his head with a sword (chap. 5), and refraining from mourning for his wife (chap. 24). Ezekiel also told a number of parables. Chapters 7; 17; 19; 21; 24; 26–32 are the main poetic sections; the rest are in Hebrew prose.

## A PRINCIPLE TO LIVE BY

**The One, True God (Ezk 6–7, *Life Essentials Study Bible*, p. 1081)**

We are to avoid any form of idolatry, acknowledging that there is only one God.

To access a video presentation of this principle featuring Dr. Gene Getz, use a Smartphone or iPad to connect to this QR code or go to http://www.bhpublishinggroup.com/handbook/ezekiel

## ENDNOTES

1. Daniel I. Block, "Ezekiel, Book of" in *Holman Illustrated Bible Dictionary* (Nashville: B&H Publishing Group, 2003), 537.

Daniel, the sixth-century Israelite prophet exiled to Babylon, has given his name to this book as its composer. His name means "God Judges" or "God's Judge" in Hebrew.

## KEY TEXT: 4:3

*"How great are His miracles, and how mighty His wonders! His kingdom is an eternal kingdom, and His dominion is from generation to generation."*

## KEY TERM: "KINGDOMS"

This book contrasts all earthly kingdoms, both in Daniel's day and those of the future, with God's glorious everlasting kingdom. Of all the Old Testament books, this one has the most sharply defined kingdom perspective.

## ONE-SENTENCE SUMMARY

Daniel demonstrated remarkable trust in God and revealed God's plans for the future, not only for his own day but also for the Maccabean period and on through the time that God's kingdom is fully established by the Son of Man.

## AUTHOR AND DATE OF WRITING

**Daniel, Perhaps Finally Compiled Around 530 BC**

The book is technically anonymous, although much of it is recorded as the first-person memoirs of Daniel. According to uniform Jewish and early Christian belief, Daniel wrote the book. In Matthew 24:15 Jesus affirmed this view.

Critical scholarship for the past two centuries has uniformly rejected that a sixth-century author could possibly have written detailed accounts of events centuries in the future. Therefore an unknown prophet living in the Maccabean era (second century BC) necessarily composed large parts of the book. The basic assumption of this critical view appears to be that Scripture does not contain true predictive prophecy. For Bible students who accept that God gave specific revelations of the distant future to His prophets, there is no reason to doubt that Daniel wrote the whole book that bears his name.

## FIRST AUDIENCE AND DESTINATION

### Israelite Exiles Living in Babylon

The first hearers were Israelites who had been taken into exile along with Daniel. After the final fall of Jerusalem, recently arriving exiles would also have heard Daniel's message. By the time of Daniel's last prophecies, Babylon was no more, and the time had come for the exiles to be permitted to return to their homeland (9:2).

## OCCASION

Daniel's early ministry as a young man was initiated by Nebuchadnezzar (chaps. 1–4). During the last years of Babylon, God initiated visions of the future (chaps. 7–8), and then Daniel was called to interpret the handwriting on the wall (chap. 5). Daniel's encounter with the lions (chap. 6) and his final visions of the future (chaps. 9–12) came when he was a very old man, shortly after the time the Persians defeated Babylon.

# GOD'S MESSAGE IN DANIEL

## PURPOSE

This book preserves the divinely inspired prophecies Daniel made during his long ministry of more than 60 years. The book looks at God's kingdom through three lenses: the lens of the present; the lens of the second century BC (the Maccabean period); and the remote lens of the completion of God's kingdom.

## FIRST PASS

### History

The first division of Daniel (chaps. 1–6) consists of historical material and some prophecy (chap. 2). Daniel was transported from Judah to Babylon in 605 BC along with other young men of nobility. Daniel and his friends were trained in the arts, letters, and wisdom in the Babylonian capital. These young men served Nebuchadnezzar (604–562 BC) while maintaining their integrity (1:9–16), even at the risk of their lives (3:1–30). Daniel rose to high rank among the Babylonian men of wisdom. To Daniel, God revealed future history (2:31–45), demonstrated His power to deliver His own (3:8–30), and gave a vivid lesson on the dangers of pride (4:28–37). Nebuchadnezzar was forced to acknowledge the sovereignty of Daniel's God. The Lord also displayed His sovereignty to subsequent rulers. He announced in dramatic fashion Belshazzar's downfall for his arrogance and lack of respect for the temple vessels (5:22–24). He demonstrated to Darius His power to deliver His faithful servants from even the worst crises (6:1–28).

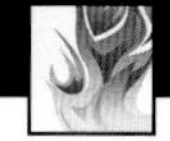

### Prophecy

The second division (chaps. 7–12) contains both history and apocalyptic messages. Through Daniel's visions the Lord demonstrated His sovereignty over history. Human empires rise and fall, but the Lord ultimately shatters Gentile opposition to His program and establishes His kingdom on earth.

In the apocalyptic section, Daniel emphasized the person and work of the Messiah (e.g., 7:13–14; 9:24–27). Eschatology was a prominent theme in Daniel's prophecies. Believers will experience tribulation in the last days (7:21,25; 9:27; 12:1), but the Messiah will appear and establish a glorious, eternal kingdom (2:44–45; 7:13–14,26–27; 9:24). In this wonderful new world, the saints will be rewarded and honored (12:2–3).

*Belshazzar's Feast* by Rembrandt Harmenszoon van Rijn (1606–1669). Belshazzar had the golden vessels that were taken from the temple in Jerusalem brought to a banquet of 1000 of his nobles. As they drank wine from these vessels they praised their own gods. Suddenly the fingers of a human hand wrote a cryptic message on the palace wall (Dn 5:1). When the Babylonian seers were unable to interpret the writing, Daniel the Hebrew was called. He interpreted the message for the king, explaining that it meant the kingdom would be taken from Belshazzar and given to the Medes and Persians (Dn 5:28). According to Daniel 5:30, Belshazzar was slain on the very night of this incident.

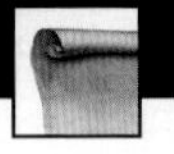


## THE RELIABILITY OF DANIEL

Critics claim the book's language, theology, position in the Hebrew Scriptures with the Writings rather than the Prophets, and inaccuracies about historical events before the second century demand a late date of composition. Evangelicals respond with arguments such as the following:

1. Daniel was not placed in the Writings because the book was late or the author's prophetic credentials were in doubt. At Qumran, the religious center from which came the Dead Sea Scrolls, the prophecy enjoyed unusual prominence and both the Septuagint and Josephus (*Against Apion*, 1.8) classified Daniel with the Prophets. Apparently those responsible for fixing the order of the Hebrew Bible did not include the book in the prophetic section because Daniel was mainly a statesman, not a preacher to the nation of Israel in the manner of an Isaiah or a Jeremiah.
2. Archaeological discoveries have confirmed the reliability of the book in many instances (e.g., the existence of Belshazzar). Alleged historical inaccuracies on close examination are found to be nonexistent or have reasonable explanations.
3. Daniel's Hebrew is consistent with a sixth-century date (it resembles the Hebrew of Ezekiel), and his Aramaic exhibits striking parallels with that of the Elephantine Papyri, also written in imperial Aramaic and dated to the fifth century BC. By contrast, the Aramaic of the book does not conform to later samples of the language found at Qumran (e.g., *Genesis Apocryphon*).
4. Against the claim that Daniel uses Persian and Greek loan words that require a late date, Daniel completed his book after the Persian conquest of Babylon and even served in the Persian administration. The Persian expressions are strong evidence for a date of composition not long after the Babylonian exile, since they are old Persian words that ceased to be used by about 300 BC.

Arguments for the traditional view include these points:

1. The New Testament writers and Jesus Himself accepted the traditional understanding of the prophecy (see Mt 24:15=Mk 13:14; Mt 26:64=Mk 14:62=Lk 22:69; Heb 11:33–34).
2. The book professes to have been written by Daniel (see Dn 7:1; 12:4), to be an account of a historical individual who experienced the exile and lived in Babylon, and to be a prediction of future events (e.g., Dn 2:29–45; 7:2,15–27; 8:15–26; 9:24–27; 10:14; 11:2–12:4).
3. One of the eight manuscripts of Daniel discovered at Qumran (4QDan[c]) has been dated to c. 125 BC and may have been written earlier. Some scholars have argued that there would have been insufficient time for the book of Daniel to

have gained such widespread acceptance if it were written only 40 years previously.

4. The Septuagint was the Greek translation of the Old Testament produced in Alexandria, Egypt, that came to be used widely by the Jews of the Diaspora. Scholars generally agree that at least the Pentateuch (first five books) was translated in the middle of the third century BC, but it is likely that all the Bible books were translated into Greek about the same time. If so, a second-century date for Daniel is impossible. According to the critical view, only 30 years after it was written, Daniel was received into the canon and carried to Alexandria, approximately 300 miles away, and there translated into Greek. Such a proposal seems unlikely.
5. Ezekiel, the sixth-century prophet, mentioned Daniel three times in his book (Ezk 14:14,20; 28:3)—seemingly clear verification of the traditional view. Critical scholars, however, insist Ezekiel was speaking of a mythological hero named Daniel who appears in the ancient Ugaritic epic "The Tale of Aqhat." A decisive argument against such a theory is that the Ugaritic Daniel was an idolater, hardly a model of faithfulness to Israel's God. Ezekiel must have been referring to the author of the book of Daniel. If so, the historicity of Daniel and his book would seem to be established.

## HOW DANIEL FITS INTO GOD'S STORY

1. Prologue: Creation, Fall, and the Need for Redemption
2. God Builds His Nation (2000–931 BC)
3. **God Educates His Nation (931–586 BC)**
4. **God Keeps a Faithful Remnant (586–6 BC)**
5. God Purchases Redemption and Begins the Kingdom (6 BC to AD 30)
6. God Spreads the Kingdom Through the Church (AD 30–?)
7. God Consummates Redemption and Confirms His Eternal Kingdom
8. Epilogue: New Heaven and New Earth

## CHRIST IN DANIEL

Daniel has a vision of "One like a son of man coming with the clouds of heaven" (7:13). This is a prophesy of Christ's second coming at which time He will be given glory and dominion over all people.

## CHRISTIAN WORLDVIEW ELEMENTS

### Teachings About God

God is both the revealer of secrets and the sovereign of the universe. His ultimate purpose is to give dominion to the Son of Man (7:13–14), fulfilled by Jesus, who deliberately called Himself "Son of Man." Daniel was recognized as having "the spirit of the holy gods," but this appears to fall short of a clear reference to the Holy Spirit.

Procession Street and the Ishtar Gate, a reconstruction. These are among the most famous structures of Babylon. Inscriptions of Nebuchadnezzar II provide understanding of the New Year's Festival of which Procession Street and the Ishtar Gate were an integral part.

#### Teachings About Humanity

Daniel and his friends modeled living as God's people in a pagan world. The kings in the book—Nebuchadnezzar, Belshazzar, and Darius—are all seen to be agents of God. Truly evil characters are predicted, yet they too are unwittingly God's agents. The clearest Old Testament statement about a future bodily resurrection is Daniel 12:2–3.

#### Teachings About Salvation

Daniel 9:26 ("After those 62 weeks the Messiah will be cut off and will have nothing") refers to Christ's crucifixion on behalf of His people. Some scholars believe that Daniel 9:27 predicts Christ's first coming, when He established the new covenant, resulting in the end of animal sacrifices. (Other scholars believe that the covenant referred to will be made not by Christ but by the Antichrist shortly before Jesus' second coming.) In any event, Daniel 9:24 anticipates "everlasting righteousness."

## GENRE AND LITERARY STYLE

#### Prophecies, Including Visions and Interpretations, Written Partly in Hebrew and Partly Aramaic

Daniel included little "forth telling," emphasizing instead "foretelling" prophecies. He predicted near events (such as the destruction of Babylon) and remote events (such as the coming of the Son of Man). The book was written in two languages. Chapters 1 and 8–12, written in Hebrew, deal with God's people and their future. Chapters 2–7, written in Aramaic, the international trade language of the day, deal with the kingdoms of the world as they carry on apart from acknowledging the true God.

In English Bibles, Daniel comes after Ezekiel as one of the "Major Prophets," following the order of the Greek translators. In Hebrew Scripture it was placed in the third section, the Writings or *Kethubim*. The Greek translation added sections with no Hebrew original. These "Additions to Daniel" are considered scriptural by Roman Catholics, but Protestants believe them to be merely interesting parts of the Apocrypha.

## A PRINCIPLE TO LIVE BY

#### Prophetic History (Dn 2;7–8;11:1–35, *Life Essentials Study Bible*, p. 1158–59)

We must understand that the Holy Spirit at times inspired prophets to record prophetic history that has been fulfilled before our time so that we will take seriously future events that are still to be fulfilled.

To access a video presentation of this principle featuring Dr. Gene Getz, use a Smartphone or iPad to connect to this QR code or go to http://www.bhpublishinggroup.com/handbook/daniel

Traditional site of Daniel's tomb in Susa, Iran. Daniel was taken from Jerusalem to Babylon around 605 BC. He was in his teens at the time. He served both Babylonian and Persian kings, including Darius I. Daniel lived over 100 years. The mostly widely accepted tradition is that he was buried in Susa, the winter capital of the Persian Empire, the setting for the events of the book of Esther some 50 years later.

Hosea, the eighth-century prophet to the northern kingdom of Israel, has given his name to this book as its composer. His name means "salvation" in Hebrew.

## KEY TEXT: 1:10

*"Yet the number of the Israelites will be like the sand of the sea, which cannot be measured or counted. And in the place where they were told: You are not My people, they will be called: Sons of the living God."*

## KEY TERM: "UNFAITHFULNESS"

The marital unfaithfulness of Gomer, Hosea's wife, became a symbol that Hosea used to proclaim his message. The people of the northern kingdom had become unfaithful to the Lord by aligning with Baal, yet God longed to take them back.

Jezreel Valley and Mount Gilboa. The Lord told Hosea to name his first son Jezreel, meaning "God sows." "Name him Jezreel, for in a little while I will bring the bloodshed of Jezreel on the house of Jehu and put an end to the kingdom of the house of Israel. On that day I will break the bow of Israel in the Valley of Jezreel" (1:4–5).

## ONE-SENTENCE SUMMARY

Hosea's marriage to an adulterous wife and the children she bore graphically demonstrated God's "marriage" to His spiritually adulterous people Israel, who must respond to His covenant love and repent or face severe judgment.

# ORIGINAL HISTORICAL SETTING

## AUTHOR AND DATE OF WRITING

**Hosea, Perhaps Around 715 BC**

Hosea was a contemporary of Isaiah and Micah. The son of Beeri, he was evidently from the northern kingdom of Israel. See *Occasion* below for information about Hosea's marriage. The book does not mention the fulfillment of Hosea's prophecies against Israel, but he witnessed the fall of Samaria and the northern kingdom. Since his prophecies also include calls for Judah to repent, it is believed that his last min-

Mount Tabor (Hs 5:1). One of the places where false religion was carried out. Hosea calls on both priests and the king to pay attention and know that their promiscuous infidelity will bring God's judgment.

istry was to people of Judah after the northern kingdom fell. He probably compiled his book during that time.

## FIRST AUDIENCE AND DESTINATION

**Israelites Living in the Northern Kingdom**

Hosea's first audience was people living in the northern kingdom—also called Ephraim or Samaria—in the mid-700s BC.

## OCCASION

Hosea's tragic marriage to Gomer—who left the prophet and became a slave, only to be bought back by her own husband—is one of the great love stories (but hardly a romance) in Scripture. Gomer bore three children: Jezreel (God Sows, a son); Lo-ruhamah (No Compassion, a daughter); and finally Lo-ammi (Not My People, a son). The last two children may have been fathered by one of Gomer's lovers; if so, it makes Hosea's personal story that much more poignant. Hosea's marriage experiences and the names of his children were at the Lord's command. Other than this, no precise occasion can be offered for his prophecies, but clearly he spoke in the name of the Lord. No one knows exactly what prompted Hosea to compile his writings at the end of his long ministry.

# GOD'S MESSAGE IN HOSEA

## PURPOSE

This book preserves the divinely inspired prophecies that Hosea made during his ministry of more than 35 years. (He and Amos were the only writing prophets to target the northern kingdom of Israel.) Hosea warned Israel that because of rebellion and idolatry, their kingdom faced destruction, yet God still loved His covenant people.

## FIRST PASS

The two broad divisions of the book of Hosea are Hosea's Marriage (Hs 1–3) and Hosea's Messages (Hs 4–14).

**Hosea's Marriage**

The first three chapters establish a parallel between the Lord and Hosea. Both are loving husbands of unfaithful wives. Hosea's prophetic ministry began with perplexing instructions from God to find a wife among the promiscuous girls of Israel (of which there were apparently many; see 4:14). This is no parable or vision but actual instructions regarding a literal marriage that would give Hosea God's perspective on Israel.

### Hosea's Messages

Hosea's three children, whose names were messages to Israel, serve as an overture to the second main division of the book, which presents its accusations and calls to repent in groups of three. Certainly the book ends on a hopeful note (Hs 14), but most of the oracles in chapters 4–13 are judgmental in nature. The dominant theme of the book is love (covenant fidelity): God's unrelenting love for His wayward people and Israel's unreliable love for God.

## THE RELIABILITY OF HOSEA

Hosea prophesied in the last years of the northern kingdom (750–722 BC). One of the important by-products of his prophecies is to show earlier Old Testament writings with which he was familiar and that were considered authoritative. Mark Rooker has demonstrated that Hosea was aware of and drew on Genesis, Exodus, Leviticus, Numbers, Deuteronomy, Joshua, and portions of Kings in his prophecies. This evidence undermines the view that these Old Testament documents weren't written until after the Babylonian exile. Not only did these documents exist in the eighth century; they were viewed as authoritative writings. These writings served as the basis for both judgment and future hope that Hosea proclaimed.

## HOW HOSEA FITS INTO GOD'S STORY

1. Prologue: Creation, Fall, and the Need for Redemption
2. God Builds His Nation (2000–931 BC)
3. **God Educates His Nation (931–586 BC)**
4. God Keeps a Faithful Remnant (586–6 BC)
5. God Purchases Redemption and Begins the Kingdom (6 BC to AD 30)
6. God Spreads the Kingdom Through the Church (AD 30–?)
7. God Consummates Redemption and Confirms His Eternal Kingdom
8. Epilogue: New Heaven and New Earth

## CHRIST IN HOSEA

Matthew tells of Joseph and Mary taking the child Jesus to Egypt to escape the wrath of Herod. Following Herod's death, Jesus' family returned to Nazareth. Matthew quoted Hosea 11:1 to show the parallel between God's calling Israel and His calling Jesus: "Out of Egypt, I called My son" (Mt 2:15).

## CHRISTIAN WORLDVIEW ELEMENTS

### Teachings About God

Hosea's doctrine of God is based mainly on the analogy of a husband-wife relationship. The Lord is jealous and will not forever tolerate His people "lusting" after other deities. He must judge unfaithfulness. At the same time, His love for His covenant people endures forever, and one day Ephraim (the northern kingdom of Israel) will be healed of rebelliousness (chap. 14). Matthew recognized Hosea's historical note about Israel's exodus from Egypt as a picture foreshadowing Jesus' coming from Egypt (Hs 11:1; Mt 2:15). The Spirit is not directly present in the book.

### Teachings About Humanity

The adultery of Gomer and the idolatry of Israel both paint rather dark portraits of human shame and sinfulness. Hosea's exceptional love for Gomer provides a stark contrast and shows something of what it means to experience the love of God.

### Teachings About Salvation

The clearest text in this book on the nature of salvation is 6:6: "For I desire loyalty and not sacrifice, the knowledge of God rather than burnt offerings." Offering sacrificial animals without an inner heart of love for God and one's neighbors was never a part of the biblical understanding of salvation. The Hebrew word *chesed* denotes loyalty to God as well as compassionate actions toward others.

## GENRE AND LITERARY STYLE

### Prophecies and a Few Historical Narratives, Written Mainly in Hebrew Poetry

Hosea's prophecies both "forth tell" and "foretell." He includes the three classic elements of Hebrew prophecy: (1) call for people to turn from their sins in the face of divine judgment, (2) predictions of near events (such as the fall of Samaria), and (3) predictions of remote events (such as the coming of ideal peacetime conditions).

The majority of the book is Hebrew poetry. The prose sections are limited to chapters 1 and 3, the narrative about Hosea's marriage and children. The Hebrew style reveals an author with rhetorical skill. In English Bibles, Hosea is the first of the 12 Minor Prophets—"minor" in the sense that they are shorter than Isaiah, Jeremiah, or Ezekiel. In the Hebrew canon the Minor Prophets were compiled as a composite book called "The Twelve." Thus "The Twelve" was the last book of the Latter Prophets (following Isaiah, Jeremiah, and Ezekiel). These four Latter Prophets balanced the four Former Prophets in the Hebrew Bible (Joshua, Judges, Samuel, and Kings).

## A PRINCIPLE TO LIVE BY

**Christ's Spotless Bride (Hs 1:1–3, *Life Essentials Study Bible*, p. 1163)**

As believers who have been chosen by God, we're to become more and more like Christ until we are presented to Him at the marriage of the Lamb.

To access a video presentation of this principle featuring Dr. Gene Getz, use a Smartphone or iPad to connect to this QR code or go to http://www.bhpublishinggroup.com/handbook/hosea

Pottery shards. "Israel is swallowed up! Now they are among the nations like discarded pottery" (8:8).

# JOEL

Joel, an otherwise unknown Israelite prophet to Judah, has given his name to this book as its composer. His name in Hebrew means "Yahweh is God."

## KEY TEXT: 1:4

*"What the devouring locust has left, the swarming locust has eaten; what the swarming locust has left, the young locust has eaten; and what the young locust has left, the destroying locust has eaten."*

## KEY TERM: "LOCUSTS"

Joel described a locust swarm that devoured the crops of Judah. He understood them to be an army sent by God to judge His people for their sins.

## ONE-SENTENCE SUMMARY

Joel proclaimed that the people of Judah should interpret a severe locust plague as a forerunner of "the Day of the LORD" that is "terrible and dreadful" (2:11) and that would consume the pagan nations—but also unfaithful Judah unless the people repented.

"What the devouring locust has left, the swarming locust has eaten; what the swarming locust has left, the young locust has eaten, and what the young locust has left, the destroying locust has eaten" (Jl 1:4).

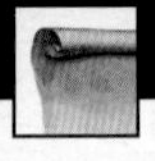

## AUTHOR AND DATE OF WRITING

**Joel, Perhaps Either Ninth or Fifth Century BC**

Although there are numerous Joels in the Old Testament, the prophet bearing this name is known only from this book. He only identified himself as "the son of Pethuel" and did not name his hometown or the kings of his ministry. Because of his frequent references to Jerusalem (six times in 73 verses), he may have lived there. No other personal details of his life are known.

## FIRST AUDIENCE AND DESTINATION

**The People of Judah Living in Jerusalem**

The first hearers were people and priests living in Judah, perhaps about 800 BC or about 500 BC.

## OCCASION

Swarms of locusts were a constant threat to farmers of the ancient Near East. Hoards consisting of millions of the creatures could strip everything green in a short period of time. The successive stages of locust life span or else four varieties of

The Valley of Jehoshaphat is mentioned only in Joel (3:12). This painting by Thomas Seddon (1854) shows the Valley with the Mount of Olives on the right and Jerusalem on the left. According to tradition, The Hill of Evil Counsel is the place where the high priest Caiaphas and his colleagues decided to arrest Jesus.

locusts that he mentioned in 1:4 and 2:25 show that this was a long-lasting scourge. Locusts easily symbolized an invading human army that could wreak utter destruction. As early as Exodus 10, locusts were a divinely sent plague, as was the swarm of Joel's day (see also Rv 9). God used the locust plague of Joel's day as the occasion to warn of a coming day of even greater disaster.

## GOD'S MESSAGE IN JOEL

### PURPOSE

This book preserves the divinely inspired prophecies that Joel made during his ministry to Judah. Although the era in which he ministered is not clear, the people were evidently assuming that the coming "Day of the Lord" would involve God's judgment on the pagan nations and not on God's people. Joel proclaimed that this view was wrong. The people of Judah would be restored only after they had been judged and repented of their sins.

### FIRST PASS

Joel's use of repetition gives the book the appearance of a series of folding doors, in some cases doors within doors. As Duane Garrett has shown, the overall structure balances the section on the locust plague (1:1–20) with a section on the land's physical restoration (2:21–27). The prophecy of an invading army (2:1–11) is balanced by the promise of the destruction of that army (2:20). In the center is the highly prominent call to repent and the promise of renewal (2:12–19). But this balanced structure overlaps with another. The prophecy of the destruction of the invading army (2:20) is also balanced with the concluding prophecy of the Lord's vengeance against all the nations (3:1–21). Finally, the assurance of the land's physical restoration through rain (2:21–27) is balanced by the promise of the people's spiritual restoration through the outpouring of God's Spirit (2:28–32).

### THE RELIABILITY OF JOEL

In the Middle East the locust (*Orthoptera*, family *Acrididae*) periodically multiplies to astronomical numbers. As the swarm moves across the land, it devours all vegetation, high and low. The Hebrew OT uses different words to describe the insect at its various stages of life, from egg to larvae to adult insect. Eaten in several ways (raw, boiled, roasted), the locust is an excellent source of protein (Lv 11:21–22; Mk 1:6). The locust plague is used as a symbol for what God's judgment will be like (Jl 2:1,11,25; Rv 9:3,7; cp. Ex 10:3–20; Dt 28:38). The image of the locust plague was also used to symbolize being overwhelmed by a large and powerful army (Jdg 6:5;

Is 33:4; Jr 46:23; 51:27; Jl 2:20; Nah 3:15). Similar imagery is used in other ancient Near Eastern literature.

## HOW JOEL FITS INTO GOD'S STORY

1. Prologue: Creation, Fall, and the Need for Redemption
2. God Builds His Nation (2000–931 BC)
3. God Educates His Nation (931–586 BC)
4. God Keeps a Faithful Remnant (586–6 BC)
5. God Purchases Redemption and Begins the Kingdom (6 BC to AD 30)
6. God Spreads the Kingdom Through the Church (AD 30–?)
7. God Consummates Redemption and Confirms His Eternal Kingdom
8. Epilogue: New Heaven and New Earth

## CHRIST IN JOEL

Peter and Paul taught that prophecies about the "Day of the Lord" applied to the second coming of Jesus (1 Th 5:2; 2 Pt 3:10). Joel also prophesied the coming of God's Spirit on all flesh: "Your sons and your daughters will prophesy, your old men will have dreams, and your young men will see visions" (2:28). According to Peter, this prediction began to be fulfilled on the day of Pentecost when the Holy Spirit filled the followers of Jesus (Ac 2:16–21).

## CHRISTIAN WORLDVIEW ELEMENTS

**Teachings About God**

God is a righteous judge, and in the coming "Day of the Lord" he will bring sure and swift devastation on all who have opposed him. Yet he also "spared His people" (2:18).

**Teachings About Humanity**

Joel explicitly denied the tendencies of God's people to presume that they are immune from God's judgment. Although God's judgment will utterly destroy the pagan nations (3:1–13), it will also be a decisive turning point that His people must go through—on the way to ultimate blessing.

**Teachings About Salvation**

This short book contains two profound passages on salvation. First, "everyone who calls on the name of Yahweh will be saved" (2:32; cp. Rm 10:13). Second, Joel describes repentance as a tearing of one's heart rather than external actions such as tearing clothes (2:12–14).

## GENRE AND LITERARY STYLE

### Prophecy Written Entirely in Hebrew Poetry

Even as one of the shortest prophetic works, the book includes two of the classic elements of Hebrew prophecy: (1) call for people to turn from their sins, and (2) predictions of remote events (the coming Day of the Lord).

Joel's poetry is vivid and visual. He also uses sarcasm, for example, when God summons the nations to assemble for their own destruction (3:9–11). In 3:10 his call to arms uses the opposite of Isaiah's and Micah's peaceful images: "Beat your plows into swords, and your pruning knives into spears."

In English Bibles, Joel is the second of the 12 Minor Prophets. In the Hebrew canon it belonged to the composite book called "The Twelve." (See *Genre and Literary Style* for **HOSEA** for more information.)

## A PRINCIPLE TO LIVE BY

### The Holy Spirit (Jl 2:28–32, *Life Essentials Study Bible*, p. 1183)

When each of us receives the Lord Jesus Christ as personal Savior, we are to claim the promise that we are all baptized by the Holy Spirit into Christ's spiritual body, the church.

To access a video presentation of this principle featuring Dr. Gene Getz, use a Smartphone or iPad to connect to this QR code or go to http://www.bhpublishinggroup.com/handbook/joel

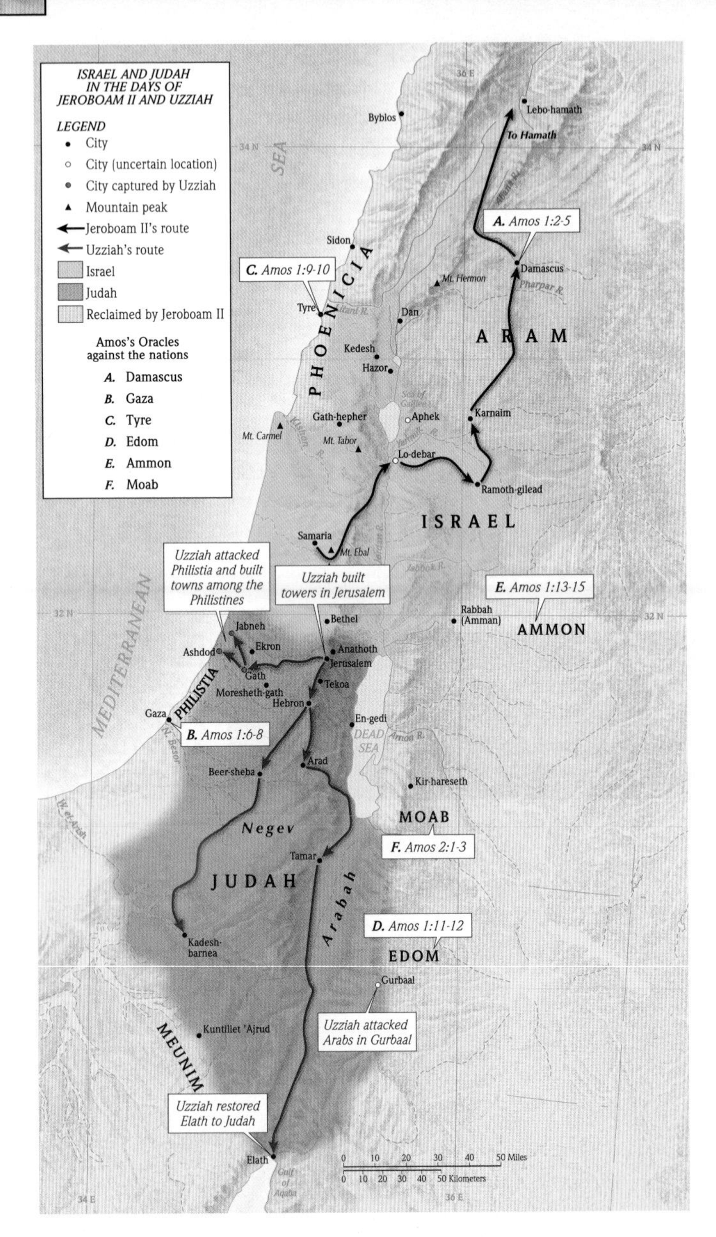

ISRAEL AND JUDAH IN THE DAYS OF JEROBOAM II AND UZZIAH
LEGEND
City
City (uncertain location)
City captured by Uzziah
Mountain peak
Jeroboam II's route
Uzziah's route
Israel
Judah
Reclaimed by Jeroboam II
Amos's Oracles against the nations
A. Damascus
B. Gaza
C. Tyre
D. Edom
E. Ammon
F. Moab
Byblos
Lebo-hamath
To Hamath
A. Amos 1:2-5
Sidon
C. Amos 1:9-10
Damascus
Mt. Hermon
Pharpar R.
Tyre
Dan
PHOENICIA
ARAM
Kedesh
Hazor
Sea of Galilee
Gath-hepher
Aphek
Karnaim
Mt. Carmel
Mt. Tabor
Lo-debar
Ramoth-gilead
ISRAEL
Samaria
Mt. Ebal
Uzziah attacked Philistia and built towns among the Philistines
Uzziah built towers in Jerusalem
E. Amos 1:13-15
Rabbah (Amman)
AMMON
Bethel
Jabneh
Ekron
Anathoth
Ashdod
Jerusalem
Gath
Tekoa
Moresheth-gath
Hebron
PHILISTIA
MEDITERRANEAN
SEA
Gaza
B. Amos 1:6-8
En-gedi
DEAD SEA
Arnon R.
Arad
Beer-sheba
Kir-hareseth
MOAB
Negev
F. Amos 2:1-3
Tamar
JUDAH
Arabah
D. Amos 1:11-12
Kadesh-barnea
EDOM
Gurbaal
Kuntillet 'Ajrud
Uzziah attacked Arabs in Gurbaal
MEUNIM
Uzziah restored Elath to Judah
Elath
Gulf of Aqaba
0 10 20 30 40 50 Miles
0 10 20 30 40 50 Kilometers
34 N
32 N
34 E
36 E

Amos, the eighth-century prophet from Judah to the northern kingdom of Israel, has given his name to this book as its composer. His name means "Burden Bearer" in Hebrew.

## KEY TEXT: 5:24

*"But let justice flow like water, and righteousness, like an unfailing stream."*

## KEY TERM: "JUSTICE"

Amos proclaimed God's disgust with both the pagan nations and the people of Israel because of their many acts of injustice. God holds all people everywhere, even those who do not recognize Him, responsible for practicing social justice.

else go into exile—but then be restored to divine favor.

# ORIGINAL HISTORICAL SETTING

## AUTHOR AND DATE OF WRITING

### Amos, Perhaps Around 750 BC

Amos was a contemporary of Jonah. He was from Tekoa, a small town about 10 miles south of Jerusalem. Amos was a rural person, by profession a shepherd and a gatherer of sycamore figs. He was not especially trained for religious work: "I was not a prophet or the son of a prophet" (7:14). Nothing is known of his family life. He evidently preached to the northern cities of Samaria (Israel's capital, 3:12; 4:1) and Bethel (a center for idolatry, 7:13). Amos's message was perhaps as startling and as well received as would be a farm boy from Nebraska preaching in Manhattan. His ministry was probably short, limited to the period "two years before the earthquake" (1:1), an event alluded to in Zechariah 5:14. The year 750 is a best-guess estimate.

## FIRST AUDIENCE AND DESTINATION

### Israelites Living in the Northern Kingdom

Amos's first audience was people living in the northern kingdom of Israel in the mid-700s BC.

## OCCASION

Amos's only explanation of what prompted his prophetic ministry was, "The Lord GOD showed me this" (7:1,4; 8:1) and "I saw the Lord" (9:1). Twenty-one times he affirmed, "This is the LORD's declaration." The only personal incident of his ministry that he recorded was his confrontation with Amaziah, the priest of Bethel (7:10–17). Amos did not explain what prompted him to commit his prophecies to writing.

# GOD'S MESSAGE IN AMOS

## PURPOSE

kingdom felt politically, economically, and religiously secure. Amos announced that these were false securities. Politically, Assyria would soon assert itself as the major threat to Israel; economically, the good times had led to social corruption, violence, and injustice; religiously, the worship of the Lord had been compromised by idolatry. Amos warned that injustice, immorality, and idolatry would bring divine judgment in the form of exile.

## FIRST PASS

### The Prophet and His Prophecy

The book of Amos opens with an introduction that provides some information about the prophet and the historical setting in which he prophesies (1:1–2).

### Judgment

Seven oracles against Israel's neighbors follow (1:3–2:5), each beginning with "The Lord says." After proclaiming judgment to seven neighboring nations, Amos turns to Israel (2:6–14).

### Five Sermons

The third section of the book gives a detailed account of God's displeasure with Israel (3:1–6:14). Amos challenged people to live by covenant standards and condemned them for their failure to reflect the covenant in daily life. He was concerned about people who "are incapable of doing right" (3:10). His word of judgment was

Sycamore fig tree in Tel Aviv, Israel. Amaziah the priest at Bethel told Amos to go back to Judah and give his prophecies there rather than in Israel. Amos responded that he was not a prophet or the son of a prophet but a herdsman and one who took care of sycamore figs (Am 7:10–17).

severe for the first ladies of Samaria who encouraged the injustice and violence of their husbands "who oppress the poor and crush the needy, who say to their husbands, 'Bring us something to drink'" (4:1). Because of such injustice and the failure to bind authentic religious experience with a social conscience, Amos claimed that the nation was already dead. One could sing Israel's funeral lament: "She has fallen; Virgin Israel will never rise again" (5:2). For individuals who were superficially and confidently "at ease in Zion and to those who feel secure on the hill of Samaria" (6:1), their only hope rested in the renewal of authentic religious experience leading to a life of justice and righteousness overflowing the land (5:24). For those who rejected that way, only judgment remained: "Israel, prepare to meet your God!" (4:12).

**Five Visions**

The fourth section contains the visions of Amos (chaps. 7–9), which may have been the earliest revelations through the prophet. The first two visions (locusts and drought, i.e., "fire") describe events that proclaim God's patience and mercy. The next two visions (the plumb line and the fruit basket) employ wordplay. Their point is that the time for God's patience and mercy is ended; Israel's apostate sanctuaries will be destroyed, and Jeroboam's dynasty will be terminated. The fourth vision of Israel's end is also followed by an explanation that Israel's lack of justice was the reason they were about to meet their end. This day will be a time of terror and great sorrow, for Israel will be abandoned by God.

In the final (and climactic) vision Amos saw the Lord standing beside this counterfeit altar of the counterfeit religion that was propping up the counterfeit kingdom of Jeroboam (see 1 Kg 12:25–13:3).

**Restoration**

The final section is a prophecy of restoration (9:11–15). This final salvation oracle collects and combines earlier trickles and streams of redemptive clues and messages (3:12; 4:6–12; 5:3,4,6,14–15; 7:1–6; 9:8–9) into a great river of celebration. "The fallen booth of David" refers to the kingdom promised to David that had suffered years of disobedience and judgment (see 2 Sm 7:5–16; Is 1:8–9; 9:6–7; 16:5; Jr 23:5; 33:15–17; Ezk 34:23–24; 37:24–25; Hs 3:5; Zch 12:8–13:1; Lk 1:32). A reuniting of northern and southern kingdoms is implied. "Possess the remnant of Edom" means that the Gentiles represented by Israel's archenemy, Edom, will be included in God's people.

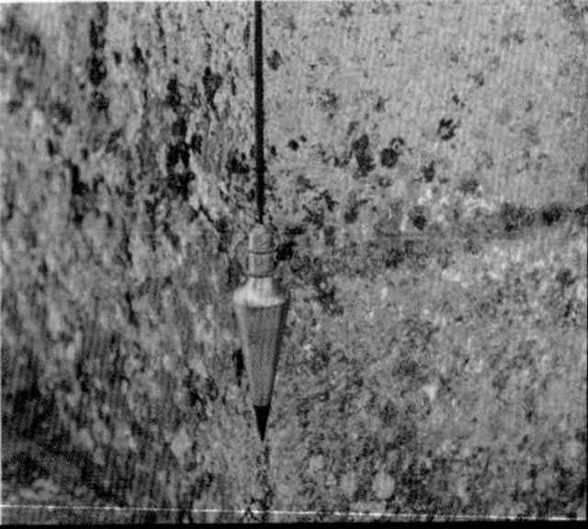

Plumb line. "He showed me this: The Lord was standing there by a vertical wall with a plumb line in His hand. The LORD asked me, 'What do you see, Amos?' I replied, 'A plumb line.' Then the Lord said, 'I am setting a plumb line among My people Israel. I will no longer spare them'" (7:7–8).

## THE RELIABILITY OF AMOS

The earthquake mentioned in Amos 1:1 apparently coincided with the beginning of Amos's ministry and probably provided the initial object lesson for his messages. It must have been especially severe since it is mentioned with recollections of terror over 200 years later in Zechariah 14:5. In his excavations at Hazor that began in 1955, Yigael Yadin found evidence of an earthquake during that period estimated to have been of a magnitude approximating 8.0.

## HOW AMOS FITS INTO GOD'S STORY

1. Prologue: Creation, Fall, and the Need for Redemption
2. God Builds His Nation (2000–931 BC)
3. God Educates His Nation (931–586 BC)
4. God Keeps a Faithful Remnant (586–6 BC)
5. God Purchases Redemption and Begins the Kingdom (6 BC to AD 30)
6. God Spreads the Kingdom Through the Church (AD 30–?)
7. God Consummates Redemption and Confirms His Eternal Kingdom
8. Epilogue: New Heaven and New Earth

## CHRIST IN AMOS

Amos proclaimed the righteousness of God and called on God's people to turn from their unrighteousness and return to God. The high standards of God's righteousness were a passion with Jesus who told His followers He had not come to put aside the law as an expression of God's righteousness. Rather He had come to fulfill God's righteous requirements.

## CHRISTIAN WORLDVIEW ELEMENTS

### Teachings About God

God is absolutely sovereign. He raises up and puts down nations. He is also a God who reveals Himself and His plans to "His servants the prophets" (3:7). Therefore, He has revealed Himself to be the judge of all, pagan and people of God alike. He is also—and not least—a God who has a wonderful future for His people when they are restored at last (9:11–15).

### Teachings About Humanity

The people of Amos's day showed the universal human tendency to do the wrong thing rather than the right thing. In particular, this often evidences itself in religious compromise and complacency (4:4–5). On the other hand, humanity will be salvaged! Both Israel and "all the nations that are called by My name" (9:12) will one day experience unmeasured blessings. (James declared that this prophecy began to be fulfilled by Gentiles turning to Jesus, Ac 15:5–18.)

**Teachings About Salvation**

In Amos, redemption is based entirely on God's initiative. God reminded them that they were "the entire clan that I brought from the land of Egypt" and that "I have known only you out of all the clans of the earth" (3:1–2). What God desires from redeemed people is righteous living and obedience. Religious rituals and festivals, even those that God commanded, cannot substitute for a right relationship with Him (5:21–24).

## GENRE AND LITERARY STYLE

**Prophecies and One Short Narrative, Written Mainly in Hebrew Poetry**

Amos may be the earliest writing prophet to complete his ministry. (Joel might have preceded him.) He includes all the elements of prophecy: a clear "this is the LORD's declaration," that includes "forth telling" and "foretelling." Amos's announcement that God despised the people's deeds implicitly included a call to repentance. Further, he predicted both near events (such as the fall of Samaria) and remote events (such as the coming restoration of "the fallen booth of David," 9:11).

Except for 7:10–16, the book is written in vigorous Hebrew poetry. Amos created startling word pictures, from his opening salvo ("The LORD roars from Zion," 1:2) to his bold reference to the women of Samaria ("cows of Bashan," 4:1). His opening chapters are memorable for repeated use of the formula, "I will not relent from punishing__________for three crimes, even four" (1:3,6,9,11,13; 2:1,4,6).

In English Bibles, Amos is the third of the 12 Minor Prophets. In the Hebrew canon it belonged to the composite book called "The Twelve." (See *Genre and Literary Style* for **HOSEA** for more information.)

## A PRINCIPLE TO LIVE BY

**Material Prosperity (Am 6:4–7, *Life Essentials Study Bible*, p. 1195–96)**

We must never conclude that material prosperity and political power are indications that God approves of our lifestyle.

To access a video presentation of this principle featuring Dr. Gene Getz, use a Smartphone or iPad to connect to this QR code or go to http://www.bhpublishinggroup.com/handbook/amos

Obadiah, the sixth-century Israelite prophet against Edom, has given his name to this book as its composer. His name means "Servant of Yahweh" in Hebrew.

## KEY TEXT: VERSE 15

*"For the Day of the* L*ORD is near, against all the nations. As you have done, so it will be done to you; what you deserve will return on your own head."*

## KEY TERM: "EDOM"

The people of Edom were descendants of Esau who lived southeast of Israel. God's wrath against Edom for its sins is the single concern of this book.

## ONE-SENTENCE SUMMARY

Obadiah prophesied that God would destroy the nation of Edom because of its pride and violence—particularly in looking down on Judah's misfortune—and ultimately "the kingdom will be the LORD's."

Caves in Edom. "Your presumptuous heart has deceived you, you who live in clefts of the rock in your home in the heights, who say to yourself, 'Who can bring me down to the ground?'" (Ob 3)

## AUTHOR AND DATE OF WRITING

### Obadiah, Perhaps Around 585–550 BC

Obadiah did not name his father or any king, and he left no personal traces in his prophecy. If the Babylonian invasions of Judah are indeed the context for Obadiah's ministry, he was a contemporary of Jeremiah. Scholars can only make a reasonable judgment about the date of composition. It could have been written in the period after the first two Babylonian invasions, but before the final disaster of 586, or following the leveling of Jerusalem and the temple in 586.

## FIRST AUDIENCE AND DESTINATION

### The Edomite People of "Mount Seir" and the Judahite People of "Mount Zion"

The first hearers of Obadiah were evidently the descendants of Esau. Ultimately, however, this was a message for the descendants of Jacob (that is, the people living

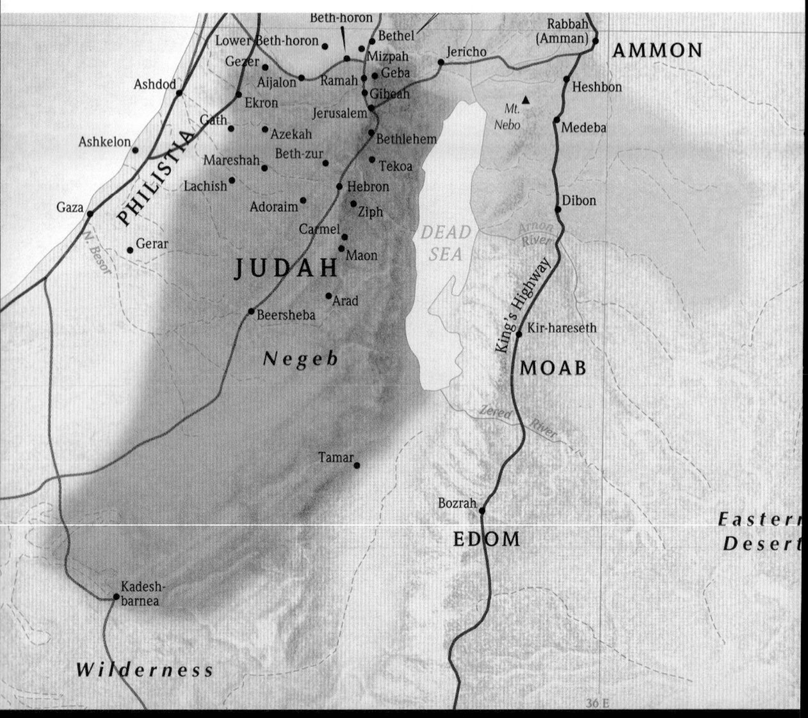


The Israelites regarded the Edomites as close neighbors, even more closely related to them than the Ammonites and Moabites. The Edomites were descendents of Esau, Jacob's brother. The King's Highway, one of the major international routes, ran through Bozrah, connecting Edom to Damascus.

in and around Jerusalem). This book was preserved by the Israelites as part of their canon of Scripture at least partly because it contained a message relevant to them.

## OCCASION

There was an ancient and bitter hatred between the Israelites and the Edomites, going all the way back to the rivalry between their respective patriarchs, Jacob and Esau (Gn 27; 32–33). The descendants of Esau had settled southeast of the Dead Sea. From there they had caused grief to the Israelites both in the last days of Moses and in the days of King Saul (Nm 20; 1Sm 22). Now they had once again demonstrated their hostility against a nation whose ethnic identity was not so different from their own.

The book of Obadiah was prompted by divine revelation. It explicitly claimed to originate as a divinely sent "vision." The prophet had no doubt that his words were simply relaying, "This is what the Lord God has said" (v. 1).

# GOD'S MESSAGE IN OBADIAH

## PURPOSE

This book preserves the divinely inspired prophecies Obadiah made during his (perhaps) brief ministry. These prophecies served a twofold purpose. First, they were meant to warn the people of Edom of their coming doom. Second they were an encouragement to the people of Judah to believe that God would punish one of their enemies for their sins against God's people.

## FIRST PASS

### Judgment on Edom

Obadiah begins with a prophetic messenger formula indicating that God is behind the message. Verses 2–9 give the divine verdict. Addressing Edom, God promised to defeat those supermen and topple the mountain capital, Bozrah, which reflected their lofty self-conceit. Edom's allies would let them down, and neither their famed wisdom nor their warriors would be able to save them. This seems to anticipate the Nabateans' infiltration from the eastern desert and their eventual takeover of Edom's traditional territory. The end of verse 1 appears to be a report from the prophet that already a coalition of neighboring groups was planning to attack Edom.

### Edom's Sin

The catalog of Edom's crimes (vv. 10–14) functions as the accusation that warranted God's verdict of punishment. The underlying thought is that Judah had been the victim of "the Day of the Lord" when God intervened in judgment and they had drunk the cup of God's wrath (vv. 15–16; cp. Lm 1:12; 2:21).

### The Day of the Lord

In OT theology the concept of the Day of the Lord embraces not only God's people but also their no-less-wicked neighbors. This wider dimension is reflected in verses 15–16 (cp. Lm 1:21). The fall of Edom was to trigger this eschatological event in which order would be restored to an unruly world. Then would come the vindication of God's people, not for their own sakes but as earthly witnesses to His glory; and so "the kingdom will be the LORD's" (Ob 21).

Like the book of Revelation, which proclaims the downfall of the persecuting Roman Empire, the aim of Obadiah is to sustain faith in God's moral government and hope in the eventual triumph of His just will. It brings a pastoral message to aching hearts that God is on the throne and cares for His own.

## THE RELIABILITY OF OBADIAH

At first glance it would seem that Obadiah has his chronology mixed up. He warned the Edomites not to carry out their (future) treachery against Judah (Ob 10–14), yet right after that warning, he pronounced judgment for what Edom (and other nations) had already done to Jerusalem. Why warn Edom not to do something and then announce that they had already done it? Possibly Obadiah penned the warning before the attack took place and then wrote the announcement of judgment later. However, it is more likely that he stated the warnings in this way for rhetorical effect. Obadiah portrayed Edom's past transgressions against Jerusalem far more vividly by placing himself at the scene and demanding, as it were, that the Edomites cease their wicked behavior. Indeed, this was a common literary technique employed elsewhere in the prophetic material (see Is 14:29; Lm 4:21; Hs 9:1; Am 3:9; Mc 7:8; Nah 2:1).

When did Edom betray the people of Jerusalem (Ob 13–14)?

A likely possibility is the invasion of the Babylonians under Nebuchadnezzar in 586 BC. In this catastrophic event the Babylonians captured Jerusalem and burned the temple. This would therefore seem to be the most likely context for the book of Obadiah. The Edomites should have been allies of Judah (Jr 27:1–11), but they sided with the Babylonians (Ps 137:7; Ezk 25:12; 35:7).

Obadiah's description is so vivid that he likely wrote his book not long after the fall of Jerusalem. He also predicted the fall of Edom as a future event, so he must have written before the late sixth century BC, when Edom was destroyed. Taking all the evidence into account, a likely date for Obadiah to have written the book would be between 585 and 550 BC.

## HOW OBADIAH FITS INTO GOD'S STORY

1. Prologue: Creation, Fall, and the Need for Redemption
2. God Builds His Nation (2000–931 BC)
3. God Educates His Nation (931–586 BC)
4. **God Keeps a Faithful Remnant (586–6 BC)**
5. God Purchases Redemption and Begins the Kingdom (6 BC to AD 30)
6. God Spreads the Kingdom Through the Church (AD 30–?)
7. God Consummates Redemption and Confirms His Eternal Kingdom
8. Epilogue: New Heaven and New Earth

## CHRIST IN OBADIAH

Obadiah prophesied that Edom would be judged and destroyed for its pride against God and its treachery against God's people. Herod the Great, who ruled Judea during the time of Jesus' birth, had Edomite ancestry. The old treachery of Edom against Israel is seen in Herod's attempt to kill Jesus when He was less than two years old.

## CHRISTIAN WORLDVIEW ELEMENTS

### Teachings About God

God's justice in dealing with human sin is displayed in Obadiah. His promised destruction of Edom will be based on the criterion noted in the *Key Text* on the previous page.

### Teachings About Humanity

On one hand Obadiah continues the biblical emphasis that there are only two kinds of people: those who belong to "Mount Zion" (God's covenant people) and all the rest. On the other hand, the book shows that when God judges people and nations, He will have enough evidence to condemn them based on their (mis)treatment of others.

### Teachings About Salvation

In Obadiah salvation is thought of in terms of God's ultimate deliverance of His people based on His sovereign care: "There will be a deliverance on Mount Zion" (v. 17). Nothing is said about personal conversion.

## GENRE AND LITERARY STYLE

### A Brief Prophecy Written in Hebrew Poetry

Obadiah is one of three prophetic books whose initial audience was outside of God's people. (The other two are Jonah and Nahum, both directed against the Assyrian capital of Nineveh.) His book "forth tells" the sins of Edom and God's displeasure. Then it "foretells" the coming ruin of Edom and the ultimate greatness of God's kingdom. Interpreters disagree about whether the prediction of Edom's destruction was fulfilled in the intertestamental period or it still waits for an end-time fulfillment.

The entire book is written in Hebrew poetry. In English Bibles, Obadiah is the fourth of the 12 Minor Prophets. In the Hebrew canon it belonged to the composite book called "The Twelve." (See *Genre and Literary Style* for **HOSEA** for more information.)

## A PRINCIPLE TO LIVE BY

**Christlike Humility (Ob 1–14, *Life Essentials Study Bible*, p. 1203–04)**

We are to evaluate our relationship with God by the extent we demonstrate true humility and compassion in all our endeavors and relationships.

To access a video presentation of this principle featuring Dr. Gene Getz, use a Smartphone or iPad to connect to this QR code or go to http://www.bhpublishinggroup.com/handbook/obadiah

Nabatean Arch in Bozrah, Edom. By NT times a people of Arabic origin known as the Nabateans had established a commercial empire with its center in the former Edomite territory east of the Arabah. Their chief city was Petra, and the whole region southeast of the Dead Sea had come to be known as Nabatea.

# JONAH

Jonah, the eighth-century Israelite prophet against Nineveh, has given his name to this book as its central character and composer. His name means "dove" in Hebrew.

## KEY TEXT: 4:11

*"Should I not care about the great city of Nineveh, which has more than 120,000 people who cannot distinguish between their right and their left, as well as many animals?"*

## KEY TERM: "FISH"

Although this book is not about the fish, clearly Jonah's being swallowed by the "huge fish" is the most exciting and memorable incident in the book. This is what keeps interest in the book alive and makes it the best known of all the minor prophets.

## ONE-SENTENCE SUMMARY

After Jonah's disobedience to God's command for him to preach in Nineveh resulted in his being swallowed by a fish, he then obeyed God and preached in Nineveh, with the result that the entire city repented and turned to God.

## AUTHOR AND DATE OF WRITING

**Jonah, Perhaps Around 780 BC**

The book is anonymous. On the other hand, according to uniform Jewish and early Christian belief, Jonah wrote this narrative of which he was the central human figure. If so, he likely wrote down the account of his ministry shortly after completing it.

Jonah was a contemporary of Amos. The only information known of his background is that his father was Amittai and he was from Gath-hepher, an Israelite town originally in the tribal allotment of Zebulun (Jos 19:13). Because critical scholars dismiss the narrative as nonhistorical, they suppose the book was composed by some unknown writer, probably after the Jews returned from exile.

## FIRST AUDIENCE AND DESTINATION

**The People of the Northern Kingdom Living in and Around Samaria**

Although the people of Nineveh heard and responded to Jonah's message, the book was written for the benefit of the people of Israel. According to 2 Kings 14:25, Jonah was involved in a prophetic ministry to Jeroboam II, presumably early in his reign.

## OCCASION

The book did not tell what prompted it to be written. Unlike all the other major and minor prophets, it is essentially a narrative. The only prophecy as such in the book is Jonah's warning, "In 40 days Nineveh will be demolished!" (3:4).

# GOD'S MESSAGE IN JONAH

## PURPOSE

Jonah was the "Missionary Prophet." This book preserves the experiences of a reluctant preacher who, of all the prophets, had the most visibly positive results. The people of Israel had forgotten that God is concerned for all people. God meant for Israel to "declare His glory among the nations, His wonderful works among all peoples" (1 Ch 16:24). Even though the people of Nineveh were a political enemy (and would destroy the northern kingdom within a century), they were not beyond God's mercy. This book teaches that the most unlikely, most evil people in the world may respond favorably when they are given an opportunity to know the one true God. It also teaches that salvation is a matter of undeserved forgiveness, a truth that God's people have sometimes forgotten.

## FIRST PASS

The book of Jonah has been called "a masterpiece of rhetoric" and a "model of literary artistry, marked by symmetry and balance." Its four chapters divide into two halves each of which opens with the Lord's command to go preach in Nineveh (1:1–2; 3:1–2).

### Jonah Flees

To avoid his divine assignment Jonah tried to get as far away from Nineveh as possible. Nineveh was about 500 miles to the east, so he headed for Tarshish, probably what is now Spain, the farthest western location he knew, about 2,000 miles. But God sent a storm and then a great fish to turn Jonah around. The sailors showed more compassion for Jonah than Jonah showed for Nineveh (1:1–16).

### Jonah Prays

Jonah, having been thrown overboard, thought his life was over. Suddenly he found himself alive inside a huge fish. The psalm of prayer Jonah uttered was an expression of thanks to God for saving his life. While Jonah was thankful for his own deliverance, he showed a different attitude toward Nineveh's deliverance. In view of his rebellion in chapter 1, his anger in chapter 4, and the pagan sailors' response to God in 1:14–16, Jonah's vow of thanks in 2:8–9 sounds rather self-serving. Also, there is no confession of sin or expression of repentance in Jonah's prayer. The "three days and three nights" of 1:17 alluded to the notion popular at that time that the journey to the land of the dead *(sheol)* took that long. So Jonah's retrieval from the fish was like a retrieval from death (Mt 12:39–40). The fish likely dropped Jonah off at Joppa, where he had started.

Jonah was not pleased when God commanded him to go to Nineveh and preach repentance. The Assyrians worshipped the vicious god Ashur and a multitude of other gods and goddesses. Assyrian brutality and cruelty were legendary. A relief from the palace of Ashurbanipal at Nineveh shows Assyrian soldiers subjecting captives to a series of tortures.

### Jonah Preaches

Perhaps about a month later, Jonah arrived in the great city of Nineveh. After Jonah preached for only one day rather than the expected three days, the people repented (3:1–10). The message God gave Jonah to preach did not explicitly call for their repentance. Rather, it told the Ninevites that they had angered Jonah's God and that punishment was on the way. The Ninevites did not presume that God could be appeased but repented in humility, hoping that "God may turn and relent" (3:9; see 1:6), which He did. That God's judgment message was conditional is clear from His sending the prophet, giving them 40 days' warning, and postponing Nineveh's destruction (see Jr 18:7–10).

### Jonah Fumes

Jonah despised the Ninevites so much that he would rather die than live, knowing he helped them escape destruction. Still hoping God would give Nineveh what they deserved, Jonah waited and watched. Through the incident of the plant and the worm (sent by God like the wind and the fish in chap. 1), the Lord chided Jonah for his double standard. Jonah was concerned for the transitory plant that gave him shade but not for the 120,000 people of Nineveh who despite their limited knowledge had trusted God (4:1–11).

## THE RELIABILITY OF JONAH

Many since the nineteenth century AD have regarded Jonah as a parable or didactic fiction, as if factual history were ruled out by literary artistry or the recounting of miraculous events. If this narrative, however, whose form bears at every point the mark of a historical account, was judged unhistorical on either of these bases, then most of the Bible would have to be so judged. It is pointless to ask whether Jonah really could have been swallowed by a great fish without also asking whether God really could communicate with a prophet. Every aspect of man's encounter with God is miraculous. Jonah is clearly didactic, but it is not presented as fiction or interpreted as such by Jesus (cp. Mt 12:40–41). Also, as Frank Page has pointed out, "If one of the lessons of Jonah, as most would admit, is that God is sovereign over and responsive to human actions, how can we employ a method in its explication that denies that message by ruling out the possibility of miracles?" We might also question the likelihood of ancient Israel's having produced and accepted as Scripture a fictional account in which the two main characters were a historical prophet and Yahweh Himself.

Some have pointed to alleged historical inaccuracies in the book as evidence of a late date of origin and lack of factual concern. One example is that 3:3 describes Nineveh as larger than we know it to have been. It is described literally as "a great city to God, a walk of three days." Although this is often said to mean that a three-day journey would be required to circumscribe it, however, the point is probably that a three-day visit was required for Jonah to spread his God-given message. This

would especially be the case if "the great city of Nineveh" referred to "greater Nineveh," that is, Nineveh and the surrounding towns. A second example is that the designation "king of Nineveh" (3:6) was not the normal way the Assyrians would refer to their king. This is true but irrelevant since we have no reason to suppose the book of Jonah was written by the Assyrians but by the Jews, who did sometimes refer to their kings in this way (1 Kg 21:1; 2 Kg 1:3).

## HOW JONAH FITS INTO GOD'S STORY

1. Prologue: Creation, Fall, and the Need for Redemption
2. God Builds His Nation (2000–931 BC)
3. **God Educates His Nation (931–586 BC)**
4. God Keeps a Faithful Remnant (586–6 BC)
5. God Purchases Redemption and Begins the Kingdom (6 BC to AD 30)
6. God Spreads the Kingdom Through the Church (AD 30–?)
7. God Consummates Redemption and Confirms His Eternal Kingdom
8. Epilogue: New Heaven and New Earth

## CHRIST IN JONAH

Some crowds who heard Jesus clamored for a sign. Jesus told them that the only sign they would be given is the sign of Jonah. As Jonah was in the belly of the fish for three days, so Jesus was in the earth for three days and then was resurrected (Lk 11:29–32).

## CHRISTIAN WORLDVIEW ELEMENTS

### Teachings About God

Jonah reveals God as Creator. He is sovereign over the storms and fish of the sea, as well as the plants and worms of the land. The book also shows God as loving and compassionate. God's unanswered question that ends the book (see *Key Text*) is meant to provoke readers to think about how His mercy relates to "the nations."

### Teachings About Humanity

God's enumeration of the vast city of Nineveh shows that each human life is valuable in the eyes of God. Jonah was personally a mass of contradictions—a prophet known mainly for disobeying God; a preacher angry at the success of his ministry; a believer more concerned about "creature comforts" than about people dying without knowing God. As such, he certainly demonstrates that God may use imperfect and reluctant persons to accomplish His plans.

### Teachings About Salvation

Jonah demonstrates the principle that those whom God saves find deliverance in response to hearing the word of God. No salvation occurs apart from the proclamation—whether willingly or reluctantly, partially or completely—of a word from God. The apostle Paul (who also knew about storms on the Mediterranean Sea) would later ask, "But how can they call on Him they have not believed in? And how can they believe without hearing about Him? And how can they hear without a preacher?" (Rm 10:14).

## GENRE AND LITERARY STYLE

### A Compact Narrative Written in Hebrew

Although this book contains almost none of the elements of Hebrew prophecy (see, for example, *Genre and Literary Style* for **ISAIAH**), this book is listed among the prophetic books for two reasons. First, its central character was a prophet (2 Kg 14:25); second, it issued a call to repentance. It contains no predictions at all. As a compact, well-written narrative, it has literary parallels with the book of Ruth or the stories about Elijah or Elisha (see 1 Kg 17–2 Kg 8).

Because taking the story as history requires believing the astonishing miracle of Jonah's survival in the fish and the otherwise unreported repentance of Nineveh, most critical scholars have suggested that the book belongs to a different genre. It has variously been called a parable or an allegory of God's love; that is, it is fictional in one way or another. Jesus Himself, however, affirmed both Jonah's being swallowed by the fish and the repentance of Nineveh (Mt 12:39–41), so there can be no doubt that the events reported in this book happened in history. If one believes in God's sovereignty over nature and history, then He can intervene supernaturally whenever it pleases Him.

The entire book is written in Hebrew prose except for Jonah's prayer. In English Bibles, Jonah is the fifth of the 12 Minor Prophets. In the Hebrew canon it belonged to the composite book called "The Twelve." (See *Genre and Literary Style* for **HOSEA** for more information.)

## A PRINCIPLE TO LIVE BY

### Transparency (Jnh 1:1–12, *Life Essentials Study Bible*, p. 1207)

When we deliberately disobey God and suffer the consequences, we should be open and honest about our sins.

To access a video presentation of this principle featuring Dr. Gene Getz, use a Smartphone or iPad to connect to this QR code or go to http://www.bhpublishinggroup.com/handbook/jonah

Micah, the eighth-century Israelite prophet from Judah, has given his name to this book as its composer. His name is a short form of Micaiah, meaning "Who is like Yahweh?" in Hebrew.

## KEY TEXT: 3:8

*"As for me, however, I am filled with power by the Spirit of the LORD, with justice and courage, to proclaim to Jacob his rebellion and to Israel his sin."*

## KEY TERM: "IDOLATRY"

The essential sin of Judah was idolatry: a rejection of the "First Table" of the Ten Commandments (the first four commandments). This brought about corruption, violence, and many other sins: a rejection of the "Second Table" (the last six commandments).

## ONE-SENTENCE SUMMARY

Although Micah also prophesied against Israel, his main message was against Judah, who must repent of idolatry and injustice or else go into exile but then be restored to divine blessing under the Ruler from Bethlehem.

## AUTHOR AND DATE OF WRITING

**Micah, Perhaps Around 700 BC**

Micah was a contemporary of Isaiah and Hosea. He was from the small town of Moresheth, probably Moresheth-gath in southern Judah (1:14). Almost nothing is known of his personal life. He saw the fulfillment of his predictions about the fall of Samaria to the Assyrians. Micah also witnessed the great religious revival initiated by Hezekiah, which delayed by a century the fulfillment of his prophecies about the coming fall of Jerusalem. Thus, he was one of the few prophets whose warnings of judgment were heeded. He probably wrote down his prophecies during the last years of Hezekiah.

## FIRST AUDIENCE AND DESTINATION

**The People of Judah Living During Micah's Lifetime**

The first hearers were people living in Judah near the end of the 700s BC.

## OCCASION

The specific occasion for Micah's prophecies is not known. They do, however, fit the period of religious and social corruption present during the rule of Ahaz (see 2 Kg 16). According to Jeremiah 26:18, Hezekiah repented in response to hearing Micah 3:12, a prophecy of the coming fall of Jerusalem. The religious revival Hezekiah instituted marked a genuine return to worship of the Lord. (Later on, Isaiah worked with Hezekiah when the Assyrian army under Sennacherib laid siege against Jerusalem in 701 BC, and God miraculously spared the city, Is 36–37.) Micah did not tell what prompted the collection of his writings.

# GOD'S MESSAGE IN MICAH

## PURPOSE

This book preserves the divinely inspired prophecies Micah made during his ministry of at least 20 years. These prophecies were originally for the people of Judah facing Assyrian invasions. Micah warned that because of idolatry and injustice, God's case against Judah (and Israel) was severe. Their kingdoms would be destroyed—even though individuals could still repent and seek the LORD. Like Isaiah his colleague Micah looked beyond the Assyrian captivity of Israel and the Babylonian captivity of Judah to the time they would be forgiven and restored in righteousness, living under the Davidic Ruler God would send.

## FIRST PASS

### From Disaster to Deliverance

God's destruction of Israel (722 BC) for their idolatry should have been a sign to Judah, and the destruction of both should be a sign to all nations that a time of retribution is coming. Micah grieved over the terrible calamity coming upon Judah for their rebellion, a punishment that included the exile of some of its inhabitants to Babylon. Micah 2:1–11 condemns those who hatched and carried out unscrupulous plots to steal houses and ancestral lands by perverting justice. The unavoidable penalty would be calamity, involving the loss of all their land, and more importantly exclusion of the guilty from the future assembly of God's redeemed people. Those wanting to hide or justify their wicked behavior tried to silence Micah and other true prophets. Those who evicted the helpless would be evicted by the Lord.

### From Predators to Shepherds

Micah denounced Israel's corrupt leaders who preyed upon God's people. Pleas for God's aid would be of no help to them. Judges, priests, and prophets abandoned

Bethlehem from Givat HaArbaa, near Hebron road, Jerusalem. "Bethlehem Ephrathah, you are small among the clans of Judah; One will come from you to be ruler over Israel for Me. His origin is from antiquity, from eternity" (5:2).

their responsibility to the truth and used their positions for personal gain. Micah, however, strengthened by God's Spirit, declared the truth, which included destruction and the ultimate darkness and silence at God's departure from them. Juxtaposed to the message of corruption and doom (chap. 3) is the message of glorious exaltation (chaps. 4–5). But even there, deliverance in the near or distant future alternates with the trials of Israel's present situation. Micah returns to Sennacherib's siege of Jerusalem and his humiliation of King Hezekiah (5:1). He then turned to the future—to the Babylonian exile and even until the coming of Messiah. God was at work to turn humiliation into glorious victory through a Messianic ruler who came not from proud Jerusalem but from insignificant Bethlehem (5:2; see Mt 2:4–8). "Bethlehem, too insignificant to be mentioned by the cartographer of the book of Joshua or in Micah's catalogue of Judah's cities of defense . . . , is today incredibly the centre of pilgrimages from around the world and is universally renowned because Jesus Christ fulfilled this verse."[1]

**From Darkness to Light**

The final section begins with an indictment against Israel in the form of a lawsuit (6:1–8). Israel is charged with forgetting the Lord's righteous acts and so losing a sense of genuine devotion to Him. Although they tried to buy God's favor with ritual sacrifices, God's primary demand was for justice, mercy, and humble obedience (v. 8; see Is 5:7; Hs 4:1; 6:6; 12:6; Am 5:24). Micah again turned accusation and sentence into lament (7:1–6). One who hunted for integrity in Israel would return empty. Micah testified (v. 7) to what the righteous remnant should do in the midst of God's judgment: They should resolve to pray and look expectantly for the Lord's deliverance that will be the fruit of His judgment (see Hab 3:1–2). He concludes with a song of victory (7:8–20). Moses' Song of the Sea in Exodus 15 has much in common with Micah's victory song, especially Exodus 15:11—"LORD, who is like You among the gods? Who is like You, glorious in holiness, revered with praises, performing wonders?" As God hurled the Egyptians into the depths of the sea (Ex 15:4–5; Neh 9:11), so He hurls our sins away.

## THE RELIABILITY OF MICAH

Many biblical scholars view key sections of Micah as having been written during or after the exile in 586 BC rather than by the eighth-century prophet for whom the book is named. Bruce Waltke argues that "there is no compelling reason to urge against the authenticity of any oracle to the prophet Micah in the book that bears his name."[2] He observes that the grammar of Micah is preexilic. Further, the theological concepts in Micah are found in documents that are generally agreed to be preexilic. The presuppositions with which one reads Micah will affect interpretation of that text. If predictive prophecy is ruled out on principle, then apparent instances of it in a text will have to be explained as something written after the event.

## HOW MICAH FITS INTO GOD'S STORY

1. Prologue: Creation, Fall, and the Need for Redemption
2. God Builds His Nation (2000–931 BC)
3. God Educates His Nation (931–586 BC)
4. God Keeps a Faithful Remnant (586–6 BC)
5. God Purchases Redemption and Begins the Kingdom (6 BC to AD 30)
6. God Spreads the Kingdom Through the Church (AD 30–?)
7. God Consummates Redemption and Confirms His Eternal Kingdom
8. Epilogue: New Heaven and New Earth

## CHRIST IN MICAH

Micah repeats (4:1–5) Israel's Messianic promise (2:2–4), focusing on the exaltation of God's temple as a worship place for all nations and on the end of war. Israel will walk in the name of the Lord (4:5). This is possible because God will once again visit David's birthplace in Bethlehem and bring forth a new, everlasting King (5:2–5a; cp. Mt 2:6).

## CHRISTIAN WORLDVIEW ELEMENTS

### Teachings About God

God's wrath in response to idolatry and all forms of human sin against others (violence, corruption, exploitation) is manifest in this book. The Assyrian and Babylonian captivities were the result of God's justice. Yet He is also a merciful God who does not retain anger forever. He will ultimately "cast all our sins into the depths of the sea" (7:19). Christ's birth in Bethlehem is specifically prophesied (5:2). The Spirit of God was present to empower the prophet (3:8).

### Teachings About Humanity

Micah painted a dark picture of humanity as all too prone to wickedness. People from small to great were lying awake at night planning evil (2:1). The only hope was divine interference, which will happen when God personally takes over shepherding His flock (2:12).

### Teachings About Salvation

In Micah, salvation is mainly corporate. It is based on God forgiving sins (7:18–20) and restoring His people under the coming King. There is, however, an individual dimension. Those in a right relationship with God in this lifetime show it in the way they live now, reflected in perhaps the most beloved text from this book: "Mankind, He has told you what is good and what it is the LORD requires of you: to act justly, to love faithfulness, and to walk humbly with your God" (6:8).

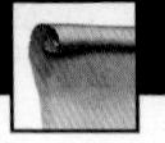


## GENRE AND LITERARY STYLE

**Prophecies Written Entirely in Hebrew Poetry**

Micah's prophecies both "forth tell" and "foretell." He includes the three classic elements of Hebrew prophecy: (1) call for people to turn from their sins in the face of divine judgment (which in fact happened), (2) predictions of near events (such as the fall of Samaria), and (3) predictions of remote events (such as the birth in Bethlehem of the coming Ruler).

Micah's poetic style alternates between a hard-charging attack against sins and the promise of a coming restoration. Sometimes he uses "I" to voice God's own words (chap. 6); sometimes the "I" is his own voice (chap. 7). He is also known for quoting both false prophets (2:6–7) and the nations that will be converted (4:2).

## A PRINCIPLE TO LIVE BY

**True Spiritual Worship (Mc 6:3–4,8, *Life Essentials Study Bible*, p. 1221)**

We are to allow the Holy Spirit to develop inner qualities that reflect the character of the Lord Jesus Christ

To access a video presentation of this principle featuring Dr. Gene Getz, use a Smartphone or iPad to connect to this QR code or go to http://www.bhpublishinggroup.com/handbook/micah

## ENDNOTES

1. Bruce K. Waltke, *Micah: An Introduction and Commentary,* Tyndale Old Testament Commentaries (Downers Grove: InterVarsity Press, 1988), 183.
2. Bruce K. Waltke, *A Commentary on Micah* (Grand Rapids: Eerdmans, 2007), 13.

Nahum, the seventh-century Israelite prophet against Nineveh, has given his name to this book as its composer. His name means "Comfort" in Hebrew.

## KEY TEXT: 1:2

*"The LORD is a jealous and avenging God; the LORD takes vengeance and is fierce in wrath. The LORD takes vengeance against His foes; He is furious with His enemies."*

## KEY TERM: "NINEVEH"

Nineveh was the capital of Assyria, the world superpower of the 600s BC. God's wrath against Nineveh for its sins is the concern of this book. Nahum, the prophet of God's judgment, followed Jonah, the prophet of God's mercy, to Nineveh.

## ONE-SENTENCE SUMMARY

Nahum prophesied that God would destroy Nineveh because of its wickedness and violence, and it would never rise again.

# ORIGINAL HISTORICAL SETTING

## AUTHOR AND DATE OF WRITING

**Nahum, Perhaps Around 650 BC**

Nahum did not name his father or any king, and he left no personal traces in his prophecy. He named himself as an "Elkoshite," that is, from the town of Elkosh, which is otherwise unknown. If Nahum prophesied soon after the fall of Thebes, the king of Judah was the idolatrous and long-reigning Manasseh, the "Ahab of Judah," who became a vassal of Assyria (2 Ch 33:11–13). At this point Assyria was at its most arrogant and imperialistic height under Ashurbanipal (669–627). The year 650 would fit the evidence for the completion of Nahum's book, but this is simply a best-guess estimate.

## FIRST AUDIENCE AND DESTINATION

**People in Nineveh or Perhaps People in Judah**

The first hearers of Nahum may have been the Ninevites themselves. Possibly the prophet traveled there to deliver his message, just as Jonah had done for an earlier generation. Ultimately, however, this was a message for God's people. Nahum was preserved by the people of Judah in their canon of Scripture at least partly because it contained a message important to them.

## OCCASION

Assyria had long terrorized the ancient world. It had conquered Samaria and Thebes and appeared invincible. Nahum did not describe the specific occasion for his prophecy other than that it came as "the vision of Nahum." Like the other prophets, he was specifically aware of the divine origin of his ministry.

# GOD'S MESSAGE IN NAHUM

## PURPOSE

This book preserves the divinely inspired prophecies that Nahum made during his (perhaps) brief ministry. These prophecies served a twofold purpose. First, they were meant to warn the people of Nineveh of their coming doom. Second, they were an encouragement to people living in the kingdom of Judah to believe that God would punish their great enemy for sins against God's people.

## FIRST PASS

### The Divine Warrior

Nahum was the only prophet whose message focused extensively on Nineveh's coming condemnation (1:1). In this way it complements the book of Jonah, in which God's judgment against Nineveh was averted. The Lord is portrayed as divine Warrior (1:2–8) vanquishing the wicked. Emphasis is placed on God's character as His vengeance demonstrates His jealousy and power, and His protection of the faithful demonstrates His goodness and compassion. The Lord is like a husband defending his wife from those who would steal her affections.

### Nineveh Attacked

The prophet had been transported in a vision to Nineveh's watchtower, where he witnessed the armies of the Babylonians (who wore red; see v. 3; Ezk 23:14) and Medes attacking, invading, and sacking the city of Nineveh. In a real sense, however, the attacker (or scatterer) was the Lord. Nahum vividly portrayed the confusion and panic of a city under attack. According to an ancient Greek historical account, Nineveh fell when the Tigris river overflowed and tore down the city walls, flooding the city (1:8; 2:6).

### Nineveh's Fall

A description of Nineveh's fall is followed by a taunt. It begins as a funerary lament for a much-deserved death. Several wordplays add to the effectiveness of this visionary portrayal of judgment. What was before an "abundance of every precious thing" (2:9) has been replaced by "mounds of corpses, dead bodies without end." Because of "the continual prostitution of the prostitute, . . . Nineveh is devastated."

For over a century the Assyrians seemed to have had an unchecked reign, but now God was responding. His judgment is likened to an approaching storm. Perhaps the people of Judah doubted God's justice since Assyria seemed to have no restraints. Through Nahum, however, God dispelled this notion.

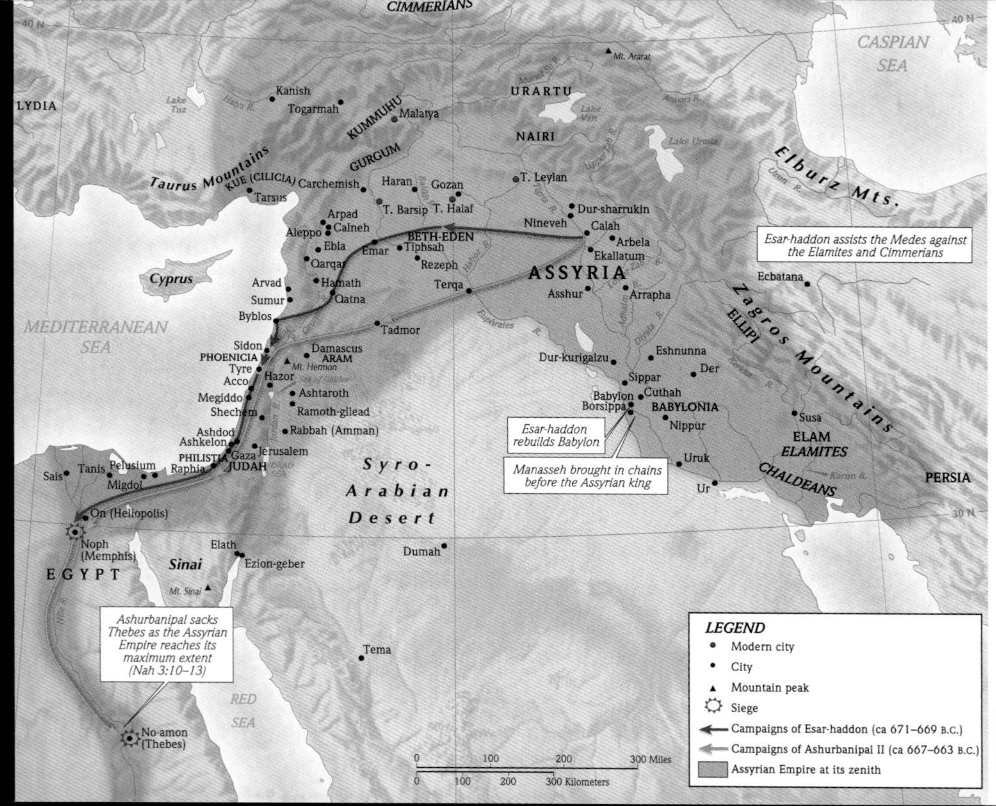

The Lord promises utter humiliation to a once proud city that trusted in her fortifications. Like Thebes, she is now desolate (3:1–19).

## THE RELIABILITY OF NAHUM

Nahum's prophecy cites the fall of Thebes (3:8–10) at the hands of the Assyrians as a historical fact (663 BC). This conquest came during the reign of Ashurbanipal who left the following record:

*This city, the whole of it, I conquered it with the help of Ashur and Ishtar. Silver, gold, precious stones, all the wealth of the palace, rich cloth, precious linen, great horses, supervising men and women, two obelisks of splendid electrum, weighing 2,500 talents, the doors of temples I tore from their bases and carried them off to Assyria. With this weighty booty I left Thebes. Against Egypt and Kush I have lifted my spear and shown my power. With full hands I have returned to Nineveh, in good health.*[1]

Nineveh wasn't destroyed until 612 BC. Nahum's use of Thebes as an example of the vulnerability of a seemingly secure city would have been most effective the closer it was in time to the destruction of Thebes. By the time of Jeremiah and Ezekiel, Thebes had been rebuilt. This argues for Nahum's prophecy being predictive and not simply a description of the fall of Nineveh in 612 BC.

## HOW NAHUM FITS INTO GOD'S STORY

1. Prologue: Creation, Fall, and the Need for Redemption
2. God Builds His Nation (2000–931 BC)
3. **God Educates His Nation (931–586 BC)**
4. God Keeps a Faithful Remnant (586–6 BC)
5. God Purchases Redemption and Begins the Kingdom (6 BC to AD 30)
6. God Spreads the Kingdom Through the Church (AD 30–?)
7. God Consummates Redemption and Confirms His Eternal Kingdom
8. Epilogue: New Heaven and New Earth

## CHRIST IN NAHUM

Nahum told Judah to look for a messenger who would bring the good news of Assyria's downfall, thus proclaiming peace for the world (1:15). The New Testament sees Jesus Christ as God's ultimate Messenger, preaching God's peace for the world (Ac 10:36). As God is the One who rebukes seas and dries up rivers (1:4), so Jesus rebukes the sea and calms the storm (Mt 8:26).

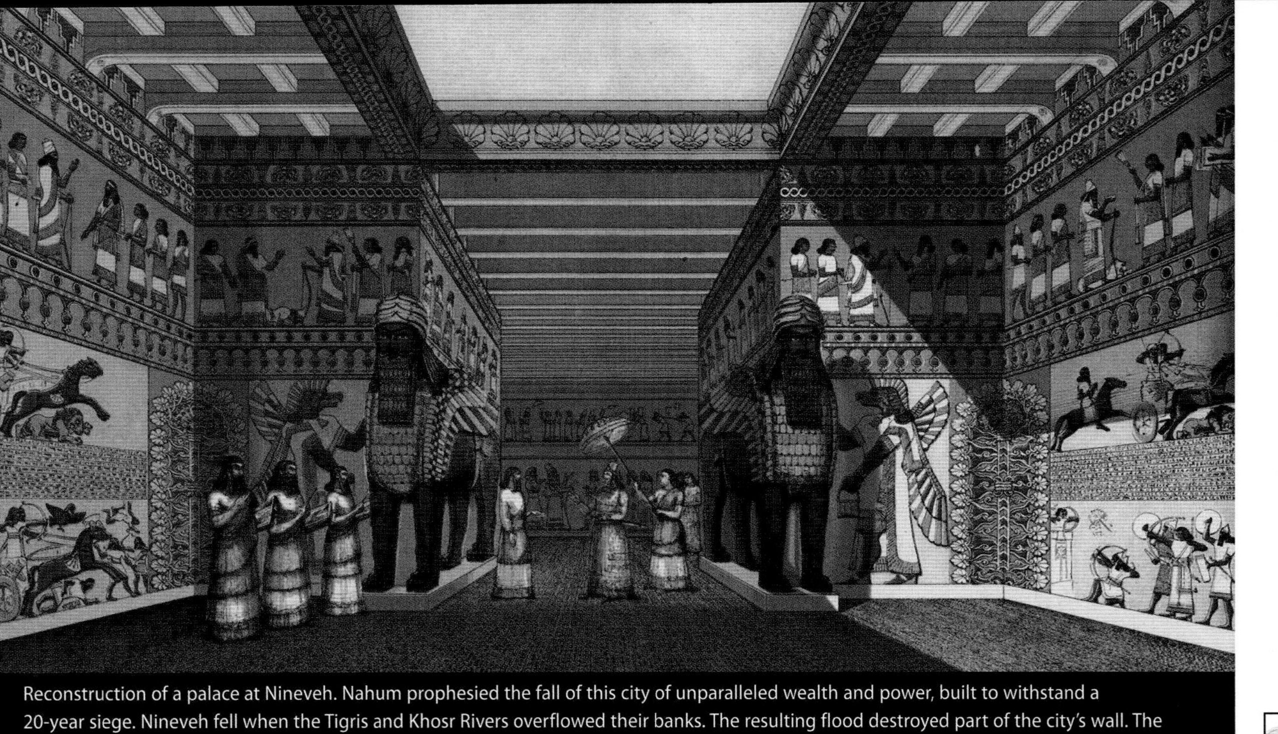

Reconstruction of a palace at Nineveh. Nahum prophesied the fall of this city of unparalleled wealth and power, built to withstand a 20-year siege. Nineveh fell when the Tigris and Khosr Rivers overflowed their banks. The resulting flood destroyed part of the city's wall. The Babylonians entered the breach in the wall, invaded the city, and destroyed it by fire. From 612 BC to the AD 1800s, Nineveh was lost in accumulating layers of dust.

## CHRISTIAN WORLDVIEW ELEMENTS

### Teachings About God

God's wrath against every affront to His holiness is on full display in Nahum. He is patient, but this should not be misunderstood as weakness. His promised destruction of Nineveh was necessary because of the divine attributes noted in the *Key Text* above.

### Teachings About Humanity

On one hand, this book shows that human beings can achieve a great deal apart from God. The Assyrian civilization was highly advanced economically and militarily. On the other hand, the Assyrians were cruel and evil, an abomination to God. The book shows that God does not recognize as great (or good) any person or nation that measures success apart from obedience to Him.

### Teachings About Salvation

In Nahum, salvation is presented as God's final rescue of His people based on His sovereign care: "The LORD is good, a stronghold in a day of distress; He cares for those who take refuge in Him" (1:7).

## GENRE AND LITERARY STYLE

### A Brief Prophecy Written in Hebrew Poetry

Nahum is written in Hebrew poetry. Nahum's style is vivid, with excellent use of metaphors and word pictures. In English Bibles, Nahum is the seventh of the 12 Minor Prophets. In the Hebrew canon it belonged to the composite book called "The Twelve." (See *Genre and Literary Style* for **HOSEA** for more information.)

## A PRINCIPLE TO LIVE BY

### God's Patience (Nah 3:19, *Life Essentials Study Bible*, p. 1230–1231)

When tempted to believe God is cruel and lacking in compassion, we should review His extraordinary patience and continual communication, both with His people Israel and with the Gentile nations.

To access a video presentation of this principle featuring Dr. Gene Getz, use a Smartphone or iPad to connect to this QR code or go to http://www.bhpublishinggroup.com/handbook/nahum

## ENDNOTES

1. See http://www.reshafim.org.il/ad/egypt/the_destruction_of_thebes.htm#rem5.

# HABAKKUK

Habakkuk, the seventh-century Israelite prophet to Judah, has given his name to this book as its composer. His name is possibly related either to the verb "embrace" in Hebrew or to an Assyrian plant called the "*hambakuku*."

## KEY TEXT: 2:4

*"Look, his ego is inflated; he is without integrity. But the righteous one will live by his faith."*

## KEY TERM: "DIALOGUE"

The book reports a dialogue between the prophet and God. The prophet asked God questions about His ways, and God answered. The book shows one righteous way to bring concerns to God when His ways appear incomprehensible.

## ONE-SENTENCE SUMMARY

When Habakkuk asked God questions about the nature of evil and its punishment, God answered by revealing His righteousness and sovereignty, and the prophet then responded with worship and faith.

"Look, I am raising up the Chaldeans, that bitter impetuous nation that marches across the earth's open spaces to seize territories not its own. They are fierce and terrifying; their views of justice and sovereignty stem from themselves. . . . They fly like an eagle, swooping to devour (Hab 1:6–8b).

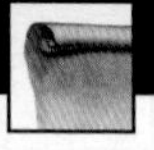



## AUTHOR AND DATE OF WRITING

### Habakkuk, Perhaps Around 610 BC

Habakkuk is unknown apart from this book. He did not name his father or town of origin. Because of what he included about the international military scene, he almost certainly prophesied near the end of the seventh century. As such, he was a contemporary of Jeremiah and Zephaniah and probably lived to see his prophecy of the Chaldean conquest of Judah fulfilled (with Jerusalem and the temple burned in 586). The year 610 fits the evidence for the completion of Habakkuk's book—after the fall of Assyria to Babylon but before King Josiah's death or the battle of Carchemish—but this is simply a best-guess estimate.

## FIRST AUDIENCE AND DESTINATION

### People in Judah Living During Habakkuk's Lifetime

The first hearers were the kings and people living in the land of Judah during the years before the Babylonian captivity.

## OCCASION

Habakkuk did not tell what prompted him to write down his book. He recorded the private dialogue of himself with God and his personal response as a written account

Gate relief of Babylon, built during the reign of Nebuchadnezzar II, when the Neo-Babylonian Empire was at its peak. The Ishtar Gate, built by Nebuchadnezzar II, was a glazed-brick structure decorated with figures of bulls and dragons, symbols of the weather god Adad and of Marduk. North of the gate the roadway was lined with glazed

for the benefit of the people. Because the last chapter contains liturgical notations (3:1,19), those verses were probably included in worship services at the temple.

## PURPOSE

This book preserves the divinely inspired dialogues and prayers of Habakkuk. These originated as a one-on-one conversation between the prophet and God, but they no doubt reflect the kinds of questions that many righteous people of Judah living in Habakkuk's time were also asking. The righteous of all eras may ask similar questions. God's people today will benefit from hearing God's replies to Habakkuk's questions: (1) Why does evil seem to go unpunished for so long? and (2) Why does God sometimes reprove a lesser evil by sending a greater evil?

## FIRST PASS

### God's Shocking Solution

The book begins with a cry to God: "How long?" The opening speech laments rampant violence and injustice in Judah (1:1–4). Habakkuk was assured that God was already at work and that he would soon see the results (v. 5). Judah's violence and injustice will be repaid by a people skilled in brutality. If Judah would not fear God, then they would soon fear the enemy He would send against them.

figures of striding lions. This relief of a lion, the animal associated with Ishtar, goddess of love and war, was thought to protect the street; its repeated design served as a guide for the ritual processions from the city to the temple.

**Retribution**

The prophet knew that because of God's covenant with Israel, His judgment of them would be redemptive rather than destructive. But the idea that the Holy God would use wickedness to punish wickedness was intolerable (1:12–17). After baring his heart to God, Habakkuk positioned himself to watch and listen for God's response (2:1). God told Habakkuk to write down the vision. Even though God would use the Babylonians to chasten His people, the Babylonians would not go unpunished. Habakkuk was called to trust and be patient (2:4).

**Psalm of Confidence**

Habakkuk 3:3–15 is a poetic portrayal of God's salvation of His people from Egypt (see Ex 15). Here metaphors of God's actions drawn from many passages of Scripture are mixed together. Habakkuk 3:16 recounts the psalmist's believing acceptance that God was active in his own moment in time as well as in the past. He would "quietly wait" for God's retribution against the tyrants. He recognized that his was a day for waiting, not for action.

Habakkuk mausoleum in Tuyserkan, Iran. There are a number of traditions outside the Bible regarding the place of Habakkuk's burial. Two of the sites are in Israel and the one pictured is in Iran. The tradition that links Habakkuk to the Persian Empire claims that he was captured by the Babylonians at Jerusalem's temple and taken to Babylon where he was a prisoner until Cyrus the Great defeated the Babylonians and freed him. Habakkuk then went to Ecbatana where he died and was buried.

## THE RELIABILITY OF HABAKKUK

The only clues for the prophecy's date come from (1) Habakkuk's complaint of great wickedness and lawlessness in Judah (1:2–4) and (2) the prophecy of a Babylonian invasion (1:5–11). From 687 BC until his repentance (perhaps in 648 BC), Manasseh led Judah in one of its worst times of wickedness (see *Author and Date of Writing* for **NAHUM**, p. 267.) Under his son Amon, from 642 to 640 BC, Judah again excelled in wickedness. This continued to some extent until Josiah's reform started in about 628 BC. Following Josiah's death in 609 BC, Judah quickly abandoned Josiah's significant reforms and continued their disastrous policies of apostasy under kings Jehoahaz (609 BC), Jehoiakim (609–597 BC), Jehoiachin (598–597 BC), and Zedekiah (597–587 BC). So the time periods for writing that best fit the first clue are 687–648, 642–628, and 609–587 BC.

A commentary on Habakkuk 1–2 was found in Cave One at Qumran in 1948. This would make unlikely the proposal that Habakkuk was written as late as the time of Alexander the Great.

## HOW HABAKKUK FITS INTO GOD'S STORY

1. Prologue: Creation, Fall, and the Need for Redemption
2. God Builds His Nation (2000–931 BC)
3. **God Educates His Nation (931–586 BC)**
4. God Keeps a Faithful Remnant (586–6 BC)
5. God Purchases Redemption and Begins the Kingdom (6 BC to AD 30)
6. God Spreads the Kingdom Through the Church (AD 30–?)
7. God Consummates Redemption and Confirms His Eternal Kingdom
8. Epilogue: New Heaven and New Earth

## CHRIST IN HABAKKUK

Habakkuk stood in awe at God's holiness and power. His reaction to the presence of God (3:16) is similar to that of the apostle John when the risen Christ appeared to him on the Isle of Patmos (Rv 1:17).

## CHRISTIAN WORLDVIEW ELEMENTS

### Teachings About God

The answers God gave the prophet show Him as the Revealer of truth. The revelations God made focus on His absolute sovereignty over human history. Habakkuk's own passion was a concern for the glory of God's name to be known among all people: "His splendor covers the heavens, and the earth is full of His praise" (3:3).

**Teachings About Humanity**

Apart from divine revelation, human reasoning will never understand the ways of God. They will always be a mystery. It is fitting for people to ask God for revelation, but they must wait for the divine answers to their questions. When God reveals Himself, people are to acknowledge His perfections by worship and praise.

**Teachings About Salvation**

The Apostle Paul quoted Habakkuk 2:4 ("the righteous one will live by his faith") twice as evidence of the doctrine of justification by faith in the Old Testament (Rm 1:17; Gl 3:11). Steadfast, persevering trust in God for deliverance has always been the hallmark of God's people. The final verses of the book, a hymn of faith in the God who saves, includes the remarkable confession, "yet I will triumph in Yahweh; I will rejoice in the God of my salvation!" (3:18).

## GENRE AND LITERARY STYLE

**Prophetic Dialogue, Woes, and Prayer Written in Hebrew Poetry**

As a prophetic writer, Habakkuk included materials in an unusual format, although he included classic elements of "forth telling" and "foretelling." His "forth telling" included great declarations of God's attributes as well as woes on the wicked (see especially 2:9–17). His "foretelling" predicted both near events (Judah's devastation by Chaldea, fulfilled in 586 BC), as well as the more remote event of the destruction of Chaldea (fulfilled in 539 BC by the Persians).

The entire book is written in Hebrew poetry. Habakkuk's style reveals him as one whose greatest concern was for the honor of God's name (1:12; 3:3). In English Bibles, Habakkuk is the eighth of the 12 Minor Prophets. In the Hebrew canon it belonged to the composite book called "The Twelve." (See *Genre and Literary Style* for **HOSEA** for more information.)

## A PRINCIPLE TO LIVE BY

**Saved by Faith (Hab 2:1–4, *Life Essentials Study Bible*, p. 1237)**

Though we do not know the answers to all of life's questions, we are to make sure we have by faith received God's gift of eternal life.

To access a video presentation of this principle featuring Dr. Gene Getz, use a Smartphone or iPad to connect to this QR code or go to http://www.bhpublishinggroup.com/handbook/habakkuk

Zephaniah, the seventh-century prophet from Judah, has given his name to this book as its composer. His name means "Yahweh hides" in Hebrew.

## KEY TEXT: 3:17

*"Yahweh your God is among you, a warrior who saves. He will rejoice over you with gladness. He will bring you quietness with His love. He will delight in you with shouts of joy."*

## KEY TERM: "DAY OF THE LORD"

Zephaniah predicted the future Day of the Lord as a time of ruin for Jerusalem. The initial coming of the Day of the Lord was manifested by Judah's fall to Babylon; its final fulfillment lies in the future in the context of Christ's return.

## ONE-SENTENCE SUMMARY

Although Zephaniah prophesied coming judgment against the nations, his main message was against Judah, whose sins were so serious that they would go into exile on "the Day of the LORD," but later they would be restored to righteousness.

"And at that time I will search Jerusalem with lamps and punish the men who settle down comfortably, who say to themselves: 'The LORD will not do us good or evil" (Zph 1:12).

## AUTHOR AND DATE OF WRITING

**Zephaniah, Perhaps Around 625 BC**

Zephaniah was a contemporary of Jeremiah and Habakkuk. He identified himself by a more complete genealogy than any other prophet (1:1), and ministered during the reign of Josiah. He was the great-great-grandson of a certain Hezekiah, probably the famous king. If so, Zephaniah belonged to the royal family. (King Josiah was Hezekiah's great-grandson.) Zephaniah's attacks on the sins of the elite—princes, priests, judges, and false prophets—suggest that he was acquainted with the powerful and that he had true boldness (see 3:3–5). The evils of Judah that he described match the religious corruption rooted out by Josiah's reform. If, as appears likely, Zephaniah preached shortly before 622, he contributed greatly to the reforms of Josiah's rule.

## FIRST AUDIENCE AND DESTINATION

**People in Judah Living During Zephaniah's Lifetime**

The first hearers were the kings and people living in Judah some 40 years before the Babylonian captivity.

## OCCASION

The specific occasion for Zephaniah's prophecies is not known. He stated only that "the word of the LORD" came to him (1:1). As noted above, however, his message fits the period of religious and social corruption during the early rule of Josiah (see 2 Kg 22–23). The revival Josiah instituted marked a genuine return to worship of the Lord. Zephaniah did not tell what prompted the collection of his writings.

# GOD'S MESSAGE IN ZEPHANIAH

## PURPOSE

This book preserves the divinely inspired prophecies that Zephaniah made during his ministry to Judah about four decades before Jerusalem's fall to Babylon. He argued that the coming "Day of the LORD" would involve God's judgment on God's people as well as on the pagan nations. God would later restore a remnant of His people, who would then worship Him forever as the King of Israel.

## FIRST PASS

The book of Zephaniah has a threefold structure governed by the three exhortations to "be silent" (1:7), "gather" and "seek the LORD" (2:1–3), and "wait" (3:8). In the

first section the exhortation is sandwiched between two announcements of the Lord's wrath. The exhortations begin the second and third sections.

**Be Silent (1:1–18)**

The prophecy opens in 1:2–6 with an announcement of total destruction for the whole "earth" (literally "ground" in 1:2–3) that would also include Judah (1:4–6). The argument is that if a universal judgment day is coming, then God will certainly judge His people. The command to "be silent" (1:7a) was often used in the presence of a person or event of great importance (Nm 13:30; Jdg 3:19; Neh 8:11; Hab 2:20; Zch 2:13). The prospect of such a horrifying outpouring of divine wrath calls for absolute silence.

**Seek the Lord (2:1–3:7)**

"Seeking" the Lord could refer either to desiring from Him a word of revelation (1:6) or to turning to Him in repentance. It is the opposite of either indifference to the Lord or abandoning Him. Judah was guilty of both, and the Lord had consequently turned His face (or favor) from them (see 1:6; Ex 33:7; Dt 4:29; 2 Ch 7:14; Jr 29:13; Hs 3:5; 5:6,15; 7:10). Genuinely seeking the Lord also means seeking righteousness and humility.

**Wait (3:8–20)**

In the face of such a dismal picture of human corruption, Zephaniah exhorted believers to "wait" for the Lord to come as witness, to pour out His wrath against all peoples, and to purify a remnant who will seek refuge in Him. To "wait" for the Lord means to "long for" Him (Jb 3:21; Is 30:18) and to place one's confident hope only in Him (Ps 33:20; Is 8:17; 64:4). God's purpose was to purify from the nations a people united to worship Him. The book concludes with a hymn of praise, an exhortation for restored Jerusalem to rejoice in the Lord's redemption.

## THE RELIABILITY OF ZEPHANIAH

Zephaniah is dated during the reign of king Josiah (1:1), who became king of Judah at age eight in 640 BC. He began to "seek the God of his ancestor David" eight years later, and four years after that he began a spiritual reformation of the land, in about 628 BC (2 Ch 34:3). The reformation became more fervent in 621 BC when the "book of the law" was discovered in the temple (2 Ch 34:8–33). Zephaniah was probably a major influence on the young king and hence predates the reforms. If the "Hezekiah" who is listed as Zephaniah's ancestor is the king by that name, that would explain the book's tracing Zephaniah's ancestry to four generations. His family connections would have given him access to the king. Zephaniah's prophecy is a tightly crafted unity with structural similarity to both Isaiah and Ezekiel.

## HOW ZEPHANIAH FITS INTO GOD'S STORY

1. Prologue: Creation, Fall, and the Need for Redemption
2. God Builds His Nation (2000–931 BC)
3. God Educates His Nation (931–586 BC)
4. God Keeps a Faithful Remnant (586–6 BC)
5. God Purchases Redemption and Begins the Kingdom (6 BC to AD 30)
6. God Spreads the Kingdom Through the Church (AD 30–?)
7. God Consummates Redemption and Confirms His Eternal Kingdom
8. Epilogue: New Heaven and New Earth

## CHRIST IN ZEPHANIAH

Zephaniah announced that the King of Israel was in their midst (3:15). Jesus was crucified as King of the Jews (Mk 15:26). As Judah did not recognize the presence of the divine King in their circumstances, so many Jewish leaders failed to recognize the presence of God in Jesus Christ.

## CHRISTIAN WORLDVIEW ELEMENTS

### Teachings About God

God is righteous and jealous for His people. In the coming "Day of the LORD," He will bring about justice on all who have shown their opposition to Him by living in violence and treachery, including those who claimed to belong to Him. Although there is no direct prediction of Christ or the coming of the Holy Spirit, Christians have understood Zephaniah's prediction of the day when "the King of Israel, Yahweh, is among you" (3:15) to refer to Jesus.

The citadel at Ashdod, one of the major cities of the Philistines. This fortress on the Mediterranean was built during the Ancient Arab Era (AD 640–1099). Zephaniah prophesied judgment for Israel and surrounding nations including the Philistines (2: 4–7), the Moabites and Ammonites (2: 8–11), the Ethiopians (2: 12), and the Assyrians (2: 13–15). Zephaniah called all nations to repent and become righteous and meek.

#### Teachings About Humanity

Zephaniah shows the universal tendency among humans toward evil. All kinds of people—Jerusalemites, Philistines, Moabites, Assyrians, and Ethiopians—will alike be condemned because of their sins against God. Arrogance, oppression, and violence deserve God's judgment, no matter what persons or nations have committed them.

#### Teachings About Salvation

Because of Zephaniah's emphasis on the Day of the Lord, his understanding of salvation focuses on God's subsequent blessing on the righteous remnant of Israel. God's restoration of the covenant people, however, also means that all the nations of the earth will know Him: "All of them may call on the name of Yahweh and serve Him with a single purpose" (3:9; cp. Rv 21:24–26).

## GENRE AND LITERARY STYLE

#### Prophecies Written Entirely in Hebrew Poetry

Zephaniah's prophecies both "forth tell" and "foretell." He includes the three classic elements of Hebrew prophecy: (1) call for people to turn from their sins in the face of divine judgment (which in fact happened); (2) predictions of near events (such as the fall of Judah and Jerusalem); and (3) predictions of remote events (such as the restoration of a remnant in righteousness).

The entire book is written in Hebrew poetry. Zephaniah's poetic style is largely dark: the coming Day of the Lord will be bitter; the penalties will be sure and severe. On the other hand, there are rays of light when he speaks of the coming time of renewal. In English Bibles, Zephaniah is the ninth of the 12 Minor Prophets. In the Hebrew canon it belonged to the composite book called "The Twelve." (See *Genre and Literary Style* for **HOSEA** for more information.)

## A PRINCIPLE TO LIVE BY

#### Judgment with Compassion (Zph 2:1–3, *Life Essentials Study Bible*, p. 1244–45)

When we speak of God's coming judgment, our primary purpose should always be to encourage unrepentant people to come to know the Lord Jesus Christ as personal Savior.

To access a video presentation of this principle featuring Dr. Gene Getz, use a Smartphone or iPad to connect to this QR code or go to http://www.bhpublishinggroup.com/handbook/zephaniah

◀ Darius I (521–486 BC), also known as Darius Hystaspes or the Great, was both extremely cruel and generous. Darius seized power following the death of Cambyses II, son of Cyrus. This is the Darius of Ezra (Ezr 4–6; Hg 1–2; Zch 1–8), under whom the temple in Jerusalem was reconstructed—completed in the sixth year of his reign. Darius continued Cyrus's policy of restoring disenfranchised peoples who were victims of Assyrian and Babylonian conquests. Darius reaffirmed Cyrus's authorization and also provided for maintenance of the temple.

▼ Darius left a record of his ancestry, lineage, and victories over enemies in what has come to be called the Behistun Inscription. This impressive inscription is carved into a massive rock over 325 feet above the ground, strategically located at the intersection of roads that connect Babylon and Ecbatana, the capitals of the Babylonian and Median empires. The inscription is written in cuneiform script in three languages: Old Persian, Elamite, and Babylonian. At great personal risk, Henry S. Rawlinson (1810–1895), scaled this massive cliff, copied, and decoded all three translations. Rawlinson's labors opened languages written in cuneiform script to scholars in much the same way that the Rosetta Stone was the key to understanding Egyptian hieroglyphs.

▶ A detailed look at part of the Behistun Inscription.

Haggai, the sixth-century prophet who returned to Judah from Babylonian exile, has given his name to this book as its composer. His name means "festive" in Hebrew.

## KEY TEXT: 1:8

*"'Go up into the hills, bring down lumber, and build the house. Then I will be pleased with it and be glorified,' says the LORD."*

## KEY TERM: "REBUILDING"

The primary focus of this book is rebuilding the Jewish temple in Jerusalem after the return from Babylonian captivity.

## ONE-SENTENCE SUMMARY

When Haggai proclaimed God's command to rebuild the temple, giving God's promises that the glory of the second temple would exceed that of the first temple, the people obeyed with a willing heart.

# ORIGINAL HISTORICAL SETTING

## AUTHOR AND DATE OF WRITING

**Haggai, Around 520 BC**

Haggai was a contemporary of Zechariah. Hardly anything is known about him. He did not note his lineage or his hometown. Presumably he was one of the exiles from Babylon that returned to Judah in the 530s. He did, however, date precisely the four occasions on which "the word of the LORD came" to him (1:1; 2:1,10,20). In modern equivalents, these dates are (1) August 29, 520; (2) October 17, 520; and (3) December 18, 520. According to Ezra 6:14, Haggai saw the successful conclusion of his ministry in the completion of the temple. Presumably he wrote down his messages as they were given to him, and he compiled them shortly thereafter.

## FIRST AUDIENCE AND DESTINATION

**Israelites in Jerusalem After They Returned from Exile**

The original hearers and destination are clearly stated. The first audience was the people of Jerusalem that had returned from exile. In particular, Zerubbabel the governor and Joshua the high priest were recipients of some of Haggai's exhortations.

## OCCASION

Ezra 4–5 describes the opposition that the returning exiles faced when they attempted to rebuild the temple. Opposition, however, became an excuse for inactivity. For more than 15 years, inertia ruled. God raised up Haggai to rouse the Jews from their inertia.

# GOD'S MESSAGE IN HAGGAI

## PURPOSE

This book preserves the divinely inspired sermons that Haggai gave during his ministry in the last months of 520 BC. These prophecies were originally for the people of Judah who had recently returned from the Babylonian captivity and were lethargic about their primary duty: to reestablish the true worship of God at His temple. Unlike most biblical prophets, Haggai's message was obeyed, and his sermons were kept as a permanent reminder of his ministry. From a broader perspective, the temple, the Jewish community, and a stable Jerusalem were important circumstances for the coming of Jesus more than five centuries later.

## FIRST PASS

The Babylonians destroyed Jerusalem and the temple 587 BC. In October 539 BC Cyrus, the Persian conquered Babylon and soon after announced that the people of Judah were free to return to their ancestral home. He even promised to help them rebuild their temple as part of a general policy of restoring foreign religious centers.

### Think Carefully About Your Ways

The leaders and people of Judah had allowed external opposition, discouragement, and self-interest to keep them from completing the task of rebuilding the Lord's temple (1:2–4; 2:3). The Lord's command through Haggai was to "build the house" for the pleasure and glory of God (1:8).

### Consider the Lord's Promises

The Lord assured His people of success through His presence (1:13–14; 2:4–5). He also promised them that He would reward their renewed work and dedication to Him by glorifying the temple and granting them peace (2:6–9) and blessing (2:18–19). Finally, He promised to restore the Davidic throne on the earth through a descendant of Zerubbabel (2:20–23).

## THE RELIABILITY OF HAGGAI

Eugene Merrill has observed that except for the prophet Ezekiel, no biblical authors have dated their activities and messages as precisely as Haggai and Zechariah.

God's message first came to Haggai in the second year of the Persian King Darius Hystaspes (522–486 BC) on the first day of the sixth month. Archaeological discoveries together with astronomical data enable us to translate this date to August 29, 520 BC. The four messages of Haggai take place within a chronological framework from this date to December 18, 520 BC.

## HOW HAGGAI FITS INTO GOD'S STORY

1. Prologue: Creation, Fall, and the Need for Redemption
2. God Builds His Nation (2000–931 BC)
3. God Educates His Nation (931–586 BC)
4. **God Keeps a Faithful Remnant (586–6 BC)**
5. God Purchases Redemption and Begins the Kingdom (6 BC to AD 30)
6. God Spreads the Kingdom Through the Church (AD 30–?)
7. God Consummates Redemption and Confirms His Eternal Kingdom
8. Epilogue: New Heaven and New Earth

## CHRIST IN HAGGAI

Through Haggai the Lord says He will shake the elements of creation and the nations. Then the nations will come to worship at the new temple that God will fill with His glory (2:6–7). Simeon saw in the baby Jesus a light for the Gentile nations and glory for Israel (Lk 2:32).

## CHRISTIAN WORLDVIEW ELEMENTS

### Teachings About God

God desires to be honored by His people (see *Key Text*). Because of this, He has the right to prescribe what pleases Him. His concern in the time of Haggai was to be worshipped properly in His temple.

### Teachings About Humanity

On one hand, the people that Haggai addressed needed to be rebuked. They were under a divine curse because of their inactivity concerning the things of God. It was not so much that they were actively evil but that they were passive when they should have been passionate. On the other hand, the book shows that people can be moved to do right things, but even this must be at God's initiative: "And the LORD stirred up . . . the spirit of all the remnant of the people" (1:14).

### Teachings About Salvation

The people who returned from exile were cured of the idolatry that took their ancestors into captivity. Haggai revived an emphasis from the era of the Davidic monarchy: the need for a temple as a place for redeemed people to worship.

## GENRE AND LITERARY STYLE

**Prophetic Sermons Written in Hebrew Prose**

Although Haggai was clearly a postexilic prophet, his prophecies both "forth tell" and "foretell" in the classic manner of the Hebrew prophets: (1) call for people to turn from their sins (in this case, the sin of unconcern for the temple) and (2) predictions of future events (such as the glory that would come to the second temple).

The book is written in Hebrew prose rather than poetry. In English Bibles, Haggai is the tenth of the 12 Minor Prophets. In the Hebrew canon it belonged to the composite book called "The Twelve." (See *Genre and Literary Style* for **HOSEA** for more information.)

## A PRINCIPLE TO LIVE BY

**Leadership Responsibility (Hg 1:1–11, *Life Essentials Study Bible*, p. 1251)**

Spiritual leaders in the church are to both model and teach the will of God.

To access a video presentation of this principle featuring Dr. Gene Getz, use a Smartphone or iPad to connect to this QR code or go to http://www.bhpublishinggroup.com/handbook/haggai

The signet ring of Cheops, king of Egypt in the early twenty-sixth century BC. The signet ring symbolizes the authority of the person. Yahweh's word to Zerubbabel that he would make him His signet ring (Hg 2:23) indicates that Zerubbabel would carry the authority to act as God's legitimate Davidic ruler.

Zechariah, the sixth-century prophet who returned to Judah from Babylonian exile, has given his name to this book as its composer. His name means "Yahweh remembers" in Hebrew.

## KEY TEXT: 8:3

*"The LORD says this: 'I will return to Zion and live in Jerusalem. Then Jerusalem will be called the Faithful City, the mountain of the LORD of Hosts, and the Holy Mountain.'"*

## KEY TERM: "JERUSALEM"

This book focuses on the city of Jerusalem, which still lay in ruins in Zechariah's day. Both the near-term rebuilding of the city and the ultimate, everlasting destiny of Jerusalem as the city in which God delights are in view.

## ONE-SENTENCE SUMMARY

Through night visions and prophetic oracles, Zechariah predicted the welfare of Jerusalem as God's beloved holy city into which the King—also called God's Servant and Branch—would enter riding a donkey.

"Then the LORD will go out to fight against those nations as He fights on a day of battle. On that day His feet will stand on the Mount of Olives, which faces Jerusalem on the east. The Mount of Olives will be split in half from east to west, forming a huge valley, so that half the mountain will move to the north and half to the south" (Zch 14:3–4).

## AUTHOR AND DATE OF WRITING

**Zechariah, Perhaps Around 518 BC**

Zechariah was a contemporary of Haggai. The only thing really known about him is that he was the son of Berechiah and grandson of Iddo (1:1). Presumably he was one of the exiles that returned to Judah in the 530s. He dated two of his visions, which enables scholars to integrate his ministry with that of Haggai. His initial call came in October or November 520 (1:1); the eight night visions came on February 15, 519 (1:7); a third message came on December 7, 518. Zechariah almost certainly did not live long enough to see the walls of Jerusalem rebuilt (in 445 BC, some 75 years after his initial call).

Most critical scholars have argued that Zechariah 9–14 was written by a later, unknown prophet, a "Deutero-Zechariah," with a different style and perspective. (This is parallel to the argument for a "Deutero-Isaiah." See *Author and Date of Writing* for **ISAIAH**.) There are, however, no really strong arguments for denying that the sixth-century prophet wrote the entire book. Presumably he wrote down his messages as they were given to him, and they were compiled shortly thereafter.

## FIRST AUDIENCE AND DESTINATION:

**Israelites in Jerusalem After They Returned from Exile**

The first audience was the people of Jerusalem that had returned from exile. In particular Zerubbabel the governor and Joshua the high priest received some of Zechariah's messages of encouragement.

## OCCASION

Zechariah described his prophetic call as simply "the word of the LORD." For more than 15 years the Jews had been back in Jerusalem, but the city was still in physical disarray. The walls were still ruined, and the people were questioning the future of the city. God raised up Zechariah to encourage these Jews with a vision of Jerusalem's glorious future. He did not tell what prompted the collection of his writings.

# GOD'S MESSAGE IN ZECHARIAH

## PURPOSE

This book preserves the divinely inspired prophecies that Zechariah received during his ministry in 520–518 BC (or possibly extending later). These prophecies were originally for the people of Judah who had recently returned from the Babylonian captivity and were uncertain about the future prospects for the city of Jerusalem,

once great but still in ruins from the Babylonian invasion. His message was essentially one of encouragement: the greatest days of Jerusalem lay in the glorious future. Because of Zechariah's messianic prophecies that Jesus fulfilled, the greatest glory of Jerusalem was that Jesus blessed the city with His presence.

## FIRST PASS

One feature of predictive prophecy in several biblical books but especially prominent in Zechariah is telescoping. Sometimes near and remote prophecies are so compressed together that it is difficult to tell whether a specific prediction is near or distant. This is like looking at two mountaintops through a telescope: they appear to be close together, but they are many miles apart. Zechariah's prophecies are like this. They include events all the way from his lifetime to the final glorious days of Jerusalem.

### Zechariah's Night Visions

The book and the visions are introduced by an initial call to "return" or repent. It was issued in October/November 520 BC about a month after work on the temple had resumed (1:1–6). The big question facing the generation of the restoration was whether they would return to faith in the Lord or repeat the sins of their fathers. The night visions apparently were all received February 15, 519 BC, about six months after the construction had resumed (1:7–6:8). The main themes of the night visions are (1) God's judgment of the nations, (2) His election and future blessing of Jerusalem, (3) the purification of the land, (4) rebuilding the temple, and (5) the leadership of Zerubbabel and Joshua.

### Crowning of Joshua

The oracle in this central and most prominent section of the book forms a hinge between the two larger sections. Like 3:1–10 it describes a messianic prototype receiving the signs of his office. The introduction, "the word of the LORD came to me" (occurring elsewhere only in Jeremiah and Ezekiel), also echoes 4:8, where it introduces an oracle promising Zerubbabel's completion of the temple. Rather than Zerubbabel, here only Joshua and "the Branch" are mentioned (6:9–15). Zechariah is told to make royal crowns (in Hebrew the word is plural) and to crown Joshua. Then the crowns are to be placed in the temple as a reminder of

Zerubbabel from one of Michelangelo's lunettes in the Sistine Chapel. The Lord's word through Zechariah to Zerubbabel: "Not by strength or by might , but by My Spirit says the LORD of Hosts" (Zch 4:6).

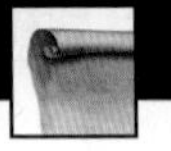


what God was going to do. This oracle spans both contemporary and future fulfillment of God's purposes. The passage's ambiguity regarding the number of crowns and the number of thrones is due to the need for both Zerubbabel and Joshua to foreshadow the Messiah, who would be both King and Priest.

**Two Oracles Concerning the Coming Kingdom**

Themes such as ceremonial days, the holiness of God's dwelling, universal worship of the Lord, the regathering of the exiles, and the repopulating of Jerusalem are introduced in chapters 7–8 and reappear in chapters 9–14. These last chapters were probably written after the temple was completed and contain two divine oracles or messages (chaps. 9–11 and 12–14). Both messages deal with God's establishing His kingdom on the earth. Both describe future events, some of which were fulfilled before Jesus' incarnation, some during Jesus' earthly ministry and some when He returns. Each oracle contains three main sections, but the first oracle concludes with a fourth section that acts as a hinge between the two oracles. It is the third of the commissioning ceremonies in Zechariah (see 3:1–10; 6:9–15).

## THE RELIABILITY OF ZECHARIAH

Zechariah's book contains three exact dates. The first two (1:1,7) pertain to the second year of Darius (Hystaspes), or 520 BC, and they correlate with the prophecies of Haggai. The third date (7:1) is from Darius's fourth year and marks the arrival of a delegation that came to worship the Lord and to ask about keeping a fast that commemorated the fall of Jerusalem. While Zechariah 1–8 deals with the rebuilding of the temple, the priesthood, and the future of Jerusalem, chapters 9–14 deal mostly with the distant future and the coming messianic kingdom. Because of this division, some have thought that these later chapters were written by another author. The evidence, however, does not require this conclusion, and the thematic unity of the book argues against it. It is just as likely that the social and political climate had changed in the country, and Zechariah's prophecies changed as a result. In this case it may be that these messianic prophecies were delivered sometime around 500 BC.

## HOW ZECHARIAH FITS INTO GOD'S STORY

1. Prologue: Creation, Fall, and the Need for Redemption
2. God Builds His Nation (2000–931 BC)
3. God Educates His Nation (931–586 BC)
4. **God Keeps a Faithful Remnant (586–6 BC)**
5. God Purchases Redemption and Begins the Kingdom (6 BC to AD 30)
6. God Spreads the Kingdom Through the Church (AD 30–?)
7. God Consummates Redemption and Confirms His Eternal Kingdom
8. Epilogue: New Heaven and New Earth

## CHRIST IN ZECHARIAH

The Gospels incorporate more passages from Zechariah than from any other prophet. In Zechariah we see foreshadowed the piercing of Jesus' body (12:10; cp. Jn 19:34,37; Rv 1:7).

## CHRISTIAN WORLDVIEW ELEMENTS

### Teachings About God

Zechariah emphasizes God's mercy—for His name's sake—on His beloved people. For this reason they will one day dwell in security and blessing in Jerusalem forever. God's Spirit is present to enable His servants (4:6). Jesus is predicted in a number of places: His royal entrance into Jerusalem (9:9); His betrayal for thirty silver pieces (11:12); and His role as Shepherd (13:7) and Branch (3:8; 6:12).

### Teachings About Humanity

In general, Zechariah looks forward to the time that God's people—having been punished for their sins—will be restored in righteousness. In particular, the book shows what God can accomplish through individuals committed to obedience. These exemplary persons are Zechariah the prophet, Joshua the priest (3:1–10), and Zerubbabel the governor (4:6–10). These men foreshadow the coming of the Messiah, the greatest Prophet, Priest, and King.

### Teachings About Salvation

Zechariah draws attention to the future redemption of God's people corporately, as they live safely in the land and He lives among them (chap. 8). This salvation will follow the horrible "Day of the LORD," when God will defeat the nations that have come against Jerusalem (chap. 14). All those who share in this salvation "will be holy to the LORD of Hosts" (14:21).

## GENRE AND LITERARY STYLE

### Prophecies, Including Visions and Words from God, Written Mainly in Hebrew Prose but with Some Poetry

Zechariah's prophecies both "forth tell" and "foretell." The book includes the three classic elements of Hebrew prophecy: (1) call for people to turn from their sins, (2) predictions of near events (such as God's blessing on Zerubbabel), and (3) predictions of remote events (such as the coming of the King to Jerusalem riding a donkey).

Like Ezekiel and Daniel, Zechariah received symbolic visions as a part of his ministry. These included both near and distant prophetic elements. The book is written mainly in good Hebrew prose, rather than poetry. Chapters 9–10 are the main poetic section. In English Bibles, Zechariah is the eleventh of the 12 Minor Prophets. In the Hebrew canon it belonged to the composite book called "The Twelve." (See *Genre and Literary Style* for **HOSEA** for more information.)

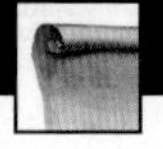


## A PRINCIPLE TO LIVE BY

**A Humble Servant (Zch 9:9, *Life Essentials Study Bible*, p. 1264)**

Though a day is coming when the Lord Jesus Christ will rule and reign as King of kings, we are to imitate His life as a humble servant when He came the first time.

To access a video presentation of this principle featuring Dr. Gene Getz, use a Smartphone or iPad to connect to this QR code or go to http://www.bhpublishinggroup.com/handbook/zechariah

The garden of Gethsemane on the Mount of Olives. Zechariah's prophecy closes by focusing on God's deliverance of Jerusalem in the last days and His coronation as King of all the earth. Jerusalem's initial defeat will be turned to victory when the Lord appears. The site of His greatest agony, the garden of Gethsemane on the Mount of Olives, will witness His greatest glory (Mt 26:30–45).

Malachi, the fifth-century prophet to Judah, has given his name to this book as its composer. His name means "My messenger" in Hebrew.

## KEY TEXT: 1:11

*"'For My name will be great among the nations, from the rising of the sun to its setting. Incense and pure offerings will be presented in My name in every place because My name will be great among the nations,' says Yahweh of Hosts."*

## KEY TERM: "MESSENGER"

Malachi, God's messenger, noted that while true priests of God served as His messengers (2:7), God would one day send "My messenger" (3:1, John the Baptist) to prepare the way for "the Messenger of the covenant" (3:1, Jesus).

## ONE-SENTENCE SUMMARY

Malachi rebuked God's people for specific violations of the covenant, such as laws concerning sacrifices, divorce, and tithes, but he also prophesied the coming of the Messenger who will set all things right.

# ORIGINAL HISTORICAL SETTING

## AUTHOR AND DATE OF WRITING

**Malachi, Perhaps Around 450 or 420 BC**

The prophet did not name his parents or the rulers of his day, which makes precise dating of his life impossible. Almost nothing is known about him. He was probably born in the land of Judah after the exiles began returning from Babylon in the 530s BC. Presumably he wrote down his messages as they were given to him, and they were compiled shortly thereafter.

## FIRST AUDIENCE AND DESTINATION

**Israelites in Judah After the Babylonian Exile**

The first audience was the people of Judah of the second or third generation after the return from captivity who had become lethargic in their relationship to God.

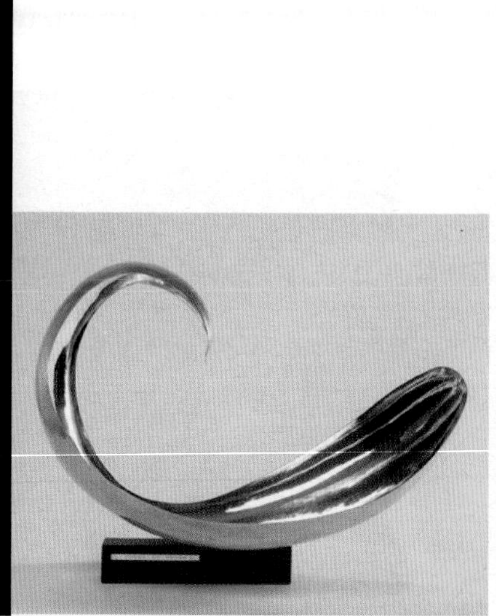

Hand-smithed silver object. "'See, I am going to send My messenger, and he will clear the way before Me. Then the Lord you seek will suddenly come to His temple , the Messenger of the covenant you desire—see, He is coming,' says the LORD of Hosts. But who can endure the day of His coming? And who will be able to stand when He appears? For He will be like a refiner's fire and like cleansing lye. He will be like a refiner and purifier of silver; He will purify the sons of Levi and refine them like gold and silver. Then they will present offerings to the LORD in righteousness" (Mal 3:1–4a).

## OCCASION

Malachi described his prophecy as "the word of the LORD to Israel" (1:1). He did not tell about receiving visions or describe the mechanism by which God spoke to him. Malachi had as strong a sense of being God's mouthpiece as any of the prophets who had preceded him, and he often spoke as the voice of God using the pronoun "I." He did not tell what prompted the collection of his writings.

# GOD'S MESSAGE IN MALACHI

## PURPOSE

The book of Malachi preserves the divinely inspired words received by the prophet during his (possibly brief) ministry around 450 or 420 BC. These prophecies were originally for the second or third generation of people in Judah after the return from the Babylonian captivity. The temple was functioning and the city was rebuilt, but people had become perfunctory in their worship and lifestyles. His message was essentially one of accusation: as God's messenger, he charged them with violations of the covenant and gave specific examples. But he also looked ahead to a time of wonderful blessing.

## FIRST PASS

### Questioning

Malachi presented Judah's sins largely on the people's own lips, quoting their words, thoughts, and attitudes (1:2, 6–7,12–13; 2:14,17; 3:7–8,13–15). Malachi was faced with the failure of the priests of Judah to fear the Lord and to serve the people conscientiously during difficult times. This neglect had contributed to Judah's

Silver ore from a rich silver vein. Even so, a high temperature is required to transform the ore to silver. For sterling silver some 1650 degrees is required; for pure silver, over 1750 degrees.

indifference toward the will of God. Blaming their economic and social troubles on the Lord's supposed unfaithfulness to them, the people were treating one another faithlessly (especially their wives) and were profaning the temple by marrying pagan women. They were also withholding their tithes from the temple.

**Turning**

Malachi called the people to turn from their spiritual apathy and correct their wrong attitudes about worship by trusting God with genuine faith as their living Lord. This included honoring the Lord's name with pure offerings, being faithful to covenants made with fellow believers, especially marriage covenants, and signifying their repentance with tithes.

**Warning**

If the priests would not alter their behavior, the Lord would curse them, shame them, and remove them from service. Malachi also announced a coming day when the Lord of justice would come to purge and refine His people. At that time He would make evident the distinction between the obedient and the wicked and would judge the wicked.

**Remembering**

Malachi based his instruction on (1) the Lord's demonstration of love for Israel (1:2), (2) their spiritual and covenant unity with God and with one another (2:10), and (3) that coming day when the Lord would also abundantly bless those who fear Him (3:1–6; 3:16–4:3).

## THE RELIABILITY OF MALACHI

Although the book is not dated by a reference to a ruler or a specific event, internal evidence, as well as its position in the canon, favors a postexilic date. Reference to a governor in 1:8 favors the Persian period when Judah was a province or subprovince of the Persian satrapy Abar Nahara, a territory that included Palestine, Syria, Phoenicia, Cyprus, and, until 485 BC, Babylon. The temple had been rebuilt (515 BC) and worship established (1:6–11; 2:1–3; 3:1,10), but the excitement and enthusiasm for which the prophets Haggai and Zechariah were the catalysts had waned. The social and religious problems Malachi addressed reflect the situation portrayed in Ezra 9–10 and Nehemiah 5 and 13, suggesting dates either just before Ezra's return (c. 460 BC) or just before Nehemiah's second term as governor (Neh 13:6–7; c. 435 BC).

## HOW MALACHI FITS INTO GOD'S STORY

1. Prologue: Creation, Fall, and the Need for Redemption
2. God Builds His Nation (2000–931 BC)
3. God Educates His Nation (931–586 BC)
4. **God Keeps a Faithful Remnant (586–6 BC)**
5. God Purchases Redemption and Begins the Kingdom (6 BC to AD 30)
6. God Spreads the Kingdom Through the Church (AD 30–?)
7. God Consummates Redemption and Confirms His Eternal Kingdom
8. Epilogue: New Heaven and New Earth

## CHRIST IN MALACHI

Malachi describes Christ as the sun of righteousness who brings healing to His people. He also comes as a refiner's fire to purify the sons of Levi so they can make an offering in righteousness.

## CHRISTIAN WORLDVIEW ELEMENTS

### Teachings About God

Malachi presents God's immutability (He does not change). For this reason His promises are enduring. Further, He is One who judges rightly, beginning with His own people. The eternal God, moreover, is personal, as frequent use of the pronoun "I" in this book emphasizes. Christ is prophesied as the Messenger who will purify priests and people alike (3:1–5). The Holy Spirit is not mentioned.

### Teachings About Humanity

God's people were addressed in this book, yet they were disheartened and disillusioned. The promises that earlier prophets had made of a coming golden age seemed empty. These people illustrate that in times when God does not appear to be acting on behalf of His people, it is easy for them to become complacent. It is even easy for them to be apathetic about obeying God's specific moral commands. This book offers God's cure for such doubtful people.

### Teachings About Salvation

Redemption in Malachi has two aspects. First is the notion of the covenant (mentioned six times). Salvation comes because God has initiated it in His covenant. Second is the work of the coming Messenger. Malachi predicted that His coming would bring cleansing: "He will be like a refiner's fire and like cleansing lye" (3:2). The implications of this prophecy would not be entirely clear until Jesus fulfilled it by His atoning death.

## GENRE AND LITERARY STYLE

**Disputations and Prophecies Written in Hebrew Prose**

As a prophetic writer, Malachi included materials in an unusual format, although he included classic elements of "forth telling" and "foretelling." His "forth telling" emphasized the sins of the people caused by their indifference to God. His "foretelling" focused on distant events (such as the coming of John the Baptist and Jesus).

The entire book is written in Hebrew prose. The prophet used a number of vivid metaphors, however. In English Bibles, Malachi is the last of the 12 Minor Prophets. In the Hebrew canon it belonged to the composite book called "The Twelve." (See *Genre and Literary Style* for **HOSEA** for more information.)

## A PRINCIPLE TO LIVE BY

**Second Coming (Mal 3:1–6, *Life Essentials Study Bible*, p. 1276)**

We are always to be prepared for the Lord's second coming.

To access a video presentation of this principle featuring Dr. Gene Getz, use a Smartphone or iPad to connect to this QR code or go to http://www.bhpublishinggroup.com/handbook/malachi

Sunrise on the Sea of Galilee. "'For My name will be great among the nations, from the rising of the sun to its setting. Incense and pure offerings will be presented in My name in every place because My name will be great among the nations,' says Yahweh of Hosts" (1:11).

*Canon* is the term used to describe the list of books approved for inclusion in the Bible. It stems from a Greek word meaning "rod," as in a straight stick that serves as a standard for measuring. Hence, to speak of the biblical canon is to speak of authoritative books, given by God, the teachings of which define correct belief and practice. Obviously, only books inspired by God should be received as canonical. The Bible before you includes 27 books in the New Testament (NT). Are these the right books? Do they reliably convey truth about Jesus Christ? This essay argues that the 27 books of the NT canon are the correct books and are fully reliable in recounting truth about Jesus and His earliest followers.

The oldest manuscript fragment of the New Testament, designated Rylands Library Papyrus P52 from the Gospel of John.

## ORIGIN AND RELIABILITY OF THE NEW TESTAMENT WRITINGS

The reliability of the NT books rests on questions about their origin: Were they written by eyewitnesses and men closely linked to them? Were the authors inspired by God as they wrote? Historic Christianity has answered yes to these questions. While skeptics maintain that the books were written by men who were inheritors of a legend that had slipped the bonds of reality, Christian confidence in the NT is well founded. Following are some lines of evidence supporting the reliability of the NT.

1. *Jesus personally groomed 12 disciples.* At the outset of His ministry, Jesus did what many gifted teachers of the ancient world did: He chose a small group of men to be His official students. For approximately three years they listened closely to Jesus' teachings and witnessed His actions. Jesus was intentional in His efforts to teach them; He used effective teaching tools such as parables, repetition, and visual aids. He also taught them *how* to spread His message (Mk 6:7–11) and then commanded them to give their lives to this task after His resurrection (Mt 28:18–20).

Despite many halts and hitches on the path to understanding, the disciples were

Jesus taught the multitudes but gave intensive training to the 12 disciples over a three-year period. Jesus' resurrection and the coming of the Holy Spirit at Pentecost were the catalysts that illuminated the teachings of Jesus and provided the disciples the lens for seeing both the power and the coherence of His teaching.

dedicated to the tasks of comprehending Jesus' teachings and remembering them with precision. But how much could they remember decades later when they and their associates wrote the four Gospels? Three considerations suggest the disciples would have had no trouble remembering Jesus' teachings.

First, note that from the time they last walked with Jesus to the time the Gospels were written, the disciples gave unbroken attention to spreading the word about Jesus. This became their purpose in life. Hence, Jesus' teachings stayed fresh in their minds through the years as they preached in city after city and were continually challenged to defend their claims.

Second, most of us today have lost touch with the potential powers of the human memory. We store reams of data not in our minds but in books and computers. Lack of such tools forced the ancients to make better use of the brain's storage capacities. The Jews in particular were impressive in this regard. As a people to whom God had revealed His will in spoken and written words, Jewish students of religion were motivated to achieve Herculean feats of memorization. It was said that advanced students were like basketfuls of books; they kept *everything* in their heads. Though Jesus' disciples lacked this level of training, it is certain that from the moment they were called to be Jesus' students they knew that they were expected to comprehend and remember His teachings. To do anything less would be to disrespect their teacher, especially since they believed He was the Messiah.

Third, it is likely that the disciples wrote down key portions of Jesus' teachings many years before the full Gospels were written. These deposits would have been available to refresh the memory, and they possibly served as handy source material for the writing of the Gospels (see Lk 1:1–4).

2. *The Holy Spirit helped the disciples understand and remember.* Jesus sent the Spirit to help His disciples comprehend and remember His teachings (Jn 14:26). Thus they were not left to their own efforts when speaking and writing about Jesus. Internal testimony in the NT shows that the disciples became aware of the Spirit's role in one another's writings. The Jews stressed the difference between inspired Scripture and ordinary writing. Rabbis even said the Scriptures "defiled the hands," a surprising phrase that encouraged Jews to consider carefully their intentions before handling Scripture and to decide if these justified the trouble of becoming ceremonially unclean. This teaching discouraged flippant handling of the Scriptures. To claim that a document is from God would be blasphemous if untrue, and yet this is the claim made by the NT itself. In 1 Timothy 5:18 Paul quotes Luke 10:7 as Scripture. Similarly, Peter affirms that Paul's writings are Scripture in 1 Peter 3:15–16. Peter's writings were in turn received as Scripture on the basis of his apostleship. While it is doubtful that NT authors were conscious at the time of writing that what they wrote was inspired Scripture (for example, see Luke's purpose statement in Lk 1:1–4), they were aware that they bore God-given authority as chosen messengers,

and the church swiftly received their writings as authoritative, inspired words from God.

3. *The NT writings stress the importance of eyewitnesses and hard facts.* The NT authors emphasize the role of eyewitnesses and hang their truth claims on the reality of the events they describe. For instance, when Luke discloses his methods and purposes at the beginning of his Gospel (Lk 1:1–4), he says his book is about "the events that have been fulfilled among us" as recounted by "the original eyewitnesses and servants" of Christ. He also says he researched these matters carefully before writing and that his reason for doing this was so his reader could "know the certainty" on which the Christian faith is based. Here is a man who has no place for legends, half-truths, or shots in the dark. His focus is on the real Jesus and on world-altering events that cannot be doubted. John similarly emphasizes the importance of *fact*. He is sure of what he has written and says he has included only a small fraction of Jesus' doings (Jn 20:30; 21:24–25). And like Luke, John wants his readers to know Jesus as Lord and thus gain eternal life (Jn 20:31; 1 Jn 5:13). Far from passing on shady legends, his goal is to convey assured truth.

Luke and John impress us with their insistence on truth, but the most striking assertion that the NT witness is truthful comes from the apostle Paul. Paul bitterly opposed the young church as it spread from Jerusalem like wildfire. As a zealot for Pharisaic doctrines and all the old ways, he wanted to eradicate Christianity. This all changed when the risen Lord appeared to him on the road to Damascus. In a stunning reversal, Paul then poured the rest of his life into spreading truth about Jesus. The foundation of Paul's preaching was Jesus' resurrection. More than just a snappy preaching point, Paul understood that the literal resurrection of Christ was the absolute basis of Christianity. For this reason, in 1 Corinthians 15:12–19, Paul said that if Christ's resurrection was not a real historical event, Christianity is a myth and Christians are liars. How could Paul dare lay his faith and personal integrity on the line like this? The answer is obvious. Like John, Luke, and every other NT author, Paul knew that Christianity is fixed on the sure foundation of historical reality. You can be confident that God the Son came in flesh, dwelt among humans, trained disciples for His service, died for us on the cross, rose on the third day, and then ascended to heaven, from which He will someday return in power.

Summing up, the NT is to be received as reliable on the basis of the following facts: Jesus trained a group of disciples to comprehend and spread His teachings. Following the established pattern among Jewish students of religion, they would have taken this task with great seriousness, including the memorization of Jesus' key teachings. For a decade or so after Christ's resurrection, these men kept His teachings alive by preaching incessantly and by grooming avid disciples such as Luke and Mark. They also accepted Paul as a bona fide apostle after his miraculous conversion (Ac 9). Then, starting in the mid 40s, the apostles and their approved

associates began writing authoritative, Spirit-inspired letters, which they circulated among the churches. Paul's writings came first and later the Gospels. These writings were received as Scripture by the earliest churches and became the standards by which doctrine and practice were judged.

## FACTORS IN THE FORMATION OF THE NEW TESTAMENT CANON

If one asks when and how the canon formed, the first thing to note is that the canon, being a list of books and not the books themselves, necessarily came into existence *after* the books were written. Thus the authoritative books were inspired Scripture prior to a list identifying them as such. Second, the canon formed as a matter of widespread consensus, not executive pronouncement. Third, in keeping with the first two points, it was several centuries before the canon emerged as a widely acknowledged fact. Critics take this relatively late emergence as proof that the books were not initially received as Scripture and that they came to be regarded as holy books only because later Christians lost sight of how they originated. In reality, however, the piecemeal development of canon consensus was a natural reflection of four conditions:

1. *The gradual creation and dissemination of the NT books.* The books of the canonical NT were written over a span of approximately 50 years (AD 45–95). Before winning universal acceptance, each newly written book had to be circulated, copied, examined, and discussed among the churches. This was not a quick process. Books that were written relatively late underwent the sort of treatment that is common for newcomers: they were vetted with especially great care before being granted a seat among the old guard. Also, the Christian faith multiplied rapidly in the early centuries, with new churches cropping up in far-flung regions at a pace that outstripped the dissemination of the Scriptures. Thus, many early churches had access to only a few NT books. Naturally, when new books came to their attention, they were cautious about embracing them as biblical, and they accepted them only after careful consideration and consultation with churches that had been founded by the apostles.

2. *Apostolic authority and the NT canon.* All the earliest churches were founded by the apostles and their associates as they fanned out from Jerusalem in the years after Jesus' resurrection. Naturally, the churches depended on these men to teach them about Jesus and the Christian life. At first these teachings were strictly oral, but over time the apostles began writing letters and Gospels for the churches, thus providing early Christians with authoritative "books" to guide them in their beliefs and practices. These apostolic churches were among the first to receive the

Scriptures as they were written, and so they were in a good position to help guide newer churches into the correct identification of a NT canon.

3. *The relative independence of each local church*. Apostolic authority was honored by all true churches at the advent of Christianity, and yet each local church was relatively independent from any centralized ecclesiastical authority. One practical result of this was that no central office pronounced the identities of the NT books or forced their use in worship abroad. Understandably, it took several centuries for churches sprawled all over the map to forge communicative ties and common consensus on the canon.

4. *The rise of heresy.* When someone came into the churches pushing ideas contrary to what had been received from the apostles, their teachings were recognized as unauthorized innovation. This happened in the second century with the advent of so-called Gnostic Christianity. Gnosticism was a popular dualistic Greek philosophy which held that the material world was created by an evil god. Hence, Gnostics stressed meditation on the secrets of a pure invisible realm, and they denied that God could take on material flesh as Christ did. A man named Marcion wedded Gnosticism with Christian elements and petitioned the church in Rome to adopt his views. Among other perversions, Marcion tried to convince Christians to reject the Old Testament Scriptures and adhere only to the writings of Paul plus a heavily edited version of Luke's Gospel that did not mention Christ's birth. As inheritors of

Irenaeus (late second century) quotes from 22

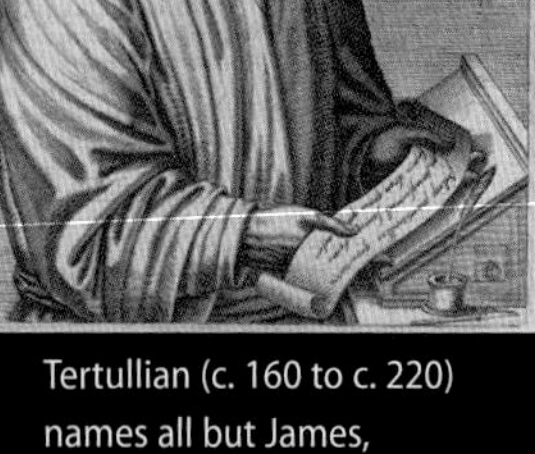

Tertullian (c. 160 to c. 220) names all but James,

Origen (c. 185–c. 254) named all 27 of the NT

the apostolic teachings, Christians in Rome and elsewhere knew that Marcion's teachings did not square with genuine Christian doctrines. As churches marked the distinction between authorized apostolic writings and the heretical innovations of men such as Marcion, and as Christians across the Roman Empire endured periodic persecutions that threatened death to anyone harboring Christian Scriptures, the NT began to emerge as a defined and defended body of books. So-called "alternative Christianities," represented in second- and third-century works such as *The Gospel of Thomas* and *The Gospel of Judas*, were never considered for adoption into the NT canon because they were written long after the apostles, and their teachings did not match the Old Testament or the apostolic traditions.

## AUTHORITATIVE WITNESSES TO THE CANON IN THE EARLY CHURCH

Though it took several centuries for the canon to emerge as a definite collection of books that were agreed upon by the majority of churches, it is certain that many of the books were widely recognized as Scripture from early on. For example, in AD 96 Clement of Rome quoted from Jesus' Sermon on the Mount (Mt 5–7) and treated it as Scripture. As a member of a church founded by an apostle, Clement probably had access to all or nearly all 27 canonical books at this time. In AD 110 Ignatius of Antioch, who was a disciple of John, claimed the Gospel materials were Scripture. By AD 180, the famed apologist Irenaeus defended Christianity by appealing to the authority of many NT writings. In total, scholars who have examined Irenaeus's surviving works believe he used 22 of our 27 NT books, including all four Gospels. A short time after Irenaeus, an apologist named Tertullian charged Gnostic Christians with misusing "the instrument," by which he meant the collection of authoritative NT books. That he would refer to the collection of NT books in this way proves that by this time the leading churches had identified a well-defined set of books as canonical. Only James, 1 Peter, and 2 and 3 John go unnamed by Tertullian. A few decades later the church father Origen named all 27 books and noted that six of them (Hebrews, James, 1 Peter, 2 and 3 John, and Jude) were disputed by some. These disputed books went on to be the subject of debate for many centuries more, though their revered position among most churches was never shaken.

In the fourth century the NT canon clearly emerged as a widely accepted set of holy books. First, Eusebius of Caesarea, known as the father of church history since he was the first to write a comprehensive history of Christianity, named 27 books that were commonly accepted as NT Scripture by the churches. He had reservations about the book of Revelation, but all in all he named the same canon we use today. In AD 367 the bishop of Alexandria, a stalwart man named Athanasius, wrote a festal letter in which he listed all 27 NT books as Scripture. He made no note about disputed books—an indication that the disputes mentioned by Origen and Eusebius had diminished in importance by this time. A little more than a decade later, the renowned scholar Jerome translated all 27 NT books into Latin and included them in his Bible, which is commonly called the Vulgate. As for the disputed books, he was convinced that their long-standing acceptance in the churches proved that they were indeed Scripture. Augustine, bishop of Hippo, agreed that the 27 were all canonical. Of the disputed books he said they are to be accepted because the majority of churches, especially those accorded great authority due to their apostolic origins, have long accepted them. Finally, in 393 and 397 the Councils of Hippo and Carthage concluded that the NT canon properly includes 27 books, no more and no less.

## THE CANON FROM THE REFORMATION TO THE PRESENT

The Reformation era was a time in which many beliefs and practices were reexamined in the light of Scripture. Men such as Luther and Calvin desired to peel away the traditions of men and take their cues only from God's authoritative Word. This emphasis highlighted the need to be certain about which books were from God and which were not. When Luther published a German translation of the NT in 1522, he included all 27 books of the traditional canon even though he sounded a few notes of disapproval over the disputed books. In the table of contents, he listed them separately from the undisputed books. For Luther, it seems, the books of the NT were divided into first-class and second-class canons. All 27 books were from God, but he did not believe Hebrews, James, Jude, and Revelation measured up to the others. Despite Luther's reservations, Christianity's long-standing acceptance of a 27-book NT canon was not seriously questioned. In 1546 the Roman Catholic Church affirmed all 27 books at the Council of Trent, and a hundred years later the Protestants did the same in the Westminster Confession of Faith. No sustained challenge to the canon has arisen in the churches since that era.

## PRESERVATION OF THE MANUSCRIPTS THROUGH THE CENTURIES

It has become popular in recent decades for skeptics to claim that the NT books have evolved beyond all recognition since the days when they were written. Amateur copyists, hapless monks, rogue theologians, sly politicians—folk from many quarters are said to have had a turn at corrupting the text by adding, deleting, and modifying at will. One popular critic famously says that the total number of variations found in the existing manuscripts exceeds the number of words in the

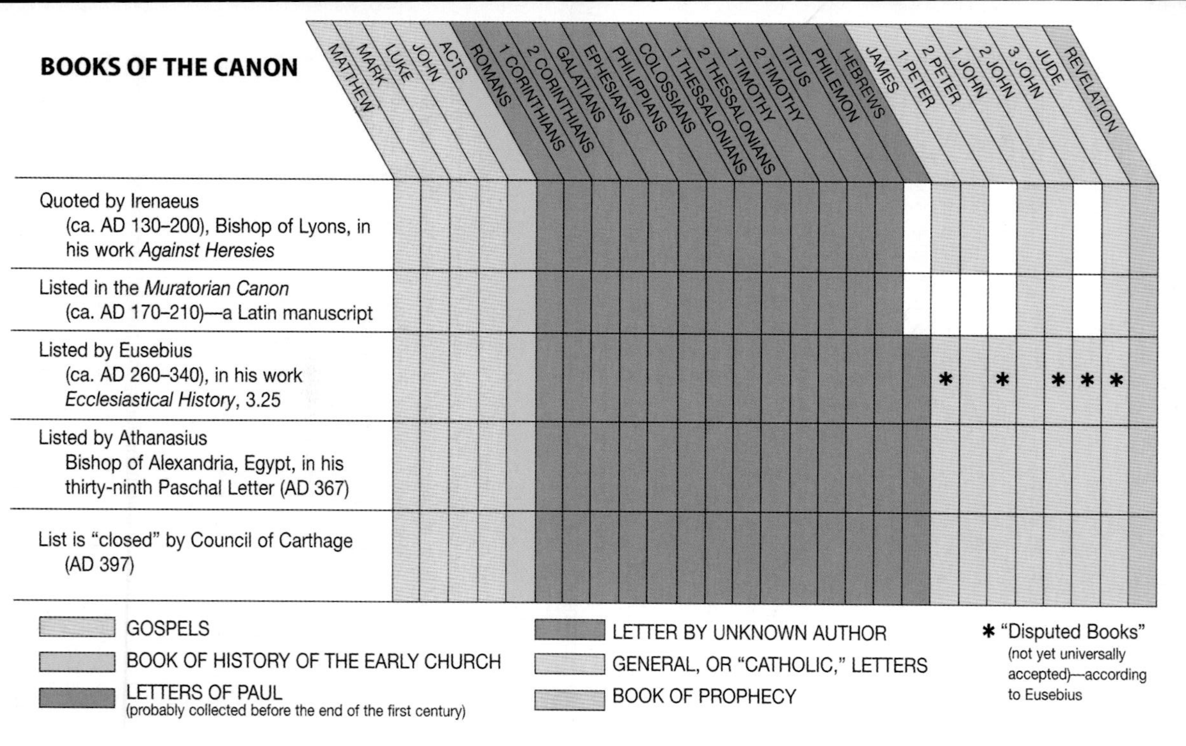
BOOKS OF THE CANON
MATTHEW
MARK
LUKE
JOHN
ACTS
ROMANS
1 CORINTHIANS
2 CORINTHIANS
GALATIANS
EPHESIANS
PHILIPPIANS
COLOSSIANS
1 THESSALONIANS
2 THESSALONIANS
1 TIMOTHY
2 TIMOTHY
TITUS
PHILEMON
HEBREWS
JAMES
1 PETER
2 PETER
1 JOHN
2 JOHN
3 JOHN
JUDE
REVELATION
Quoted by Irenaeus (ca. AD 130–200), Bishop of Lyons, in his work Against Heresies
Listed in the Muratorian Canon (ca. AD 170–210)—a Latin manuscript
Listed by Eusebius (ca. AD 260–340), in his work Ecclesiastical History, 3.25
*
*
*
*
*
Listed by Athanasius Bishop of Alexandria, Egypt, in his thirty-ninth Paschal Letter (AD 367)
List is "closed" by Council of Carthage (AD 397)
GOSPELS
BOOK OF HISTORY OF THE EARLY CHURCH
LETTERS OF PAUL
(probably collected before the end of the first century)
LETTER BY UNKNOWN AUTHOR
GENERAL, OR "CATHOLIC," LETTERS
BOOK OF PROPHECY
* "Disputed Books"
(not yet universally accepted)—according to Eusebius

entire NT! Technically his claim is true, but the conclusions to be drawn from it are far less drastic than he would have us believe. The fact is the vast majority of all changes are easily detected, and they amount to nothing more than simple misspellings and other minor alterations that have no impact whatsoever on the meaning of the NT. In the few places where the changes potentially have theological importance, scholars are often able to trace the text back to its original reading with confidence. In cases where the original reading is in greater dispute, textual scholars have rightly said that you could eliminate all such verses from the NT and not detract from a single vital doctrine of Christianity. In other words, none of the corrupted verses serve as the sole basis for any NT doctrine. So even if we dropped such verses from the Bible, we could always point to undisputed verses elsewhere in the NT as support for the doctrine in question. In this light we see that the variants are not very important. A fair assessment of the evidence reveals that the NT manuscripts have been preserved remarkably well through centuries of transmission. Aside from inconsequential alterations, the NT manuscripts on which our translation is based are close replications of the original writings.

## CONCLUSION

The churches that initially received the letters and Gospels written by the apostles and their commissioned associates understood that the writings were Scripture, for they came from men who were recognized as the authorized exponents of Jesus' life and message. These writings were copied with care and circulated to other churches. Awareness of the approved books among Christians increased as the decades clicked away, for slowly the copies reached churches that sprang up far from the point of Christian origins in Israel. It is nevertheless true that many sincere Christian devotees in the early centuries would have been unaware of several or even many of the inspired works since many newer churches had little or no access to Scripture. Hence, the fact that the canon was not widely described until the fourth century does not mean the canon itself was an open question among those who were in a good position to judge the matter. After all, we find clear references to most of the canonical books in the writings of the early church fathers, and certainly Christians who worshipped at churches founded by the apostles had an early grasp of the NT canon since their churches were among those that received the original writings in the first century. It is no exaggeration to say that once the practical obstacles to travel, communication, and dissemination of the manuscripts were alleviated, the 27-book NT canon quickly became the consensus position in Christendom.

Looking back, it is apparent that all the books that were admitted into the canon met the following criteria: (a) they were written either by an apostle or a sanctioned associate of the apostles; (b) they had enjoyed wide and long-standing usage in the churches, especially churches that were founded by the apostles; (c) they reflected high praise for Jesus, were true to the apostolic tradition that had been handed down to the churches, and fit with the overall theology of the other biblical books in both testaments.

In summary, church history shows that great care was taken when candidate books were assessed; the fact that a number of the books in our canon were repeatedly quizzed for their merits proves this beyond all doubt. Our NT canon is a well-proven, carefully protected heritage in which Christians can rejoice and place their full confidence.

This title has been associated with the first Gospel as long as it has been known. It was named this because its author was believed to be Matthew, the apostle of Jesus.

## KEY TEXT: 16:16,18

*"Simon Peter answered, 'You are the Messiah, the Son of the living God!'"*
*"And I also say to you that you are Peter, and on this rock I will build My church, and the forces of Hades will not overpower it."*

## KEY TERM: "MESSIAH"

This book shows Jesus' fulfillment of the Scriptures as the promised Messiah more emphatically than any other Gospel.

## ONE-SENTENCE SUMMARY

In His life, death, and resurrection, Jesus fulfilled the prophecies about the Jewish Messiah and created the church.

The Herodium, a fortress-palace built by Herod the Great about four miles southeast of Bethlehem, 7.5 miles south of Jerusalem. Herod was buried there. In 40 BC, Herod retreated to Masada after the Parthians took Syria. On this location near Bethlehem, he clashed with and defeated the Parthians. To commemorate his victory, Herod built a town on the site of the battle and named it for himself. Herod plays an important role in Matthew's account of Jesus' birth and early childhood (2:1–23).

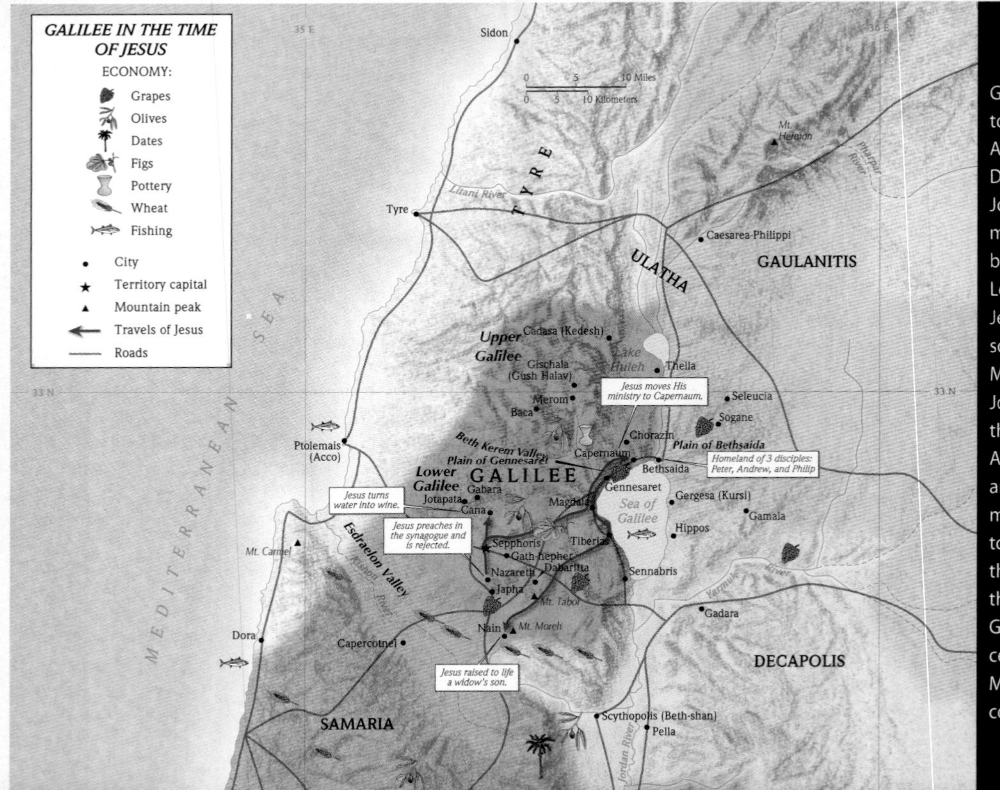


Galilee was the region given to the tribes of Naphtali, Asher, Issachar, Zebulun, and Dan during the time of Joshua. It covered approximately the 45-mile stretch between the Litani River in Lebanon and the Valley of Jezreel in Israel north to south and from the Mediterranean Sea to the Jordan River west to east. In the time of Jesus, Herod Antipas governed Galilee and Perea. Jesus devoted most of His earthly ministry to Galilee, being known as the Galilean (Mt 26:69). After the fall of Jerusalem in AD 70, Galilee became the major center of Judaism. The Mishnah and Talmud were collected and written there.

# ORIGINAL HISTORICAL SETTING

## AUTHOR AND DATE OF WRITING

**Matthew the Apostle, Perhaps Around AD 55–65**

The book is anonymous, but early Christian tradition uniformly affirmed that Matthew composed this Gospel. He was also known as Levi, a tax collector ("publican") whom Jesus called to be an apostle (Mt 9:9; Mk 2:14). The organization and fondness for numbers in the book point to an author interested in mathematical precision. Many scholars of the past two centuries have denied that Matthew wrote this book, partly because of their belief that the author fabricated many of the

Waterfall at Banias in the vicinity of Caesarea Philippi where Jesus asked His disciples the famous question about His identity. When He asked them who men said He was, they answered that people were identifying Him with Elijah, John the Baptist, or one of the prophets (Mk 8:27–33; Mt 16:13–23). Jesus then asked them, "Who do you say that I am?" (Mt 16:15). Peter, acting as the group's spokesman, replied with his famous statement that Jesus is the Messiah.

details, such as the miracles of Jesus. Such invention is harder to explain if the account was written by an eyewitness to Christ's life. The Christian tradition of authorship by Matthew is surely correct.

Because most scholars believe Matthew used Mark's Gospel as a source, Matthew should be dated in the AD 50s or later. Matthew quoted Jesus' prophecy of the coming destruction of the temple (24:2; fulfilled in AD 70) without mentioning that it had come to pass as Jesus said. This leads many conservative scholars to conclude that Matthew published his Gospel before 70. Others, however, accept the decade of the 70s. Critical scholars uniformly date Matthew after 70, perhaps near the end of the first century. A typical conservative estimate for its composition is the decade from 55 to 65.

## FIRST AUDIENCE AND DESTINATION

### Jewish Christians, Perhaps Living in Antioch of Syria

Matthew did not directly mention his audience, but his interest in showing that Jesus fulfilled the Scriptures points to a Jewish-Christian audience. He began his Gospel with a genealogy that recalls the entire history of the Jewish people, also pointing in this direction. This understanding has generally been held throughout Christian history.

Antioch of Syria is a best-guess deduction. This major Roman city had a significant number of Greek-speaking Jewish Christians involved in carrying out Jesus' missionary commission (Mt 28:18–20; Ac 11:19; 13:1–3). Further, the first known quotation from this Gospel was made by Ignatius of Antioch in three of his letters in the early second century.

## OCCASION

Matthew did not explain what prompted him to write. The assessment of many students is that he composed his Gospel largely to help Jewish Christians interpret Jesus as the fulfillment of the Scriptures. Most scholars believe that the author was prompted by reading Mark's Gospel plus a (now lost) record of Jesus' teachings (sometimes called "Q"). There is much to commend the view that Matthew interwove Mark, "Q," his own research, and eyewitness memories into his own careful account.

# GOD'S MESSAGE IN MATTHEW

## PURPOSE

The original purpose of this Gospel was to provide a written proclamation of the redemption God brought about through Jesus with an emphasis suitable for Jewish Christians: *Jesus is the promised Messiah*. God's people who read and study Matthew today should view it with this original purpose in mind.

## FIRST PASS

### Introduction to Jesus' Ministry

Matthew began his Gospel by recounting selected events surrounding Jesus' birth around 6–4 BC (1:18–2:12). The genealogy establishes Jesus' ancestry by which He was a legitimate descendant of David and rightful candidate for the messianic throne (1:2–17). The rest of Matthew's introduction comprises five quotations from the Old Testament and a narrative that illustrates how those texts were fulfilled in Jesus. Matthew then moved abruptly to Jesus' adulthood, passing over in silence the intervening years of His life (3:1–4:16). The events of this section set the stage for and culminate in Jesus' baptism and temptation, both of which would prepare Him for His approximately three-year ministry.

### Development of Jesus' Ministry

"From then on Jesus began to preach" marks the beginning of His major public ministry, mostly spent in Galilee. "Repent, because the kingdom of heaven has come near" epitomizes His message in one sentence. With Jesus' ministry, death, and resurrection, God's saving reign would be inaugurated in the hearts and lives of those who became

Mount Hermon, the place where some scholars believe Jesus' transfiguration occurred a week following Simon Peter's confession at Caesarea Philippi. Hermon, 9,100 feet above sea level, is the highest mountain in Syria. It can be seen from as far away as the Dead Sea—120 miles. The range is approximately 28 miles in length and reaches a width of 15 miles. Its peak is covered with snow two-thirds of the year. Water from its melting snow flows into the rivers of the Hauran and provides the principal source for the Jordan River. Although Hermon receives about 60 inches of precipitation (dew, snow, rain) per year, practically no vegetation grows above the snow line, where there is an almost complete absence of soil.

His disciples. Universal acknowledgment of God's sovereignty in Jesus must await His Second Coming, but the kingdom has been inaugurated. He began to call to Himself those who would be His most intimate associates and trainees. Matthew then previewed the essence of Christ's ministry with the key terms *preaching*, *teaching*, and *healing*, which characterized His activity wherever He went (4:17–16:20).

**The Sermon on the Mount: Authority in Word**

Perhaps no portion of Scripture is as well known as Jesus' great sermon (5:1–7:29). It begins with the well-loved Beatitudes that classically exemplify God's inversion of the world's values. These countercultural values could suggest that Jesus intended His followers to withdraw from the world and form separate communities. Matthew 5:13–16 immediately belies any such notion. Disciples must be salt and light, arresting decay and providing illumination for a lost and dying world. Such radical ideas understandably would have raised the question of the relationship between Jesus' teaching and the Old Testament. Jesus addressed this topic next. He had not come to abolish the law, yet neither had He come to preserve it but rather to "fulfill" it—to bring to completion everything to which it originally pointed.

Jesus turned to the theme of true versus hypocritical piety. In three closely parallel examples, He treated the practices of almsgiving, prayer, and fasting (6:1–18). He then addressed the themes of wealth and worry (6:19–34). Here Jesus contrasted transient, earthly riches with permanent, heavenly riches. Jesus boldly asserted that money may be the single biggest competitor with God for ultimate allegiance in our lives, particularly for those who are not in the poorest classes of society (6:22–24).

Jesus called His followers not to be judgmental in their relationships with others. But His illustrations also underlined that once we have properly dealt with our own sins, we have the right and responsibility to evaluate others' behavior and to help them deal with their shortcomings (7:1–12).

Jesus concluded with a warning (7:14–27). There are only two possible responses

Roman denarius bears the image of Tiberius Caesar who reigned AD 14–37.

to Jesus' preaching—obedience or rejection. The narrow versus the wide roads, the good versus the bad fruit, and the wise versus the foolish builders illustrate this warning in three parallel ways. Professions of faith without appropriate changes of lifestyle prove empty. But mere works by themselves do not save; a relationship with Jesus is needed. On judgment day many will cry, "Lord, Lord" and appeal to their deeds. Christ will reply, "I never knew you."

#### Authority in Deed

Jesus demonstrated His authority over disease, natural catastrophes, demons, and death with a series of 10 miracles (8:1–10:42). What He had demonstrated verbally in the teachings on the mount, Jesus acted out through displays of power. His disciples were amazed; "even the winds and the sea obey Him!" (8:27), and the crowds stood amazed that He had the authority to forgive sins (9:8). Matthew then showed a variety of responses to Jesus' authority (11:1–18:35).

#### From Galilee to Jerusalem

Matthew 19:1–25:46 makes the transition from Galilee to Jerusalem. Jesus dramatically presented His kingly authority by His triumphal entry into Jerusalem (21:1–9) and by cleansing the temple (21:10–17). Then, while He was teaching, the chief priests and elders challenged Him by asking, "By what authority are You doing these things?" (21:23). Jesus answered with parables and other teachings (21:28–22:46). Jesus warned the people about the examples of the Pharisees and Sadducees (23:1–38). He then concentrated His teaching only on His disciples (24:1–25:46). They could recall this when He commanded them to teach what He taught.

#### From Death to Life

Matthew 26:1–28:20 has no teaching situations, but it tells of the conspiracy ending in Jesus' crucifixion. In the midst of the trial scene Jesus was asked if He was the Messiah. Jesus responded by affirming His authority: "You have said it" (26:64). Pilate, a Gentile, recognized Jesus' kingly authority, placing over His head, "THIS IS JESUS THE KING OF THE JEWS" (27:37). The Gentile centurion proclaimed, "This man really was God's Son!" (27:54). As in the birth story, so in the end, the author stressed Jesus' divine, kingly authority and emphasized the inclusion of the Gentiles.

When the resurrected Lord declared His authority to His disciples in 28:18, they understood because they had seen His authority displayed as they lived with Him.

## THE RELIABILITY OF MATTHEW

The Gospel of Matthew contains clear evidence that the author possessed a strong command of both Aramaic and Greek, something that would be a prerequisite for most tax collectors. Furthermore, the author of Matthew used the more precise term *nomisma* for the coin used in the dispute over tribute (Mt 22:19) than Mark's and Luke's *denarion* (Mk 12:15; Lk 20:24). This linguistic specificity strongly implies that the author was conversant in the fine details of money and finance, a point that would lend credence to the proposition that the author was a tax collector.

## HOW MATTHEW FITS INTO GOD'S STORY

1. Prologue: Creation, Fall, and the Need for Redemption
2. God Builds His Nation (2000–931 BC)
3. God Educates His Nation (931–586 BC)
4. God Keeps a Faithful Remnant (586–6 BC)
5. **God Purchases Redemption and Begins the Kingdom (6 BC to AD 30)**
6. God Spreads the Kingdom Through the Church (AD 30–?)
7. God Consummates Redemption and Confirms His Eternal Kingdom
8. Epilogue: New Heaven and New Earth

## CHRIST IN MATTHEW

When the wise men came to Jerusalem, they asked, "Where is He who has been born King of the Jews?" (2:2). "This is Jesus the King of the Jews" (27:37) was placed in writing

Reconstruction of a typical first-century synagogue in Israel (Mt 12:9; 13:54; Mk 1:21; 3:1; 5:22,35; 6:2; Lk 4:16,33; 6:6, 7:5; Jn 6:59).

above Jesus as He was crucified. Matthew presents Jesus as King and Israel's Messiah. More than any Gospel writer, he quotes from the Old Testament to make his case.

## CHRISTIAN WORLDVIEW ELEMENTS

### Teachings About God

The first Gospel shows God in action, taking the initiative in fulfilling the Scriptures about the coming Messiah. It teaches about the Trinity, and it contributes greatly to the Christian understanding of the deity of Christ. Jesus' constant reference to Himself as the Son of Man plays a key role in understanding Jesus' earthly mission.

### Teachings About Humanity

The author documented the sinfulness of humans in stark terms: Both Jews and Romans were responsible for Jesus' crucifixion. Yet he also showed that humans committed to following Jesus can accomplish great good. Matthew noted the importance of people putting faith in Jesus; he also showed Jesus' criticism of those with little faith.

### Teachings About Salvation

Salvation is presented mainly in terms of belonging to the kingdom of God that arrived in a fresh way in the person of Jesus (12:28). The death and resurrection of

"'When they came to a place called Golgotha (which means Skull Place), they gave Him wine mixed with gall to drink. But when He tasted it, He would not drink it" (Mt 27:33–34). One of two sites said to be the place of Jesus' crucifixion.

Jesus were the divine means by which God provided salvation. Although Jesus took the message of the kingdom only to Jews during His lifetime, His last act in this Gospel was to commission His followers to go to Gentiles ("all nations") as well (28:18–20).

## GENRE AND LITERARY STYLE

### A Gospel Composed in Ordinary Greek

The question, What, exactly, are the Gospels in comparison to other literary genres? has been discussed at length by scholars. The Gospels are more like biographies than any other ancient literary type. Yet they lack many features common to biography (such as regular attention to place and date), and they omit many years of the central character's life. The best suggestion is that the Gospels are a unique literary genre brought into being by the coming of the unique Son of God to the world. As such, the Gospels may be defined as "kerygmatic history." The Greek term *kerygma* meant "proclamation," a reminder that the Gospels proclaim the good news about Jesus in written form—just as the apostles orally proclaimed the good news and called people to commitment to Jesus. The term *history* indicates that the author—like every historian—selected and arranged his material to suit his own purposes.

Matthew wrote in the ordinary (*Koinē*) Greek spoken throughout the Roman world of the first century. His style is both more concise and more polished than Mark's; it is less sophisticated in vocabulary and precision than Luke's. Christian tradition records that Matthew composed material in Hebrew or Aramaic, but the present Gospel bears no marks of being a translated document.

## A PRINCIPLE TO LIVE BY

### The Great Commission (Mt 28:16–20, *Life Essentials Study Bible*, p. 1338)

Since the Lord Jesus Christ died and rose again to bring salvation to all who believe, we are to do what we can to deliver this message to the whole world.

To access a video presentation of this principle featuring Dr. Gene Getz, use a Smartphone or iPad to connect to this QR code or go to http://www.bhpublishinggroup.com/handbook/matthew

This title has been associated with the second Gospel as long as it has been known. It was named this because its author was believed to be (John) Mark, the first-century Christian associated especially with Peter and Paul.

## KEY TEXT: 10:45

*"For even the Son of Man did not come to be served, but to serve, and to give His life—a ransom for many."*

## KEY TERM: "SERVANT"

Omitting Jesus' birth and reporting relatively few of His teachings, this Gospel emphasizes Jesus as One who actively served the needs of people through His deeds.

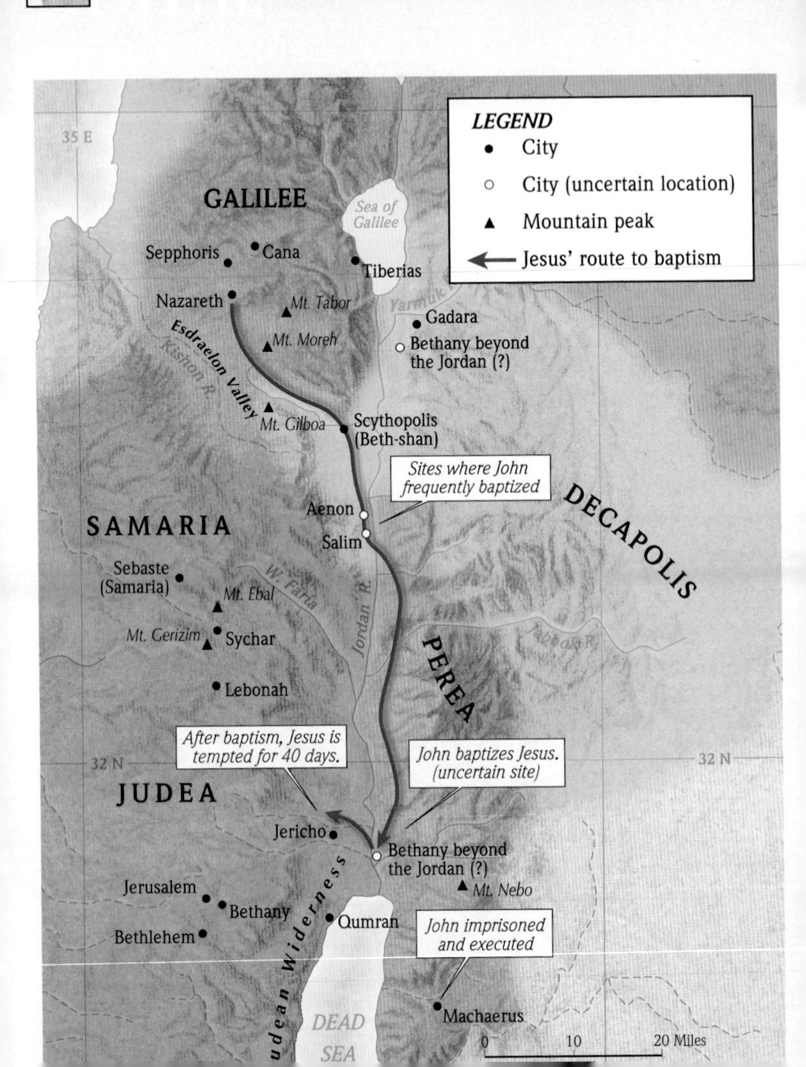
LEGEND
City
City (uncertain location)
Mountain peak
Jesus' route to baptism
35 E
GALILEE
Sea of Galilee
Sepphoris
Cana
Tiberias
Nazareth
Mt. Tabor
Yarmuk R.
Gadara
Bethany beyond the Jordan (?)
Esdraelon Valley
Kishon R.
Mt. Moreh
Mt. Gilboa
Scythopolis (Beth-shan)
Sites where John frequently baptized
DECAPOLIS
Aenon
Salim
SAMARIA
Sebaste (Samaria)
W. Far'a
Mt. Ebal
Mt. Gerizim
Sychar
Jordan R.
Jabbok R.
PEREA
Lebonah
After baptism, Jesus is tempted for 40 days.
John baptizes Jesus. (uncertain site)
32 N
32 N
JUDEA
Jericho
Bethany beyond the Jordan (?)
Mt. Nebo
Jerusalem
Bethany
Qumran
Bethlehem
Judean Wilderness
John imprisoned and executed
Machaerus
DEAD SEA
0
10
20 Miles

## ONE-SENTENCE SUMMARY

In His life, death, and resurrection, Jesus did the deeds of the (suffering) Servant of the Lord, notably through His death as "a ransom for many."

# ORIGINAL HISTORICAL SETTING

## AUTHOR AND DATE OF WRITING

**John Mark, Perhaps Around AD 50–60**

The book is anonymous, but early Christian tradition uniformly asserted that Mark composed this Gospel in conjunction with Peter's memories. He was a secondary figure in Acts. Mark became infamous for deserting Paul and Barnabas on their first missionary journey (Ac 12:25; 13:5). He later did mission work with Barnabas and eventually won his way back into Paul's good graces (Col 4:10; 2Tm 4:11). At the time Peter wrote his first letter, perhaps a few years after Mark wrote his Gospel, the aged apostle called Mark "my son" (1 Pt 5:13). Most critical scholars deny that Mark was the author or that he wrote on the basis of Peter's recollections, but a number of incidental details in the book support this conclusion. In particular, Bible students have noted that Mark's outline is identical to the outline Peter used in his preaching (Ac 3:13–15; 10:36–41).

During the past two centuries a general, but not universal, consensus has emerged (among all kinds of scholars, both critical and conservative, Protestant and Roman Catholic) that Mark was the first Gospel written. The reasons focus on Mark's more elementary chronology and style of writing as compared to the other Gospels. In any event, most conservative scholars conclude that Mark finished his Gospel before AD 70, prior to the temple's destruction (Mk 13:2). A good estimate for its composition is the decade from 50 to 60, when both Peter and Mark were still alive and certainly had opportunities for collaboration on this project.

## FIRST AUDIENCE AND DESTINATION

**Probably Gentile Christians Living Around Rome**

The original hearers and destination are not stated but are accepted based on tradition. Irenaeus and Clement of Alexandria (both late second century) each identified Rome as the place of origin. A number of details in the Gospel support this conclusion, such as the quick, businesslike pace with which Jesus is presented, heightened by Mark's frequent use of "immediately." Several terms with Latin origins also point in this direction.

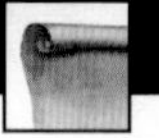

## OCCASION

Scholars have long debated the human factors that prompted the composition of this Gospel. Frankly this is all a matter of conjecture. Some have suggested that the impetus was the growing realization that Jesus' return might be in the distant future. Until then His followers had a need for a written account of the life of their Master. Since Peter was an eyewitness to almost everything recorded in this Gospel, his memories provided Mark with an outstanding historical basis for writing. Another suggestion is that this Gospel was written for Christians facing persecution, perhaps the Roman persecution instigated by Emperor Nero in AD 64. The Christians would thus be encouraged. Since their Master had faced the injustice of religious and political authorities victoriously, they too could triumph no matter what they had to suffer.

"Who then is this?" is the central question of Mark's Gospel. Jesus' disciples asked this question of one another just after Jesus spoke to and calmed what seemed a life-threatening storm on the Sea of Galilee (4:35–41). At the turning point of this Gospel, Jesus asked, "Who do people say that I am?" Ironically, the Roman centurion in charge of the crucifixion detail answered the question when he observed the way Jesus breathed His last (15:39).

## PURPOSE

The main purpose of this Gospel was to provide a written proclamation of the redemption brought about through Jesus with an emphasis suitable for Gentile Christians: *Jesus is the perfect Servant of the Lord*. God's people who read and study Mark today should view it with its original purpose in mind.

## FIRST PASS

### Introduction

In introducing his Gospel (1:1), Mark gave his readers the answer to a question that is implicit throughout the Gospel: "Who then is this?" (4:41). The Greek term "Christ" corresponds to the Hebrew "Messiah," meaning *anointed king*. For Mark the "gospel of Jesus Christ" begins with John the Baptist to whom Jesus came for baptism. On receiving John's baptism, Jesus was confirmed as the beloved Son who pleased God by His identification with sinners (1:9–11). The experience of God's affirmation quickly gave way to Satan's temptations in the wilderness of Judea (1:12–13).

### Jesus' Authority Revealed

The first major section of Mark highlights Jesus' role as authoritative teacher, healer, and exorcist (1:14–3:6). Jesus began His ministry following John's arrest (6:14–18). The "fulfilled time" was the era the prophets anticipated when God's rule would become a reality. The necessary response to God's work in Jesus was repentance (a radical turning from self to God) and trust in the good news of God's reign.

### Jesus' Authority Rejected

The Herodians' and Pharisees' rejection of Jesus contrasted with the common people's acceptance. Jesus' popularity exceeded John's (1:5), extending into the Gentile areas of Lebanon and Transjordan (3:7–6:6a). The parable of the soils (4:1–34) provided a framework for interpreting responses to Jesus' message. Jesus' preaching evoked (1) the disciples' obedient following (1:18,20; 2:14); (2) the crowd's amazement; (3) His family's suspicion of insanity (3:21); and (4) the Jewish leaders' opposition (2:7,16,24; 3:6,22).

### Gathering a New Community

Jesus' rejection by "His own" prepared for the gathering of His new people anticipated in 3:35 (6:6b–8:21) . The mission of the Twelve brackets the account of John's martyrdom, underscoring the danger of preaching repentance. Jesus set the pattern for the mission of the Twelve by His preaching, healing, and exorcisms. Though the authority given the disciples to heal and exorcise demons was a sign of the kingdom, Jesus only commissioned them to preach repentance, not the good news of the kingdom (1:15). The mission instructions are evidence of absolute dependence on God for support and allude to the exodus. The disciples, like Jesus before them, were to experience rejection as well as welcome.

**Equipping the New Community**

Mark's central section is preceded and followed by two accounts of Jesus' giving sight to blind men (8:22–26; 10:46–52). This core teaching emphasizes the cost of discipleship and the suffering/glorification of the Son of Man. The healing of the blind man at Bethsaida is distinct from other miracles in the Gospel traditions in being two-part healing. The man at first saw distorted images—people who looked like walking trees. Only after a "second touch" from Jesus did he see clearly. Similarly Peter correctly answered Jesus' question, "Who do you say that I am?" but Peter's understanding of Messiah was badly distorted, even Satanic. In this larger section of Mark, Jesus reminded His disciples repeatedly of the necessity of His suffering and death (8:31; 9:31; 10:32,45).

**Judgment on Jerusalem**

Jesus' coming to Jerusalem was the occasion for escalating conflict with the religious leaders (11:1–13:37). Their failure to see and respond to what God was doing would result in the destruction of Jerusalem and the temple. Jesus' teaching on the destruction of the temple/Jerusalem and the coming of the Son of Man in Mark 13 are challenging to untangle. Despite these difficulties, two primary pastoral emphases are clear in the warnings to beware of deception and to be prepared for Christ's return.

*The Siege and Destruction of Jerusalem* by David Roberts (1850). As Jesus was in Jerusalem for the last time, He and His disciples were leaving the temple complex. One of the disciples observed the massive stones and impressive structure that were part of the temple complex. "Jesus said to him, 'Do you see these great buildings? Not one stone will be left here on another that will not be thrown down!'" (Mk 13:2). Less that 40 years after Jesus spoke these words, the Roman general Titus led his legions in the destruction of Jerusalem to put down

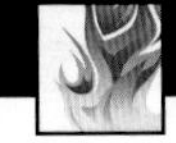

### Jesus' Passion and Resurrection

Mark's final section concerns events surrounding the human judgment *against* Jesus (14:1–15:47) and God's judgment *for* Jesus (16:1–8). Mark's account of the Lord's Supper repeatedly emphasizes its Passover setting. As Son of Man, Jesus would go to His death in accordance with Scripture just as the Passover lambs were sacrificed. At Gethsemane Jesus responded to crisis with prayer. Mark showed a frankly human Jesus, "deeply distressed and horrified," repeatedly falling on the ground in anguished prayer. Despite the test of faith, Jesus emerged reaffirming faith in God's possibilities and obeying His Father's will. Judas, one of the Twelve, betrayed Jesus. While Jesus was in the Jewish phase of His trial, Peter denied Him. The religious leaders were pressing for execution. Only the Romans had the authority to carry out capital punishment, so Jesus was taken to Pilate, prefect of the Roman province of Judea. Pilate was not convinced of Jesus' guilt but gave in to the pressure of the religious leaders and the mob they had incited. Pilate handed Jesus over to be crucified. Before Jesus died, He cried out, "My God, my God, why have you forsaken Me?" Witnessing the manner of Jesus' death, the Roman centurion in charge of the execution detail confessed, "This man really was God's Son!" giving a strong affirmative answer to the question that recurs in Mark's Gospel: "Who then is this?" The centurion's affirmation was strongly punctuated in what followed. Early Sunday morning, three women strongly devoted to Jesus came to the tomb to anoint His body with spices. To their amazement they found the tomb empty. A young man sitting to the right of the entrance told them not to be alarmed. "You are looking for Jesus the Nazarene, who was crucified. He has been resurrected!" They were then invited to explore the tomb for themselves.

## THE RELIABILITY OF MARK

Ghostwriters are persons who write letters, speeches, articles, and even books on behalf of another person. The document carries the name of the person for whom it is written rather than the person who wrote it. A well-known person or one whose name carries weight with a given audience may not take the time to do his own writing. Some scholars believe something like this was practiced in the early church. Documents like gospels and letters were ascribed to one of the apostles or to a person whose name carried significant weight to the document. Mark D. Roberts[1] has pointed out that this was certainly the case with *The Gospel of Peter*, *The Gospel of Thomas*, *The Gospel of Philip*, *The Gospel of Judas*, and *The Gospel of Mary Magdalene*, among others. Roberts and others have made a strong case in support of the early tradition that the second Gospel was written by Mark. The earliest mention of Mark as the author of a Gospel comes from Papias, the bishop of Hierapolis, in Asia Minor, writing around AD 130. The early church historian Eusebius quoted Papias's words to the effect that Mark, as a follower of Peter, recorded stories about Jesus that Peter used in his preaching and that the stories were accurate but not in proper order. Papias added that he received this information from "the elder," by which he possibly meant the apostle John. If the early church had followed the practice the Gnostics, it would have called the second Gospel "The Gospel According to Peter." This would have carried far more weight and authority than calling this "The Gospel According to Mark," after a minor character in the early church. Mark Roberts argues that the church attributed the second Gospel to Mark because Mark wrote it and the church was concerned more about truth than about the status of the human author.

## HOW MARK FITS INTO GOD'S STORY

1. Prologue: Creation, Fall, and the Need for Redemption
2. God Builds His Nation (2000–931 BC)
3. God Educates His Nation (931–586 BC)
4. God Keeps a Faithful Remnant (586–6 BC)
5. **God Purchases Redemption and Begins the Kingdom (6 BC to AD 30)**
6. God Spreads the Kingdom Through the Church (AD 30–?)
7. God Consummates Redemption and Confirms His Eternal Kingdom
8. Epilogue: New Heaven and New Earth

## CHRIST IN MARK

Mark's presentation of Jesus is action packed and fast paced. He emphasizes Jesus' mighty acts and His role as Suffering Servant who calls followers to take up their own cross and follow Him.

## CHRISTIAN WORLDVIEW ELEMENTS

### Teachings About God

Jesus emphasized God as "your Father" in this Gospel. He is also the Father of Jesus, and from his opening words Mark declared Jesus to be "the Son of God." The Holy Spirit is present, empowering Jesus' ministry and mission. This is seen especially in His triumph over every unholy spirit.

### Teachings About Humanity

Jesus encountered both the sick and the sinful in this Gospel. He healed the sick and forgave the sinful. Multitudes (at the feeding of the 5,000 and the triumphal entry) and small groups (the apostles) were transformed by Jesus. Yet other large crowds (at Jesus' trial and crucifixion) and small groups (Jewish religious leaders) utterly rejected him. Mark emphasized that humans could not remain neutral about Jesus. They had to decide either for Him or against Him.

### Teachings About Salvation

A higher percentage of this book is given over to the events of Jesus' suffering and death than any other Bible book. By quoting the three times that Jesus' predicted His death, Mark emphasized the necessity of the cross, that He "must" die (8:31; 9:31; 10:33). At the Last Supper, Jesus explained His death was as a substitute: "for many" (14:24).

## GENRE AND LITERARY STYLE

### A Gospel Composed in Ordinary Greek

See *Genre and Literary Style* for **MATTHEW** for information about what a "Gospel" is. Assuming Mark was the first to compose a Gospel, he may be credited as the one who innovated this genre. Mark wrote in ordinary (*Koinē*) Greek, in a style characterized by frequent use of the present tense to describe the action. His vigorous, vivid vocabulary is generally wordier than Matthew or Luke (when these Gospels are parallel). The style is consistent with someone who is writing down the memories of another as they are recounted to him.

## A PRINCIPLE TO LIVE BY

### Christ's Authority (Mk 9:1–8, *Life Essentials Study Bible*, p. 1356)

In a world that is permeated with many religious and philosophical messages, we must discern truth from error by listening carefully to the words of Jesus Christ.

To access a video presentation of this principle featuring Dr. Gene Getz, use a Smartphone or iPad to connect to this QR code or go to http://www.bhpublishinggroup.com/handbook/mark

## ENDNOTE

1. "Gospel Authorship by Mark and Luke: Some Implications," part 4 of series: *Are the New Testament Gospels Reliable? Further Thoughts*, Posted for Thursday, July 20, 2006.

This title has been associated with the third Gospel as long as it has been known. Its author was believed to be Luke, the first-century Christian physician who was a traveling companion of Paul.

## KEY TEXT: 19:10

*"For the Son of Man has come to seek and to save the lost."*

## KEY TERM: "SAVIOR"

The saving activity of Jesus, both in His ministry and in His death, is the focus of this book. Because His mission was to save others, He did not save Himself (23:35).

## ONE-SENTENCE SUMMARY

Jesus not only lived and ministered as the perfect human, but He also died and rose to new life as the Savior for sinners.

## AUTHOR AND DATE OF WRITING

**Luke, Perhaps Around AD 60–61**

The book is anonymous, but early Christian tradition uniformly affirmed that Luke composed this Gospel as well as Acts. See *Author and Date of Writing* for **ACTS** for reasons supporting Luke's authorship of Acts. The dedications to Theophilus, the similar Greek style and vocabulary, and special shared emphases of the books (such as prayer and joy) all point to common authorship.

Luke was a secondary figure in the book of Acts, known not by name but by his use of the pronouns "we" and "us" when he was present during the actions he was describing. Paul named him three times in his letters (Col 4:14; 2Tm 4:11; Phm 24). He was a Gentile, a medical doctor, and a loyal supporter of Paul. His home city and the nature of his conversion are unknown. Most critical scholars believe the author of the third Gospel and Acts was someone other than the Luke of Paul's letters or the "we" of Acts.

The date of Luke must be after Mark, which Luke almost certainly used as a source, but before Acts, which was perhaps published around AD 61–62. If Luke researched his Gospel while Paul was imprisoned in Caesarea, then perhaps he wrote and published from Caesarea (c. AD 59) or possibly after he arrived in Rome with Paul after the famous shipwreck (c. AD 61). Other scholars have argued that Luke, like all the Gospels, must be dated later, from the AD 70s or 80s.

## FIRST AUDIENCE AND DESTINATION

**Theophilus, a Gentile Whose Residence is Unknown**

Luke explicitly dedicated this Gospel to Theophilus ("God's friend"), whom he called "most honorable." Mentioned only in the prefaces to Luke and Acts, he appears to have been a Gentile of high social status who had been "instructed" in Christianity but wanted more detailed information about Jesus. Theophilus may have provided financial patronage for Luke, underwriting his research expenses.

## OCCASION

The needs of Theophilus provided the immediate prompting for Luke's writing. Already "many" had written of Jesus' life, and in his preface Luke said that he used sources, including eyewitnesses. Luke possibly used the two years Paul was imprisoned in Caesarea (Ac 24:26–27; 27:1) to research the Gospel. He had access to any number of witnesses to Jesus' life, possibly including Jesus' mother (Lk 2:19,51). Most scholars believe he was also aided by reading Mark's Gospel plus a (now lost) record of Jesus' teachings (sometimes called "Q"). There is much to commend the view that Luke interwove Mark, "Q," and his own research findings into his own careful account.

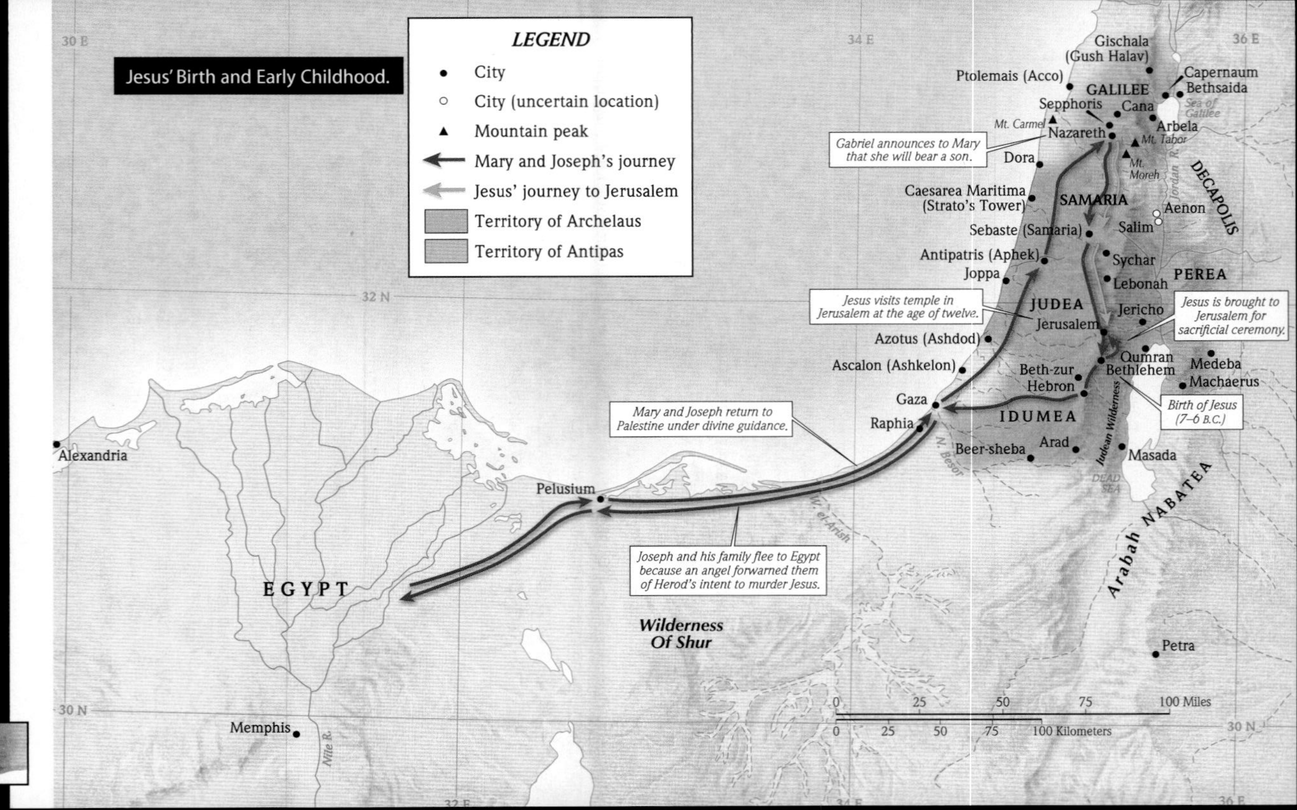

Jesus' Birth and Early Childhood.
LEGEND
City
City (uncertain location)
Mountain peak
Mary and Joseph's journey
Jesus' journey to Jerusalem
Territory of Archelaus
Territory of Antipas
Gabriel announces to Mary that she will bear a son.
Jesus visits temple in Jerusalem at the age of twelve.
Jesus is brought to Jerusalem for sacrificial ceremony.
Birth of Jesus (7–6 B.C.)
Mary and Joseph return to Palestine under divine guidance.
Joseph and his family flee to Egypt because an angel forwarned them of Herod's intent to murder Jesus.
Gischala (Gush Halav)
Ptolemais (Acco)
GALILEE
Capernaum
Bethsaida
Sea of Galilee
Sepphoris
Cana
Mt. Carmel
Nazareth
Arbela
Mt. Tabor
Mt. Moreh
Dora
Jordan R.
DECAPOLIS
Caesarea Maritima (Strato's Tower)
SAMARIA
Aenon
Salim
Sebaste (Samaria)
Antipatris (Aphek)
Sychar
Joppa
Lebonah
PEREA
JUDEA
Jericho
Jerusalem
Azotus (Ashdod)
Qumran
Medeba
Ascalon (Ashkelon)
Beth-zur
Bethlehem
Machaerus
Hebron
Gaza
IDUMEA
Raphia
Judean Wilderness
Beer-sheba
Arad
Masada
N. Besor
DEAD SEA
NABATEA
Arabah
Alexandria
Pelusium
W. el-Arish
EGYPT
Wilderness Of Shur
Petra
Memphis
Nile R.
30 E
34 E
36 E
32 N
30 N
32 E
0 25 50 75 100 Miles
0 25 50 75 100 Kilometers

## PURPOSE

The author explicitly stated his purpose in the preface (1:1–4). He wrote his Gospel to provide an orderly account of the beginnings of Christianity so the reader will have reliable information about Jesus Christ. Every fair understanding of this Gospel accepts this as a beginning point for understanding.

## FIRST PASS

### Luke's Purpose: Certainty

Of the four Gospel writers, Luke and John (20:31) expressly state their purpose in writing (1:1–4). Luke's prologue is addressed to "most honorable Theophilus" for whom he intended to provide certainty regarding the matters in which he had been instructed. Luke acknowledged other narratives. He likely consulted these and supplemented these accounts with his own careful, firsthand research with "original eyewitnesses." Drawing on these sources, Luke provided Theophilus with an orderly account.

### John the Baptist and Jesus

Following his prologue, Luke launched into a unique comparison of John and Jesus by showing how both represent the fulfillment of promises made by God. John was like Elijah, but Jesus had Davidic roles to fulfill and possessed a unique supernatural origin. John was forerunner, but Jesus was fulfillment (1:5–2:52). This section narrates the birth announcements of John and Jesus as well as their births. Jesus' own self-awareness concludes the introductory overture in the Gospel. Here the young boy declared to religious leaders in the temple that He must be about the work of His Father in the temple.

### Preparation for Ministry

Only Luke contains the section where the ethical dimensions of John's call to repentance in terms of compassionate response to others is made clear. John also warns about judgment, calls for repentance, and promises the coming of One who brings God's Spirit. John baptized Jesus, but the main feature of the baptism is one of two heavenly testimonies to Jesus (9:35 has the other).

The universal character of Jesus' relationship to humankind is highlighted in the list of His ancestors. He is "son of Adam, son of God." (3:23–38). Jesus not only has connections to heaven but also connections with those created from the dust of the earth.

Following Jesus' baptism, Jesus' first actions were to overcome temptations from Satan, something Adam had failed to do. So this section shows Jesus as anointed by God, representative of humanity and faithful to God (4:1–13).

### Galilean Ministry

Luke turns to Jesus' 18-month public ministry in Galilee (4:14–9:50). The account of this ministry is shared by Matthew, Mark, and Luke; however Luke provides a unique perspective on these months. Only Luke includes Jesus' declaration of the fulfillment of God's promise in His hometown synagogue and the Sermon on the Plain (6:17–49). His interpretation of Isaiah 61 in the synagogue represents Jesus' self-description of His mission, while the sermon sets forth His fundamental ethic presented without concerns for Jewish tradition that Matthew's Sermon on the Mount possesses. Jesus' ability to bring salvation is pictured in a series of miracles. These miracles show His total authority by exhibiting sovereignty over nature, over demons, and over disease and death. Beyond deliverance is mission. Disciples are called to be fishers of men. Unlike fishermen, who catch fish to devour them, disciples fish to snatch people from the grip of death and damnation.

At this point the narrative moves from Jesus' teaching and demonstration of authority to confession and call to discipleship. Peter confessed Jesus to be the Christ. Then Jesus explained what kind of Messiah He would be: He would suffer. Those who follow Jesus must have total and daily commitment in order to survive the path of rejection that comes with following Him.

Mount Precipice in Nazareth. "When they heard this, everyone in the synagogue was enraged. They got up, drove Him out of town, and brought Him to the edge of the hill that their town was built on, intending to hurl Him over the cliff. But He passed right through the crowd and went on His way"(4:28–30).

### Journey to Jerusalem

This section is often referred to as the "travel narrative" since it roughly outlines the final journey of Jesus to Jerusalem (9:51–19:44). Luke 10:38–42 and 17:11 seem to indicate that the narrative is only broadly chronological, and this may account for some of the variations with the settings in Matthew, though it is also possible Jesus repeated these teachings on multiple occasions. A significant amount of material in this section is unique to Luke and can be seen as an extended opportunity for Jesus to prepare His disciples for their mission following His death and resurrection.

### Jerusalem

In this concluding section Luke explained how Jesus died and why apparent defeat became victory (19:45–24:53). Luke showed how God revealed who Jesus was. In addition, the task of disciples in light of God's acts becomes clear. Luke mixed fresh material with that present in the other Gospels. The final battles in Jesus' earthly ministry occur here, recalling earlier confrontations in Luke 11–13. Jesus cleansed the temple, signaling His displeasure with official Judaism.

In light of the nation rejecting Him, Jesus predicted the fall of the temple and of Jerusalem—events that themselves are a foretaste of the end. The fall of Jerusalem would be a terrible time for the nation, but it was not yet the end, when the Son of Man returns on the clouds with authority to redeem His people (Dn 7:13–14). The

Zacchaeus's sycamore tree in Jericho. As Jesus came to Jerusalem for the last time, He came through Jericho where he encountered Zacchaeus who had climbed a sycamore tree to better see Jesus, perhaps without being seen. Zacchaeus's response to Jesus' invitation was life-changing (Lk 19:1–10).

## The Apostles and Their History

| Name | Surname | Parents | Home | Business | Writings |
|---|---|---|---|---|---|
| Simon | Peter or Cephas = Rock | Jonah | ***Early life***: Bethsaida; ***Later***: Capernaum | Fisherman | 1 & 2 Peter |
| Andrew = manhood or valor | | Jonah | ***Early life***: Bethsaida; ***Later***: Capernaum | Fisherman | |
| James the greater or the elder | Boanerges or Sons of Thunder | Zebedee and Salome | Bethsaida, Capernaum, and Jerusalem | Fisherman | |
| John, the beloved disciple | Boanerges or Sons of Thunder | Zebedee and Salome | Bethsaida, Capernaum, and Jerusalem | Fisherman | Gospel, three epistles, and Revelation |
| James the less | | Alphaeus and Mary | Galilee | | |
| Judas (not Iscariot) | Same as Thaddaeus and Lebbaeus | James | Galilee | | |
| Philip | | | Bethsaida | | |
| Bartholomew | Nathaniel | | Cana of Galilee | | |
| Matthew | Levi | | Galilee | Tax Collector | Gospel |
| Thomas | Didymus | | Galilee | | |
| Simon | The Zealot | | Galilee | | |
| Judas | Iscariot | Simon Iscariot | Kerioth of Judea | | |

| Work | Death |
|---|---|
| Peter may have ministered in the provinces of Pontus, Galatia, Cappadocia, Asia, perhaps in Corinth, and finally in Rome. | According to tradition, attested by Tertullian and Origin, Peter was crucified "with his head downwards" in Rome. The date of his death is likely between AD 64 and 68. |
| Uncertain but tradition says he ministered in Cappadocia, Galatia, Bithynia; later in the Sythian deserts and Byzantium; and finally in Thrace, Macedonia, Thessaly, and Achaia. | The traditional view is that he was crucified at Patrae in Achaia by order of the Roman governor Ageas. |
| Preached in Jerusalem and Judea | Beheaded by Herod in AD 62 or 66 in Jerusalem |
| Labored among the churches of Asia Minor, especially in Ephesus | Banished to Patmos AD 95. Recalled; died a natural death |
| Preached in Judea and Egypt | According to tradition, he was martyred in Egypt. |
| Preached in Mesopotamia and Armenia | Was martyred in present-day Iran and buried near Tabriz |
| Preached in Phrygia | Was martyred in Phrygia; tradition says he was buried in Hierapolis. |
| One tradition says he preached in India. Others say he ministered in Mesopotamia, Persia, Egypt, Armenia, Lycaonia, Phrygia, and on the shores of the Black Sea. | One tradition says King Astyages of Babylon had him flayed and beheaded because the king's brother had been converted under Bartholomew's preaching. |
| There is strong consensus that he preached to his own people for nearly two decades. He is also associated with Ethiopia to the south of the Caspian Sea, Parthia, Macedonia, and Syria. | Some sources say Matthew was martyred; others say he died a natural death. |
| Tradition says Thomas brought the gospel to India. | He is said to have been killed with a spear. Later his remains were taken to Edessa. |
| Preached in Persia | Tradition says Simon was tortured and sawed in two. |
| Betrayed Jesus | Suicide |

events of AD 70 are a guarantee that the end will also come, since the one set of events pictures the other.

Luke 22–23 describes the moments before Jesus' death. Jesus directed the setting for the Last Supper and told the disciples to prepare it. Jesus, though betrayed, was innocent, but His death would bring the new covenant and was a sacrifice on behalf of others. In His last discourse Jesus announced the betrayal, pointed out that greatness is in service, appointed the Eleven to authority, predicted Peter's denials, and warned of rejection. Jesus was in control, even as His death approached.

Luke made clear that Jesus died unjustly, yet in the face of injustice God still works. Luke described Jesus' death with Old Testament allusions that picture Jesus as an innocent sufferer who relied on God (Pss 19; 22:8–9; 31:6). The injustice is transcended in God's plan through the coming resurrection.

Luke closes with three scenes of resurrection and vindication. First, 24:1–12 announces the empty tomb, but the news of the excited women is greeted with skepticism. Second, the experience of the Emmaus disciples pictures the reversal the resurrection brought to the disciples' despair. Third, Luke reported Jesus' final commission, instruction, and ascension. Just as Luke 12 opened with the hope of Old Testament promise fulfilled, so Luke 24:43–47 returns to the central theme of Jesus the Messiah as the fulfillment of God's plan and promise. Jesus' final Gospel appearance yields a commission, a plan, and a promise.

## THE RELIABILITY OF LUKE

Most scholars from the second century to the eighteenth century read the Gospel of Luke as a historically accurate document. During and following the Enlightenment, many scholars came to view Luke and Acts as primarily theological documents in which the author fabricated events, speeches, and dialogue to serve his theological agenda. One instance of such "creativity" is Luke's introduction to Jesus' ministry where he provides chronological and geopolitical markers (3:1) for the commencement of John the Baptist's ministry: "In the fifteenth year of the reign of Tiberius Caesar, while Pontius Pilate was governor of Judea, Herod was tetrarch of Galilee, his brother Philip tetrarch of the region of Iturea and Trachonitis, and Lysanias tetrarch of Abilene." The problem is that Lysanias was tetrarch of Chalcis from 40 to 36 BC. According to Josephus, as Cleopatra "passed through Syria with him (Marc Antony), she contrived to get it into her possession; so he slew Lysanias, the son of Ptolemy, accusing him of his bringing the Parthians upon those countries" (*Antiquities of the Jews,* 15.4.1). Based on this evidence, it appeared that Luke was wrong. Lysanias had been dead for half a century, and he had been ruler of Calcis and not Abilene. However, an inscription was later found at Abila from the time of Tiberius Caesar (AD 14–29) that names another Lysanias as tetrarch of Abila.

## HOW LUKE FITS INTO GOD'S STORY

1. Prologue: Creation, Fall, and the Need for Redemption
2. God Builds His Nation (2000–931 BC)
3. God Educates His Nation (931–586 BC)
4. God Keeps a Faithful Remnant (586–6 BC)
5. God Purchases Redemption and Begins the Kingdom (6 BC to AD 30)
6. God Spreads the Kingdom Through the Church (AD 30–?)
7. God Consummates Redemption and Confirms His Eternal Kingdom
8. Epilogue: New Heaven and New Earth

## CHRIST IN LUKE

Luke writes primarily for Gentiles and focuses on Jesus as offering salvation to Jew and Gentile alike. Luke shows Jesus' compassion for the poor and the oppressed.

## CHRISTIAN WORLDVIEW ELEMENTS

### Teachings About God

In this Gospel, God initiates everything concerning salvation. The glory of God is especially emphasized from the song of the angels (2:14) to the triumphal entry (19:38). Equally important is the glory of Jesus Himself, from the transfiguration (9:32) to His resurrection splendor (24:26). Jesus is, of course, the virgin-born Son of God in this book. The Spirit is active from Jesus' conception to the great power of His ministry (1:35; 4:14). The Spirit is also the gift Jesus promised to His followers (11:13).

### Teachings About Humanity

This Gospel focuses on humanity in two ways. First, Jesus is the ideal or perfect Human. Luke shows what a Spirit-filled person, wholly obedient to God, is like. (Note the centurion's confession at Jesus' death: "This man really was righteous!" 23:47). Second, Luke painted a vivid portrait of a number of individuals Jesus impacted, showing the value of each human life.

### Teachings About Salvation

The turning point in this Gospel is 9:51, when "He determined to journey to Jerusalem." Jerusalem was the proper place for Jesus to offer Himself as a sacrifice. In His own words, "Didn't the Messiah have to suffer these things and enter into His glory?" (24:26). On the night He was betrayed, He taught his disciples that His death was a substitute and that it brought about the new covenant (see Jr 31:31–34).

## New Testament Jerusalem

ca. AD 30 (VIEW IS LOOKING WESTWARD, FROM A VANTAGE POINT ABOVE THE MOUNT OF OLIVES)

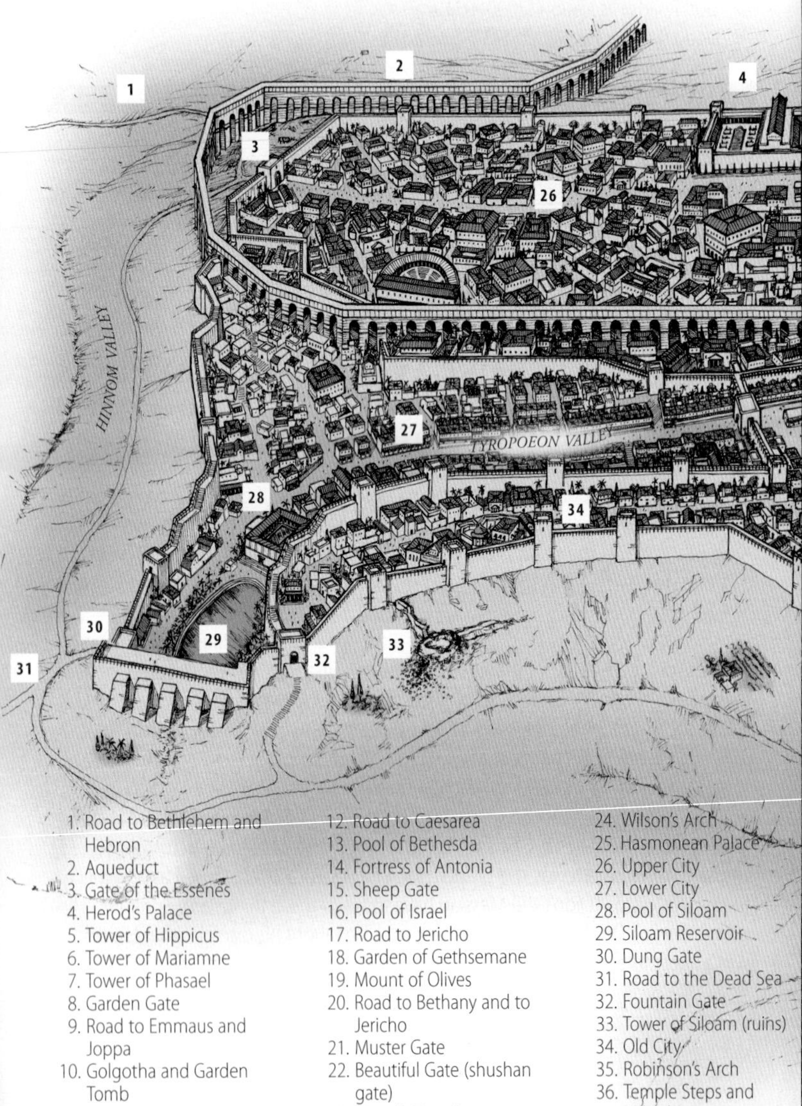


1. Road to Bethlehem and Hebron
2. Aqueduct
3. Gate of the Essenes
4. Herod's Palace
5. Tower of Hippicus
6. Tower of Mariamne
7. Tower of Phasael
8. Garden Gate
9. Road to Emmaus and Joppa
10. Golgotha and Garden Tomb
11. Fish Gate
12. Road to Caesarea
13. Pool of Bethesda
14. Fortress of Antonia
15. Sheep Gate
16. Pool of Israel
17. Road to Jericho
18. Garden of Gethsemane
19. Mount of Olives
20. Road to Bethany and to Jericho
21. Muster Gate
22. Beautiful Gate (shushan gate)
23. Herod's Temple
24. Wilson's Arch
25. Hasmonean Palace
26. Upper City
27. Lower City
28. Pool of Siloam
29. Siloam Reservoir
30. Dung Gate
31. Road to the Dead Sea
32. Fountain Gate
33. Tower of Siloam (ruins)
34. Old City
35. Robinson's Arch
36. Temple Steps and Mikveh

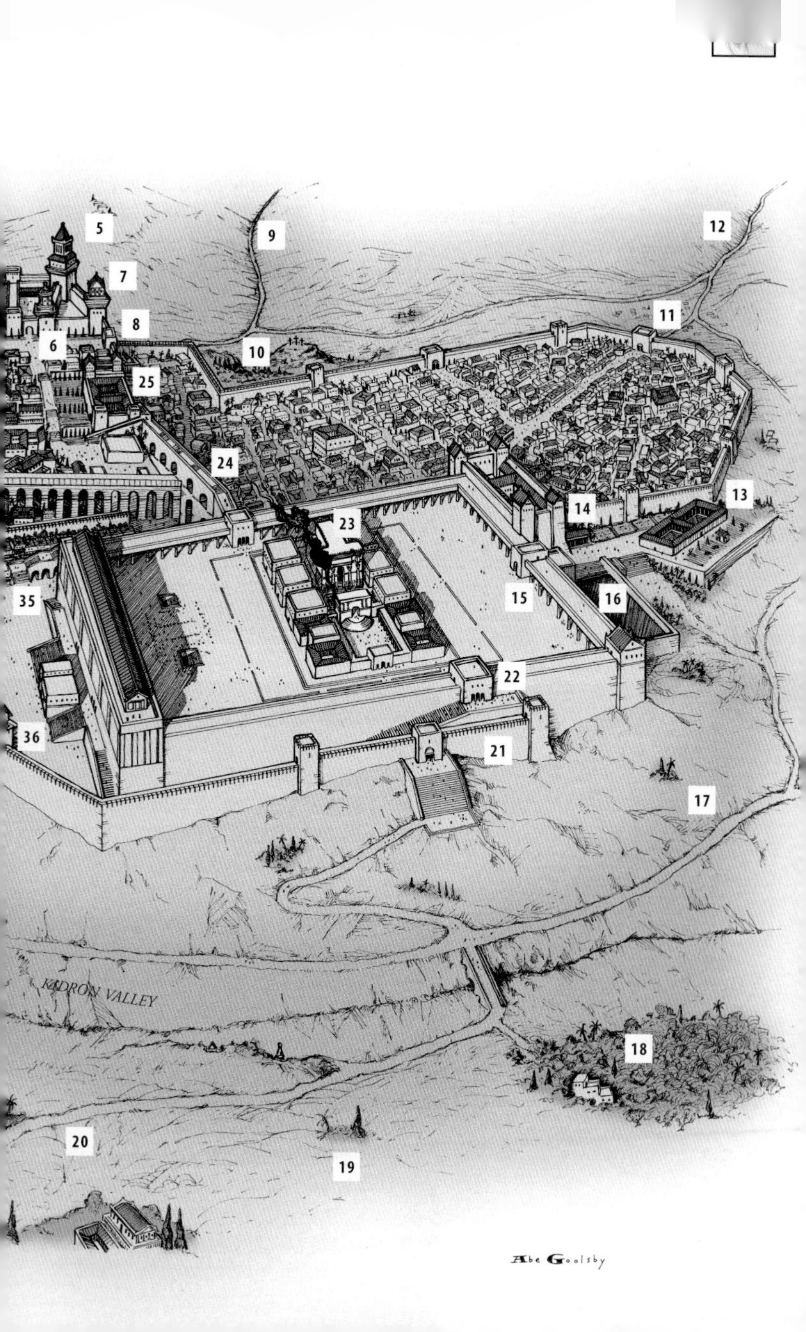
5
7
8
6
9
10
25
24
12
11
13
14
23
15
16
35
22
36
21
17
KIDRON VALLEY
18
20
19
Abe Goolsby

## GENRE AND LITERARY STYLE

### A Gospel Composed in Outstanding *Koinē* Greek

See *Genre and Literary Style* for **MATTHEW** for information about what a "Gospel" is. Luke was the most versatile of all the Gospel writers. The preface is classical Greek, and the rest of chapters 1–2 resembles a Hebrew style. The body of the Gospel is in excellent *Koinē* Greek. Luke's large vocabulary and careful style mark him as an educated "man of letters." Luke was more self-conscious that he was writing "a history" than the other Gospel writers, as his attention to dating certain events shows.

## A PRINCIPLE TO LIVE BY

### Universal Grace (Lk 19:1–9, *Life Essentials Study Bible*, p. 1418)

We must never forget Jesus' primary mission: to provide salvation for all people.

To access a video presentation of this principle featuring Dr. Gene Getz, use a Smartphone or iPad to connect to this QR code or go to http://www.bhpublishinggroup.com/handbook/luke

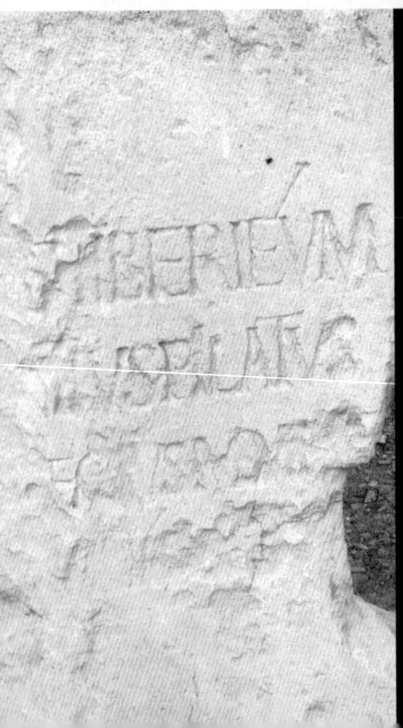

The "Pilate Inscription" from Caesarea Maritima, Israel. The dedicatory inscription to Tiberius Caesar is from Pontius Pilate, prefect of Judea. This inscription was found in 1961 by a team led by Dr. Antonio Frova. The NT refers to Pilate as "governor," while other sources call him "procurator" or "prefect," as in the inscription. Pilate served as prefect of the Roman province of Judea from AD 26 to 36. He greatly outraged the religious sensibilities of both Jews and Samaritans and for the latter was recalled to Rome. In view of his attitude toward and actions against the Jews, it is surprising that he allowed himself to be pressured by a group of Jewish religious authorities into allowing Jesus to be executed. A possible explanation is that he already felt his position in the empire to be in jeopardy (note the threat implicit in John 19:12). Pilate seems to have had no personal inclination to put Jesus to death, and the NT writers are eager to show that he did not (Lk 23:4,14,22; Jn 18:38; 19:4,6; cp. Mt 27:19).

# JOHN

## THE GOSPEL ACCORDING TO JOHN

This title has been associated with the fourth Gospel as long as it has been known. It was named this because its author was believed to be John, the apostle of Jesus.

### KEY TEXT: 3:16

*"For God loved the world in this way: He gave His One and Only Son, so that everyone who believes in Him will not perish but have eternal life."*

### KEY TERM: "LORD"

From the opening prologue to the end of the Gospel, Jesus is portrayed as Lord and God, with a proportionately greater emphasis on His deity than in the other Gospels.

### ONE-SENTENCE SUMMARY

Jesus is the sign-working Son of God who gives eternal life on the basis of His death and resurrection to all who believe in Him.

Ruins of the fishing village of Bethsaida on the northern end of the Sea of Galilee. Bethsaida was home of three of Jesus' disciples, Peter, Andrew, and Philip. Peter and Andrew later lived in the nearby village of Capernaum.

## AUTHOR AND DATE OF WRITING

**John The Apostle, Perhaps Around AD 80–90**

As with all the Gospels, the book is anonymous. Early Christian tradition uniformly affirmed that John composed this Gospel. He was a fisherman from Galilee, son of Zebedee and brother of James, whom Jesus called to be an apostle (Mk 1:19; 3:17). According to Acts, John and Peter were the prominent leaders of the early church.

Many scholars of the past two centuries have denied that John wrote this book, partly because of their belief that the author fabricated many details, such as the miracles and the discourses of Jesus. Such invention is harder to explain if the account was written by an eyewitness of Jesus' life. The author, however, claimed to be an eyewitness (21:24) and referred to himself in the third person as "the disciple He loved" (13:23; 19:26; 20:2; 21:7,20). The tradition of authorship by John is undoubtedly correct.

This Gospel was the last to be written, for it assumes knowledge of many events in Jesus' ministry (which are omitted). On the other hand, it offers much new material. The decade of the AD 80s is a good estimate for the composition of this Gospel.

## FIRST AUDIENCE AND DESTINATION

**Probably Christians Living in Roman Asia**

This issue has been vigorously debated by scholars. According to strong and consistent Christian tradition, John lived a long life and ministered in Ephesus, the largest city in the Roman province of Asia. There is no good reason to doubt this original destination. Scholars, however, are divided as to whether the first audience was Greek, Jewish, or simply Christian. Those who see a Greek (non-Christian) audience note, among other things, that John began with emphasizing Jesus as the Logos, "the Word," a concept from Greek philosophy. The Jewish audience view emphasizes that John wanted people to believe Jesus was the Messiah (20:31). The similarities between this book and the letters of John that were clearly written for believers probably mean that this Gospel was first intended for the benefit of believers. In God's providence it has become remarkably effective in moving unbelievers to embrace Jesus as Lord and Savior.

## OCCASION

John did not relate the human factors that prompted him to write. It appears evident, however, that he was prompted to give a fuller account of some aspects of Jesus' ministry than the other Gospels related. This may have been prompted by John's advancing age and awareness that he had a unique perspective on Jesus' life.

## PURPOSE

The author explicitly states his purpose near the end of his book (20:30–31). He wrote his Gospel to provide an account of Jesus' life and the signs He performed so that people will believe in Him and experience eternal life. Because the verb "believe" may be translated "continue to believe," his purpose no doubt included building up Jesus' followers as well as converting unbelievers.

## FIRST PASS

### Prologue: Christ as the Eternal Word

One does not have to read far into the Gospel of John to realize significant differences with Matthew, Mark, and Luke. Mark opened his Gospel at the beginning of Jesus' ministry. Matthew and Luke began with Jesus' birth. John stretched his readers' minds by taking them beyond the horizon of creation where the Word has always existed. Moreover, the Word was with God and was God. The Word became flesh—a human being—and lived among us showing forth a glory that belongs to the One and Only Son of God. Matthew and Luke gave two different perspectives on Jesus' human genealogy. John began by presenting Jesus' uniquely divine nature and then affirmed His full humanity (1:1–18).

### Presentation of Christ as the Son of God

The role of John the Baptist is explained with clarity in relation to Jesus. John the Baptist was sent from God (1:6). John was not himself the Light (1:8). He came as a witness to Jesus (1:7,15). John the Baptist confessed upon seeing Jesus that here is "the Lamb of God, who takes away the sin of the world!" The calling of Andrew, Simon Peter's brother, was the direct result of John the Baptist's testimony concerning Jesus as the Lamb of God.

This section of John's Gospel is sometimes called the Book of Signs (1:19–12:50), the first of which is Jesus' turning water to wine at a wedding feast in Cana of Galilee. As is the pattern of this Gospel, miracles are referred to as "signs" (*semeion*), intimating that they served as authentication for Jesus' nature and mission. The other six signs are healing an official's son (4:46–54), healing the man at the Pool of Bethesda (5:1–15), feeding 5,000 (6:1–15), walking on water (6:16–21), healing a man born blind (9:1–41), and raising Lazarus from the dead (11:1–57). The disciples see the signs and believe (2:11). Some see the signs and still reject Jesus, as is illustrated by those who knew of the raising of Lazarus and yet did not believe (11:47). Moreover, there are some like Nicodemus who seem to be "secret believers" (3:1–2; 7:50–51).

### Instruction of the Twelve by the Son of God

After Jesus raised Lazarus from death, He performed no other signs but concentrated on preparing His disciples for the events that soon followed, for their new relationship with Him, and for the mission they shared (13:1–17:26). Gathering for Passover meal, the disciples were first cleansed literally (foot-washing; 13:1–17), then figuratively through the removal of the betrayer (13:18–30). Jesus' farewell discourse (13:31 to 16:33) conveys instructions to His followers, particularly about the coming Helping Presence (Gk. *parakletos*), the Holy Spirit, and the disciples' need to remain in Jesus spiritually after His physical departure from earth. This discourse, unique to John's Gospel, concludes with Jesus' prayer for Himself, His disciples, and all believers (chap. 17).

**Jesus' Death, Burial, and Resurrection**

John's passion narrative (18:1–19:42) begins with Jesus' betrayal by Judas (18:1–11), His informal hearing before Annas (18:12–14,19–24), Peter's denials (18:15–18,25–27), Jesus' Roman trial before Pilate (18:28–19:16a), and His crucifixion and burial (19:16b-42). John covered Jesus' appearance before Annas and His Roman trial in considerably more detail than in the other three Gospels.

In John's account Mary Magdalene, Peter, and John became aware that the tomb where Jesus was placed was empty even though it had been sealed by a large stone. When John saw the configuration of grave clothes, he believed. After Peter and John left the scene, Jesus appeared to Mary Magdalene. That evening, the disciples, except for Thomas, were gathered in a room where the doors were locked. Jesus appeared to them and commissioned them. A week later He appeared to the disciples with Thomas present and provided Thomas with more than enough evidence of His resurrection. Jesus later appeared to seven of His disciples on the shore of the Sea of Tiberias. There He commissioned Peter.

The traditional site of Lazarus's tomb in Bethany. Jesus' raising Lazarus from death was the seventh sign in the Gospel of John.

The concluding statement in 20:30–31 rehearses some of the major themes of the Gospel, particularly Jesus' identity as the Messiah and Son of God, His messianic

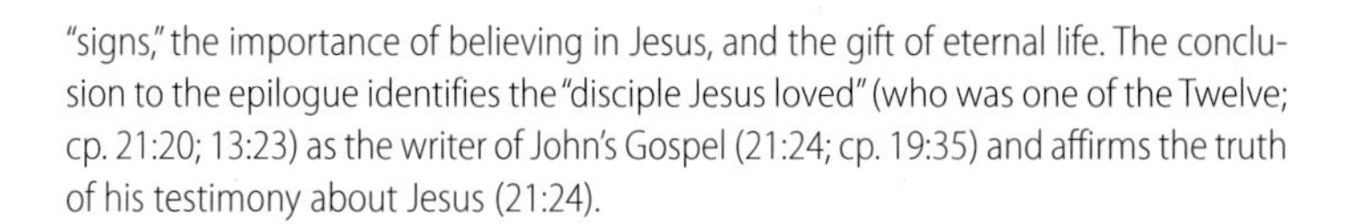

"signs," the importance of believing in Jesus, and the gift of eternal life. The conclusion to the epilogue identifies the "disciple Jesus loved" (who was one of the Twelve; cp. 21:20; 13:23) as the writer of John's Gospel (21:24; cp. 19:35) and affirms the truth of his testimony about Jesus (21:24).

## THE RELIABILITY OF JOHN

Those who read the four Gospels are often impressed by the differences between John and the Synoptics. John includes no parables, few kingdom teachings, no exorcisms, and no pronouncement stories (short debates with hostile questioners ending in climactic pronouncements). Parables seem to have been a distinctively Jewish form of teaching not known to the Greeks. The kingdom was an Old Testament theocratic concept that likewise could have misled a largely Gentile church. Exorcisms were viewed almost magically in the Greco-Roman world, and John does include plenty of more extended controversies with Jewish leaders.

More telling are examples of "interlocking" between John and the Synoptics—places where details in one Gospel help explain what might have remained mysterious in another. For example, John refers to the imprisonment of the Baptist ever so briefly (Jn 3:24), but only the Synoptics narrate the actual story (Mk 6:14–29). John 11:2 distinguishes Mary the sister of Lazarus from Mary the mother of Jesus by alluding to a story John has not yet narrated but that Mark said would be recounted whenever the gospel is preached (Mk 14:9). And the references to Jesus' trial before Caiaphas (Jn 18:24,28) are so short as to presuppose the fuller detail known from the first three Gospels (Mk 14:53–65)

In other instances John clarifies something the Synoptics leave puzzling. Why did the garbled charges against Jesus at His trial claim that He had predicted He would destroy the temple (Mk 14:58–59)? Presumably, because of what He said two years earlier about destroying the temple, when His audience didn't understand He was talking about His own body (Jn 2:19). Why did the Jewish Sanhedrin involve the Roman authorities with Jesus' execution in the first place, since their law prescribed stoning for blasphemy (Mk 15:1–3)? Most probably it was because Rome prevented the Jews from carrying out capital punishment in most instances (Jn 18:31). How could the Synoptics describe Jesus as often wanting to gather the children of Jerusalem together (Mt 23:37) when they narrate only one trip the adult Jesus took to the Holy City—that of His final Passover? Doubtless because He did in fact go there regularly at festival times, as John repeatedly indicates (chaps. 2; 5; 7–9; 10). Indeed, only in John we learn that Jesus' ministry lasted for roughly three years, a claim most scholars accept as accurate. Plenty of additional examples of interlocking in each direction could be given.

A key feature of John's literary genre provides further explanation of the book's distinctives. John was less literal in his reporting than the authors of the Synoptics, in large measure due to writing in a style somewhat akin to ancient Greco-Roman drama. But his recurring emphasis on themes like truth and witness shows that he believed he was faithfully reproducing the life and times of Jesus even through this genre.

A detailed analysis of the historical reliability of John proceeds through the Gospel, verse by verse, looking for compatibility with the Synoptic data and applying standard historical criteria for authenticity to each text in turn. The most helpful criterion is what has been called *double similarity and dissimilarity*. When a teaching or event from Jesus' life fits plausibly into the Jewish world of Israel during the first third of the first century but differs in some respect from most conventional Judaism of the day, it is not likely to have been invented by some Jew other than

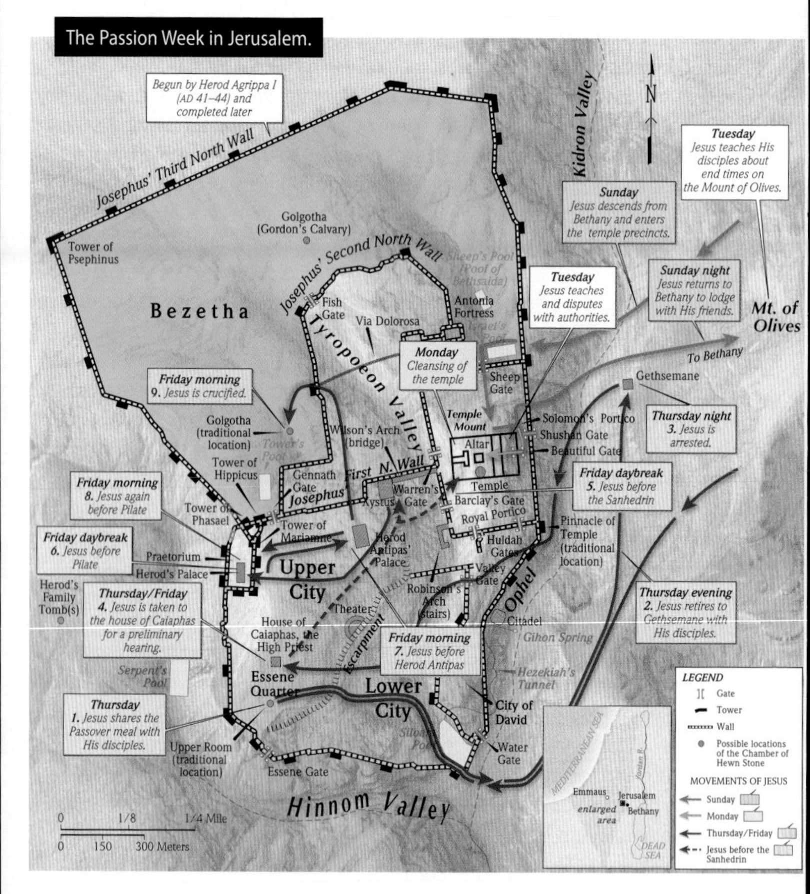

The Passion Week in Jerusalem.

Jesus. When that same teaching or event also shows some continuity with later Christian belief or practice and yet likewise proves distinctive at some telling point, it is not likely to have been manufactured by any later Christian. Usually at least one central element, if not several, emerge in each passage in John to satisfy this four-part criterion.

Much scholarship today continues to dismiss John as not nearly as valuable for recovering the "historical Jesus" as the Synoptics, but this scholarship rarely interacts in detail with the studies that demonstrate the points briefly summarized here.[1]

None of this suggests that historical research can "prove" the reliability of every last detail in John (or any other portion of Scripture). But when writers prove repeatedly reliable where they can be tested, they should be given the benefit of the doubt where they cannot be checked. Christian belief in the full trustworthiness, authority, and inspiration or inerrancy of the text requires a leap of faith beyond what historical evidence alone can demonstrate. But it is not a leap in the dark, flying in the face of the evidence. It is a conscious choice consistent with the evidence that does exist.

## HOW JOHN FITS INTO GOD'S STORY

1. Prologue: Creation, Fall, and the Need for Redemption
2. God Builds His Nation (2000–931 BC)
3. God Educates His Nation (931–586 BC)
4. God Keeps a Faithful Remnant (586–6 BC)
5. **God Purchases Redemption and Begins the Kingdom (6 BC to AD 30)**
6. God Spreads the Kingdom Through the Church (AD 30–?)
7. God Consummates Redemption and Confirms His Eternal Kingdom
8. Epilogue: New Heaven and New Earth

## CHRIST IN JOHN

In John, Jesus is the Logos, the Word of God who was with God and was God. Jesus is God in flesh. Jesus' deity is further amplified in His seven "I am" sayings (I am the bread of life; the light of the world; the door of the sheep; the good shepherd; the resurrection and the life; the way, the truth, and the life; the true vine).

## CHRISTIAN WORLDVIEW ELEMENTS

### Teachings About God

John emphasized the sovereignty and the love of God in sending Jesus. Jesus perfectly reveals God (1:18). In particular, Jesus' astounding proclamations that begin with "I am" are remarkable claims about both His person and His work. Jesus' teaching on the Spirit ("the Counselor") is more extensive than in any other Gospel (chaps. 14–16). This Gospel especially reveals the glory and the name of the Father and the Son.

**Teachings About Humanity**

Humans are sinners in need of a Savior. They are unable to save themselves but are wholly dependent on God's initiative through Jesus. Many individuals demonstrate this: Nicodemus, the Samaritan woman, the man born blind.

**Teachings About Salvation**

This Gospel, more than the others, emphasizes strongly a personal relationship with Jesus that's built on faith in Him and His sacrificial death. Faith in Jesus *is* salvation and eternal life. One such text is 10:27–28: "My sheep hear My voice, I know them, and they follow Me. I give them eternal life, and they will never perish—ever!" John affirms both God's sovereign election of some for eternal life (6:44) and the invitation to "everyone who believes" (3:16).

The Garden Tomb. "There was a garden in the place where He was crucified. A new tomb was in the garden; no one had yet been placed in it. They placed Jesus there because of the Jewish preparation and since the tomb was nearby" (Jn 19:41–42).

## GENRE AND LITERARY STYLE

**A Gospel Composed in Simple but Elegant *Koinē* Greek**

See *Genre and Literary Style* for **MATTHEW** for information about what a "Gospel" is. John wrote with a limited vocabulary, joining his sentences with "and." His style lent itself to developing a number of contrasting concepts: love versus hate; light versus dark; life versus death; truth versus falsehood; above versus below.

## A PRINCIPLE TO LIVE BY

**Acceptance or Rejection (Jn 9:1–41, *Life Essentials Study Bible*, p. 1454)**

We should not be surprised when the message of Christ's deity leads either to saving faith or to total rejection of the salvation story .

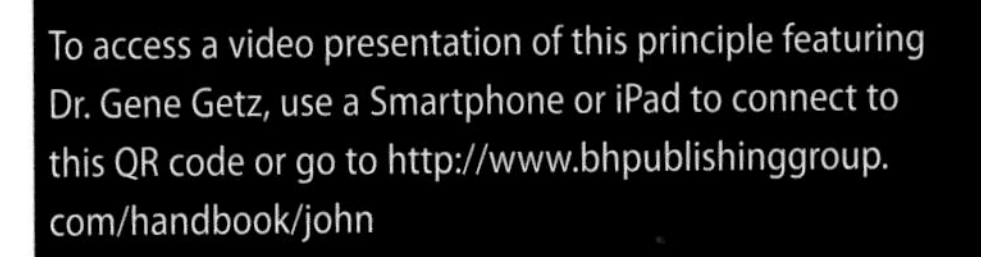

## ENDNOTE

1. Craig L. Blomberg, *The Historical Reliability of John's Gospel: Issues and Commentary* (Downers Grove, IL: InterVarsity Press, 2011).

This title has always been associated with this book. It refers to the deeds Jesus' apostles did in the 30 or so years following His return to heaven.

## KEY TEXT: 1:8

*"But you will receive power when the Holy Spirit has come on you, and you will be My witnesses in Jerusalem, in all Judaea and Samaria, and to the ends of the earth."*

## KEY TERM: "SPIRIT"

This book records what the apostles and early Christians accomplished as they were empowered by the Holy Spirit. The author understood that none of this would have been possible apart from the Holy Spirit.

## ONE-SENTENCE SUMMARY

Christianity spread from Jerusalem to Rome and from Jews to Gentiles by the power of the Holy Spirit, working especially through Peter and Paul.

# ORIGINAL HISTORICAL SETTING

## AUTHOR AND DATE OF WRITING

### Luke, Perhaps Around AD 61–62

Like the Gospel according to Luke, this book is anonymous. On the other hand, uniform Christian tradition affirms that Luke wrote both. The evidence for Lukan authorship within the book is found in three "we sections" in which "we" and "us" occurs (16:10–17; 20:5–21:18; 27:1–28:16). At these times the writer was an eyewitness of Paul's ministry (from Troas to Philippi on Paul's second journey; from Philippi to Jerusalem on the third journey; and from Caesarea to Rome). By a process of deduction, all the associates of Paul except for Luke can be eliminated. If Luke was the author of the "we sections," then by extension he wrote the rest of Acts (since the Greek style and vocabulary are noticeably the same). By further extension Luke must also be the author of the third Gospel. (See *Author and Date of Writing* for **LUKE** for more information.)

Determining the date for Acts depends on what to make of the end of the book. From Acts 25:11 the primary historical question raised by the book is, What happened to Paul when he appeared before Caesar? Yet Acts does not tell. Many Bible students are persuaded that, in his desire to publish, Luke was unwilling to wait on the

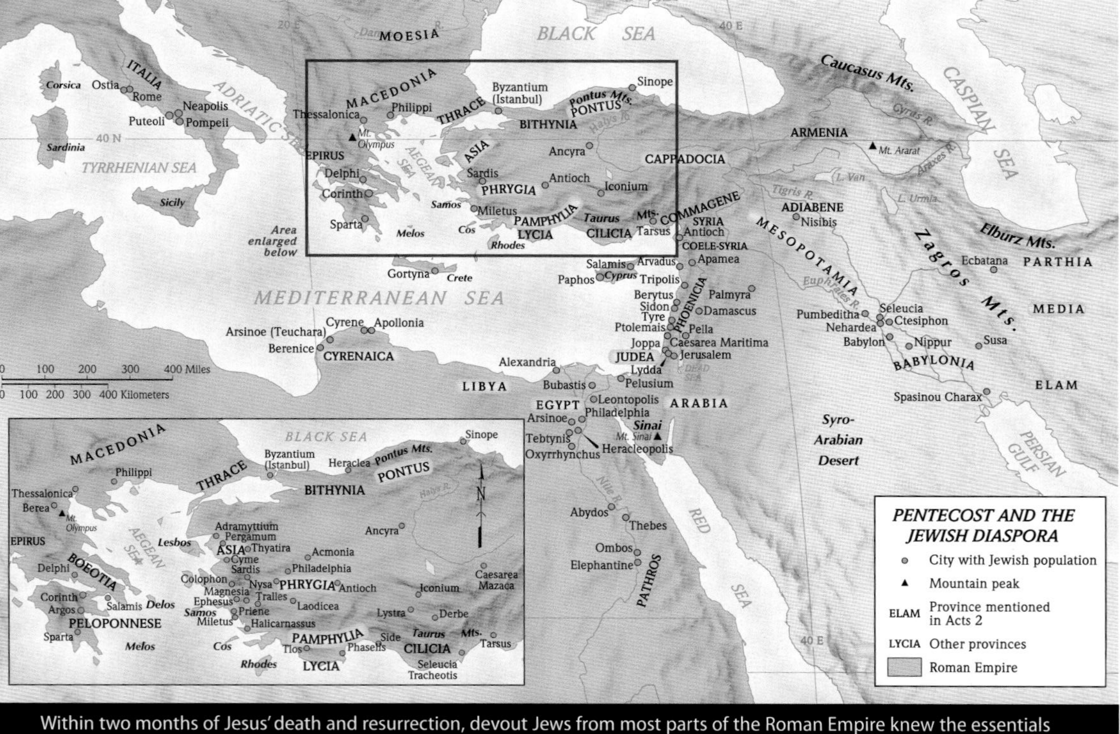


Within two months of Jesus' death and resurrection, devout Jews from most parts of the Roman Empire knew the essentials of the gospel and witnessed the power of the Holy Spirit at the feast of Pentecost.

outcome of Paul's case. He went ahead with publication at the end of Paul's two-year detention described in 28:30. If this is true, Acts is to be dated at 61 or 62. Other scholars, particularly those that reject the traditional understanding of authorship, date the book in the 80s. (The influential nineteenth-century radical critic F. C. Baur believed Acts was written in the second century as an imaginative fiction.)

## FIRST AUDIENCE AND DESTINATION

**Theophilus, a Gentile Whose Residence Is Unknown**

Both Luke and Acts were written for Theophilus. See *First Audience and Destination* for **LUKE**.

## OCCASION

The needs of Theophilus and perhaps his ongoing financial patronage provided the immediate occasion for Acts. If Luke began researching Acts while Paul was detained in Caesarea (see *Occasion* for **LUKE**), then he had direct access to Philip, who was an eyewitness of most of the events for chapters 1–12 (21:8; 23:33; 24:27). Luke also had direct access to Paul, the central character for chapters 13–28, and was himself an eyewitness of some of the events he recorded.

# GOD'S MESSAGE IN ACTS

## PURPOSE

The author's purpose was twofold. First, he wrote as a historian, penning "volume 2" of his two-part work. The first part told what Jesus "began both to do and to teach" (Acts 1:1); the second part is a selective record of what Jesus continued to do through His Spirit and His apostles. The second aspect of his purpose was theological. He showed that Christianity and the church had become the legitimate heir of Israel (and of the Scriptures of Israel). This is seen especially in the biblical quotations in the book, for example "this is that" in Peter's citation of Joel (Ac 2:16–21), James's quotation of Amos (Ac 15:16–17), and Paul's reference to Isaiah (Ac 28:25–28).

## FIRST PASS

**Spirit-Empowered Church**

Acts opens by linking the book with the Gospel, Luke's "first narrative." Like the Gospel (Luke 1:3), the book is dedicated to Theophilus. The first two chapters of Acts in many ways correspond to the first two chapters of the Gospel of Luke: Luke 1–2 dealing with the birth of the Savior, Acts 1–2 with the birth of the church. Just as Jesus was born of the Holy Spirit (Luke 1:35), the same Spirit is the vital force in the life of the church. Acts 1 and 2 relate the coming of the Spirit to the church. Acts 1

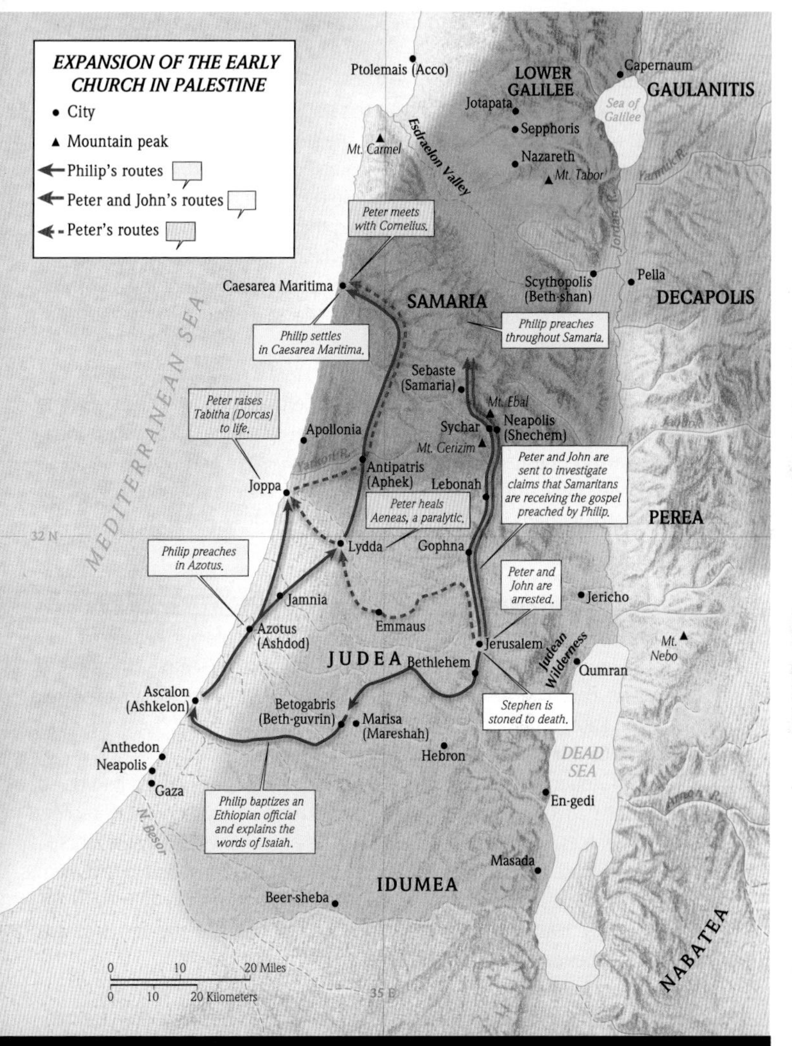


"But you will receive power when the Holy Spirit has come on you, and you will be My witnesses in Jerusalem, in all Judea, and Samaria, and to the ends of the earth" (1:8).

deals with the events leading up to the Spirit's coming, and chapter 2 relates that coming at Pentecost.

**Apostles' Witness**

The setting is still Jerusalem (3:1–5:42). At this point in the life of the church, their witness was solely to the Jews of Jerusalem. The story begins with a healing in the temple complex. This attracted a crowd to whom Peter preached. The crowd made the Jewish authorities uneasy, and they arrested Peter and John. Peter and John were interrogated by the Sanhedrin regarding the healing of the man and were dismissed with a warning to desist from preaching Christ. The Christians did not heed the warning of the Sanhedrin and continued their witness of Jesus. Now *all* the apostles were arrested and hauled before the Sanhedrin for their failure to observe its prohibition.

**Wider Witness**

At this point the gospel began to move beyond Jerusalem in fulfillment of Jesus' commission (1:8). The key figures in this widening mission were the Hellenists, non-Palestinian Jewish Christians who had settled in Jerusalem and whose language and ways were Greek. They are introduced in 6:1–7. Then the witness of two of them is related: Stephen's in 6:8–8:3, and Philip's in 8:4–40.

**In All Judea**

Acts 9–12 completes the narrative of the church's witness in Jerusalem and all Judea. The conversion of Paul and the witness of the Antioch church link with the work of the Hellenists and prepare for the Gentile mission of Paul. Peter's ministry to Cornelius results in Peter's endorsing the witness to the Gentiles. The twelfth chapter gives a final glimpse into the Jerusalem church before the narrative focuses altogether on Paul and his mission to the Gentiles.

**Mission to the Gentiles: First and Second Missionary Journeys**

The church at Antioch was ready to expand its outreach. The Spirit led it to do so through a mission undertaken by Paul and Barnabas. They had great success among the Gentiles. This stirred a debate over the extent to which Gentiles should be made to embrace the Jewish law. A formal meeting was convened in Jerusalem to discuss the issue. After that Paul began a second mission (15:36–18:22). Accompanied by Silas and Timothy, Paul for the first time left the east and witnessed in the cities of Macedonia and Greece.

**Third Missionary Journey**

For the most part Paul's third missionary journey was an extensive three-year ministry in Ephesus. Luke devoted only one chapter to that ministry, but we know from Paul's letters that it was a time when many churches were established and many of his letters written (18:23–21:16).

**Paul's Witness in Judea**

Coming to Jerusalem for the purpose of bringing offerings from churches across the

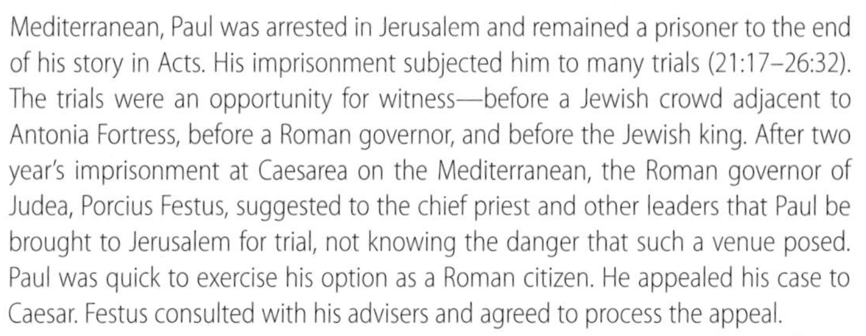

Mediterranean, Paul was arrested in Jerusalem and remained a prisoner to the end of his story in Acts. His imprisonment subjected him to many trials (21:17–26:32). The trials were an opportunity for witness—before a Jewish crowd adjacent to Antonia Fortress, before a Roman governor, and before the Jewish king. After two year's imprisonment at Caesarea on the Mediterranean, the Roman governor of Judea, Porcius Festus, suggested to the chief priest and other leaders that Paul be brought to Jerusalem for trial, not knowing the danger that such a venue posed. Paul was quick to exercise his option as a Roman citizen. He appealed his case to Caesar. Festus consulted with his advisers and agreed to process the appeal.

**Rome**

Paul's voyage to Rome was difficult, particularly the shipwreck. Much of the narrative merely relates in detail the whole life-threatening experience. Through it all, the providence of God shone. God was with Paul and all his traveling companions so that Paul could bear his witness in the imperial city of Rome (27:1–28:31).

## THE RELIABILITY OF ACTS

From the second through the eighteenth century, most scholars read Acts as a historical document. Jerome (AD 340–420) called it "unadorned history." But in the early nineteenth century the historical reliability of Acts was called into question by W. M. L. de Wette in his *Introduction to the New Testament*. Many scholars followed de Wette's rejection of the traditional view. A number came to see Acts as having

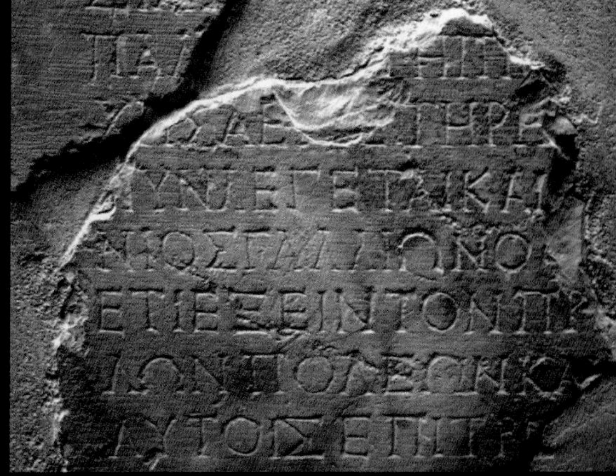

View of the portion of the "Gallio Inscription" from Delphi that mentions Gallio. In the large fragment, in the fourth line from the top, the Greek form of "Gallio" is clearly visible. Gallio was the proconsul of Achaia while Paul was in Corinth (Ac 18:12). The inscription is written in Greek and is a copy of a decree of the Roman Emperor Claudius (AD 41–54) who commanded L. Iunius Gallio, the governor, to assist in settling additional elite persons in Delphi—in an effort to revitalize it. The inscription dates between April and July AD 52, and from it, it can be deduced that Gallio was the proconsul of Achaia in the previous year. Thus Paul's 18 month stay in Corinth (Ac 18:1–18) included the year 51. This inscription is critical in helping to establish the chronology of Paul as presented in the book of Acts.

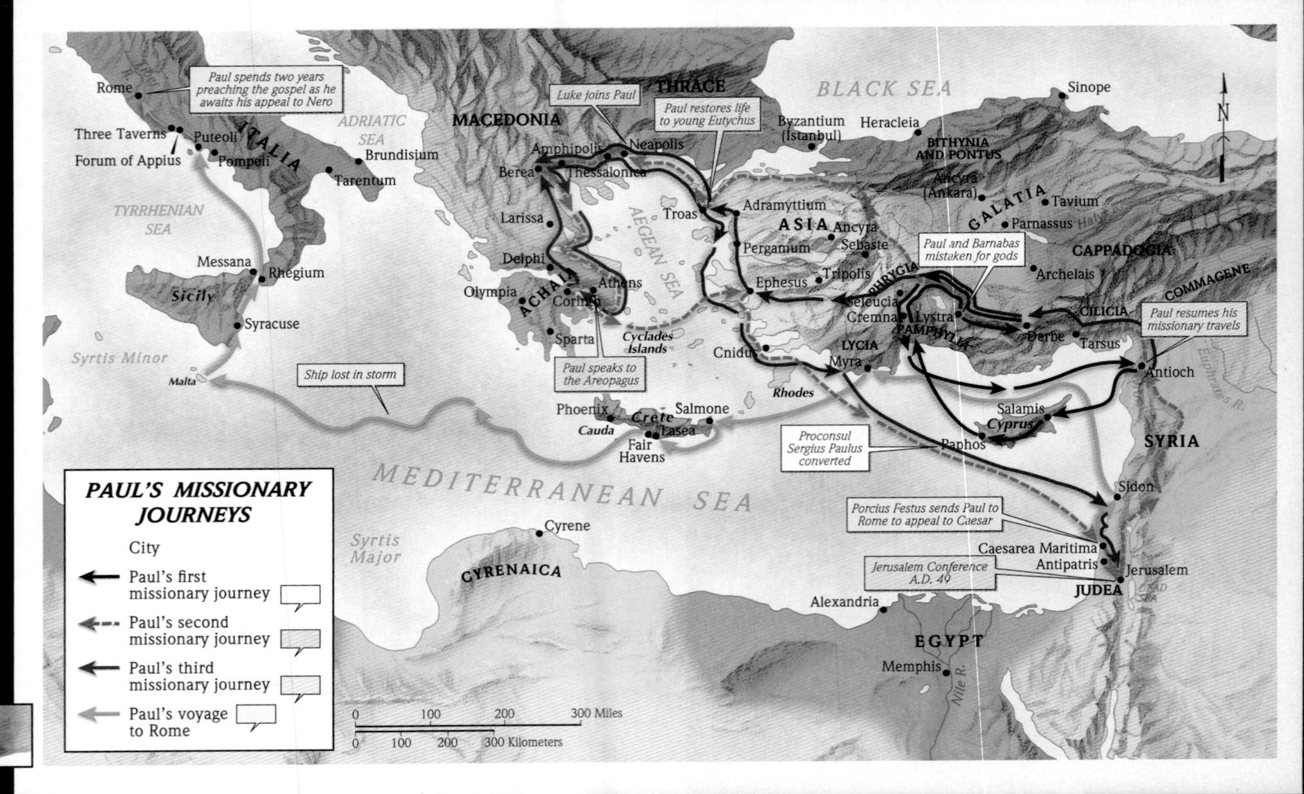

PAUL'S MISSIONARY JOURNEYS
City
Paul's first missionary journey
Paul's second missionary journey
Paul's third missionary journey
Paul's voyage to Rome
0 100 200 300 Miles
0 100 200 300 Kilometers
Paul spends two years preaching the gospel as he awaits his appeal to Nero
Luke joins Paul
Paul restores life to young Eutychus
Paul and Barnabas mistaken for gods
Paul resumes his missionary travels
Ship lost in storm
Paul speaks to the Areopagus
Proconsul Sergius Paulus converted
Porcius Festus sends Paul to Rome to appeal to Caesar
Jerusalem Conference A.D. 49
Rome
Tiber R.
Three Taverns
Forum of Appius
Puteoli
Pompeii
ITALIA
ADRIATIC SEA
Brundisium
Tarentum
TYRRHENIAN SEA
Messana
Rhegium
Sicily
Syracuse
Syrtis Minor
Malta
MACEDONIA
THRACE
Amphipolis
Neapolis
Berea
Thessalonica
Larissa
Delphi
Olympia
ACHAIA
Corinth
Athens
Sparta
AEGEAN SEA
Cyclades Islands
Troas
BLACK SEA
Sinope
Byzantium (Istanbul)
Heracleia
BITHYNIA AND PONTUS
Ancyra (Ankara)
GALATIA
Tavium
Parnassus
Halys
Adramyttium
ASIA
Ancyra
Pergamum
Sebaste
CAPPADOCIA
Ephesus
Tripolis
PHRYGIA
Archelais
COMMAGENE
Seleucia
Cremna
Lystra
PAMPHYLIA
Derbe
CILICIA
Tarsus
Cnidus
LYCIA
Myra
Antioch
Euphrates R.
Rhodes
Phoenix
Crete
Salmone
Cauda
Lasea
Fair Havens
Salamis
Cyprus
Paphos
SYRIA
MEDITERRANEAN SEA
Sidon
Cyrene
Syrtis Major
CYRENAICA
Caesarea Maritima
Antipatris
Jerusalem
JUDEA
Dead Sea
Alexandria
EGYPT
Memphis
Nile R.
N

been written in the early to mid-second century by someone who did not have firsthand acquaintance with his subject or access to eyewitnesses and who had a different agenda than writing history.

Some ancient literary works simply can't be tested for their historical reliability. British New Testament scholar J. B. Lightfoot observed that of all ancient literary works, Acts is the most testable for accuracy. This testability is a two-edged sword: Acts has greater potential for confirmation but also greater potential for being shown to be historically inaccurate.

Scottish archaeologist and New Testament scholar Sir William Ramsay (1851–1939) was educated in the view that Acts was not a historically accurate document. But when he read Acts alongside firsthand research in Asia Minor and Greece, he came to the view "that Luke's history is unsurpassed in respect of its trustworthiness." In Luke's literary prologue to his Gospel, he speaks of having "carefully investigated everything from the very first." This statement of his intention and manner of working describes the way the minute details of Acts are borne out in the evidence that has been brought to light. This growing body of evidence for the historicity of Acts has been substantially augmented by the work of Colin J. Hemer in *The Book of Acts in the Setting of Hellenistic History*.

Antonia Fortress in Jerusalem. Paul came to Jerusalem with brothers from a number of the churches of Asia, Macedonia, and Lycaonia. While in Jerusalem, some Jews from Asia saw Paul in the temple and wrongly concluded that he had brought Gentiles with him into parts of the temple where only Jews were allowed. A riot resulted. The Roman regimental commander had Paul taken into Antonia Fortress adjacent to the temple in order to spare his life and to question him (Ac 21:26–23:27).

## HOW ACTS FITS INTO GOD'S STORY

1. Prologue: Creation, Fall, and the Need for Redemption
2. God Builds His Nation (2000–931 BC)
3. God Educates His Nation (931–586 BC)
4. God Keeps a Faithful Remnant (586–6 BC)
5. God Purchases Redemption and Begins the Kingdom (6 BC to AD 30)
6. **God Spreads the Kingdom Through the Church (AD 30–?)**
7. God Consummates Redemption and Confirms His Eternal Kingdom
8. Epilogue: New Heaven and New Earth

## CHRIST IN ACTS

Jesus, triumphant over death, spends 40 days in conversation with His disciples. He then ascends to the Father and sends, 10 days later, the Holy Spirit to indwell and empower believers. Acts is an account of what Jesus continued to do through His church in the wisdom and power of the Holy Spirit.

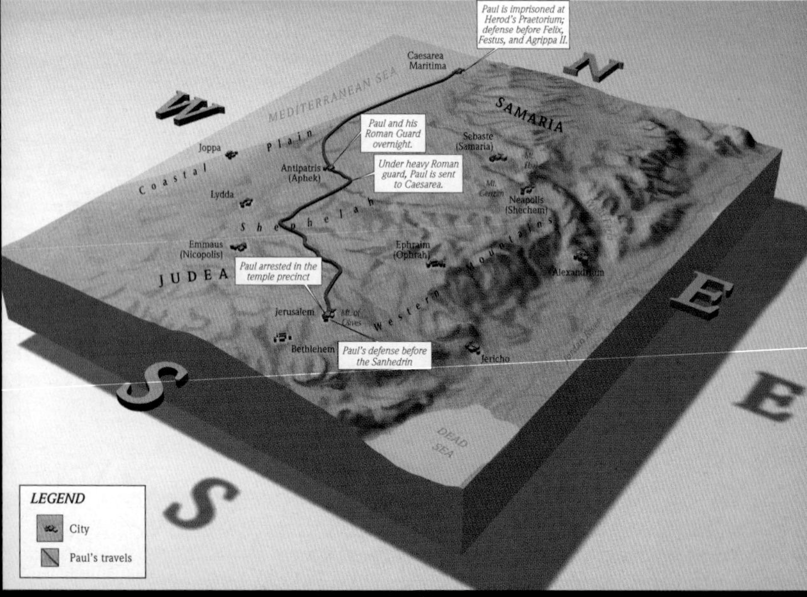


Claudius Lysias, the regimental commander, learned of a plot to kill Paul. He had him taken from Jerusalem to the Roman provincial capital of Judea at Caesarea Maritima where there

## CHRISTIAN WORLDVIEW ELEMENTS

### Teachings About God

The Father is in particular the Sender of the Holy Spirit. The book shows that from the beginning of Christianity Jesus has been the center of proclamation. His life, death, and resurrection were the essence of the good news. Above all, however, this book reveals the person and work of the Holy Spirit more extensively than any other book in the Bible.

### Teachings About Humanity

Particularly by tracing the spread of Christianity from Jews to Samaritans and then to Gentiles, this book shows that all kinds of people are included in salvation. A Pharisee that persecuted Jesus' followers, an African official, a Roman centurion, and a slave girl in Philippi were all touched by the power of Jesus. On the other hand, some leading authorities (both Jewish and Gentile) rejected the proclamation about Jesus.

### Teachings About Salvation

Over and over in this book the basic Christian message is presented: Jesus fulfilled the prophecies of Scripture by His deeds and life; He was crucified; God raised Him;

Sunset on St. Paul's Bay, Malta. The ship on which Paul was sailing to Rome encountered a violent storm that battered the ship over a two-week period. The ship struck a sandbar and ran aground on Malta (27:13–28:19).

the necessary human response is to repent of sins and believe in Him; those who do so receive God's good gift of the Spirit. Salvation in Acts focuses on the Spirit's filling believers so that they live holy lives and do God's will.

## GENRE AND LITERARY STYLE

### A Historical Narrative Written in Excellent *Koinē* Greek

The overall genre of Acts is "historical narrative." In this sense Acts parallels other works from antiquity, especially those also known as "Acts." Luke's work (like his Gospel) was not simply a recounting of facts but a careful theological interpretation. He included summaries of important early Christian speeches, giving samples of a variety of speakers (Peter, Stephen, Paul), audiences (Jewish, Greek, Christian), and circumstances (friendly, hostile). Luke used a large vocabulary and carefully polished Greek style.

## A PRINCIPLE TO LIVE BY

### Waiting and Working (Ac 1:6–14, *Life Essentials Study Bible*, p. 1480)

Though we always should be prepared for Christ's return, we are to focus on being His witnesses in this world.

To access a video presentation of this principle featuring Dr. Gene Getz, use a Smartphone or iPad to connect to this QR code or go to http://www.bhpublishinggroup.com/handbook/acts

The last leg of Paul's journey to Rome was likely the Appian Way that he would have accessed several miles from the port of Puteoli (Ac 28:11–16).

# ROMANS

## THE EPISTLE TO THE ROMANS

As with all the New Testament letters written by Paul the apostle, this epistle is titled according to its first recipients, in this case the Christians in Rome.

### KEY TEXT: 1:16–17

*"For I am not ashamed of the gospel, because it is God's power for salvation to everyone who believes, first to the Jew, and also to the Greek. For in it God's righteousness is revealed from faith to faith, just as it is written: The righteous will live by faith."*

### KEY TERM: "RIGHTEOUSNESS"

The Greek noun translated "righteousness" is *dikaiosunē*. It is closely related to the verb *dikaioō*, usually translated "justify." This book is a long theological argument about how unrighteous sinners may receive right standing with God (are justified).

### ONE-SENTENCE SUMMARY

Righteousness with God is given freely (imputed) to all those who have faith in Jesus Christ for salvation according to God's eternal plan.

The Pantheon is one of the most complete ancient Roman structures to have survived. It was first built in 27–25 BC by Marcus Vipsanius Agrippa, son-in-law of Caesar Augustus. The inscription on the architrave says the structure was built by Agrippa during his third term as consul. Historians disagree over the Pantheon's stages of development. Nevertheless, it has stood for two millennia as the world's largest unreinforced concrete dome.

## AUTHOR AND DATE OF WRITING

**Paul the Apostle, Around AD 57**

This book claims to be written by "Paul, a slave of Christ Jesus." All New Testament scholars accept this claim. He was a devout Pharisee converted to faith in Jesus and called to become apostle to the Gentiles on the famous "Road to Damascus" (Acts 9). Paul's ministry may be divided into three parts:

- The period of personal growth in discipleship, about AD 33–47 (Acts 9–12)
- The period of three missionary journeys, about AD 48–57 (Acts 13–21)
- The period of consolidating the churches, about AD 58–65 (Acts 22–28)

Romans was written near the end of Paul's third missionary journey, which culminated in his arrest in Jerusalem.

## FIRST AUDIENCE AND DESTINATION

**Christians Worshipping in House Churches in Rome**

Little is known about how Christianity first arrived in Rome. No biblical evidence supports the tradition that Peter was the first to preach the gospel in Rome. The gospel may have been taken there by Jews from Rome who believed in Jesus on Pentecost (Ac 2:10). It was already present in AD 49, when the Emperor Claudius expelled Jews from the city, among whom were the Christian couple Priscilla and Aquila (Ac 18:2).

By the time Paul wrote Romans, the majority of believers there were probably Gentile. Paul knew a number of Roman Christians by name (chap. 16), and his greeting pattern indicates that they met in house churches scattered throughout the city (16:5,14, and 15 probably each reflect a house church group).

The city of Rome was a splendid if corrupt monument to centuries of Roman military success. It may have had a million people, half of them slaves. Rome was the economic and political center of the world. Truly all roads led to Rome.

## OCCASION

Paul had never preached in Rome, and he had long desired this privilege. He had finished his great endeavor of the third missionary journey, the collection for the saints in Jerusalem (see *Occasion* for **2 CORINTHIANS**). He was at this time spending the winter in Corinth (AD 56–57), for the Mediterranean Sea was unsafe for travel for three months (Ac 20:3). Paul's mind was now turning to Rome (where he wanted to preach and to encourage the Roman Christians) and to Spain. With "time on his hands" in Corinth, he penned this letter to the Roman Christians in order to introduce himself and his theology. He was aided by Tertius the scribe (16:22).

## PURPOSE

Paul wrote to the Roman Christians in order to give them a substantial resume of his theology. This epistle stands as Paul's "theological self-confession." Behind this was his concern to prepare the Roman believers for his intended ministry there and to create interest in the preaching mission to Spain that he planned.

## FIRST PASS

### The Righteousness of God

God's righteousness is a paramount theme throughout this the longest of Paul's letters. This motif is introduced at the outset in 1:16–17 (Hab 2:4). Gentiles (1:18–2:16) and Jews (2:17–29) have both sinned, and the atonement of Christ is applicable to both (3:21–31). God's way of justifying sinners, both Gentiles and Jews, is seen in the case of Abraham who lived before the law was given (4:1–25). Paul expounded the meaning of this gift of righteousness. Whether Jew or Gentile, those who trust in the redemptive work of God in Jesus Christ will have "peace with God" (5:1), will be freed from the penalty and power of sin (chap. 6), but will still struggle experientially with reality of sin and the power of the law (chap. 7). Chapter 8 gloriously describes the believer's freedom from condemnation, futility, alienation from God, and eternal death.

### Israel's Place in God's Purposes

Paul agonized over Israel's rejection of God's Messiah (9:1–5). He recalled God's gracious election of Israel (9:6–13) and affirmed God's freedom and His justice in His choices. For Paul this was not just abstract theology but a matter that troubled him at the deepest

The interior of the Pantheon. Since the seventh century the Pantheon has served as a Roman Catholic church, Santa Maria della Rotonda.

levels of his being (10:1). Gentiles who believed had been grafted into the cultivated olive tree, but God did not cast off Israel (11:1–2). God will graft them back into the tree from which they have been temporarily separated because of their unbelief. This God will do if they trust in Jesus as the true Messiah and Savior (11:23). God continues to have a believing "remnant"(11:5) "until the full number of the Gentiles has come in" (11:25).

**The Fruits of God's Righteousness**

God's righteousness is to be expressed in the lives of believers within the family, the church, and in the larger society (12:1–15:13). Paul concluded his letter by revealing his plans to come to Rome en route to Spain. He then greeted 27 people, including a significant number of women. Paul appealed for the church to avoid divisions and disunity. He offered greetings from his colleagues and closed with an appropriate doxology: "To the only wise God, through Jesus Christ—to Him be glory forever! Amen."

Baptistry at Emmaus Nicopolis, Israel, the site to which Jesus accompanied Cleopas and another disciple, on the day of His resurrection (Lk 24:13–35). "Therefore we were buried with Him by baptism into death, in order that, just as Christ was raised from the dead by the glory of the Father, so we too may walk in a new way of life" (Rm 6:4).

## THE RELIABILITY OF ROMANS

Some geographical and temporal markers shed light on Paul's letter to the Romans. The gospel probably came to Rome in the early 30s when pilgrims from Pentecost returned to Rome. The first Jewish community in Europe was that in Rome dating to 161 BC when Judas Maccabeus sent envoys to Rome. Twelve synagogues existed in Rome during the first century, although not all 12 simultaneously. Those Jewish pilgrims who had embraced Jesus as Messiah at Pentecost probably practiced their faith within the context of their Jewish community just as their Judean brothers and sisters were fully engaged in worship within the temple.

In AD 49, the Roman emperor Claudius expelled the Jews from Rome. In his *Life of Claudius* (25.4), Seutonius says, "As the Jews were making constant disturbances at the instigation of Chrestus, he expelled them from Rome." Some have interpreted *Chrestus* to be a variant of *Christus* and have conjectured that there was a division within the Jewish community of Rome over Jesus Christ.

Olive trees with harvest moon rising over the hills. Paul, speaking to Gentiles, likens them to wild olive branches that have been grafted into a cultivated olive tree (Israel). He charges them not to be arrogant but to "consider God's kindness and severity: severity towards those who have fallen but God's kindness toward you—if you remain in His kindness. Otherwise you too will be cut off" (11:22).

Two of those expelled were a couple, Aquila and Priscilla, who travelled to Corinth where they met Paul. Claudius lived only five years after the edict of 49, and following his death many Jews returned to Rome. During the five years when Claudius's edict was in effect, the church(es) in Rome would have been predominantly Gentile. The return of Jewish believers to Rome could well have created tensions within the church at Rome that Paul addressed in his letter.[1]

## HOW ROMANS FITS INTO GOD'S STORY

1. Prologue: Creation, Fall, and the Need for Redemption
2. God Builds His Nation (2000–931 BC)
3. God Educates His Nation (931–586 BC)
4. God Keeps a Faithful Remnant (586–6 BC)
5. God Purchases Redemption and Begins the Kingdom (6 BC to AD 30)
6. **God Spreads the Kingdom Through the Church (AD 30–?)**
7. God Consummates Redemption and Confirms His Eternal Kingdom
8. Epilogue: New Heaven and New Earth

## CHRIST IN ROMANS

In this letter to the Romans, Paul presents Christ as "a descendant of David according to the flesh and who has been declared to be the powerful Son of God by the resurrection from the dead according to the Spirit of holiness" (1:3–4). Through Jesus' death we are reconciled to God, and by His life we are saved (5:10).

## CHRISTIAN WORLDVIEW ELEMENTS

### Teachings About God

In Romans God is supreme in all matters of salvation, which serves His glory and the good of His people. He is both the One who is righteous and the One who declares righteous (3:26). There is no fuller presentation of the person and work of Christ. The Holy Spirit is the One by whose indwelling believers are enabled to live holy lives (chap. 8).

### Teachings About Humanity

There are only two kinds of human beings: sinners who are condemned "in Adam" and believing sinners "in Christ" who are therefore declared righteous. Those who have been justified by faith are expected to live holy lives and to live in Christian community with one another by the power of the Spirit.

### Teachings About Salvation

Salvation is a complex concept that includes past, present, and future. For individual believers, Christ has saved from the penalty of sin (justification, chaps. 4–5); He is

saving from the power of sin (sanctification, chaps. 6–7); and He will save from the presence of sin (glorification, chap. 8). For the community of believers, salvation came first to Israel (chaps. 9–10), and in the present era it is coming to Gentiles (and some Jews) who make up the church (chap. 11).

## GENRE AND LITERARY STYLE

**A Long, Formal Epistle Written in *Koinē* Greek**

See *Genre and Literary Style* for **1 THESSALONIANS** for information about the genre "epistle." All four standard parts of a first-century epistle appear in Romans: salutation (1:1–7); thanksgiving (1:8–17); main body (1:18–16:18); and farewell (16:19–24). Some scholars designate Romans as a tractate (a formal treatise rather than a pastoral letter). Paul's Greek is careful, and Romans reflects Paul at his most typical writing style.

## A PRINCIPLE TO LIVE BY

**Salvation Through Faith (Rm 3:21–26, *Life Essentials Study Bible*, p. 1538)**

Since we all fall short of God's perfect standard of righteousness, in order to be saved we must put our faith in the Lord Jesus Christ.

To access a video presentation of this principle featuring Dr. Gene Getz, use a Smartphone or iPad to connect to this QR code or go to http://www.bhpublishinggroup.com/handbook/romans

## ENDNOTE

1. Craig L. Blomberg, *From Pentecost to Patmos: An Introduction to Acts Through Revelation* (Nashville: B&H Publishing Group, 2006), 235.

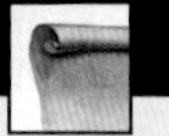


The Acrocorinth, a massive rock (1,886 feet) that overlooked Corinth, a principal Greek city that dated to the 10th century BC. Julius Caesar rebuilt Corinth in 44 BC, and it quickly became an important city in the Roman Empire. An overland shiproad across the isthmus connected the ports of Lechaion and Cenchreae. Cargo from large ships was unloaded, transported across the isthmus, and reloaded on other ships. Small ships were moved across on a system of rollers. Ships were able, therefore, to avoid 200 miles of stormy travel around the southern part of the Greek peninsula. (See p. 378,381.)

The Lechaion road entered Corinth from the north, connecting it with the port on the Gulf of Corinth. As the road entered the city, it widened to more than 20 feet with walks on either side. From the southern part of the city a road ran southeast to Cenchreae. Approaching the city from the north, the Lechaion road passed through the Propylaea, the beautiful gate marking the entrance into the agora (market).

This book is so named because it is the first canonical letter that Paul the apostle wrote to the Christians in Corinth.

## KEY TEXT: 15:58

*"Therefore, my dear brothers, be steadfast, immovable, always excelling in the Lord's work, knowing that your labor in the Lord is not in vain."*

## KEY TERM: "LOVE"

Although this letter reflects a church facing many difficult issues, the solution always involves love ("charity" in the KJV; *agapē* in Greek). The "Love Chapter" (13) is the best known and most beloved part of the letter.

## ONE-SENTENCE SUMMARY

The many problems a congregation may have, whether doctrinal or practical, will be resolved as that church submits properly to the lordship of Christ and learns to love one another genuinely.

## AUTHOR AND DATE OF WRITING:

**Paul the Apostle, Around AD 55**

This book claims to be written by "Paul, called as an apostle of Christ Jesus by God's will." All New Testament scholars accept this claim. See *Author and Date of Writing* for **ROMANS** for more information about Paul. The apostle wrote this letter around AD 55, probably near the end of his long ministry in Ephesus on his third missionary journey (Ac 19).

## FIRST AUDIENCE AND DESTINATION

**Christians in Corinth**

Acts 18 describes how Christianity first came to Corinth through Paul's preaching. Silas, Timothy, Priscilla, Aquila, and Apollos also helped establish the church in Corinth. The members had come from both Jewish and pagan backgrounds.

Corinth was a large and splendid commercial city, with Greek roots and a Roman overlay in the first century. Its population was perhaps 500,000. Because of its location at the Corinthian isthmus, it benefited from both land and sea routes. Corinth, rather than Athens, was chosen as the Roman capital of Achaia. Like all large cities of the Roman Empire, Corinth was both religious (with a number of pagan temples) and immoral (with the worship of Aphrodite sanctioning religious prostitution).

## OCCASION

Paul's ministry in Corinth had resulted in a well-established, thriving congregation. He had moved on from there and now was living in Ephesus. Several factors converged to make this letter necessary.

1. Paul had written a (now lost) letter advising the believers not to associate with people claiming to be Christians but living immorally. The church misunderstood Paul's meaning (5:9–11).
2. Paul had received an oral report that the church had divided into several competing factions (1:11–12).
3. Paul had learned that the church was tolerating open sexual immorality (5:1).
4. Paul had received a "committee" (composed of Stephanas, Fortunatus, and Achaicus) sent by the Corinthians. They brought him more information about the church and had a list of written questions for Paul to respond to (7:1; 16:17).

Paul therefore wrote this letter to respond to this great variety of issues. He apparently used the professional secretarial help of Sosthenes and sent the letter by Timothy (1:1; 4:17).

# GOD'S MESSAGE IN 1 CORINTHIANS

## PURPOSE

Paul wrote to the Corinthian Christians in order to address the difficulties they were facing (see *Occasion* above). His desire, of course, was for the church to change where it needed to change and to be encouraged where it was doing the right things.

## FIRST PASS

The focus of 1 Corinthians is pastoral theology occasioned by real problems in and questions from the church at Corinth. Although the church was gifted (1:4–7), it was equally immature and unspiritual (3:1–4). Paul wanted to restore the church in its areas of weakness. The letter begins by dealing with the problem of those who bring division to the body of Christ (1:11–3:4). Second, Paul addressed a case of immorality in the church (chaps. 5–6). Third, he answered the church's list of questions brought to him by a committee (16:12). A recurring literary device is expressions like "about" or "concerning" to move through the list of questions about male and female in marriage (7:1), virgins (7:25), food offered to idols (8:1), spiritual gifts

(12:1), the collection for the saints in Jerusalem (16:1), and Apollos (16:12). Although 1 Corinthians is not a doctrinal treatise like Romans, it contains the Bible's clearest exposition on the Lord's Supper (11:17–34), the resurrection (15:1–58).

## THE RELIABILITY OF 1 CORINTHIANS

First Corinthians 15 contains a concise summary of the gospel and some of the strongest evidence for Jesus' resurrection as a historical event. Paul had a fragmentary knowledge of the gospel even before his conversion. He knew what the apostles claimed regarding Jesus: that He had been crucified and raised from death and that He was God's Messiah. The apostles' claims fueled Paul's intense opposition to the early church. The claims that Jesus had been crucified and raised from death were equally provocative to Paul. Crucifixion indicated the person crucified was under a divine curse (Dt 21:23; Gl 3:13). Paul believed the second claim to be patently false. He wholeheartedly defended God's truth as he understood it. His reversal came in a firsthand experience of Jesus on the road to Damascus. In the list of witnesses to the resurrection, Paul listed himself as "one abnormally born" (15:8).

▲ Bronze head of a boxer crowned with olive wreath for Olympic Games victor (only stem remains). Probably famous boxer Satyros of Elis. Work of Athenian bronze-sculptor Silanion, about 330–320 BC. "I do not run like one who runs aimlessly or box like one beating the air. Instead, I discipline my body and bring it under strict control, so that after preaching to others, I myself will not be disqualified" (1Co 9:26–27).

Paul probably received this confessional statement (15:3–4) at his baptism in Damascus. In his first visit to Jerusalem that came about three years following his conversion, he talked with others who had witnessed firsthand the risen Christ prior to His ascension: Peter, the Twelve, James. From these conversations he learned of an appearance of Jesus "to over 500 brothers at one time." In effect, Paul was inviting Corinthian skeptics concerning the resurrection to check the evidence. The late Pinchas

Lapide, Orthodox Jewish scholar and former chairman of the applied linguistics department at Jerusalem's Bar-Han University, believed Paul's summary of the gospel to be a statement of eyewitness. Although he did not accept Jesus as Israel's Messiah, he believed the evidence for His resurrection was compelling.

## HOW 1 CORINTHIANS FITS INTO GOD'S STORY

1. Prologue: Creation, Fall, and the Need for Redemption
2. God Builds His Nation (2000–931 BC)
3. God Educates His Nation (931–586 BC)
4. God Keeps a Faithful Remnant (586–6 BC)
5. God Purchases Redemption and Begins the Kingdom (6 BC to AD 30)
6. **God Spreads the Kingdom Through the Church (AD 30–?)**
7. God Consummates Redemption and Confirms His Eternal Kingdom
8. Epilogue: New Heaven and New Earth

## CHRIST IN 1 CORINTHIANS

To a church fascinated by wisdom and power, Paul declares Christ to be both the power (1:18,24) and the wisdom (1:21,24,30) of God.

## CHRISTIAN WORLDVIEW ELEMENTS

### Teachings About God

God the Father is the supreme Lord, for whose glory all things are to be done (10:31). The theological centrality of Jesus' bodily resurrection is developed in the sustained argument of the "Resurrection Chapter" (chap. 15). His lordship over the church means that He has the right to order its life and worship. The Spirit's life-giving presence has brought the church into existence, has given each of its members "spiritual gifts," and enables its members to live *holy* lives because He is the *Holy* Spirit.

### Teachings About Humanity

Humanity in this book is seen mainly within the context of Christian community. Redeemed people have been transformed by Christ, are called and enabled to love one another, and are destined for resurrection. Such persons, however, still struggle with sins such as divisiveness, sexual immorality, and disorder in worship.

### Teachings About Salvation

This letter contains what may be the first-composed written summary of the New Testament understanding of redemption: "For I passed on to you as most important what I also received: that Christ died for our sins according to the Scriptures" (15:3).

Further, this book emphasizes that God saves only those individuals who believe in Christ's death (1:21).

## GENRE AND LITERARY STYLE

### A Long Epistle Written in *Koinē* Greek

See *Genre and Literary Style* for **1 THESSALONIANS** for information about the genre "epistle." The four standard parts of a first-century epistle all appear in 1 Corinthians: salutation (1:1–3); thanksgiving (1:4–9); main body (1:10–16:18); and farewell (16:19–21). Like most of Paul's writings, this is a pastoral letter, driven by the occasion and needs of the recipients rather than a tractate (a formal treatise). Paul's Greek is careful, and 1 Corinthians reflects the typical Pauline writing style.

## A PRINCIPLE TO LIVE BY

### Reflections of Love (1Co 13:1–13, *Life Essentials Study Bible*, p. 1585–86)

To build up one another, we must demonstrate Christ's love in all of our relationships.

To access a video presentation of this principle featuring Dr. Gene Getz, use a Smartphone or iPad to connect to this QR code or go to http://www.bhpublishinggroup.com/handbook/1corinthians

This book is so named because it is the second canonical letter Paul the apostle wrote to the Christians in Corinth.

## KEY TEXT: 12:9

*"But He said to me, 'My grace is sufficient for you, for power is perfected in weakness.' Therefore, I will most gladly boast all the more about my weaknesses, so that Christ's power may reside in me."*

## KEY TERM: "DEFENSE"

Of all Paul's letters, this is the most personal and the most defensive. In it Paul mounted a defense ("apology" in the good sense) of his apostolic authority and ministry.

## ONE-SENTENCE SUMMARY

True Christian ministry, although it may have to be defended against false attacks, is commissioned by Christ and empowered by His Spirit.

The Corinth Canal.

## AUTHOR AND DATE OF WRITING

**Paul the Apostle, About AD. 56**

This book claims to be written by "Paul, an apostle of Christ Jesus by God's will." All biblical scholars accept this claim. See *Author and Date of Writing* for **ROMANS** for more information about Paul. The apostle wrote this letter around AD 56, after he had concluded his ministry in Ephesus on his third missionary journey and had arrived in Macedonia (Ac 20:1–2; 2Co 7:5–7).

## FIRST AUDIENCE AND DESTINATION

**The Christians in Corinth**

See *First Audience and Destination* for **1 CORINTHIANS**.

## OCCASION

See *Occasion* for **1 CORINTHIANS**. Careful study of 2 Corinthians has resulted in the following understanding of the events that led to its composition.

1. First Corinthians was not well received by the congregation. Timothy evidently returned to Paul in Ephesus with a report that the church was still greatly troubled. This was partly caused by the arrival in Corinth of "false apostles" (11:13–15). (These were evidently Jewish Christians who emphasized sophisticated rhetoric; perhaps also they were Judaizers, asking the Corinthians to live according to Mosaic regulations.)
2. Paul visited Corinth, an experience he described as "painful" (2:1; 13:2–3). Evidently the "false apostles" led the Corinthians to disown Paul.
3. Paul then wrote a (now lost) "severe letter" of stinging rebuke to Corinth from Ephesus. He sent this letter by Titus (2:3–4). Sometime shortly after this, Paul left Ephesus and traveled on, first to Troas and then to Macedonia (2:12–13).
4. Titus finally tracked Paul down in Macedonia with good news: Most of the church had repented and returned to the gospel and accepted Paul's authority (7:5–7).

Paul decided to write the Corinthians one more time, his fourth known letter to them, expressing his relief but still pleading with the unrepentant minority. He apparently used the professional secretarial help of Timothy and sent the letter by Titus (1:1; 8:17).

# GOD'S MESSAGE IN 2 CORINTHIANS

## PURPOSE

Paul wrote to the Corinthian Christians in order to express his relief at the success of his severe letter and the mission of Titus, to ask for money for the poor saints in

Jerusalem, and to defend his ministry as an apostle to the minority of unrepentant Corinthians (see *Occasion* above). His desire, of course, was to encourage the majority and to lead the minority to change its mind.

## FIRST PASS

### Authentic Ministry

Praise to God for His mercy and comfort is the note Paul struck in opening this letter. Paul opened his heart to the Corinthians, explaining why he was not able to visit them as he had intended (1:15–22), and giving an account of his ministry as one of integrity and suffering (1:8–12; 6:3–10; 11:23–29), marks of a true apostle. His ministry was a continuing triumph in Christ (2:14), empowered by the risen life of Christ (4:10–11). At the same time he gloried in suffering and was content with weaknesses, persecutions, and calamities for the sake of Christ (12:9).

### A Call to Generosity

In the context of restored relationships, Paul turned to the topic of the collection for the church in Jerusalem (8:1–9:15). Paul had earlier appealed to the Corinthians (1 Co 16:1–4) to join with other churches across the Mediterranean in supporting the church in Jerusalem. Famine and perhaps economic sanctions had left many Judean believers impoverished. The Corinthians had promised to give and had failed to follow through. Paul now appealed for the Corinthians to complete what they said they would do. In this context Paul articulated principles of stewardship that are valid at all times.

### Paul's Apostolic Authority

At this point there is an abrupt change in tone and content. The "superapostles" who had exalted themselves and deprecated Paul in the eyes of the Corinthians had to be challenged. Paul had been commissioned by Christ and was given authority for planting and building up the churches (10:8).

Paul had planted the church in Corinth. His love for the Corinthians took the form of a godly jealousy for their well-being in the face of those who would take advantage of them and lead them astray (11:1–15). The eloquence and self-promotion of the "superapostles" gave Paul the appearance of not measuring up as an apostle. The irony is that his tenderness and pastoral concern was used against him as a supposed weakness. They claimed Paul was a false apostle and knew it; thus he did not receive their money. Paul turned the argument around and suggested the true sign of an apostle was a form of weakness, for true apostles suffer. With some reluctance Paul then chronicled his experiences of suffering and weakness that paradoxically were his strength in leading him to place his reliance on Christ rather than himself (11:16–12:10).

Remnants of the Diolkos, the paved road built in ancient times across the Isthmus of Corinth. This was a rudimentary form of a railway over which ships were transported from one side of the isthmus to the other, saving significant navigational time and effort.

**Conclusion**

Paul claimed he would without fail make another trip to visit them. He warned them at this time that he would have to deal with their sin. He would do so firmly with the power of God. He admonished them to examine their faith and to restore fellowship with him and with one another. The letter concludes without the usual greetings but with a beautiful benediction (13:1–14).

## THE RELIABILITY OF 2 CORINTHIANS

Some have suggested that chapters 10–13 were the severe letter, written prior to chapters 1–9, but strong evidence for this hypothesis is lacking. Most likely the severe letter has not survived. The letter, as we now have it, forms a coherent whole as the structure and outline indicate. The history of the church has been nearly unanimous in affirming the letter's unity. No existing Greek manuscripts present the letter in any other form.

Further evidence for unity between chapters 1–9 and 10–13 can be found in seven distinct vocabulary patterns that are rarely used in Paul's letters but are employed in both major parts of 2 Corinthians.[1] Some interpreters have defended the unity of 2 Corinthians as a rhetorical strategy Paul used to affirm believers who had repented. This would have been important in laying the foundation for calling the Corinthians to make good on their intention to contribute to the offering for the church in Jerusalem. Not all the Corinthians had repented, and chapters 10–13 are designed to speak to that minority. Colin Hemer suggested that delay in the process of composing 2 Corinthians may explain the apparent shift in tone between chapters 1–9 and chapters 10–13.

## HOW 2 CORINTHIANS FITS INTO GOD'S STORY

1. Prologue: Creation, Fall, and the Need for Redemption
2. God Builds His Nation (2000–931 BC)
3. God Educates His Nation (931–586 BC)
4. God Keeps a Faithful Remnant (586–6 BC)
5. God Purchases Redemption and Begins the Kingdom (6 BC to AD 30)
6. **God Spreads the Kingdom Through the Church (AD 30–?)**
7. God Consummates Redemption and Confirms His Eternal Kingdom
8. Epilogue: New Heaven and New Earth

## CHRIST IN 2 CORINTHIANS

Jesus Christ, God's Son, is not an ambiguous, fickle word from God, not "yes and no" but "yes." Conformity to Christ's image is the goal of the Christian life. Christ, working through the Spirit, brings this about.

## CHRISTIAN WORLDVIEW ELEMENTS

### Teachings About God

God is the Father of Jesus Christ (1:3; 11:31) who sovereignly sent Him as the great "indescribable gift" (9:15). Jesus is the source of all comfort for His people. By His death and resurrection, Jesus is Lord of the new creation (5:14–17). The life-giving Spirit has come as the "down payment," guaranteeing the believer's future (5:5). "Where the Spirit of the Lord is, there is freedom" (3:17).

Chapel of St. Paul in Damascus, the site of Paul's escape from the city. "In Damascus, the governor under King Aretas guarded the city of the Damascenes in order to arrest me, so I was let down in a basket through a window in the wall and escaped his hands" (2Co 11:32–33).

### Teachings About Humanity

There were two kinds of people in the Corinthian church: those who submitted to genuine apostolic authority and those who did not. Paul sent blistering criticism on the latter (chaps. 10–11). This book contains the most extensive teaching in Scripture about the status of redeemed humans between the death of the body and the resurrection. This is referred to as the "intermediate state," when persons are "with the Lord" in conscious bliss while waiting for the consummation (5:1–8).

### Teachings About Salvation

This letter contains Paul's most extensive discussion on the contrast between the "old covenant" and the "new covenant" (chap. 3). Although salvation was real in the Mosaic era, it came with fading glory, for the old covenant was meant to be temporary. The new covenant arrived with Jesus Christ, and its glory can never be surpassed. The benefit to the believer in the new covenant era is incomparable (3:18).

## GENRE AND LITERARY STYLE

### A Long Epistle Written in *Koinē* Greek

See *Genre and Literary Style* for **1 THESSALONIANS** for information about the genre "epistle." The standard parts of a first-century epistle appear in Corinthians, except that the thanksgiving is missing: salutation (1:1–2); main body (1:3–13:10); and farewell (13:11–14). Like most of Paul's writings, this is a pastoral letter, driven by the occasion and needs of the recipients, rather than a tractate (a formal treatise).

## A PRINCIPLE TO LIVE BY

### Self Defense (2Co 10:7–18, *Life Essentials Study Bible*, p. 1605–06)

When we are falsely accused, it is not wrong to defend ourselves, but when we do, we should always reflect the fruit of the Holy Spirit .

To access a video presentation of this principle featuring Dr. Gene Getz, use a Smartphone or iPad to connect to this QR code or go to http://www.bhpublishinggroup.com/handbook/2corinthians

## ENDNOTE

1. See http://paulbarnett.info/2011/09/paul-chronology-and-the-unity-of-2-corinthians/#_ftn33.

As with all the New Testament letters written by Paul, this epistle is titled according to its first recipients, in this case Christians in the Roman province of Galatia.

## KEY TEXT: 2:16

*"[We] know that no one is justified by the works of the law but by faith in Jesus Christ. And we have believed in Christ Jesus so that we might be justified by faith in Christ and not by the works of the law, because by the works of the law no human being will be justified."*

## KEY TERM: "FAITH"

"Faith alone" is the heartbeat of this book. Paul's insistence that no human work can contribute to a person's right standing with God makes this book critical for all those who cherish the doctrine of salvation as a gift of God's grace.

## ONE-SENTENCE SUMMARY

Sinners are justified (and live out a godly life) by trusting in Jesus Christ alone, not by keeping the law or by counting on good works.

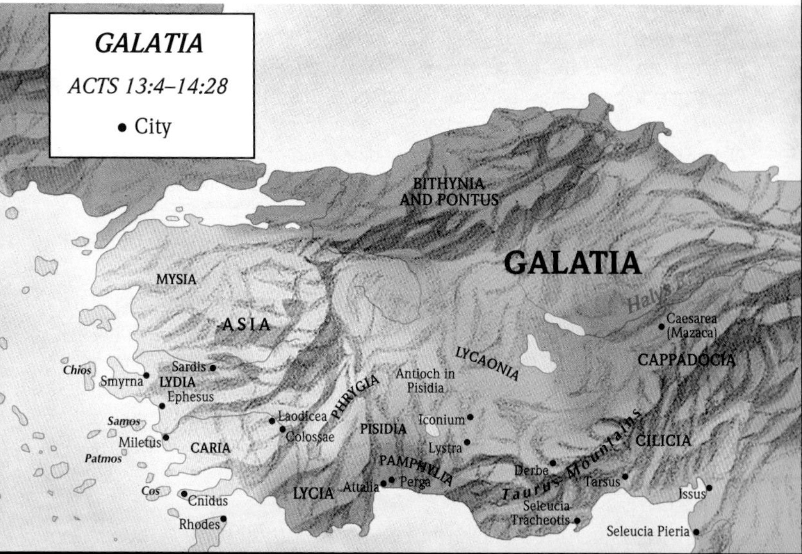


The map shows both north and south Galatia. Paul's letter was likely directed to the churches that he and Barnabas had planted on their first missionary journey: Derbe, Lystra, Iconium, and Pisidian Antioch.

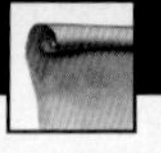



## AUTHOR AND DATE OF WRITING

**Paul the Apostle, Around AD 49 (or Around 52–55)**

The book claims to be written by Paul, and no one doubts that he wrote this letter. See *Author and Date of Writing* for **ROMANS** for more information about Paul's life.

The date of writing depends on whether the North or the South Galatian View is true. The South Galatian View seems preferable because (1) Acts specifically mentions Paul's preaching only in southern Galatia; (2) the alternate view asserts that Paul deliberately omitted referring to his Jerusalem visit of Acts 11:29–30; and (3) the vehemence of the epistle makes better sense if it preceded the Jerusalem Council.

## FIRST AUDIENCE AND DESTINATION

**Christians Living in the Roman Province of Galatia**

These Christians came mainly from a Gentile background. They had been believers in Christ for a few years at most. Galatia was a large Roman province in the center of modern Turkey. "Galatians" was originally an ethnic term for the original settlers of the northern part of the region who had migrated from Gaul. The Romans had extended the original Galatian region southward to make it a large province whose capital was Ancyra in the north.

## OCCASION

After Paul left the Galatian churches, troublemakers had come there proclaiming a different version of the gospel (1:6–9; 5:7–12). These agitators evidently wanted Christianity to be a sect within current Judaism. Gentiles, they said, had to become Jews (accepting circumcision and living according to Mosaic laws—for example, dietary rules) before they could be saved and be a part of God's people. These false teachers are called "Judaizers," based on the verb translated "to live as do the Jews" in Galatians 2:14.

Paul understood the gospel as fundamentally incompatible with Judaism as it was practiced by most Jews in the first century, especially in the matter of how human beings stand in right relationship with God. He reacted violently against the Judaizers by penning this letter (5:12). If Paul wrote at the earlier date, he probably composed from Antioch of Syria, his "home base," and Galatians is his earliest letter (written between his first and second missionary journeys). If he wrote to churches in northern Galatia, he probably composed from Corinth or Ephesus (during the second or third missionary journeys).

## PURPOSE

Galatians was written to accomplish three purposes. First, Paul defended his authority as an apostle of Jesus. Second, he argued the doctrinal case for salvation by faith alone. Third, he showed that everyday Christian living is based on freedom from the law in the power of the Holy Spirit.

## FIRST PASS

### Greeting

Like the introduction of most letters in the New Testament era, the name of the writer ("Paul") and readers ("the churches of Galatia") are given, as well as Paul's standard greeting ("grace to you and peace"). Unlike some of his introductions, Paul did not affirm commendable qualities in the churches of Galatia. He quickly cut to the chase (1:1–5).

### Error

Paul was astounded that so soon after his ministry among the Galatians they had defected from the gospel of grace. To turn away from Paul's message was, in effect, to turn away from God and to turn to a perversion of the gospel. It was being passed off by the false teachers as an alternate gospel but was, in reality, merely a confusing counterfeit. Paul was so concerned by this development that he twice pronounced a curse (Greek *anathema*) on any being, including angels, who distorted the gospel among his readers (1:6–10).

### Apostolic Authority

Paul did not receive the gospel he preached from any human source. It came as a revelation from Jesus Christ (1:12). When Paul met some of the original 12 apostles, they affirmed the gospel as Paul had received it and preached it to the Gentiles.

### Right with God

Paul asked the Galatians if they received the Holy Spirit and experienced God's miraculous work among them by keeping the law or by faith in Christ (3:2). Paul then went back to Abraham who lived before the law was given. He reminded the Galatians that the basis of Abraham's right standing with God was that he believed God (3:6–9). The problem with the law is that it carries with it a curse. If a person does not keep the law perfectly, he is under a curse (3:10). But by God's grace Christ became a curse so that those who trust Him no longer bear the curse that comes with failing to keep the law perfectly (3:13).

### What About the Law?

The law convicted all people of sin, holding them in captivity until the message of faith in Christ was revealed. The law played the role of both a jailer and a guardian of underage children in preparing believers to be full-fledged children of God, on equal footing spiritually and joint heirs of God's promise no matter their gender or their ethnic and social backgrounds (3:19–25). To go back to the law as the way of being made right with God is like a child becoming a slave in the family rather than a member of that family (4:1–7). As the capstone of his argument concerning

justification by faith, Paul created an allegory from the two sons of Abraham: Ishmael and Isaac (4:21–31).

**The Freedom of the Christian**

Having secured the argument for freedom in Christ through justifying faith alone, Paul examined the nature of that liberty. While again rebuking the tendency to turn back to legalism, he also deplored the opposite extreme of license.

**Conclusion**

At this point Paul began the conclusion to Galatians by taking the manuscript from his unnamed scribe and writing with large, bold script. He then effectively summarized the issues of the entire letter (6:11–18).

## THE RELIABILITY OF GALATIANS

God told Abraham over 2000 years before Christ that his offspring would be enslaved and oppressed in a foreign land for a period of 400 years (Gn 15:13). In Galatians 3:17 Paul speaks of the law that came 430 years after the promise came to Abraham and his seed. This 430-year period matches the time between God's last affirmation of the promise to Abraham's seed, Jacob (Gn 46:1–4), and the day Israel went out of Egypt (Ex 12:40). The 400 years in Genesis 15 is a rounding of the 430 years.

## HOW GALATIANS FITS INTO GOD'S STORY

1. Prologue: Creation, Fall, and the Need for Redemption
2. God Builds His Nation (2000–931 BC)
3. God Educates His Nation (931–586 BC)
4. God Keeps a Faithful Remnant (586–6 BC)
5. God Purchases Redemption and Begins the Kingdom (6 BC to AD 30)
6. **God Spreads the Kingdom Through the Church (AD 30–?)**
7. God Consummates Redemption and Confirms His Eternal Kingdom
8. Epilogue: New Heaven and New Earth

## CHRIST IN GALATIANS

Christ became a curse for us so that He could redeem us from the curse of the law (3:13). Believers are crucified with Christ and yet they live. Christ Himself becomes their very life (2:19–20).

## CHRISTIAN WORLDVIEW ELEMENTS

**Teachings About God**

God is the Father of Jesus who brings about all things related to salvation (including setting apostles apart for service, 1:15). Jesus is the Son of God by whose death

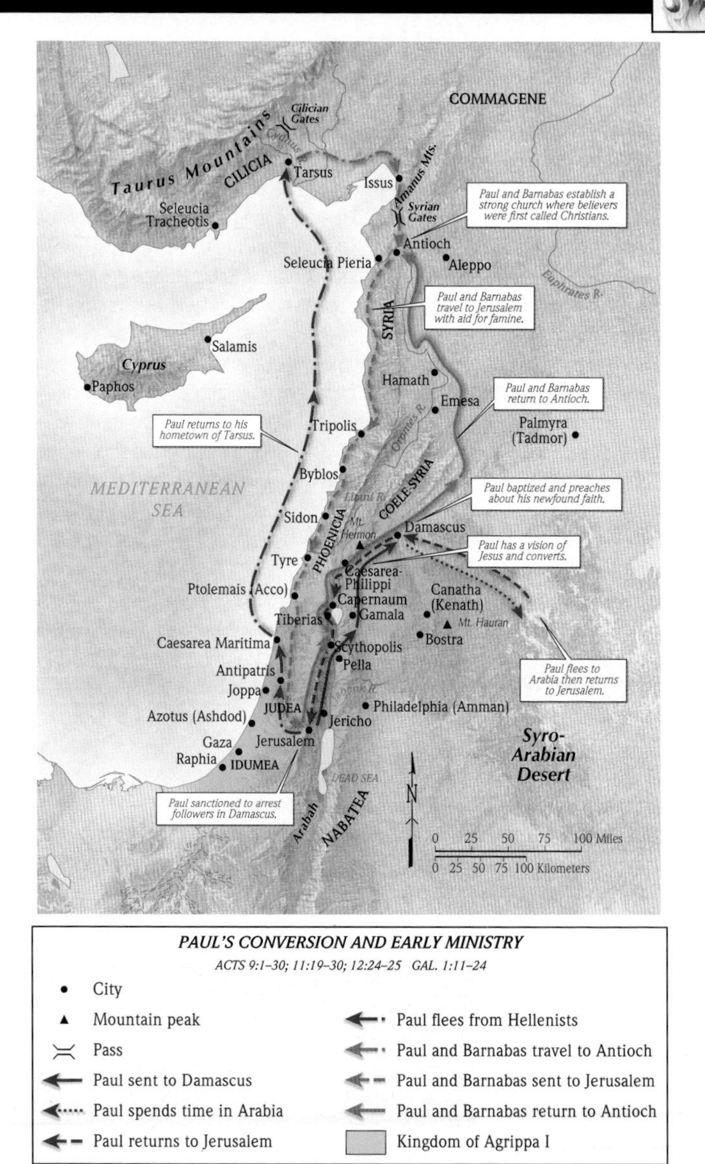


The "three years" Paul mentions (1:18) could be three full years or one year and portions of the year preceding and the year following. His journey to Jerusalem to meet Peter and other apostles was of great importance in his future work.

righteousness is provided (2:21). The Holy Spirit is given to all believers, enabling them to subdue "the flesh" and to grow in Christian character ("the fruit of the Spirit").

### Teachings About Humanity

Galatians contrasts two kinds of people in the world. First, there are those under God's curse (3:10). This includes persons who suppose that they can attain salvation by doing good works. They are doomed to live according to the evil works of the flesh and will not be part of God's kingdom. Second, there are those who, by God's grace, have been set free from the curse by faith in Christ who bore the curse by His death (3:13). Such persons live according to the Spirit's power and will "reap eternal life" (6:8).

### Teachings About Salvation

Galatians stands as Paul's passionate testimony that salvation is a gift of God's grace. It is unearned and undeserved and must be received by faith alone. Paul is careful not to turn faith into a work, for he argues that "faith came" (3:23–25) to those who were helpless slaves (see also Eph 2:8; Php 1:29). This view of salvation so strongly gripped the apostle that if someone offered a different doctrine, let "a curse be on him" (1:8).

## GENRE AND LITERARY STYLE

### An Epistle Written in *Koinē* Greek

See *Genre and Literary Style* for **1 THESSALONIANS** for information about the genre "epistle." The standard parts of a first-century epistle appear, except that the thanksgiving is missing: salutation (1:1–5), main body (1:6–6:15), and farewell (6:16–18). This is a pastoral letter, driven by the occasion and needs of the recipients, rather than a tractate (a formal treatise). Paul's Greek is at its most passionate in this letter.

## A PRINCIPLE TO LIVE BY

### Justification by Faith (Gl 3:24–25, *Life Essentials Study Bible*, p. 1616–17)

When explaining that salvation is a free gift, we must also clarify that this gift can only be received by faith in Jesus Christ.

To access a video presentation of this principle featuring Dr. Gene Getz, use a Smartphone or iPad to connect to this QR code or go to http://www.bhpublishinggroup.com/handbook/galatians

As with all New Testament letters written by Paul the apostle, this epistle is titled according to its first recipients, in this case Christians in the city of Ephesus.

## KEY TEXT: 3:10–11

*"This is so God's multifaceted wisdom may now be made known through the church to the rulers and authorities in the heavens. This is according to His eternal purpose accomplished in the Messiah, Jesus our Lord.*

## KEY TERM: "UNITY"

Ephesians focuses on the unity between Christ the head of the church and the church as the body of Christ, as well as the unity between Jew and Gentile in God's greatest masterpiece, the church.

## ONE-SENTENCE SUMMARY

In God's eternal plan God's great masterpiece the church has now been manifested, in which Christ is united with all the redeemed whether Jew or Gentile, transforming relationships in this life and leading to a glorious future.

A replica of the Temple of Artemis (Diana) in Istanbul, Turkey. The original temple was in Ephesus and was one of the seven wonders of the world until it was destroyed by the Goths in AD 263. Silversmiths in Ephesus created and sold silver shrines of Artemis. Paul's preaching against idolatry led to a riot in Ephesus (Ac 19:21–41).

## AUTHOR AND DATE OF WRITING

**Paul, About AD 61**

The letter claims to be written by "Paul, an apostle of Christ Jesus by God's will." For the last two centuries, critical scholars have argued that Paul was not the author. The arguments against Pauline authorship of Ephesians include the following: (1) The Greek style and vocabulary are different from the undisputed Pauline letters. (2) The doctrine of the church is too advanced for Paul's time. (3) The parallels between Ephesians and Colossians open the possibility that a sincere admirer of Paul used Colossians as a source for writing a letter in his own (later) day, claiming Paul's name to lend his work greater authority. Each of these points may be refuted. The letter's self-claim and the unbroken Christian tradition of Pauline authorship should be accepted.

Assuming that Paul is the author, he wrote from Roman imprisonment as described at the end of Acts, around AD 60–61. Those who reject Pauline authorship date the letter toward the end of the first century.

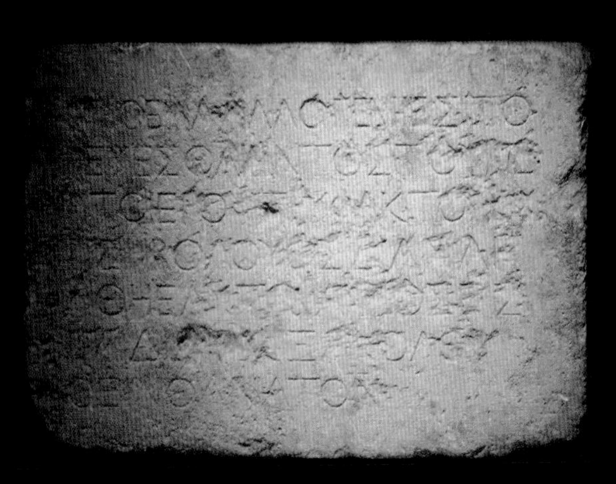

The Soreg inscription—an inscription in Greek from the late first century BC or the beginning of the first century AD, found in Jerusalem, warning non-Jews from entering the sanctuary where the Jewish temple was located. If they failed to heed this warning, they would be killed and have only themselves to blame for the consequences. This inscription now stands at the National Archaeological Museum in Istanbul. In addition, archaeologists have found two fragmentary copies of this warning that were in both Latin and Greek. The Soreg Inscription bears witness to the wall of hostility that has been torn down. "For He (Jesus) is our peace, who made both groups one and tore down the dividing wall of hostility" (Eph 2:14).

## FIRST AUDIENCE AND DESTINATION

**Christians Living in (and Around) the City of Ephesus**

The gospel came to Ephesus on Paul's third missionary journey. He stayed longer in Ephesus than he did in any other city (Ac 19:10). Paul's Ephesian work was the most visibly successful of all the places of his ministry. The church included both Jews and Gentiles. Because the words "in Ephesus" are missing from Ephesians 1:1 in some of the earliest and best manuscripts, many believe this was originally a circular letter, intended for several cities (as was Galatians). This would account for Paul's lack of referring to individuals and his note that he had only heard of the readers' faith (1:15). For further discussion of this possibility, see *The Reliability of Ephesians* below.

## OCCASION

Paul had ample opportunity to think over the full implications of Christianity and the church during his Roman imprisonment. He had evidently just written the Colossians (to deal with the Colossian heresy; see *Occasion* for **COLOSSIANS**). He concluded that the doctrinal message of that letter was worth expanding and distributing to a wider audience. Thus he composed this letter and had it sent with the help of Tychicus (6:21) to Ephesus (and perhaps to other nearby churches; compare Rv 1:11).

# GOD'S MESSAGE IN EPHESIANS

## PURPOSE

Paul wrote to the Christians in and around Ephesus in order to develop fully in writing his magnificent understanding of the doctrine of the church and to instruct believers about the importance of holy conduct, particularly in Christian family relationships. Ephesians presents the church as the focal point of displaying God's glory forever (3:21).

## FIRST PASS

### Introduction

Paul identified himself by name and calling. He offered greetings in the manner common to the Pauline letters. Absent is the usual mention of Paul's companions.

### God's Purposes in Christ

Paul offered praise to God for His glorious blessings in Christ and for salvation provided for sinful humanity. This work is accomplished by Father, Son, and Holy Spirit (1:3–14). He wanted his readers to know that he prayed for them. He wanted them to have an enlarged understanding of the hope that was theirs in Christ and the power available to them through Christ (1:15–19). This power comes to persons who were dead in sin but are saved by grace—saved to do good works (2:1–10). Paul reminded his Gentile readers that apart from Christ, they were hopeless. But in Christ both Jews and Gentiles are reconciled to God and to each other (2:11–3:21). Jews and Gentiles are joined together in Christ's church, built on the foundation of the apostles and serving as the residence of God the Spirit. This good news is a mystery—a mystery God calls people to share with other people through His grace and a mystery that allows all people to approach God in confidence and freedom. Paul turned to prayer to conclude this section and reveal the goal of redemption (3:14–21). His prayer was that Christ may dwell in the believers, who will be rooted in love and who can grasp the marvelous greatness of that love.

### God's Purposes in the Church

Paul turned to the application of redemption to the church, to personal life, and to family life (4:1–6:24). To complete his letter, Paul called his readers to put on God's armor to avoid Satan's temptations, resulting in a life of prayer for self and for other servants of God. This would lead to concern for and encouragement from other Christians (6:10–20). As usual, Paul concluded his letter with a benediction, praying for peace, love, faith, and grace for his readers.

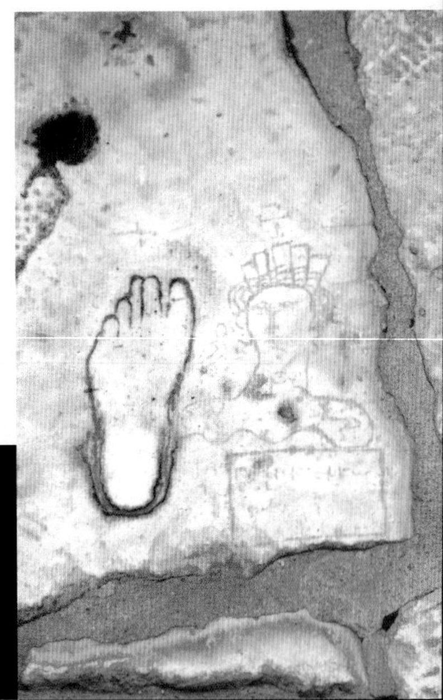

Directions to a brothel in Ephesus. Those made alive in Christ would evince a lifestyle contrary to the prevailing culture in Ephesus. "Sexual immorality and any impurity or greed should not even be heard of among you, as is proper for saints" (Eph 5:3).

## THE RELIABILITY OF EPHESIANS

Paul's authorship of Ephesians wasn't questioned until the nineteenth century. One of the features of the letter that doesn't seem to add up with other information we have about Paul is his prayer for the Ephesians: "This is why, since I heard about your faith in the Lord Jesus and your love for all the saints, I never stop giving thanks for you as I remember you in my prayers" (1:15–16). Paul spent nearly three years in Ephesus, perhaps his longest ministry in any one location. He experienced great persecution and danger in Ephesus that would have forged a strong relationship with believers there. Given Paul's experience in Ephesus, he wouldn't use the phrase "since I heard about your faith." He didn't just hear about it but saw it up close.

A plausible explanation that accepts Paul's authorship and explains the language of 1:15–16 is suggested first by Marcion (AD 85–160), who said that the letter we call Ephesians was originally intended for the church at Laodicea, a church we know about from Revelation. Tychicus, who was with Paul during his house arrest in Rome, carried this letter first to Laodicea (6:21–22). Paul instructed Tychicus to give a verbal report to church at Laodicea, giving believers a more complete account of Paul's situation. At the same time, Tychicus was carrying Paul's letters for the Colossians and for Philemon to Colossae. Paul instructed Tychicus to read the Laodicean letter to the Colossians and the Colossian letter to the Laodiceans.

This lends weight to the view that the Laodicean letter was a circular letter written to be delivered to a number of churches in Asia Minor, including Ephesus. It could well be that the only extant copy of this letter available when the churches began to collect Paul's letters was the one for Ephesus, though it may not have borne the phrase "in Ephesus" in 1:1.

## HOW EPHESIANS FITS INTO GOD'S STORY

1. Prologue: Creation, Fall, and the Need for Redemption
2. God Builds His Nation (2000–931 BC)
3. God Educates His Nation (931–586 BC)
4. God Keeps a Faithful Remnant (586–6 BC)
5. God Purchases Redemption and Begins the Kingdom (6 BC to AD 30)
6. **God Spreads the Kingdom Through the Church (AD 30–?)**
7. God Consummates Redemption and Confirms His Eternal Kingdom
8. Epilogue: New Heaven and New Earth

## CHRIST IN EPHESIANS

Christ, through His death, brought peace between God and man and between Jew and Gentile. He is the cornerstone and head of the church, which is His body.

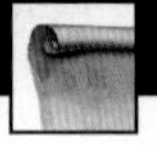


## CHRISTIAN WORLDVIEW ELEMENTS

### Teachings About God

Ephesians is filled with texts that contribute to a fully orbed doctrine of the Trinity. God the Father is the One whose eternal plan for the church has now been revealed. Jesus the Son is the exalted Head of the body, the church, and the One for whose glory the church exists. The church is a house or temple in which God's Spirit lives, yet the Spirit fills each believer individually.

### Teachings About Humanity

Ephesians shows the dreadful condition of all who are still in their natural condition: "dead in your trespasses and sins" (2:1). Paul summarizes this as "without hope, and without God" (2:12). The alternate group is those whom God has changed and who are in a supernatural state: made alive together with Christ (2:5). Old distinctions between Jew and Gentile used to count for something, but now in the church they no longer apply.

### Teachings About Salvation

The best-known and most-loved New Testament summary of the gospel is Ephesians 2:8–9, with its emphasis on grace and faith. Ephesians also notes God's delight in electing persons to salvation. The language of predestination to eternal life is pronounced (1:5,11), as is Paul's notion that "Christ loved the church, and gave Himself for her" (5:25). (The long-standing theological dispute about divine election—predestination—is a matter of discerning the basis of God's choice. All students who take the Bible seriously affirm divine predestination; the debate is simply over its basis.)

## GENRE AND LITERARY STYLE

### An Epistle Written in *Koinē* Greek

See *Genre and Literary Style* for **1 THESSALONIANS** for information about the genre "epistle." All four standard parts of a first-century epistle appear in Ephesians: salutation (1:1–2), thanksgiving (1:3–23), main body (2:1–6:20), and farewell (6:20–24). Some scholars designate Ephesians as a "tractate" (a formal treatise rather than a pastoral letter). Paul's Greek is at its most composed and dispassionate in this letter.

## A PRINCIPLE TO LIVE BY

### Oneness in Christ (Eph 2:11–22, *Life Essentials Study Bible*, p. 1628.

Regardless of our ethnic backgrounds, social status, gender, or race, when we become believers we are to function as members of one family.

To access a video presentation of this principle featuring Dr. Gene Getz, use a Smartphone or iPad to connect to this QR code or go to http://www.bhpublishinggroup.com/handbook/ephesians

As with all New Testament letters written by Paul the apostle, this epistle is titled according to its first recipients, in this case Christians in the city of Philippi.

## KEY TEXT: 3:10

*"My goal is to know Him and the power of His resurrection and the fellowship of His sufferings, being conformed to His death."*

## KEY TERM: "JOY"

Forms of the noun "joy" and the verb "rejoice" occur 16 times in this short letter. Philippians is the biblical book that most extensively defines and describes joy.

## ONE-SENTENCE SUMMARY

Knowing Jesus Christ is much more joyful and important than anything else because God has exalted Jesus, the crucified Servant, with the name above every name.

Philippi's acropolis seen from the hill where Cassius's forces camped in 42 BC. The Battle at Philippi was one of the strategic engagements between Julius Caesar's assassins, Brutus and Cassius, and his avengers, Marc Antony and Octavian. The victory of the latter forces was a critical step toward Octavian becoming Caesar Augustus (Lk 2:1).

## AUTHOR AND DATE OF WRITING

**Paul, Around AD 61**

The letter claims to be written by Paul, and all biblical students accept this testimony. See *Author and Date of Writing* for **ROMANS** for more information about Paul's life. Some scholars have argued that all or part of Philippians 3 was written at a different time than the main letter, but no Greek manuscript evidence supports this. It is much better to accept that Philippians was first written in the form it now appears.

According to tradition, Philippians is one of the four "Prison Epistles" written from Rome. In the twentieth century some scholars argued that the many travels implied in the letter make better sense if Paul wrote from Ephesus a few years earlier. They have conjectured an otherwise unknown imprisonment (not mentioned in Acts or anywhere in Paul's letters) during his third missionary journey, around 55–56. While this theory remains possible, it is an argument based on silence, and the traditional view that Philippians was written from Rome around 60–61 appears much more plausible.

## FIRST AUDIENCE AND DESTINATION

**Christians Living in the City of Philippi**

The gospel came to Philippi on Paul's second missionary journey. This was the first church Paul planted after his Macedonian vision (Acts 16:9). Because Luke was an eyewitness of the founding of this church (as the "we's" of Acts 16 indicate), a great deal is known about the individuals that made up the original core of the congregation, such as Lydia and the city jailer. Paul did not stay in Philippi very long, but Luke himself probably stayed behind as the church's spiritual leader (the "we's" stop after Acts 16:17). By reading Acts and Philippians carefully, one discovers that Paul had visited the church at least twice since its beginning and that it was a source of joy for him.

Philippi was an important commercial city in the province of Macedonia. (The capital was Thessalonica.) The city had a privileged status as a colony of Rome, so its citizens were considered citizens of Rome (note Paul's emphasis on heavenly citizenship in 3:20–21). According to Acts there were evidently not enough Jews in the city to support a synagogue, so the city and the church were primarily Gentile. Like other cities of its day, Philippi was very religious and very immoral.

## OCCASION

While Paul was imprisoned in Rome, the Philippian church had sent him a financial gift, perhaps to assist with his living expenses or his legal fees, through Epaphroditus, one of their leaders (4:10–20). While Epaphroditus was with Paul, he experienced a near-fatal illness. The Philippians had received word of this, and Paul had learned

that they were gravely concerned about Epaphroditus. At last, however, Epaphroditus had recovered, and Paul was ready to send him home (2:25–29). He took this occasion, therefore, to write the Philippians a thank-you letter in which he complimented Epaphroditus and brought them up-to-date on his own ministry. The doctrinal and practical emphases in the letter are probably a response to information brought by Epaphroditus. Thus, Paul composed this letter (probably with Timothy's help, whom he also wanted to send to Philippi at a later time, 1:1; 2:19–24) and sent it to Philippi with Epaphroditus.

## PURPOSE

Paul wrote to the Philippians to thank them for the financial gift they had sent through Epaphroditus. He further wanted to report on Epaphroditus and to tell about Timothy's probable visit to them. As an added bonus Paul wanted to give them some important doctrinal teaching about Christ (and knowing Him) as well as to offer practical advice on living the Christian life vigorously and joyfully.

## FIRST PASS

### Greeting

Philippians is structured much like a typical personal letter of that day. The introduction identifies the sender(s): Paul and Timothy, and the recipients: the saints, overseers, and deacons. This typical letter form, however, is filled with Christian content. The usual secular greeting and wish for good health is transformed into a blessing (v. 2), a thanksgiving for the Philippian church's faithful participation in the work of the gospel (1:3–8), and a prayer that they may be blessed with an ever growing, enlightened, Christian love (1:9–11).

### Paul's Present Circumstances

Paul explains his current situation (1:12–26). He revealed that his primary concern—the proclamation of the gospel—was being accomplished in spite of his difficult circumstances (1:12–18). His captors were being evangelized (vv. 12–13). His compatriots had gained confidence through his bold example (v. 14). Even those who were working with wrong motives were sharing the good news actively; Paul rejoiced in their work (vv. 15–18). The severity of Paul's imprisonment is reflected (1:19–26). His death appears to be a real possibility. Death would unite him with Christ. Life would give him the joys of continued productive ministry. He found cause for genuine rejoicing in both. Paul seemed confident, however, that he would eventually be released and reunited with the Philippians.

### The Mind of Christ as the Foundation for Unity

When Paul returned to Philippi, he hoped to find a church united in Christ. Philippians 1:27–4:9 is a multifaceted call for unity in the church. The great cause of the proclamation of the gospel calls for them to be united in spirit, in task, and in confidence (1:27–30). Their common Christian experience (2:1) and purpose (2:2) should also rule out a self-centered, self-serving attitude (2:3–4). Those who follow Christ must follow Him in selfless service to others (2:5–11). Christ's preexistence, incarnation, passion, resurrection, and exaltation are all summarized in a masterful fashion to highlight the humility and selfless service demonstrated by Jesus.

**Lights in the World**

Paul was concerned that the Philippians demonstrate the reality of their Christian profession in action. Neither the grumbling so characteristic of Israel in the wilderness or the perversity of a world that does not know God should characterize the church. His desire for them and for himself was that he be able to rejoice that his labor on their behalf was not in vain (2:12–18).

**Epaphroditus**

Philippians 2:25–30 explained to the church why Epaphroditus was returning to Philippi. The church had sent him to take a gift to Paul (Php 4:10–20) and minister to him in his imprisonment. Paul probably feared that some would criticize Epaphroditus for returning earlier than planned.

**Warning**

The encouragement to rejoice (3:1) unexpectedly becomes a stern warning (3:2). The change is so marked that some scholars think chapter 3 is a later addition to the letter. A problem was threatening the church at Philippi that had the potential of destroying the foundation of unity and the basis of joy.

The exact nature of the problem is unclear. Jewish legalism (3:2–11), Christian or gnostic perfectionism (3:12–16), and pagan libertinism (3:17–21) are all attacked. What is clear, however, is that Paul countered the heretical teachings with Christian truths: Jesus Christ is the only avenue to righteousness (3:2–11); the stature of Christ is the goal of Christian maturity (3:12–16); and the nature of Christ and His kingdom is the standard by which the Christian must live (3:17–21).

**Agree in Christ**

Two women, Euodia and Syntyche (4:2–3), were exhorted to end their conflict, for personal disagreements may be as damaging to the unity of the church as false doctrine. General exhortations to rejoice and to remain faithful (4:4–9) led to Paul's expression of gratitude for the Philippians' faithful support of him and of the ministry (4:10–20). The letter closes in typical Pauline fashion, with an exchange of greetings and a prayer for grace.

## THE RELIABILITY OF PHILIPPIANS

In spite of Pauline authorship, many have questioned the letter's integrity: Is it a unified document or two or three documents woven into one? The arguments for multiple sources primarily appeal to claims of variation in the style of writing and supposed changes in content. For example, some scholars argue that 3:2–4:1 does

not fit the patterns established by the remainder of the letter with its harsh tone and invective argument. They propose that perhaps this was a different letter inserted into Philippians.

Two observations help here. First, Paul's opponents denied the gospel, also harshly criticizing Paul's apostleship. Paul responded energetically to such challenges (see 2 Co 10–12). Second, Paul could not respond in person to the impending threat; so the letter is candid, disclosing inner thoughts and evaluations. Indicative of their relationship, Paul also instructed his original readers by appealing to his spiritual pilgrimage.

Other scholars suggest that 4:10–20 is an insertion, assuming such an important note of thanks would not be delayed to the end. However, modern readers must take care in second-guessing first-century writing forms. Further, Paul naturally included the other expressions of appreciation before turning to financial issues. All forms of support were equally appreciated.

Questions regarding the literary integrity of the letter raise a more central issue. Are contemporary scholars better able to detect supposed seams in the fabric of the letter than could its early readers? Given the care we know characterized the transmission of Scripture, theories about literary fragments present far more difficulties than they presume to solve.

## HOW PHILIPPIANS FITS INTO GOD'S STORY

1. Prologue: Creation, Fall, and the Need for Redemption
2. God Builds His Nation (2000–931 BC)
3. God Educates His Nation (931–586 BC)
4. God Keeps a Faithful Remnant (586–6 BC)
5. God Purchases Redemption and Begins the Kingdom (6 BC to AD 30)
6. **God Spreads the Kingdom Through the Church (AD 30–?)**
7. God Consummates Redemption and Confirms His Eternal Kingdom
8. Epilogue: New Heaven and New Earth

## CHRIST IN PHILIPPIANS

Christ, who existed in the form of God, emptied Himself of His privileges as God and became a human being and a slave. After this, God exalted Him and gave Him the name that is above every name. At the name of Jesus all creatures will bow and confess Him as Lord.

## CHRISTIAN WORLDVIEW ELEMENTS

### Teachings About God

For His glory God the Father has both exalted Jesus Christ and called a people to know Him. Jesus, by very nature God, humbled Himself by death on a cross but thereby has been exalted with the greatest name. The Spirit of God enables all true worship and provides help for God's people.

**Teachings About Humanity**

In Philippians there are two essential categories of human beings: enemies of the cross of Christ and those who know Him (3:18–20). The former are destined for destruction, the latter for resurrection. Among those who know Him, however, some proclaim Him purely, but others do so from false motives (1:15–18).

**Teachings About Salvation**

Salvation is presented from the viewpoint of knowing Christ. Knowing Christ, more than just the remedy for sins, is a valuable treasure, for which everything else in life is to be happily cast aside. This applies not only to whatever good things one was and did before, but it also means that His followers will joyfully suffer (as He did). They will ultimately share in His resurrection.

## GENRE AND LITERARY STYLE

**An Epistle Written in *Koinē* Greek**

See *Genre and Literary Style* for **1 THESSALONIANS** for information about the genre "epistle." All four standard parts of a first-century epistle appear in Philippians: salutation (1:1–2); thanksgiving (1:3–11); main body (1:12–4:20); and farewell (4:21–23). This is a pastoral letter, driven by the occasion and needs of the recipients, rather than a tractate (a formal treatise). Paul's Greek is at its most typical in this letter.

## A PRINCIPLE TO LIVE BY

**Expressing Appreciation (Php 2:3–8, *Life Essentials Study Bible*, p. 1639–40)**

Spiritual leaders should express sincere appreciation to those who partner with them in the ministry.

To access a video presentation of this principle featuring Dr. Gene Getz, use a Smartphone or iPad to connect to this QR code or go to http://www.bhpublishinggroup.com/handbook/philippians

As with all New Testament letters written by Paul the apostle, this epistle is titled according to its first recipients, in this case Christians in the town of Colossae.

## KEY TEXT: 1:18

*"He is also the head of the body, the church; He is the beginning, the firstborn from the dead, so that He might come to have first place in everything."*

"For everything was created by Him, in heaven and on earth, the visible and the invisible. . . . All things have been created through Him and for Him. He is before all things, and by Him all things hold together" (Col 1:16–17). This photo by Yuri Beletsky at the European Southern Observatory in Chile's Atacama Desert. One of the most conducive places on earth for studying the stars. In this photo a laser from the Very Large Telescope (VLT) enables astronomers to observe the center of our galaxy, the Milky Way. The Milky Way has between 200 and 400 billion stars. It's estimated that the universe has as many galaxies as the Milky Way has stars.

## KEY TERM: "FIRST PLACE"

Colossians declares the supremacy of Christ in all things, whether of creation or redemption. This teaching was the cure to a deadly heresy facing early believers.

## ONE-SENTENCE SUMMARY

Jesus Christ is supreme Lord of the universe and head of the church, and therefore He is the only One through whom forgiveness is possible, making legal obligations or philosophical studies irrelevant in matters of salvation.

# ORIGINAL HISTORICAL SETTING

## AUTHOR AND DATE OF WRITING

**Paul the Apostle, Around AD 61**

The letter claims to be written by Paul the apostle. For the past two centuries some (but not all) critical scholars have denied that Paul wrote this letter. They have argued that Colossians reflects the issues of a later time than Paul and was written by an unknown later Christian who used Paul's name to bolster his own authority. The basic arguments are (1) that the false teaching attacked is Gnosticism, which did not become a destructive influence until the end of the first century and (2) that the Christology is too highly developed for Paul. In response, (1) there is no proof that the Colossian heresy was directly related to Gnosticism, and (2) the Christology is no more exalted than Philippians 2:9–11, which is clearly Pauline. The letter's self-claim and the unbroken Christian tradition of Pauline authorship should be accepted.

Paul wrote from Roman imprisonment as described at the end of Acts, around AD 60–61. Those who reject Pauline authorship date it toward the end of the first century.

## FIRST AUDIENCE AND DESTINATION:

**Christians Living in the Town of Colossae**

Christianity came to Colossae through the ministry of Epaphras (1:7). He evidently brought the gospel while Paul was in Ephesus on his third missionary journey. Paul had only "heard" of the Colossians (1:4,9). The false teaching mixed Jewish and Greek elements, suggesting that the believers were probably from both Jewish and Gentile backgrounds.

Colossae was an unimportant town in the province of Asia in the Lycus River Valley, about a hundred miles inland (east) from Ephesus. Its better known sister cities were Hierapolis and Laodicea (2:1; 4:13–16).

## OCCASION

While Paul was imprisoned in Rome, Epaphras had visited him and brought news

about the churches in the Lycus River Valley (4:12). Paul had learned from him about the presence of false teachers in the Colossian congregation that were threatening the survival of the church. He therefore wrote this letter, evidently with the secretarial assistance of Timothy, using Tychicus as the letter carrier. This is one of four letters, called "The Prison Epistles," written while Paul was waiting to make his appeal to Caesar. Careful reading shows the following relationships:

- Colossians and Philemon were both sent to Colossae (Col 1:1; 4:17; Phm 2).
- Colossians and Ephesians were carried by Tychicus (Col 4:7; Eph 6:21).
- Ephesians reflects a theological development of Colossians.

All three of these were probably written not long after Paul arrived in Rome; and all three were perhaps carried together by Tychicus, who was also accompanying Onesimus (see *Occasion* for **PHILEMON**). Philippians was likely the last of the four to be written because Paul was expecting to be released soon (Php 1:19).

# GOD'S MESSAGE IN COLOSSIANS

## PURPOSE

Paul wrote the Colossian Christians to combat a dangerous teaching, known only through his criticism of it in this letter (see *Occasion* above). Although he condemned this heresy, his main approach was to exalt the person of Jesus Christ and to urge the Colossians to give up anything that denied Jesus His preeminent position as Lord.

## FIRST PASS

Colossians may be divided into two main parts. The first (1:3–2:23) is a polemic against false teachings. The second (3:1–4:17) is made up of exhortations to proper Christian living.

### Introduction

The introduction (1:1–2) is in the form of a Hellenistic, personal letter. The senders (Paul and Timothy) and the recipients (the Colossian church) are identified, and a greeting is expressed. Typical of Paul, a lengthy thanksgiving (1:3–8) and prayer (1:9–14) lead into the body of the letter. Paul thanked God for the faith, hope, and love (1:4–5) the Colossians had by virtue of their positive response to the gospel. He prayed that they might have a full knowledge and understanding of God's will and lead a life worthy of redeemed saints, citizens of the kingdom of Christ (1:9–14).

### The Centrality of Christ

Paul described the grandeur of Christ (1:15–20) and in so doing set the standard against which unworthy views of Christ and the triune God would be compared as he developed the letter. Christ is God's agent of creation (v. 16), the One to whom creation owes its continued existence (v. 17), the head of the church (v. 18), fully God in human form (v. 19), and through His sacrificial death the agent of redemption and reconciliation. Believers in Colossae had experienced the benefits of Christ. Paul urged them not to be distracted from the truth by which they had been forgiven and set on a path of hope (1:21–2:3).

**Christ and the Colossian Heresy**

Paul gave a summary description of the heresy that failed to measure up to Christ as He was revealed in time and space. He warned the Colossians of plausible sounding "philosophies" that were anti-christ (2:8). The heresy apparently involved the legalistic observance of traditions, rites, dietary laws, and religious festivals (2:8,11,16,21; 3:11). The worship of angels and lesser spirits was encouraged by the false teachers (2:8,18). Asceticism, the deprivation or harsh treatment of one's "evil" fleshly body, was promoted (2:20–23). Finally, the false teachers claimed to possess special insight, perhaps special revelations, that made them, rather than the Scriptures and the apostles' testimony, the ultimate source of truth (2:18–19).

**Put on Christ**

Understanding Christ is indissolubly linked to how believers live a life that is distinctive and reflective of the glory and grandeur of Christ. Believers are to "put to death" (3:5) and to "put away" those practices that incur the wrath of God (3:5–11). They are then to "put on" (3:12) those things characteristic of God's chosen people (3:12–17). The changes are far from superficial, however. They stem from the Christian's new nature and submission to the rule of Christ in every area of one's life (3:9–10,15–17).

**Christ in the Family**

Rules for the household appear in 3:18–4:1. The typical first-century household is assumed; thus the passage addresses wives and husbands, fathers and children, masters and slaves. Paul made no comment about the rightness or wrongness of the social structures; he accepted them as givens. Paul's concern was that the structures as they existed be governed by Christian principles. Submission to the Lord (3:18,20,22; 4:1), Christian love (3:19), and the prospect of divine judgment (3:24–4:1) must determine the way people treat one another regardless of their social station. This Christian motivation distinguishes these house rules from those that can be found in Jewish and pagan sources.

**Conclusions**

A final group of exhortations (4:2–6) and an exchange of greetings (4:7–17) bring the letter to a close. Notable in this final section are the mention of Onesimus (4:9), which links this letter with Philemon; the mention of a letter at Laodicea (4:16), which may have been Ephesians; and Paul's concluding signature, which indicates that the letter was prepared by a secretary (4:18).

## THE RELIABILITY OF COLOSSIANS

Colossians 4:7–18 brings together a number of threads that strengthen the claim that Paul wrote the letter to the Colossians. He had not been to Colossae, a city about 100 miles east of Ephesus, but he knew a lot about the church and had close friends there (Philemon and his family; 4:9). Paul spent AD 54–56 planting the church in Ephesus, the principal city of the Roman province of Asia. With Ephesus as a center and a base, the gospel was heard and received, and churches were planted throughout the province (Acts 19:10; 26). Epaphras, who likely became a believer as Paul taught in Ephesus, planted the church in Colossae (1:7–8). He had come to Paul with concerns about the direction the church was taking. Paul's letter is written to deal with these concerns. Paul dispatched this letter, the letter we now call Ephesians, and the short letter to Philemon with Tychicus, who was traveling from Rome to Laodicea and Colossae with Onesimus. Ephesians was to be delivered to the church at Laodicea and Colossians and Philemon to the church at Colossae.

## HOW COLOSSIANS FITS INTO GOD'S STORY

1. Prologue: Creation, Fall, and the Need for Redemption
2. God Builds His Nation (2000–931 BC)
3. God Educates His Nation (931–586 BC)
4. God Keeps a Faithful Remnant (586–6 BC)
5. God Purchases Redemption and Begins the Kingdom (6 BC to AD 30)
6. **God Spreads the Kingdom Through the Church (AD 30–?)**
7. God Consummates Redemption and Confirms His Eternal Kingdom
8. Epilogue: New Heaven and New Earth

## CHRIST IN COLOSSIANS

Christ is Creator of all things, whether visible or invisible. He is the One who holds all creation together. The fullness of God lived in Him, and through Christ's death God reconciled everything to Himself.

## CHRISTIAN WORLDVIEW ELEMENTS

**Teachings About God**

God is the Father of Jesus, and His fullness is in His Son (1:19; 2:9). Jesus is especially the "firstborn" (1:15,18). Colossians 1:15–18 is the most elevated passage in Paul's letters presenting the identity of Christ. When Jesus returns, His people will appear with Him in glory (3:4). The Spirit is mentioned only once (1:8), as the source of love.

### Teachings About Humanity

Because Colossians was first written to stop false teachings, it shows just how easy it is for people to be led astray from truth, particularly in matters of eternal destiny. In every age powerful enemies of truth oppose genuine understanding of God and the human condition. Apart from Christ, all are "dead in trespasses" (2:13). Christ brings new life and transformation of relationships, particularly within the home (3:18–4:1).

### Teachings About Salvation

Any understanding of salvation which is "Jesus plus" is defective. Good works, keeping Jewish law, accepting certain philosophical principles, and other positive human accomplishments cannot add anything to what Jesus has already achieved. Therefore salvation is a matter of being rightly related to Him by faith and refusing to trust anything else, no matter how valuable. Christ allows nothing to rival Him in redeeming sinners.

## GENRE AND LITERARY STYLE

### An Epistle Written in *Koinē* Greek

See *Genre and Literary Style* for **1 THESSALONIANS** for information about the genre "epistle." The standard parts of a first-century epistle appear: salutation (1:1–2); thanksgiving (1:3–8); main body (1:9–4:6); and farewell (4:7–18). This is a pastoral letter, driven by the occasion and needs of the recipients, rather than a tractate (a formal treatise). This letter was written in Paul's typical style.

## A PRINCIPLE TO LIVE BY

### Putting Christ First (Col 1:15–20, *Life Essentials Study Bible*, p. 1651)

To walk in God's will, Jesus Christ must always be the central focus in our personal and corporate lives.

To access a video presentation of this principle featuring Dr. Gene Getz, use a Smartphone or iPad to connect to this QR code or go to http://www.bhpublishinggroup.com/handbook/colossians

# 1 THESSALONIANS

## THE FIRST EPISTLE TO THE THESSALONIANS

This book is so named because it is the first canonical letter Paul the apostle wrote to the Christians in Thessalonica.

### KEY TEXT: 4:16–17

*"For the Lord Himself shall descend from heaven with a shout, with the voice of the archangel, and with the trump of God: and the dead in Christ shall rise first: Then we which are alive and remain shall be caught up together with them in the clouds, to meet the Lord in the air: and so shall we ever be with the Lord."*

### KEY TERM: "COMING"

This book mentions the return of Christ in every chapter. The Greek noun *parousia*, here rendered "coming," can also be translated "arrival" or "presence."

### ONE-SENTENCE SUMMARY

Whatever difficulties and sufferings believers experience in this life, the coming of Christ is the true hope of the Christian.

The seafront promenade of Thessaloniki, Greece, on a clear spring day.

# ORIGINAL HISTORICAL SETTING

## AUTHOR AND DATE OF WRITING

**Paul the Apostle, About AD 50**

All New Testament scholars accept the claim of the letter to be written by Paul. See *Author* and *Date of Writing* for **ROMANS** for more information about Paul. The apostle wrote this letter around AD 50 from Corinth (see *Occasion* below).

## FIRST AUDIENCE AND DESTINATION

**Christians in Thessalonica**

Acts 17:1–8 describes how Christianity first came to Thessalonica through Paul's preaching. Silas, Timothy, and Paul left Philippi and traveled the Via Egnatia to Thessalonica, the capital of Macedonia and numbered perhaps 200,000 in the first century. It was a seaport and commercial center lying at the intersection of the Egnatian Way and the road leading north toward the Danube River.

The believers had come from both Jewish and pagan backgrounds. Having been beaten and jailed in Philippi, Paul was forced by persecution to leave Thessalonica early, possibly staying there only three months. These new believers had enthusiastically embraced the gospel but were not taught in the way of the Lord.

## OCCASION

After Paul fled Macedonia, Timothy and Silas finally caught up with him in Athens. Paul was so concerned to learn about the spiritual state of the Thessalonians that he dispatched Timothy to them (1Th 3:1–5). Timothy stayed there for a time, strengthening and encouraging these new believers. At last Timothy caught up with Paul a second time, this time in Corinth (Ac 18:5; 1Th 3:6). Timothy's report was essentially positive. The congregation was thriving and growing in virtue, although they were enduring persecution of some kind. Paul's ministry there had emphasized that Christ's coming could be soon. Thus the Thessalonians had some concern when some of their members died (4:13). Had those who died missed the kingdom? Would they see the King? Paul found it important to expand his teaching on "eschatology" (end times) and to clarify their confusion. He penned this letter perhaps within months of first preaching in Thessalonica.

# GOD'S MESSAGE IN 1 THESSALONIANS

## PURPOSE

Having to leave Thessalonica so abruptly and before he intended, Paul wanted to communicate many things to these new believers. He writes to encourage these new converts in their understanding of the gospel and its implications for how they lived.

He also sought to correct a deficiency in their understanding of the second coming of Christ.

## FIRST PASS

Paul begins with heartfelt thanksgiving for what God had done among the Thessalonians when the gospel was proclaimed to them in the power of the Spirit. They rapidly became imitators of Paul and the Lord and thus became a model to all believers throughout Macedonia and Achaia (1:1–10).

### Personal Relations

In Paul's absence his critics suggest that he operated out of ulterior motives (2:3–13). Paul addressed his readers' concerns most affectionately.

### The Call to Please God

Serving God stems from the desire to please Him in the details of life. Paul gave general guidelines concerning pleasing God and then specific ones focused on sexual morality (4:1–12).

### Questions About Christ's Second Coming

The question of what happens to believers who die before Christ's return concerned the Thessalonians (4:8–18). Paul said the living believer will not have an advantage at the Lord's appearing. In fact, the Christian dead will rise first. After that those "who are still alive" will be "caught up together with them in the clouds to meet the Lord in the air." These encouraging words provided great comfort to those whose family members had already died. Just as people today want to know more about "end times" so did the Thessalonians.

### The Day of the Lord

In this section Paul continued his discussion about the Lord's return with particular emphasis on the meaning of the Day of the Lord (5:1–11). Since the Day of the Lord will come suddenly and unexpectedly, bringing destruction on those who walk in darkness, believers should maintain spiritual alertness.

### Concluding Exhortations

Paul next stressed the responsibilities to the different people in the Christian community (5:14–15). They were to warn when necessary, encourage the timid, and show kindness to one another. Then in staccato-like fashion, he gives eight commands designed to enhance their worship of and walk with God (5:16–22).

## RELIABILITY OF 1 THESSALONIANS

The authenticity of 1 Thessalonians is almost universally accepted. It bears Paul's style and is mentioned in early Christian writings such as the lists of NT books given by Marcion (mid second century) and by the Muratorian Canon (late second century). Irenaeus (130–200), Tertullian, and Clement of Alexandria all viewed the letter as one of Paul's epistles. In the nineteenth century F. C. Baur argued that 1 Thessalonians was spurious. Baur's views carried weight with a number of scholars for a time. This trend was reversed in large measure by the careful statistical analysis of 1 Thessalonians by J. E. Frame (1912) who demonstrated that the vocabulary and concepts of 1 Thessalonians are strongly consistent with letters universally held to be written by Paul.

## HOW 1 THESSALONIANS FITS INTO GOD'S STORY

1. Prologue: Creation, Fall, and the Need for Redemption
2. God Builds His Nation (2000–931 BC)
3. God Educates His Nation (931–586 BC)
4. God Keeps a Faithful Remnant (586–6 BC)
5. God Purchases Redemption and Begins the Kingdom (6 BC to AD 30)
6. God Spreads the Kingdom Through the Church (AD 30-?)
7. God Consummates Redemption and Confirms His Eternal Kingdom
8. Epilogue: New Heaven and New Earth

## CHRIST IN 1 THESSALONIANS

Christ is a source of comfort because He is coming again. At His coming those who have died in Him will rise first. Then believers who are living will be caught up to join those who have died and be together with Him.

## CHRISTIAN WORLDVIEW ELEMENTS

### Teachings About God

God is the Father who actively works to bring about salvation. He is presently working holiness into his children. Jesus died and rose again at His first coming, and He will return in glory at His Second Coming. The Spirit, the active agent by whom God makes the gospel alive, is God's gift enabling His people to have great joy (1:5–6; 4:8).

### Teachings About Humanity

There are only two kinds of people: those who have received the word of God and those who have rejected it (2:13–16). The destiny of the one group is the experience of the wrath of God, leading to their destruction. The destiny of the other group is to be with the Lord forever. This latter group is called on to live a holy life that pleases God.

### Teachings About Salvation

The basis of salvation is Jesus' death and resurrection (4:14; 5:10). The letter summarizes salvation as past, present, and future in this way: "You turned to God from idols to serve the living and true God and to wait for His Son from heaven, whom He raised from the dead—Jesus, who rescues us from the coming wrath" (1:9–10).

## GENRE AND LITERARY STYLE

### An Epistle Written in *Koinē* Greek

Unlike the Gospels, which were a new literary genre inspired by Christianity, epistles were a well-known first-century literary form. First Thessalonians is one of the earliest of Paul's letters to survive, although Galatians may be earlier. This is the earliest Pauline epistle that contains all four standard elements of an epistle, of which many secular examples have been discovered.

- **Salutation** (1:1). The form is "from sender to recipient: greetings." Paul always identified himself as the author and named the recipient. In place of the conventional word greetings, Paul always used "grace and peace."
- **Thanksgiving** (1:2–3). This was a prayer directed to God on behalf of the readers. The secular examples invoked a variety of deities, depending on which god was served.
- **Body** (1:4–5:22). This obviously was the main point of the letter. Paul typically wrote a doctrinal argument followed by a shorter practical application.
- **Farewell** (5:23–28). The writer gave greetings and otherwise concluded the document. Paul always used the word "grace" (Greek, *charis*) in his farewell.

Like most of Paul's writings, this is a pastoral letter, driven by the occasion and needs of the recipients, rather than a tractate (a formal treatise). First Thessalonians represents Paul's typical careful use of the Greek language.

## A PRINCIPLE TO LIVE BY

### Understanding Doctrinal Truths (1 Th 4:13–18, *Life Essentials Study Bible*, p. 1664)

To help new converts have a clear understanding of the Scriptures, we should develop a plan to teach basic doctrinal truths.

To access a video presentation of this principle featuring Dr. Gene Getz, use a Smartphone or iPad to connect to this QR code or go to http://www.bhpublishinggroup.com/handbook/1thessalonians

This book is so named because it is the second canonical letter Paul the apostle wrote to the Christians in Thessalonica.

## KEY TEXT: 2:15

*"Therefore, brothers, stand firm and hold to the traditions you were taught, either by our message or by our letter."*

## KEY TERM: "STAND"

This book was written to believers who had been shaken by false teaching concerning the end times. The apostle's advice to "stand firm" applies no matter what doctrinal or practical challenge believers face.

## ONE-SENTENCE SUMMARY

Whatever difficulties believers face, they should stand firm and continue living useful lives since Christ's return may be in the distant future.

Thessaloniki in the late 1800s.

## AUTHOR AND DATE OF WRITING

**Paul the Apostle, Around AD 50**

The letter claims to be written by Paul the apostle. For the past two centuries some (but not all) critical scholars have rejected that Paul wrote this letter. They have argued that the eschatology (end-times doctrine) of this letter contradicts the eschatology of 1 Thessalonians. This letter was therefore written by an unknown later Christian who used Paul's name to bolster his own authority. The basic argument is that in 2 Thessalonians, Christ's coming appears to be distant, and a number of signs must precede it. Yet in the first epistle, His return appears to be imminent and without warning. Clearly the letters have differing emphases, but they are not incompatible. Through the centuries Christians have held that the Day of the Lord may come at any time (imminence), but that it is not necessarily immediate. For further discussion of authorship, see *The Reliability of 2 Thessalonians.* Paul wrote from Corinth just a few months after he wrote 1 Thessalonians. Those who reject Pauline authorship date the letter toward the end of the first century.

## FIRST AUDIENCE AND DESTINATION

**Christians in Thessalonica**

See *First Audience and Destination* for **1 THESSALONIANS**.

## OCCASION

After Paul sent 1 Thessalonians, the church had received a further report that the "Day of the Lord"—the end times—had come. The return of Christ was immediate. This had come as if from Paul himself (2:2). The church was thrown into turmoil, and many of the members had quit their jobs and were waiting for the Second Coming. Paul therefore had to write them again to correct the doctrinal error and to urge them to settle down and get back to work.

# GOD'S MESSAGE IN 2 THESSALONIANS

## PURPOSE

Paul wrote this letter mainly to correct a new deficiency in the Thessalonians' understanding of the coming of Christ and related events (see *Purpose* for **1 THESSALONIANS**). He also wanted to correct the problem brought about because some had stopped working (in light of their belief that the Day of the Lord had come).

## FIRST PASS

### The Thessalonians Commended

Paul commended the Thessalonians for their growing faith, maturing love, and patience in the face of persecution (1:3–5). He reminded them of the great reversal that would come with the appearance of the Lord Jesus Christ. God's people can be encouraged by knowing they will be vindicated at the Lord's coming and will realize they have neither believed nor suffered in vain (1:6–10).

### The Day of the Lord

With much focus on Jesus' second coming, some were wrongly teaching that the Day of the Lord had already occurred. Paul countered these false teachers by noting that a full-scale rebellion must precede the second coming of Christ. Before the Lord's coming the lawless one must be revealed. He is one who exalts himself over God. Those who are themselves lawless will be so deluded as to believe what is false (2:5–12).

### Request for Prayer

Paul requested that the Thessalonians pray that he would be delivered from evil men and that the message of Christ would spread rapidly. He, in turn, assured them of his prayers on their behalf. Paul then urged those who had had stopped working in view of imminence of Jesus' return to go back to work and reminded them of his own practice of working to support himself rather than being a burden to the Thessalonians.

## THE RELIABILITY OF 2 THESSALONIANS

Paul's authorship of 2 Thessalonians has been questioned frequently in recent years in spite of the fact that it has extremely strong support throughout church history. The objections to Pauline authorship are threefold: (1) The style of 2 Thessalonians is said to be more formal than 1 Thessalonians. (2) The vocabulary is supposedly too different from the rest of Paul's writings. (3) The unique approach to eschatology in 2 Thessalonians (the "man of lawlessness" is not mentioned elsewhere).

However, these arguments are not convincing in light of the similarity of content between 1 and 2 Thessalonians. The interval between 1 and 2 Thessalonians must have been rather short, for the second epistle does not presuppose major changes in the inner constitution of the Thessalonian church or in the conditions under which Paul was writing. The second letter may have been written more quickly and with more urgency to address the claim that the Day of the Lord had already occurred. Since a more personal letter had preceded the second letter, Paul was concerned to move to the pressing issues within the church.

The views of the Second Coming in the two letters are not logically incompatible. It can be shown that the differences concerning the Second Coming are differences of emphasis rather than substance. Both letters view the second coming of

Christ as imminent but not necessarily immediate. In 2:5 Paul reminded the Thessalonians that during his short time with them, part of his message was that an apostasy and the appearance of the man of lawlessness would precede the Day of the Lord.

## HOW 2 THESSALONIANS FITS INTO GOD'S STORY

1. Prologue: Creation, Fall, and the Need for Redemption
2. God Builds His Nation (2000–931 BC)
3. God Educates His Nation (931–586 BC)
4. God Keeps a Faithful Remnant (586–6 BC)
5. God Purchases Redemption and Begins the Kingdom (6 BC to AD 30)
6. God Spreads the Kingdom Through the Church (AD 30–?)
7. God Consummates Redemption and Confirms His Eternal Kingdom
8. Epilogue: New Heaven and New Earth

## CHRIST IN 2 THESSALONIANS

Christ came the first time as a baby. His Second Coming will be different. He will come with His powerful angels who will punish God's enemies, those who refuse peace with God made possible by the death of Christ.

## CHRISTIAN WORLDVIEW ELEMENTS

### Teachings About God

God's supremacy in all things, particularly concerning salvation and the consummation of the world, is taught in this letter. His justice is especially taught in the way He will ultimately punish all evildoers. Jesus' coming is taught in this book, and He will easily overcome "the man of lawlessness" (2:3) as a display of His glory on "the Day of the Lord." The Holy Spirit, mentioned only at 2:13, sanctifies (makes holy) those God has chosen to save.

### Teachings About Humanity

This letter shows two sharply opposed groups of humanity. On one hand are those who know God and have come to obey the gospel. On the other hand are all others, who will pay the penalty of eternal destruction away from the Lord's presence" (1:9).

### Teachings About Salvation

In 2 Thessalonians, salvation is seen from the future perspective of deliverance from judgment and destruction on the Day of the Lord. In the end those who perish do so "because they did not accept the love of the truth in order to be saved" (2:10).

## GENRE AND LITERARY STYLE

### An Epistle Written in *Koinē* Greek

See *Genre and Literary Style* for **1 THESSALONIANS** for information about the genre "epistle." The standard parts of a first-century epistle appear: salutation (1:1–2); thanksgiving (1:3–11); main body (2:1–3:15); and farewell (3:16–18). This is a pastoral letter, driven by the occasion and needs of the recipients, rather than a tractate (a formal treatise). It was written in Paul's typical style.

## A PRINCIPLE TO LIVE BY

### Preparation or Speculation (2Th 2:13–17, *Life Essentials Study Bible*, p. 1669)

No matter what happens in the future, we are to encourage believers to stand firm in their faith, hope, and love, always being ready for Christ's return.

To access a video presentation of this principle featuring Dr. Gene Getz, use a Smartphone or iPad to connect to this QR code or go to http://www.bhpublishinggroup.com/handbook/2thessalonians

This book is so named because it is the first canonical letter that Paul the apostle wrote to Timothy.

### KEY TEXT: 6:11

*"But you, man of God, run from these things, and pursue righteousness, godliness, faith, love, endurance, and gentleness."*

### KEY TERM: "GODLINESS"

Godliness (Greek, *eusebeia*) is the virtue that sums up all others. Timothy's many ministry challenges would succeed only if he proceeded from godly character.

### ONE-SENTENCE SUMMARY

Whatever challenges Christian leaders face in life and ministry, they are to make progress in godliness and help maintain order in congregational life.

## ORIGINAL HISTORICAL SETTING

### AUTHOR AND DATE OF WRITING

**Paul the Apostle, about AD 63**

The book claims explicitly to be written by "Paul, an apostle of Christ Jesus" (1:1). Until about two centuries ago, all Bible students affirmed this belief. With the rise of critical approaches to Scripture, nonconservative scholars have adopted the position that an unknown admirer of Paul wrote 1 Timothy (as well as 2 Timothy and Titus). Opinions vary whether these letters contain any genuine Pauline fragments. The chief objection is historical. The travels mentioned in these three epistles do not fit into the framework provided by Acts. If Paul indeed perished at the end of Acts, he could not be the author of these books. It is also held that the congregational form encouraged in these letters (with overseers and deacons officially recognized) is too advanced for Paul's day. The Greek style is also noticeably different from that of the undisputed Pauline letters.

These objections may be satisfactorily answered: (1) It is by no means certain that Paul died at the end of the Acts 28 imprisonment. In fact, the evidence from Philippians 1:25 is that Paul expected to be released. (2) Little is actually known about the congregational form of the Pauline churches. Overseers and deacons certainly functioned in Philippi years before 1 Timothy was written (Php 1:1). (3) The difference in Greek style does not prove anything, for the Greek of 1 and 2 Timothy and Titus are more like the Greek of the undisputed Pauline letters than any other part of the Bible. For additional discussion of authorship, see *The Reliability of 1 Timothy* below.

Paul wrote after he was released from the Roman imprisonment described at the end of Acts, around AD 63. Those who reject Pauline authorship date the letter toward the end of the first century.

## FIRST AUDIENCE AND DESTINATION

### Timothy, Paul's Dearest Friend, Who Was in Ephesus

Timothy had the task of being an apostolic representative. He was from Lystra (in modern Turkey). His father was Gentile, but his mother Eunice was a Jewish Christian (Ac 16:1; 2Tm 1:5). Timothy had probably come to the gospel through Paul during his first visit to Lystra (1Tm 1:2). Timothy joined Paul on his second missionary journey, helping Paul in Macedonia and Achaia (Ac 17–18). He traveled with Paul later on and was with him during his Roman imprisonment (Php 1:1; Col 1:1).

After Paul was released, he assigned Timothy the responsibility of helping the church of Ephesus with its difficulties. Paul's comments about Timothy in Philippians 2:19–24 and his statements in 1 and 2 Timothy show Paul's affection for his loyal associate. Paul later asked Timothy to rejoin him (2Tm 4:9,21), and Hebrews 13:23 indicates that Timothy was later imprisoned. (For information about Ephesus, see *First Audience and Destination* for **EPHESIANS**.)

Bust of Nero, Roman emperor AD 54–68 during whose reign both Paul and Peter were martyred. Paul instructed Timothy to pray for kings and all those who are in authority (1 Tm 2:1–2).

## OCCASION

Paul had left Timothy in Ephesus when he found that false teaching had upset the stability of the church there. The exact nature of this teaching is impossible to determine, but it included both Jewish speculative elements ("myths and endless genealogies," 1:4) as well as Greek philosophical elements ("irreverent, empty speech and contradictions from the 'knowledge' that falsely bears that name," 6:20). Timothy had to deal with false teachers as well as organize the church along sound principles.

# GOD'S MESSAGE IN 1 TIMOTHY

## PURPOSE

Paul wrote his dear friend Timothy to accomplish a number of objectives. First, he wished to encourage Timothy in his growth as a Christian and as a leader. Second, he offered instructions about church organization, particularly congregational officers.

## FIRST PASS

### Sound Teaching

When Paul went to Macedonia, he left Timothy to provide leadership with the church at Ephesus. Some in Ephesus had moved away from sound doctrine and narrowly focused on the Jewish law, genealogies, and myths and were involved more in speculation than on God's clear plan. Two leaders among the false teachers were Hymenaeus and Alexander; Paul said he "delivered them to Satan, so that they may be taught not to blaspheme" (1:20; cp. 1 Co 5:5). The purpose of this and all Christian discipline was the eventual restoration of the offender.

### Christian Worship

From his concerns about false teachers Paul turned to worship in the church. He began with instructions concerning prayer (2:1–7) and then moved to matters regarding the roles of men and women (vv. 8–15). Prayer is given priority in public worship services. Seven different Greek words appear in the NT for prayer, and four of them occur in verse 1.

### Leadership

Paul affirmed that church leadership is a noble task. Here Paul described the qualifications for those who aspire to such leadership (3:1–7). He then moved to discuss the qualification of deacons, which are virtually the same as those for elders. Generally the service of deacons was meant to free the overseers to give full attention to prayer and the ministry of the Word (Ac 6:2–4).

**Correction**

Paul returned to the false teaching that Timothy must be aware of and address. The false teaching was demonic in nature. It had the appearance of hyper-religiosity, teaching a false asceticism, forbidding marriage and the eating of various foods. But Paul maintained that God has given these things to be enjoyed and used for God's glory (4:1–5). To take the corrective action required, Timothy must be a leader of godly character. He was to lead as a servant (4:6) and "be an example to the believers in speech, in conduct, in love, in faith, in purity" (4:12).

**Widows**

Paul addressed the care of widows. Specifically he offered guidelines for helping widows in need, for enabling widows as workers in the church, and suggestions for the younger widows. Younger widows were to be encouraged to marry again. The church, then, would only have the responsibility to care for the older widows who had no families to take care of them (5:3–16).

**Elders**

The elders were not only to teach but to provide oversight for the church. These leaders who work hard were worthy of "an ample honorarium." Early church leaders were not perfect. Their imperfections needed to be dealt with. Criticisms of leaders should be rejected unless they can be proven to be true. Formal discipline should be exercised with care and caution when needed. These leaders must be examined thoroughly. They should not be chosen or ordained too quickly (5:17–25).

**Masters, Slaves, and Money**

How Christian masters and slaves treat each other is a reflection on the God whom they serve. Money can be made into a false god and bring all kinds of evil to those with misplaced affections.

**Closing Challenge**

Timothy had been a partaker of eternal life since he had first believed the gospel, but Paul encouraged him to claim the gospel's benefits in greater fullness. Timothy should fight a good fight as a soldier of God in his pursuit of holiness, his persistence in service, and in the protection of the gospel. In order to do this Timothy, like all believers, must focus his adoration on the glorious Christ. The letter concludes with a brief benediction, "Grace be with you" (6:11–21).

## THE RELIABILITY OF 1 TIMOTHY

One reason some scholars have denied Paul wrote 1 Timothy is because they assume he was executed following his first imprisonment in Rome and couldn't have been in either Ephesus or Macedonia as indicated in the letter (1:3). It has been noted (*Author and Date of Writing*) that in his letter to Philippi (Php 2:23–24) and to Philemon (Phm 22), he expected to be released soon. Luke's description of the manner of Paul's confinement makes plausible his release (Ac 28:17–31). The

way Paul is treated on his arrival in Rome doesn't have the appearance of a person who has committed a capital offense against Rome. From the time he embarked the Adramyttium ship at Caesarea, he was under the supervision of Julius, a centurion of the Imperial Regiment. In Rome his guard was an ordinary soldier (28:16) and not a centurion. Paul was chained, but he was not placed in a military or criminal prison but was "permitted to stay by himself" (28:16), "at his lodging" (28:23), that he rented (28:30).

Three days after his arrival in Rome, he called the Jewish leaders in Rome to come and meet with him. Paul's access to visitors over a two-year period further underscores the fact that Roman authorities didn't view him as a security risk. Brian Rapske[1] argues that the Roman official(s) who made the arrangements for Paul's confinement based their decisions on "the trial documents . . . indicating that there were no grounds for the Roman charges" against him.

## HOW 1 TIMOTHY FITS INTO GOD'S STORY

1. Prologue: Creation, Fall, and the Need for Redemption
2. God Builds His Nation (2000–931 BC)
3. God Educates His Nation (931–586 BC)
4. God Keeps a Faithful Remnant (586–6 BC)
5. God Purchases Redemption and Begins the Kingdom (6 BC to AD 30)
6. **God Spreads the Kingdom Through the Church (AD 30–?)**
7. God Consummates Redemption and Confirms His Eternal Kingdom
8. Epilogue: New Heaven and New Earth

## CHRIST IN 1 TIMOTHY

Christ's purpose for coming into the world is to save sinners. Paul said Christ took him as a worst-case scenario. He argued that if Christ can save him, He can save anyone.

## CHRISTIAN WORLDVIEW ELEMENTS

### Teachings About God

This epistle contains the classic biblical summary of God's attributes: "the King eternal, immortal, invisible, the only God" (1:17). He is also "the blessed and only Sovereign, the King of kings, and the Lord of lords" (6:15). Jesus is the only Mediator between God and mankind (2:5). The Holy Spirit's person is clearly affirmed (3:16; 4:1).

### Teachings About Humanity

As one of the six New Testament letters first written to a single individual (1 and 2 Timothy, Titus, Philemon, 2 and 3 John), this book shows the importance of what one person can be and do. The individuals addressed in these books (Timothy, Titus, Philemon, "the elect lady," and Gaius) were all redeemed sinners working for the kingdom of God in one way or another. They all benefited from the advice and encouragement offered by the letter they received. These persons stand as examples of living out one's life for the glory of God and in the hope of eternal life.

**Teachings About Salvation**

Salvation in this letter, as everywhere in Paul's writings, focuses on Jesus Christ. Paul summarized his understanding by reminding Timothy of "the mystery of godliness," evidently an early Christian hymn or poem: "He was manifested in the flesh, vindicated in the Spirit, seen by angels, preached among the nations, believed on in the world, taken up in glory" (3:16).

## GENRE AND LITERARY STYLE

**An Epistle Written in *Koinē* Greek**

See *Genre and Literary Style* for **1 THESSALONIANS** for information about the genre "epistle." The standard parts of a first-century epistle appear in 1 Timothy, except that the thanksgiving is missing: salutation (1:1–2); main body (1:3–6:19); and farewell (6:20–21). This letter, 2 Timothy, and Titus share certain vocabulary and style elements that make these three books distinctive. So clearly do they belong together that they are often considered as a unit, "The Pastoral Epistles."

## A PRINCIPLE TO LIVE BY

**A Profile for Christian Maturity (1 Tm 3:1–13, *Life Essentials Study Bible*, p. 1676)**

Leaders who are appointed to serve in shepherding roles in the church are to be selected based on comprehensive biblical criteria for measuring Christian maturity.

To access a video presentation of this principle featuring Dr. Gene Getz, use a Smartphone or iPad to connect to this QR code or go to www.bhpublishinggroup.com/handbook/1timothy

## ENDNOTE

1. Brian Rapske, *The Book of Acts and Paul in Roman Custody* (Grand Rapids: William B. Eerdmans, 1994), 189–91.

This book is so named because it is the second canonical letter Paul the apostle wrote to Timothy.

## KEY TEXT: 2:2

*"And what you have heard from me in the presence of many witnesses, commit to faithful men who will be able to teach others also."*

## KEY TERM: "COMMITTED"

Timothy was to commit (entrust) the treasure of the gospel that had been committed to him to those who would faithfully transmit it to the next generation, just as he had committed his eternal destiny to the One who would keep it for "that day" (1:12).

## ONE-SENTENCE SUMMARY

Christian leaders are to be unashamed of the gospel and to carry on faithfully with the message about Christ entrusted to them.

# ORIGINAL HISTORICAL SETTING

## AUTHOR AND DATE OF WRITING

**Paul the Apostle, Around AD 66**

See *Author and Date of Writing* for **1 TIMOTHY** for information about objections to Pauline authorship. Assuming Paul is the author, he wrote from his final Roman imprisonment, around AD 66. Those who reject Pauline authorship date the letter toward the end of the first century. For further discussion of authorship, see *The Reliability of 2 Timothy* below.

## FIRST AUDIENCE AND DESTINATION

**Timothy, Paul's Dearest Friend, Possibly in Ephesus**

See *First Audience and Destination* for **1 TIMOTHY**. There is no definite indication in this letter concerning Timothy's location. Many students think it likely that he was still serving the Lord in Ephesus (1Tm 1:3).

## OCCASION

Paul had been rearrested in an unknown place and was back in Rome. The Roman government's official hostility to Christianity that arose after the great fire of Rome in AD 64 when Nero decided to make Christians his scapegoats was probably the context for Paul's final imprisonment. Paul was evidently in an imperial prison. He was not even given the benefit of adequate clothing as the cold and damp of winter approached (4:13).

Paul was virtually alone. Only Luke had access to him; others had abandoned him or been sent out in ministry (4:10–12). Paul had been through a preliminary hearing that persuaded him that he would soon be executed (4:16). He therefore wanted company before he died and twice begged Timothy to come (4:9,21). He also wanted his books, his coat, and the fellowship of Mark (4:12–13). It is not known whether Timothy arrived in Rome in time to say good-bye to his beloved mentor face-to-face.

# GOD'S MESSAGE IN 2 TIMOTHY

## PURPOSE

Paul wrote this letter as his "last will and testament." He wished to remind Timothy of what mattered most to him in case he did not survive his imprisonment until Timothy arrived. He also urged Timothy and Mark to come to him in haste in order to be with him in his last days.

## FIRST PASS

### Introduction

Paul began this letter with a highly personal greeting as he did in 1 Timothy. In this letter he referred to Timothy as "my dearly loved son." Paul offered thanks for Timothy's heritage and for the gift God had planted in Timothy. He urged Timothy to appropriate the rich heritage that was his and to stir up the gift God had given him.

### Keep the Faith

Paul offered a strong admonition to Timothy to keep the faith in the midst of suffering. During this time the apostle had been deserted by Phygelus and Hermogenes. This may have taken place when Paul was arrested and taken to Rome for his final imprisonment. In contrast to the actions of the majority, some, such as Onesiphorus, befriended Paul and wasn't ashamed of the fact that he was a prisoner.

### Be Strong

Paul exhorted Timothy to be strong in the grace of Jesus Christ and to convey the

truth he had received from Paul to faithful men who, in turn, would teach others. Paul gave three examples for Timothy to follow: (1) a soldier who wants to please his commander, (2) an athlete who follows the rules of the game, and (3) a farmer who toils faithfully (1 Co 9:6,24–27).

### False Teachers

Hymenaeus and Philetus were examples of false teachers. They were disturbing the faith of some by claiming the resurrection had already taken place. Confronting false teachers requires careful preparation as one who seeks God's approval. This preparation is one of mind, heart, and relational skill that desires of a change of heart on the part of those who have strayed from the truth.

### Last Days

Paul described an intensification of evil in the last days, an era that has just begun. Paul listed 18 characteristics of evil men in 3:2–5. He compared them to Jannes and Jambres (3:8). Although these two individuals are not mentioned in the OT, Jewish

Snow on some sycamore (platanus) trees near the Tiber, in Rome. In closing his letter, Paul wrote, "When you come bring the cloak I left in Troas with Carpus, as well as the scrolls, especially the parchments" (2Tm 4:13). Likely winter was approaching and the Mamertine Prison would not have afforded protection as the temperature dropped.

tradition maintains that these men were two Egyptian magicians who opposed Moses and Aaron.

**Scripture**

In times of rampant evil, Timothy was to stay with the truth he had learned and believed. This truth was not just abstract but had been incarnated in the lives of those who had been vital in Timothy's formation as a believer. The source of this teaching was the Scriptures, which are God inspired and designed to make every believer complete in Christ.

**Preach the Word**

Paul's concluding charge stressed the need not only to know the word but to preach it (4:1–5). Like Timothy, all believers are to be prepared in any situation to speak a needed word, whether of correction, rebuke, or encouragement. Christian workers must be ready to endure hardship as Paul had done.

Paul viewed his approaching death as the pouring out of a "drink offering." A drink offering referred to the offering of wine poured around the base of the altar during the Old Testament sacrifices (see Nm 15:1–12; 28:7; Php 2:17). Paul's plea to Timothy closed with personal requests and reference to his "first defense."

**Final Greeting**

The letter concludes with greetings to Priscilla and Aquila and the household of Onesiphorus. Paul then sent greetings from four members of the church at Rome and all the brothers. Paul pronounced a personal benediction on Timothy ("your spirit" in 4:22a is singular) before concluding with a corporate blessing: "Grace be with you" ("you" in 4:22 is plural).

## THE RELIABILITY OF 2 TIMOTHY

Many scholars have argued that 2 Timothy was not written by Paul in spite of the ascription: "Paul, an apostle of Christ Jesus by God's will . . . to Timothy, my dearly loved son" (1:1–2). Their view is that 1, 2 Timothy and Titus were written by someone in the second century, addressing situations in a way that Paul would have if he had been living. For 2 Timothy, their primary reasons for ascribing the letter to the late first century or early second century have to do with the vocabulary of 2 Timothy and the fact that 2 Timothy contains information that is difficult to reconcile with the closing chapter of Acts.

Second Timothy contains 81 words that don't occur in any of the 10 letters widely believed to have been written by Paul. This in itself is not sufficient evidence to deny that Paul wrote 2 Timothy. The difference in vocabulary may be explained by the fact that a scribe had considerable freedom in shaping the final form of the letter. In Romans, Paul's scribe, Tertius, inserts his own greeting to the Romans: "I Tertius, who wrote this letter, greet you in the Lord." Other letters show evidence of having been written by a scribe. At the end of 1 Corinthians, Paul writes: "This greet-

ing is in my own hand—Paul." After Sosthenes or some other scribe had finished the letter, Paul inserted a greeting in his handwriting.

Many who hold that 2 Timothy was written early in the second century believe Paul was executed at the end of his first imprisonment in Rome. This would make it difficult to account for some of the geographical references in 2 Timothy. Paul's initial imprisonment or house arrest was around 61–62. Eusebius (AD 265–339), the early church historian, says that Paul was martyred in the fourteenth year of Nero's reign, AD 67–68. Eusebius also maintains, "Paul's martyrdom was not accomplished during the sojourn in Rome which Luke describes." This leaves a gap of several years during which Paul could have ministered in Macedonia, Asia Minor, Achaia, Crete, and Nicopolis.

The number of personal references in 2 Timothy makes it highly unlikely than anyone but Paul wrote this letter. Pseudepigraphers—those who wrote letters in the name of a well-known person—rarely included these kinds of details in such letters because such details didn't serve the purpose of the letter. The abundance of personal references in 2 Timothy is strong evidence that the letter was written by Paul.

## HOW 2 TIMOTHY FITS INTO GOD'S STORY

1. Prologue: Creation, Fall, and the Need for Redemption
2. God Builds His Nation (2000–931 BC)
3. God Educates His Nation (931–586 BC)
4. God Keeps a Faithful Remnant (586–6 BC)
5. God Purchases Redemption and Begins the Kingdom (6 BC to AD 30)
6. **God Spreads the Kingdom Through the Church (AD 30–?)**
7. God Consummates Redemption and Confirms His Eternal Kingdom
8. Epilogue: New Heaven and New Earth

## CHRIST IN 2 TIMOTHY

God's saving grace through Christ was not an afterthought, a response to unforeseen developments in the world. It was planned before time. Christ has abolished death and brought life and immortality through His death and resurrection.

## CHRISTIAN WORLDVIEW ELEMENTS

### Teachings About God

God is the powerful Father who has graciously gifted His servants for ministry. Scripture is itself "God-breathed" (Greek, *theopneustos*; "inspired by God," 3:16). Jesus is both God and man: "Keep your attention on Jesus Christ as risen from the dead and descended from David" (2:8). The Holy Spirit is the powerful presence of God indwelling believers and enabling them to continue their ministry (1:14).

### Teachings About Humanity

See *Teachings about Humanity* for **1 TIMOTHY**.

### Teachings About Salvation

Salvation is both sovereignly determined by God and the divine gift to all who believe. Paul summarized the evangelistic aspect of his ministry with a statement combining both emphases: "I endure all things for the elect: so that they also may obtain salvation, which is in Christ Jesus, with eternal glory" (2:10).

## GENRE AND LITERARY STYLE

### An Epistle Written in *Koinē* Greek

See *Genre and Literary Style* for **1 THESSALONIANS** for information about the genre "epistle." The standard parts of a first-century epistle appear in 2 Timothy: salutation (1:1–2); thanksgiving (1:3–7); main body (1:8–4:18); and farewell (4:19–22). This letter, like 1 Timothy and Titus, has certain vocabulary and style elements that make these three books distinctive. So clearly do they belong together that they are often considered as a unit, "The Pastoral Epistles."

## A PRINCIPLE TO LIVE BY

### Mentoring Others (2 Tm 2:1–6, *Life Essentials Study Bible*, p. 1685)

Spiritual leaders should develop a core of faithful men and women who can multiply their efforts.

To access a video presentation of this principle featuring Dr. Gene Getz, use a Smartphone or iPad to connect to this QR code or go to http://www.bhpublishinggroup.com/handbook/2timothy

This book is so named as the letter Paul the apostle wrote to Titus.

## KEY TEXT: 2:1

*"But you must say the things that are consistent with sound teaching."*

## KEY TERM: "TEACHING"

This book emphasizes that sound teaching is the necessary foundation for everything worthwhile in the life of a congregation or an individual.

## ONE-SENTENCE SUMMARY

Whatever challenges they face in life and ministry, Christian leaders are to maintain order in the congregation, but only according to sound teaching.

View of Crete's Psiloritis Mountains. Crete is an incomparably beautiful island. Nevertheless, Titus had a challenging task in view of the character of the people whom Paul described as rebellious, full of empty talk and deception (1:10). Cretans were among those listed as present in Jerusalem on the day of Pentecost (Ac 2:11), and the gospel may first have reached the island through them.

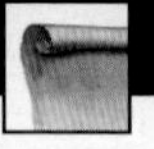


## AUTHOR AND DATE OF WRITING

**Paul the Apostle, Around AD 63**

See *Author and Date of Writing* for **1 TIMOTHY** for information about critical objections to Pauline authorship. Assuming that Paul is the author, he wrote after he was released from the Roman imprisonment described at the end of Acts, around AD 63. Those who reject Pauline authorship date the letter toward the end of the first century.

## FIRST AUDIENCE AND DESTINATION

**Titus, Paul's Trusted Friend, Who Was on Crete**

Titus had the task of being an apostolic representative. He was one of Paul's early converts (1:4), a Gentile, and may have been from Antioch of Syria. Paul took Titus with him to Jerusalem to discuss the nature of the gospel (Gl 2:1–3). Titus was so vibrant a disciple that the Jerusalem leaders were persuaded that Paul's law-free gospel was acceptable (Gl 2:3–5). Titus was with Paul in Ephesus on his third missionary journey and was Paul's ambassador to the troubled church in Corinth, carrying both the "severe letter" and 2 Corinthians (see *Occasion* for **2 CORINTHIANS**).

After Paul was released from his Roman imprisonment, he assigned Titus the responsibility of helping the churches on the island of Crete put sound leadership in place. After this letter was written, Paul sent him to Dalmatia (2Tm 4:10). Titus proved to be a courageous and strong leader.

Crete is one of the largest islands in the Mediterranean Sea, lying directly south of the Aegean Sea. It is about 160 miles across, with a long history of civilization. In the Old Testament it was called Caphtor, and the Philistine people probably migrated from there to southern Palestine. Paul's shipwreck adventure occurred after the captain of the ship on which he was a passenger declined to spend the winter in Crete (Ac 27). Life in Crete was distressing because of the lying and laziness of the people (1:12).

## OCCASION

It is not known when the gospel first came to Crete. Paul had left Titus there when he discovered that false teaching had upset the stability of the churches there. The exact nature of this teaching is impossible to determine, but it was probably similar to the error facing the Ephesian church about the same time (see *Occasion* for **1 TIMOTHY**). Both the false teaching and the Cretan character made Titus's task a big one. From an undisclosed location, possibly Macedonia or Ephesus, Paul wrote this letter to encourage Titus and to remind him of the responsibilities he faced on Crete.

## PURPOSE

Paul wrote his friend in ministry Titus to accomplish a number of objectives. First, he wished to encourage Titus in his Christian growth. Second, he offered instructions about church organization, particularly congregational officers and various age groups. Finally, he wanted Titus to come to Nicopolis to spend the winter with him.

## FIRST PASS

### Paul's Charge to Titus

Paul had left Titus on Crete to appoint leaders in every town where there were believers. He set forth the qualifications for these overseers. Strong, godly leadership was vital in the early stages of the churches on Crete to respond to a wave of false teaching that had elements of Jewish mythology and legalistic ritualism. The lifestyles of these false teachers indicated that they didn't know God in spite of their claim to the contrary (1:5–9).

### Response to False Teaching

Paul urged two approaches in contending with the false teaching. The first was verbal rebuke (1:13). The second was sound teaching. Such teaching accurately conveys God's revelation in Scripture (Old Testament) and in Jesus Christ and moves to application in the details of peoples' lives (2:1). Paul articulated application for various segments of the fledgling churches including men, women, and slaves (2:2–10). The focus is on what God has done in Christ and what He will yet do when Christ returns (2:11–14).

### The Difference Christ Makes

Paul articulated the difference Christ makes in the lives of people, transforming them from being contentious in words and actions to being persons that enrich the society of which they are a part (3:1–3). He clearly stated that this transformation is an act of God's mercy, effected by the Holy Spirit. Good works within the family of faith and in the larger community are the fruit of this act of washing and regeneration (3:4–7).

## THE RELIABILITY OF TITUS

As with 1 and 2 Timothy, Paul's authorship of Titus has been called into question and rejected by many scholars since the nineteenth century. One of the reasons for rejecting Paul's authorship of Titus stems from the fact that Acts does not report Paul's having planted churches on Crete. According to Acts, the ship on which Paul traveled from Caesarea Maritima to Rome put in at Fair Havens, Crete, a port unsuitable for spending the winter. The plan of the ship's captain was to sail west to Phoenix, Crete, and spend the winter. These plans went awry when the severe Mediterranean storm battered the ship over a period of two weeks, driving it as far west as Malta.

There is credible evidence that Paul was released from his first imprisonment in Rome around AD 62. At least two of his prison letters, Philippians and Philemon, reflect the confidence that he would be released and that he would come to Philippi and Colossae. Crete is on the sea route to both Macedonia and Asia Minor. Paul could have spent time on Crete as he traveled east to the destinations indicated in Philippians and Philemon.

The letter to Titus was likely written from Macedonia or Nicopolis (3:12–13). Paul dispatched Zenas and Apollos to carry the letter to Titus on Crete. He was preparing Artemas and Tychicus to come to Crete as replacements so Titus could come to Nicopolis where he and Paul would plan a mission to Dalmatia (2Tm 4:10).

## HOW TITUS FITS INTO GOD'S STORY

1. Prologue: Creation, Fall, and the Need for Redemption
2. God Builds His Nation (2000–931 BC)
3. God Educates His Nation (931–586 BC)
4. God Keeps a Faithful Remnant (586–6 BC)
5. God Purchases Redemption and Begins the Kingdom (6 BC to AD 30)
6. **God Spreads the Kingdom Through the Church (AD 30–?)**
7. God Consummates Redemption and Confirms His Eternal Kingdom
8. Epilogue: New Heaven and New Earth

## CHRIST IN TITUS

Christ came to redeem human beings from lawlessness, to create a special people, eager to do good works now and to look forward to Christ's appearing a second time.

## CHRISTIAN WORLDVIEW ELEMENTS

### Teachings About God

"God our Savior" promised us the hope of eternal life, which He revealed through "Christ Jesus our Savior" (1:2–4). God regenerated and renewed us through the work of the Holy Spirit (3:5). He poured out the Holy Spirit on us abundantly, again through Jesus Christ our Savior (3:6).

### Teachings About Humanity

See *Teachings About Humanity* for **1 TIMOTHY**.

### Teachings About Salvation

Salvation is sovereignly determined by God for "the elect" (1:1), by grace (2:11), through God's goodness and love (3:4). It is offered to "all people" (2:11). Those who

believe God should respond in good works, which are "good and profitable for everyone" (3:8).

## GENRE AND LITERARY STYLE

### An Epistle Written in *Koinē* Greek

See *Genre and Literary Style* for **1 THESSALONIANS** for information about the genre "epistle." The standard parts of a first-century epistle appear in Titus, except that the thanksgiving is missing: salutation (1:1–4); main body (1:5–3:14); and farewell (3:15). This letter, like 1 and 2 Timothy, shares certain vocabulary and style elements that make these three books distinctive. So clearly do they belong together that they are often considered as a unit, "The Pastoral Epistles."

## A PRINCIPLE TO LIVE BY

### Knowing and Living (Ti 2:1–10, *Life Essentials Study Bible*, p. 1696)

We must not assume that teaching believers biblical truths about God, Jesus Christ, the Holy Spirit, salvation, and the second coming of Christ will cause them to live in God's will.

To access a video presentation of this principle featuring Dr. Gene Getz, use a Smartphone or iPad to connect to this QR code or go to http://www.bhpublishinggroup.com/handbook/titus

you will do even more than I say," are a strong hint for Philemon to set Onesimus free. Paul also asked Philemon for hospitality when he visited.

## FIRST PASS

The subject of this letter is a slave, Onesimus, who had left his master, Philemon, and traveled to Rome. There Onesimus found Paul who was under house arrest awaiting a judicial hearing before Caesar. Paul sent Onesimus back to Colossae with Tychicus, who carried this letter, Colossians, and probably Ephesians.

Paul indicated that Onesimus had come to faith in Christ. Paul requested that Philemon forgive and receive Onesimus not as a slave but as a brother (v. 16). This request was not made from Paul's apostolic authority but tenderly as a Christian brother (v. 17).

Paul expressed a willingness to pay any damages caused by Onesimus. Some scholars indicate that Paul may have been asking subtly that Philemon release Onesimus so that he could return and aid Paul in his evangelistic endeavors. Philemon had a judicial right to punish severely or even kill Onesimus.

## THE RELIABILITY OF PHILEMON

Based on its vocabulary, style, and content, most scholars view Philemon as having been written by Paul. The closings of Colossians and Philemon indicate they were written at the same time and place. Tychicus carried this letter and the letter to the Colossians as he accompanied Onesimus in returning to Colossae.

## HOW PHILEMON FITS INTO GOD'S STORY

1. Prologue: Creation, Fall, and the Need for Redemption
2. God Builds His Nation (2000–931 BC)
3. God Educates His Nation (931–586 BC)
4. God Keeps a Faithful Remnant (586–6 BC)
5. God Purchases Redemption and Begins the Kingdom (6 BC to AD 30)
6. **God Spreads the Kingdom Through the Church (AD 30–?)**
7. God Consummates Redemption and Confirms His Eternal Kingdom
8. Epilogue: New Heaven and New Earth

## CHRIST IN PHILEMON

Christ's grace is offered to master and slave alike. In Christ master and slave become brothers.

## CHRISTIAN WORLDVIEW ELEMENTS

### Teachings About God

In this epistle God the Father is the source of grace and peace and the one to whom Christians pray (vv. 3–4). Jesus is the center of faith, on whose account Paul was in prison (vv. 5,9). The Holy Spirit is not specifically mentioned.

### Teachings About Humanity

Philemon addresses slavery, a widely accepted social arrangement in the ancient world. Paul does not attack the institution of slavery head on. Such a challenge could not have gained a hearing in the first century. Instead, Paul's teaching that in Christ both master and slave are to consider each other as brothers and equals undermines the concept of slavery and lays the foundation for eliminating slavery as an institution. The fact that in the twenty-first century slavery still exists in parts of the world is evidence of the power of sin in human lives and societies.

### Teachings About Salvation

Salvation is seen through the perspective of two individuals, the master (Philemon) and the slave (Onesimus). Philemon was indebted to the apostle because Paul had brought the message of salvation to him (v. 19). Onesimus is a classic example of transformation because of the message of salvation: "Once he was useless to you, but now he is useful both to you and to me" (v. 11).

## GENRE AND LITERARY STYLE

### A Brief Epistle Written in *Koinē* Greek

See *Genre and Literary Style* for **1 THESSALONIANS** for information about the genre "epistle." This letter has all four standard parts of a first-century epistle: salutation (vv. 1–3); thanksgiving (vv. 4–7); main body (vv. 8–22); and farewell (vv. 23–25). The Greek of this letter is typical for Paul.

## A PRINCIPLE TO LIVE BY

### Demonstrating Wisdom (Phm 8–22, *Life Essentials Study Bible*, p. 1702)

To carry out Christ's mission to the world, we must demonstrate wisdom toward all people.

To access a video presentation of this principle featuring Dr. Gene Getz, use a Smartphone or iPad to connect to this QR code or go to http://www.bhpublishinggroup.com/handbook/philemon

# HEBREWS

## THE EPISTLE TO THE HEBREWS

This title is based on the belief that the first recipients were Hebrew (or Jewish) believers in Jesus as the Messiah.

## KEY TEXT: 1:1–3

*"Long ago God spoke to the fathers by the prophets at different times and in different ways. In these last days, He has spoken to us by His Son. God has appointed Him heir of all things and made the universe through Him. The Son is the radiance of God's glory and the exact expression of His nature, sustaining all things by His powerful word. After making purification for sins, He sat down at the right hand of the Majesty on high."*

## KEY TERM: "BETTER"

This book repeatedly makes the case that Christ and Christianity are better or superior to the old way of the old covenant. The word "better" (Greek, *kreittōn* or *kreissōn*) appears 12 times.

"The Son is the radiance of God's glory and the exact expression of His nature, sustaining all things by His powerful word" (Heb 1:3). The VLT Survey Telescope (VST) has captured in sharp detail the beauty of the nearby spiral galaxy NGC 253. This new portrait is probably the best wide-field view of this object and its surroundings ever taken. It demonstrates that the VST, the newest telescope at ESO's Paranal Observatory, provides broad views of the sky while also offering impressive image quality. Luminous regions of ongoing star formation are spread throughout NGC 253, which is pumping out new stars at a furious pace.

## ONE-SENTENCE SUMMARY

Jesus Christ, who is better than the angels, Moses, Joshua, and the Hebrew high priests, made a better sacrifice and established a better covenant, ensuring that the old way is obsolete and that faith is the better way to live.

# ORIGINAL HISTORICAL SETTING

## AUTHOR AND DATE OF WRITING

**Unknown, Perhaps Around AD 66**

The secret of this book's authorship is one of the longest ongoing challenges for Bible students. In fact, scholarship has hardly advanced farther today than Origen of the third century, who said that God alone knew who wrote the epistle. In the earliest centuries, Barnabas and Luke were mentioned as possible authors; in the Reformation era Luther made the brilliant suggestion that Apollos may have been the author. From the fifth to the sixteenth centuries, Paul was believed to be the author, and many handwritten Greek manuscripts added Paul's name to the title, as did many translations.

The consensus of contemporary scholarship is that Paul could not have been the author. The strongest argument is historical: the author put himself in second-generation Christianity, distancing himself from eyewitnesses. In the eyes of many Bible students, it is impossible that the one who wrote Hebrews 2:3–4 could also have written Galatians 1:11–12, Paul's vehement claim that he was an eyewitness.

The author was an expert in Scripture, quoting extensively from the Greek translation (the Septuagint). He was almost certainly Jewish, with an outstanding ability in Greek composition. Although knowing his name would be interesting, it would add little to the interpretation of the book's message. The date of composition may be around AD 66, almost certainly before the destruction of Jerusalem (AD 70).

## FIRST AUDIENCE AND DESTINATION

**Jewish Believers, Perhaps in Rome**

As the title suggests, the letter was first "to the Hebrews." A number of features point in this direction, particularly the detailed arguments about the sacrificial system and the priesthood of the Old Testament. They were, however, now Christians. The greeting of 13:24 was sent from persons with the author to their fellow Italians "back home." This and the first citation of the epistle, by Clement of Rome about AD 96, suggests that the original recipients were Christians in Italy, perhaps Rome itself.

## OCCASION

The precise occasion has been debated because interpreters are limited to the data provided by the epistle, which is not entirely clear. These Jewish believers had been persecuted for their new religion (10:32–39). They were now, however, considering giving up Christianity and returning to Judaism, which was legally recognized, unlike Christianity. Hebrews 10:25 may refer to some who had already withdrawn from meeting with fellow believers from different ethnic backgrounds. The author, who knew their situation well, composed this letter about the superiority of Christ and Christianity and the danger of turning away to something that was clearly inferior.

## GOD'S MESSAGE IN HEBREWS

## PURPOSE

Hebrews was written to Jewish believers in Jesus to set forth the superiority of Jesus Christ to angels, Moses, the covenant at Sinai, the Aaronic priesthood, and its sacrifices. The author also showed that the essential weakness of the old covenant was its "planned obsolescence" in God's purposes.

## FIRST PASS

### God Has Spoken

In the past God spoke to the fathers through the prophets. More recently, He spoke through His Son. The Son was God's agent of creation, the Sustainer of the universe, and the One for whom the worlds were created. The Son is the exact expression of God's nature, was the perfect sin offering, and is now enthroned at God's right hand (1:1–4).

### Angels

From the author's description of the Son, it is clear that the Son is superior to angels since angels are created beings, and the Son is eternal. And yet the Son was, for a time, made lower than the angels so that He could atone for the sins of human beings and help those who are being tested (1:5–2:18). The author reminds his readers of the awesomeness of the giving of the law at Sinai mediated by angels. Ignoring or disobeying this revelation had severe consequences. How much greater the judgment for those who neglect the salvation offered by the Son (2:1–4).

### Moses

The Son is superior to Moses, who was merely a servant within God's household. Jesus' superiority to Moses made it a more serious matter to reject Jesus than to reject Moses (3:1–19). The writer referred to Israel's rebellion against God and Moses during the journey from Egypt to the Promised Land (Nm 14:1–35) and the severe judgment the rebellion brought.

### The Call to Rest

The invitation to enter God's rest was issued to those whom Moses and Joshua led. This standing invitation is repeated in the psalms, "Today, if you hear His voice, do not harden your hearts." In urging his readers on, the writer reminds them of the awesomeness of God and His word (4:1–13).

### Jesus: Our Great High Priest

The writer has compared Jesus to the prophets, angels, and Moses. He now introduces a section that compares Jesus as high priest with Aaron, Israel's first high priest, and Aaron's successors. Jesus is incomparably greater than Aaron in the covenant He effects (7:22; 8:6; 9:15), the ministry He has obtained (8:6), and His perfect sacrifice for sin (10:12). Jesus' superiority and His place at the right hand of God might seem to make Him far removed from human need, but the writer is quick to point out that He is sympathetic with human weaknesses. He has been thoroughly tested yet without sin. Given Jesus' sympathetic identification with sinful human beings, the writer urges his readers not to come cowering before Jesus but to come boldly to the throne of grace to find timely help (4:14–16).

The extended comparison of Jesus as high priest with Aaron and his successors is interspersed with warnings against regression (6:1–12; 10:26–31) and exhortations to press on to maturity (5:11–6:1).

### Heroes of Faith

To give his exhortations flesh and blood, the writer brings to mind specific men and women who received God's approval by their faith (11:1–40). He urges his readers to press on as if they were in a race with these heroes watching from the stands. They should cast off anything that hinders their running. They should keep their eyes on Jesus, the Source of their faith and the One who brings faith to maturity (12:1–2).

### Sinai and Mount Zion

Once again the writer contrasts the old covenant with the new—God's revelation to Moses and Israel and the heavenly Jerusalem. If God's appearance at Sinai invoked awe and reverence, how much more the heavenly Jerusalem should inspire obedience and reverence. The letter opens with an emphasis on God's speaking. As he closes, the writer urges his readers not to reject the One who speaks (12:14–29).

### Final Exhortations

Faith expresses itself in hospitality, care for those in prison, and honoring one's own marriage and that of others. Christians must follow the faith of their leaders. When Christians submit to those who care for their spiritual needs, this allows the leaders to do their jobs with joy and not with hardship or frustration. God is pleased with spiritual sacrifices that Christians offer. These sacrifices are commitment, praise, and unselfish sharing of goods (13:1–16).

## THE RELIABILITY OF HEBREWS

Hebrews is the only letter in the New Testament for whom no author is given. It was included in the New Testament canon later than some books. What did the early church see in this letter that prompted them to include it in the New Testament canon?

Key criteria for canonicity were that it had been (a) written by or under the authority of an apostle, (b) universally accepted by the churches, (c) used in public worship, and (d) congruent with universally accepted Christian writings.

The Eastern church, centered in Alexandria, Egypt, grouped Hebrews with Paul's letters long before the Western church centered in Rome did. If the letter was originally sent to Rome, then the knowledge of the identity of the author may have prompted that hesitancy. In the West, the Muratorian Canon, Irenaeus, and Hipppolytus of Rome did not acknowledge Paul as the author. In 419, the Sixth Synod of Carthage viewed Paul as the writer of Hebrews. This became the majority view in the churches, both East and West, until the time of the Reformation.

With early disagreement as to authorship, the connection to an apostle was absent. In light of that, the other three major criteria for canonicity became all the more important in the decision to include Hebrews in the canon.

If Hebrews were not in the New Testament, some vital emphases would be missing from the church's theology and worship. A major challenge of those who followed Jesus as Savior and Lord was connecting the events of Jesus' life, teachings, death, resurrection, and ascension to what God had done through Abraham and his offspring. For both Jews and Gentiles, it was vital to see those lines of connection to what God had done before with His people Israel. With great power and clarity Hebrews enables those who follow Jesus to see the wealth and strength of these connections and how they are to be interpreted in light of the covenant Jesus effected. Early in the second century, Marcion sought to sever those connections to the Hebrew Scriptures. The church, over time, had the wisdom to see that Hebrews performed a number of unique functions, including showing the relationship between what God had done before with what He did in His Son.

## HOW HEBREWS FITS INTO GOD'S STORY

1. Prologue: Creation, Fall, and the Need for Redemption
2. God Builds His Nation (2000–931 BC)
3. God Educates His Nation (931–586 BC)
4. God Keeps a Faithful Remnant (586–6 BC)
5. God Purchases Redemption and Begins the Kingdom (6 BC to AD 30)
6. **God Spreads the Kingdom Through the Church (AD 30–?)**
7. God Consummates Redemption and Confirms His Eternal Kingdom
8. Epilogue: New Heaven and New Earth

## CHRIST IN HEBREWS

Christ is both God's agent of creation and the One for whom the universe is created. He is superior to angels, Moses, the priesthood, the old covenant, and the Levitical sacrificial system. Christ is both the source of our faith and the One who brings it to perfection. He is the same yesterday, today, and forever.

## CHRISTIAN WORLDVIEW ELEMENTS

### Teachings About God

God is the Father of Jesus Christ. He is wholly other and is to be approached with reverence and fear, "for our God is a consuming fire" (12:29). The superiority of Jesus to all possible rivals is the theme of the entire book. The full deity and complete humanity of Jesus is explicitly taught. The Holy Spirit in Hebrews is both the One who speaks in Scripture (3:7; 10:15) and the One alive among believers in the present age (6:4; 10:29).

"Therefore, since we also have such a large cloud of witnesses surrounding us, let us lay aside every weight and the sin that so easily ensnares us. Let us run with endurance the race that lies before us, keeping our eyes on Jesus, the source and perfecter of our faith, who for the joy that lay before Him endured a cross and despised the shame and has sat down at the right hand of God's throne" (Heb 12:1–2). Pictured is Eric Liddell who won the gold (400 meters) and bronze (200) meters in the 1924 Paris Olympics. From 1924 to 1945, Eric served as a missionary in China. With the Japanese invasion in 1941, he was interred in Weihsien Internment Camp. He died of a brain tumor five months before the camp was liberated. His last words: "It's complete surrender."

### Teachings About Humanity

A number of prominent Old Testament persons are mentioned in Hebrews, and the "roll call of faith" in chapter 11 is an impressive reminder of what believing humans can do. The emphasis in Hebrews, however, is that Jesus has the glory and honor of being humanity at its best. In Psalm 8 God declared "man" as the crown of creation; Hebrews 2 declares that this "Man" is none other than Jesus Christ.

### Teachings About Salvation

Jesus is a better high priest than the high priests of the old covenant. Further, Jesus' death was a superior sacrifice to any that had been made before, "For it is impossible for the blood of bulls and goats to take away sins" (10:4). At the same time, however, Hebrews affirms that the human response to God's redemptive actions, faith, has always and forever been the single way that pleases God. This Bible book, more clearly than any other, shows the permanence of the new covenant state of affairs and the impermanence of the old covenant.

## GENRE AND LITERARY STYLE

### A Long, Formal Epistle Written in Excellent *Koinē* Greek

Some scholars designate Hebrews as a tractate (a formal treatise rather than a pastoral letter). Two of the usual features of an epistle (salutation and thanksgiving) are missing, although there is a body (1:1–13:17) and a farewell (13:18–25). In addition, it has a number of sermon-like features. It begins with a rhetorical statement of its thesis (1:1–3) and develops step-by-step arguments. The farewell shows that in its present form it was sent as a letter. The style of argument has parallels to the figurative interpretations made by Philo, the Jewish scholar of Alexandria. The Greek of Hebrews is outstanding, with a large vocabulary and excellent style, suggesting that the author was highly educated. The style is more like that of Luke and Acts than any other New Testament book.

## A PRINCIPLE TO LIVE BY

### The Person of Christ (Heb 1:1–4, *Life Essentials Study Bible*, p. 1707)

To be truly Christian, we must believe in Jesus Christ—who He is and what He has done for us through His life, death, resurrection, and ascension.

To access a video presentation of this principle featuring Dr. Gene Getz, use a Smartphone or iPad to connect to this QR code or go to http://www.bhpublishinggroup.com/handbook/hebrews

# JAMES

## THE EPISTLE TO JAMES

This letter is titled according to its author, James, who was probably the half brother of Jesus.

### KEY TEXT: 2:26

*"For just as the body without the spirit is dead, so also faith without works is dead."*

### KEY TERM: "WORKS"

This book focuses on the importance of good works as the evidence of genuine faith. As such, it perfectly complements Galatians.

### ONE-SENTENCE SUMMARY

True faith must be lived out in everyday life by good deeds, especially in the face of trials or persecution, and such good works demonstrate the presence of faith and justification before God.

Forest fire at Beit Oren, in the heart of Israel's Carmel mountain range. "Consider how large a forest a small fire ignites. And the tongue is a fire. The tongue, a world of unrighteousness is placed among the parts of our bodies. It pollutes the whole body, sets the course of life on fire, and is set on fire by hell" (Jms 3:5b–6).

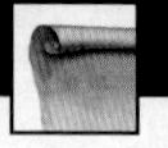


## AUTHOR AND DATE OF WRITING:

**James, Perhaps Around AD 45**

The author identified himself as "James, a slave of God and of the Lord Jesus Christ" (1:1). James is the English translation of the Hebrew name "Jacob" when it appears in the New Testament, *Iakōbos* in Greek. There were several Jameses in the New Testament, including two apostles (Mt 10:2–3). This letter was almost certainly written by the James who rose to prominence in the church of Jerusalem (Ac 12:17; 15:13; 21:18). This was "James, the Lord's brother" (Gl 1:19; 2:9). The son of Mary and Joseph, James had not believed that Jesus, his older half brother, was the Messiah until after the resurrection, when Jesus appeared to him (Mt 13:55; Jn 7:5; 1 Co 15:7).

James was an effective leader as Acts and this letter show. He apparently rose to leadership in the Jerusalem church around the time Peter left Jerusalem, about AD 44 (see Acts 12, especially v. 17). The tenor of his letter is such that it must predate the Jerusalem Council of AD 49 that opened Christianity officially and fully to Gentiles (Ac 15). The epistle may well have been the first New Testament book written—between AD 44 and 49, with the year 45 being a reasonable estimate. It was perhaps composed in Jerusalem.

According to the Jewish historian Josephus, James was martyred in AD 62. Christian tradition indicates that he was thrown from the pinnacle of the temple.

## FIRST AUDIENCE AND DESTINATION

**Jewish Believers Living Somewhere Outside Palestine**

This letter was written to Jewish followers of Jesus. Their meeting was called a "synagogue" in the original (2:2), and they were led by "elders" (5:14). They were part of "the 12 tribes in the Dispersion" (1:1), meaning Jews living outside Palestine. They lived in an unknown city of the Roman Empire where they spoke Greek. No reference is made to Gentiles.

## OCCASION

No one knows how James came to know about these believers. They had been victims of harassment of some kind and were being taken advantage of by their rich neighbors (1:2; 2:6).

## PURPOSE

James was originally composed to let (Jewish) believers in Jesus know the importance of having a practical, living, everyday faith. For James, practical faith equaled good works.

## FIRST PASS

### Trials

After a brief salutation, James moved quickly to the reality of trials. He invited his readers to see trials as occasions for joy. This joy stems from seeing trials in long-term perspective. Trials can build endurance, and endurance maturity (1:2–4). Trials call for wisdom. God stands ready to give such wisdom generously to those who ask with confidence in God's willingness and His full provision (1:5–8). After all, God has taken the initiative in making believers His own, radically changing them at the core by His truth (1:18).

### Hearing, Doing, and Speaking

God's Word should be heard and acted on. Just hearing takes a person down the path of self-deception (1:22–25). Really hearing God's Word changes the way one speaks, treats persons who are especially vulnerable, and views persons considered inferior to oneself (2:1–12). In amplifying his warning about speech, James painted a series of vivid pictures of the potential evil of the tongue and what is required to bring the tongue in check (3:1–12).

### Wisdom

Sinful speech is a symptom of a heart governed by envy and selfish ambition. Humbly acknowledging one's condition before God is an important step in living a life governed by wisdom that is pure and peace loving (3:13–18). Also, recognizing total dependence on God in every detail of life will increase one's humility and diminish arrogance, greed, and injustice to neighbors. Since we are completely dependent on God, patience and endurance are needed to realize the fruits of righteousness (4:1–5:6).

### Prayer

Just as James began by focusing on trials, he closed with our needy condition and how that prompts us to pray and to ask for others to pray on our behalf. He reminds his readers of Elijah, a man thoroughly human but one whose prayer was powerful in its effect. James closed his letter with a reminder of the life-and-death consequences of turning a straying brother or sister back to the truth (5:13–20).

## THE RELIABILITY OF JAMES

The Latin church father, Jerome (AD 345–420), in his work *On Illustrious Men*, affirms that James the Just, the half brother of Jesus, was author of one letter whose authority was only gradually recognized. Jerome and Augustine, the two most prolific authors of the Latin church, were influential in the letter of James being recognized as belonging to the New Testament canon.

One of the factors in the late recognition of James was the fact that it was so different from the letters of Paul. While some viewed James's uniqueness and difference from Paul as counting against it, a strong case can be made that its differences stem from the fact that it was written earlier than most of Paul's letters and that the environments out of which James and Paul were writing were considerably different. Over the last 500 years, Martin Luther's low view of James's letter has amplified the perceived differences between James and Paul. On a major point of theology, James's expression is highly compressed but is at one with Paul's understanding expressed in different terms and at great length. Says James: "By His own choice, He gave us a new birth by the message of truth so that we would be the firstfruits of His creatures" (1:18). This choice and God's gift of new birth are prior to both faith and works.

## HOW JAMES FITS INTO GOD'S STORY

1. Prologue: Creation, Fall, and the Need for Redemption
2. God Builds His Nation (2000–931 BC)
3. God Educates His Nation (931–586 BC)
4. God Keeps a Faithful Remnant (586–6 BC)
5. God Purchases Redemption and Begins the Kingdom (6 BC to AD 30)
6. **God Spreads the Kingdom Through the Church (AD 30–?)**
7. God Consummates Redemption and Confirms His Eternal Kingdom
8. Epilogue: New Heaven and New Earth

## CHRIST IN JAMES

Salvation made James a slave of his half brother Jesus, the resurrected Lord (1:1). Jesus the Lord shares God's unique glory (2:1). Looking forward to His return will be a source of patience with the trials and tests of life.

## CHRISTIAN WORLDVIEW ELEMENTS

**Teachings About God**

God is good and the Father of His redeemed children. James often calls him "the Lord," evidently parallel to the Old Testament usage of "the LORD" (Yahweh), in particular calling him "the Lord of Hosts"(5:4). Jesus is mentioned only twice (1:1; 2:1), which contributes to the distinctive Old Testament feel to this book. The indwelling Spirit is described as yearning jealously (4:5).

**Teachings About Humanity**

James had a realistic—some would say pessimistic—view of the effects of sin in human life. The rich oppress the poor; temptation is a constant danger; all persons are possessed of an evil tongue. Even believers can be called "adulteresses" (4:4) for being too friendly with the evil world, like the people of Israel who "prostituted themselves with other gods" (Jdg 2:17; 8:33). The advice James offered was to sub-

mit to God's sovereign goodness, to seek to live a life of true religion, and to do good deeds.

**Teachings About Salvation**

God saves through the action of "the implanted word" (1:21), bringing the response of faith. While Paul emphasized that faith alone saves, James emphasized that saving faith is never alone. For Paul, justification is a legal declaration of righteousness before God (see **ROMANS**, p. 367). James, however, used justification in the sense of being righteous before people. Thus he can say, "You see that a man is justified by works and not by faith alone" (2:24). Good works are open to observation by others; faith is not; therefore good works make faith visible. Good works are never the root cause of salvation, but they are always the fruit (result) of salvation.

## GENRE AND LITERARY STYLE

**An Epistle Written in *Koinē* Greek**

James is the first of seven "General Epistles" in the New Testament, all of which are titled according to their authors. Two of the usual features of an epistle (thanksgiving and farewell) are missing, although there is a salutation (1:1) and a body (1:2–5:20). James is a pastoral letter, driven by the occasion and needs of the recipients, rather than a tractate (a formal treatise). Many scholars have noted the parallels in style between Proverbs and James. Many practical truths are presented, but they are only loosely connected by the general theme of everyday Christian living. The Greek style is considered above average for the books of the New Testament.

## A PRINCIPLE TO LIVE BY

**Good Works (Jms 2:14–17, *Life Essentials Study Bible*, p. 1732)**

If our profession of faith does not eventuate in good works, we should evaluate the validity of our salvation experience.

To access a video presentation of this principle featuring Dr. Gene Getz, use a Smartphone or iPad to connect to this QR code or go to http://www.bhpublishinggroup.com/handbook/james

Titled according to its author, this is the first canonical letter by Simon Peter, the apostle of Jesus.

## KEY TEXT: 4:13

*"Instead, rejoice as you share in the sufferings of the Messiah, so that you may also rejoice with great joy at the revelation of His glory."*

## KEY TERM: "HOPE"

This epistle emphasizes hope for suffering believers. Hope (Greek, *elpis*) means "future certainty" rather than a vague expectation of some future occurrence.

## ONE-SENTENCE SUMMARY

As Christians grow in understanding their privileges in salvation, their blessings of election, and the theology of suffering, they will live in holiness and humility, waiting for their great future hope of sharing Christ's glory.

*The Fire of Rome*, 18 July 64 AD by Hubert Roberts (1733–1808). "Dear friends, don't be surprised when the fiery ordeal comes among you to test you as if something unusual were happening to you" (1Pt 4:12).

## AUTHOR AND DATE OF WRITING

**Simon Peter the Apostle, Perhaps Around AD 64**

The author called himself "Peter, an apostle of Jesus Christ" (1:1). He was the son of Jonah (or John), the brother of Andrew, and a Galilean fisherman by trade when Jesus called him to become an apostle. His birth name, Simeon (often shortened to Simon), was transformed by Jesus to "Rock" ("Peter" in Greek; "Cephas" in Aramaic).

Peter's role as one of the three most prominent apostles (along with James and John) is well known from the Gospels. Peter rose to become the most visible leader of Christianity in Jerusalem. According to Paul, Peter was the apostle to Jews (Gl 2:8). Peter's contribution to the New Testament was two epistles and probably collaboration with John Mark in producing the second Gospel. In this letter Peter mentioned that he was in Rome (called "Babylon," as in Revelation) and that Mark was with him (5:13). According to tradition, he was later crucified in Rome during the last years of Nero. For further discussion on authorship, see *The Reliability of 1 Peter* below.

## FIRST AUDIENCE AND DESTINATION

**Believers Living in Roman Provinces of Asia Minor**

This letter was addressed "to the temporary residents dispersed in Pontus, Galatia, Cappadocia, Asia, and Bithynia" (1:1). These five Roman provinces make up roughly the northern half of modern Turkey. The order is probably the route the letter carrier followed. Evidence within the letter suggests that these believers were primarily Gentile (and therefore pagan, 1:18) in background, although there was probably also a Jewish minority (accounting for the frequent Old Testament references).

## OCCASION

Peter knew a great deal about what these believers had gone through, but he did not tell his source of information. They had been victims of serious persecution and unjust suffering, something Peter called a "fiery ordeal" (4:12). This in all likelihood was the first official Roman persecution of Christians, instigated by Nero after the great fire in Rome of AD 64. These disciples needed to be encouraged not to lose heart. He wanted to remind them of a number of important doctrinal truths (about God and salvation) as well as to help them see that suffering within the plan of God serves His glory. Thus, Peter wrote this letter with the help of Silvanus (Silas).

## PURPOSE

First Peter was written to encourage suffering Christians to live in light of the future. The apostle wanted to give a number of doctrinal insights and also provided many practical instructions, such as how to submit to those in authority. This book contains the most extensive New Testament development of a "theology of suffering," and it echoes the teaching of Job that God's glory is served when suffering is permitted.

## FIRST PASS

### Greetings

Peter addressed his readers as "temporary residents dispersed" throughout five provinces, away from their heavenly home. They were a people chosen by the Father's foreknowledge, sanctified by the Spirit and redeemed by the blood of Jesus Christ (1:1–2).

### Salvation

Peter praised God for the resurrection of Jesus that has wrought in believers a new birth and given them a living hope and an indestructible inheritance (1:3–5). Even in the great trials of the present age, believers are protected by God's power. The suffering that they experience can serve to strengthen and purify their faith in the way that fire purifies gold (1:6–7).

### A Call to Holiness

Salvation that comes as a gift purchased at a great price carries with it a call to a holy life. Believers are to forsake malicious attitudes and to love one another with a pure heart (1:13–2:3). They are more than individuals. They are members of the church that Peter described with three images: a living body, a building, and nation God has chosen (2:4–10).

### Witness

Believers are called upon to glorify God in their daily lives and to imitate Christ, who suffered on the cross for the sake of His people. Peter called his readers to live as Christians, explaining how believers are to relate to governing authorities (2:13–17), to cruel masters (2:18–25), and to unbelieving husbands (3:1–6). He warned believers that suffering may be intense, but believers should rely upon God's grace, knowing there is a heavenly reward (4:12–19).

### Leaders

Peter called on elders to shepherd God's people willingly, from right motives, and not for the money, leading by example rather with arrogance. He called on others to be subject to elders and for all believers to exercise humility toward one another (5:1–7). Peter called on believers to be alert to and resist the Devil, whom he likened to a prowling lion (5:8–9).

## THE RELIABILITY OF 1 PETER

For the past two centuries, many critical scholars have argued that Peter could not be the author of this epistle, primarily for two reasons. First, the excellent Greek of this letter is thought to be beyond what a Galilean fisherman could produce (Acts 4:13). Second, the persecutions are thought to belong to a later era than Nero's. These objections may be satisfactorily answered. First, significant evidence exists that Greek was spoken in Palestine and especially in Galilee. As a fisherman in Galilee, Peter would have engaged in business with other Greek speakers. The notion that Peter was uneducated or illiterate is a myth. Acts 4:13 merely means that he was not trained rabbinically and does not imply that he was unable to read. Since Peter knew Greek, it is not surprising that he used the Septuagint, the Greek translation of the Old Testament. Like any good pastor, Peter quoted from the Bible that his readers used. The Greek style is probably due to the help of Silvanus (Silas), whom Peter acknowledged (5:12). Second, the suffering of the believers could just as easily have occurred in Nero's time as in a later era. There is no persuasive reason to deny that Simon Peter wrote this epistle.

## HOW 1 PETER FITS INTO GOD'S STORY

1. Prologue: Creation, Fall, and the Need for Redemption
2. God Builds His Nation (2000–931 BC)
3. God Educates His Nation (931–586 BC)
4. God Keeps a Faithful Remnant (586–6 BC)
5. God Purchases Redemption and Begins the Kingdom (6 BC to AD 30)
6. **God Spreads the Kingdom Through the Church (AD 30–?)**
7. God Consummates Redemption and Confirms His Eternal Kingdom
8. Epilogue: New Heaven and New Earth

## CHRIST IN 1 PETER

The Spirit of Christ was present in the Hebrew prophets pointing them to the sufferings of Christ and the glory that followed His sufferings. Christ is like a lamb without defect or blemish. His precious blood redeems believers from their futile ways. Believers can expect to suffer as He suffered and anticipate the joy of His coming in glory.

## CHRISTIAN WORLDVIEW ELEMENTS

### Teachings About God

This book notes many attributes of God, from His foreknowledge (1:2) to His grace (5:12). The glory of God is the goal of all things (4:11). Jesus' suffering and death for sinners is strongly emphasized, as is His resurrection and return in glory. The Holy Spirit, who inspired the prophets of old, has now been sent to God's people (1:11; 4:14). First Peter 1:2 is an important text for understanding the Trinity.

**Teachings About Humanity**

First Peter dignifies all classes of human life by showing that living by the gospel makes a great difference in relationships. Christians submit both to government and to masters to the glory of God. In the Christian family husbands and wives have a mutual responsibility to respect each other. In the congregation spiritual leaders ("elders," 5:1) lead their flocks by being humble servants, creating a context of mutual submission.

**Teachings About Salvation**

Salvation in this book is past, present, and future. The past aspect involves God's sovereign election as well as Jesus' suffering and death to purchase salvation (2:9; 3:18). The present aspect involves the regeneration and the ongoing faith of God's people (1:3,21; 5:9). At Christ's return those who "are being protected by God's power through faith" will receive the "salvation that is ready to be revealed in the last time" (1:5).

## GENRE AND LITERARY STYLE

**An Epistle Written in *Koinē* Greek**

First Peter is the second of seven "General Epistles" in the New Testament, all of which are titled according to their authors. All four of the usual features of an epistle are present: salutation (1:1–2); thanksgiving (1:3–5); body (1:6–5:11); and farewell (5:12–14). Some scholars designate 1 Peter as a tractate (a formal treatise rather than a pastoral letter), particularly since it originated as a circular letter intended for several churches. The Greek style is excellent, on a par with Luke, Acts, and Hebrews.

## A PRINCIPLE TO LIVE BY

**Christian Suffering (1Pt 4:1–19, *Life Essentials Study Bible*, p. 1748–49)**

When we suffer because of our Christian faith, we should draw strength from Christ's sufferings.

To access a video presentation of this principle featuring Dr. Gene Getz, use a Smartphone or iPad to connect to this QR code or go to http://www.bhpublishinggroup.com/handbook/1peter

Titled according to its author, this is the second canonical letter by Simon Peter, the apostle of Jesus.

## KEY TEXT: 1:12

*"Therefore I will always remind you about these things, even though you know them and are established in the truth you have."*

## KEY TERM: "RETURN"

This epistle shows the importance of holding firmly to the truth in the face of false teachings, particularly the truth that Jesus will visibly, bodily, and gloriously return and bring about the consummation of all things.

## ONE-SENTENCE SUMMARY

As Christians grow in understanding, they will be safeguarded from false teachers, especially those who deny the return of Christ and the end of the world as it now exists.

## AUTHOR AND DATE OF WRITING

### Simon Peter the Apostle, Perhaps Around AD 67

The author identified himself as "Simon Peter," and after hesitation on the part of a few, this book was accepted as apostolic in the fourth century. See *Author and Date of Writing* for **1 PETER**. For the past two centuries, however, almost all critical scholars have denied that Peter could be the author of this epistle. Both the style and content of this letter are noticeably different from 1 Peter. The difference in style, however, may be accounted for by the loss of Silas's secretarial assistance (1 Pt 5:12), and the difference in content may surely be attributed to the differing occasions of the two letters. Another argument has been based on the reference to Paul's epistles (3:15–16), which supposedly refer to a time after Paul's letters had been collected, which in turn must be after Peter's lifetime. Yet this reference only means that Peter knew some of Paul's letters.

There is no persuasive reason to deny that Simon Peter wrote this epistle. The date of 67 is a best guess, determined by noting the strong tradition that Peter died during the last part of Nero's reign (ruled AD 54–68).

## FIRST AUDIENCE AND DESTINATION

### Believers Living in an Unknown Location

attacked concerned whether Christ's return and the end of the world would really happen.

## FIRST PASS

### Purpose and Theology

Peter felt strongly that his death was near (1:14–15). He wanted to leave a spiritual testament that would provide helpful instruction after his departure. He provided warning against the character and false teaching of heretics who would infiltrate the church (2:1–19; 3:1–4). To provide protection against their errors, he urged a development of proper Christian virtues (1:3–11) and a constant growth in God's grace (3:17–18). Peter held to a high view of Scripture (1:19–21), and he viewed Paul's writings as "Scripture" (3:16). He designated Jesus Christ as "Savior" and "Lord" (1:1–2), and he outlined his observation of Jesus' transfiguration (1:16–18). He affirmed the return of Christ (3:1–4) and asserted God's sovereign control of the events of history (3:13). He used the certainty of Christ's return as an incentive to appeal for godly living (3:14).

### Growth in the Faith

Peter fortified his readers with the truth that in Christ's power are all the resources needed for life and godliness. These resources enable believers to share in the divine nature and to escape the corruption of the world. Those who have experienced the new birth have the capacity to cultivate eight qualities. Cultivating these qualities will result in increased usefulness, greater knowledge of Christ, and entrance into Christ's eternal kingdom (1:3–11).

### The Trustworthy Prophetic Word

Peter's message was not a cleverly crafted myth but an eyewitness testimony to the majesty of Christ. Here he refers to the transfiguration of Jesus on the mountain when Moses and Elijah appeared to them (1:16–17). What Peter witnessed firsthand is that to which the prophetic word, the Scriptures, bears witness. The testimony of the apostles and the Old Testament Scriptures are not ultimately of human origin but are God's Word (1:18–21).

### The Judgment of False Teachers

As there had been false prophets in Israel's history, so now there were false teachers leading believers astray. Their departure from sound teaching was motivated by greed and by corrupt desires. To strengthen his warning, Peter gave his readers three examples of God's judgment of lawlessness (2:4–17).

### The Day of the Lord

The false teachers labored under the assumption that there will be no accountability to God—no judgment. The apostles had taught that Christ will return, but the false teachers point to everyday experience and say things will continue to go on as they have from the beginning of creation. In response to this, Peter had his readers consider the vast difference between God's perspective and that of humans. God's sense of time is far different from that of human beings. Using the same picture Jesus used, Peter says the Day of the Lord will come like a thief. The universe as we know it will be thoroughly destroyed. This conflagration will be followed by "the new heavens and a new earth, where righteousness will dwell" (3:1–13).

**Closing Commands**

Peter reminded his readers that an anticipation of Christ's future return carried with it the incentive to live a holy life. He referred to Paul's writings as a support for Peter's belief that divine patience was a factor in the delay of Jesus' return. Many see a reference by Peter to Romans, but Peter left his Pauline source unstated. Peter acknowledged the difficulty of some of Paul's teachings, but he suggested their authority by naming them as "Scripture." Peter boldly stated that his recipients could protect themselves spiritually by mature Christian growth. The "knowledge" they needed was a development in personal acquaintance with Christ (3:14–18).

## THE RELIABILITY OF 2 PETER

Many scholars deny that 2 Peter was written by the apostle Peter, claiming the letter is pseudonymous. This view is defended by the following arguments: (1) Peter used Jude as a source in his second chapter, and the letter of Jude is too late to have been used by the historic Peter who died in the 60s. Further, some insist that Peter would have never borrowed from a writer like Jude. (2) The Hellenistic vocabulary and theology in the letter show that Peter, a Galilean fisherman, could not be the author. The style and syntax are quite different from 1 Peter, demonstrating a different author from the first epistle. (3) The false teachers in the letter are second-century gnostics, and obviously Peter could not have written the letter in the second century. (4) Paul's letters are considered to be Scripture (2 Pt 3:15–16), but it is impossible that Paul's letters could have been collected together and viewed as Scripture while Peter was alive. (5) The letter lacks clear attestation in the second century, and even in the fourth century its canonicity was questioned.

Despite the objections of many, Petrine authorship is still the most convincing view. (1) Most important, the letter claims to be written by Peter (1:1). He claimed that his death is imminent (1:14). Even more striking, he claims to have heard and seen Jesus' transfiguration (1:16–18). The author is obviously open to a charge of deception and fraud if he was not Peter. (2) The use of Jude as a source is not certain but only a theory. Furthermore, even if Peter used Jude, there is no problem. Jude likely wrote before Peter died. Nothing in Jude demands a late date, and there is no reason an apostle would not use another source. (3) The idea that the opponents were second-century gnostics is not verified by the data of the letter. No evidence exists of the cosmological dualism that was typical of Gnosticism. Nor is it clear that

the opponents rejected the material world. (4) It is unnecessary to conclude from 2 Peter 3:15–16 that all of Paul's letters were collected and stamped as canonical. Peter obviously knows some of the Pauline letters and considers them to be authoritative, but that is not the same thing as a collected canon of Pauline writings. (5) The vocabulary and style of 2 Peter are distinct from 1 Peter, and the language has a Hellenistic flavor. But this is not an insuperable problem. We need first to observe that the corpus of Petrine writings is incredibly small. Hence, judgments about "Petrine style" should be made with humility. Second, Peter may have adapted his style to speak to the situation of his readers, just as Paul did in Athens (Ac 17:16–34). Finally, Peter may have instructed a secretary (amanuensis) to compose the writing, and this may account for some of the stylistic differences. (6) The argument that Peter uses a different theology does not stand either. We need to recall that the letter is occasional and hence is not a summary of all of Peter's theology. Furthermore, the differences between 1 and 2 Peter theologically have often been overemphasized. (7) Second Peter is not as strongly attested by external evidence as many other letters. Still, some evidence for the letter's use exists even in the second century, and we ought to remember that the letter was ultimately judged to be authentic and canonical.

## HOW 2 PETER FITS INTO GOD'S STORY

1. Prologue: Creation, Fall, and the Need for Redemption
2. God Builds His Nation (2000–931 BC)
3. God Educates His Nation (931–586 BC)
4. God Keeps a Faithful Remnant (586–6 BC)
5. God Purchases Redemption and Begins the Kingdom (6 BC to AD 30)
6. God Spreads the Kingdom Through the Church (AD 30–?)
7. God Consummates Redemption and Confirms His Eternal Kingdom
8. Epilogue: New Heaven and New Earth

## CHRIST IN 2 PETER

Christ came to live, die, and rise again in space and time. This is not some myth cleverly made up by men. Peter says that he was an eyewitness of Christ's glory on the Mount of Transfiguration when he, James, and John heard the voice of the Father say, "This is My beloved Son. I take delight in Him!" (2 Pt 1:17).

## CHRISTIAN WORLDVIEW ELEMENTS

### Teachings About God

God is the Father of Jesus, and He glorified His Son (1:17). He is the judge of all beings, human and superhuman (2:4). This is the only Bible book that uses the full title "our Lord and Savior Jesus Christ" ( 2:20; 3:18), a magnificent confession by one who knew Him face-to-face during His earthly life. The single reference to the Holy Spirit mentions His role in the inspiration of Scripture (1:21).

### Teachings About Humanity

Second Peter shows the great evil of those who are enslaved by error and sin: "like irrational animals—creatures of instinct born to be caught and destroyed—speak blasphemies about things they don't understand, and in their destruction they too will be destroyed" (2:12). On the other hand, redeemed humanity can grow in every virtue (1:5–8).

### Teachings About Salvation

This book provides an important definition of heresy as "denying the Master who bought them" (2:1). In other words, a heresy is a serious error about the person or work of Christ, in particular a denial that His death involved the purchase of salvation. There is little that the letter develops about Christ's work, but God's people are described as those "who have obtained a faith of equal privilege" with the apostle (1:1). The future dimension of salvation will be revealed on "the Day of the Lord" and the coming of "the new heavens and a new earth, where righteousness will dwell" (3:10,13).

## GENRE AND LITERARY STYLE

### An Epistle Written in *Koinē* Greek

Second Peter is the third of seven "General Epistles" in the New Testament, all of which are titled according to their authors. One of the usual features of an epistle (thanksgiving) is missing, although there is a salutation (1:1–2), a body (1:3–3:18a), and a farewell (in this letter, a brief doxology, 3:18b). Second Peter is a pastoral letter, driven by the occasion and needs of the recipients, rather than a tractate (a formal treatise). The Greek style is awkward but more like 1 Peter than any other part of the Scriptures.

## A PRINCIPLE TO LIVE BY

### Life and Godliness (2 Pt 1:3–7, *Life Essentials Study Bible*, p. 1752)

Drawing on God's power, we are to do all we can to become mature followers of Jesus Christ .

To access a video presentation of this principle featuring Dr. Gene Getz, use a Smartphone or iPad to connect to this QR code or go to http://www.bhpublishinggroup.com/handbook/2peter

# 1 JOHN

## THE FIRST EPISTLE OF JOHN

Titled according to its author, this is the first canonical letter by John, the apostle of Jesus.

### KEY TEXT: 1:3

*"What we have seen and heard we also declare to you, so that you may have fellowship along with us; and indeed our fellowship is with the Father and with His Son Jesus Christ."*

### KEY TERM: "FELLOWSHIP"

Fellowship (Greek, *koinōnia*) is partnership with Jesus and partnership with other believers in Jesus. The best preventive against false doctrine is true fellowship.

The traditional site of the tomb of John the apostle in the ancient city of Ephesus, an important religious center of early Christianity. Ephesus is today located in Turkey.

## ONE-SENTENCE SUMMARY

Christians have fellowship with Christ, who is God incarnate, through walking in the light and through living in love, and as a result they are secure in the eternal life that Christ has given them.

# ORIGINAL HISTORICAL SETTING

## AUTHOR AND DATE OF WRITING

**John the Apostle, Perhaps Around AD 80–90**

This letter is actually anonymous, but the style and approach are so much like the Fourth Gospel that the epistle and the Gospel are generally acknowledged to be written by the same person. Thus, the rejection of John's authorship of the fourth Gospel by critical scholars also applies to this epistle. Christian tradition, however, has uniformly asserted that this author was John the apostle, which certainly fits the claim that the writer personally saw Jesus (1:1–4). See *Author and Date of Writing* for **JOHN** for more information. Most scholars believe this epistle was written somewhat after the Gospel, but it is impossible to be certain. The decade of the AD 80s is a good estimate.

## FIRST AUDIENCE AND DESTINATION

**Probably Christians Living in Roman Asia**

This letter was written to Christians (2:12–14,19; 3:1; 5:13). It makes the best sense if it is seen as addressed to the same believers, living in and around Ephesus, who had earlier received the fourth Gospel. See *First Audience and Destination* for **JOHN** for a discussion.

## OCCASION

John was intimately acquainted with these believers, whom he repeatedly called "my little children." He had become aware of dangerous false teachings that threatened these believers. The foundational error appears to be the belief that "matter is sinful." If this is true, then: (1) Jesus could not have had a material body or else He was necessarily sinful, and (2) human beings are sinful because they have material bodies (rather than because of their sinful deeds or sinful nature), which in turn leads to errors about the relationship of believers to sin. Such dualism (spirit = good; matter = evil) later developed into Gnosticism, a heresy that challenged Christianity in the second and third centuries. John did not say how he became aware of this teaching. He penned his letter, however, as the response of an aged, beloved apostle to Christians in desperate need of his advice.

## PURPOSE

First John was written mainly to combat the false doctrines of denying either the incarnation of Jesus Christ (that He came with real humanity and a truly physical body) or the messiahship of Jesus (that He is the Christ). These heresies led to certain false behaviors, in particular a denial of the seriousness of sin. John wrote not only to correct these dangers but also to give positive encouragement about true beliefs and true Christian behavior, centered around fellowship with Jesus Christ.

## FIRST PASS

### Fellowship with God and with One Another

Complete joy of John and his readers was his aim as he wrote this letter. This joy grew as he communicated who God is and what He has done in His Son Jesus Christ. This message is not just words on papyrus but is dynamic, pulsating with life, though which God brings John and his readers into God's own life and in which they experience fellowship and communion (1:1–4). This fellowship with God is not a natural phenomenon. Fellowship depends on some shared characteristics, but God is light and humans are sinful by nature. The blood of Christ is the agent that transforms sinful humans into the likeness of God, providing forgiveness and cleansing from all unrighteousness (1:5–2:2).

### How Can I Know?

John set forth a test by which people can discern whether they know God. Are they obeying God's commands? Do they walk as Jesus walked (2:3–6)? Evidence that a person doesn't know God is hatred of a brother (2:9–11). Further evidence is the love of the world that excludes loving God supremely (2:15–17). John warned of the coming of Antichrist and said that already many antichrists had come. Antichrists are those who deny Jesus is Messiah. One's appraisal of and affection for Jesus determines knowledge of and relationship to the Father (2:18–23).

### Marks of God's Children

As a skilled teacher John used repetition with his readers—a repetition that further elucidates sin as breaking the law and as having its source in the Devil. Sin presents an attractive face. John wanted his readers to peer behind the façade. Cain's murder of his brother Abel shows the full development of sin. Jesus has appeared to destroy the works of the Devil. Those born of God cannot sin habitually. God's life has entered them, and they are incapable of habitual sin. The actions of the children of God and the Devil's children will be different. Rather than being murders and lawbreakers, God's children will look like Jesus in laying down their lives for others (2:28–3:15). This may mean complete death, or it may begin by seeing a brother in need and providing the material sustenance he lacks (3:16–17).

### Finding Assurance

Sometimes believers may not feel love in their hearts. Their heart condemns them.

They wonder if they are really children of God. John pointed questioning believers to their actions and then took them into the presence of an omniscient God who is greater than their condemning hearts (3:21–24).

### Test the Spirits

John warned of false prophets and urged his readers not to believe every spirit but to test the spirits. The spirit that confesses that Jesus has come in the flesh is of God (4:1–6). John once again emphasized the supremacy of love. The measure of love is not human love for God but God's love for His children. God's love is original, unsurpassed, and fully effective through the propitiatory sacrifice of Jesus for sin (4:7–19).

### Joy in Obedience

In closing, John reminded his readers that those who believe Jesus is Messiah are born of God. They show their love of God by obeying His commands. Because they have the very life of God, obedience is no longer a burden. Those who don't believe God's testimony about His Son are, in effect, calling God a liar. Humanity divides into those who have the Son and those who don't. Those who have the Son have eternal life. One of John's key purposes for writing this letter was to give his readers the assurance that they have eternal life. In the here and now they can be confident that God hears them as they pray according to His will. As they pray in this way, they can know that their prayer is answered (4:20–5:13).

## THE RELIABILITY OF 1 JOHN

### Internal Evidence

The author of 1 John claimed to be an eyewitness of Christ (1 Jn 1:1–3). Throughout the book, he wrote with an authoritative tone that is virtually apostolic.

A comparison of 1 John and the Gospel of John reveals numerous similarities in theology, vocabulary, and syntax. There are contrasting pairs such as life and death, truth and falsehood, light and darkness, children of God and children of the devil, and love and hate.

The term *paraklētos* occurs only five times in Scripture and all are in the Johannine material (John 14:16,26; 15:26; 16:7; 1 Jn 2:1). The word *monogenēs* as an expression of the Son's unique relationship to the Father occurs in John 1:14,18; 3:16,18; and 1 John 4:9.

### External Evidence

The early church was consistent in ascribing the authorship of the Fourth Gospel and 1 John to the apostle John. Papias, who knew John (and was born c. AD 60), is the first second-century writer to make specific reference to a Johannine letter as the work of the apostle John. Irenaeus (c. AD 180) specifically makes reference to 1 and 2 John, and he clearly attributes both, as well as the Fourth Gospel, to the apostle John. Indeed, the early Christian tradition is unanimous in ascribing 1 John to John, the disciple and apostle of the Lord.

## HOW 1 JOHN FITS INTO GOD'S STORY

1. Prologue: Creation, Fall, and the Need for Redemption
2. God Builds His Nation (2000–931 BC)
3. God Educates His Nation (931–586 BC)
4. God Keeps a Faithful Remnant (586–6 BC)
5. God Purchases Redemption and Begins the Kingdom (6 BC to AD 30)
6. **God Spreads the Kingdom Through the Church (AD 30–?)**
7. God Consummates Redemption and Confirms His Eternal Kingdom
8. Epilogue: New Heaven and New Earth

## CHRIST IN 1 JOHN

Jesus is the Word of life who has come to earth and has been seen, heard, and touched. He reveals to us who God is and what God has done for our salvation. He came to make it possible for us to have fellowship with the Father (1:3) and to have fellowship with other believers (1:7). That fellowship is possible because Christ's blood cleanses us and takes away the sin that separates us from God (1:7).

## CHRISTIAN WORLDVIEW ELEMENTS

### Teachings About God

God is seen especially in His relationship to Jesus Christ. Thus, He is "the Father." Jesus Christ is, in perfect complement, "the Son" (1:3). He is as well "the Messiah" (2:22) who came "in the flesh" (4:2–3). The Holy Spirit has been given to believers (3:24; 4:13), and He enables believers to recognize and reject every false spirit (4:1–6).

### Teachings About Humanity

First John recognizes only two categories of human beings: those who believe in Jesus Christ and all others (who belong to the spirit of the Antichrist). Believers confess when they sin, but their lives are not characterized by sin (1:7–9; 5:16–18). They live in fellowship with God and with one another. Those who continue to live in sin are giving evidence that they have never known God (3:6).

### Teachings About Salvation

One of the great texts about salvation is 1 John 2:2: "He Himself is the propitiation for our sins, and not only for ours, but also for those of the whole world." The term "propitiation" refers to removal of divine wrath because of sin, as also in Romans 3:25. Christ's death propitiated God's wrath not only for "our sins," referring to the people to whom John was writing, but also for persons from all ethnic, economic, and social groups (Gl 3:28; Rv 7:9–10). The benefits of Christ's death come only to those who believe (5:13).

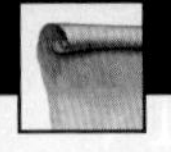



## AUTHOR AND DATE OF WRITING

**John the Apostle, Perhaps Around AD 80–90**

This letter claims to be written by "the elder," who is otherwise unnamed. Some have speculated that he was an unknown Christian leader, but the style and content are so much like 1 John that these letters are acknowledged to be written by the same person. Christian tradition has uniformly asserted that this author was John the apostle. See *Author and Date of Writing* for **JOHN** for more information. Most scholars believe this epistle was written somewhat after the Gospel, but it is impossible to be certain. The decade of the AD 80s is a good estimate for the composition of this letter.

## FIRST AUDIENCE AND DESTINATION

**A Christian Lady or a Congregation, Somewhere in Roman Asia**

The letter was written to "the elect lady and her children." If this refers to an individual, she is otherwise unknown, but she had taught her children to follow the gospel. Those who support this view point out that this letter is parallel to 3 John, which was also written to an individual. Since John seems to have known this "dear lady" well (v. 5), she was evidently someone he had met during his ministry, which was centered in Ephesus.

Alternatively, "the elect lady" may be a figurative expression to refer to a particular congregation. The "children" are members of that church.

## OCCASION

John was prompted to write because he had recently become aware of the excellent Christian reputation of the "children" (v. 4). They had apparently related to him facts about a heresy they had faced, identical to the false doctrine facing the recipients of his first epistle. (See *Occasion* for **1 JOHN**.) He penned this letter as a personal note to advise the "lady" about the heresy and to urge her to continue in Christian love.

# GOD'S MESSAGE IN 2 JOHN

## PURPOSE

Second John was written to combat the same false doctrines that were written about in 1 John. In the first letter the teachings were to be applied to a congregational setting; in the second letter they were applied either the same way or to a personal family setting.

## FIRST PASS

### Greeting

John described himself as "the elder." The term may either refer to an official title (see 1 Pt 5:1), or it may describe John affectionately as an old man. John designated his recipients as "the elect lady and her children." If the recipient were an individual, she would likely be anonymous. The phrase is more likely a reference to some local church over which the elder had authority. The "children" were members of that church. John's statement of love and the command to love would be more suitable for a church than for a person. The command not to host false teachers is also more suitable for a local church than for a single home.

### Encouragement

John had met some of the children of the lady, perhaps members of the church, in his travel. Their conduct had impressed him. The meeting led to a single charge: Love one another. John then sets forth the link between love and obedience. If we love God, we will obey Him. Our love for Him expresses itself in our obedience (vv. 4–6).

### Warning

John warned against deceivers who led others astray. The doctrine they stressed involved a denial of the incarnation. Christians affirmed the genuine humanity of Jesus when they said, "Christ has come in the flesh" (1 Jn 4:2; 2 Jn 7). Jesus did not become Christ at the baptism or cease to be Christ before His death. He was Christ come in the flesh from conception to ascension. John warned his readers against losing their reward for faithful service by falling into doctrinal error (v. 8). He affirmed that one who erred at this important point did not have God. John included an additional warning in verses 10–11. He warned against providing any sort of official welcome for those who erred in their doctrine of Christ. John was not promoting intolerance, nor was he violating his earlier appeal to "love one another." He was warning against extending any form of support for those who erred at the point of the genuine humanity of Christ.

### Looking Ahead

Although John had much he desired to communicate to his readers, he did not want to use another sheet of papyrus for writing. He preferred to speak face-to-face so that he could not be misunderstood. He anticipated a future visit that would be an occasion of joy. John's concluding word in verse 13 sounds like a message of greeting from members of one church to another.

## THE RELIABILITY OF 2 JOHN

The 27-book New Testament canon dates to Athanasius's Easter letter of AD 367. Included in that list of 27 books was 2 John. Just the fact of 2 John's inclusion in the canon is one of the strongest arguments for its authenticity and its having been written by the apostle John. This second shortest book in the New Testament, 245 words in the Greek text, faced severe tests before being included in the canon.

Unlike Paul's letters, 2 John was not widely quoted, so references to this short letter were few. In his book *Against Heresies* (3.16.8) (c. AD 180), Irenaeus quotes 2 John 7–8 in the context of referring to 1 John. This may be evidence that the three letters of John circulated together.

This letter would have been of special interest to Irenaeus who, during his youth, had heard Polycarp (AD 69–155). Polycarp, in turn, had been a disciple of the apostle John. Given Irenaeus' proximity to the generation that followed that of the apostles and his passion for truth, if he had doubts about the authenticity of 2 John, it would likely never have been received into the canon.

## HOW 2 JOHN FITS INTO GOD'S STORY

1. Prologue: Creation, Fall, and the Need for Redemption
2. God Builds His Nation (2000–931 BC)
3. God Educates His Nation (931–586 BC)
4. God Keeps a Faithful Remnant (586–6 BC)
5. God Purchases Redemption and Begins the Kingdom (6 BC to AD 30)
6. **God Spreads the Kingdom Through the Church (AD 30–?)**
7. God Consummates Redemption and Confirms His Eternal Kingdom
8. Epilogue: New Heaven and New Earth

## CHRIST IN 2 JOHN

John's key concern in this letter was to affirm that Christ had come in the flesh. John warned his readers not to go beyond this teaching about Christ and not to associate with people who modify this teaching.

## CHRISTIAN WORLDVIEW ELEMENTS

### Teachings About God

God is the Father of Jesus and is the One who has issued commands that His children are to live by. Jesus is the Messiah, the Son of the Father, who came "in the flesh." The Holy Spirit is not mentioned.

### Teachings About Humanity

This book shows (negatively) that many deceivers and antichrists are out to oppose God's people. It also shows (positively) the great good that one Christian or one congregation ("the elect lady") can accomplish. See also *Teachings About Humanity* for **1 TIMOTHY**.

#### Teachings About Salvation

The only teaching directly related to salvation is the crucial importance of the incarnation of the Son of God. Those who deny this doctrine are cut off from salvation (v. 7). Redeemed people "walk in" love and "remain in Christ's teaching" as a way of living.

## GENRE AND LITERARY STYLE

#### A Brief Epistle Written in *Koinē* Greek

Second John is the fifth of seven "General Epistles" in the New Testament, all of which are titled according to their authors. One of the usual features of an epistle (thanksgiving) is missing. There is a salutation (vv. 1–3), a body (vv. 4–11), and a farewell (vv. 12–13). This is a pastoral letter, driven by the occasion and needs of the recipient, rather than a tractate (a formal treatise). The Greek style is identical to that of 1 John.

## A PRINCIPLE TO LIVE BY

#### Rejecting False Teaching (2 Jn 9–10, *Life Essentials Study Bible*, p. 1771)

As communities of faith, we must not allow anyone to preach and teach if they deny that Jesus Christ is God who became flesh.

To access a video presentation of this principle featuring Dr. Gene Getz, use a Smartphone or iPad to connect to this QR code or go to http://www.bhpublishinggroup.com/handbook/2john

# 3 JOHN

## THE THIRD EPISTLE OF JOHN

Titled according to its author, this is the third canonical letter by John, the apostle of Jesus.

## KEY TEXT: VERSE 8

*"Therefore, we ought to support such men so that we can be coworkers with the truth."*

## KEY TERM: "TRUTH"

The word "truth" (Greek, *alētheia*) is used six times. Christians are called on to be committed to the truth and to show hospitality to Christian leaders involved in ministering the truth.

## ONE-SENTENCE SUMMARY

Christians are to recognize and to work for the truth of the gospel, and one way they do this is to show hospitality to Christian ministers that are hard at work.

Bust of Roman Emperor Traianus (Trajan) who reigned from AD 98 to 117. The bust is on display in Ankara's Museum of Anatolian Civilizations. Irenaeus affirmed that John lived in Asia until the reign of Trajan (98–117).

## AUTHOR AND DATE OF WRITING

**John the Apostle, Perhaps Around AD 80–90**

See *Author and Date of Writing* for **2 JOHN**.

## FIRST AUDIENCE AND DESTINATION

**Gaius, a Christian Living in Roman Asia**

Gaius is known only through this letter. He was a fine Christian that John loved and knew well ("dear friend," v. 5). He probably had leadership responsibility in the congregation John mentioned in his letter. Where he lived is not known, but it was probably near Ephesus, where John lived during his last years.

## OCCASION

The occasion for this letter is entirely different than the occasion for 1 and 2 John.

John wrote his friend Gaius a short note. In it he commended the practice of showing hospitality for the sake of the gospel.

# GOD'S MESSAGE IN 3 JOHN

## PURPOSE

Gaius was also warned to beware of a troublemaker (Diotrephes) and to welcome a newcomer (Demetrius).

**First Pass**

Third John is a personal letter that provides insight into a personality conflict that arose at the end of the first century and the strategy John adopted to resolve it. John opened with a word of exhortation to Gaius encouraging him not to imitate the bad example of Diotrephes but to continue the good work he was doing of receiving and supporting the traveling teachers/missionaries.

## THE RELIABILITY OF 3 JOHN

Similarity of style and vocabulary among the three letters of John have led most modern scholars to the conclusion that they were written by the same person, even if they don't believe that person was John the apostle. Couple that recognition with the early external evidence that strongly supports John's authorship of both the Gospel and 1 John, and the conclusion is reasonable that John the apostle wrote the Gospel and all three letters ascribed to him.

Charles E. Hill cites several lines of evidence that the Gospel, John's three letters, and the Revelation were viewed as a literary corpus that may have existed in physical form. Beyond this possibility, "these books existed as a definite conceptual corpus, for writers use them as if they belong together and emanated from a single, authoritative source."[1]

One fascinating piece of indirect evidence that these five documents may have existed together is found in Codex Bezae, one of the five most important manuscripts of the Greek New Testament, which dates to the late fourth or early fifth centuries. It is actually a bilingual manuscript with Greek on the left-hand pages and Latin on the right. This manuscript has the four Gospels in the following order: Matthew, John, Luke, Mark. There is then a gap in which a number of pages is missing. The next document is a fragment of 3 John (verses 11–15) in Latin followed by Acts.[2]

The gap is not large enough to have accommodated either Paul's letters or all of the General Epistles. What would fit the missing space well are Revelation and 1, 2, 3 John. This does not prove that the five writings traditionally assigned to John the apostle were bound together in a single codex but is indirect evidence that such codices may have existed in the second century.

## HOW 3 JOHN FITS INTO GOD'S STORY

1. Prologue: Creation, Fall, and the Need for Redemption
2. God Builds His Nation (2000–931 BC)
3. God Educates His Nation (931–586 BC)
4. God Keeps a Faithful Remnant (586–6 BC)
5. God Purchases Redemption and Begins the Kingdom (6 BC to AD 30)
6. **God Spreads the Kingdom Through the Church (AD 30–?)**
7. God Consummates Redemption and Confirms His Eternal Kingdom
8. Epilogue: New Heaven and New Earth

## CHRIST IN 3 JOHN

John describes a man named Diotrephes, who had to be first in everything. This man is the opposite of Christ who humbled Himself, became a slave, and suffered an ignominious death. John then urges his readers not to imitate evil but to imitate good. Christ is the supreme example of goodness.

## CHRISTIAN WORLDVIEW ELEMENTS

### Teachings About God

God is mentioned three times (vv. 6,11) as the source of good, not evil, who expects His people to live worthy of Him. The essence of God's glory is summarized by calling Him "the Name" (v. 7).

### Teachings About Humanity

This letter is full of contrasts. On one hand, there are several shining examples of

what people committed to the truth can accomplish (Gaius, Demetrius, John himself, the traveling ministers). On the other hand, Diotrephes is a negative example of someone who obstructs the truth. See also *Teachings about Humanity* for **1 TIMOTHY**.

### Teachings About Salvation

Salvation is addressed indirectly in John's constant use of "the truth" (vv. 1,3,4,8,12). "The truth" is evidently his paraphrase for "the gospel of Jesus Christ," thought of in broad terms. This truth is nowhere defined, but its importance is evident.

## GENRE AND LITERARY STYLE

### A Brief Epistle Written in *Koinē* Greek

Third John is the sixth of seven "General Epistles" in the New Testament, all of which are titled according to their authors. This letter has all four standard parts of a first-century epistle: salutation (v. 1); thanksgiving (in this letter, a brief petition, v. 2); main body (vv. 3–12); and farewell (vv. 13–14). Third John is a pastoral letter, driven by the occasion and needs of the recipient, rather than a tractate (a formal treatise). The Greek style is identical to that of 1 John.

## A PRINCIPLE TO LIVE BY

### Hospitality and Generosity (3 Jn 5–8, *Life Essentials Study Bible*, p. 1774)

Those qualified believers who devote large amounts of time to ministry and have personal financial needs should be cared for by the church body.

To access a video presentation of this principle featuring Dr. Gene Getz, use a Smartphone or iPad to connect to this QR code or go to http://www.bhpublishinggroup.com/handbook/3john

## ENDNOTES

1. Charles E. Hill, *The Johannine Corpus in the Early Church* (New York: Oxford University Press, 2004), 461.
2. Ibid., 454.

# JUDE

## THE EPISTLE OF JUDE

This letter is titled according to its author, Jude, who was probably the half brother of Jesus.

### KEY TEXT: VERSE 3

*"Dear friends, although I was eager to write you about the salvation we share, I found it necessary to write and exhort you to contend for the faith that was delivered to the saints once for all."*

### KEY TERM: "CONTEND"

This letter is a reminder that Christians are soldiers engaged in spiritual warfare. They are called to contend for the truth of the gospel.

### ONE-SENTENCE SUMMARY

Christians must defend the faith against false teachings and false teachers, and at the same time they must build up their own faith in Christ.

## ORIGINAL HISTORICAL CENTER

### AUTHOR AND DATE OF WRITING

**Jude, Perhaps in the AD 60s**

The author was "Jude, a slave of Jesus Christ and a brother of James" (v. 1). Jude is the English translation of the Hebrew name "Judah." (The name "Judas" is identical, *Ioudas* in Greek, but most English translators reserve "Judas" for Jesus' betrayer because of the negative connotations of that name.) There were several Judes in the New Testament, but the only one who was James's brother was also the brother of Jesus (Mt 13:15). He was the son of Mary and Joseph, and, like all Jesus' brothers, had not believed in Jesus until after the resurrection (Ac 1:14). Little is known about him as a Christian leader beyond his authorship of this letter. The decade of the AD 60s fits because of the connection of this epistle with 2 Peter (see *Occasion* below).

### FIRST AUDIENCE AND DESTINATION:

**Believers Living in an Unknown Location**

This letter contains no specific information that permits identification of the first audience. They were Christians that Jude knew well ("dear friends," v. 3) and wanted to warn. His quotation of Jewish sources suggests that the recipients were Jewish, but beyond that nothing can be determined.

## OCCASION

Jude had intended to write on one subject but changed his mind when he learned about dangerous false teachers. They had already infiltrated the congregation, and Jude heaped condemnation on them (v. 13). Their problem was that they were "turning the grace of our God into promiscuity" (v. 4). This evidently referred to a libertine understanding that God's grace entitles believers to do whatever they want without reference to God's commandments. The false teachers were motivated by their own sensual lust and desire for financial gain (v. 16). Thus, Jude wrote this letter of warning. Not only did he attack falsehood, but he also encouraged these believers to stay true to the faith and to reach out compassionately to those who were tempted to compromise with the false teachers (vv. 20–22).

# GOD'S MESSAGE IN JUDE

## PURPOSE

Jude was written to condemn false teachers who were trying to persuade Christians that they were free to sin since they had been forgiven and were under God's grace. Jude wanted his readers to oppose this teaching with the truth about God's grace.

## FIRST PASS

### Introduction

Jude had prepared to write a letter on the theme of "salvation" when he learned of the influence of false teachers. He urged his readers to contend for the faith by living godly, obedient lives. He described the false teachers as ungodly men, who stood condemned before God because of their denial of Jesus' lordship (vv. 3–4).

### Apostates: Past and Present

Jude pictured the false teachers as deserving to receive God's judgments just as the unbelieving Israelites, the rebellious angels, and the cities of Sodom and Gomorrah had merited judgment. He showed that the false teachers were arrogantly defying God by their perverse moral behavior. They disdained angelic creatures, whom they failed to understand. Jude commended the example of the angel Michael, who did not deal with the devil's protests on his own authority. Jude used this story from the apocryphal *Assumption of Moses* to demonstrate a proper attitude toward the supernatural (vv. 5–9).

The false teachers had the murderous spirit of Cain, were as greedy as Balaam and were as rebellious as Korah (vv. 10–13). Citing a passage from *1 Enoch*, a book that isn't Scripture but may have been highly regarded by the false teachers, Jude emphasized the reality of divine judgment (vv. 14–15).

### Encouragement

Jude reminded his readers that the apostles had warned against false teachers who would be spiritually empty and would promote divisiveness (vv. 17–19). He encouraged his readers to remain in God's love by building on the faith delivered once for all, praying in the Holy Spirit, and expecting God's mercy for eternal life (vv. 20–21). They were to have mercy on those who doubted and those caught up in sin (vv. 22–23).

**Blessing**

Jude closed by commending his readers to the power of God, who alone can provide the strength needed for full obedience. To God alone through Jesus Christ he ascribes "glory, majesty, power, and authority before all time, now and forever. Amen."

## THE RELIABILITY OF JUDE

The author is identified in the first verse as "Jude, a slave of Jesus Christ and a brother of James" (v. 1). The James mentioned is almost certainly James, the brother of the Lord Jesus Christ and the author of the letter from James (cp. also Ac 15:13–21; 1 Co 15:7; Gl 2:9). We can conclude from this that Jude was well known by his association with his famous brother who played a significant role in the apostolic church. Hence, Jude was also the half brother of Jesus Christ (Mt 13:55; Mk 6:3). External evidence from the early church also supports the view that Jude, the brother of Jesus, wrote the letter.

Some scholars have argued that another Jude wrote the letter. Calvin identified the author as the apostle "Judas of James" (Lk 6:16; Ac 1:13). But if this were correct, the author would probably call himself an apostle. Others have speculated that the writer is "Judas Barsabbas" (Ac 15:22,27,32), but there is no evidence that the latter was James's brother. Even more unlikely is the theory that the author was the apostle Thomas. Still others maintain that the letter is pseudonymous, but support for pseudonymity in canonical writings is lacking. To sum up, there are good reasons to accept the view that Jude, the brother of Jesus, is the author of the letter.

## HOW JUDE FITS INTO GOD'S STORY

1. Prologue: Creation, Fall, and the Need for Redemption
2. God Builds His Nation (2000–931 BC)
3. God Educates His Nation (931–586 BC)
4. God Keeps a Faithful Remnant (586–6 BC)
5. God Purchases Redemption and Begins the Kingdom (6 BC to AD 30)
6. God Spreads the Kingdom Through the Church (AD 30–?)
7. God Consummates Redemption and Confirms His Eternal Kingdom
8. Epilogue: New Heaven and New Earth

##  CHRIST IN JUDE

Jude looks to the day when Jesus will reward His followers. He looks from the present perspective, talking about believers being kept for Jesus (v. 1). He knows eternal life is based on Jesus' mercy (v. 21).

## CHRISTIAN WORLDVIEW ELEMENTS

### Teachings About God

God is referred to as Father, Savior, and Lord (vv. 1,5,9,25). The grace of God is the attribute that comes to the fore in this book (v. 4). Jesus is also called Lord, and He is the One who keeps His people and brings them to eternal life (vv. 1,21,25). The Spirit, never given to those who reject the truth, enables the prayers of the saints (vv. 19–20).

### Teachings About Humanity

Jude shows the great evil of those who are enslaved by falsehood: "wild waves of the sea, foaming up their shameful deeds; wandering stars for whom the blackness of darkness is reserved forever!" (v. 13). On the other hand, redeemed humanity looks forward to everlasting joy: "Now to Him who is able to protect you from

Jude warns against lawless men who have infiltrated the church. He likens them to "trees in late autumn—fruitless, twice dead, pulled out by the roots" (Jd 12).

stumbling and to make you stand in the presence of His glory, blameless and with great joy" (v. 24).

**Teachings About Salvation**

Jude had intended to write about the "the salvation we share," but he wrote instead about false teachers (v. 3). He refers to God as "Savior" (v. 25). Verse 24 makes clear that salvation is God's doing from start to finish (see also v. 1).

## GENRE AND LITERARY STYLE

**An Epistle Written in *Koinē* Greek**

Jude is the last of seven "General Epistles" in the New Testament, all of which are titled according to their authors. One of the usual features of an epistle (thanksgiving) is missing, although there is a salutation (vv. 1–2), a body (vv. 3–23), and a farewell (in this letter, a doxology, vv. 24–25). Jude is a pastoral letter, driven by the occasion and needs of the recipients, rather than a tractate (a formal treatise). The Greek style is awkward and is hard to read. (The repetition of the word "ungodly" in v. 15 is an example of the stylistic difficulty.)

Jude quoted noncanonical Jewish sources, both *The Assumption of Moses* (v. 9) and *1 Enoch* (vv. 14–15), to back up his arguments. He did not call them Scripture or imply that they were inspired. Rather, he used them as sources of information. The apostle Paul sometimes used noncanonical sources as well (Ac 17:28; 1Co 15:33; Ti 1:12; 2Tm 3:8).

## A PRINCIPLE TO LIVE BY

**Love That Confronts (Jd 3–4, *Life Essentials Study Bible*, p. 1777)**

Though it is easier and more enjoyable to give positive feedback to our fellow Christians, there are times when we must address difficult and painful situations very directly .

To access a video presentation of this principle featuring Dr. Gene Getz, use a Smartphone or iPad to connect to this QR code or go to http://www.bhpublishinggroup.com/handbook/jude

# REVELATION

## THE APOCALYPSE

The first word in the Greek text of this book is *apokalypsis*, which means "revelation" or "unveiling." Although some English Bibles title it "The Revelation of John," the work is manifestly a revelation to John by Jesus Christ.

### KEY TEXT: 1:7

*"Look! He is coming with the clouds, and every eye will see Him, including those who pierced Him. And all the families of the earth will mourn over Him. This is certain. Amen."*

### KEY TERM: "PROPHECY"

This book self-consciously calls itself a prophecy at both its beginning and its end (1:3; 22:18–19). It is the only New Testament book that is essentially prophetic.

### ONE-SENTENCE SUMMARY

Jesus, the Lord of history, will return to earth, destroy all evil and all opposition to Him, and bring the kingdom of God to its glorious culmination.

*St. John the Evangelist on Patmos* by Jocopo Vignali (1592–1664).

## AUTHOR AND DATE OF WRITING

**The Apostle John, Around AD 95**

The book was written by John. He had great authority, even from his place of banishment, the tiny island of Patmos some 35 miles out in the Aegean Sea. Most (but not all) early Christian references to the authorship of Revelation affirmed that this was Jesus' apostle of that name. See *Author* and *Date of Writing* for **JOHN** for more information. Tradition records that John had a long and successful ministry in and around the city of Ephesus during his later life. Some scholars believe the author of Revelation was some other (unknown) John. There is no good reason, however, to deny that the author was indeed the apostle—also the composer of the Fourth Gospel and three epistles. See *The Reliability of Revelation*, p. 488.

Revelation originated during a time of Roman persecution of Christians. Some have suggested the last days of the Emperor Nero (ruled AD 54–68) as the time of composition. The severity of the persecution as well as the spiritual decline of the churches in Revelation 2–3 suggests a later date to most scholars. The last years of Domitian (ruled AD 81–96) are a more likely date for the origin of this book. If this is so, Revelation was the last book of the New Testament to be written.

## FIRST AUDIENCE AND DESTINATION

**Persecuted Christians Living in Seven Cities in the Roman Province of Asia**

The recipients and destination of Revelation were not John's choice. He was following divine orders. This is explicit in Revelation 1:10–11: "I was in the Spirit on the Lord's day, and I heard a loud voice behind me like a trumpet saying, 'Write on a scroll what you see and send it to the seven churches: Ephesus, Smyrna, Pergamum, Thyatira, Sardis, Philadelphia, and Laodicea.'" The list follows the order the letter carrier traveled after arriving on the mainland from Patmos.

## OCCASION

John explained what prompted him to write. While he was exiled on Patmos, the exalted Lord appeared to him and gave him visions that he was instructed to write down. The recipients were Christians living through vicious persecution. All Bible books are inspired by God, but this one, more than any other, bears a sense of divine dictation.

# GOD'S MESSAGE IN REVELATION

## PURPOSE

This prophetic book originally intended to teach that faithfulness to Jesus ultimately triumphs over all the evils of this world and that Jesus will return to earth as

King and Lamb-Bridegroom. God's people who read and study Revelation today should view it with this original purpose in mind.

## FIRST PASS

### Prologue

Written to "the seven churches" of the Roman province of Asia, John's work is a "revelation" of "what must quickly take place." The theme is clear: the Lord God Himself has guaranteed the final vindication of the crucified Jesus (1:7–8). A blessing, the first of seven, is promised to those who hear and heed its message (1:3).

The Seven Churches of the Revelation.

**John's Vision of the Risen Lord**

While in exile on Patmos, John saw the risen Lord (1:9–20). Appearing clothed in power and majesty, the Living One revealed Himself as the Lord of the churches and instructed John to send not only the seven letters, but also an account of the things which he had seen and would see, a revelation of "what will take place after this" (1:19).

**The Recipients: The Seven Churches in Asia**

The letters to the churches of Ephesus, Smyrna, Pergamum, Thyatira, Sardis, Philadelphia, and Laodicea have a fairly consistent format. First, after designating the recipients, the risen Lord describes Himself using a portion of the description in 1:9–20. Then follows an "I know" section of commendation and/or criticism. Next, typically, is some form of exhortation: to those receiving criticism, an exhortation to repent; however, to the churches of Smyrna and Philadelphia, for whom the Lord had only praise, the exhortation is one of assurance (2:10; 3:10–13). Each letter concludes with both an exhortation to "listen to what the Spirit says to the churches" and a promise of reward to the "victor," the one who conquers by persevering in the cause of Christ. Each promise finds its source in the glorious consummation (Rv 19–22).

**Coming Judgments**

Chapters 4 and 5 are pivotal, tying the risen Lord's exhortations to the churches (chaps. 2–3) to the judgments and final triumph of the Lamb (chaps. 6–22). The crucified Lord Jesus is the risen and exalted Lion and Lamb of God who is all-powerful, all-knowing, and present everywhere (5:6). He and He alone is worthy to take the book and open its seven seals. When the Lamb begins to break the seals, the climactic events of history begin to unfold.

**Seven Seals, Seven Trumpets, and Seven Bowls**

A careful reading of Revelation shows that both the seventh seal and the seventh trumpet are empty of content. Some suggest that the three series of judgments (seals, trumpets, and bowls) have a telescopic relationship, so that the seventh seal contains the seven trumpets, and the seventh trumpet contains the seven bowls, accounting for the intensity and rapidity of the judgments toward the end.

**Preparation for the Lord's Appearance**

Although John has withheld a description of the coming of the Lord on at least three earlier occasions (8:5; 11:15–19; 16:17–21; cp. 14:14–16), he was now prepared to describe the glories of the Lord's appearance. All of heaven rejoices over the righteous judgment of God upon evil (19:1–2). The Lamb's bride, the people of God, has made herself ready by her faithfulness to her Lord through the hour of suffering (19:7–8).

**Final Conflicts**

Heaven is opened, and the One whose coming has been faithfully anticipated from ages past appears to battle the enemies of God, a conflict whose outcome is not in

doubt (19:11–16). The first beast (the Antichrist) and the second beast (the false prophet) are thrown into the lake of fire from which there is no return (19:20), a place of everlasting punishment and torment, not annihilation.

### A Thousand Years

The dragon (Satan) is cast into the abyss, which is shut and sealed for a thousand years (20:1–3). Christ will reign for a thousand years on the earth as King of kings and Lord of lords. The dead in Christ are raised to govern with Him (20:4–6), and God's rightful rule over the earth is vindicated.

### Satan's Destiny

At the end of the thousand years, the final disposition of Satan will occur (20:7–10). Though Satan will have one last deception, his final insurrection will be short. In one final battle Satan and his followers are overcome, and the Devil joins the beast and the false prophet in the lake of fire where "they will be tormented day and night forever and ever" (20:10). Then the final judgment takes place, at which Death, Hades, and all not included in "the book of life" are thrown into the lake of fire (20:11–15).

### New Heavens and a New Earth

The creation of the new heavens and a new earth follows (21:1). The Holy City, new Jerusalem, comes down from heaven (21:2). She is an exquisitely beautiful bride prepared for marriage to her Husband, the Lamb. Within this beautiful city, God's people are secure and removed from the presence of evil and sin (21:22–27). The

Patmos from the chapel at the entrance to the Cave of the Apocalypse.

throne of God and of the Lamb is there, and there His slaves shall serve Him and reign with Him forever and ever (22:1–5).

**Final Affirmation and Exhortation**

John concluded his prophecy by declaring the utter faithfulness of his words. Those who heed his prophecy will receive the blessings of God. Those who ignore the warnings will be left outside the gates of God's presence (22:6–15). Solemnly and praying in hope for the Lord to come, John closed his book (22:17,20). The churches must have ears to hear what the Spirit has said (22:16). The people of God must, by His grace (22:21), persevere in the hour of tribulation, knowing their enthroned Lord will return in triumph.

## THE RELIABILITY OF REVELATION

Revelation is one of a few New Testaments books that were widely debated before being recognized as Scripture. It differs from other so-called disputed books in an important way. Revelation was accepted early as a work of the apostle John and then later disputed and debated before becoming one of the 27 books we call the New Testament.

Excavation of a synagogue that dates to the third century AD. A vital Jewish community existed in Sardis from the third century BC. Indications are that the relationships between the Jewish community and Roman authorities were positive. The church at Sardis was challenged to repent. They had a reputation for being alive but were dead (Rv 3:1–6).

Early support for John's authorship of Revelation includes Papias (AD 60–130), Hegisippus (second century), Justin Martyr (100–165), Irenaeus (c. 115–c. 202, Clement of Alexandria (c. 155–c. 220), Tertullian (c. 160–c. 215), Hippolytus (d. 236), and Origen (c. 185–c. 254). Papias is the earliest second-century witness to apostolic authorship, but his writings come in fragments through later writers, Irenaeus and Eusebius.

In his *Dialogue with Trypho* (81.4), Justin Martyr is the earliest and clearest witness to John's authorship of Revelation:

> We have perceived, moreover, that the expression, 'The day of the Lord is as a thousand years,' is connected with this subject. And further, there was a certain man with us, whose name was John, one of the apostles of Christ, who prophesied, by a revelation that was made to him, that those who believed in our Christ would dwell a thousand years in Jerusalem; and that thereafter the general, and, in short, the eternal resurrection and judgment of all men would likewise take place.

Like Papias and Justin, Irenaeus affirms that John the apostle wrote Revelation. In his writings Irenaeus makes a clear distinction between elders and Christ's disciples.[1] For Irenaeus elders were disciples of Christ's apostles. In a passage on the millennium, he wrote:

> The predicted blessing, therefore, belongs unquestionably to the times of the kingdom, when the righteous shall bear rule upon their rising from the dead; when also the creation, having been renovated and set free, shall fructify with an abundance of all kinds of food, from the dew of heaven, and from the fertility of the earth: as the elders who saw John, the disciple of the Lord, related that they had heard from him how the Lord used to teach in regard to these times.[2]

In addition to the elders who heard John and affirmed his authorship of Revelation, Irenaeus mentions Papias specifically as one who bore witness to these matters. In that context Irenaeus stated the Papias heard John and was a friend of John's disciple, Polycarp.[3]

Justin, Papias, Irenaeus, and other second-century writers accepted a literal thousand-year reign of Christ on earth (Rv 20:1–7). This interpretation became a stumbling block for some interpreters in the third century and was one factor in later disputing the claim that Revelation was written by the apostle John. Dionysius (d. 264), a student of Origen, head of the Alexandria's Catechetical School, and later bishop of Alexandria, called attention to the great differences between the Gospel of John and Revelation. He came to the conclusion that they couldn't have been written by the same person. Dionysius didn't deny that Revelation was inspired—only that it couldn't have been written by John, the beloved disciple.

R. H. Charles's analysis of Revelation[4] underscores what Dionysius observed. The Greek of Revelation is evidence that the author was a Palestinian Jew from the region of Galilee. The context contains numerous instances of grammatical irregularity that could be expected from a writer whose first language was Hebrew. The Greek of Revelation is more complex than that of the Gospel of John. This doesn't preclude Revelation's having been written by John the apostle. The Greek of Revelation is what might be expected from John. If the Gospel and Revelation were written at different times and in different circumstances, John may have had a different scribe for the two works, which could account for the differences in style and linguistic patterns.

## HOW REVELATION FITS INTO GOD'S STORY

1. Prologue: Creation, Fall, and the Need for Redemption
2. God Builds His Nation (2000–931 BC)
3. God Educates His Nation (931–586 BC)
4. God Keeps a Faithful Remnant (586–6 BC)
5. God Purchases Redemption and Begins the Kingdom (6 BC to AD 30)
6. God Spreads the Kingdom Through the Church (AD 30–?)
7. God Consummates Redemption and Confirms His Eternal Kingdom
8. Epilogue: New Heaven and New Earth

## CHRIST IN REVELATION

Christ is the Alpha and the Omega, the first and the last, the One who was coming, is coming, and will come. When He appeared to John on Patmos, the sight was so overwhelming, John fell at his feet like a dead man. Jesus told him not to be afraid but to write down the things He would show him, the things that will take place.

## CHRISTIAN WORLDVIEW ELEMENTS

**Teachings About God**

Revelation teaches the supremacy and glory of God in all things. God is the primary mover who will bring about the return of Christ and the end of the world. The righteous wrath of a holy God is fully displayed in Revelation. The book teaches about the Trinity and contributes greatly to an understanding of the deity of Christ.

**Teachings About Humanity**

Revelation shows the sinfulness of humans in stark terms. There are only two kinds of people in Revelation: those who follow the Lamb (and bear His special mark) and those who follow the beast (and bear his mark). Those who follow the Lamb are given unimaginably great blessings, but they are a minority. The majority that follows evil is destined for eternal damnation.

### Teachings About Salvation

Salvation from sin in Revelation is presented mainly in terms of something God purchased through the death of the Lamb (the first coming of Christ). Those who are saved oppose evil "by the blood of the Lamb and by the word of their testimony, for they did not love their lives in the face of death" (12:11). Final salvation after the resurrection is presented mainly in terms of "the Holy City, new Jerusalem" (21:2).

## GENRE AND LITERARY STYLE

### A Prophecy Composed in *Koinē* Greek

Some students of Revelation have classed Revelation as apocalyptic literature. This kind of writing, then popular among Jews, had a number of features: (1) the claim to originate from God through a mediating being; (2) the use of symbolic creatures and actions; (3) conflict between this evil age and the coming age. However,

Bust of Domitian, brother and successor to Emperor Titus. The fourth-century historian Eusebius reported that the apostle John was exiled to Patmos (Rv 1:9) in the reign of Domitian. Eusebius also claimed that in Nerva's reign the senate took away Domitian's honors and freed exiles to return home, thus letting John return to Ephesus. Nerva's reign was brief, lasting little more than a year (AD 96–98). He was succeeded by Trajan (AD 98–117), who bathed the empire red in the blood of Christians. His persecution was more severe than that instituted by Domitian. Irenaeus wrote in the second century that John died in Ephesus in the reign of Trajan.

Revelation lacks certain other apocalyptic features: (1) claim to be written by a famous Old Testament character; (2) extensive angelic interpretation; (3) belief that the Messiah was still future.

Revelation is better seen as a prophecy, a message to God's people exhorting them to remain faithful to Him. Unlike the apocalyptic literature, Revelation contains serious calls for God's people to repent of sin. Like Isaiah and Jeremiah, it predicts both near and remote future events. The apocalyptic elements are secondary to the book's prophetic message.

The Greek style of Revelation is more like the Greek of the fourth Gospel and the three epistles of John than any other part of the New Testament. The book has a number of grammatical peculiarities that make its Greek unusual in places. This may be accounted for by either the author's loss (or change) of a secretary or the author's eagerness to write down his experiences, causing him to write in haste.

## A PRINCIPLE TO LIVE BY

**The Second Coming (Rv 1:7–8, *Life Essentials Study Bible*, p. 1782)**

Since Jesus Christ will return, we are always to be ready for that great event.

To access a video presentation of this principle featuring Dr. Gene Getz, use a Smartphone or iPad to connect to this QR code or go to http://www.bhpublishinggroup.com/handbook/revelation

## ENDNOTES

1. Eugenia Scarvelis Constantiou, "Andrew of Caesarea and the Apocalypse in the Ancient Church of the East," PhD diss., Université Laval, 2008, 58–59.
2. *Against Heresies*, 5.33.3.
3. *Against Heresies*, 5.33.4
4. Andreas Köstenberger, L. Scott Kellum, and Charles L. Quarles, *The Cradle, the Cross, and the Crown: An Introduction to the New Testament* (Nashville: B&H Academic, 2009), 812.

## MILLENNIAL PERSPECTIVES ON REVELATION

| POINT OF INTERPRETATION | AMILLENNIAL | HISTORICAL PREMILLENNIAL | DISPENSATIONAL PREMILLENNIAL |
|---|---|---|---|
| Description of View | Viewpoint that the present age of Christ's rule in the church is the millennium; holds to one resurrection and judgment marking the end of history as we know it and the beginning of life eternal | Viewpoint that Christ will reign on earth for a thousand years following His second coming; saints will be resurrected at the beginning of judgment | Viewpoint that after the battle of Armageddon, Christ will rule through the Jews for a literal thousand years accompanied by two resurrections and at least three judgments |
| Book of Revelation | Current history written in code to confound enemies and encourage Asian Christians; message applies to all Christians | Immediate application to Asian Christians; applies to all Christians throughout the ages, but the visions also apply to a great future | "Unveiling" of theme of Christ among churches in present dispensation, also as Judge and King in dispensations to come |
| Seven candlesticks (1:13) | Churches | | Churches, plus end-time application |
| Seven stars (1:16,20) | Pastors | Symbolizes heavenly or supernatural character of the church (some believe refers to pastors) | Pastors or saints |
| Churches addressed (chaps. 2–3) | Specific historical situations, truths apply to churches throughout the ages; do not represent periods of church history | | Specific historical situations and to all churches throughout the ages; shows progress of churches' spiritual state until end of church age |
| Twenty-four elders (4:4,10; 5:8,14) | Twelve patriarchs and twelve apostles; together symbolize all the redeemed | Company of angels who help execute God's rule (or elders represent twenty-four priestly and Levitical orders) | The rewarded church; also represents twelve patriarchs and twelve apostles |
| Sealed book (5:1-9) | Scroll of history; shows God carrying out His redemptive purpose in history | Contains prophecy of end events of chapters 7–22 | Title deed to the world |
| 144,000 (7:4-8) | Redeemed on earth who will be protected against God's wrath | Church on threshold of great tribulation | Jewish converts of tribulation period who witness to Gentiles (same as 14:1) |
| Great multitude (7:9-10) | Uncountable multitude in heaven praising God for their salvation | Church, having gone through great tribulation, seen in heaven | Gentiles redeemed during tribulation period through witness of 144,000 |
| Great tribulation (first reference in 7:14) | Persecution faced by Asian Christians of John's time; symbolic of tribulation that occurs throughout history | Period at end time of unexplained trouble, before Christ's return; church will go through it; begins with seventh seal (18:1) which includes trumpets 1–6 (8:2–14:20) | Period at end time of unexplained trouble referred to in 7:14 and described in chapters 11–18; lasts three and a half years, the latter half of seven-year period between rapture and millennium |

## MILLENNIAL PERSPECTIVES ON REVELATION, cont.

| POINT OF INTERPRETATION | AMILLENNIAL | HISTORICAL PREMILLENNIAL | DISPENSATIONAL PREMILLENNIAL |
|---|---|---|---|
| "Star" (9:4) | Personified evil | Represents an angelic figure divinely commissioned to carry out God's purpose | The leader of apostasy during the great tribulation |
| Forty-two months (11:2);1,260 days (11:3) | Indefinite duration of pagan desolation | A symbolic number representing period of evil with reference to last days of age | Half of seven-year tribulation period |
| Two witnesses (11:3-10) | Spread of gospel in first century | Two actual historical persons at end of time who witness to Israel | A witnessing remnant of Jews in Jerusalem testifying to the coming kingdom and calling Israel to repent |
| Sodom and Egypt (11:8) | Rome as seat of Empire | Earthly Jerusalem | |
| Woman (12:1-6) | True people of God under Old and New Covenants (true Israel) | | Indicates Israel, not church; key is comparison with Gen. 37:9 |
| Great red dragon (12:3) | All views identify as Satan | | |
| Manchild (12:4-5) | Christ at His birth, life events, and crucifixion, whom Satan sought to kill | Christ, whose work Satan seeks to destroy | Christ but also the church (head and body); caught up on throne indicates rapture of church |
| 1,260 days (12:6) | Indefinite time | Symbolic number representing period of evil with special reference to last days of age | First half of great tribulation after church is raptured |
| Sea beast (13:1) | Emperor Domitian, personification of Roman Empire (same as in chap. 17) | Antichrist, here shown as embodiment of the four beasts in Daniel 7 | A new Rome, satanic federation of nations that come out of old Roman Empire |
| Seven heads (13:1) | Roman emperors | Great power, shows kinship with dragon | Seven stages of Roman Empire; sixth was imperial Rome (John's day); last will be federation of nations |
| Ten horns (13:1) | Symbolize power | Kings, represent limited crowns (ten) against Christ's many | Ten powers that will combine to make the federation of nations of new Rome |
| Earth beast (13:11) | *Concilia*, Roman body in cities responsible for emperor worship | Organized religion as servant of first beast during great tribulation period; headed by a false prophet | Antichrist, who will head apostate religion, a Jewish leader described in Daniel 11:36-45 (some identify as assistant to the Antichrist) |

Note: Postmillennialism is the viewpoint that Christ's reign on earth is spiritual not physical. Christ returns after the millennium that is established by gospel preaching.

## MILLENNIAL PERSPECTIVES ON REVELATION, cont.

| POINT OF INTERPRETATION | AMILLENNIAL | HISTORICAL PREMILLENNIAL | DISPENSATIONAL PREMILLENNIAL |
|---|---|---|---|
| 666 (13:18) | Imperfection, evil; personified as Domitian | Symbolic of evil, short of 777; if a personage meant, he is unknown but will be known at the proper time | Not known but will be known when time comes |
| 144,00 on Mount Zion (14:1) | Total body of redeemed in heaven | | Redeemed Jews gathered in earthly Jerusalem during millennial kingdom |
| River of blood (14:20) | Symbol of infinite punishment for the wicked | Means God's radical judgment crushes evil thoroughly | Scene of wrath and carnage that will occur in Palestine |
| Babylon (woman–17:5) | Historical Rome | Capital city of future Antichrist | Apostate church of the future |
| Beast | Domitian | Antichrist | Head of satanic federation of nations of revived Roman Empire; linked with apostate church (seventh head) |
| Seven mountains (17:9) | Pagan Rome, which was built on seven hills | Indicate power, so here means a succession of empires, last of which is end-time Babylon | Rome, revived at end time |
| Seven heads (17:7) and seven kings (17:10) | Roman emperors from Augustus to Titus, excluding three brief rules | Five past godless kingdoms; sixth was Rome; seventh would arise in end time | Five distinct forms of Roman government prior to John; sixth was imperial Rome; seventh will be revived Roman Empire |
| Ten horns (17:7) and ten kings (17:12) | Vassal kings who ruled with Rome's permission | Symbolic of earthly powers that will be subservient to Antichrist | Ten kingdoms arising in future out of revived Roman Empire |
| Waters (17:15) | People ruled by Roman Empire | Indicates complex civilization | People dominated by apostate church |
| Bride, wife (19:7) | Total of all the redeemed | | The church; does not include Old Testament saints or tribulation saints |
| Marriage supper (19:9) | Climax of the age; symbolizes complete union of Christ with His people | Union of Christ with His people at His coming | Union of Christ with His church accompanied by Old Testament saints and tribulation saints |
| One on white horse (19:11-16) | Vision of Christ's victory over pagan Rome; return of Christ occurs in connection with events of 20:7-10 | Second coming of Christ | |

## MILLENNIAL PERSPECTIVES ON REVELATION, cont.

| POINT OF INTERPRETATION | AMILLENNIAL | HISTORICAL PREMILLENNIAL | DISPENSATIONAL PREMILLENNIAL |
|---|---|---|---|
| Battle of Armageddon (19:19-21; see 16:16) | Not literally at end of time but symbolizes power of God's Word overcoming evil; principle applies to all ages | Literal event of some kind at end time but not literal battle with military weapons; occurs at Christ's return at beginning of millennium | Literal bloody battle at Armageddon (valley of Megiddo) at end of great tribulation between kings of the East and federation of nations of new Rome; they are all defeated by blast from Christ's mouth and then millennium begins |
| Great supper (19:17) | Stands in contrast to marriage supper | | Concludes series of judgments and opens way for kingdom to be established |
| Binding of Satan (20:2) | Symbolic of Christ's resurrection victory over Satan | Curbing of Satan's power during the millennium | |
| Millennium (20:2-6) | Symbolic reference to period from Christ's first coming to His second | A historical event, though length of one thousand years may be symbolic, after Armageddon during which Christ rules with His people | A literal thousand-year period after the church age during which Christ rules with His people but especially through the Jews |
| Those on thrones (20:4) | Martyrs in heaven; their presence with God is a judgment on those who killed them | Saints and martyrs who rule with Christ in the the millennium | The redeemed ruling with Christ, appearing and disappearing on earth at will to oversee life on earth |
| First resurrection (20:5-6) | The spiritual presence with Christ of the redeemed that occurs after physical death | Resurrection of saints at beginning of millennium when Christ returns | Includes three groups: (1) those raptured with church (4:1); (2) Jewish tribulation saints during tribulation (11:11); (3) other Jewish believers at beginning of millennium (20:5-6) |
| Second death (20:6) | Spiritual death, eternal separation from God | | |
| Second resurrection (implied) | All persons, lost and redeemed, rise when Christ returns in only resurrection that takes place | Nonbelievers, resurrected at end of millennium | |
| New heavens and earth (21:1) | A new order; redeemed earth | | |
| New Jerusalem (21:2-5) | God dwelling with His saints in the new age after all other end-time events | | |
| New Jerusalem (21:10– 22:5) | Same as 21:2-5 | | Millennial Jerusalem from which the world will be ruled; the bride as well as the home of the saints |

# Table of Weights and Measures

## WEIGHTS

| BIBLICAL UNIT | LANGUAGE | BIBLICAL MEASURE | U.S. EQUIVALENT | METRIC EQUIVALENT | VARIOUS TRANSLATIONS |
|---|---|---|---|---|---|
| Gerah | Hebrew | $^1/_{20}$ shekel | $^1/_{50}$ ounce | .6 gram | gerah; oboli |
| Beqa' | Hebrew | $^1/_2$ shekel or 10 gerahs | $^1/_5$ ounce | 5.7 grams | bekah; half a shekel; quarter ounce; fifty cents |
| Pim | Hebrew | $^2/_3$ shekel | $^1/_3$ ounce | 7.6 grams | $^2/_3$ of a shekel; quarter |
| Shekel | Hebrew | 2 bekahs | $^2/_5$ ounce | 11.5 grams | shekel; piece; dollar; fifty dollars |
| Litra (pound) | Greco-Roman | 30 shekels | 12 ounces | .4 kilogram | pound; pounds |
| Mina | Hebrew/Greek | 50 shekels | $1^1/_4$ pounds | .6 kilogram | mina; pound |
| Talent | Hebrew/Greek | 3,000 shekels or 60 minas | 75 pounds/ 88 pounds | 34 kilograms/ 40 kilograms | talent/talents; 100 pounds |

## LENGTH

| BIBLICAL UNIT | LANGUAGE | BIBLICAL MEASURE | U.S. EQUIVALENT | METRIC EQUIVALENT | VARIOUS TRANSLATIONS |
|---|---|---|---|---|---|
| Handbreadth | Hebrew | $^1/_6$ cubit or $^1/_3$ span | 3 inches | 8 centimeters | handbreadth; three inches; four inches |
| Span | Hebrew | $^1/_2$ cubit or 3 handbreadths | 9 inches | 23 centimeters | span |
| Cubit/Pechys | Hebrew/Greek | 2 spans | 18 inches | .5 meter | cubit/cubits; yard; half a yard; foot |
| Fathom | Greco-Roman | 4 cubits | 2 yards | 2 meters | fathom; six feet |
| Kalamos | Greco-Roman | 6 cubits | 3 yards | 3 meters | rod; reed; measuring rod |
| Stadion | Greco-Roman | $^1/_8$ milion or 400 cubits | 1/8 mile | 185 meters | miles; furlongs; race |
| Milion | Greco-Roman | 8 stadia | 1,620 yards | 1.5 kilometer | mile |

# DRY MEASURE

| BIBLICAL UNIT | LANGUAGE | BIBLICAL MEASURE | U.S. EQUIVALENT | METRIC EQUIVALENT | VARIOUS TRANSLATIONS |
|---|---|---|---|---|---|
| Xestes | Greco-Roman | $^1/_2$ cab | 1 1/6 pints | .5 liter | pots; pitchers; kettles; copper pots; copper bowls; vessels of bronze |
| Cab | Hebrew | $^1/_{18}$ ephah | 1 quart | 1 liter | cab; kab |
| Choinix | Greco-Roman | $^1/_{18}$ ephah | 1 quart | 1 liter | measure; quart |
| Omer | Hebrew | $^1/_{10}$ ephah | 2 quarts | 2 liters | omer; tenth of a deal; tenth of an ephah; six pints |
| Seah/Saton | Hebrew/Greek | $^1/_3$ ephah | 7 quarts | 7.3 liters | measures; pecks; large amounts |
| Modios | Greco-Roman | 4 omers | 1 peck or $^1/_4$ bushel | 9 liters | bushel; bowl; peck-measure;corn-measure; meal-tub |
| Ephah [Bath] | Hebrew | 10 omers | $^3/_5$ bushel | 22 liters | bushel; peck; deal; part; measure; six pints; seven pints |
| Letek | Hebrew | 5 ephahs | 3 bushels | 110 liters | half homer; half sack |
| Kor [Homer]/ Koros | Hebrew/Greek | 10 ephahs | 6 bushels or 200 quarts/15 bushels or 550 quarts | 220 liters/525 liters | cor; homer; sack; measures; bushels |

# LIQUID MEASURE

| BIBLICAL UNIT | LANGUAGE | BIBLICAL MEASURE | U.S. EQUIVALENT | METRIC EQUIVALENT | VARIOUS TRANSLATIONS |
|---|---|---|---|---|---|
| Log | Hebrew | $^1/_{72}$ bath | $^1/_3$ quart | .3 liter | log; pint; cotulus |
| Xestes | Greco-Roman | $^1/_8$ hin | $1^1/_6$ pints | .5 liter | pots; pitchers; kettles; copper pots; copper bowls; vessels of bronze |
| Hin | Hebrew | $^1/_6$ bath | 1 gallon or 4 quarts | 4 liters | hin; pints |
| Bath/Batos | Hebrew/Greek | 1 ephah | 6 gallons | 22 liters | gallon(s); barrels; liquid measure |
| Metretes | Greco-Roman | 10 hins | 10 gallons | 39 liters | firkins; gallons |

# ART CREDITS

B&H Publishing Group is grateful to the following persons and institutions for use of the graphics in ***Holman Illustrated Bible Handbook.*** Where we have inadvertently failed to give proper credit for any graphic used in the ***Handbook***, please contact us (bhcustomerservice@lifeway.com) and we will make the required correction on the next printing. B&H gratefully acknowledges the contributions of G. B. Howell, Brent Bruce, James McLemore, and the staff of the ***Biblical Illustrator*** for their counsel. We also thank Dr. Gene A. Getz , President of the Center for Church Renewal and General Editor of ***Life Essentials Study Bible*** for making available a video presentation from each of the sixty-six books of the Bible to readers of the *Holman Illustrated Bible Handbook*.

## PHOTOGRAPHS

### PHOTOGRAPHERS

***Biblical Illustrator***, Nashville, Tennessee: p. 162.

***Biblical Illustrator*** (James McLemore, photographer), Nashville, Tennessee: pp. 57, 332, 334.

***Biblical Illustrator*** (Bob Schatz, photographer), Nashville, Tennessee: pp. 57, 76, 87, 90 (lower left), 246.

***Biblical Illustrator*** (Ken Touchton, photographer), Nashville, Tennessee: pp. 61, 159, 296.

***Biblical Illustrator*** (Jerry Vardaman, photographer), Nashville, Tennessee: p. 82.

**Brisco, Thomas V.**, Dean and Professor of Biblical Backgrounds and Archaeology, Logsdon School of Theology, Hardin-Simmons University, Abilene, Texas: pp. 96, 326.

**HolyLandPhotos**, Dr. Carl Rasmussen (www.holylandphotos.org): p. 359.

*Illustrated World of the Bible:* **pp. 31, 257.**

**iStock**: pp. x, 10, 65, 167, 201, 215, 237, 261, 273, 279, 457, 481.

**Scofield Collection**, E. C. Dargan Research Library, LifeWay Christian Resources, Nashville, Tennessee: pp. 403, 1830.

**Trainor, Rev. Dr. Michael**, Senior Lecturer at Flinders University, Adelaide, Australia, Principal Researcher, Colossae Project and **Rosemary Canavan**, Associate Dean (Postgraduate & Research) Catholic Theological College, MCD University of Divinity, p. 436.

**Wikimedia Commons**: pp. xii, lower left (Jayel Aheram), xii lower right (Zee Prime at cs.wikipedia), 1, 8 (Patrick Hawks), 12 (ElVacilando), 15 (The WB), 17 (John Bodsworth), 20 (Lancastermerrin88), 27 (2MASS/UMass/IPAC-Caltech/NASA/NSF), 29, 35 (Jacques Descloitres, MODIS Rapid Response Team, NASA/GSFC), 56, 63 (Bernard Werner), 81 (Egyptian Museum, Cairo/Webscribe), 90 lower right (Henri Sivonen/The Louvre), 92 (Olaf Tausch), 95 (Deror Avi), 113 (British Museum/London/Steven G. Johnson, 114 (Mike Peel; www.mikepeel.net), 116 (David Castor), 128 (Wilson44691), 129 (British Museum/Mike Peel; ; www.mikepeel.net), 131 (Jayel Aheram), 134 (Mike Peel; ; www.mikepeel.net), 143 (Göttingen, Stadtmuseum/Jewish life/Esther-Rolle/Ingersoll), 148 (Infrogmation of New Orleans), 149 (Chefallen), 151 (Fir0002), 152 (NASA, ESA, AURA/Caltech, Palomar Observatory), 155 (NASA, ESA, M. Robberto (Space Telescope Science Institute/ESA) and the Hubble Space Telescope Orion Treasury Project Team), 156 (Schuyler Shepherd/(Ununtunium272), 160 (amoruso) , 175 (My Lev-ari Eilat), 176 (Ernst Rosca, Moscow, Russia), 182 (Joe Sarembe), 183 (metsilomi yehudit gera'in kol), 185 (Fir0002), 189 (Jeff Belmonte, Cuiabá, Brazil), 196 (Tamar Hayardeni), 197 (Tamar Hayardeni), 202 ( Sd Abubakr), 203 (Dr. Avishai Teicher), 204 (Nenya Aleks), 207, 210 (Aziz1005), 216 (© Guillaume Piolle), 228 (Gryffindor), 230 (Blitz1980), 231 (Tal Oz), 232 (Eli Zahavi), 236 (Institute for the Study of the Ancient World), 245 (Lior Golgher), 249 (Bernard Gagnon), 254, 263 (Deror

Avi), 274-75 (Rosemania), 276 (Betta27), 282 (Ashdod), 284 upper (O. Mustafin), 284 middle (Patrick C., aka dynamomosquito), 284 lower (KendallKDown), 288, 289 (Deror Avi), 294 (Chad Rosenthal), 295 (Tjibbe), 296 (Mieke Vranken), 297 (Rob Lavinski/iRocks.com), 300 (Ilana Shckolnick-Backal), 301 (Papyrologist Bernard Grenfell /John Rylands Library), 306 lower left, 306 lower middle, 306 lower right, 313 (Asaf T.), 315 (Matanya), 317 (Almog), 321 (Yucatan), 336 (Almog), 337 (Bonio), 344, (Marion Doss), 345 (Chmee2), 352 (Berthold Werner), 361 (Berthold Werner), 363 (Erik 1980), 364 (Kleuske at nl.wikipedia), 365 (Njaker), 367 (Emilio Labrador), 368 (Avishai Teicher), 369 (Kucharz), 372 upper (Jeanhousen), 372 lower (Jeanhousen), 375 (Sharon Mollerus), 378 (Frank van Mierlo), 381 (Dan Diffendale), 383 (Pufacz), 391 (Zee Prime at cs.wikipedia), 392 (Tamar Hayardeni), 394 (Rensi), 397 (Marsyas), 403 (ESO/Y. Beletsky), 409 (Anjči), 414 (Philly boy 92), 420 (Mister Sunshine), 427 (Barbaking), 431 (Jerzy Strzelecki), 440 (ESO/INAF-VST Acknowledgement: A. Grado/L. Limatola/INAF-Capodimonte Observatory), 445, 447 (Flame Center Tirat Carmel Ori Gonen family album), 463 (Me, but logged in at en.wikipedia), 469 (Marsyas), 474 (Bjørn Christian Tørrissen), 487 (Aboumael at fr.wikipedia), 488 (AtilimGunesBaydin), 491 (Jastrow 2006).

## ILLUSTRATIONS AND RECONSTRUCTIONS

### ILLUSTRATORS

*Biblical Illustrator*, Linden Artists, London: p. 47.
**Goolsby, Abe**, Principal, Officina Abrahae, Nashville, TN: pp. ix, 40–41, 51, 120, 127, 342–43.
**Latta, Bill**, Latta Art Services, Mt. Juliet, TN: pp. 243, 320, 323.
**Layard, Austen Henry**: p. 271.

## PAINTINGS

### ARTISTS

**Berruguete, Pedro** (1450–1504), ***Salomon,*** Santa Eulalia, Parades de Nava, Web Gallery of Art: p. 169.
**Bloch, Carl Heinrich** (1844–1890), ***The Sermon on the Mount***: p. 302.
**Brueghel, Jan the Elder** (1568–1625), ***Jonah Emerging from the Throat of the Whale***: p. 255.
**Feuerbach, Anselm** (1829–80), ***Mirjam***: p. 52.
**Francisco Collantes** (1599–1656), ***The Vision of Ezekiel***: p. 217.
**Hoet, Gerard**, (1648–1733),***Israel at Sinai***: p. 168 lower.
**Kozenitzky, Lidia**, ***Splitting of the Red Sea***: p. 168 upper.
**Michelangelo Buonarroti** (1475–1564), ***Zerubbabel***: p. 291.
**Pskov Historical, Architectural and Art Museum Complex**, Pskov, Russia (Shakko): p. 110.
**Rembrandt Harmenszoon van Rijn** (1606–1669), ***Belshazzar's Feast***: p.225.
**Rembrandt Harmenszoon van Rijn** (1606–1669), ***Jeremiah Lamenting the Destruction of Jerusalem***: p. 211.
**Roberts, David** (1796–1864), ***The Siege and Destruction of Jerusalem***: p. 328.
**Roberts, Hubert** (1733–1808), ***The Fire of Rome***: p. 452.
**Seddon, Thomas** (1821–1856), ***The Valley of Jehoshaphat***: p. 238.
**Vignali: Jacopo** (1592–1664), ***St. John the Evangelist on Patmos***: p. 483.

Great Illustrated Classics

# CINDERELLA
## & Other Stories

BARONET BOOKS, New York, New York

**GREAT ILLUSTRATED CLASSICS**

**edited by**
**Rochelle Larkin**



BARONET BOOKS is a trademark of Playmore Inc., Publishers
and Waldman Publishing Corp., New York, N.Y.



Printed in the United States of America

# Contents

She Could Not Bear This Pretty Girl.

# CINDERELLA

Once there was a gentleman who married, for his second wife, the proudest and most haughty woman that was ever seen. She had, by a former husband, two daughters who were, indeed, exactly like her in all things. He had likewise, by his first wife, a young daughter, but of unparalleled goodness and sweetness of temper, which she took from her mother, who had been the best creature in the world.

No sooner were the wedding ceremonies over but the new mother began to show herself in her true colors. She could not bear the good qualities of this pretty girl, and the less because they made her own daughters appear the worst.

She employed her in the work of the house: the girl scoured the dishes, tables, and madam's chamber, and those of her daughters; she slept in a sorry garret, upon a wretched straw bed, while her sisters lay in fine rooms, with floors all inlaid, upon beds of the very newest fashion, and where they had looking-glasses so large that they might see themselves from head to foot.

The poor girl bore all patiently, and dared not tell her father, for his wife governed him entirely. When she had done her work, she used to go into the chimney-corner, and sit down among cinders and ashes, which made her be called Cinderella. However, Cinderella, notwithstanding her mean apparel, was a hundred times prettier than her sisters, though they were always dressed very richly.

It happened that the King's son gave a ball, and invited all persons of fashion to it. Our young misses were also invited, for they cut a very grand figure. They were mightily delighted at this invitation, and wonderfully busy in choosing out such gowns, petticoats, and headdresses as might become them. This was a new trouble for Cinderella; for it was she who ironed her sisters' linen, and smoothed their ruffles; they talked all day long of nothing but how they should be dressed.

"For my part," said the eldest, "I will wear my red velvet suit with French trimming."

"And I," said the youngest, "shall have my usual petticoat; but then, to make amends for that, I will put on my gold-flowered mantle, and my diamond belt, which is far from being the most ordinary one in the world."

They sent for the best woman they could get to make up their headdresses and adjust their skirts, and make them look as good as they possibly could.

Cinderella was likewise called up to them to be consulted in

A New Trouble for Cinderella

all these matters, for she had excellent notions, and advised them always for the best, and offered her services to dress their hair, which they were very willing she should do. As she was doing this, they said to her:

"Cinderella, would you not be glad to go to the ball?"

"Alas!" said she. "You only jeer at me; it is not for such as I am to go."

"You are right," replied they; "it would make the people laugh to see a cindergirl at a ball."

Anyone but Cinderella would have dressed their heads awry, but she was very good, and dressed them perfectly well. They were almost two days without eating, so much they were transported with joy. They broke above a dozen laces in trying to be laced up close, that they might have fine slender shapes, and they were continually at their looking-glass. At last the happy day came; they went to court, and Cinderella followed them with her eyes as long as she could, and when she had lost sight of them, she fell a-crying.

Her godmother, who saw her all in tears, asked her what was the matter.

"I wish I could — I wish I could — " she was not able to speak the rest, being interrupted by her tears and sobbing.

This godmother of hers, who was a fairy, said to her, "Thou wishest thou couldst go to the ball, is it not so?"

"Y—es," cried Cinderella, with a great sigh.

"Well," said her godmother, "be a good girl, and I will make

Her Godmother Asked What Was the Matter.

it that thou shalt go." Then she took her into her chamber, and said to her, "Run into the garden, and bring me a pumpkin."

Cinderella went immediately to gather the finest she could get, and brought it to her godmother, not being able to imagine how this pumpkin could help her go to the ball. Her godmother scooped out all the inside of it, having left nothing but the rind; which done, she struck it with her wand, and the pumpkin was instantly turned into a fine coach, gilded all over with gold.

She then went to look into her mouse-trap, where she found six mice, all alive, and ordered Cinderella to lift up a little the trap-door; then, giving each mouse, as it went out, a little tap with her wand, the mouse was that moment turned into a fine horse, which altogether made a very fine set of six horses of a beautiful mouse-colored dapple-grey.

"Being at a loss for a coachman, I will go and see," Cinderella said, "if there is a rat in the rat-trap — we may make a coachman of him."

"Thou art in the right," replied her godmother; "go and look." Cinderella brought the trap to her, and in it there were three huge rats. The fairy picked the one which had the largest beard, and, having touched him with her wand, he was turned into a fat, jolly coachman, who had the smartest whiskers eyes ever beheld.

After that, she said to her: "Go again into the garden, and you will find six lizards behind the watering-pot. Bring them to me."

Cinderella had no sooner done so but her godmother turned

“Bring Me a Pumpkin.”

them into six footmen, who skipped up immediately behind the coach, with their liveries all gold and silver, and clung as close behind each other as if they had done nothing else their whole lives. The fairy then said to Cinderella:

"Well, you see here an equipage fit to go to the ball with; are you not pleased with it?"

"Oh! Yes," cried Cinderella; "but must I go thither as I am, in these nasty rags?"

Her godmother only just touched her with her wand, and, at the same instant, her clothes were turned into cloth of gold and silver, all set with jewels. This done, she gave her a pair of glass slippers, the prettiest in the whole world.

Being thus dressed, she got up into her coach; but her godmother commanded her not to stay after midnight, above all things telling her, at the same time, that if she stayed one moment longer, the coach would be a pumpkin again, her horses mice, her coachman a rat, her footmen lizards, and her clothes become just as they were before.

She promised her godmother she would not fail to leave the ball before midnight; and then away she drove, scarce able to contain herself for joy.

The King's son, who was told that a great Princess, whom nobody knew, was come, ran out to receive her; he gave her his hand as she alighted out of the coach, and led her into the hall, among all the company.

A Pair of Glass Slippers

There was immediately a profound silence. They left off dancing, and the violins ceased to play, so attentive was everyone to contemplate the singular beauties of the unknown newcomer.

Nothing was then heard but a murmured noise of: "How handsome she is! How handsome she is!"

The King himself, old as he was, could not help watching her, and telling the Queen softly that it was a long time since he had seen so beautiful and lovely a creature.

All the ladies were busied in considering her clothes and headdress, that they might have some made next day after the same pattern, provided they could meet with such fine materials and as able hands to make them.

The King's son conducted her to the most honorable seat, and afterwards took her out to dance with him; she danced so very gracefully that they all more and more admired her. A fine dinner was served up, whereof the young Prince ate not a morsel, so intently was he busied in gazing on her.

She went and sat down by her sisters, showing them a thousand civilities, giving them part of the oranges and citrons which the Prince had presented her with, which very much surprised them, for they did not know her. While Cinderella was thus amusing her sisters, she heard the clock strike eleven and three-quarters, whereupon she immediately made a curtsey to the company and hastened away as fast as she could.

Being home, she ran to seek out her godmother, and, after

The King's Son Took Her Out to Dance.

having thanked her, she said she could not but wish she might go next day to the second ball, as the King's son had desired her to.

As she was eagerly telling her godmother whatever had passed at the ball, her two sisters knocked at the door, which Cinderella ran and opened.

"How long you have stayed!" cried she, gaping and rubbing her eyes and stretching herself as if she had been just waked out of her sleep.

"If thou hadst been at the ball," said one of her sisters, "thou wouldst not have been tired of it. There came thither the finest Princess, the most beautiful ever seen with mortal eyes; she showed us a thousand civilities, and gave us oranges and citrons."

Cinderella seemed very indifferent in the matter; indeed, she asked them the name of that Princess; but they told her they did not know it, and that the King's son was very uneasy on that account and would give all the world to know who she was.

At this Cinderella, smiling, replied: "She must, then, be very beautiful indeed; how happy you have been! Could not I see her? Ah! Dear Miss Charlotte, do lend me your yellow suit of clothes which you wear every day."

"Ay, to be sure!" cried Miss Charlotte. "Lend my clothes to such a dirty cindergirl as thou art! I should be a fool."

Cinderella, indeed, well expected such an answer, and was very glad of the refusal; for she would have been sadly put to it if her sister had lent her what she asked for in jest!

"How Long You Have Stayed!"

The next day the two sisters were at the ball, and so was Cinderella, but dressed more magnificently than before. The King's son was always by her, and never ceased his compliments and kind speeches to her; for Cinderella this was so far from being tiresome that she quite forgot what her godmother had told her; so that she counted the clock striking twelve when she took it to be no more than eleven; she then rose up and fled, as nimble as a deer.

The Prince followed, but could not overtake her. She left behind one of her glass slippers, which the Prince took up most carefully.

She got home, but quite out of breath, and in her nasty old clothes, having nothing left her of all her finery but one of the little slippers, the mate to that she dropped.

The guards at the palace gate were asked if they had not seen a Princess go out. But they said they had seen nobody go out but a young girl, very meanly dressed, and who had more the air of a poor country wench than a gentlewoman.

When the two sisters returned from the ball, Cinderella asked them if they had been well entertained, and if the fine lady had been there.

They told her yes, but that she hurried away immediately at midnight, and with so much haste that she dropped one of her little glass slippers, which the King's son had taken up; that he had done nothing but look at her all the time at the ball, and that most

One of Her Glass Slippers

certainly he was very much in love with the beautiful person who owned the glass slipper.

What they said was very true; a few days after, the King's son caused it to be proclaimed, by sound of trumpet, that he would marry her whose foot this slipper would fit. They whom he employed began to try it upon the Princesses, then the Duchesses and all the court, but in vain; it was brought to the two sisters, who did all they possibly could to thrust a foot into the slipper, but they could not do it.

Cinderella, who saw all this, and knew her slipper, said to them, laughing: "Let me see if it will not fit me."

Her sisters burst out a-laughing, and began to banter her. The gentleman who was sent to try the slipper looked earnestly at Cinderella, and, finding her very handsome, said it was but just that she should try, and that he had orders to let everyone make trial.

He obliged Cinderella to sit down, and, putting the slipper to her foot, he found it went on very easily, and fitted her as if it had been made for her. The astonishment her two sisters were in was excessively great, but still abundantly greater when Cinderella pulled out of her pocket the other slipper, and put it on her foot.

Thereupon, in came her godmother, who, having touched with her wand Cinderella's clothes, made them richer and more magnificent than any of those she had before.

And now her two sisters found her to be that fine, beautiful lady whom they had seen at the ball. They threw themselves at her

Putting the Slipper to Her Foot

feet to beg pardon for all the ill treatment they had made her undergo.

Cinderella took them up, and, as she embraced them, cried that she forgave them with all her heart, and desired them always to love her.

She was conducted to the young Prince, dressed as she was; he thought her more charming than ever, and, a few days after, married her. Cinderella, who was no less good than beautiful, gave her two sisters lodgings in the palace, and that very same day married them to two great lords of the court.

No Less Good Than Beautiful

Cormoran!

# JACK • THE • GIANT-KILLER

When good King Arthur reigned, there lived near the Land's End of England, in the county of Cornwall, a farmer who had only one son called Jack. He was brisk and of a ready lively wit, so that nobody or nothing could best him.

In those days the Mount of Cornwall was kept by a huge giant named Cormoran. He was eighteen feet in height, and about three yards round the waist, of a fierce and grim countenance, the terror of all the neighboring towns and villages. He lived in a cave in the midst of the Mount, and whenever he wanted food he would wade over to the mainland, where he would furnish himself with whatever came in his way. Everybody at his approach ran out of their houses, while he seized their cattle, making nothing of carrying half-a-dozen oxen on his back at a time; and as for their sheep and hogs, he would tie them round his waist like a bunch of tallow-dips. He had done this for many years, so that all Cornwall was in despair.

One day Jack happened to be at the town-hall when the magistrates were sitting in council about the giant. He asked: "What reward will be given to the man who kills Cormoran?"

"The giant's treasure," they said, "will be the reward."

Quoth Jack: "Then let me undertake it."

So he got a horn, shovel, and pickax, and went over to the Mount in the beginning of a dark winter's evening, when he fell to work, and before morning had dug a pit twenty-two feet deep, and nearly as broad, covering it over with long sticks and straw. Then he strewed a little mold over it, so that it appeared like plain ground.

Jack then placed himself on the opposite side of the pit, farthest from the giant's lodging, and, just at the break of day, he put the horn to his mouth, and blew, *Tantivy, Tantivy.*

This noise roused the giant, who rushed from his cave, crying: "You incorrigible villain, are you come here to disturb my rest? You shall pay dearly for this. Satisfaction I will have, and this it shall be, I will take you whole and broil you for breakfast."

He had no sooner uttered this, than he tumbled into the pit, and made the very foundations of the Mount shake.

"Oh, Giant," quoth Jack, "where are you now? Oh, faith, you are now in Lob's Pound, where I will plague you for your threatening words: what do you think now of broiling me for your breakfast? Will no other diet serve you but poor Jack?" Then having teased the giant for a while, he gave him a most weighty knock

Rousing the Giant

with his pickax on the very crown of his head, and killed him on the spot.

Jack then filled up the pit with earth, and went to search the cave, which he found contained much treasure. When the magistrates heard of this they made a declaration he should henceforth be termed

**JACK THE GIANT-KILLER**

and presented him with a sword and a belt, on which were written these words embroidered in letters of gold:

"Here's the right valiant Cornish man,
Who slew the giant Cormoran."

The news of Jack's victory soon spread over all the West of England, so that another giant, named Blunderbore, hearing of it, vowed to be revenged on Jack, if ever he should meet him. This giant was the lord of an enchanted castle situated in the midst of a lonesome wood.

Now Jack, about four months afterwards, walking near this wood in his journey to Wales, being weary, seated himself near a pleasant fountain and fell fast asleep. While he was sleeping, the giant, coming there for water, discovered him, and knew him to be the far-famed Jack the Giant-killer by the lines written on the belt.

He took Jack on his shoulders and carried him towards his castle. Now, as they passed through a thicket, the rustling of the boughs awakened Jack, who was strangely surprised to find him-

He Took Jack on His Shoulders.

self in the clutches of the giant. His terror had only begun, for, on entering the castle, he saw the ground strewed with human bones, and the giant told him his own would before long be among them.

After this the giant locked poor Jack in an immense chamber, leaving him there while he went to fetch another giant, his brother, living in the same wood, who might share in the meal of Jack.

After waiting some time, Jack, on going to the window, beheld afar off the two giants coming towards the castle. "Now," quoth Jack to himself, "my death or my deliverance is at hand."

Now there were strong cords in a corner of the room in which Jack was, and two of these he took, and made a strong noose at the ends; and while the giants were unlocking the iron gate of the castle he threw the ropes over each of their heads. Then he drew the other ends across a beam, and pulled with all his might, so that he throttled them. When he saw they were black in the face, he slid down the rope, and drawing his sword, slew them both. Then, taking the giant's keys, and unlocking the rooms, he found three fair ladies tied by the hair of their heads, almost starved to death. "Sweet ladies," quoth Jack, "I have destroyed this monster and his brutish brother, and obtained your liberties." This said, he presented them with the keys, and so proceeded on his journey to Wales.

Jack made the best of his way by travelling as fast as he could, but lost his way, and was confused, and could find no habitation until, coming into a narrow valley, he found a large house, and in

Fetching His Brother Giant

order to get shelter took courage to knock at the gate.

But what was his surprise when there came forth a monstrous giant with two heads; yet he did not appear so fiery as the others were, for he was a Welsh giant, and what bad he did was by secret malice under the false show of friendship.

Jack, having told his condition to the giant, was shown into a bedroom, where, in the dead of night, he heard his host in another apartment muttering these words:

"Though here you lodge with me this night,
You shall not see the morning light:
My club shall find your head outright!"

"Say'st thou so," quoth Jack; "that is one of your tricks, yet I hope to be cunning enough for you." Then, getting out of bed, he laid a bundle in the bed in his stead, and hid himself in a corner of the room. At the dead time of the night in came the giant, who struck several heavy blows on the bed with his club, thinking he had broken every bone in Jack's skin.

The next morning Jack, laughing in his sleeve, gave him hearty thanks for his night's lodging.

"How have you rested?" quoth the giant. "Did you not feel anything in the night?"

"No," quoth Jack, "nothing but a rat, which gave me two or three slaps with her tail."

With that, greatly wondering, the giant led Jack to breakfast, bringing him a bowl containing four gallons of thick pudding.

Monstrous!

Not wanting to let the giant think it too much for him, Jack put a large leather bag under his loose coat, in such a way that he could convey the pudding into it without its being perceived.

Then, telling the giant he would show him a trick, taking a knife, Jack ripped open the bag, and out came all the pudding. Whereupon, saying, "Odds splutters, I can do that trick myself," the monster took the knife, and ripping open his own belly, fell down dead.

Now, it happened in these days that King Arthur's only son asked his father to give him a large sum of money, in order that he might go and seek his fortune in the principality of Wales, where lived a beautiful lady possessed with seven evil spirits. The King did his best to persuade his son from it, but in vain; so at last gave way and the Prince set out with two horses, one loaded with money, the other for himself to ride upon.

Now, after several days' travel, he came to a market-town in Wales, where he beheld a vast crowd of people gathered together.

The Prince asked the reason of it, and was told that they had arrested a corpse for several large sums of money which he owed when he died. The prince replied that it was a pity creditors should be so cruel, and said: "Go bury the dead, and let his creditors come to my lodging, and their debts shall be paid." They came in such great numbers that before night he had only twopence left for himself.

Now Jack the Giant-killer, coming that way, was so taken

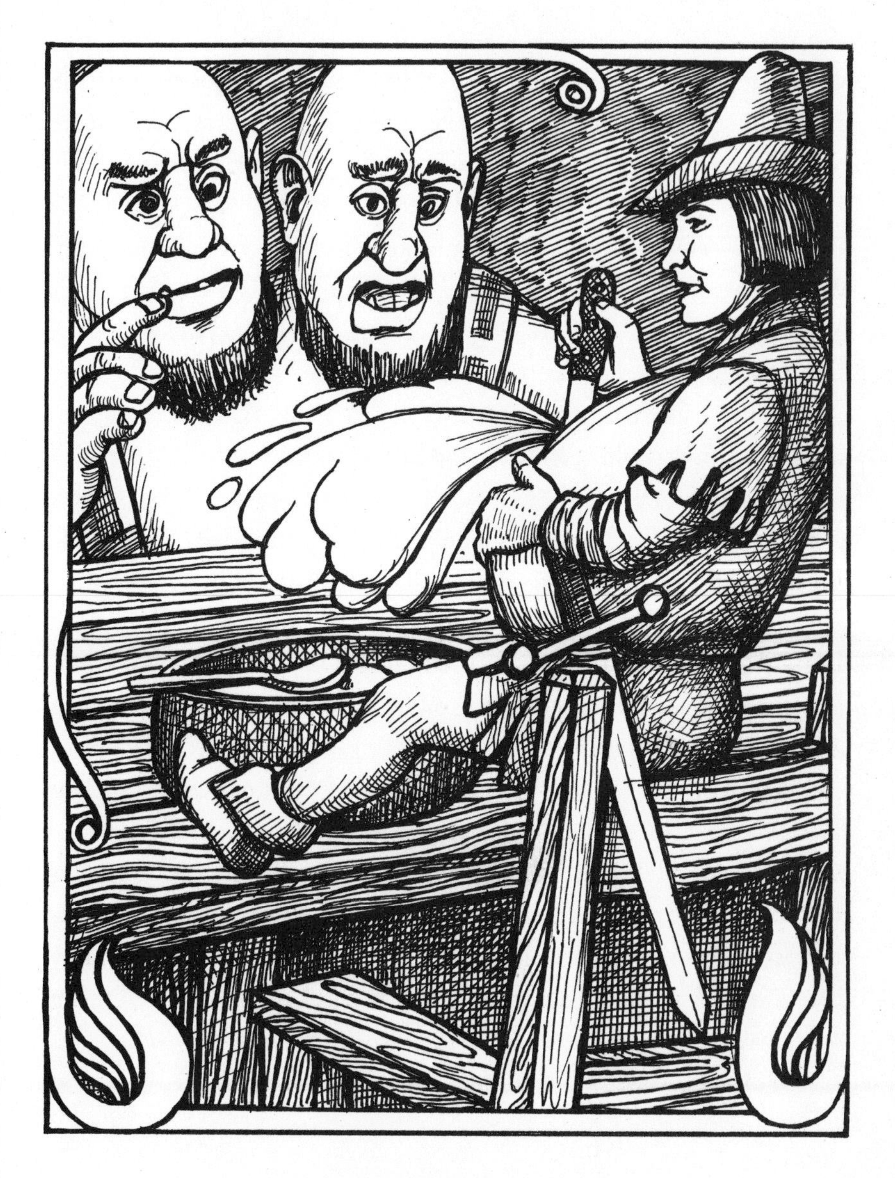

Jack Ripped Open the Bag.

with the generosity of the Prince, that he desired to be his servant. This being agreed upon, the next morning they set forward on their journey together, when, as they were riding out of the town, an old woman called after the Prince, saying, "He has owed me twopence these seven years; pray pay me as well as the rest." Putting his hand to his pocket, the Prince gave the woman all he had left, so that after their day's food, which cost what small store Jack had by him, they were without a penny between them.

When the sun got low, the King's son said: "Jack, since we have no money, where can we lodge this night?"

But Jack replied: "Master, we'll do well enough, for I have an uncle who lives within two miles of this place; he is a huge and monstrous giant with three heads; he'll fight five hundred men in armor, and make them fly before him."

"Alas!" quoth the Prince, "what shall we do there? He'll certainly chop us up at a mouthful. Nay, we are scarce enough to fill one of his hollow teeth!"

"It is no matter for that," quoth Jack; "I myself will go before and prepare the way for you; therefore stop here and wait till I return."

Jack then rode away at full speed, and coming to the gate of the castle, he knocked so loud that he made the neighboring hills resound.

The giant roared out at this like thunder: "Who's there?"

Jack answered: "None but your poor cousin Jack."

"Where Can We Lodge This Night?"

Quoth he: "What news has my poor cousin Jack?"

Jack replied: "Dear uncle, heavy news, I fear!"

"Prithee," quoth the giant, "what heavy news can come to me? I am a giant with three heads, and besides thou knowest I can fight five hundred men in armor, and make them fly like chaff before the wind."

"Oh, but," quoth Jack, "here's the King's son a-coming with a thousand men in armor to kill you and destroy all that you have!"

"Oh, cousin Jack," said the giant, "this is heavy news indeed! I will immediately run and hide myself, and thou shalt lock, bolt, and bar me in, and keep the keys until the Prince is gone."

Having secured the giant, Jack fetched his master, and they made themselves heartily merry whilst the poor giant lay trembling in a vault under the ground.

Early in the morning Jack furnished his master with a fresh supply of gold and silver, and then sent him three miles forward on his journey, at which time the Prince was pretty well out of the smell of the giant.

Jack then returned, and let the giant out of the vault, who asked what he should give Jack for keeping the castle from destruction.

"Why," quoth Jack, "I want nothing but the old coat and cap, together with the old rusty sword and slippers which are at your bed's head."

Quoth the giant: "You know not what you ask; they are the

What Heavy News Can Come to Me?

most precious things I have. The coat will keep you invisible, the cap will tell you all you want to know, the sword cuts asunder whatever you strike, and the shoes are of extraordinary swiftness. But you have been very serviceable to me, therefore take them with all my heart."

Jack thanked his uncle, and then went off with them. He soon overtook his master and they quickly arrived at the house of the lady the Prince sought, who, finding the Prince to be a suitor, prepared a splendid banquet for him.

After the repast was concluded, she told him she had a task for him. She wiped his mouth with a handkerchief, saying, "You must show me that handkerchief to-morrow morning, or else you will lose your head." With that she put it in her pocket.

The Prince went to bed in great sorrow, but Jack's cap of knowledge informed him how it was to be obtained. In the middle of the night she called upon a spirit to carry her to a demon. But Jack put on his coat of darkness and his shoes of swiftness, and was there as soon as she was.

When she entered the place of the demon, she gave the handkerchief to him, and he laid it upon a shelf, whence Jack took it and brought it to his master, who showed it to the lady next day, and so saved his life.

On that, she gave the Prince a kiss and told him he must show her the lips tomorrow morning that she would kiss that night, or lose his head.

The Coat of Darkness, the Shoes of Swiftness

"Ah!" he replied, "if you kiss none but mine, I will."

"That is neither here nor there," said she; "if you do not, death's your portion!"

At midnight she went as before, and was angry with the demon for letting the handkerchief go. "But now," quoth she, "I will be too hard for the King's son, for I will kiss thee, and he is to show me thy lips." Which she did, and Jack, when she was not standing by, cut off the demon's head and brought it under his invisible coat to his master, who the next morning pulled it out by the horns before the lady.

This broke the enchantment and the evil spirit left her, and she appeared in all her beauty. They were married the next morning, and soon after went to the court of King Arthur, where Jack, for his many great exploits, was made one of the Knights of the Round Table.

Jack soon went searching for giants again, but he had not ridden far when he saw a cave, near the entrance of which he beheld a giant sitting upon a block of timber, with a knotted iron club by his side. His eyes were like flames of fire, his countenance grim and ugly, and his cheeks like a couple of large flitches of bacon, while the bristles of his beard resembled rods of iron wire, and the locks that hung down upon his brawny shoulders were like curled snakes or hissing adders.

Jack alighted from his horse, and, putting on the coat of darkness, went up close to the giant, and said softly: "Oh! are you

The Enchantment Broken

: It will not be long before I take you fast by the beard."

The giant all this while could not see him, on account of his invisible coat, so that Jack, coming up close to the monster, struck a blow with his sword at his head, but, missing his aim, he cut off the nose instead. At this, the giant roared like claps of thunder, and began to lay about him with his iron club like one stark mad.

But Jack, running behind, drove his sword up to the hilt in the giant's back, so that he fell down dead. This done, Jack cut off the giant's head, and sent it to King Arthur, by a wagoner he hired for that purpose.

Jack now resolved to enter the giant's cave in search of his treasure, and, passing along through a great many windings and turnings, he came at length to a large room paved with freestone, at the upper end of which was a boiling caldron, and on the right hand a large table, at which the giant used to dine. Then he came to a window, barred with iron, through which he looked and beheld a vast number of miserable captives, who, seeing him, cried out: "Alas! young man, art thou come to be one amongst us in this miserable den?"

"Ay," quoth Jack, "but pray tell me what is the meaning of your captivity?"

"We are kept here," said one, "till such time as the giants have a wish to feast, and then the fattest among us is slaughtered! And many are the times they have dined upon men!"

"Say you so," quoth Jack, and straightway unlocked the gate

In Search of Treasure

and let them free, who all rejoiced like condemned men at sight of a pardon. Then searching the giant's coffers, he shared the gold and silver equally amongst them and took them to a neighboring castle, where they all feasted and made merry over their deliverance.

But in the midst of all this mirth a messenger brought news that one Thunderdell, a giant with two heads, having heard of the death of his kinsmen, had come from the north to be revenged on Jack, and was within a mile of the castle, the country people flying before him like chaff.

But Jack was not a bit daunted, and said: "Let him come! I have a tool to pick his teeth; and you, ladies and gentlemen, walk out into the garden, and you shall witness this giant Thunderdell's death and destruction."

The castle was situated in the midst of a small island surrounded by a moat thirty feet deep and twenty feet wide, over which lay a drawbridge. So Jack employed men to cut through this bridge on both sides, nearly to the middle; and then, dressing himself in his invisible coat, he marched against the giant with his sword of sharpness.

Although the giant could not see Jack, he smelled his approach, and cried out in these words:

"Fee, fi, fo, fum!
I smell the blood of an Englishman!
Be he alive or be he dead,
I'll grind his bones to make my bread!"

“I Smell the Blood of an Englishman!”

"Say'st thou so," said Jack; "then thou art a monstrous miller indeed."

The giant cried out again: "Art thou that villain who killed my kinsmen? Then I will tear thee with my teeth, and grind thy bones to powder."

"You'll have to catch me first," quoth Jack, and throwing off his invisible coat, so that the giant might see him, and putting on his shoes of swiftness, he ran from the giant, who followed like a walking castle, so that the very foundations of the earth seemed to shake at every step.

Jack led him a long dance, in order that the gentlemen and ladies might see; and at last to end the matter, ran lightly over the drawbridge, the giant, in full speed, pursuing him with his club. Then, coming to the middle of the bridge, the giant's great weight broke it down, and he tumbled headlong into the water, where he rolled and wallowed like a whale.

Jack, standing by the moat, laughed at him all the while; but though the giant foamed to hear him scoff, and plunged from place to place in the moat, yet he could not get out to be revenged. Jack at length got a cart-rope and cast it over the two heads of the giant, and drew him ashore by a team of horses, and then cut off both his heads with his sword of sharpness, and sent them to King Arthur.

After some time spent in mirth and pastime, Jack, taking leave of the knights and ladies, set out for new adventures. Through many woods he passed, and came at length to the foot of a high

"You'll Have to Catch Me First!"

mountain. Here, late at night, he found a lonesome house, and knocked at the door, which was opened by an aged man with a head as white as snow.

"Father," said Jack, "can you lodge a benighted traveller that has lost his way?"

"Yes," said the old man; "you are right welcome to my poor cottage."

Whereupon Jack entered, and down they sat together, and the old man began to speak as follows:

"Son, I see by your belt you are the great conqueror of giants, and behold, my son, on the top of this mountain is an enchanted castle, kept by a giant named Galligantua, and he by the help of an old conjurer, betrays many knights and ladies into his castle, where by magic art they are transformed into sundry shapes and forms.

"But above all, I grieve for a duke's daughter, whom they fetched from her father's garden, carrying her through the air in a burning chariot drawn by fiery dragons, and when they secured her within the castle, they transformed her into a white hare. And though many knights have tried to break the enchantment, and work her deliverance, yet no one could accomplish it, on account of two dreadful griffins which are placed at the castle gate and which destroy every one who comes near. But you, my son, may pass by them undiscovered, where on the gates of the castle you will find engraven in large letters how the spell may be broken."

An Enchanted Castle

Jack gave the old man his hand, and promised that in the morning he would venture his life to free the lady.

In the morning Jack arose and put on his invisible coat and magic cap and shoes, and prepared himself for the fray. Now, when he had reached the top of the mountain he soon discovered the two fiery griffins, but passed them without fear, because of his invisible coat. When he had got beyond them, he found upon the gates of the castle a golden trumpet hung by a silver chain, under which these lines were engraved:

"Whoever shall this trumpet blow,
Shall soon the giant overthrow,
And break the bad enchantment straight;
So all shall be in happy state."

Jack had no sooner read this but he blew the trumpet, at which the castle trembled to its vast foundations, and the giant and conjurer were in horrid confusion, biting their thumbs and tearing their hair, knowing their wicked reign was at an end.

Then the giant stooping to take up his club, Jack at one blow cut off his head; whereupon the conjurer, mounting up into the air, was carried away in a whirlwind. Then the enchantment was broken, and all the lords and ladies who had so long been transformed into birds and beasts returned to their proper shapes, and the castle vanished away in a cloud of smoke.

This being done, the head of Galligantua was likewise, in the usual manner, conveyed to the court of King Arthur, where, the

Two Fiery Griffins

very next day, Jack followed, with the knights and ladies who had been delivered. Whereupon, as a reward for his good services, the King prevailed upon the duke to bestow his daughter in marriage on honest Jack.

So married they were, and the whole kingdom was filled with joy at the wedding. Furthermore, the King bestowed on Jack a noble castle, with a very beautiful estate, where he and his lady lived in great joy and happiness all the rest of their days.

A Reward for Good Services

The Mighty Merlin

# The · History · of · Tom · Thumb

In the days of the great King Arthur, there lived a mighty magician, called Merlin, the most learned and skillful enchanter the world has ever seen.

This famous magician, who could take any form he pleased, was travelling about as a poor beggar, and being very tired, he stopped at the cottage of a ploughman to rest himself, and asked for some food.

The countryman bade him welcome, and his wife, who was a very good-hearted woman, soon brought him some milk in a wooden bowl, and some coarse brown bread on a platter.

Merlin was much pleased with the kindness of the ploughman and his wife; but he could not help noticing that though everything was neat and comfortable in the cottage, they both seemed to be very unhappy. He therefore asked them why they were so melancholy, and learned that they were miserable because they had no children.

The poor woman said, with tears in her eyes: "I should be the happiest creature in the world if I had a son; although he was no bigger than my thumb, I would be satisfied."

Merlin was so much amused with the idea of a boy no bigger than a thumb, that he determined to grant the poor woman's wish. Accordingly, in a short time after, the ploughman's wife had a son, who, wonderful to relate! was not a bit bigger than his mother's thumb.

The Queen of the fairies, wishing to see the little fellow, came in at the window while the mother was sitting up in the bed admiring him. The Queen kissed the child, and, giving him the name of Tom Thumb, sent for some of the fairies, who dressed her little godson according to her orders;

"An oak-leaf hat he had for his crown;
His shirt of web by spiders spun;
With jacket wove of thistle's down;
His trousers were of feathers done.
His stockings, of apple-rind, they tie
With eyelash from his mother's eye:
His shoes were made of mouse's skin,
Tann'd with the downy hair within."

Tom never grew any larger than a thumb of only ordinary size; but as he got older he became very cunning and full of tricks. When he was old enough to play with the boys, and had lost all his own cherry stones, he used to creep into the bags of his playfellows, fill his pockets, and, getting out without their noticing him,

A Boy no Bigger than a Thumb!

would again join in the game.

One day, however, as he was coming out of a bag of cherry-stones, where he had been stealing as usual, the boy to whom it belonged chanced to see him. "Ah, ah! my little Tommy," said the boy, "so I have caught you stealing my cherry-stones at last, and you shall be rewarded for your thievish tricks." On saying this, he drew the string tight round Tom's neck, and gave the bag such a hearty shake, that poor little Tom's legs, thighs, and body were sadly bruised. He roared out with pain, and begged to be let out, promising never to steal again.

A short time afterwards his mother was making a batter pudding, and Tom, being very anxious to see how it was made, climbed up to the edge of the bowl; but his foot slipped, and he plumped over head and ears into the batter, without his mother noticing him, who stirred him into the pudding, and put him in the pot to boil.

The batter filled Tom's mouth, and prevented him from crying; but, on feeling the hot water, he kicked and struggled so much in the pot that his mother thought that the pudding was bewitched, and, pulling it out of the pot, she threw it outside the door. A poor tinker, who was passing by, lifted up the pudding, and, putting it into his bag, he then walked off.

As Tom had now got his mouth cleared of the batter, he then began to cry aloud, which so frightened the tinker that he flung down the pudding and ran away. The pudding being broke to

Into the Batter!

pieces by the fall, Tom crept out covered all over with the batter, and walked home. His mother, who was very sorry to see her darling in such a woeful state, put him into a teacup, and soon washed off the batter; after which she kissed him, and laid him in bed.

Soon after the adventure of the pudding, Tom's mother went to milk her cow in the meadow, and she took him along with her. As the wind was very high, for fear of his being blown away she tied him to a thistle with a piece of fine thread. The cow soon observed Tom's oak-leaf hat, and liking the appearance of it, took poor Tom and the thistle at one mouthful. While the cow was chewing the thistle Tom was afraid of her great teeth, which threatened to crush him in pieces, and he roared out as loud as he could: "Mother, mother!"

"Where are you, Tommy, my dear Tommy?" asked his mother.

"Here, mother," replied he, "in the red cow's mouth."

His mother began to cry and wring her hands; but the cow, surprised at the odd noise in her throat, opened her mouth and let Tom drop out. Fortunately his mother caught him in her apron as he was falling to the ground, or he would have been dreadfully hurt. She then ran home with him.

Tom's father made him a whip out of a barley straw to drive the cattle with, and having one day gone into the fields, he slipped and rolled into the furrow. A raven, which was flying over, picked him up, and flew with him over the sea, and there dropped him.

A large fish swallowed Tom the moment he fell into the sea,

Liking the Look of It

which was soon after caught, and bought for the table of King Arthur. When they opened the fish in order to cook it, every one was astonished at finding such a little boy, and Tom was quite delighted at being free again.

They carried him to the King, who made Tom his dwarf, and he soon grew a great favorite at court; for by his tricks and gambols he not only amused the King and Queen, but also all the Knights of the Round Table.

It is said that when the King rode out on horseback, he often took Tom along with him, and if a shower came on, he used to creep into his majesty's waistcoat-pocket, where he slept till the rain was over.

King Arthur one day asked Tom about his parents, wishing to know if they were as small as he was, and whether they were well off. Tom told the King that his father and mother were as tall as anybody about the court, but in rather poor circumstances. On hearing this, the King carried Tom to his treasury, the place where he kept all his money, and told him to take as much money as he could carry home to his parents, which made the poor little fellow caper with joy. Tom went immediately to procure a purse, which was made of a water-bubble, and then returned to the treasury, where he received a silver threepenny piece to put into it.

Our little hero had some difficulty in lifting the burden upon his back; but he at last succeeded in getting it placed to his mind, and set forward on his journey. However, without meeting with

Astonished at Finding Tom

any accident, and after resting himself more than a hundred times by the way, in two days and two nights he reached his father's house in safety.

Tom had travelled forty-eight hours with a huge silver piece on his back, and was almost tired to death, when his mother ran out to meet him, and carried him into the house. But he soon returned to King Arthur's court.

As Tom's clothes had suffered much in the batter pudding, and the inside of the fish, his majesty ordered him a new suit of clothes, and to be mounted as a knight on a mouse.

Of Butterfly's wings his shirt was made,
His boots of chicken's hide;
And by a nimble fairy blade,
Well learned in the tailoring trade,
His clothing was supplied.
A needle dangled by his side;
A dapper mouse he used to ride,
Thus strutted Tom in stately pride!

It was certainly very diverting to see Tom in this dress and mounted on the mouse, as he rode out a-hunting with the King and nobility, who were all ready to expire with laughter at Tom and his fine prancing charger.

The King was so charmed with his appearance that he ordered a little chair to be made, in order that Tom might sit upon his table, and also a palace of gold, a span high, with a door an inch wide, to

Tom at Court

live in. He also gave him a coach, drawn by six small mice.

The Queen was so enraged at the honors conferred on Sir Thomas that she resolved to ruin him, and told the King that the little knight had been saucy to her.

The King sent for Tom in great haste, but being fully aware of the danger of royal anger, Tom crept into an empty snail-shell, where he lay for a long time until he was almost starved with hunger; but at last he ventured to peep out, and seeing a fine large butterfly on the ground, near the place of his concealment, he got close to it and jumping astride on it, was carried up into the air.

The butterfly flew with him from tree to tree and from field to field, and at last returned to the court, where the King and nobility all strove to catch him; but at last poor Tom fell from his seat into a watering-pot, in which he was almost drowned.

When the Queen saw him she was in a rage, and said he should be beheaded; and he was again put into a mouse trap until the time of his execution.

However a cat, observing something alive in the trap, patted it about till the wires broke, and set Thomas at liberty.

The King received Tom again into favor, which he did not live to enjoy, for a large spider one day attacked him; and although he drew his sword and fought well, the spider's poisonous breath at last overcame him.

He fell dead on the ground where he stood,
And the spider spilt every drop of his blood.

Jumping Astride

The End of Tom Thumb

King Arthur and his whole court were so sorry at the loss of their little favorite that they went into mourning and raised a fine white marble monument over his grave with the following epitaph:

Here lies Tom Thumb, King Arthur's knight,
Who died by a spider's cruel bite.
He was well known in Arthur's court,
Where he afforded gallant sport;
He rode at tilt and tournament,
And on a mouse a-hunting went.
Alive he filled the court with mirth;
His death to sorrow soon gave birth.
Wipe, wipe your eyes, and shake your head
And cry, — Alas! Tom Thumb is dead!

Here Sat a Duck on Her Nest.

# The · Ugly · Duckling

by Hans Christian Andersen

It was a glorious day in the country. It was summer, the cornfields were yellow, the oats green, the hay had been put up in the green meadows, and the stork went about on his long red legs and chattered in Egyptian, the language he had learned from his mother. All around the fields and meadows were great forests, and in the midst of the forests were deep lakes.

In the midst of the sunshine lay an old farm, with deep canals, and from the wall down to the water grew great hedges, so high that little children could stand upright under the tallest of them. It was just as wild there as in the deepest wood.

Here sat a duck on her nest to hatch her ducklings. She was already tired even before the little ones came; and she seldom had visitors. The other ducks preferred to swim about rather than sit down under a hedge to gossip with her.

At last one eggshell after another burst open. "Peep! Peep!"

they cried, and soon in all the eggs there were little creatures that stuck out their heads.

"Quack! quack!" they said, and they all came quacking out as fast as they could, looking all round them at the green leaves. Their mother let them look as much as they chose, for green is good for the eye.

"How big the world is!" said all the ducklings, for they certainly had much more room now than when they were in the eggs.

"D'ye think this is all the world?" said the mother. "That stretch goes far across the other side of the garden, into the parson's field; I have never even been there yet. I hope you are all here," and she stood up. "No, not all. The largest egg still lies there. How long is that to last? I am really tired." And she sat down again.

"Well, how goes it?" asked an old duck who had come to pay her a visit.

"It's taking a long time with this one egg," said the mother duck. "It will not burst. Now, only look at the others. Are they not the prettiest little ducks one could possibly see? They are all like their father; the rogue never comes to see me."

"Let me see the egg which will not burst," said the old visitor. "You may be sure it is a turkey's egg. I was once cheated in that way, and had much trouble with the young ones, for they are afraid of the water. I could not get them to venture in. I quacked and I clacked, but it was no use. Let me see the egg. Yes, that's a turkey's egg. Let it lie there and go teach the other children to swim."

"The Largest Egg Still Lies There."

"I think I will sit on it a little longer," said the duck. "I've sat so long now that I can sit a few days more."

"Just as you please," said the old duck; and away she went.

At last the great egg burst. "Peep! peep!" said the little one, and crept forth. It was very large and ugly. The duck looked at it.

"It's a very large duckling," said she, "none of the others look like that: can it really be a turkey chick? Well, we shall soon find out. It must go into the water, even if I have to thrust it in myself."

The next day it was bright, beautiful weather; the sun shone on all the green trees. The mother duck went down to the canal with all her family. Splash! She jumped into the water. "Quack! quack!" she said, and one duckling after another plunged in. The water closed over their heads, but they came up in an instant, and swam; their legs went of themselves, and they were all in the water. The ugly gray duckling swam with them.

"No, it's not a turkey," said the mother, "look how well it can use its legs, and how straight it holds itself. It is my own child! On the whole it's quite pretty, if one looks at it rightly. Quack! quack! Come with me, and I'll lead you out into the great world, and present you in the duck yard; but keep close to me, so that no one may tread on you; and take care of the cats!"

And so they came into the duck yard. There was a terrible riot going on in there, for two families were quarreling about an eel's head, and the cat got it after all.

"See, that's how it goes in the world!" said the mother duck;

Can It Be a Turkey Chick?

and she whetted her beak, for she too wanted the eel's head. "Only use your legs," she said. "See that you all bustle about, and bow your heads before the old duck yonder. She's the grandest of all here; she's of royal blood — that's why she's so fat; and d'ye see? She has a red rag round her leg; that's something particularly fine, and the greatest distinction a duck can enjoy; it signifies that one does not want to lose her, and that she's to be known by animals and by men, too. Shake yourselves, don't turn in your toes; a well-brought-up duck turns its toes quite out, just like — so! Now bend your necks and say 'Quack!' "

And they did so: but the other ducks round about looked at them, and said quite boldly — "Look there! Now we're to have these hanging on, as if there were not enough of us already! And how that duckling yonder looks; we won't stand that!" And one duck flew up at it, and bit it in the neck.

"Let it alone," said the mother; "it does no harm to anyone."

"Yes, but it's too large and peculiar," said the duck who had bitten it; "and therefore it must be put down."

"Those are pretty children that the mother has there," said the old duck with the rag round her leg. "They're all pretty but that one; that was rather unlucky. I wish she could bear it over again."

"That cannot be done, my lady," replied the mother duck. "It is not pretty, but it has a really good disposition, and swims as well as any other; yes, I may even say, it swims better. I think it will

"Let It Alone, It Does No Harm."

grow up pretty, and become smaller in time; it has lain too long in the egg, and therefore is not properly shaped." And then she pinched it in the neck, and smoothed its feathers. "Moreover it is a drake," she said. "I think he will be very strong: he makes his way already."

"The other ducklings are graceful enough," said the old duck. "Make yourself at home, and if you find an eel's head, you may bring it to me."

And now they were at home. But the poor duckling which had crept last out of the egg, and looked so ugly, was bitten and pushed and jeered, as much by the ducks as by the chickens.

"It is too big!" they all said. And the turkey-cock, who had been born with spurs, and therefore thought himself an emperor, blew himself up like a ship in full sail, and bore straight down upon it; then he gobbled and grew quite red in the face. The poor duckling did not know where it should stand or walk; it was quite melancholy because it looked ugly, and was the butt of the whole duck yard.

So it went on the first day, and afterwards it became worse and worse. The poor duckling was hunted about by everyone; even its brothers and sisters were quite angry with it, and said, "If the cat would only catch you, you ugly creature!" And the mother said, "If you were only far away!" and the ducks bit it, and the chickens beat it, and the girl who had to feed the poultry kicked at it with her foot.

It Became Worse and Worse.

Then it ran and flew over the fence, and the little birds in the bushes flew up in fear.

"That is because I am so ugly!" thought the duckling. It shut its eyes, but flew on farther; and so it came out into the great moor, where the wild ducks lived. Here it lay the whole night long, and it was weary and downcast.

Toward morning the wild ducks flew up, and looked at their new companion.

"What sort of a one are you?" they asked, and the duckling turned in every direction, and bowed as well as it could. "You are remarkably ugly!" said the wild ducks. "But that is nothing to us."

Poor thing! It only hoped to obtain leave to lie among the reeds and drink some of the swamp water.

Thus it lay two whole days; then there came two wild ganders. It was not long since each had crept out of an egg, and that's why they were so saucy.

"Listen, comrade," said one of them. "You're so ugly that I like you. Will you go with us, and become a bird of passage? Near here, in another moor, there are a few sweet lovely wild geese, all unmarried, and all able to say, 'Rap.' You've a chance of making your fortune, ugly as you are."

"Piff! paff!" resounded through the air; and the two ganders fell down dead in the swamp, and the water became blood red. "Piff! paff!" it sounded again, and the whole flock of wild geese rose up from the reeds. A great hunt was going on. The sportsmen

The Wild Ducks Flew Up.

were all round the moor, some even sitting in the trees. Blue smoke rose up among the trees, and wafted across the water; the hunting dogs came into the swamp, and bent the rushes and reeds.

That frightened the poor duckling! It turned its head under its wing; but at that moment a frightful dog stood close by. His tongue hung out of his mouth, and his eyes gleamed; he thrust out his nose close to the duckling, showed his sharp teeth and away he went, without touching it.

"Oh, thank heaven!" said the duckling. "I am so ugly even a dog does not like me!"

It lay quiet, while gun after gun fired. Late in the day, all was still; the poor duckling did not dare rise, but waited several hours before it hastened out of the moor as fast as it could. It ran on and on, but there was such a raging storm that it was difficult to get anywhere.

The duck came to a miserable little hut, so dilapidated that it did not itself know on which side to fall; that's why it stood. The storm raged around the duckling so that the poor creature had to sit down, to stand it; the wind blew worse and worse. The duckling saw that the hinges of the door had given way, and the door hung so that the duckling could slip through the crack and into the room.

Here lived a woman, with cat and hen. And the cat, whom she called Flixx, could arch his back and purr, and give out sparks; but for that one had to stroke his fur the wrong way. The hen had

Frightful Dog Stood Close By.

short legs, and she was called Little Biddie; she laid good eggs, and the woman loved her well.

In the morning the strange duckling was spotted at once, causing the cat to purr and the hen to cluck.

"What's this?" said the woman. She thought the duckling was a fine catch. "This one is a prize! I hope to have duck's eggs."

The duckling was on trial for three weeks; but no eggs came. The cat was master of the house, and the hen the lady, and they always said, "We and the world!" for they thought they were half the world, and the better half by far. The duckling might have a different opinion, but the hen would not permit that.

"Can you lay eggs?" she asked.

"No."

"Then hold your tongue!"

And the cat said, "Can you curve your back, or give out sparks?"

"No," said the duckling, who sat sadly in a corner.

But when the fresh air and warm sunshine streamed in, it was seized with a strong longing to swim, and could not help telling the hen about it.

"What can you be thinking?" cried the hen. "You have nothing to do, that's why you dream of things. Lay eggs, purr, or do something useful and it will pass."

"But to swim on the water," said the duckling wistfully, "to let it flow over one's head, and to dive to the bottom."

"I fancy you must have gone crazy," said the hen.

The Cat Was Master; the Hen the Lady.

"You don't understand me," said the duckling. "I think I will go out into the wide world."

"Yes, do," replied the hen.

So the duckling went. It swam and dove, but it was snubbed by everyone because of its looks.

Soon it was autumn. The leaves turned gold and red and brown; the wind caught them about, and the air was very cold. The clouds hung heavy with hail and snow. The poor little duckling watched one evening as there came a flock of great, handsome birds, white, with long, flexible necks: swans.

They spread their great wings, and flew away from that cold region to warmer lands, to fair open lakes. They mounted high and the ugly duckling felt strange as it watched them. It turned in the water like a wheel, stretched its neck toward them, and uttered strange cries, loud and longing.

Then it could see them no longer and it dived down and when it came up again, it was quite sad. It knew not those birds, nor whither they flew; but it loved them more than it had ever thought to have loved any one.

The winter grew very cold. The duckling would swim about in the water, but every night the hole in which it swam became smaller. It froze so hard that the icy covering crackled, and the duckling used its legs continually to keep the hole from entirely freezing. At last it was too exhausted, and lay quite still, and froze into the ice.

There Came a Flock of Great, Handsome Birds.

The next morning a peasant passing by saw what had happened. He broke the ice and carried the duckling home. Then it came to life again. The children wanted to play, but the duckling thought they wanted to hurt it, and in its terror the poor creature slipped out into the snow where it lay exhausted.

It lay among the reeds until the sun began to shine and it was beautiful spring once again.

All at once the duckling could flap its wings, and more strongly than before, and before it knew how it happened, it found itself in a great garden, where the willows bent their long green branches down to the stream.

From the thicket there came three white swans; they rustled their wings, and swam on the water. The duckling remembered the splendid creatures, and felt a peculiar sadness.

"I will fly to them and they will beat me, because I dare to come near them. Better am I to be killed by *them* than by ducks, and fowls, and pushed about by the girl who cares for the poultry yard, and to suffer in winter!"

It flew out into the water, and swam toward the beautiful swans who looked at it, and came sailing with outspread wings. "Kill me!" said the poor creature, and bent its head down upon the water, expecting its death.

But what it saw in the clear water was its own image; and no longer was it a clumsy bird, ugly and hateful to look at, but a swan!

The Duckling Could Flap Its Wings Again.

It felt quite glad now as the great swans swam around it, and stroked it.

In the garden little children threw bread and corn seeds into the water, and cried, "There is a new one!" and they shouted joyously, "Yes, a new one has arrived!" They clapped their hands and ran to their parents; now bread and cake were thrown into the water: "The new one is the most beautiful of all! So young and handsome!" they said, and the old swans bowed to him.

He felt quite ashamed, his head under his wings, and did not know what to do, he was so happy. He had been persecuted; now he heard them saying he was most beautiful of all the birds. Even the willow bent its branches into the water before him, and the sun shone warm and mild. Then he lifted his slender neck, and cried rejoicingly from the depths of his heart, "I never dreamed of so much happiness when I was the ugly duckling!"

"The Most Beautiful of All!"

A Fiery Dragon Came Flying Through the Air.

# The · Dragon · and · his · Grandmother

There was once a great war, and the King had a great many soldiers, but he gave them so little pay that they could not live on it. Then three of them took counsel together and determined to desert.

One of them said to the others, "If we are caught, we shall be hanged on the gallows; how shall we get out of it?"

Another said, "Do you see that large cornfield there? If we were to hide ourselves in that, no one could find us. The army cannot come into it, and tomorrow it is to march on."

They crept into the corn, but the army did not march on and remained encamped close around them. They sat for two days and two nights in the corn, and grew so hungry that they nearly died; but if they were to venture out, it was certain death.

They said at last, "What use was it our deserting? We must perish here miserably."

Whilst they were speaking a fiery Dragon came flying through the air. It hovered near them, and asked why they were hidden there.

They answered, "We are three soldiers, and have deserted because our pay was so small. Now if we remain here we shall die of hunger, and if we move out we shall be strung up on the gallows."

"If you will serve me for seven years," said the Dragon, "I will lead you through the midst of the army so that no one shall catch you."

"We have no choice, and must take your offer," said they.

Then the dragon seized them in his claws, took them through the air over the army, and set them down on the earth a long way from it.

He gave them a little whip, saying, "Whip and slash with this, and as much money as you want will jump up before you. You can then live as great lords, keep horses, and drive about in carriages. But after seven years you are mine." Then he put a book before them, which he made all three of them sign. "I will then give you a riddle," he said; "if you guess it, you shall be free and out of my power." The dragon then flew away, and they journeyed on with their little whip.

They had as much money as they wanted, wore grand clothes, and made their way into the world. Wherever they went they lived in merrymaking and splendor, drove about with horses and carriages, ate and drank, but did nothing really wrong.

The time passed quickly away, and when the seven years were nearly ended, two of them grew terribly anxious and frightened, but the third made light of it, saying, "Don't be afraid, brothers, I wasn't born yesterday; I will guess the riddle."

The Dragon Seized Them in His Claws.

They went into a field, sat down, and the two pulled long faces. An old woman passed by, and asked them why they were so sad. "Alas! What have you to do with it? You cannot help us."

"Who knows?" she answered. "Only confide your trouble in me."

They told her that they had become the servants of the Dragon for seven long years, and how he had given them money as plentiful as blackberries; but as they had signed their names they were his, unless when the seven years had passed they could guess a riddle.

The old woman said, "If you would help yourselves, one of you must go into the wood, and there he will come upon a tumble-down building of rocks which looks like a little house. He must go in, and there he will find help."

The two melancholy ones thought, "That won't save us!" and they remained where they were. But the third merry one jumped up and went into the wood till he found the rock hut.

In the hut sat a very old woman, who was the Dragon's grandmother. She asked him how he came, and what was his business there. He told her all that happened, and because she was pleased with him she took compassion on him, and said she would help him.

She lifted up a large stone which lay over the cellar, saying, "Hide yourself there; you can hear all that is spoken in this room. Only sit still and don't stir. When the Dragon comes, I will ask

In the Hut Sat a Very Old Woman.

him what the riddle is, for he tells me everything; then listen carefully what he answers."

At midnight the Dragon flew in, and asked for his supper. His grandmother laid the table, and brought out food and drink till he was satisfied, and they ate and drank together. Then in the course of the conversation she asked him what he had done in the day, and how many souls he had conquered.

"I haven't had much luck today," he said, "but I have a tight hold on three soldiers."

"Indeed! Three soldiers!" said she. "Who cannot escape you?"

"They are mine," answered the Dragon scornfully, "for I shall only give them one riddle which they will never be able to guess."

"What sort of a riddle is it?" she asked.

"I will tell you this. In the sea lies a dead sea-cat — that shall be their roast meat; and the rib of a whale — that shall be their silver spoon; and the hollow foot of a dead horse — that shall be their wineglass."

When the Dragon had gone to bed, his old grandmother pulled up the stone and let out the soldier.

"Did you pay attention to everything?"

"Yes," he replied, "I know it all, and can help myself splendidly."

Then he went out through the window secretly, and in all haste back to his comrades. He told them how the Dragon had been outwitted by his grandmother, and how he had heard from his own lips the answer to the riddle.

The Dragon Flew In and Asked for His Supper.

They were all delighted and in high spirits, and took out their whip, and cracked so much money that it came jumping up from the ground. When the seven years had quite gone, the Dragon came with his book, and pointing at the signatures, said to the first soldier, "I will take you underground with me; you shall have a meal there. If you can tell me what you will get for your roast meat, you shall be free, and shall also keep the whip."

Then said the first soldier, "In the sea lies a dead sea-cat; that shall be the roast meat."

The Dragon was much annoyed, and hemmed and hawed a good deal, and asked the second, "But what shall be your spoon?"

"The rib of a whale shall be our silver spoon."

The Dragon made a face, and growled again three times, "Hum, hum, hum," and said to the third, "Do you know what your wineglass shall be?"

"An old horse's hoof shall be our wineglass."

Then the Dragon flew away with a loud shriek, and had no more power over them. But the three soldiers took the little whip, whipped as much money as they wanted, and lived happily to their lives' end.

The Money Came Jumping Up from the Ground.

“Spin All Night Till Early Dawn.”

# RUMPELSTILTSKIN

There was once upon a time a poor miller who had a very beautiful daughter. Now it happened one day that he had an audience with the King, and in order to appear a person of some importance he told him that he had a daughter who could spin straw into gold.

"Now that's a talent worth having," said the King to the miller; "if your daughter is as clever as you say, bring her to my palace tomorrow, and I'll put her to the test."

When the girl was brought to him he led her into a room full of straw, gave her a spinning-wheel and spindle, and said: "Now set to work and spin all night till early dawn, and if by that time you haven't spun the straw into gold you shall die." Then he closed the door behind him and left her alone inside.

So the poor miller's daughter sat down, and didn't know what in the world she was to do. She hadn't the least idea of how to spin straw into gold, and became at last so miserable that she began to cry. Suddenly the door opened, and in stepped a tiny little man and said: "Good-evening, Miss Miller-maid; why are you crying so bitterly?"

"Oh!" answered the girl, "I have to spin straw into gold, and haven't a notion how it's done."

"What will you give me if I spin it for you?" asked the manikin.

"My necklace," replied the girl.

The little man took the necklace, sat himself down at the wheel, and whir, whir, whir, the wheel went round three times, and the bobbin was full. Then he put on another, and whir, whir, whir, the wheel went round three times, and the second too was full; and so it went on till the morning, when all the straw was spun away, and all the bobbins were full of gold.

As soon as the sun rose the King came, and when he perceived the gold he was astonished and delighted, but his heart only yearned more than ever after the precious metal.

He had the miller's daughter put into another room full of straw, much bigger than the first, and bade her, if she valued her life, spin it all into gold before the following morning.

The girl didn't know what to do, and began to cry; then the door opened as before, and the tiny little man appeared and said: "What'll you give me if I spin the straw into gold for you?"

"The ring from my finger," answered the girl.

The manikin took the ring, and whir! round went the spinning-wheel again, and when morning broke he had spun all the

"What Will You Give Me?"

straw into glittering gold.

The King was pleased beyond measure at the sight, but his greed for gold was still not satisfied, and he had the miller's daughter brought into a yet bigger room full of straw, and said: "You must spin all this away in the night; but if you succeed this time you shall become my wife."

"She's only a miller's daughter, it's true," he thought; "but I could not find a richer wife if I were to search the whole world over."

When the girl was alone the little man appeared for the third time, and said: "What'll you give me if I spin the straw for you once again?"

"I've nothing more to give," answered the girl.

"Then promise me when you are Queen to give me your first child."

"Who knows what may happen before that?" thought the miller's daughter; and besides, she saw no other way out of it, so she promised the manikin what he demanded, and he set to work once more and spun the straw into gold.

When the King came in the morning, and found everything as he had desired, he straightway made her his wife, and the miller's daughter became a Queen.

When a year had passed a beautiful son was born to her, and she thought no more of the little man, till all of a sudden one day he stepped into her room and said: "Now give me what you promised."

"When You Are a Queen . . ."

The Queen was in a great state, and offered the little man all the riches in her kingdom if he would only leave her the child.

But the manikin said: "No, a living creature is dearer to me than all the treasures in the world."

Then the Queen began to cry and sob so bitterly that the little man was sorry for her, and said: "I'll give you three days to guess my name, and if you find it out in that time you may keep your child."

Then the Queen pondered the whole night over all the names she had ever heard, and sent a messenger to scour the land, and to pick up far and near any names he should come across. When the little man arrived on the following day she began with Kasper, Melchior, Belshazzar, and all the other names she knew, in a string, but at each one the manikin called out: "That's not my name."

The next day she sent to inquire the names of all the people in the neighborhood, and had a long list of the most uncommon and extraordinary ones for the little man when he made his appearance.

"Is your name, perhaps, Sheepshanks, Cruickshanks, Spindleshanks?"

But he always replied: "That's not my name."

On the third day the messenger returned and announced: "I have not been able to find any new names, but as I came upon a high hill round the corner of the wood, where the foxes and hares bid each other good night, I saw a little house, and in front of the

A Messenger to Scour the Land

house burned a fire, and round the fire sprang the most grotesque little man, hopping on one leg and crying:

'Tomorrow I brew, today I bake,
And then the child away I'll take;
For little deems my royal dame
That Rumpelstiltskin is my name!' "

You may imagine the Queen's delight at hearing the name, and when the little man stepped in shortly afterwards and asked: "Now, my lady Queen, what's my name?" she asked first: "Is your name Conrad?"

"No."

"Is your name Harry?"

"No."

"Is your name, perhaps, Rumpelstiltskin?"

"Some demon has told you that, some demon has told you that!" screamed the little man, and in his rage drove his right foot so far into the ground that it sank in up to his waist; then in a passion he seized the left foot with both hands and tore himself apart.

The King, the Queen, and the little Prince lived happily ever after.

"Some Demon Has Told You That!"

Pinkel Made Himself Useful.

# Pinkel · the · Thief

Long, long ago there lived a widow who had three sons. The two eldest were grown up, and though they were known to be idle fellows, some of the neighbors had given them work to do on account of the respect in which their mother was held. But at the time this story begins they had both been so careless and idle that their masters declared they would keep them no longer.

So home they went to their mother and youngest brother, of whom they thought little, because he made himself useful about the house, and looked after the hens, and milked the cow. "Pinkel," they called him. And by-and-by "Pinkel" became his name throughout the village.

The two young men thought it was much nicer to live at home and be idle than to be obliged to do a quantity of disagreeable things they did not like; idle they would have stayed till the end of their lives had not the widow lost patience with them and said that since they would not look for work at home they must seek it elsewhere, for she would not have them under her roof any longer.

But she repented bitterly of her words when Pinkel told her that he too was old enough to go out into the world, and that when he had made a fortune he would send for his mother to keep house for him.

The widow wept many tears at parting from her youngest son, but as she saw that his heart was set upon going with his brothers, she did not try to keep him. So the young men started off one morning in high spirits, never doubting that work such as they might be willing to do would be had for the asking, as soon as their little store of money was spent.

But a very few days of wandering opened their eyes. Nobody seemed to want them, or, if they did, the young men declared that they were not able to undertake all that the farmers or millers or woodcutters required of them.

The youngest brother, Pinkel, who was wiser, would gladly have done some of the work that the others refused, but he was small and slight, and no one thought of offering him any. Therefore they went from one place to another, living only on the fruit and nuts they could find in the woods, and getting hungrier every day.

One night, after they had been walking for many hours and were very tired, they came to a large lake with an island in the middle of it. From the island streamed a strong light, by which they

The Young Men Started Off One Morning.

could see everything almost as clear as if the sun had been shining, and they perceived that, lying half hidden in the rushes, was a boat.

"Let us take it and row over to the island, where there must be a house," said the eldest brother; "and perhaps they will give us food and shelter." And they all got in and rowed across in the direction of the light.

As they drew near the island they saw that it came from a golden lantern hanging over the door of a hut, while sweet tinkling music proceeded from some bells attached to the golden horns of a goat which was feeding near the cottage.

The young men's hearts rejoiced as they thought that at last they would be able to rest their weary limbs, and they entered the hut, but were amazed to see an ugly old woman inside, wrapped in a cloak of gold which lighted up the whole house. They looked at each other uneasily as she came forward with her daughter, as they knew by the cloak that this was a famous witch.

"What do you want?" asked she, at the same time signing to her daughter to stir the large pot on the fire.

"We are tired and hungry, and would fain have shelter for the night," answered the eldest brother.

"You cannot get it here," said the witch, "but you will find both food and shelter in the palace on the other side of the lake. Take your boat and go; but leave this boy with me — I can find work for him, though something tells me he is quick and cunning, and will do me ill."

A Cloak of Gold Lighted Up the House.

"What harm can a poor boy like me do a great witch like you?" answered Pinkel. "Let me go, I pray you, with my brothers. I will promise never to hurt you." And at last the witch let him go, and he followed his brothers to the boat.

The way was further than they thought, and it was morning before they reached the palace.

Now, at last, their luck seemed to have turned, for while the two eldest were given places in the King's stables, Pinkel was taken as page to the little Prince. Pinkel was a clever and amusing boy, who saw everything that passed under his eyes, and the King noticed this, and often employed him in his own service, which made his brothers very jealous.

Things went on in this way for some time, and Pinkel every day rose in the royal favor. At length the envy of his brothers became so great that they could bear it no longer, and consulted together how best they might ruin his credit with the King. They did not wish to kill him — though, perhaps, they would not have been sorry if they had heard he was dead — but merely wished to remind him that he was after all only a child, not half so old and wise as they.

Their opportunity soon came. It happened to be the King's custom to visit his stables once a week, so that he might see that his horses were being properly cared for. The next time he entered the stables the two brothers managed to be in the way, and when the King praised the beautiful satin skins of the horses under their

Pinkel Was Page to the Little Prince.

charge, and remarked how different was their condition when his grooms had first come across the lake, the young men at once began to speak of the wonderful light which sprang from the lantern over the hut.

The King, who had a passion for collecting all the rarest things he could find, fell into the trap directly, and inquired where he could get this marvelous lantern.

"Send Pinkel for it, Sire," said they. "It belongs to an old witch, who no doubt came by it in some evil way. But Pinkel has a smooth tongue, and he can get the better of any woman, old or young."

"Then bid him go this very night," cried the King; "and if he brings me the lantern I will make him one of the chief men about my person."

Pinkel was much pleased at the thought of his adventure, and without more ado he borrowed a little boat which lay moored to the shore, and rowed over to the island at once. It was late by the time he arrived, and almost dark, but he knew by the savory smell that reached him that the witch was cooking her supper.

He climbed softly on to the roof, and, peering, watched till the old woman's back was turned, when he quickly drew a handful of salt from his pocket and threw it into the pot. Scarcely had he done this when the witch called her daughter and bade her lift the pot off the fire and put the stew into a dish, as it had been cooking quite long enough and she was hungry.

"Bid Him Go This Very Night."

But no sooner had she tasted it than she put her spoon down, and declared that her daughter must have been meddling with it, and it was impossible to eat anything that was all salt.

"Go down to the spring in the valley, and get some water, that I may prepare a fresh supper," cried she, "for I feel half-starved."

"But, mother," answered the girl, "how can I find the well in this darkness? For you know that the lantern's rays do not reach down there."

"Well, then, take the lantern with you," answered the witch, "for supper I must have, and there is no water that is nearer."

So the girl took her pail in one hand and the golden lantern in the other, and hastened away to the well, followed by Pinkel, who took care to keep out of the way of the rays. When at last she stooped to fill her pail at the well, Pinkel pushed her into it, and snatching up the lantern, hurried back to his boat and rowed off from the shore.

He was already a long distance from the island when the witch, who wondered what had become of her daughter, went to the door to look for her. Close around the hut was thick darkness, but what was that bobbing light that streamed across the water? The witch's heart sank as all at once it flashed upon her what had happened.

"Is that you, Pinkel?" cried she; and the youth answered:

"Yes, dear mother, it is I!"

"Take the Lantern with You."

"And are you not a knave for robbing me?" cried she.

"Truly, dear mother, I am," replied Pinkel, rowing faster than ever, for he was half afraid that the witch might come after him.

But she had no power on the water, and turned angrily into the hut, muttering to herself all the while: "Take care! Take care! A second time you will not escape so easily!"

The sun had not yet risen when Pinkel returned to the palace, and, entering the King's chamber, he held up the lantern so that its rays might fall upon the bed. In an instant the King awoke, and seeing the golden lantern shedding its light upon him, he sprang up, and embraced Pinkel with joy.

"O cunning one," cried he, "what treasure hast thou brought me!" And calling for his attendants he ordered that rooms next to his own should be prepared for Pinkel, and that the youth might enter his presence at any hour. And besides this, he was to have a seat on the council.

It may easily be guessed that all this made the brothers more envious than they were before, and they cast about in their minds afresh how best they might destroy him. At length they remembered the goat with the golden horns and the bells, and they rejoiced; "For," said they, "this time the old woman will be on the watch, and let him be as clever as he likes, the bells on the horns are sure to warn her."

So when, as before, the King came down to the stables and praised the cleverness of their brother, the young men told him of

"You Will Not Escape So Easily!"

that other marvel possessed by the witch, the goat with the golden horns.

From this moment the King never closed his eyes at night for longing after this wonderful creature. He understood something of the danger that there might be in trying to steal it, now that the witch's suspicions were aroused, and he spent hours in making plans for outwitting her. But somehow he never could think of anything that would do, and at last, as the brothers had foreseen, he sent for Pinkel.

"I hear," he said, "that the old witch on the island has a goat with golden horns, from which hang bells that tinkle the sweetest music. That goat I must have! But, tell me, how am I to get it? I would give the third part of my kingdom to anyone who would bring it to me."

"I will fetch it myself," answered Pinkel.

This time it was easier for Pinkel to approach the island unseen, as there was no golden lantern to throw its beams over the water. But, on the other hand, the goat slept inside the hut, and would therefore have to be taken from under the very eyes of the old woman. How was he to do it?

All the way across the lake he thought and thought, till at length a plan came into his head which seemed as if it might do, though he knew it would be very difficult to carry out.

The first thing he did when he reached the shore was to look about for a piece of wood, and when he had found it he hid himself

The Goat with the Golden Horns

close to the hut, till it grew quite dark and near the hour when the witch and her daughter went to bed. Then he crept up and fixed the wood under the door, which opened outwards, in such a manner that the more you tried to shut it the more firmly it stuck.

And this was what happened when the girl went as usual to bolt the door and make all fast for the night:

"What are you doing?" asked the witch, as her daughter kept tugging at the handle.

"There is something the matter with the door; it won't shut," answered she.

"Well, leave it alone; there is nobody to hurt us," said the witch, who was very sleepy; and the girl did as she was bid, and went to bed. Very soon they both were heard snoring, and Pinkel knew that his time was come.

Slipping off his shoes, he stole into the hut on tiptoe, and taking from his pocket some food of which the goat was particularly fond, he laid it under his nose.

Then, while the animal was eating it, he stuffed each golden bell with wool which he had also brought with him, stopping every minute to listen, lest the witch should awaken, and he should find himself changed into some dreadful bird or beast. But the snoring still continued, and he went on with his work as quickly as he could.

When the last bell was done he drew another handful of food out of his pocket, and held it out to the goat, which instantly rose

He Fixed the Wood Under the Door.

to its feet and followed Pinkel, who backed slowly to the door, and directly when he got outside he seized the goat in his arms and ran down to the place where he had moored his boat.

As soon as he had reached the middle of the lake, Pinkel took the wool out of the bells, which began to tinkle loudly. Their sound awoke the witch, who cried out as before:

"Is that you, Pinkel?"

"Yes, dear mother, it is I," said Pinkel.

"Have you stolen my golden goat?" asked she.

"Yes, dear mother, I have," answered Pinkel.

"Are you not a knave, Pinkel?"

"Yes, dear mother, I am," he replied. And the old witch shouted in a rage:

"Ah! Beware how you come hither again, for next time you shall not escape me!"

But Pinkel only laughed and rowed on.

The King was so delighted with the goat that he always kept it by his side, night and day; and, as he had promised, Pinkel was made ruler over the third part of the kingdom. As may be supposed, the brothers were more furious than ever, and grew quite thin with rage.

"How can we get rid of him?" said one to the other. And at length they remembered the golden cloak.

"He will need to be clever if he is to steal that!" they cried with a chuckle. And when next the King came to see his horses,

"Is That You, Pinkel?"

the brothers began to speak of Pinkel and his marvelous cunning, and how he had contrived to steal the lantern and the goat, which nobody else would have been able to do.

"But as he was there, it is a pity he could not have brought away the golden cloak," added they.

"The golden cloak! What is that?" asked the King.

The young men described its beauties in such glowing words that the King declared he should never know a day's happiness till he had wrapped the cloak round his own shoulders.

"And," added he, "the man who brings it to me shall wed my daughter, and shall inherit my throne."

"None can get it save Pinkel," said they; for they did not imagine that the witch, after two warnings, could allow their brother to escape a third time. So Pinkel was sent for, and with a glad heart he set out.

He passed many hours inventing first one plan and then another, till he had a scheme ready which he thought might prove successful.

Thrusting a large bag inside his coat, he pushed off from the shore, taking care this time to reach the island in daylight. Having made his boat fast to a tree, he walked up to the hut, hanging his head, and putting on a face that was both sorrowful and ashamed.

"Is that you, Pinkel?" asked the witch when she saw him, her eyes gleaming savagely.

"Yes, dear mother, it is I," answered Pinkel.

"The Golden Cloak! What Is That?"

"So you have dared, after all you have done, to put yourself in my power!" cried she. "Well, you shan't escape me this time!" And she took down a large knife and began to sharpen it.

"Oh! Dear mother, spare me!" shrieked Pinkel, falling on his knees, and looking wildly about him.

"Spare you, indeed, you thief! Where are my lantern and my goat? No! No! There is only one fate for robbers!" And she brandished the knife in the air so that it glittered in the firelight.

"Then, if I must die," said Pinkel, who by this time was getting really rather frightened, "let me at least choose the manner of my death. I am very hungry, for I have had nothing to eat all day. Put some poison, if you like, into the porridge, but at least let me have a good meal before I die."

"That is not a bad idea," answered the woman; "as long as you do die, it is all one to me." And ladling out a large bowl of porridge, she stirred some poisonous herbs into it, and set about some work that had to be done. Then Pinkel hastily poured all the contents of the bowl into his bag, and made a great noise with his spoon, as if he was scraping up the last morsel.

"Poisoned or not, the porridge is excellent. I have eaten it, every scrap; do give me some more," said Pinkel, turning towards her.

"Well, you have a fine appetite, young man," answered the witch; "however, it is the last time you will ever eat it, so I will give you another bowlful." And rubbing in the poisonous herbs,

She Took Down a Large Knife.

she poured him out half of what remained, and then went to the window to call her cat.

In an instant Pinkel again emptied the porridge into the bag, and the next minute he rolled on the floor, twisting himself about as if in agony, uttering loud groans the while. Suddenly he grew silent and lay still.

"Ah! I thought a second dose of that poison would be too much for you," said the witch, looking at him. "I warned you what would happen if you came back. I wish that all thieves were as dead as you! But why does not my lazy girl bring the wood I sent her for? It will soon be too dark for her to find her way. I suppose I must go and search for her. What a trouble girls are!"

And she went to the door to see if there were any signs of her daughter. But nothing could be seen of her, as heavy rain was falling.

"It is no night for my cloak," she muttered; "it would be covered with mud by the time I got back." So she took it off her shoulders and hung it carefully up in a cupboard in the room. After that she put on her clogs and started to seek her daughter.

Directly after the last sound of the clogs had ceased, Pinkel jumped up and took down the cloak, and rowed off as fast as he could.

He had not gone far when a puff of wind unfolded the cloak, and its brightness shed gleams across the water. The witch, who was just entering the forest, turned round at that moment and saw the golden rays.

Pinkel Jumped Up and Took the Cloak.

She forgot all about her daughter, and ran down to the shore, screaming with rage at being outwitted a third time.

"Is that you, Pinkel?" cried she.

"Yes, dear mother, it is I."

"Have you taken my gold cloak?"

"Yes, dear mother, I have."

"Are you not a great knave?"

"Yes, truly dear mother, I am."

And so indeed he was!

But, all the same, he carried the cloak to the King's palace, and in return he received the hand of the King's daughter in marriage. People said that it was the bride who ought to have worn the cloak at her wedding feast; but the King was so pleased with it that he would not part from it; and to the end of his life was never seen without it.

After his death, Pinkel became King, and let us hope that he gave up his bad and thievish ways, and ruled his subjects well. As for his brothers, he did not punish them, but left them in the stables, where they grumbled all day long.

The King's Daughter in Marriage

They Were Wet Through.

# The · Enchanted · Wreath

Once upon a time there lived near a forest a man and his wife and two girls; one girl was the daughter of the man, and the other the daughter of his wife; and the man's daughter was good and beautiful, but the woman's daughter was cross and ugly. However, her mother did not know that, but thought her the most bewitching maiden that ever was seen.

One day the man called to his daughter and bade her come with him into the forest to cut wood. They worked hard all day, but in spite of the chopping they were very cold, for it rained heavily, and when they returned home, they were wet through.

Then, to his vexation, the man found that he had left his ax behind him, and he knew that if it lay all night in the mud it would become rusty and useless. So he said to his wife: "I have dropped my ax in the forest. Bid your daughter go and fetch it, for mine has worked hard all day and is both wet and weary."

But the wife answered:

"If your daughter is wet already, it is all the more reason that *she* should go and get the ax. Besides, she is a great strong girl, and a little rain will not hurt her, while *my* daughter would be sure to catch a bad cold."

By long experience the man knew there was no good saying any more, and with a sigh he told the poor girl she must return to the forest for the ax.

The walk took some time, for it was very dark, and her shoes often stuck in the mud; but she was brave as well as beautiful and never thought of turning back merely because the path was both difficult and unpleasant. At last, with her dress torn by brambles that she could not see, and her face scratched by the twigs on the trees, she reached the spot where she and her father had been cutting in the morning, and found the ax in the place he had left it.

To her surprise, three little doves were sitting on the handle, all of them looking very sad.

"You poor little things," said the girl, stroking them. "Why do you sit there and get wet? Go and fly home to your nest, it will be much warmer than this; but first eat this bread, which I saved from my dinner, and perhaps you will feel happier. It is my father's ax you are sitting on, and I must take it back as fast as I can, or I shall get a terrible scolding from my stepmother."

She crumbled the bread on the ground, and was pleased to see the doves flutter quite cheerfully towards it. "Good-bye," she said, picking up the ax, and went on her way homewards.

By the time they had finished all the crumbs, the doves felt

Three Little Doves Were Sitting on the Handle.

much better, and were able to fly back to their nest in the top of a tree.

"That is a good girl," said one; "I really was too weak to stretch out a wing before she came. I should like to do something to show how grateful I am."

"Well, let us give her a wreath of flowers that will never fade as long as she wears it," cried another.

"And let the tiniest singing birds in the world sit amongst the flowers," rejoined the third.

"Yes, that will do beautifully," said the first. And when the girl stepped into her cottage a wreath of rosebuds was on her head, and a crowd of little birds were singing unseen.

The father, who was sitting by the fire, thought that, in spite of her muddy clothes, he had never seen his daughter looking so lovely; but the stepmother and the other girl grew wild with envy.

"How absurd to walk about on such a pouring night, dressed up like that," she remarked crossly, and roughly pulled off the wreath as she spoke, to place it on her own daughter. As she did so the roses became withered and brown, and the birds flew out of the window.

"See what a useless thing it is!" cried the stepmother. "And now take your supper and go to bed, for it is near upon midnight."

But though she pretended to despise the wreath, she longed none the less for her daughter to have one like it.

Now it happened that the next evening the father, who had been alone in the forest, came back a second time without his ax.

A Wreath of Rosebuds on Her Head

The stepmother's heart was glad when she saw this, and she said quite mildly:

"Why, you have forgotten your ax again, you careless man! But now *your* daughter shall stay at home, and *mine* shall go and bring it back;" and throwing a cloak over the girl's shoulders, she bade her hasten to the forest.

With a very ill grace the damsel set forth, grumbling to herself as she went; for though she wished for the wreath, she did not at all want the trouble of getting it.

By the time she reached the spot where her stepfather had been cutting the wood, the girl was in a very bad temper indeed, and when she caught sight of the ax, there were the three little doves, with drooping heads and soiled, bedraggled feathers, sitting on the handle.

"You dirty creatures," cried she, "get away at once, or I will throw stones at you." And the doves spread their wings in a fright and flew up to the very tip of a tree, their bodies shaking with anger.

"What shall we do to revenge ourselves on her?" asked the smallest of the doves, "we were never treated like that before."

"Never," said the biggest dove. "We must find some way of paying her back in her own coin!"

"I know," answered the middle dove; "she shall never be able to say anything but 'dirty creatures' to the end of her life."

"Oh, how clever of you! That will do beautifully," exclaimed

"Mine Shall Go and Bring It Back."

the other two. And they flapped their wings and clucked so loud with delight, and made such a noise, that they woke up all the birds in the trees close by.

"What in the world is the matter?" asked the birds sleepily.

"That is *our* secret," said the doves.

Meanwhile the girl had reached home crosser than ever; as soon as her mother heard her lift the latch of the door, she ran out to hear her adventures. "Well, did you get the wreath?" cried she.

"Dirty creatures!" answered her daughter.

"Don't speak to me like that! What ever do you mean?" asked the mother.

"Dirty creatures!" repeated the daughter, and nothing else could she say.

Then the woman saw that something evil had befallen her, and turned in her rage to her stepdaughter.

"*You* are at the bottom of this, I know," she cried; and as the father was out of the way she took a stick and beat the girl till she went to bed sobbing.

If the poor girl's life had been miserable before, it was ten times worse now, for the moment her father's back was turned, the others teased and tormented her from morning till night; and their fury was increased by the sight of the wreath, which the doves had placed again on her head.

Things went on like this for some weeks, when, one day, as the King's son was riding through the forest, he heard some

"Dirty Creatures!"

strange birds singing more sweetly than birds had ever sung before. He tied his horse to a tree, and followed where the sound led him, and, to his surprise, he saw before him a beautiful girl chopping wood, with a wreath of pink rose-buds, out of which the singing came.

Standing in the shelter of a tree, he watched her a long while, and then, hat in hand, he went up and spoke to her. "Fair maiden, who are you, and who gave you that wreath of singing roses?" asked he, for the birds were so tiny that till you looked closely you never saw them.

"I live in a hut on the edge of the forest," she answered, blushing, for she had never spoken to a Prince before. "And as to the wreath, I know not how it came, unless it may be the gift of some doves whom I fed when they were starving."

The Prince was delighted with this answer, which showed the goodness of the girl's heart, and besides he had fallen in love with her beauty, and would not be content till she promised to return with him to the palace, and become his bride.

The old King was disappointed at his son's choice of a wife, as he wished him to marry a neighboring Princess; but as from his birth the Prince had always done exactly as he liked, nothing was said and a splendid wedding feast was got ready.

The day after her marriage the bride sent a messenger bearing handsome presents to her father, and telling him of the good fortune which had befallen her. As may be imagined, the step-

She Had Never Spoken to a Prince Before.

mother and her daughter were so filled with envy that they grew quite ill, and had to take to their beds, and nobody would have been sorry if they had never got up again; but that did not happen.

At length, they began to feel better, for the mother invented a plan by which she could be revenged on the girl who had never done her any harm.

Her plan was this: In the town where she had lived before she was married there was an old witch, who had more skill in magic than any other witch she knew. To this witch she would go and beg her to make her a mask with the face of her stepdaughter, and when she had the mask the rest would be easy.

She told her daughter what she meant to do and although the daughter could only say "dirty creatures" in answer, she nodded and smiled and looked well pleased.

Everything fell out exactly as the woman had hoped. By the aid of her magic mirror, the witch beheld the new Princess walking in her gardens in a dress of green silk, and in a few minutes had produced a mask so like her that very few people could have told the difference.

However, she counseled the woman that when her daughter first wore it — for that, of course, was what she intended her to do — she had better pretend that she had a toothache, and cover her head with a lace veil. The woman thanked her and paid her well, and returned to her hut, carrying the mask under her cloak.

In a few days she heard that a great hunt was planned, and the

By the Aid of Her Magic Mirror

Prince would leave the palace very early in the morning, so that his wife would be alone all day. This was a chance not to be missed, and taking her daughter with her, she went up to the palace, where she had never been before.

The Princess was too happy in her new home to remember all that she had suffered in the old one, and she welcomed them both gladly, and gave them quantities of beautiful things to take back with them.

At last she took them down to the shore to see a pleasure boat which her husband had made for her; and here, the woman seizing her opportunity, stole softly behind the girl and pushed her off the rock on which she was standing, into the deep water, where she instantly sank to the bottom.

She fastened the mask on her daughter, flung over her shoulders the velvet cloak which the Princess had let fall, and finally arranged a lace veil over her head.

"Rest your cheek on your hand, as if you were in pain, when the Prince returns," said the mother; "and be careful not to speak, whatever you do. I will go back to the witch and see if she cannot take off the spell laid on you by those horrible birds. Ah! Why did I not think of it before!"

No sooner had the Prince entered the palace than he hastened to the Princess's apartments, where he found her lying on a sofa apparently in great pain.

"My dearest wife, what is the matter with you?" he cried,

She Pushed Her Off the Rock.

kneeling down beside her, and trying to take her hand; but she snatched it away, and pointing to her cheek murmured something he could not catch.

"What is it? Tell me! Is the pain bad? When did it begin? Shall I send for your ladies to bathe the place?" asked the Prince, pouring out these and a dozen other questions, to which the girl only shook her head.

"But I can't leave you like this," he continued, starting up. "I must summon all the court physicians to apply soothing balms to the sore place." And as he spoke, he sprang to his feet to go in search of them.

This so frightened the pretended wife, who knew that if the physicians once came near her the trick would at once be discovered, that she forgot her mother's counsel not to speak, and forgot even the spell that had been laid upon her, and catching hold of the Prince's tunic, she cried in tones of entreaty: "Dirty creatures!"

The young man stopped, not able to believe his ears, but supposed that pain had made the Princess cross, as pain sometimes does. However, he guessed somehow that she wished to be left alone, so he only said:

"Well, I dare say a little sleep will do you good, if you can manage to get it, and that you will wake up better tomorrow."

Now, that night happened to be very hot and airless, and the Prince, after vainly trying to rest, went to the window. Suddenly he beheld in the moonlight a form, with a wreath of roses on her

Her Trick Would at Once Be Discovered.

head, rise out of the sea below him and step on to the sands, holding out her arms towards the palace.

"That maiden is strangely like my wife," thought he; "I must see her closer." And he hastened down to the water. But when he got there, the Princess, for she indeed it was, had disappeared completely, and he began to wonder if his eyes had deceived him.

The next morning he went to the false bride's room, but her ladies told him she would neither speak nor get up, though she ate everything they set before her. The Prince was sorely perplexed as to what could be the matter with her, for naturally he could not guess that she was expecting her mother to return every moment, and to remove the spell the doves had laid upon her, and meanwhile was afraid to speak lest she should betray herself.

At length he made up his mind to summon all the court physicians. He did not tell her what he was going to do, lest it should make her worse, but he went himself and begged the four learned men attached to the King's person to follow him to the Princess's apartments.

Unfortunately for her, as they entered, the Princess was so enraged at the sight of them that she forgot all about the doves, and shrieked out: "Dirty creatures! Dirty creatures!" which so offended the physicians that they left the room at once, and nothing that the Prince could say would prevail on them to remain.

He tried to persuade his wife to send them a message that she was sorry for her rudeness, but not a word would she say.

He Beheld a Form in the Moonlight.

Late that evening, when he had performed all the tiresome duties which fall to the lot of every Prince, the young man was leaning out of his window, refreshing himself with the cool breezes that blew off the sea. His thoughts went back to the scene of the morning, and he wondered if, after all, he had not made a great mistake in marrying a low-born wife, however beautiful she might be.

How could he have imagined that the quiet, gentle girl who had been so charming a companion to him during the first days of their marriage, could have become in a day the rude, sulky woman, who could not control her temper even to benefit herself?

One thing was clear, if she did not change her conduct very shortly he would have to send her away from court.

He was thinking these thoughts, when his eyes fell on the sea beneath him, and there, as before, was the figure that so closely resembled his wife, standing with her feet in the water, holding out her arms to him.

"Wait for me! Wait for me! Wait for me!" he cried, not even knowing he was speaking. But when he reached the shore there was nothing to be seen but the shadows cast by the moonlight.

A state ceremonial in a city some distance off caused the Prince to ride away at daybreak, and he left without seeing his wife again.

"Perhaps she may have come to her senses by tomorrow," said he to himself; "and, anyhow, if I am going to send her back to her

The Prince Rode Away at Daybreak.

father, it might be better if we did not meet in the meantime." Then he put the matter from his mind, and kept his thought on the duty that lay before him.

It was nearly midnight before he returned to the palace, but, instead of entering, he went down to the shore and hid behind a rock. He had scarcely done so when the girl came out of the sea, and stretched out her arms towards his window. In an instant the Prince had seized her hand, and though she made a frightened struggle to reach the water — for she in her turn had a spell laid upon her — he held her fast.

"You are my own wife, and I shall never let you go!" he said. But the words were hardly out of his mouth when he found that it was a hare that he was holding by the paw. Then the hare changed into a fish, and the fish into a bird, and the bird into a slimy wriggling snake. This time the prince's hand nearly opened of itself, but with a strong effort he kept his fingers shut, and drawing his sword, cut off its head, and the spell was broken. The girl stood before him as he had first seen her, the wreath upon her head and the birds singing for joy.

The very next morning the stepmother arrived at the palace with an ointment that the old witch had given her to place upon her daughter's tongue, which would break the dove's spell, if the rightful bride had really been drowned in the sea; if not, then it would be useless.

The mother assured her that she had seen her stepdaughter

"I Shall Never Let You Go!"

sink, and that there was no fear that she would ever come up again; but, to make all quite safe, the old woman might bewitch the girl; and so she did.

After that the wicked stepmother traveled all through the night to get to the palace as soon as possible, and made her way straight into her daughter's room. "I have got it! I have got it!" she cried triumphantly, and laid the ointment on her daughter's tongue. "*Now* what do you say?" she asked proudly.

"Dirty creatures! Dirty creatures!" answered the daughter; and the mother wrung her hands and wept, as she knew that all her plans had failed.

At this moment the Prince entered with his real wife. "You both deserve death," he said, "and if it were left to me, you should have it. But the Princess has begged me to spare your lives, so you will be put into a ship and carried off to a desert island, where you will stay till you die."

Then the ship was made ready and the wicked woman and her daughter were placed in it, and it sailed away, and no more was heard of them. But the Prince and his wife lived together long and happily, and ruled their people well.

The Prince and His Wife Lived Long and Well.

From the Four Corners of the World

# Princess Mayblossom

Once upon a time there lived a King and Queen whose children had all died, first one and then another, until at last only one little daughter remained, and the Queen was at her wits' end to know where to find a really good nurse who would take care of her, and bring her up.

A herald was sent who blew a trumpet at every street corner, and commanded all the best nurses to appear before the Queen, that she might choose one for the little Princess.

So on the appointed day the whole palace was crowded with nurses, who came from the four corners of the world to offer themselves, until the Queen declared that if she was ever to see the half of them, they must be brought out to her, one by one, as she sat in a shady wood near the palace.

This was accordingly done, and the nurses, after they had made their curtsey to the King and Queen, ranged themselves in a line before her that she might choose. Most of them were fair and fat and charming, but there was one who was ugly, and spoke a strange language which nobody could understand.

The Queen wondered how she dared offer herself, and she was told to go away, as she certainly would not do. Upon which she muttered something and passed on, but hid herself in a hollow tree, from which she could see all that happened.

The Queen, without giving her another thought, chose a pretty rose-faced nurse, but no sooner was her choice made than a snake, which was hidden in the grass, bit that very nurse on her foot, so that she fell down as if dead.

The Queen was very much vexed by this accident, but she soon selected another, who was just stepping forward when an eagle flew by and dropped a large tortoise upon her head, which was cracked in pieces like an egg shell.

At this the Queen was much horrified; nevertheless, she chose a third time, but with no better fortune, for the nurse, moving quickly, ran into the branch of a tree and blinded herself with a thorn.

Then the Queen in dismay cried that there must be some malignant influence at work, and that she would choose no more that day; and she had just risen to return to the palace when she heard peals of malicious laughter behind her, and turning round saw the ugly stranger whom she had dismissed, who was making very merry over the disasters and mocking everyone, but especially the Queen.

This annoyed Her Majesty very much, and she was about to

She Hid Herself in a Hollow Tree.

order that she should be arrested, when the witch — for she was a witch — with two blows from a wand summoned a chariot of fire drawn by winged dragons, and was whirled off through the air uttering threats and cries.

When the King saw this he cried:

"Alas! Now we are ruined indeed, for that was no other than the Fairy Carabosse, who has had a grudge against me ever since I was a boy and put sulphur into her porridge one day for fun."

Then the Queen began to cry.

"If I had only known who it was," she said, "I would have done my best to make friends with her; now I suppose all is lost."

The King was sorry to have frightened her so much, and proposed that they should go and hold a council as to what was best to be done to avert the misfortunes which Carabosse certainly meant to bring upon the little Princess.

So all the counsellors were summoned to the palace, and when they had shut every door and window, and stuffed up every keyhole that they might not be overheard, they talked the affair over, and decided that every fairy for a thousand leagues round should be invited to the christening of the Princess, and that the time of the ceremony should be kept a profound secret, in case the Fairy Carabosse should take it into her head to attend it.

The Queen and her ladies set to work to prepare presents for the fairies who were invited: for each one a blue velvet cloak, a petticoat of apricot satin, a pair of high-heeled shoes, some sharp

Whirled Through the Air

needles, and a pair of golden scissors.

Of all the fairies the Queen knew, only five were able to come on the day appointed, but they began immediately to bestow gifts upon the Princess.

One promised that she should be perfectly beautiful, the second that she should understand anything — no matter what — the first time it was explained to her, the third that she should sing like a nightingale, the fourth that she should succeed in everything she undertook, and the fifth was opening her mouth to speak when a tremendous rumbling was heard in the chimney, and Carabosse, all covered with soot, came rolling down, crying:

"I say that she shall be the unluckiest of the unlucky until she is twenty years old."

Then the Queen and all the fairies began to beg and beseech her to think better of it, and not be so unkind to the poor little Princess, who had never done her any harm. But the ugly old Fairy only grunted and made no answer. So the last Fairy, who had not yet given her gift, tried to mend matters by promising the Princess a long and happy life after the fatal time was over.

At this Carabosse laughed maliciously, and climbed away up the chimney, leaving them all in great consternation, especially the Queen. However, she entertained the fairies splendidly, and gave them beautiful ribbons, of which they are very fond, in addition to the other presents.

When they were going away the oldest Fairy said that they

"Unluckiest of the Unlucky"

were of opinion that it would be best to shut the Princess up in some place, with her waiting-women, so that she might not see anyone else until she was twenty years old.

So the King had a tower built for that purpose. It had no windows, so it was lighted with wax candles, and the only way into it was by an underground passage, which had iron doors only twenty feet apart, and guards were posted everywhere.

The Princess had been named Mayblossom, because she was as fresh and blooming as Spring itself, and she grew up tall and beautiful, and everything she did and said was charming. Every time the King and Queen came to see her they were more delighted with her than before, but though she was weary of the tower, and often begged them to take her away from it, they always refused. The Princess's nurse, who had never left her, sometimes told her about the world outside the tower, and though the Princess had never seen anything for herself, yet she always understood exactly, thanks to the second Fairy's gift.

Often the King said to the Queen:

"We were cleverer than Carabosse after all. Our Mayblossom will be happy in spite of her predictions."

And the Queen laughed until she was tired, at the idea of having outwitted the old Fairy. They had caused the Princess's portrait to be painted and sent to all the neighboring courts, for in four days she would have completed her twentieth year, and it was time to decide whom she should marry.

The King Had a Tower Built.

All the town was rejoicing at the thought of the Princess's approaching freedom, and when the news came that King Merlin was sending his ambassador to ask her in marriage for his son, they were still more delighted.

The nurse, who kept the Princess informed of everything that went forward in the town, did not fail to repeat the news that so closely concerned her, and gave such a description of the splendor in which the ambassador Fanfaronade would enter the town, that the Princess was wild to see the procession for herself.

"What an unhappy creature I am," she cried, "to be shut up in this dismal tower as if I had committed some crime! I have never seen the sun, or the stars, or a horse, or a monkey, or a lion, except in pictures, and though the King and Queen tell me I am to be set free when I am twenty, I believe they only say it to keep me amused when they never mean to let me out at all."

And then she began to cry, and her nurse, and the nurse's daughter, and the cradle-rocker, and the nursery-maid, who all loved her dearly, cried too for company, so that nothing could be heard but sobs and sighs. It was a scene of woe.

When the Princess saw that they all pitied her she made up her mind to have her own way. So she declared that she would starve herself to death if they did not find some means of letting her see Fanfaronade's grand entry into the town.

"If you really love me," she said, "you will manage it, somehow or other, and the King and Queen need never know

The Princess Was Wild to See the Procession.

anything about it."

Then the nurse and all the others cried harder than ever, and said everything they could think of to turn the Princess from her idea. But the more they said the more determined she was, and at last they consented to make a tiny hole in the tower on the side that looked towards the city gates.

After scratching and scraping all day and all night, they presently made a hole through which they could, with great difficulty, push a very slender needle, and out of this the Princess looked at the daylight for the first time. She was so dazzled and delighted by what she saw, that there she stayed, never taking her eyes away from the peep-hole for a single minute, until presently the ambassador's procession appeared in sight.

At the head of it rode Fanfaronade himself upon a white horse, which pranced and caracoled to the sound of the trumpets. Nothing could have been more splendid than the ambassador's attire. His coat was nearly hidden under an embroidery of pearls and diamonds, his boots were solid gold, and from his helmet floated scarlet plumes. At the sight of him the Princess lost her wits entirely, and determined that Fanfaronade and nobody else would she marry.

"It is quite impossible," she said, "that his master should be half as handsome and delightful. I am not ambitious, and having spent all my life in this tedious tower, anything — even a house in the country — will seem a delightful change. I am sure that bread

Fanfaronade Himself Upon a White Horse

and water shared with Fanfaronade will please me far better than roast chicken and sweetmeats with anybody else."

And so she went on talk, talk, talking, until her waiting-women wondered where she got it all from. But when they tried to stop her, and suggested that her high rank made it perfectly impossible that she should do any such thing, she would not listen, and ordered them to be silent.

As soon as the ambassador arrived at the palace, the Queen started to fetch her daughter.

All the streets were spread with carpets, and the windows were full of ladies who were waiting to see the Princess, and carried baskets of flowers and sweetmeats to shower upon her as she passed.

They had hardly begun to get the Princess ready when a dwarf arrived, mounted upon an elephant. He came from the five fairies, and brought for the Princess a crown, a scepter, and a robe of golden brocade, with a petticoat marvelously embroidered with butterflies' wings. They also sent a casket of jewels, so splendid that no one had ever seen anything like it before, and the Queen was perfectly dazzled when she opened it.

But the Princess scarcely gave a glance to any of these treasures, for she thought of nothing but Fanfaronade. The Dwarf was rewarded with a gold piece, and decorated with so many ribbons that it was hardly possible to see him at all.

The Princess sent to each of the fairies a new spinning-wheel

Waiting to See the Princess

with a distaff of cedar wood, and the Queen said she must look through her treasures and find something very charming to send them also.

When the Princess was arrayed in all the gorgeous things the Dwarf had brought, she was more beautiful than ever, and as she walked along the streets the people cried: “How pretty she is! How pretty she is!”

The procession consisted of the Queen, the Princess, five dozen other Princesses, her cousins; and ten dozen who came from the neighboring kingdoms; and as they proceeded at a stately pace the sky began to grow dark, then suddenly the thunder growled, and rain and hail fell in torrents.

The Queen put her royal mantle over her head, and all the Princesses did the same with their trains. Mayblossom was just about to follow their example when a terrific croaking, as of an immense army of crows, rooks, ravens, screech-owls, and all birds of ill-omen was heard, and at the same instant a huge owl skimmed up to the Princess, and threw over her a scarf woven of spiders' webs and embroidered with bats' wings.

And then peals of mocking laughter rang through the air, and they knew that this was another of the Fairy Carabosse's unpleasant jokes.

The Queen was terrified at such an evil omen, and tried to pull the black scarf from the Princess's shoulders, but it really seemed as if it must be nailed on, it clung so closely.

A Huge Owl Skimmed Up to the Princess.

"Ah!" cried the Queen, "Can nothing appease this enemy of ours? What good was it that I sent her more than fifty pounds of sweetmeats, and as much again of the best sugar, not to mention two hams? She is as angry as ever."

While she lamented in this way, and everybody was as wet as if they had been dragged through a river, the Princess still thought of nothing but the ambassador, and just at this moment he appeared before her, with the King, and there was a great blowing of trumpets, and all the people shouted louder than ever.

Fanfaronade was not generally at a loss for something to say, but when he saw the Princess, she was so much more beautiful and majestic than he had expected that he could only stammer out a few words, and entirely forgot the harangue which he had been learning for months, and knew well enough to have repeated it in his sleep.

To gain time to remember at least part of it, he made several low bows to the Princess, who on her side dropped half-a-dozen curtseys without stopping to think, and then she said, to relieve his evident embarrassment:

"Sir Ambassador, I am sure that everything you intend to say is charming, since it is you who mean to say it; but let us make haste into the palace, as it is pouring cats and dogs, and the wicked Fairy Carabosse will be amused to see us all stand dripping here. When we are once under shelter we can laugh at her."

Upon this the ambassador found his tongue, and replied

The Ambassador Appeared Before Her.

gallantly that the Fairy had evidently foreseen the flames that would be kindled by the bright eyes of the Princess, and had sent this deluge to extinguish them.

Then he offered his hand to conduct the Princess, and she said softly: "As you could not possibly guess how much I like you, Sir Fanfaronade, I am obliged to tell you plainly that, since I saw you enter the town on your beautiful prancing horse, I have been sorry that you came to speak for another instead of for yourself. So, if you feel as I do, I will marry you instead of your master. Of course I know you are not a Prince, but I shall be just as fond of you as if you were, and we can go and live in some cozy little corner of the world, and be as happy as the days are long."

The ambassador thought he must be dreaming, and could hardly believe what the lovely Princess had said. He dared not answer, but only squeezed the Princess's hand until he really hurt her little finger, but she did not cry out.

When they reached the palace the King kissed his daughter on both cheeks, and said: "My little lambkin, are you willing to marry the great King Merlin's son, as this ambassador has come on his behalf to fetch you?"

"If you please, sire," said the Princess, dropping a curtsey.

"I consent also," said the Queen; "so let the banquet be prepared."

This was done with all speed, and everybody feasted except Mayblossom and Fanfaronade, who looked at one another and

"You Came to Speak for Another."

forgot everything else.

After the banquet came a ball, and after that a ballet, and at last they were all so tired that everyone feel asleep just where he sat. Only the lovers were as wide awake as mice, and the Princess, seeing that there was nothing to fear, said to Fanfaronade:

"Let us be quick and run away, for we shall never have a better chance than this."

Then she took the King's dagger, which was in a diamond sheath, and the Queen's neck-handkerchief, and gave her hand to Fanfaronade, who carried a lantern, and they ran out together into the muddy street and down to the seashore.

Here they got into a little boat in which the poor old boatman was sleeping, and when he woke up and saw the lovely Princess, with all her diamonds and her spiders'-web scarf, he did not know what to think, and obeyed her instantly when she commanded him to set out.

They could see neither moon nor stars, but in the Queen's neck-handkerchief there was a carbuncle which glowed like fifty torches.

Fanfaronade asked the Princess where she would like to go, but she only answered that she did not care where she went as long as he was with her.

"But, Princess," said he, "I dare not take you back to King Merlin's court. He would think hanging too good for me."

"Oh, in that case," she answered, "we had better go to Squirrel

She Took the King's Dagger and They Ran Out Together.

Island; it is lonely enough, and too far for anyone to follow us there."

So she ordered the old boatman to steer for Squirrel Island.

Meanwhile the day was breaking, and the King and Queen and all the courtiers began to wake up and rub their eyes, and think it was time to finish the preparations for the wedding. And the Queen asked for her neck-handkerchief, that she might look richly dressed for her daughter's ceremony.

Then there was a scurrying hither and thither, and a hunting everywhere: they looked into every place, from the wardrobes to the stoves, and the Queen herself ran about from the garret to the cellar, but the handkerchief was nowhere to be found.

By this time the King had missed his dagger, and the search began all over again. They opened boxes and chests of which the keys had been lost for a hundred years, and found numbers of curious things, but not the dagger, and the King tore his beard, and the Queen tore her hair, for the handkerchief and the dagger were the most valuable things in the kingdom.

When the King saw that the search was hopeless he said:

"Never mind, let us make haste and get the wedding over before anything else is lost." And then he asked where the Princess was. Upon this her nurse came forward and said: "Sire, I have been seeking her these two hours, but she is nowhere to be found."

This was more than the Queen could bear. She gave a shriek of alarm and fainted away, and they had to pour two barrels of eau-

The Handkerchief Was Nowhere to Be Found.

de-cologne over her before she recovered.

When she came to herself everybody was looking for the Princess in the greatest terror and confusion, but as she did not appear, the King said to his page: "Go and find the Ambassador Fanfaronade, who is doubtless asleep in some corner, and tell him the sad news."

So the page hunted hither and thither, but Fanfaronade was no more to be found than the Princess, the dagger, or the neck-handkerchief!

Then the King summoned his counsellors and his guards, and, accompanied by the Queen, went into his great hall. As he had not had time to prepare his speech beforehand, the King ordered that silence should be kept for three hours, and at the end of that time he spoke as follows:

"Listen, great and small! My dear daughter Mayblossom is lost: whether she had been stolen away or has simply disappeared I cannot tell. The Queen's neck-handkerchief and my sword, which are worth their weight in gold, are also missing, and worst of all, the Ambassador Fanfaronade is nowhere to be found. I fear the King, his master, will come to seek him, and accuse us of having made mince-meat of him. I could bear even that if I had any money, but I assure you that the expenses of the wedding have completely ruined me. Advise me, then, my dear subjects, what had I better do to recover my daughter, Fanfaronade, and the other things."

This was the most eloquent speech the King had been known

Silence for Three Hours

to make, and when everybody had done admiring it the Prime Minister made answer:

"Sire, we are all very sorry to see you so sorry. We would give everything we value in the world to take away the cause of your sorrow, but this seems to be another of the tricks of the Fairy Carabosse. The Princess's twenty unlucky years were not quite over, and really, if the truth must be told, I noticed that Fanfaronade and the Princess appeared to admire one another greatly. Perhaps this may give us some clue to the mystery of their disappearance."

Here the Queen interrupted him, saying, "Take care what you say, sir. Believe me, the Princess Mayblossom was far too well brought up to think of falling in love with an ambassador."

At this moment the nurse came forward, and, falling on her knees, confessed how they had made the little needle-hole in the tower, and how the Princess had declared when she saw the ambassador that she would marry him and nobody else.

Then the Queen was very angry, and gave the nurse, and the cradle-rocker, and the nursery-maid, such a scolding that they shook in their shoes.

But the Admiral Cocked-Hat interrupted her, crying: "Let us be off after this good-for-nothing Fanfaronade, for without a doubt he has run away with our Princess."

Then there was a great clapping of hands, and everybody shouted, "By all means let us be after him."

So while some embarked upon the sea, the others ran from

The Nurse Came Forward.

kingdom to kingdom beating drums and blowing trumpets, and wherever a crowd collected they cried:

"Whoever wants a beautiful doll, sweetmeats of all kinds, a little pair of scissors, a golden robe, and a satin cap has only to say where Fanfaronade has hidden the Princess Mayblossom."

But the answer everywhere was, "You must go farther, we have not seen them."

However, those who went by sea were more fortunate, for after sailing about for some time they noticed a light before them which burned at night like a great fire. At first they dared not go near it, not knowing what it might be, but by-and-by it remained stationary over Squirrel Island, for, as you have guessed already, the light was the glowing of the carbuncle.

The Princess and Fanfaronade on landing upon the island had given the boatman a hundred gold pieces, and made him promise solemnly to tell no one where he had taken them; but the first thing that happened was that, as he rowed away, he got into the midst of the fleet, and before he could escape the Admiral had seen him and sent a boat after him.

When he was searched they found the gold pieces in his pocket, and as they were quite new coins, struck in honor of the Princess's wedding, the Admiral felt certain that the boatman must have been paid by the Princess to aid her in her flight. But he would not answer any questions, and pretended to be deaf and dumb.

Then the Admiral said: "Oh! Deaf and dumb is he? Lash him

A Light Like a Great Fire

to the mast and give him a taste of the cat-o'-nine-tails. I don't know anything better than that for curing the deaf and dumb!"

And when the old boatman saw that he was in earnest, he told all he knew about the cavalier and the lady whom he had landed upon Squirrel Island, and the Admiral knew it must be the Princess and Fanfaronade; so he gave the order for the fleet to surround the island.

Meanwhile the Princess Mayblossom, who was by this time terribly sleepy, had found a grassy bank in the shade, and throwing herself down had already fallen asleep into a profound slumber, when Fanfaronade, who happened to be hungry and not sleepy, came and woke her up, saying very crossly:

"Pray, madam, how long do you mean to stay here? I see nothing to eat, and though you may be very charming, the sight of you does not prevent me from famishing."

"What! Fanfaronade," said the Princess, sitting up and rubbing her eyes, "is it possible that when I am here with you you can want anything else? You ought to be thinking all the time how happy you are."

"Happy!" cried he; "Say rather unhappy. I wish with all my heart that you were back in your dark tower again."

"Darling, don't be cross," said the Princess. "I will go and see if I can find some wild fruit for you."

"I wish you might find a wolf to eat you up," growled Fanfaronade.

The Old Boatman Told All He Knew.

The Princess, in great dismay, ran hither and thither all about the wood, tearing her dress, and hurting her pretty hands with the thorns and brambles, but she could find nothing to eat, and at last she had to go back sorrowfully to Fanfaronade.

When he saw that she came empty-handed he got up and left her, grumbling to himself.

The next day they searched again, but with no better success.

"Alas!" said the Princess, "If only I could find something for you to eat, I should not mind being hungry myself."

"No, I should not mind that either," answered Fanfaronade.

"Is it possible," said she, "that you would not care if I died of hunger? Oh, Fanfaronade, you said you loved me!"

"That was when we were in quite another place and I was not hungry," said he. "It makes a great difference in one's ideas to be dying of hunger and thirst on a desert island."

At this the Princess was dreadfully vexed, and she sat down under a white rose bush and began to cry bitterly.

"Happy roses," she thought to herself, "they have only to blossom in the sunshine and be admired, and there is nobody to be unkind to them."

And the tears ran down her cheeks and splashed on to the rose-tree roots. Presently she was surprised to see the whole bush rustling and shaking, and a soft little voice from the prettiest rose-bud said:

"Poor Princess! Look in the trunk of that tree, and you will

The Princess Ran Hither and Thither.

find a honeycomb, but don't be foolish enough to share it with Fanfaronade."

Mayblossom ran to the tree, and sure enough there was the honey. Without losing a moment she ran with it to Fanfaronade, crying gaily:

"See, here is a honeycomb that I have found. I might have eaten it up all by myself, but I had rather share it with you."

But without looking at her or thanking her he snatched the honeycomb out of her hands and ate it all up — every bit, without offering her a morsel. Indeed, when she humbly asked for some he said mockingly that it was too sweet for her, and would spoil her teeth.

Mayblossom, more downcast than ever, went sadly away and sat down under an oak tree, and her tears and sighs were so piteous that the oak fanned her with his rustling leaves, and said:

"Take courage, pretty Princess, all is not lost yet. Take this pitcher of milk and drink it up, and whatever you do, don't leave a drop for Fanfaronade."

The Princess, quite astonished, looked round, and saw a big pitcher full of milk, but before she could raise it to her lips the thought of how thirsty Fanfaronade must be, after eating at least fifteen pounds of honey, made her run back to him and say: "Here is a pitcher of milk; drink some, for you must be thirsty, I am sure; but pray save a little for me, as I am dying of hunger and thirst."

But he seized the pitcher and drank all it contained at a single

"Here Is a Honeycomb I Have Found."

draught, and then broke it to atoms on the nearest stone, saying, with a malicious smile: "As you have not eaten anything you cannot be thirsty."

"Ah!" cried the Princess, "I am well punished for disappointing the King and Queen, and running away with this ambassador, about whom I knew nothing."

And so saying she wandered away into the thickest part of the wood, and sat down under a thorn tree, where a nightingale was singing. Presently she heard him say: "Search under the bush, Princess; you will find some sugar, almonds, and some tarts there. But don't be silly enough to offer Fanfaronade any."

And this time the Princess, who was fainting with hunger, took the nightingale's advice, and ate what she found all by herself. But Fanfaronade, seeing that she had found something good, and was not going to share it with him, ran after her in such a fury that she hastily drew out the Queen's carbuncle, which had the property of rendering people invisible if they were in danger, and when she was safely hidden from him she reproached him gently for his unkindness.

Meanwhile Admiral Cocked-Hat had despatched Jack-the-Chatterer-of-the-Straw-Boots, Courier in Ordinary to the Prime Minister, to tell the King that the Princess and the ambassador had landed on Squirrel Island, but that not knowing the country he had not pursued them, for fear of being captured by concealed enemies. Their Majesties were overjoyed at the news, and the

“You Cannot Be Thirsty.”

King sent for a great book, each leaf of which was eight ells long. It was the work of a very clever Fairy, and contained a description of the whole earth. He very soon found that Squirrel Island was uninhabited.

"Go," said he to Jack-the-Chatterer, "tell the Admiral from me to land at once. I am surprised at his not having done so sooner." As soon as this message reached the fleet, every preparation was made for war, and the noise was so great that it reached the ears of the Princess, who at once flew to protect her ambassador. As he was not very brave he accepted her aid gladly.

"You stand behind me," said she, "and I will hold the carbuncle which will make us invisible, and with the King's dagger I can protect you from the enemy."

So when the soldiers landed they could see nothing, but the Princess touched them one after another with the dagger, and they fell insensible upon the sand, so that at last the Admiral, seeing that there was some enchantment, hastily gave orders for a retreat to be sounded, and got his men back into their boats in great confusion.

Fanfaronade, being once more left with the Princess, began to think that if he could get rid of her, and possess himself of the carbuncle and the dagger, he would be able to make his escape.

So as they walked back over the cliffs he gave the Princess a great push, hoping she would fall into the sea; but she stepped aside so quickly that he only succeeded in overbalancing himself,

Every Preparation Was Made for War.

and over he went, and sank to the bottom of the sea like a lump of lead, and was never heard of any more.

While the Princess was still looking after him in horror, her attention was attracted by a rushing noise over her head, and looking up she saw two chariots approaching rapidly from opposite directions.

One was bright and glittering, and drawn by swans and peacocks, while the Fairy who sat in it was beautiful as a sunbeam; but the other was drawn by bats and ravens, and contained a frightful little Dwarf, who was dressed in a snake's skin, and wore a great toad upon her head for a hood.

The chariots met with a frightful crash in mid-air, and the Princess looked on in breathless anxiety while a furious battle took place between the lovely Fairy and her golden lance, and the hideous little Dwarf and her rusty pike. But very soon it was evident that the beauty had the best of it, and the Dwarf turned her bats' heads and flickered away in great confusion.

The Fairy came down to where Mayblossom stood, and said, smiling: "You see, Princess, I have completely routed that malicious old Carabosse. Will you believe it! She actually wanted to claim authority over you forever, because you came out of the tower four days before the twenty years were ended. However, I think I have settled her pretensions, and I hope you will be very happy and enjoy the freedom I have won for you."

The Princess thanked her heartily, and then the Fairy

Two Chariots Approaching

despatched one of her peacocks to her palace to bring a gorgeous robe for Mayblossom, who certainly needed it, for her own was torn to shreds by the thorns and briars. Another peacock was sent to the Admiral to tell him that he could now land in perfect safety, which he at once did, bringing all his men with him, even to Jack-the-Chatterer, who, happening to pass the spit upon which the Admiral's dinner was roasting, snatched it up and brought it with him.

Admiral Cocked-Hat was immensely surprised when he came upon the golden chariot, and still more so to see two lovely ladies walking under the trees a little farther away. When he reached them, of course he recognized the Princess, and he went down on his knees and kissed her hand quite joyfully. Then she presented him to the Fairy, and told him how Carabosse had been finally routed, and he thanked and congratulated the Fairy, who was most gracious to him.

While they were talking, she cried suddenly: "I declare I smell a savory dinner."

"Why yes, Madam, here it is," said Jack-the-Chatterer, holding up the spit, where all the pheasants and partridges were frizzling. "Will Your Highness please to taste any of them?"

"By all means," said the Fairy, "especially as the Princess will certainly be glad of a good meal."

So the Admiral sent back to his ship for everything that was needful, and they feasted merrily under the trees. By the time they

Another Peacock Was Sent to the Admiral.

had finished, the peacock had come back with a robe for the Princess, in which the Fairy arrayed her. It was of green and gold brocade, embroidered with pearls and rubies, and her long golden hair was tied back with strings of diamonds and emeralds, and crowned with flowers.

The Fairy made her mount beside her in the golden chariot, and took her on board the Admiral's ship, where she bade her farewell, sending many messages of friendship to the Queen, and bidding the Princess tell her that she was the fifth Fairy who had attended the christening. Then salutes were fired, the fleet weighed anchor, and very soon they reached the port.

Here the King and Queen were waiting, and they received Mayblossom with such joy and kindness that she could not get a word in edgewise, to say how sorry she was for having run away with such a very poor spirited ambassador. But, after all, it must have been all Carabosse's fault.

Just at this lucky moment who should arrive but King Merlin's son, who had become uneasy at not receiving any news from his ambassador, and so had started out himself with a magnificent escort of a thousand horsemen, and thirty body-guards in gold and scarlet uniforms, to see what could have happened.

As he was a hundred times handsomer and braver than the ambassador, the Princess found she could like him very much. So the wedding was held at once, with so much splendor and rejoicing that all the previous misfortunes were quite forgotten.

King Merlin's Son

Always Smashing, Upsetting, Breaking!

# How · Moti · Won · The · War

Once upon a time there was a youth called Moti, who was very big and strong, but the clumsiest creature you can imagine. So clumsy was he that he was always putting his great feet into the bowls of sweet milk which his mother set out on the floor to cool, always smashing, upsetting, breaking, until at last his father said to him:

"Here, Moti, are fifty silver pieces which are the savings of years; take them and go and make your living or your fortune if you can."

Then Moti started off early one spring morning with his thick staff over his shoulder, singing gaily to himself as he walked along.

In one way and another he got along very well until a hot evening when he came to a certain city where he entered the travelers' serai, or inn, to pass the night. Now a serai is generally just a large square enclosed by a high wall with an open colonnade along the inside all round to accommodate both men and beasts, and with perhaps a few rooms in towers at the corners for those who are too rich or too proud to sleep by their own camels and horses.

Moti, of course, was a country lad and had lived with cattle all his life, and he wasn't rich and he wasn't proud, so he just borrowed a bed from the innkeeper, set it down beside an old buffalo who reminded him of home, and in five minutes was fast asleep.

In the middle of the night he woke, feeling that he had been disturbed, and putting his hand under his pillow found to his horror that his bag of money had been stolen!

He jumped up quietly and began to prowl around to see whether anyone seemed to be awake, but, though he managed to arouse a few men and beasts by falling over them, he walked in the shadow of the archways round the whole serai without coming across a likely thief.

He was just about to give up when he overheard two men whispering, and one laughed softly, and, peering behind a pillar, he saw two Afghan horsedealers counting out his bag of money! Then Moti went back to bed.

In the morning Moti followed the two dealers outside the city to the horsemarket in which their horses were offered for sale. Choosing the best-looking horse amongst them he went up to it and said:

"Is this horse for sale? May I try it?" and, the merchants assenting, he scrambled up on its back, dug in his heels, and off they flew. Now Moti had never been on a horse in his life, and had

His Money Had Been Stolen!

so much to do to hold on with both hands as well as with both legs that the animal went just where it liked, and very soon broke into a break-neck gallop and made straight back to the serai where it had spent the last few nights.

"This will do very well," thought Moti as they whirled in at the entrance. As soon as the horse had arrived at its stable it stopped of its own accord and Moti immediately rolled off; but he jumped up at once, tied the beast up, and called for some breakfast. Presently the dealers appeared, out of breath and furious, and claimed the horse.

"What do you mean?" cried Moti, with his mouth full of rice. "It's my horse; I paid you fifty pieces of silver for it — quite a bargain, I'm sure!"

"Nonsense! It is *our* horse," answered one of the Afghans, beginning to untie the bridle.

"Leave off," shouted Moti, seizing his staff; "if you don't let my horse alone I'll crack your skulls! You thieves! *I* know you! Last night you took my money, so today I took your horse; that's fair enough!"

Now they began to look a little uncomfortable, but Moti seemed so determined to keep the horse that they resolved to appeal to the law, so they went off and laid a complaint before the King that Moti had stolen one of their horses and would not give it up nor pay for it.

Presently a soldier came to summon Moti to the King; and,

"It Is *Our* House!"

when he arrived and made his obeisance, the King began to question him as to why he had galloped off with the horse in this fashion. But Moti declared that he had got the animal in exchange for fifty pieces of silver, whilst the horse merchants vowed that the money they had on them was what they had received for the sale of other horses.

In one way and another the dispute got so confusing that the King (who really thought that Moti had stolen the horse) said at last: "Well, I tell you what I will do. I will lock something into this box before me, and if he guesses what it is, the horse is his, and if he doesn't, then it is yours."

To this Moti agreed, and the King arose and went out alone by a little door at the back of the court, and presently came back clasping something closely wrapped up in a cloth under his robe, slipped it into the little box, locked the box, and set it up where all might see.

"Now," said the King to Moti, "guess!"

It happened that when the King had opened the door behind him, Moti noticed that there was a garden outside: without waiting for the King's return he began to think what could be got out of the garden small enough to be shut in the box.

"Is it likely to be a fruit or a flower? No, not a flower this time, for he clasped it too tight. Then it must be a fruit or a stone. Yet not a stone, because he wouldn't wrap a dirty stone in his nice clean cloth.

“Now,” said the King, “Guess!”

"Then it is a fruit! And a fruit without much scent, or else he would be afraid that I might smell it. Now what fruit without much scent is in season just now?

"When I know that I shall have guessed the riddle!"

Moti was a country lad, and used to work in his father's garden. He knew all the common fruits, so he thought he ought to be able to guess right; but not to let it seem too easy, he gazed up at the ceiling with a puzzled expression, looked at the floor with an air of wisdom, his fingers pressed against his forehead, and then he said, slowly, with his eyes on the king:

"It is freshly plucked! It is round and it is red! It is a pomegranate!"

Now the King knew nothing about fruits except that they were good to eat; and, as for seasons, he asked for whatever fruit he wanted whenever he wanted it, and saw that he got it; so to him Moti's guess was like a miracle, and clear proof not only of his wisdom but of his innocence, for it *was* a pomegranate that he had put into the box!

Of course when the King marveled and praised Moti's wisdom, everybody else did so, too; and, whilst the horsetraders went off crestfallen, Moti took the horse and entered the King's service.

Very soon after this, Moti, who continued to live in the serai, came back one wet and stormy evening to find that his precious horse had strayed. Nothing remained of him but a broken halter cord, and no one knew what had become of him. After inquiring

"It Is a Pomegranate!"

of everyone who was likely to know, Moti seized the cord and his big staff and sallied out to look for him.

Away and away he tramped out of the city and into the neighboring forest, tracking hoof-marks in the mud.

Presently it grew late, but still Moti wandered on until suddenly in the gathering darkness he came right upon a tiger who was contentedly eating his horse.

"You thief!" shrieked Moti, and ran up, and, just as the tiger, in astonishment, dropped a bone — *whack* came Moti's staff on his head with such good will that the beast was half-stunned and could hardly breathe or see. Then Moti continued to shower upon him blows and abuse until the poor tiger could hardly stand, whereupon Moti tied the broken halter round his neck and dragged him back to the serai.

"If you had my horse," he said, "I will at least have you, that's fair enough!" And he tied him up securely by the head and heels, much as he used to tie the horse; then, the night being far gone, he flung himself beside him and slept soundly.

You cannot imagine anything like the fright of the people in the serai, when they woke up and found a tiger — very battered but still a tiger — securely tethered amongst themselves and their beasts!

Men gathered in groups talking and exclaiming, and finding fault with the innkeeper for allowing such a dangerous beast into the serai, and all the while the innkeeper was just as troubled as the

"You Thief!"

rest, and none dared go near the place where the tiger stood blinking miserably on everyone, and where Moti lay stretched out snoring like thunder.

At last news reached the King that Moti had exchanged his horse for a live tiger; and the monarch himself came down, half disbelieving the tale, to see if it were really true. Someone at last awaked Moti with the news that his royal master was come; and he arose yawning, and was soon delightedly explaining and showing off his new possession.

The King, however, did not share his pleasure at all, but called up a soldier to shoot the tiger, much to the relief of all the inmates of the serai except Moti.

If the King, however, was before convinced that Moti was one of the wisest of men, he was now still more convinced that he was the bravest, and he increased his pay a hundredfold, so that our hero thought that he was the *luckiest* of men.

A week or two after this incident the King sent for Moti, who on arrival found his master in despair. A neighboring monarch, he explained, who had many more soldiers than he, had declared war against him, and he was at his wits' end, for he had neither money enough to buy him off nor soldiers enough to fight him — what was he to do?

"If that is all, don't you trouble," said Moti. "Turn out your men, and I'll go with them, and we'll soon bring this robber to reason."

The Monarch Himself Came Down.

The King began to revive at these hopeful words, and took Moti off to his stable where he bade him choose for himself any horse he liked. There were plenty of fine horses in the stalls, but to the King's astonishment Moti chose a poor little rat of a pony that was used to carry grass and water for the rest of the stable.

"But why do you choose that beast?" said the King.

"Well, you see, your majesty," replied Moti, "there are so many chances that I may fall off, and if I choose one of your fine big horses I shall have so far to fall that I shall probably break my leg or my arm, if not my neck, but if I fall off this little beast I can't hurt myself much."

A very comical sight was Moti when he rode out to the war. The only weapon he carried was his staff, and to help him to keep his balance on horseback he had tied to each of his ankles a big stone that nearly touched the ground as he sat astride the little pony.

The rest of the King's cavalry were not very numerous, but they pranced along in armor on fine horses. Behind them came a great rabble of men on foot armed with all sorts of weapons, and last of all was the King with his attendants, very nervous and ill at ease. So the army started.

They had not very far to go, but Moti's little pony, weighted with a heavy man and two big rocks, soon began to lag behind the cavalry, and would have lagged behind the infantry too, only they were not very anxious to be too early in the fight, and hung back so as to give Moti plenty of time.

A Poor Little Rat of a Pony

Moti jogged along more and more slowly for some time, until at last, getting impatient at the slowness of the pony, he gave him such a tremendous thwack with his staff that the pony completely lost his temper and bolted. First one stone became untied and rolled away in a cloud of dust to one side of the road, whilst Moti nearly rolled off, too, but he clasped his steed valiantly by its ragged mane, and, dropping his staff, held on for dear life.

Then fortunately the other rock broke away from his other leg and rolled thunderously down a neighboring ravine. Meanwhile the advanced cavalry had barely time to draw to one side when Moti came dashing by, yelling bloodthirsty threats to his pony: "You wait till I get hold of you! I'll skin you alive! I'll wring your neck! I'll break every bone in your body!"

The cavalry thought that this dreadful language was meant for the enemy, and were filled with admiration for his courage. Many of their horses were quite upset by this whirlwind that galloped howling through their midst, and in a few minutes, after a little plunging and rearing and kicking, the whole troop were following on Moti's heels.

Far in advance, Moti continued his wild career. Presently he came to a great field of castor-oil plants, ten or twelve feet high, big and bushy, but quite green and soft. Hoping to escape from the back of his fiery steed, Moti grasped one in passing, but its roots gave way, and he dashed on, with the whole plant looking like a young tree flourishing in his grip!

The Pony Bolted.

The enemy was in battle array, advancing over the plain, their King with them confident and cheerful, when suddenly from the front came a desperate rider at a furious gallop.

"Sire!" he cried, "Save yourself! The enemy is coming!"

"What *do* you mean?" said the King.

"Oh, sire!" panted the messenger, "Fly at once, there is no time to lose. Foremost of the enemy rides a mad giant at a furious gallop. He flourishes a tree for a club and is wild with anger, for as he goes he cries: 'You wait till I get hold of you! I'll skin you alive! I'll wring your neck! I'll break every bone in your body!' Others ride behind, and you will do well to retire before this whirlwind of destruction comes upon you!"

Just then out of a cloud of dust in the distance, the King saw Moti approaching at a hard gallop, looking indeed like a giant compared with the little beast he rode, whirling his castor-oil plant, which in the distance might have seemed an oak tree, and the sound of his revilings and shoutings came down upon the breeze!

Behind him the dust cloud moved to the sound of the thunder of hoofs, whilst here and there flashed the glitter of steel. The sight and the sound struck terror into the King, and, turning his horse, he fled at top speed, thinking that a regiment of yelling giants was upon him; and all his force followed him as fast as they might go.

One fat officer alone could not keep up on foot with that mad rush, and as Moti came galloping up he flung himself on the

“Sire! Save Yourself!”

ground in abject fear. This was too much for Moti's excited pony, who shied so suddenly that Moti went flying over his head like a sky rocket, and alighted right on the top of his fat foe.

Quickly regaining his feet, Moti began to swing his plant round his head and to shout:

"Where are your men? Bring them up and I'll kill them. My regiments! Come on, the whole lot of you! Where's your King? Bring him to me. Here are all my fine fellows coming up and we'll each pull up a tree by the roots and lay you all flat and your houses and towns and everything else! Come on!"

But the poor fat officer could do nothing but squat on his knees with his hands together, gasping. At last, when he got his breath, Moti sent him off to bring his King, and to tell him that if he was reasonable his life should be spared.

Off the poor man went, and by the time the troops of Moti's side had come up and arranged themselves to look as formidable as possible, he returned with his King. The latter was very humble and apologetic, and promised never to make war any more, to pay a large sum of money, and altogether do whatever his conqueror wished.

So the armies on both sides went rejoicing home, and this was really the making of the fortune of clumsy Moti, who lived long and contrived always to be looked up to as a fountain of wisdom, valor, and discretion by all except his own relatives, who could never understand what he had done to be considered so much wiser than anyone else!

Moti the Wise